ANATOMY AND HUMAN MOVEMENT
STRUCTURE AND FUNCTION

NIGEL PALASTANGA   BA, MA, MCSP, DMS, Dip TP
Principal, School of Physiotherapy, University Hospital of Wales, Cardiff

DEREK FIELD   Grad Dip Phys, MCSP, Dip TP, SRP
Vice Principal, North London School of Physiotherapy, London

ROGER SOAMES   BSc, PhD
Senior Lecturer in Anatomy, King's College, University of London

With a contribution *The Nervous System* by
Nikolai Bogduk   MB, BS, PhD
Senior Lecturer, Faculty of Medicine, University of Newcastle, New South Wales, Australia

HEINEMANN MEDICAL BOOKS

Heinemann Medical Books
An imprint of Heinemann Professional Publishing Ltd
Halley Court, Jordan Hill, Oxford OX2 8EJ

OXFORD   LONDON   SINGAPORE   NAIROBI   IBADAN   KINGSTON

First published 1989

British Library Cataloguing in Publication Data
Palastanga, Nigel
   Anatomy and human movement.
   1. Man. Anatomy
   I. Title II. Field, Derek III. Somes, Roger
   612'.76

ISBN 0 433 00032 5

Typeset and printed in Great Britain by
The Bath Press, Avon

Contents

ACKNOWLEDGEMENTS

We would like to thank Dr Nikolai Bogduk of the University of Newcastle, New South Wales, Australia for his extremely valuable contribution *The Nervous System*.

We would especially like to thank Mike Duffy who prepared the illustrations and Roger Soames who drew his own diagrams for the joints and biomechanics sections. We also thank Bruce Keogh and Stephen Ebbs who kindly gave us permission to reproduce some of the figures and x-rays from their book *Normal Surface Anatomy* (Heinemann Medical Books, 1985).

We are most grateful to Richard Barling, Stephen Bishop and Caroline Creed of Heinemann Medical Books for all their help and advice, and to Dot Palastanga, Penny de Magry and Marcia Eedle for typing the manuscript.

Preface

We have designed and written this book for the student of anatomy who is concerned with the study of the *living* body, and who wishes to use this knowledge functionally for a greater understanding of the mechanisms which allow movement to take place. Traditional anatomy texts are written as an adjunct to the study of the human body in the dissecting room; but only the surgeon has the advantage of directly viewing living musculoskeletal structures. The vast majority of students interested in musculoskeletal anatomy as well as those involved with human movement and its disorders are confronted by an intact skin, and therefore must visualize the structures involved by palpation and analysis of movement. *Anatomy and Human Movement* presents the musculoskeletal structures as a living dynamic system – an approach lacking in many existing textbooks. The applied anatomy of the musculoskeletal system occupies the greater part of the book, and is built up from a study of the bones and muscles (which are grouped according to their major functions, rather than as seen in the dissecting room) to a consideration of joints and their biomechanics. Anatomical descriptions of each joint are given with a detailed explanation of how it functions, the forces generated across it and how it might fail. We have placed great emphasis on the joints as these are of major concern to those interested in active movement and passive manipulation, and we give examples of common traumatic or pathological problems affecting the structures described. Where possible we describe palpation and analyze movement with respect to the joints and muscles involved, as well as any accessory movements. The course and distribution of the major peripheral nerves and blood vessels, together with the lymphatic drainage of the region are given at the end of each relevant section. There are separate chapters on embryology, the skin and its appendages, and we have included, in the introduction, a section on the terminology used in the book. There is also an account of the structure and function of the nervous system written by Nikolai Bogduk whose contribution has been extremely valuable.

The format of the book matches a page of text to a page of illustrations, whenever possible, and we hope that this will allow the reader to confirm his or her understanding of the text with the visual information provided. The book is extensively illustrated with large, clear, fully-labelled diagrams, all of which have been specially prepared. In the sections covering the joints and biomechanics the illustrations have been drawn by Roger Soames, and these are particularly detailed as they pull together the anatomy from the previous parts of that chapter.

We hope that this new approach to the teaching of anatomy will serve to fill the gap which has always existed for those who have to learn their anatomy on a living subject, and eventually have to determine their diagnoses and apply their treatments through an intact skin.

Nigel Palastanga, Derek Field, Roger Soames
1989

Introduction and terminology

Introduction and terminology

Anatomy and Human Movement is written for the student of anatomy who wishes to use this knowledge functionally and desires greater understanding of the mechanisms which allow movement to take place. For this reason some sections of the book have been expanded giving greater detail, whereas others are considered in outline only.

EXPLANATION OF THE LAYOUT OF THE BOOK

The book has three sections dealing with the musculoskeletal system: the upper limb, the lower limb, and the head, neck and trunk. In addition there is a fourth section on the nervous system. Some degree of overlap between these sections is inevitable as they are artificial and merely serve to make description easier. It is difficult to determine where the movements of the upper limb or lower limb end and those of the trunk begin, as movement of one is usually dependent on the control and stability of the other two.

Nevertheless, each musculoskeletal section is presented in a similar manner. It starts with a study of the bones, to provide the basic framework of the section. This is followed by a description of the muscles, which are considered in functional groups in an attempt to explain how movement is produced. Finally, the joints are described and discussed, building on the knowledge gained from a consideration of the bones and muscles. The last part of each section also serves to bring together the preceding parts. At the end of each of the limb and trunk sections a review of the relevant peripheral nervous system is presented, which outlines the innervation of the various joints, muscle groups and cutaneous supply to the skin. There is also a brief description of the blood supply and lymphatic drainage of each region.

An important feature of the book is that it is written in terms of living anatomy, unlike so many of the standard anatomy textbooks which tend to be for use with cadaveric material. This book describes how many of the structures can be palpated through an intact skin, as well as how movements can be tested and analyzed with respect to joint movement, muscle work and function. Where possible the clinical significance and functional importance of the anatomical features discussed is stressed.

Anatomical detail has been kept to that only considered to be essential, and is supplemented by illustrations of the structures described (usually on the page opposite the written text). Photographs and radiographs of the normal anatomy are used to aid understanding when appropriate. The student should bear in mind, however, that there may be individual variation between the anatomical structures described here and those that they find in practice.

TERMINOLOGY

It is essential for the student beginning their study of anatomy that they become familiar with as many relevant anatomical terms as possible prior to studying the descriptive sections of the book. Some of these terms have an English or Arabic origin, but by far the majority come from Latin or Greek. Over the years an internationally accepted vocabulary, allowing communication and understanding between all members of the medical and paramedical professions throughout the world, has been established. Perhaps the single, most important descriptive feature of this vocabulary is the adoption of an unequivocal position of the human body. This is known as *the anatomical position*. It is described as follows: the body is standing erect and facing forwards; the legs are together with the feet parallel so that the toes point forwards; the arms hang loosely by the sides with the palm of the hand facing forward so that the thumb is lateral (Fig. A.1). All positional terminology is used with reference to this position, irrespective of the actual position of the body when performing an activity.

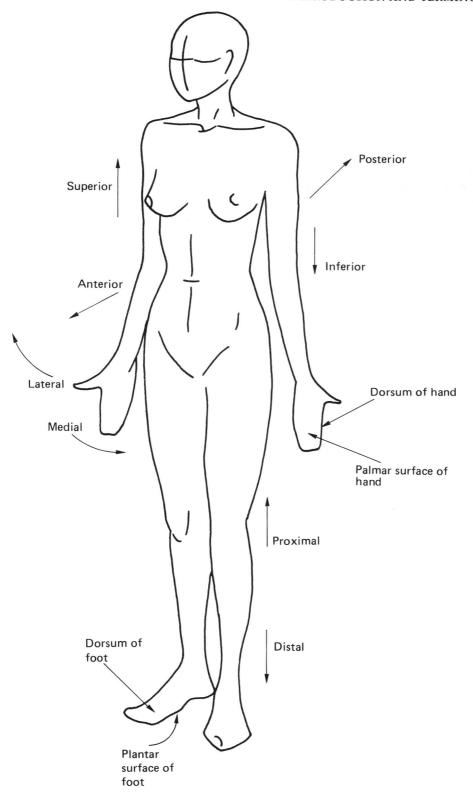

Fig. A.1 The anatomical position.

The following is a list of more commonly used terms which describe the position of anatomical structures:

Anterior (ventral)	To the front or in front, e.g. the patella lies anterior to the knee joint.
Posterior (dorsal)	To the rear or behind, e.g. gluteus maximus lies posterior to the hip joint. (Ventral and dorsal are used more commonly in four-legged animals.)
Superior (cephalic)	Above, e.g. the head is superior to the trunk.
Inferior (caudal)	Below, e.g. the knee is inferior to the hip.
Cephalic (the head) *Caudal* (the tail)	May be used in relation to the trunk.
Lateral	Away from the median plane or midline, e.g. the little toe lies lateral to the big toe.
Medial	Towards the median plane or midline, e.g. the little finger lies medial to the thumb.
Distal	Away from the trunk or root of the limb, e.g. the foot is distal to the knee.
Proximal	Close to the trunk or root of the limb, e.g. the wrist is proximal to the hand.
Superficial	Closer to the surface of the body or skin, e.g. the ulnar nerve passes superficial to the flexor retinaculum of the wrist.
Deep	Further away from the body surface or skin, e.g. the tendon of tibialis posterior passes deep to the flexor retinaculum at the ankle.

PLANES AND AXES OF THE HUMAN BODY

To facilitate the understanding of the relation of structures one to another and the movement of one segment with respect to another, imaginary reference planes pass through the body in such a way that they are mutually perpendicular to each other (Fig. A.2). Passing through the body from front to back and dividing it into two symmetrical right and left halves is the *sagittal (median) plane*. Any plane parallel to this is also known as a *sagittal (paramedian) plane*.

A plane passing through the body from top to bottom and lying at right angles to the sagittal plane is the *coronal (frontal) plane*. This divides the body into anterior and posterior parts. All planes that divide the body in this way are known as coronal planes. Finally, a plane passing through the body at right angles to both the previous planes dividing it into upper and lower parts is known as a *transverse (horizontal) plane*. A whole family of parallel transverse planes exist, it is therefore usual when presenting a particular transverse section to specify the level at which it is taken. This may be conveniently done by specifying the vertebral level or the position within the limb, e.g. C6 or midshaft of humerus respectively.

Within each plane a single axis can be identified, usually in association with a particular joint, about which movement takes place. An anteroposteriorly directed axis in the sagittal (or a paramedian) plane allows movement in a coronal plane. Similarly, a vertical axis in a coronal plane allows movement in a transverse plane. Lastly a transverse (right to left) axis in a coronal plane provides movement in a paramedian plane. By arranging that these various axes intersect at the centre of joints, the movements possible at the joint can be broken down into simple components. It also becomes easier to understand how specific muscle groups produce particular movements, as well as determining the resultant movement of combined muscle actions.

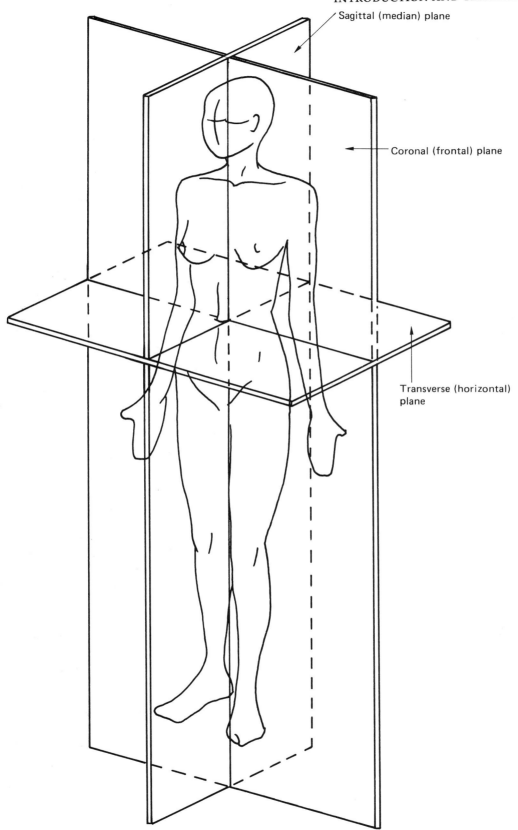

Sagittal (median) plane

Coronal (frontal) plane

Transverse (horizontal) plane

Fig. A.2   Anatomical planes.

Rarely do movements of one body segment with respect to another take place in a single plane. They almost invariably occur in two or three planes simultaneously producing a complex pattern of movement. However, it is convenient to consider movements about each of the three defined axes separately. Movement about a transverse axis occurring in the paramedian plane is referred to as *flexion* and *extension*; that about an anteroposterior axis in a coronal plane is termed *abduction* and *adduction*; and finally, that about a vertical axis in a transverse plane are *medial* and *lateral rotation*.

Terms used in describing movement

All movements are described, unless otherwise stated, with respect to the anatomical position as the position of reference. In this position joints are often referred to as being in a 'neutral position'.

Flexion   The bending of adjacent body segments in a paramedian plane so that their two anterior/posterior surfaces are brought together, e.g. bending the elbow so that the anterior surfaces of the forearm and arm are opposed.

(For the knee joint the posterior surfaces of the leg and thigh are opposed.)

Extension   The moving apart of two opposing surfaces in a paramedian plane, e.g. the straightening of the flexed knee or elbow. Extension also refers to movement beyond the neutral position in a direction opposite to flexion, e.g. extension at the wrist occurs when the posterior surfaces of the hand and forearm move towards each other.

Flexion and extension of the foot at the ankle joint may be referred to as plantarflexion and dorsiflexion respectively.

Plantar-flexion   Moving the top (dorsum) of the foot away from the anterior surface of the leg.

Dorsi-flexion   Bringing the dorsum of the foot towards the front of the leg.

Abduction   The movement of a body segment in a coronal plane such that it moves away from the midline of the body, e.g. movement of the upper limb away from the side of the trunk.

Adduction   The movement of a body segment in a coronal plane such that it moves towards the midline of the body, e.g. movement of the upper limb back towards the side of the trunk.

Lateral flexion (bending)   A term used to denote bending of the trunk (vertebral column) to one side, e.g. lateral bending of the trunk to the left. The movement occurs in the coronal plane.

Medial rotation   Rotation of a limb segment about its longitudinal axis such that the anterior surface comes to face towards the midline of the body, e.g. turning the lower limb inwards so that the toes point towards the midline.

Lateral rotation   Rotation of a limb segment about its longitudinal axis so that its anterior surface faces away from the midline plane, e.g. turning the lower limb so that the toes point outwards away from the midline.

Supination and *pronation* are terms used in conjunction with the movements of the forearm and foot.

Supination   Movement of the forearm so that the palm of the hand faces forwards. In the foot it is the movement whereby the forefoot is turned so that the sole faces medially; it is always accompanied by adduction of the forefoot.

Pronation   Movement of the forearm which brings the palm of the hand to face backwards. In the foot it is a movement of the forefoot which causes the sole to face laterally; it is always accompanied by abduction of the forefoot.

Inversion and *eversion* are terms used to describe composite movements of the foot.

Inversion   Movement of the whole foot to bring the sole to face medially. It consists of supination and adduction of the forefoot, with plantarflexion at the ankle joint.

Eversion   Movement of the whole foot so that the sole comes to face laterally. It consists of pronation and abduction of the forefoot in conjunction with dorsiflexion at the ankle joint.

LEVERS

An understanding of the action and principle of levers is of considerable use when considering the application of the forces applied to bones. The following is a simplified description of the mechanics of levers and how they are applied in the human body.

A lever may be considered to be a simple, rigid bar, with no account taken of its shape or structure. Most long bones appear as rigid bars but although many bones, such as those of the skull, are far from the usual concept of a lever they can, nevertheless, still act in this way.

The fulcrum is the point around which the lever rotates. That part of the lever between the fulcrum and point of force application is known as the *force arm*, and that between the fulcrum and the point of load application is known as the *load arm*. This concept is easy to understand when applied to a child's see-saw (Fig. A.3a). Different arrangements of the fulcrum, load and force arms produce different *classes of lever*. There are three possible arrangements: a *first class lever* has the fulcrum between the load and force arms; a *second class lever* has the fulcrum at one end and the applied force at the other, with the load situated between them; a *third class lever* again has the fulcrum at one end but the load at the other with the applied force between (Fig. A.3b).

All three classes of lever are found within the human body; the fulcra are usually situated at the joints, the load may be body weight or some external resistance, with the force usually being produced by muscular effort. It is the complex arrangement of all three classes of lever within the human body that produce movement.

A *first class lever* is used in balancing weight and/or changing the direction of pull. There is usually no gain in mechanical advantage, e.g. when standing on the right lower limb the fulcrum is the right hip joint, the load being body weight to the left of the hip, while the force is provided by the contraction of the right gluteus medius and minimus muscles.

A *second class lever* (the principle on which weight is lifted in a wheelbarrow), gains mechanical advantage thereby allowing large loads to be moved, but with a loss of speed. Raising up onto the toes is a good example of such a system, the metatarsal heads act as the fulcrum, the weight of the body acting down through the tibia is the load while the calf muscles contract to produce the required force. The load arm is thus the distance from the tibia to the metatarsal heads, while the force arm is the distance between the attachment of the calf muscles to the calcaneus and the metatarsal heads.

A *third class lever* is the most commonly found within the body. It works at a mechanical disadvantage moving less weight but often at great speed. The biceps brachii acting across the elbow is a good example of this class of lever. The elbow is the fulcrum, the weight is the forearm and hand being supported; with the force being provided by biceps. In this example the load arm is the distance between the elbow and centre of mass of the forearm and hand, whereas the force arm is the distance between the elbow joint and the attachment of biceps.

All movements of the human body are dependent on the interaction of these three classes of lever. It is well to remember when studying the structure of the human body the relationship between the joints, the attachment of relevant muscles and the load to be moved. This will lead to an understanding of functional anatomy and with it human movement.

Fig. A.3 Levers: **a** = child's see-saw; **b** = classes of lever.

1

Components of the musculoskeletal system

Components of the musculoskeletal system

As this book is concerned essentially with the musculoskeletal system a brief account of the major tissues of the system, i.e. connective, skeletal and muscular tissue, and of the type of joints which enable varying degrees of movement to occur, is given below in the hope that it will aid in the understanding of the mobility and inherent stability of various segments. The initiation and coordination of movement is the responsibility of the nervous system; an account of the basic components of that system is reserved until the appropriate section.

CONNECTIVE TISSUE

Connective tissue is of mesodermal origin and in the adult has many forms, the character of the tissue depending on the organization of its constituent cells and fibres.

Fat

Fat is a packing and insulating material, however, in some circumstances it can act as a shock absorber, an important function as far as the musculoskeletal system is concerned. Under the heel, the buttock and the palm of the hand, the fat is divided into lobules by fibrous tissue septa thereby stiffening it for the demands made upon it.

Fibrous tissue

Fibrous tissue is of two types. In *white fibrous tissue* there is an abundance of collagen bundles, whereas in *yellow fibrous tissue* there is a preponderance of elastic fibres.

White fibrous tissue is dense thereby providing considerable strength without being rigid or elastic. It forms: (1) ligaments, which pass from one bone to another in the region of joints, uniting the bones and limiting joint movement; (2) tendons for attaching muscles to bones, and (3) protective membranes around muscle (*perimysium*), bone (*periosteum*) and many other structures.

Yellow fibrous tissue, on the other hand, is highly specialized, being capable of considerable deformation and yet returning to its original shape. It is found in the ligamenta flava associated with the vertebral column as well as in the walls of arteries.

SKELETAL TISSUE

Skeletal tissues are modified connective tissues, whereby the cells and fibres have a particular organization which becomes condensed so that the tissue is rigid.

Cartilage

Cartilage is supplementary to bone, being formed wherever strength, rigidity and some elasticity are required. In fetal development, cartilage is often a temporary tissue being later replaced by bone. However, in many places cartilage persists throughout life. Although a rigid tissue cartilage is not as hard or strong as bone. It is also relatively non-vascular being nourished by tissue fluids. A vascular invasion of cartilage often results in the death of the cells during the process of ossification of the cartilage and its eventual replacement by bone. Except for the articular cartilage of synovial joints, cartilage possesses a fibrous covering layer, the *perichondrium*.

There are three main types of cartilage: *hyaline cartilage*, *white fibrocartilage* and *yellow fibrocartilage*.

Hyaline cartilage

This forms the temporary skeleton of the fetus from which many bones develop. Its remnants can be seen as the articular cartilages of synovial joints, the epiphyseal growth plates between parts of an ossifying bone during growth, and the costal carti-lages of the ribs. At joint surfaces it provides a certain degree of elasticity to offset and absorb shocks, as well as providing a relatively smooth surface permitting free movement to occur.

With increasing age, hyaline cartilage tends to become calcified and sometimes ossified.

White fibrocartilage

White fibrocartilage contains bundles of white fibrous tissue which give it great tensile strength combined with some elasticity so that it is able to resist considerable pressure. It is found at many sites within the musculoskeletal system: (1) within the intervertebral discs between adjacent vertebrae; (2) in the menisci of the knee joint; (3) in the labrum deepening the glenoid fossa of the shoulder joint and the acetabulum of the hip joint; (4) in the articular discs of the wrist, sternoclavicular, acromioclavicular and temporomandibular joints, and (5) as the articular covering of bones which ossify in membrane, e.g. the clavicle and mandible.

White fibrocartilage may calcify and ossify.

Yellow fibrocartilage

Yellow fibrocartilage contains bundles of elastic fibres with little or no white fibrous tissue. It does not calcify or ossify, and is not found within the musculoskeletal system.

Bone

Bone is extremely hard with a certain amount of resilience. It is essentially an organic matrix of fibrous connective tissue impregnated with mineral salts. The connective tissue gives the bone its toughness and elasticity, while the mineral salts provide hardness and rigidity, the two being skillfully blended together. It must be remembered that the mineral component provides a ready store of calcium, which is continuously exchanged with that in body fluids, with the rate of exchange and overall balance of these mineral ions being influenced by several factors including hormones.

Each bone is enclosed in a dense layer of fibrous tissue, the *periosteum*, with its form and structure adapted to the function of support and the resistance of mechanical stresses. Being a living tissue, bone is continually being remodelled to meet these demands, this is particularly so during growth. The structure of any bone cannot be satisfactorily considered in isolation, for it is dependent upon its relationship to adjacent bones and the type of articulation between them, as well as the attachment of muscles, tendons and ligaments to it.

The internal architecture of bone reveals systems of *trabeculae* running in many directions (Fig. 1.1), arranged to resist compressive, tensile and shearing stresses. Surrounding these trabecular systems, which tend to be found at the ends of long bones, is a thin layer of condensed or compact bone (Fig. 1.1). The network of the trabeculae, because of its appearance, is known as *cancellous* or *spongy bone*. In the region of the shaft of a long bone is an outer, relatively thick ring of *compact bone* surrounding a cavity, which in life contains bone marrow.

Red and white blood cells are formed in red bone marrow, which after birth is the only source of red blood cells and the main source of white blood cells. In infants, the cavities of all of the bones contains red marrow. However, this gradually becomes replaced by yellow fat marrow, so that at puberty red marrow is only found in the cavities associated with cancellous bone. With increasing age many of these regions containing red marrow are replaced by yellow marrow. Nevertheless, red marrow tends to persist throughout life in the vertebrae, the ribs and sternum, and the proximal ends of the femur and humerus.

For descriptive purposes bones can be classified according to their shape:

1. *Long bones* are found within the limbs, and consist of a shaft (*diaphysis*) and two expanded ends (*epiphyses*).
2. *Short bones* are the bones of the wrist and part of the foot, the carpal and tarsal bones respectively.
3. *Flat bones* are thin and tend to be curved in spite of their classification; they include the bones of the skull vault and the ribs. Structurally, they consist of two layers of compact bone enclosing cancellous bone.
4. *Irregular bones* are those which fit none of the above categories, and include the vertebrae and many of the bones of the skull and face.

Both irregular and short bones consist of a thin layer of compact bone surrounding cancellous bone.

Bone development

Bone develops either directly in mesoderm by the deposition of mineral salts, or in a previously formed cartilage model. When the process of calcification and then ossification takes place without an intervening cartilage model, the process is known as *intramembranous ossification*, with the bone being referred to as *membrane bone*. However, if there is an intervening cartilage model, the process is known as *endochondral ossification*, with the bone being referred to as *cartilage bone*. This latter process is by far the most common.

Intramembranous ossification

The site of bone formation is initially indicated by a condensation of cells and collagen fibres accompanied by the laying down of organic bone matrix, which becomes impregnated with mineral salts. The formation of new bone continues in a similar manner to bone developed in cartilage (see p. 16). Intramembranous ossification occurs in certain bones of the skull, the mandible and the clavicle.

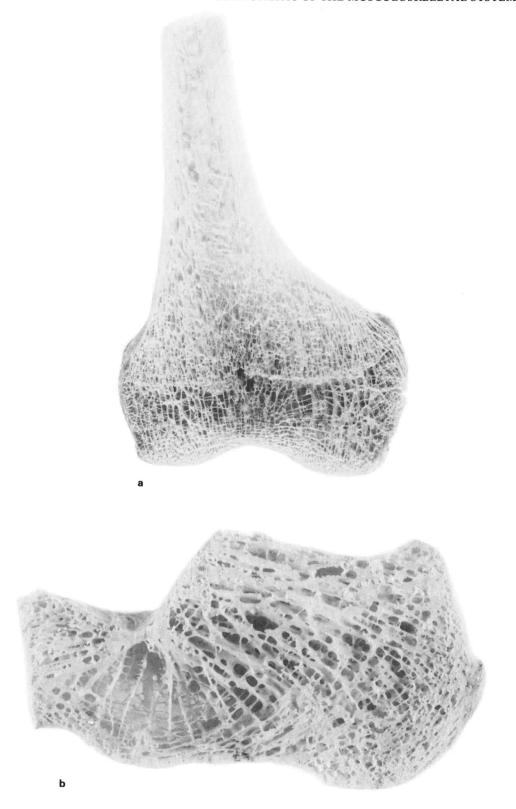

Fig. 1.1 Trabecular arrangement within bone: **a** = coronal section through the lower end of the femur; **b** = sagittal section through the calcanelus.

Endochondral ossification

Again the first step in the process is the accumulation of mesodermal cells in the region where the bone is to develop. A cartilage model of the future bone develops from these mesodermal cells (Fig. 1.2a). In long bones the cartilage model grows principally at its ends, so that the oldest part of the model is near the middle. As time progresses, the cartilage matrix in this older region is impregnated with lime salts so that it becomes calcified. Consequently the cartilage cells, being cut off from their nutrient supply, die. The greater part of the calcified cartilage is subsequently removed and bone is formed around its few remaining spicules (Fig. 1.2a). Ultimately, the continual process of excavation of calcified cartilage and laying down of bone leads to the complete removal of the calcified cartilage (Fig. 1.2a).

The cartilage at the ends of the bone continues to grow due to the multiplication of its cells. However the deeper layers gradually become calcified and replaced by bone. Therefore the increase in length of a long bone is due to active cartilage at its ends, while increases in width is by deposition of new bone on that already existing.

When first laid down, bone is cancellous in appearance, having no particular pattern of organization. It is referred to as woven bone. In the repair of fractures, the newly formed bone also has this woven appearance. However, in response to stresses applied to the bone by muscles, tendons, ligaments and the forces transmitted across joints, the woven bone gradually assumes a specific pattern in response to these stresses.

Growth and remodelling of bone

During growth there is an obvious change in the shape of the bone. However, it should be remembered that even in the adult, bone is being continuously remodelled, principally under the direct control of hormones to stabilize blood calcium levels, but also in response to long-term changes in the force patterns applied to the bone.

Both growth and remodelling depends on the balanced activity of two cell types, one of which removes bone tissue (osteoclasts) and the other which lays down new bone (osteoblasts). In a growing bone, for example, new bone is laid down around the circumference of the shaft in order to increase its diameter. At the same time the deepest layers of bone are being removed, thereby maintaining a reasonable thickness of cortical bone and enlarging the marrow cavity (Fig. 1.2b). Should the combined process of deposition and absorption fail to match, then either a very thick or a very thin shaft results.

Ossification centres

The regions where bone begins to be laid down are known as ossification centres. It is from these centres that the process of ossification spreads. The earliest, and usually the principal, centre of ossification in a bone is referred to as a *primary centre*. Primary centres of ossification appear at different times in different bones, but are relatively constant between individuals, and also appear in an orderly sequence. The majority of such centres appear between the seventh and twelfth week of intrauterine life. They are virtually all present before birth. In long bones, the primary ossification centre appears in the shaft of the bone (Fig. 1.2c).

Secondary ossification centres appear much later than primary ones, usually after birth, being formed in parts of the cartilage model into which ossification from the primary centre has not spread (Fig. 1.2c). All of the long bones in the body, and many others, have secondary ossification centres. The bone formed from these centres is almost entirely cancellous.

That part of a long bone which ossifies from the primary centre is called the *diaphysis*, while that from the secondary centre is called an *epiphysis*. The plate of cartilage between these two regions is where the diaphysis continues to grow in length. Consequently, it is referred to as the *epiphyseal growth plate* (Fig. 1.2c). When this growth plate disappears the diaphysis and epiphysis become fused and growth of the bone ceases.

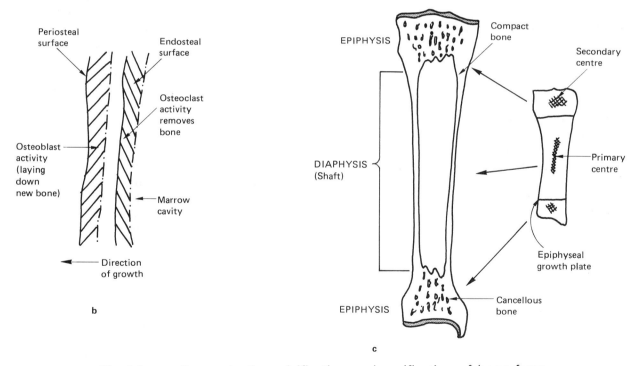

Fig. 1.2 **a** = Stages in the calcification and ossification of bone from a cartilage model. **b** = Schematic representation of osteoblast and osteoclast activity. **c** = Sites of ossification centres in long bones, and the parts of the bone each forms.

MUSCULAR TISSUE

Within the body there are three varieties of muscle: (1) *smooth muscle*, also referred to as involuntary or non-striated muscle; (2) *cardiac muscle*, and (3) *skeletal muscle*, also known as *voluntary* or *striated* muscle. Smooth muscle forms the muscular layer of the walls of blood vessels and of hollow organs such as the stomach. It is not under voluntary control, contracting slower and less powerfully than skeletal muscle. However, it is able to maintain its contraction longer. Cardiac muscle is also not under voluntary control, but although it exhibits striations it is considered to be different from skeletal muscle.

Skeletal muscle

Skeletal muscle constitutes over one-third of the total human body mass. It consists of non-branching striated muscle fibres, bound together by loose areolar tissue. Muscles have various forms; some are flat and sheet-like, some are short and thick, while others are long and slender. The length of a muscle, exclusive of tendons, is closely related to the distance through which it is required to contract. Experiment has shown that muscle fibres have the ability to shorten to almost half their resting length. Consequently, the arrangement of fibres within a muscle determines how much it can shorten when it contracts. Irrespective of muscle fibre arrangement, it has to be remembered that all movement is brought about by muscle shortening, with the consequent action of pulling across joints changing the relative positions of the bones involved.

Muscle forms

The arrangement of the individual fibres within a muscle can be in one of two ways only; either parallel or oblique to the line of pull of the whole muscle. When the fibres are parallel to the line of pull they are grouped in a discrete bundle giving a *fusiform muscle* (Fig. 1.3a) (e.g. biceps brachii) or spread as a broad, thin sheet (Fig. 1.3b), (e.g. external oblique of the abdomen). When contraction occurs it does so through the maximal distance allowed by the length of the muscle fibres. However, it is of limited power.

Muscles whose fibres are oblique to the line of pull cannot shorten to the same degree, but because of the increased number of fibres packed into the same unit area they are much more powerful. Such arrangements of fibres are known as *pennate*, of which there are three main patterns (Fig. 1.3c). In *unipennate muscles* the fibres attach to one side of the tendon only (e.g. flexor pollicis longus). *Bipennate muscles* have a central septum with the muscle fibres attaching to both sides of the septum and to its continuous central tendon (e.g. rectus femoris). Finally, some muscles possess several intermediate septa, each of which has associated with it a bipennate arrangement of fibres. The whole is known as a *multipennate muscle* (e.g. deltoid (Fig. 1.3c)).

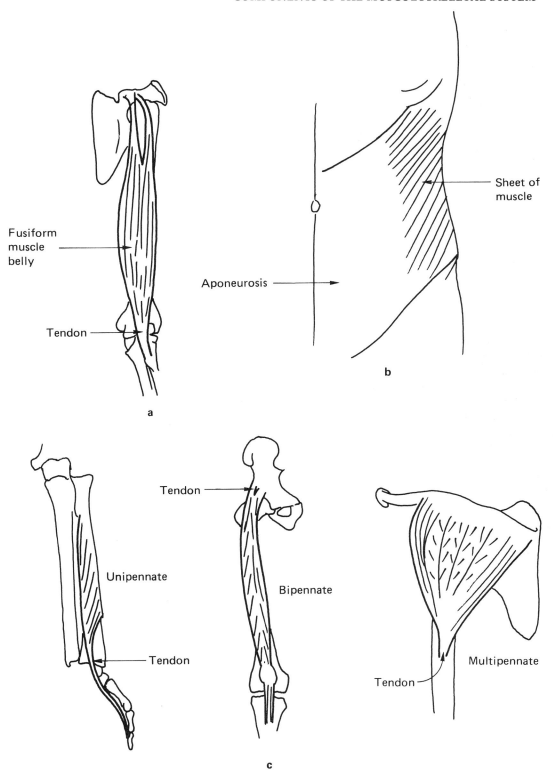

Fig. 1.3 Various arrangements of fibres within muscles:
    a = Fusiform.
    b = Sheets.
    c = Pennate.

Muscle structure (Fig. 1.4)

Muscle is composed of many individual fibres, each of which is a long, cylindrical, multinucleated cell of varying length and width. Each fibre has a delicate connective tissue covering, the *endomysium*, separating it from its neighbours, yet connecting them together. Bundles of parallel fibres are known as *fasciculi*, which in turn are bound together by a more dense connective tissue covering known as the *perimysium*. It is groups of fasciculi which are bound together to form whole muscles, being enclosed in a fibrous covering called the *epimysium*, which may be thick and strong or thin and relatively weak.

Muscle attachments

The attachment of a muscle to a bone or some other tissue is always indirect, being via the connective tissue elements of the muscle. Sometimes the perimysium and epimysium unite directly with the periosteum (outer covering) of bone or with joint capsules. Where this connective tissue element cannot readily be seen, the muscle is said to have a fleshy attachment. Such attachments leave no mark on the bone, although the area is often flattened or depressed. In many instances the connective tissue elements of the muscle fuse together forming an intervening tendon, which consists of bundles of collagen fibres. It must be remembered, however, that there is no direct continuity between the fibres of the muscle and those of the tendon. Tendons can take various forms, all of which are generally strong. They can be round cords, flattened bands or thin sheets of dense connective tissue. The latter is known as an *aponeurosis*. Attachments of pure tendon to bone nearly always leave a smooth mark, which may be raised or depressed. It is only when the attachment to bone is by a mixture of fleshy and tendinous fibres, or when the attachment is via a long aponeurosis, that the surface is roughened.

Where a muscle or tendon passes over and/or around the edge of a bone, sometimes using it to change direction, it is usually separated from the bone by a *bursa*, which serves to reduce friction between the structures during movement. Bursae are sac-like dilatations which may communicate directly with an adjacent joint cavity or they may exist independently; they contain a fluid similar to synovial fluid.

Fig. 1.4 The organization of individual muscle fibres into whole muscles, together with their investing connective layers.

When a tendon is subjected to friction it may develop in its substance a *sesamoid bone*. Sesamoid bones once formed have the general effect of increasing the lever arm of the muscle, as well as acting as pulleys thereby enabling a slight change in the direction of pull of the muscle, e.g. the patella (sesamoid bone) and the quadriceps tendon (Fig. 1.5a).

Because each end of a muscle attaches to different bones, observation of its principal action led to the designation of one end being the origin and the other the insertion; the insertion being to the bone which showed the freest movement. Such a designation is however misleading, since the muscle can, in certain circumstances, cause either of the two attachments to move relatively freely. The term *attachment* is therefore the preferred one to use.

Muscle action

When stimulated, a muscle contracts so as to bring its two ends closer together. If this is allowed to happen the muscle length obviously changes, although the tension generated usually remains approximately constant; such contractions are termed *isotonic*. If however, the length of the muscle remains unaltered (due to some externally applied force for example) then the tension it develops usually increases in an attempt to overcome the resistance; such contractions are termed *isometric*.

Isotonic contractions can be of two types, *concentric*, in which the muscle shortens, or *eccentric*, in which the muscle lengthens. Eccentric contraction is used in situations in which the muscle is being used to control the movement of a body segment against an applied force.

When a muscle, or group of muscles, contracts to produce a specific movement, it is termed a *prime mover*. Muscles which directly oppose this action are called *antagonists*. A further group of muscles which prevent unwanted movements associated with the action of the prime movers are known as *synergists*.

In all actions, a part (often the larger) of the muscle activity is directed across the joint, thereby stabilizing it by pulling the two articular surfaces together (Fig. 1.5b).

When testing the action of a muscle to determine whether it is weakened or paralysed, the subject is usually asked to perform the principal action of the muscle against resistance. However, this in itself may be insufficient to confirm the integrity of the muscle. The only infallible guide is to palpate over the muscle belly or its tendons to determine whether it is contracting during the manouevre.

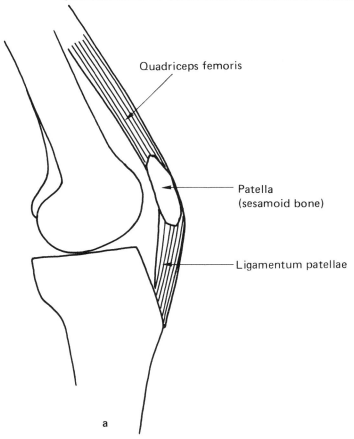

Quadriceps femoris

Patella
(sesamoid bone)

Ligamentum patellae

a

Stability
component of muscular
contraction

Direction of
muscle pull

Movement of distal bone

Movement component
of muscular contraction

b

Fig. 1.5   a = Arrangement of a sesamoid bone within a tendon.
b = The components of muscle action across a joint.

JOINTS

The bones of the body come together to form joints. It is through these articulations that movement occurs. However, the type and extent of the movement possible depends on the structure and function of the joint, these latter can, and do, vary considerably. Nevertheless, the variation that exists in the form and function of the various joints of the body allow them to be grouped into well-defined classes: *fibrous*, *cartilaginous* and *synovial*, with the degree of mobility gradually increasing from fibrous to synovial.

Fibrous joints

Fibrous joints are of three types: *suture*, *gomphosis* and *syndesmosis*.

Suture (Fig. 1.6a)

This is a form of fibrous joint that exists between the bones of the skull. They permit no movement as the edges of the articulating bones are often highly serrated, as well as being united by an intermediate layer of fibrous tissue. Either side of this fibrous tissue the inner and outer periosteal layers of the bones are continuous, and in fact constitute the main bond between them.

The sutures are not permanent joints, as they usually become partially obliterated when age increases beyond 30 years.

Gomphosis (Fig. 1.6b)

In this form of fibrous joint a peg fits into a socket, being held in place by a fibrous ligament or band; the roots of the teeth being held within their sockets in the maxilla and mandible are such examples.

Syndesmosis (Fig. 1.6c)

In a syndesmosis the uniting fibrous tissue is greater in amount than in a suture, forming a ligament or an interosseous membrane. Examples in the adult are the inferior tibiofibular joint where the two bones are joined together by an interosseous ligament, and the interosseous membrane between the radius and ulna. Flexibility of the membrane or twisting and stretching of the ligament permit movement at the joint. However, the movement allowed is restricted and controlled.

Cartilaginous joints

In cartilaginous joints the two bones are united by a continuous pad of cartilage. There are two types of such joint, *primary* and *secondary cartilaginous* (*synchondrosis* and *symphysis* respectively).

Primary cartilaginous (Fig. 1.7a)

Between the ends of the bone involved in the joint is a continuous layer of hyaline cartilage. These joints occur at the epiphyseal growth plates of growing and developing bone, and obviously become obliterated with fusion of the two parts (diaphysis and epiphysis). Because the plate of hyaline cartilage is relatively rigid, such joints exhibit no movement. However there is one such joint in the adult, which is slightly modified because, by virtue of its structure, it enables slight movement to occur. This is the first sternocostal joint.

Secondary cartilaginous (Fig. 1.7b)

These joints occur in the midline of the body and are slightly more specialized. Moreover, their structure enables a small amount of controlled movement to take place. Hyaline cartilage covers the articular surfaces of the bones involved in the joint, but interposed between these hyaline coverings is a pad of fibrocartilage. Examples are the joints between the bodies of adjacent vertebrae, where the fibrocartilaginous pad is in fact the intervertebral disc, and the joint between the two bodies of the pubic bones.

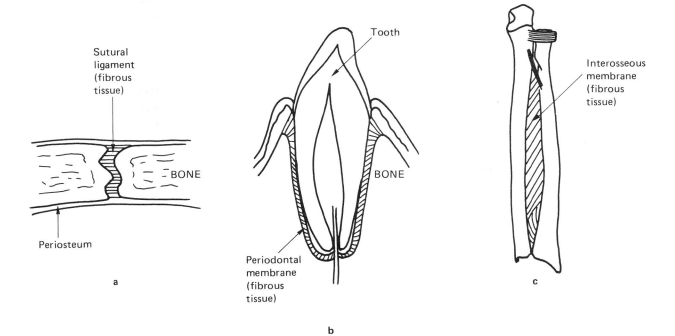

Fig. 1.6   Fibrous joints:
  a = Suture.
  b = Gomphosis.
  c = Syndesmosis.

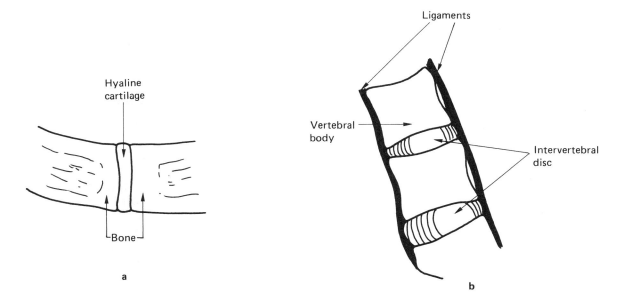

Fig. 1.7   Cartilaginous joints:
  a = Primary cartilaginous joint.
  b = Secondary cartilaginous joint.

Synovial joints

Synovial joints are a class of freely mobile joints, with movement being limited by muscles, ligaments and the associated joint capsules. The majority of the joints of the limbs are synovial. In synovial joints the articular surfaces of the bones involved are covered with articular (hyaline) cartilage, which because of its hardness and smoothness enable the bones to move against each other with minimum friction. Passing between the two bones, either attaching at or away from the articular margins, is a fibrous articular capsule. The capsule may be strengthened by the blending of ligaments or the deeper parts of muscles crossing the joint. Lining the deep surface of the capsule is the synovial membrane, which covers all the surfaces within the capsule except the articular cartilage (Fig. 1.8a). The synovial membrane secretes synovial fluid into the joint space (cavity) enclosed by the capsule, and serves to lubricate and nourish the articular cartilage as well as the opposing joint surfaces.

If the bones involved in the articulation originally ossified in membrane (see p. 14), then the articular cartilage has a large fibrous element. In addition there is enclosed within the capsule an intra-articular disc, which may not be complete (Fig. 1.8b).

Bursae are often associated with synovial joints, sometimes communicating directly with the joint space.

Because of the large number of synovial joints within the body and their differing forms they can be subdivided according to the shape of their articular surfaces and the movements possible at the joint.

Plane joint

The joint surfaces are flat, or at least relatively flat, and of approximately equal extent. The movement possible is of a single gliding type or a twisting of one bone against the other, usually within narrow limits. An example is the acromioclavicular joint.

Saddle joint

The two surfaces are reciprocally concavo-convex, as a rider sitting on a saddle. The principal movements possible at the joint occur about two mutually perpendicular axes. However, because of the nature of the joint surfaces there is usually a small amount of movement about a third axis. The best example in the body is the carpometacarpal joint of the thumb.

Hinge joint

The surfaces are so arranged to allow movement about one axis only. Consequently, the 'fit' of the two articular surfaces is usually good, but in addition the joint is supported by strong collateral ligaments. The elbow is a typical hinge joint. The knee joint is considered to be a modified hinge joint, as it permits some movement about a second axis. In this case the movement is possible because of the poor fit of the articular surfaces.

Pivot joint

Again movement occurs about a single axis, with the articular surfaces arranged so that one bone rotates within a fibro-osseous ring. The atlantoaxial joint is a good example of a pivot joint.

Ball and socket joint

As the name suggests the 'ball' of one bone fits into the 'socket' of the other. This type of joint allows movement about three principal mutually perpendicular axes. The hip joint is a ball and socket joint.

Condyloid joint

This is a modified form of a ball and socket joint, which only allows active movement to occur about two perpendicular axes. However, passive movement may occur about the third axis. The metacarpophalangeal joints are examples of such joints.

Ellipsoid joint

This is another form of a ball and socket joint, although in this case the surfaces are ellipsoid in nature. Consequently, movement only occurs about two perpendicular axes. The radiocarpal joint is an ellipsoid joint.

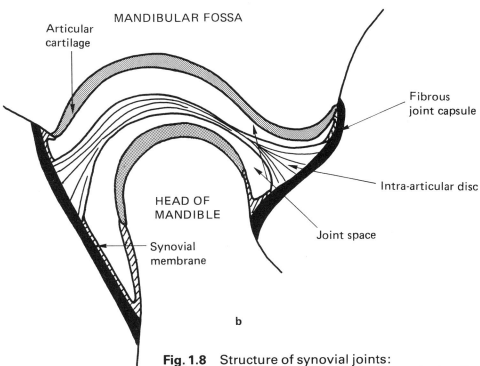

Fig. 1.8 Structure of synovial joints:
a = Without the presence of an intra-articular disc.
b = With the presence of an intra-articular disc.

2

Embryology

Embryology

STAGES IN DEVELOPMENT

The process of development begins with the penetration of the zona pellucida of the ovum (egg) by the head of the sperm—this is fertilization. It is this event which activates the ovum biochemically and leads, some 40 weeks later, to the birth of an infant. Between fertilization and birth, however, a series of complicated changes, involving both differentiation and reorganization, occur which gradually build up different tissues, organs and organ systems to create a viable individual. This account is intended as an introduction designed to help in the understanding of early human development. Unfortunately many new, and sometimes confusing, terms are used particularly when describing early development. These new terms are kept to a minimum.

Fertilization and cleavage

Fertilization usually occurs within the fallopian tubes, and it is not until some 6 days later that the resulting cell mass implants itself in the uterine wall. However, during this time considerable differentiation and organization has already taken place. Within 12 hours of fertilization the male and female pronuclei have met and fused near the centre of the ovum, forming a *zygote*. Within another 12 hours cleavage occurs; this consists of repeated mitotic divisions of the zygote (still within the zona pellucida) with the consequent formation of an increasing number of cells (now called *blastomeres*) without an increase in total cytoplasmic mass, which obviously becomes partitioned among the blastomeres. By the time there are 16 cells, i.e. after four divisions, the mass of cells is known as a *morula* (Fig. 2.1a).

The morula

Evidence from submammalian species suggests that the nuclei of individual cells come to lie in quantitatively and qualitatively different cytoplasmic environments, thus the initial circumstances of cellular differentia-

tion have been created. Furthermore, the blastomeres of the future inner cell mass are able to move with respect to one another. Consequently, the ground-work for the movements of gastrulation and the possibility of inductive cellular interaction, resulting from the acquisition of a new microenvironment by an individual cell, are established.

At the 16-cell stage, the morula enters the uterus and the process of compaction occurs, as a result of which individual blastomeres become less distinct. The cells on the outside of the morula become adherent to one another and a topographical difference is established between these surface cells and those inside. The outer cells, under the influence of the inner cell mass, form the *trophoectoderm* which eventually forms the *fetal membranes*. The inner cell mass forms the *embryonic cells*, and may also contribute to the *extra-embryonic membranes*.

The blastocyst

Some 4–6 days after fertilization the morula takes in uterine fluid, which passes through the zona pellucida, eventually forming a *blastocyst cavity* (Fig. 2.1b). This separates the inner cell mass from the trophoblast except in the region of the *polar trophoblast*, which overlies the inner cell mass (Fig. 2.1b). During blastocyst formation the zona pellucida thins and is eventually shed, exposing the cells. The polar trophoblast becomes adherent to the uterine wall and the process of implantation begins.

Implantation

During the early stages of implantation (6–8 days) the inner cell mass begins a process of differentiation which will eventually form the complete embryo. First, those cells facing the blastocyst cavity form a single layer of *primary embryonic endoderm*. The remaining cells form another layer which constitutes the precursor of the *embryonic ectoderm*,

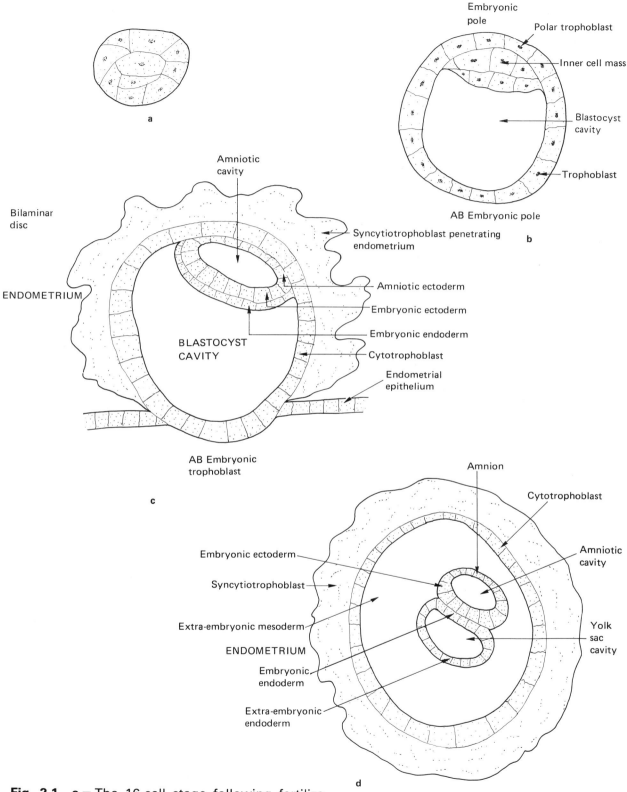

Fig. 2.1   **a** = The 16-cell stage following fertilization—the morula; **b** = the blastocyst; **c** = implantation; **d** = the appearance of the yolk sac.

also giving rise later to the *embryonic meso-derm* (see Fig. 2.1c). The *amniotic cavity* appears between these cells and an overlying layer of cells which form the *amniotic ecto-derm*, derived from the deep aspect of the polar trophoblast (see Fig. 2.1c). The trophoblast has formed the *cytotrophoblast* surrounding the *blastocyst cavity*, and the *syncytiotrophoblast* which penetrates the endometrial lining of the uterus (see Fig. 2.1c). Thus the inner cell mass, from which the cells of the future embryo arise, forms no more than a *bilaminar disc* while the remainder of the blastocyst forms the fetal membranes.

Development of the yolk sac

While the amniotic cavity is being formed, the blastocyst cavity becomes lined by cells of extra-embryonic endoderm. Consequently, the blastocyst wall now consists of three layers: an outer trophoblast (the extra-embryonic ectoderm), consisting of cyto-trophoblast and syncytiotrophoblast, a loose reticular layer of extra-embryonic mesoderm, and an inner cell layer of extra-embryonic endoderm. The space remaining is the *yolk sac* (see Fig. 2.1d).

Prochordal plate

In a localized area in the roof of the yolk sac the *prochordal plate* is formed. It occurs at the cranial end of the future embryo and gives the bilaminar disc bilateral symmetry. At the same time the extra-embryonic meso-derm begins to develop fluid-filled spaces, which join together forming a large cavity surrounding the whole of the yolk sac and the amnion, except for the mesodermal *con-necting stalk* (Fig. 2.2a). This space is the *extra-embryonic coelom*, which splits the extra-embryonic mesoderm into visceral and parietal layers and separates the amniotic and yolk cavities from the outer wall of the conceptus (Fig. 2.2a).

The primary germ layers

The primary germ layers as well as the supporting membranes have now been established. From the embryonic ectoderm the outer covering of the embryo is formed. This includes the outer layers of the skin and its derivatives (hair, nails); the mucous membrane of the cranial and caudal ends of the alimentary canal; the central and peripheral nervous systems, including the retina; and part of the iris of the eye. In general terms, the embryonic endoderm forms epithelial tissues in the adult; these being the epithelial lining of the alimentary canal, the parenchyma of its associated glands (liver, pancreas), the lining of the respiratory system, and most of the epithelium of the bladder and urethra.

About 15 days after fertilization, the trilaminar disc begins to form as a heaping up of cells in the upper layer of the bilaminar disc towards the posterior part of the midline, forming the *primitive streak* (Fig. 2.2b). The heaping up is due mainly to a medial and backward migration of actively proliferating ectodermal cells which spread laterally and forward between the ectoderm and endoderm layers as *intra-embryonic mesoderm* (Fig. 2.2c). At the lateral extremes of this migration, the mesodermal cells become continuous with the *extra-embryonic meso-derm* (splanchnopleuric) covering the yolk sac and that covering the amnion (somato-pleuric). Anteriorly, the embryonic meso-dermal cells become continuous across the midline in front of the prochordal plate.

Soon after the appearance of the primitive streak, which forms as a line on the surface, a further heaping of cells occurs at the anterior end. This is the *primitive knot* from which the notochordal process extends forwards to the posterior edge of the prochordal plate. The ectoderm overlying the notochordal process, as well as that immediately anterior to it, becomes thickened to form the *neural plate*, from which the neural tube, and eventually the brain and spinal cord, develop.

On either side of the notochord the meso-derm forms two longitudinal strips known as the *paraxial mesoderm* (Fig. 2.2d). Each of these becomes segmented forming approximately 44 blocks of mesoderm—these are the *somites*, none of which are formed anterior to the notochord. Lateral to the paraxial mesoderm is a thinner layer, the *lateral plate mesoderm*, which is continuous at its edges with the extra-embryonic mesoderm. Connecting the edge of the paraxial mesoderm to the lateral plate mesoderm is a longitudi-

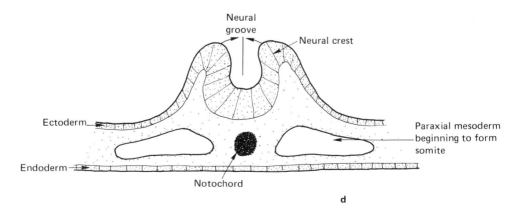

Fig. 2.2 **a** = Site of development of the prochordal plate; **b** = further development of the prochordal plate and appearance of the primitive streak; **c** = the trilaminar disc; **d** = formation of the neural groove.

nal tract, the *intermediate mesoderm*, from which arises the *nephrogenic cord*.

Within the lateral plate mesoderm small, fluid-filled spaces appear which join together to form the intra-embryonic mesoderm, continuous across the midline (Fig. 2.3a). The intra-embryonic mesoderm forms the pericardial (heart), pleural (lung) and peritoneal (abdominal) cavities.

During the fourth week following fertilization the trilaminar disc bulges further into the amniotic cavity. Under the cranial and caudal parts of the disc a head and tail fold appear, at the same time marked folding occurs along the lateral margins of the embryo (Fig. 2.3b).

As the theme of this book is movement, the remaining part of this section is concerned only with the development of the musculoskeletal system.

DEVELOPMENT OF THE MUSCULOSKELETAL SYSTEM

Mesodermal somites

By the end of the third week following fertilization the paraxial mesoderm begins to become divided up into *mesodermal somites* which are easily recognizable during the fourth and fifth weeks (Fig. 2.3c). Eventually some 44 pairs of somites develop, although not all are present at the same time, however the paraxial mesoderm at the cranial end of the embryo remains unsegmented. There are 4 occipital somites, followed by 8 cervical, 12 thoracic, 5 lumbar, 5 sacral and 8–10 coccygeal somites. The growth and migration of these somitic cells is responsible for the thickening of the body wall that occurs, as well as the development of bone and muscle. The deeper layers of the skin are also of somitic origin. Somite-derived tissue spreads medially to form the vertebrae, dorsally to form the musculature of the back, and ventrally into the body wall to form the ribs, and the intercostal and abdominal muscles.

Soon after its formation each somite becomes differentiated into three parts. The ventromedial part forms the *sclerotome*, which migrates medially towards the noto-

chord and neural tube to take part in the formation of the vertebrae and ribs (Fig. 2.3b). The remainder of the somite is known as the *dermomyotome*. The cells of the dorsal and ventral edges proliferate and move medially to form the *myotome*, whose cells migrate widely and become differentiated into myoblasts (primitive muscle cells). The thin layer of remaining cells form the *dermatome* which spreads out to form the dermis of the skin.

The myotome of each somite receives a single spinal nerve which innervates all the muscle derived from that myotome, no matter how far it eventually migrates. The dorsal aortae lie adjacent to the somites and give off a series of intersegmental arteries which lie between them.

Development of the limbs

The limbs make their appearance as flipper-like projections (the limb buds), with the fore-limbs appearing first, between 24 and 26 days, each bud consisting of a mass of mesenchyme covered by ectoderm with a thickened ectodermal ridge at the tip. It is the ectodermal ridge which controls the normal development of the limb. Consequently, damage to it will result in some trauma to the limb. At the beginning of the second month the elbow and knee prominences can be seen projecting laterally and backwards. At about the same time, the hand and foot plates appear as flattened expansions at the end of the limb bud. Between 36 and 38 days, five radiating thickenings forming the fingers and toes can be distinguished. The webs between the thickenings disappear freeing the digits. Appropriate spinal nerves grow down to the limbs; C5, 6, 7, 8 and T1 for the upper limb, and L4, 5, S1, 2 and 3 for the lower limb. Bones differentiate from the mesenchyme of the bud. The limbs grow in such a way that they rotate in opposite directions, the upper limb laterally and the lower limb medially. Consequently, the thumb becomes the lateral digit of the hand and the great toe the medial digit of the foot.

Development of the vertebrae

The sclerotomes come to surround the noto-

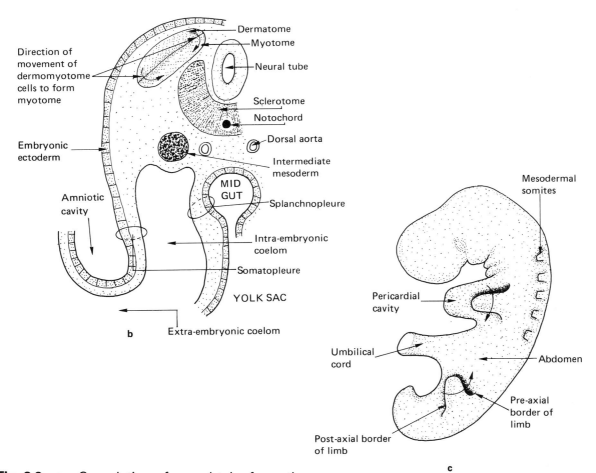

Fig. 2.3 **a** = Completion of neural tube formation, appearance of paraxial mesoderm (somite) and intermediate mesoderm; **b** = differentiation and migration of the somite mesoderm; **c** = portion of somites in embryo, also showing limb buds and the direction in which they will rotate.

chord, followed by the myotomes. Each vertebra is formed from the two adjacent parts of the sclerotome (Fig. 2.4), with the intervening part forming the outer part (*annulus fibrosus*) of the intervertebral disc. The *nucleus pulposus* of the disc is derived from the

notochord. As there are eight cervical somites, there are also eight cervical nerves, similarly in the thoracic, lumbar and sacral regions. However, because each vertebra is formed from adjacent somites the cervical nerves come to lie above their correspond-

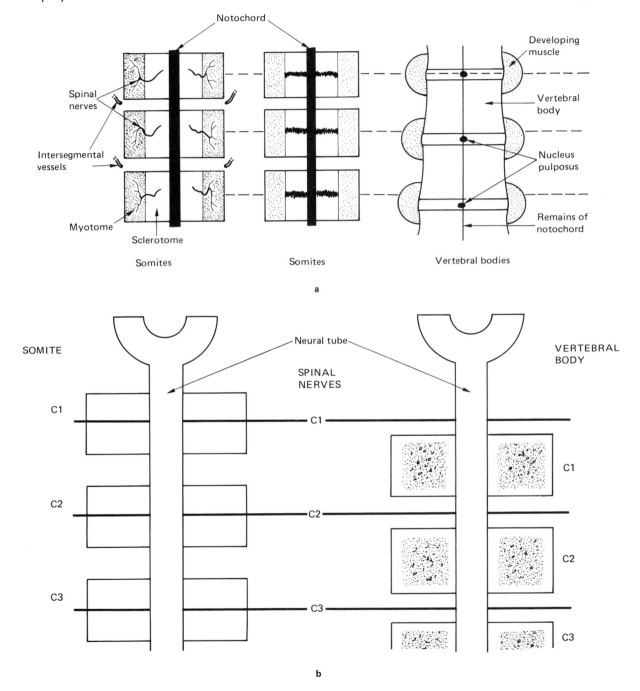

Fig. 2.4   **a** = Development of the vertebrae from the sclerotome component of the somite; **b** = the relationship of spinal nerves to the vertebrae.

ingly numbered vertebrae, with the eighth cervical nerve lying below the seventh cervical vertebra. The thoracic, lumbar and sacral spinal nerves all lie below their correspondingly numbered vertebrae.

The dermomyotome breaks up with cells moving both ventrally and dorsally. The original spinal nerve supplying the myotome divides into an anterior and posterior primary ramus supplying the ventral part of the myotome (the *hypomere*) and the dorsal part (the *epimere*) respectively. The epimeres come to lie between the transverse and spinous processes giving rise to the musculature of the trunk and neck. The hypomeres give rise to the prevertebral muscles (the scalenes, quadratus lumborum, psoas and piriformis) and the musculature of the thoracic and abdominal walls.

The occipital myotomes do not participate in the formation of the musculature of the trunk or neck. They give rise to the muscle mass of the tongue. That part of the paraxial mesoderm that does not become segmented eventually becomes incorporated into the branchial arches, each of which is innervated by a cranial nerve. The musculature derived from these arches form the muscles of the face, those around the mandible and those of the larynx and pharynx.

SUMMARY OF THE STAGES IN DEVELOPMENT

This is given in Table 2.1 below.

Table 2.1   A summary of development

Time from ovulation	Event
Within 24 hours	Fertilization
72 hours	Passage of conceptus through isthmus of fallopian tubes
80 hours	Entry of conceptus into uterus
4–6 days	Blastocyst formation
7 days	Implantation
9–13 days	Bilaminar embryonic disc
14–15 days	Beginning of primitive streak; appearance of extra-embryonic coelom
16 days	Beginning of notochord process
17–18 days	Neural plate appears
19–20 days	Intra-embryonic coelom begins to appear
20–30 days	Formation of somites
24 days	Head, tail and lateral body folds have established basic embryonic shape
24–26 days	Limb buds appear
5 weeks	Hands and feet begin to develop
8 weeks	Primary ossification centres appear in long bones
12 weeks	Formation of definitive body wall complete
3 months	Nails appear
4 months	Hair (lanugo) appears
5 months	Whitish slippery coating (vernix caseosa) begins to develop—probably makes skin more waterproof
7 months	Scalp and eyebrow hair develops
Birth	Vertebrae in three parts (centrum and two neural arches); nails have grown to end of digits; shafts of long bones completely ossified; secondary ossification beginning to appear (distal end femur, proximal end tibia)

3

Skin and its appendages

Skin and its appendages

INTRODUCTION

The skin is a tough, pliable waterproof covering of the body, blending with the more delicate lining membranes of the body at the mouth, nose, eyelids, urogenital, and anal openings. It is the largest single organ in the body. Not only does it provide a surface covering, it is also a sensory organ endowed with a host of nerve endings which provide sensitivity to touch and pressure, changes in temperature and painful stimuli. As far as general sensations are concerned, the skin is their principal source. The waterproofing function of the skin is essentially concerned with the prevention of fluid loss from the body. To this end, fatty secretions from the sebaceous glands help to maintain this waterproofing, as well as being acted upon to produce vitamin D. However, the efficient waterproofing mechanism does not prevent the skin having an absorptive function when certain drugs, vitamins and hormones are applied to it in a suitable form. Nor does it prevent the excretion of certain crystalloids through sweating. (If sweating is copious as much as 1 g of non-protein nitrogen may be eliminated in an hour.) Because human beings are warmblooded, the body temperature must be kept within relatively narrow limits despite enormous variations in environmental temperature. Reduction of body temperature is a special function of the skin because of the variability in its blood supply and the presence of sweat glands. Heat is lost through radiation, convection and evaporation. Together with the lungs, the skin accounts for over 90% of total heat loss from the body. As well as the ability of the blood vessels to 'open up' to promote heat loss, they can also be 'closed down' in an attempt to conserve body heat in cool environments.

The metabolic functions of the skin require a large surface area for effective functioning. In an adult, this area is approximately $1.8\,m^2$, being seven times greater than at birth. Skin thickness also varies, not only with age but also from region to region. It is thinnest over the eyelids (0.5 mm) and thickest over the back of the neck and upper trunk, the palm of the hand and the sole of the foot. It generally tends to be thicker over posterior and extensor surfaces, than over anterior and flexor surfaces, being between 1 and 2 mm thick for the most part.

The total thickness of the skin depends on the thickness of both the epidermis and the dermis. On the palms of the hands and soles of the feet the epidermis is responsible for the thickness of the skin, the dermis being relatively thin. This arrangement provides protection for the underlying dermis, as these are regions of great wear and tear. The character of flexor and extensor skin differs in more respects than just thickness. The extensor skin of the limbs tends to be more hairy than the flexor skin, while the flexor skin is usually far more sensitive in that it has a rich nerve supply.

The skin is loosely applied to underlying tissues so that it is easily displaced. However, in some regions it may be firmly attached to the underlying structures, e.g. the cartilage of the ear and nose, the subcutaneous periosteal surface of the tibia, and the deep fascia surrounding joints. In response to continued friction, skin reacts by increasing the thickness of its superficial layers. When wounded it responds by increased growth and repair.

The skin of young individuals is extremely elastic, rapidly returning to its original shape and position. However, this elasticity is increasingly lost with age so that unless it is firmly attached to the underlying tissues it stretches. The stretching tends to occur in one direction because of the orientation of the collagen in the deeper layers, which runs predominantly at right angles to the direction of stretch, being therefore parallel to the communicating grooves present on the skin surface. In some places the skin must be bound down to the underlying deep fascia to allow freedom of movement without interference from subcutaneous fat and otherwise highly mobile skin. For example, at flexion creases of joints the skin is bound down to the underlying fibrous tissue. Where the skin has to be pulled around a joint when it is flexed, it is bound down in loose folds which are taken up in flexion. The joints of the fingers clearly show this arrangement.

In adjusting to allow movement, the skin follows the contours of the body. Although this is enabled by its intrinsic elasticity the skin is nevertheless subjected to internal stresses, which vary from region to region. These stress lines are often referred to as Langer's lines or cleavage lines (Fig. 3.1). They are important because incisions along these lines heal with a minimum of scar, whereas in wounds across them the scar may become thicker, with the possible risk of scar contraction, because the wound edges are being pulled apart by the internal stresses of the skin. Langer's lines do not always correspond with the stress lines of life, they merely reflect the stresses within the skin at rest.

The colour of the skin depends on the presence of pigment (melanin) and the vascularity of the dermis. When hot the skin appears reddened due to the reflection of large quantities of blood through the epidermis. Similarly when cold the skin appears paler due to the reduction of blood flow to it. The degree of oxygenation of the blood also influences skin colour; anaemic individuals generally appear pale. Individual and racial variations in skin colour is dependent upon the presence of melanin in the deepest layers of the epidermis. In darker skinned races, the melanin is distributed throughout the layers of the epidermis. In response to sunlight and heat the skin increases its degree of pigmentation, thereby making it appear darker. This physiological increase in pigment formation, i.e. tanning from exposure to sunlight, is widely sought after in caucasian populations. Some areas of the body show a constant deeper pigmentation, these being the external genital regions, the perianal region, the axilla and the areola of the breast.

On the pads of the fingers and toes, and extending over the palm of the hand and sole of the foot are a series of alternating ridges and depressions. The arrangement of these ridges and depressions are highly individual, so much so that even identical twins have different patterns. It is this patterning which forms the basis for identification through finger prints. They are due to the specific arrangement of the large dermal papillae under the epidermis. They act to improve the grip and prevent slippage. Along the summits of these ridges sweat glands open. Sebaceous glands and hair are absent on these surfaces.

Fig. 3.1 Cleavage line orientation.

The skin and subcutaneous tissues camouflage the deeper structures of the body. Nevertheless, it is often necessary to identify and manipulate these deeper structures through the skin, and also to test their function, effectiveness and efficiency. To do this the examiner relies heavily on sensory information provided by his or her own skin, particularly that of the digits and hands. Indeed, the skin of this region is so richly endowed with sensory nerve endings that it allows objects to be identified by touch alone, culminating in the ability of the blind to read with their fingers.

As well as all of the functions of skin referred to above, nails, hair, sebaceous and sweat glands are all derived from the epidermis. The delicate creases extending in all directions across the skin form irregular diamond-shaped regions. It is at the intersections of these creases that hairs typically emerge.

STRUCTURE

The skin consists of a superficial layer of ectodermal origin known as the *epidermis*, and a deeper mesodermal-derived layer known as the *dermis* (Fig. 3.2a).

Epidermis

The epidermis is a layer of stratified squamous epithelium of varying thickness (0.3–1.0 mm), being composed of many layers of cells. The deeper cells are living and actively proliferating, with the cells produced gradually passing toward the surface. As they do so they become cornified (*keratinized*). They are ultimately shed as the skin rubs against the clothing and other surfaces. The epidermis is avascular but is penetrated by sensory nerve endings. Its deep surface is firmly locked to the underlying dermis by projections into it known as *epidermal pegs*, with the reciprocal projections from the dermis being known as *dermal papillae* (Fig. 3.2a).

It is usually convenient to consider the epidermis as being divided into a number of layers, particularly in the so-called thick skin of the palm or sole of the foot. These layers are from within outwards known as the *stratum basale, stratum spinosum, stratum granulosum, stratum lucidum* and finally the *stratum corneum* (Fig. 3.2a).

The stratum basale consists of a single layer of cells adjacent to the dermis. It is in this layer, as well as in the stratum spinosum that new cells are produced to replace those lost from the surface. The stratum spinosum itself consists of several layers of irregularly shaped cells, which become flattened as they approach the stratum granulosum. The stratum basale and stratum spinosum together are often referred to as the germinal zone, because of their role in new cell production.

Collectively, the remaining layers of the epidermis (granulosum, lucidum and corneum) are often referred to as the horny layer. In the stratum granulosum the cells become increasingly flattened and the process of keratinization begins. The cells in this layer are in the process of dying. A relatively thin transparent layer (the stratum lucidum) lies between the granulosum and the superficial stratum corneum. It is this latter layer from which the cells are shed, and also which is mainly responsible for the thickness of the skin.

The *epidermal melanocytes*, which are responsible for the pigmentation of the skin, lie within the deepest layers of the epidermis.

Dermis

The dermis is the deeper interlacing feltwork of collagen and elastic fibres, which generally comprises the greater part of total skin thickness. It can be divided into a superficial finely-textured *papillary layer*, which, although clearly separated from it, interdigitates with the epidermis, and a deeper coarser *reticular layer*, which gradually blends into the underlying subcutaneous connective tissue.

The projecting dermal papillae usually contain capillary networks which bring the blood into close association with the epidermis (Fig. 3.2a). The ability to open up or close down these networks is responsible for the regulation of heat loss through the skin, as well as causing the individual to

Duct of sweat gland

Stratum corneum

Stratum lucidum
Stratum granulosum
Stratum spinosum
Stratum basale

Dermis

Capillary loops
in dermal ridge

Dermal papillae

Meissner's corpuscle

a

EPIDERMIS

Tactile corpuscle

DERMIS

Subcutaneous
papilla

Sweat gland

SUBCUTANEOUS
CONNECTIVE
TISSUE

b

Free nerve
endings

Dermal papilla

Hair

Sebaceous gland

Blood vessel

Arrector pili
muscle

Hair follicle

Hair papilla

Blood vessel

Pacinian corpuscle

Nerve bundle

Fig. 3.2 **a** = Arrangement of the epidermal and dermal layers of the skin. **b** = Three-dimensional representation of the skin and subcutaneous connective tissue layer showing the arrangement of hair, glands and blood vessels.

blush in moments of embarrassment. Some of the papillae contain tactile receptors, these obviously being more numerous in regions of high tactile sensitivity (e.g. fingers, lips) and less so in other regions (e.g. back).

The reticular layer of dermis consists of a dense mass of interweaving collagen and elastic connective tissue fibres. It is this layer which gives the skin its toughness and strength. The tissue fibres run in all directions, but are generally tangential to the surface. However, there is a predominant orientation of fibre bundles, with respect to the skin surface, which varies in different regions of the body. It is this orientation which gives rise to the cleavage lines of the skin (see Fig. 3.1).

The dermis contains the numerous blood vessels and lymphatic channels, nerves and sensory nerve endings as well as a small amount of fat. In addition to these it also contains hair follicles, sweat and sebaceous glands, and smooth muscle (*arrectores pilorum*). The deep surface of the dermis is invaginated by projections of subcutaneous connective tissue, which serve partly for the entrance of the nerves and blood vessels into the skin (see Fig. 3.2b).

Subcutaneous connective tissue

This is a layer of loosely arranged connective tissue containing fat and some elastic fibres. The amount of subcutaneous fat varies in different parts of the body, being completely absent in only a few regions (eyelid, scrotum, penis, nipple and areola). The distribution of subcutaneous fat also differs between men and women, constituting a secondary sexual characteristic in women, e.g. the breast as well as the rounded contour of the hips. The subcutaneous connective tissue contains blood and lymph vessels, the roots of hair follicles, the secretory parts of sweat glands, cutaneous nerves, and sensory endings (particularly *Pacinian (pressure) corpuscles*) (see Figs. 3.2b, 3.5).

In the subcutaneous tissue overlying joints, subcutaneous bursae exist, which contain a small amount of fluid, and thereby facilitate movement of the skin in these regions.

APPENDAGES OF THE SKIN

These are nails, hairs, sebaceous, sweat and mammary glands, and are all derived from the epidermis.

Nails (Fig. 3.3)

The nail consists of an approximately rectangular plate of horny tissue found on the dorsum of the terminal phalanx of the fingers, thumb and the toes. They are a special modification of the two most superficial layers of the epidermis, particularly the stratum lucidum. Its transparency allows the pinkness of the underlying highly vascular nail bed to show through. The nail is partly surrounded by a fold of skin, the nail wall, and is firmly adherent to the underlying nail bed with some fibres ending in the periosteum of the distal phalanx. It is this firm attachment which enables the nails to be used for scratching and as instruments for prizing open various objects.

The distal end of the nail is free, while the proximal covered part constitutes the nail root. There is an abundant supply of sensory nerve endings and blood vessels to the nail bed. The nails grow at approximately 1 mm per week, being faster in summer than in winter.

Hairs (see Fig. 3.2b)

Hairs are widely distributed over the body surface, notable exceptions being the palm of the hand and the sole of the foot. Hairs vary as to their thickness and length. Most of them are extremely fine so that the skin may appear hairless. There is a marked sexual difference in the distribution of coarse hair, particulary on the face and trunk, and in its loss from the scalp. This coarse hair tends to become more prominent after puberty, particulary in the axilla, over the pubes, and on the face in males.

Except for the eyelashes, all hairs emerge obliquely from the skin surface, with the hairs in any one region doing so in the same direction. The part of the hair which projects from the skin surface is the shaft, with that part under the skin being the root, which is ensheathed in a sleeve of epidermis

Superior aspect

Lateral aspect

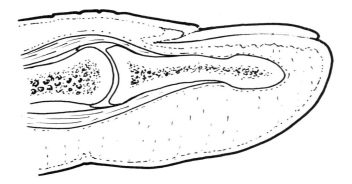

Fig. 3.3   Nails.

known as the *follicle* extending into the subcutaneous tissue. The shaft appears circular in cross-section. Throughout most of its length the hair consists of the keratinized remains of cells. Hair colour is due to pigment in the hair cells (melanin and a subtle red pigment), and to air within the shaft of the hair. The hair of the head has a life of between 2 and 4 years, but that of the eylashes is only 3 to 5 months. All hairs are intermittently shed and replaced.

In the growing hair, the deepest part of the hair follicle expands to form a cap, known as the bulb of the hair, which almost completely surrounds some loose, vascular connective tissue, known as the papilla. The cells of the follicle around the papilla proliferate to form the various layers of the hair. In the resting hair follicle the bulb and papilla shrink, with the deepest part of the follicle being irregular in shape.

Associated with each hair are one or more sebaceous glands, which lie in the angle between the slanting hair follicle and the skin surface with their ducts opening into the neck of the follicle. Bundles of smooth muscle fibres (the arrectores pilorum) attach to the sheath of the hair follicle, deep to the sebaceous gland, and pass to the papillary layers of the dermis on the side towards which the hair slopes (see Fig. 3.2b). Contraction of the muscle causes the hair to stand away from the skin, elevating the skin around the opening of the hair follicles thereby producing 'goose flesh'. This action also compresses the sebaceous glands causing them to empty their secretions onto the skin surface. Elevation of the hairs traps a layer of air against the skin surface in an attempt to produce an insulating layer to reduce heat loss, while the sebaceous secretions are important in 'waterproofing' the skin surface and in aiding the absorption of fat-soluble substances through the skin.

GLANDS

Sebaceous glands

These are associated with all hairs and hair follicles, there being between one and four associated with each hair. They may also exist where there is no hair, such as the corner of the mouth and adjacent mucosa, the lips, the areola and the nipple, opening directly onto the skin surface. However, they are absent from the skin of the palm and sole and the dorsum of the distal segments of the digits. The glands vary in size between 0.2 and 2.0 mm in diameter. The cells of the glands are continuously destroyed in the production of the oily secretions, known as sebum. This mode of secretion production is known as *holocrine secretion*.

Inflammation and accumulation of secretion within the sebaceous glands gives rise to acne. If plugging of the outlet is permanent, a sebaceous cyst may be formed in the duct and follicles. These may become so enlarged that they require surgical removal. Sebaceous glands do not appear to be under nervous control.

Sweat glands

These have a wide distribution throughout the body (Fig. 3.4), being more numerous on its exposed parts, especially on the palms, soles and flexor surfaces of the digits. Here the ducts open onto the summits of the epidermal ridges. Each gland has a long tube extending into the subcutaneous tissue, where it becomes coiled forming the secretory body of the gland (see Fig. 3.2b). The glands produce sweat, which is a clear fluid without any cellular elements, for secretion (*eccrine secretion*). The production of sweat is important in temperature regulation, as its evaporation from the skin surface promotes heat loss. These eccrine sweat glands are innervated by sympathetic nerves. Consequently, any disturbance in the sympathetic system will result in a dry warm skin (anhydrosis) either locally or extensively.

In the axilla, groin and around the anus there are large modified sweat glands, being between 3 and 5 mm in diameter and lying deeply in the subcutaneous layer. Their ducts may be associated with a hair follicle or they may open directly onto the skin surface. The secretions of the glands include some disintegration products of the gland cells (*apocrine secretions*). The odour associ-

Sweat glands

Eccrine   Apocrine

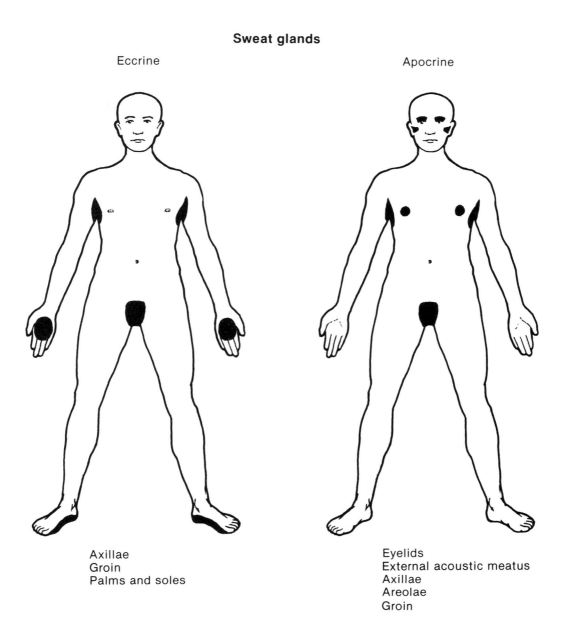

Axillae   Eyelids
Groin   External acoustic meatus
Palms and soles   Axillae
                                 Areolae
                                 Groin

Fig. 3.4   The distribution of eccrine and apocrine sweat glands.

ated with these glands is not from the secretion itself, but is due to bacterial invasion and contamination from the skin. Pigment granules associated with axillary glands produce a slight colouration of the secretion. The apocrine glands vary with sexual development, enlarging at puberty. In females they show cyclical changes associated with the menstrual cycle.

The glands which open at the margins of the eyelid (*ciliary glands*) are modified, uncoiled sweat glands, as are the glands of the external auditory meatus (*ceruminous glands*). The cells of these latter glands contain a yellowish pigment which colours the wax secretion (*cerumin*).

Mammary gland (breast)

The mammary glands are modified sweat glands, being accessory to the reproductive function in females, secreting milk (lactation) for the nourishment of the infant. In children prior to puberty and the adult male, the glands are rudimentary and functionless.

BLOOD SUPPLY AND LYMPHATIC DRAINAGE OF THE SKIN

The arterial supply of the skin is derived from vessels in the subcutaneous connective tissue layer, which form a network at the boundary between the dermis and subcutaneous tissue (see Fig. 3.2b). Branches from the network supply the fat, sweat glands and deep parts of the hair follicles. Branches within the dermis form a subpapillary plexus. The epidermis is avascular. Abundant arteriovenous anastomoses occur within the skin. Lymphatics of the skin begin in the dermal papillae as networks or blind outgrowths which form a dense mesh of lymphatic capillaries in the papillary layer. Larger lymphatic vessels pass deeply to the boundary between dermis and subcutaneous tissue to accompany the arteries as they pass centrally.

NERVES OF THE SKIN

The nerves of the skin are of two types, afferent somatic fibres mediating pain, touch, pressure, heat and cold (general sensations), and efferent autonomic (sympathetic) fibres supplying blood vessels, arrectores pilorum and sweat glands. The sensory (afferent) endings have several forms. Free nerve endings extend between cells of the basal layer of the epidermis, terminating around and adjacent to hair follicles. They are receptive to general tactile sensation as well as painful stimuli. Enclosed tactile corpuscles lie in the dermal papillae, being sensitive to touch. Pacinian corpuscles (Fig. 3.5) exist in the subcutaneous tissue, being particularly plentiful along the sides of the digits, and act as pressure receptors. Specific endings for heat and cold have been described, although general agreement as to their identity has not been reached. Details of all of the above receptors are given on pp. 858–860.

APPLICATION

The majority of physiotherapy techniques are applied either directly or indirectly via the patient's skin. Manual manipulations, such as massage manipulations, and thermal treatments both have an effect on the skin. The skin provides an extremely important barrier as it restricts the penetration of damaging electromagnetic radiations in the ultraviolet spectrum. All but the very longest ultraviolet wavelengths are absorbed by the skin, and if sufficiently high levels of ultraviolet have been absorbed then the characteristic effects of erythema, thickening of the epidermis, increased pigmentation and finally peeling will all be seen.

The general dryness and natural greasiness of the skin surface means that it has a high electrical resistance. Consequently, if electrical currents are to be applied directly to body tissues this resistance must be reduced. This is usually successfully achieved by the application of moist pads or conducting gels to the skin below the site of electrode attachment.

Free nerve endings

Hair follicle afferents

Merkel's discs

Meissner's corpuscle

Krause's end bulb

Ruffini's corpuscle

Fig. 3.5   Types of receptors found in skin.

Pacinian corpuscle

4

The upper limb

The upper limb

INTRODUCTION

The human upper limb has almost no locomotor function. It is instead an organ for grasping and manipulating. With the evolutionary adaptation of bipedalism the upper limb acquired a great degree of freedom of movement. During this adaptation, however, the upper limb has still retained its ability to act as a locomotor prop, as when grasping an immobile object and pulling the body towards the hand. Alternatively, the upper limb may be used in conjunction with a walking aid to support the body during gait. Nevertheless, the bones of the upper limb are not as robust as their counterparts in the lower limb.

The upper limb is attached to the trunk by the pectoral girdle, which consists of the scapula and the clavicle. The only point of articulation with the axial skeleton is at the sternoclavicular joint. The scapula rides in a sea of muscles attaching it to the head, neck and thorax, while the clavicle acts as a strut holding the upper limb away from the trunk. Between the trunk and the hand are a series of highly mobile joints and a system of levers. These enable the hand to be brought to any point in space and to hold it there steadily and securely while it performs its task. However, it is the development of the hand as a sensitive instrument of precision, power and delicacy which is the acme of human evolution. The importance of the opposability of the thumb in providing effective grasping and manipulating skills makes the hand the most efficient tool in the animal kingdom. In grasping, the thumb is equal in value to the other four digits; loss of the thumb is as disabling as the loss of all four fingers. For these skills the hand has a rich motor and sensory nerve supply. It is no coincidence that the hand has large representations in both the motor and sensory regions of the cerebral cortex. The adoption of a bipedal gait during human evolution freed the upper limbs for functions other than locomotion, this is one of the reasons why the brain developed and enlarged to its present form. Not to be overlooked in the functional effectiveness of the hand is the important contribution made by the extensive vascular network in supporting its metabolic requirements.

As the upper limb is also used for carrying loads and supporting the body, the question arises as to how these forces are transmitted to the axial skeleton. The usual means is by tension developed in the muscles and ligaments crossing the various joints. In addition, because the upper limb itself is heavy, every movement that it makes has to be accompanied by postural contractions of the muscles of the trunk and lower limb to compensate for shifts in the body's centre of gravity.

During development the upper limb bud appears as a swelling from the body wall at about 4 weeks (Fig. 4.1a). It develops at the level of the lower cervical and first thoracic segments. At first the limb buds project at right angles to the surface of the body, having ventral and dorsal surfaces and cephalic (preaxial) and caudal (postaxial) borders (Fig. 4.1b). As the limb increases in length it becomes differentiated during which time it is folded ventrally so that the ventral surface becomes medial (Fig. 4.1c), with the convexity of the elbow directed laterally (Fig. 4.1d). At a later stage the upper and lower limbs rotate in opposite directions so that the convexity of the elbow is directed towards the caudal end of the body (Fig. 4.1e). As the limb bud develops the primitive muscle mass gradually becomes compartmentalized foreshadowing the adult pattern. Intermuscular septa, extending outwards from the periosteum of the humerus, divide the arm into anterior and posterior compartments. As in the lower limb, some of the anterior compartment musculature has become separated into an adductor group. However, in the upper limb this muscle mass has degenerated phylogenetically so that all that remains is coracobrachialis. Adduction of the upper limb is a powerful action in humans, being served by great sheets of muscle that have

Fig. 4.1 The development of the upper limb.

migrated into it, these are latissimus dorsi posteriorly and pectoralis major anteriorly. In the forearm, the radius (preaxial bone) and the ulna (postaxial bone) are connected by an interosseous membrane, and to the investing fascia by intermuscular septa. The compartments so formed enclose muscles of similar or related functions.

With the upper limb in the anatomical position the anterior preaxial compartments are in a continuous plane with the muscles being supplied by branches from the lateral and medial cords of the brachial plexus, which are all derived from the anterior divisions of the nerve trunks. Similarly, the posterior postaxial compartment muscles are all supplied by branches of the posterior cord, derived from the posterior divisions of the nerve trunks.

The median, musculocutaneous and ulnar nerves are responsible for preaxial innervation, whereas the radial nerve supplies all of the postaxial musculature of the upper limb below the shoulder. Within the pectoral girdle the clavicle is the anterior preaxial bone and the scapula, with the exception of the coracoid process (which is also an anterior bone), is the posterior postaxial bone. The distinction with respect to the coracoid process is that phylogenetically it is a separate bone, its fusion with the scapula is secondary. Consequently, muscles arising from the clavicle or coracoid process belong to the preaxial group, and are therefore supplied by preaxial branches of the brachial plexus. Similarly, muscles arising from the remainder of the scapula are part of the postaxial group and are innervated by postaxial branches of the plexus.

Furthermore, there is a serial arrangement of the nerves in the brachial plexus, both with respect to their motor innervation and their sensory supply. The order is retained from the primitive serial morphology of the embryo. Remembering that the skin has essentially been stretched over the developing limb, the fifth cervical nerve in the adult is sensory to the cranial part of the limb, and the first thoracic to its caudal part, with the seventh cervical nerve lying in the middle of the limb. This pattern of motor innervation, in simple terms, progresses from C5 for shoulder movements to T1 for intrinsic hand movements, with the elbow being served by C5 and 6, the forearm by C6, the wrist by C6 and 7, and the fingers and thumb by C7 and 8.

As in the lower limb, many muscles cross two or more joints, and can therefore act on all of them. Consequently, a complex system of synergists and fixators is provided in order to cancel out unwanted movements. Procedures for testing for loss of muscle action, as in paralysis, can thus be fairly complicated.

The upper limit of the upper limb is not so easily defined as in the lower limb. In spite of muscular attachments to the head, neck and thorax, the upper limits can be conveniently considered as the superior surface of the clavicle anteriorly and the superior border of the scapula posteriorly. The free upper limb is divided into the arm between the shoulder and elbow, the forearm between the elbow and the wrist, and the hand beyond the wrist. The hand has an anterior or palmar surface, and a posterior or dorsal surface (Fig. 4.2).

The bones of the upper limb are the clavicle and scapula of the pectoral girdle, the humerus in the arm, the lateral radius and medial ulna in the forearm, the eight carpal bones of the wrist, the five metacarpals of the hand and the phalanges of the digits– two in the thumb and three in each finger (Fig. 4.2).

Fig. 4.2 The regions, bones and joints of the upper limb.

REGIONS

BONES

Clavicle

JOINTS

Sternoclavicular

Scapula

Pectoral

Humerus

Acromioclavicular

Shoulder

Arm

Elbow

Superior radioulnar

Forearm

Radius

Ulna

Inferior radioulnar

Carpal bones

Radiocarpal

Midcarpal

Carpometacarpal

Metacarpophalangeal

Interphalangeal

Hand

Palmar surface

Dorsal surface

Metacarpal

Phalanges

Fig. 4.2

Bones

THE PECTORAL GIRDLE AND ARM

The scapula

The scapula is a large, flat, triangular plate of bone on the posterolateral aspect of the thorax, overlapping the second to the seventh ribs. Suspended in muscles, the scapula is held in its lateral position by the strut-like clavicle, but has great mobility relative to the thorax. As it is a triangular bone it presents three angles, three borders and two surfaces which support three bony processes (Fig. 4.3, see Fig. 4.4a).

The costal surface which faces the ribs is slightly hollowed and ridged with a smooth, narrow strip along its entire medial border. It is also known as the *subscapular fossa*.

The dorsal surface faces posterolaterally and is divided into a smaller *supraspinous fossa* above and a larger *infraspinous fossa* below the *spine of the scapula*. The supraspinous and infraspinous fossae communicate via the *spinoglenoid notch* between the lateral end of the spine and the neck of the scapula. The spine of the scapula has two free borders, lateral and posterior, and where they come together laterally it is continuous with the acromion.

The thin *medial border* ascends from the inferior to the superior angle, being slightly angled at the medial end of the spine. The *lateral border* is thicker, being deeply invested in muscles, and runs down from the *infraglenoid tubercle* below the *glenoid fossa* to meet the medial border at the inferior angle. The *superior border*, which is thin and sharp, is the shortest of the three, and has the *scapular notch* marking the junction with the root of the coracoid process.

Inferiorly, the thick *inferior angle* lies over the seventh rib and is easily palpated. The *superior angle* lies at the junction of the medial and superior borders, whilst the *lateral angle* is truncated and broadened to support the *head* and glenoid fossa of the scapula.

The *head* of the scapula is an expanded part of the bone joined to a flat blade by a short inconspicuous neck. The *glenoid fossa*

(or cavity) is found on the head as a shallow, pear-shaped concavity, facing anterolaterally. The glenoid fossa is broader below and articulates with the head of humerus thereby forming the shoulder joint. Immediately above the glenoid fossa is the *supraglenoid tubercle*, which gives attachment to biceps brachii.

The *acromion process*, which is the expanded lateral end of the spine, is large and quadrilateral, projecting forwards at right angles to the spine. The lower border of the crest of the spine continues as the lateral border of the acromion, the junction of these two borders forming the palpable *acromial angle*. The upper border of the crest becomes continuous with the medial border of the acromion and presents an oval facet for articulation with the clavicle at the acromioclavicular joint. The superior surface of the acromion is flattened.

The *coracoid process* is a hook-like projection with a broad base directed upwards and forwards from the upper part of the head, and a narrow more horizontal part which passes anterolaterally from the upper edge of the base. The tip lies below the junction of the middle and lateral thirds of the clavicle.

Palpation

Starting at the lowest point, the *inferior angle* can readily be gripped between thumb and index finger and, if the subject relaxes sufficiently, can be lifted away from the thorax. The *medial border* can be followed along its whole length from inferior to superior angles. The *spine of the scapula* can be palpated as a small triangular area medially which increases in size as the fingers are moved laterally along it. The flat crest with its upper and lower borders can be identified. Continuing along the lower border of the crest to its most lateral point, the sharp 90° *acromial angle* can be felt. This continues as the palpable *lateral border* of the *acromion*. Running onto this lateral border the flat upper surface of the acromion can be felt above the shoulder joint. The *coracoid process* can be felt as an anterior projection below the lateral part of the clavicle, and therefore is a useful reference point for surface marking the shoulder joint.

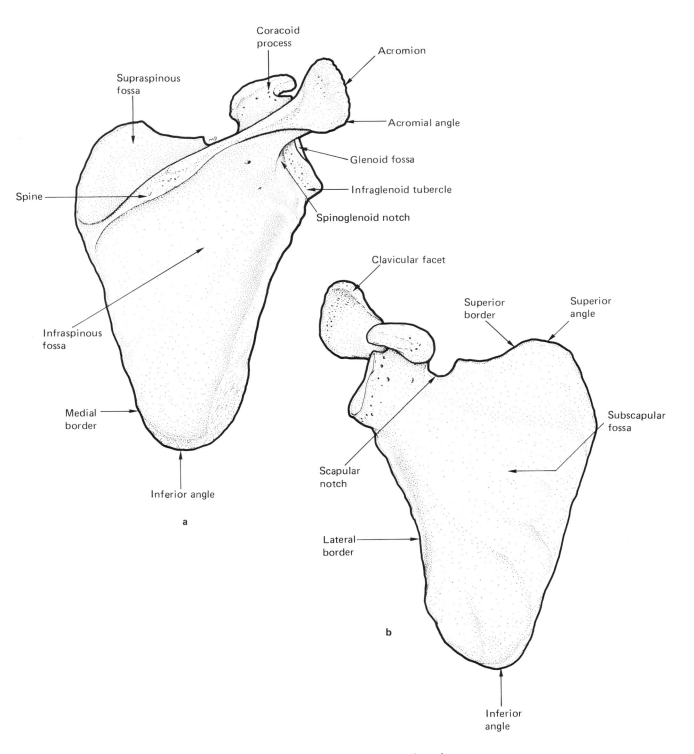

Fig. 4.3 The right scapula: **a** = posterior view; **b** = anterior view.

Ossification

The scapula ossifies from a considerable number of centres. The primary ossification centre appears in the region of the neck by the eighth week *in utero*, so that at birth the coracoid process, acromion, glenoid cavity, medial border and inferior angle are still cartilaginous. Secondary centres appear in each of these regions except the coracoid between the ages of 12 and 14 years, fusing with the body between 20 and 25. The secondary centre for the coracoid process, however, appears during the first year and fuses with the body between 12 and 14 years.

The clavicle

The clavicle (Fig. 4.4b and c) is a subcutaneous bone running horizontally from the sternum to the acromion. It acts as a strut holding the scapula laterally, thus enabling the arm to be clear of the trunk—an essential feature in primates. The scapula and clavicle together form the pectoral or shoulder girdle, transmitting the weight of the upper limb to the axial skeleton and facilitating a wide range of movement of the upper limb.

The *medial two-thirds* of the clavicle is convex forwards and is roughly triangular in cross-section. The *lateral third* is concave forwards and flattened from above downwards. The medial convexity conforms with the curvature of the superior thoracic aperture, the lateral concavity with the shape of the shoulder.

The *lateral* (acromial) *end* of the clavicle is the most flattened part of the bone and has a small *deltoid tubercle* on its anterior border. Inferiorly, the rounded *conoid tubercle* is present at the posterior edge of the bone, with the rough *trapezoid line* (Fig. 4.4c) running forwards and laterally away from it. The conoid tubercle and trapezoid line give attachment to the conoid and trapezoid parts of the coracoclavicular ligament binding the clavicle and scapula together. Laterally is a small oval *articular facet* for the acromion process. It is set obliquely facing downwards and laterally.

The *medial* (sternal) *end* of the clavicle is enlarged and faces downwards and medially. The lower three-quarters is bevelled and articulates with the clavicular notch of the manubrium and the costal cartilage of the first rib, forming the sternoclavicular joint. The cylindrical clavicle projects above the shallow notch on the sternum, this can be confirmed by palpation. The superior quarter of the sternal end is roughened for the attachment of the intra-articular disc and ligaments. Between the lateral and medial ends, the superior surface of the clavicle is smooth, while the inferior surface is marked by a rough groove for subclavius and a large oval roughened impression for the costoclavicular ligament medially. The anterior and posterior borders are roughened by muscle attachments.

The clavicle is often fractured by the direct violence of a blow, or by indirect forces transmitted up the limb following a fall on an outstretched arm. The fracture usually occurs at the junction of the two curvatures, and the resultant fracture deformity is caused by the weight of the arm pulling the shoulder downwards and medially.

Palpation

In a slender subject the whole length of the clavicle can often be seen pressing against the skin. Initially, the enlarged medial end of the clavicle can be palpated with the fingers, and the line of the sternoclavicular joint can also be identified. Moving laterally, almost the whole length of the shaft of the clavicle can be gripped between finger and thumb. At the lateral end, the bulk of deltoid may require deeper pressure, nevertheless the line of the acromioclavicular joint should be palpable, particularly from above.

Ossification

The clavicle ossifies in membrane, being the first bone in the body to begin ossification. Two primary centres appear during the fifth week *in utero*. These centres unite and ossification spreads towards the ends of the bone. A secondary centre appears in the medial end between 14 and 18 years, fusing with the main part of the bone as early as 18 to 20 years in females and 23 to 25 years in males. An additional centre may appear in the lateral end at puberty, however it soon fuses with the main bone.

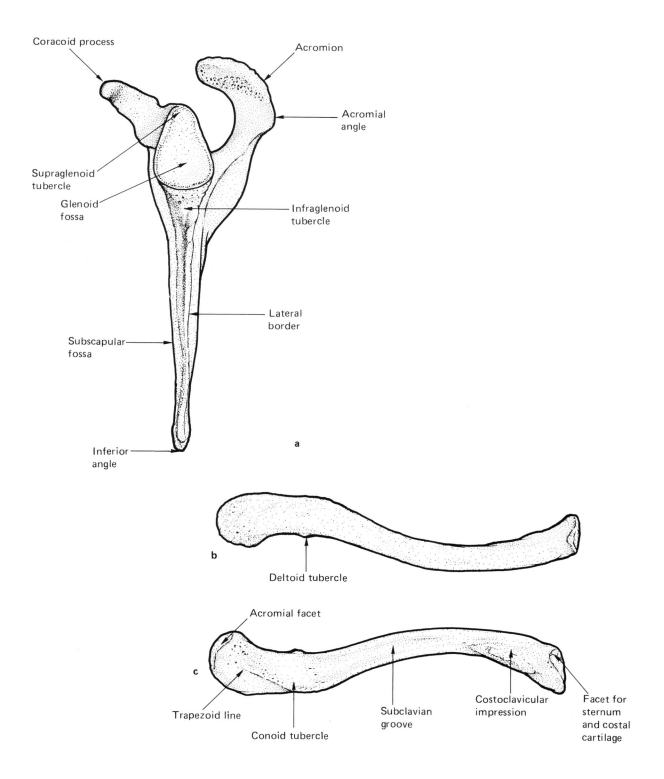

Coracoid process

Acromion

Acromial angle

Supraglenoid tubercle

Glenoid fossa

Infraglenoid tubercle

Lateral border

Subscapular fossa

Inferior angle

a

b

Deltoid tubercle

Acromial facet

c

Trapezoid line

Conoid tubercle

Subclavian groove

Costoclavicular impression

Facet for sternum and costal cartilage

Fig. 4.4   a = Right scapula, lateral view; **b** = right clavicle, superior view; **c** = right clavicle, inferior view.

The humerus

The humerus is the largest of the bones in the upper limb. It is a typical long bone having a shaft (body) and two extremities. Proximally, the humerus articulates with the glenoid fossa of the scapula forming the shoulder joint, and distally with the radius and ulna forming the elbow joint (Fig. 4.5).

Upper end of the humerus

The major feature, proximally, is the *head* of the humerus with its smooth, rounded articular surface facing upwards, medially and backwards. It is almost hemispherical, being considerably larger than the socket formed by the glenoid fossa. The head is joined to the upper end by the *anatomical neck*, a slightly constricted region encircling the bone at the articular margin, separating it from the tubercles.

The *greater tubercle* is a prominence on the upper lateral part of the bone, next to the head. It merges with the shaft below and is marked by three distinct impressions for muscular attachment. The greater tubercle projects laterally past the margin of the acromion and is the most lateral bony point at the shoulder.

The smaller *lesser tubercle* is a distinct prominence on the anterior aspect below the anatomical neck. It has a well-marked impression on its medial side for muscular attachment. Between these two tubercles, and passing onto the shaft of the humerus, is the deep *intertubercular sulcus* (groove). The crests of the greater and lesser tubercles continue down from the anterior borders of the tubercles to form the lateral and medial lips of the groove. Between the two lips is the floor of the groove.

Below the head and tubercles, where they join the shaft, there is a definite constriction. This region is termed the *surgical neck* because fractures often occur here, particularly in the elderly.

Shaft (body) of the humerus

The shaft of the humerus is almost cylindrical above, becoming triangular in its lower part with distinct medial and lateral borders. It presents three borders and surfaces, although the borders are frequently rounded and indistinct. They are described as anterior, medial and lateral. Between the three borders are the three surfaces of the shaft. The intertubercular groove is continuous with the anteromedial surface; the medial border beginning as the crest of the lesser tubercle and ending by curving towards the medial epicondyle. The smooth anterolateral surface is marked about its middle by the *deltoid tuberosity*. The posterior surface is crossed obliquely from superomedial to inferolateral by the *spiral groove* (radial groove). It reaches the lateral border below the deltoid tuberosity, but is often poorly marked.

Lower end of the humerus

The lower end of the humerus is expanded laterally, flattened anteroposteriorly, and bent slightly forwards. It presents two articular surfaces separated by a ridge. The lateral articular surface, the *capitulum*, is situated on the anteroinferior aspect and is a rounded, convex surface, being less than a hemisphere in size. The capitulum articulates with the radius, making its greatest contact with the radius when the elbow is fully flexed.

Medial to the capitulum is the *trochlea*, the articular surface for the ulna. The trochlea is a grooved surface rather like a pulley, the medial edge projecting further distally and anteriorly than the lateral. This causes the ulna also to project laterally and results in a carrying angle between the humerus and ulna (see p. 193).

On the medial side of the trochlea is the large *medial epicondyle*. Its posterior surface is smooth and has a shallow groove for the ulnar nerve. The sharp *medial supracondylar ridge*, comprising the lower third of the medial border, runs upwards onto the shaft. On the lateral side of the capitulum is the *lateral epicondyle* with the *lateral supracondylar ridge*, comprising the lower third of the lateral border, running upwards onto the shaft.

Just above the articular surfaces, the lower end of the humerus presents three fossae for the bony processes of the radius and ulna. Situated posteriorly is the deep *olecranon fossa* which receives the olecranon

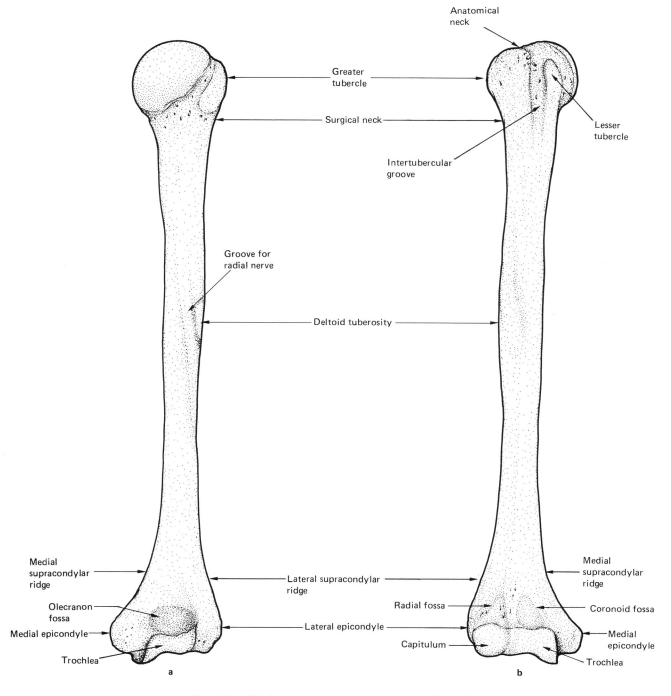

Fig. 4.5 Right humerus **a** = posterior view; **b** = anterior view.

process of the ulna when the elbow is extended. Anteriorly, there are two fossae: the lateral *radial* and medial *coronoid* fossae, which receive the head of the radius and coronoid process of the ulna respectively on full flexion of the elbow.

Many of the bony features previously described can be seen in Figs. 4.6 and 4.7.

Palpation

At the upper end of the humerus the most lateral bony point at the shoulder is the *greater tubercle*, whose quadrilateral superior, anterior and posterior surfaces can be felt. Further differentiation can be made by palpating the lateral margin of the acromion (see p. 56) and then running the fingers off its edge onto the greater tubercle. The rounded *lesser tubercle* can be felt through deltoid, and is just lateral to the tip of the coracoid process. To the lateral side of the lesser tubercle the impression of the *intertubercular sulcus* can usually be felt. The *shaft* of the humerus is covered with thick muscle, but can be palpated on its medial and lateral sides. At the lower end, the prominent *medial epicondyle* is the most obvious bony landmark. The ulnar nerve can be rolled in the groove behind it (the 'funny bone'). Running upwards from the medial epicondyle the sharp *medial supracondylar ridge* can be palpated. The *lateral epicondyle* can be palpated at the base of a dimple on the lateral aspect of the elbow, as can the *lateral supracondylar ridge* running upwards from it. Posteriorly, the *olecranon fossa* can be felt through the triceps tendon, if the relaxed elbow is flexed.

Ossification

A primary ossification centre appears in the shaft in the eighth week *in utero* and spreads until, at birth, only the ends are cartilaginous. Secondary centres appear in the head early in the first year, in the greater tubercle at about 3 years and in the lesser tubercle at about 5 years. These fuse to form a single cap of bone between the ages of 6 and 8 years, finally fusing with the shaft between 18 and 20 in females and 20 and 22 years in males.

At the lower end of the humerus, secondary centres appear for the capitulum during the second year, for the trochlea between 9 and 10 years, and for the lateral epicondyle between 12 and 14 years. These join together at about 14 years, fusing with the shaft at 15 years in females and 18 years in males. A separate centre for the medial epicondyle appears between 6 and 8 years and fuses between 15 and 18 years with a spicule of bone projecting down from the shaft medial to the trochlea. This latter ossification centre lies entirely outside the joint capsule. Most of the growth in length of the humerus occurs at its upper end.

Fig. 4.6 X-ray of the shoulder in the anatomical position, oblique view:

1 = Coracoid process
2 = Acromion
3 = Acromioclavicular joint
4 = Head of humerus
5 = Rim of glenoid fossa
6 = Blade of scapula (end on)
7 = Lesser tubercle

Fig. 4.7 X-ray of left shoulder, anteroposterior view with the arm externally rotated and slightly abducted:

1 = Cortex of vertebral border
2 = Bone in infraspinous fossa
3 = Lateral border of scapula
4 = Acromion
5 = Spine of scapula
6 = Coracoid process
7 = Glenoid fossa
8 = Head of humerus
9 = Greater tubercle
10 = Lesser tubercle

Fig. 4.6

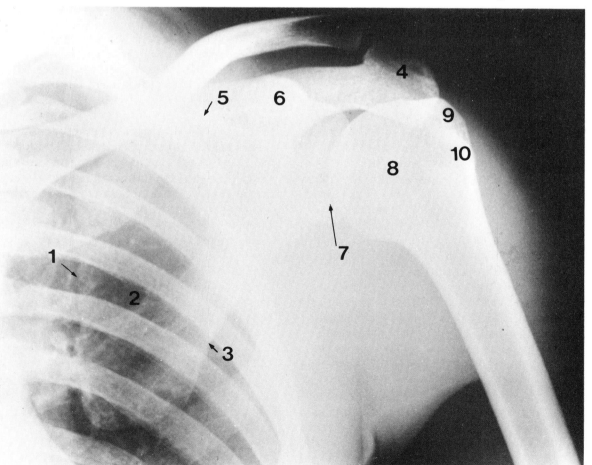

Fig. 4.7

THE FOREARM

There are two bones in the forearm, the *radius* laterally, and the *ulna* medially. Both bones articulate proximally with the humerus at the elbow joint and contribute to the wrist joint distally. They are connected by a strong interosseous membrane between their shafts, and synovial pivot joints at their proximal and distal ends. Both are long bones with the ulna being expanded proximally and the radius distally (Fig. 4.8). The shaft of the radius is markedly convex laterally, allowing it to move around the ulna, thus carrying the hand with it into pronation.

The radius

The radius lies lateral to the ulna and is the shorter of the two bones. It articulates above with the capitulum of the humerus, distally with the scaphoid and lunate bones of the proximal row of the carpus, and at each end with the ulna. It has a shaft and two ends, the inferior end being the larger.

The *head* is a thick disc with a concave superior surface for articulation with the capitulum. The outer, articular surface of the head is flattened, articulating inside a fibro-osseous ring formed by the radial notch of the ulna and the annular ligament. Below the head is the constricted *neck*, which slopes medially as it approaches the shaft. Where the shaft joins the neck it is round, but becomes triangular lower down. Together with the neck, the shaft has a slight medial convexity on its upper quarter, with a lateral convexity in its remaining lower part. The *radial tuberosity* lies anteromedially on the upper part of the shaft at the maximum convexity of the medial curve. The majority of the shaft presents three borders and three surfaces.

The *interosseous border*, to which the interosseous membrane attaches, is sharp and faces medially. It extends from just below the radial tuberosity to the medial side of the lower end of the radius, splitting into two ridges which become continuous with the anterior and posterior margins of the ulnar notch. The *anterior* and *posterior borders* descend either side of the radial tuberosity and roughened area for pronator teres lower

down. The anterior border becomes distinct lower down, while the posterior border becomes more rounded. These borders enclose the lateral, anterior and flatter posterior surfaces.

The inferior end of the radius is expanded having five distinct surfaces. The *lateral surface*, which extends down to the styloid process, has a shallow groove for the tendons of abductor pollicis longus and extensor pollicis brevis. The *medial surface* forms the concave ulnar notch for articulation with the head of the ulna. The *posterior surface* is convex and grooved by tendons. The prominent ridge in the middle of this surface is the *dorsal (Lister's) tubercle*. The lateral half of this surface continues down onto the styloid process. The *anterior surface* is smooth and curves forward to a distinct anterior margin. The *distal* articular *surface* is concave and extends onto the styloid process. It is divided by a ridge into two areas, a lateral triangular area for articulation with the scaphoid and a medial quadrilateral area for the lunate (see Fig. 4.9). Many of the bony features around the elbow can be seen in Fig. 4.10 (p. 67).

Palpation

The *head* of the radius can be palpated in a deep 'dimple' on the posterolateral aspect of the elbow, particularly when the elbow joint is extended because it overhangs the capitulum. The head can be felt to rotate during pronation and supination. The *shaft* of the radius can be palpated on the lateral side in the lower half of the forearm. On the posterior aspect of the lower end, the *dorsal tubercle* can be identified above the wrist, as can the *styloid process* on the lateral aspect inside the 'anatomical snuff-box' between the extensor tendons of the thumb.

Ossification

A primary ossification centre appears in the shaft during the eighth week *in utero*, so that at birth only the head, inferior end and radial tuberosity are cartilaginous. The first secondary centre appears in the inferior end during the first year of life, fusing with the shaft between the ages of 20 and 22 years. The secondary centre for the head appears

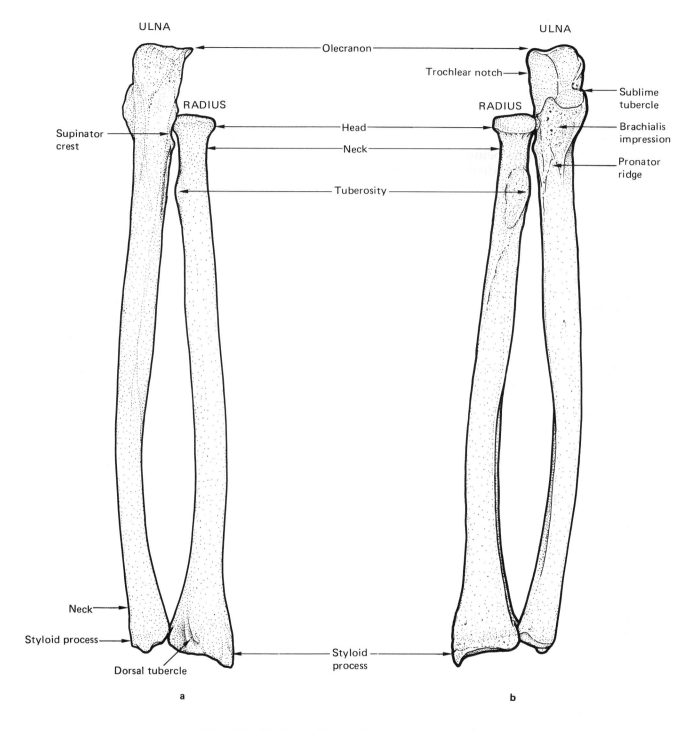

Fig. 4.8 Right radius and ulna: **a** = posterior view; **b** = anterior view.

at about 6 years and fuses with the shaft between 15 and 17 years. A secondary centre usually appears in the radial tuberosity between 14 and 15 years, but soon fuses with the shaft.

The ulna

The ulna lies medial to the radius and is the longer of the two bones. It has a shaft and two ends, of which the superior is the larger presenting as a hook-like projection for articulation with the trochlea of the humerus. The smaller rounded distal end is the *head* of the *ulna* (see Figs. 4.8 and 4.9). It does not articulate directly with the carpus. The ulna articulates at each end with the radius.

The upper end of the ulna is large with two projecting processes, enclosing a concavity. The *olecranon process* is the larger of the two processes and forms the proximal part of the bone. It is beak-shaped and points forwards, being continuous inferiorly with the shaft. Posteriorly, it is smooth and subcutaneous while anteriorly it is concave, forming the upper part of the articular surface of the *trochlear notch*. The borders of the olecranon are thickened and rough.

The *coronoid process* projects from the front of the shaft and has an upper articular surface which completes the trochlear notch. These two surfaces are often separated by a roughened non-articular area running horizontally across the notch. The trochlear notch is divided by a vertical ridge into a larger medial part and a smaller lateral part, the latter being continuous over its outer edge with the articular surface of the radial notch on the lateral side of the coronoid process. There is a small tubercle where the medial and anterior edges of the articular surface of the coronoid process meet. This gives attachment to the anterior part of the

ulnar collateral ligament. The irregular, anterior surface of the coronoid ends inferiorly as the rough tuberosity of the ulna. Both this surface and the tuberosity give attachment to brachialis.

On the lateral side of the coronoid process, the concave radial notch receives the head of the radius. Below this and extending onto the shaft is the triangular supinator fossa. It is bound posteriorly by the distinct *supinator crest*. The medial border of this area forms a prominent ridge which has a small tubercle at its upper end.

The prominent *interosseous border*, to which the interosseous membrane attaches, runs down from the apex of the supinator fossa. The *anterior border* runs down from the medial margin of the coronoid process but is indistinct. The sinuous, subcutaneous *posterior border*, prominent in its upper part, is continuous with the subcutaneous region of the olecranon and upper part of the shaft. Between these borders are three surfaces, the anterior and medial surfaces being continuous at the rounded anterior border. The lower quarter of the anterior surface is marked by an oblique ridge running downwards and medially. On the posterior surface, an oblique ridge runs downwards and backwards from the radial notch to the posterior border. The remaining posterior surface has faint ridges laterally and is smooth medially.

The lower end of the ulna shows a narrowed neck which expands into a small, rounded head. From the posterior part of the head of the ulna, the conical *styloid process* projects downwards. The head has a smooth articular surface for the radius on its anterior and lateral aspects. The distal surface of the head is smooth and almost flat, and articulates with an articular disc which intervenes between it and the triquetral.

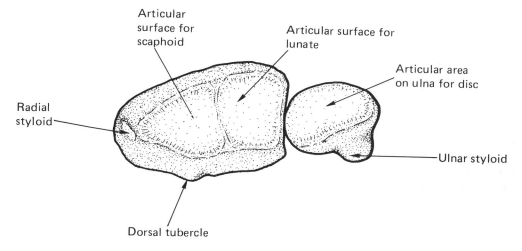

Fig. 4.9 Right radius and ulna viewed distally.

Posterior view

Lateral view

Fig. 4.10 X-rays of elbow region of the right arm.

a = Posterior view in full extension:

  1 = Lateral epicondyle
  2 = Medial epicondyle
  3 = Superimposed olecranon and coronoid fossae
  4 = Coronoid process
  5 = Joint space between coronoid and trochlea
  6 = Head of radius
  7 = Tuberosity of radius

b = Lateral view:

  1 = Supracondylar ridges
  2 = Capitulum
  3 = Olecranon
  4 = Coronoid process
  5 = Radial head

Palpation

At the upper and posterior aspect of the elbow the outline of the olecranon can be identified; it forms the 'point' of the elbow seen in flexion. Running downwards from this point the posterior border can be palpated throughout its length. At the lower end, the neck, head and styloid process can all be palpated, with the styloid process being the most posterior. When the forearm is fully pronated the rounded head of the ulna stands out from the back of the wrist.

Ossification

A primary ossification centre appears in the shaft during the eighth week *in utero*. The body, coronoid process and major part of the olecranon ossify from this primary centre. A secondary centre appears in the head during the fifth year and fuses with the shaft between 20 and 22 years. The secondary centre for the remainder of the olecranon appears at about 11 years, with fusion occuring between 16 and 19 years. There may be several secondary centres for the olecranon.

THE WRIST

The carpus

The carpus is composed of eight separate bones arranged around the capitate, but commonly described as forming two rows each of four bones. Three of the bones in the proximal row articulate above with the radius or articular disc at the radiocarpal joint, whilst below they articulate with the distal row of bones forming the midcarpal joint. The four carpal bones of the distal rows articulate with the bases of the five metacarpal bones via the carpometacarpal joints. There are also articulations between the adjacent carpal bones in each of the rows, the intercarpal joints.

The bones are bound together by ligaments and so form a compact mass, which is curved to give a posterior convexity and a pronounced anterior concavity (the *carpal sulcus*). This sulcus is converted into a canal (*carpal tunnel*) by the flexor retinaculum.

The individual carpal bones are clinically important because they are often injured, especially the scaphoid and lunate, and because they provide recognizable bony landmarks in the wrist region.

From lateral to medial the proximal and distal rows are arranged as follows (Fig. 4.11 see also Fig. 4.12):

Proximal: Scaphoid, lunate, triquetral, pisiform
Distal: Trapezium, trapezoid, capitate, hamate

Proximal row

The three lateral bones of the proximal row are so arranged as to form a convex articular surface facing proximally to fit into the concavity formed by the radius and the articular disc. Individually, each of the bones has a characteristic shape and its own set of articular surfaces.

Scaphoid The scaphoid is marked anteriorly by a prominent palpable tubercle and a narrowed waist around its centre. Articular surfaces are present on the scaphoid: proximally for the radius, medially for the lunate and more distally for the head of the capitate, and lateral to the tubercle for the trapezium and trapezoid. The small, non-articular surface of the tubercle is the only region available for the entry of blood vessels. It is a common site of fracture.

Lunate The lunate has a smooth convex palmar surface which is larger than its dorsal surface. On its medial side is a square articular surface for the triquetral, and on its lateral side a crescent-shaped area for the scaphoid. Distally, there is a deep concavity for the head of the capitate, while proximally the bone is convex where it articulates with the radius and articular disc.

Triquetral The triquetral lies in the angle between the lunate and hamate, with which it articulates via a sinuous surface. The square lateral articular surface is for the lunate. The triquetral is distinguished by a circular surface for the pisiform. The proximal part enters the radiocarpal joint during adduction of the hand.

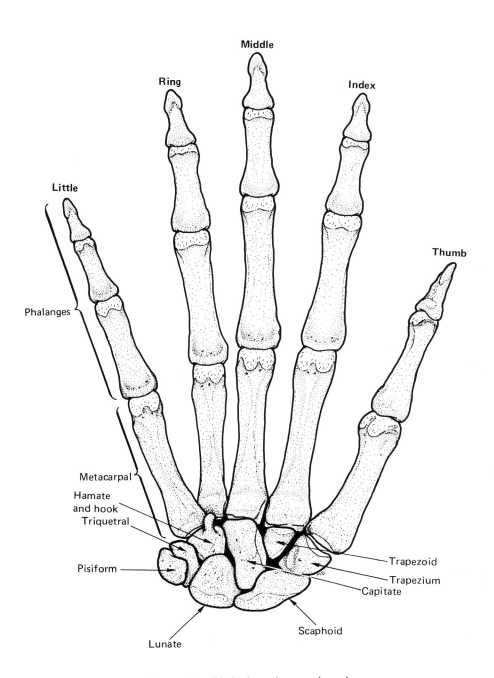

Fig. 4.11   Right hand, anterior view.

Pisiform   The pisiform is a small round sesamoid bone found in the tendon of flexor carpi ulnaris. It articulates with the palmar surface of the triquetral. The anterior surface projects distally and laterally forming the medial part of the carpal tunnel.

Distal row

The distal row of carpal bones presents a more complex proximal articular surface, being flat laterally and convex medially. Individually, the bones all have a characteristic shape.

Trapezium   The trapezium is the most irregular of the carpal bones, with a palpable tubercle and groove medially on its anterior surface. It has articular surfaces proximally for the scaphoid and trapezoid, which are set at an angle to each other. Its main feature is the articular surface for the base of the first metacarpal. This articular surface is saddle-shaped and faces distally, laterally and slightly forwards, contributing greatly to the mobility of the carpometacarpal joint of the thumb.

Trapezoid   The trapezoid is a small and irregular bone which articulates with the second metacarpal. It lies in the space bounded by the metacarpal, scaphoid, capitate and trapezium, articulating with each.

Capitate   The capitate is the largest of the carpal bones being centrally placed with a rounded head articulating with the concavities of the lunate and scaphoid. Medially and laterally there are flatter articular surfaces for the hamate and trapezoid respectively. The dorsal surface is flat, but the palmar aspect is roughened by ligamentous attachments. The distal surface articulates mainly with the base of the third metacarpal, but also by narrow surfaces with the bases of the second and fourth metacarpals.

Hamate   The hamate is wedge-shaped with a large curved palpable hook projecting from its palmar surface near the base of the fifth metacarpal. The *hook* is concave on its lateral side forming part of the carpal tunnel. The distal base of the wedge articulates with the bases of the fourth and fifth metacarpals. The wedge passes up between the capitate and triquetral to reach the lunate. The articular surface for the capitate is flat and that for the triquetral is sinuous.

Overall the carpus presents a deep transverse concavity on the palmar surface. The *flexor retinaculum* bridges the concavity, attaching to the tubercles of the scaphoid and trapezium laterally, and the pisiform and hook of hamate medially, forming the roof of the *carpal tunnel*.

Palpation

Starting on the medial side of the palmar aspect of the wrist at the proximal part of the hypothenar eminence, the *pisiform* can be distinguished easily with the tendon of flexor carpi ulnaris running proximally from it. Immediately distal and slightly lateral to the pisiform, the *hook of the hamate* can be palpated if sufficient pressure is applied through the hypothenar muscles.

On the lateral side of the carpus just proximal to the distal wrist crease, the prominent *tubercle* of the *scaphoid* can be palpated, and immediately beyond this, the *tubercle* of the *trapezium*. The scaphoid can be 'pinched' between the palpating thumb and index finger if these are placed on the tubercle and in the 'anatomical snuff-box' at the base of the thumb on its dorsal surface.

Ossification

Each carpal bone ossifies from a single centre, all of which appear after birth. During the first year of life the centres for the capitate and hamate appear. These are followed by centres for the triquetral between 2 and 4 years, the lunate between 3 and 5 years, the scaphoid, trapezium and trapezoid all between 4 and 6 years, and finally the pisiform between 9 and 14 years. Ossification is not complete until between 20 and 25 years. The hook of hamate may be separate. Small additional nodules may also be present. The shape of the individual carpal bones, and not their size, can be used to age an individual.

THE HAND

The metacarpus

The metacarpus consists of five bones, the metacarpals, one corresponding to each digit and numbered in sequence from the lateral side. Each is a long bone with a proximal quadrilateral base, a shaft and a distal rounded head (see Fig. 4.11). The variations in shape of the bases provide a means of distinguishing them. The base of the first metacarpal has a saddle-shaped articular surface which fits a corresponding surface on the trapezium. The base of the second metacarpal articulates with the trapezium, trapezoid and capitate. The base of the third has a single articulation with the capitate. The bases of the fourth and fifth metacarpals articulate with the hamate. The bases of the second to fifth also articulate with the adjacent metacarpal bones, having articular facets in appropriate positions.

The heads of the metacarpals are smooth and rounded, extending further onto the palmar surface. The palmar articular margin is notched in the midline. The head of the first metacarpal is wider than the others. Two sesamoid bones, usually found in the short tendons crossing the joint, articulate with the palmar part of the joint surface occasionally grooving it. The heads fit into a concavity on the base of the proximal phalanx at the metacarpophalangeal joints. The shaft of the metacarpals is slightly curved with a longitudinal palmar concavity. That of the first metacarpal is nearly as wide as the base and has a rounded dorsal surface. The palmar surface is divided by a blunt ridge into a larger lateral part and a smaller medial part.

Palpation

If the fingers are flexed to form a fist, the heads of the metacarpals can easily be palpated as the knuckles. Running proximally on the dorsal surface of the hand the shafts can also be distinguished. At the proximal end of the shaft the gap between the base of the metacarpal and the carpus can be palpated as the line of the carpometacarpal joint.

Ossification

Primary ossification centres appear in the shaft in the ninth week *in utero*, so that the bones are well ossified at birth. Secondary centres appear in the heads of the second to fifth metacarpals between 2 and 3 years. The secondary centre for the base of the first metacarpal appears slightly later. Fusion of the epiphysis with the shaft occurs between 17 and 19 years for all metacarpals. Occasionally, a secondary centre may appear in the head of the first metacarpal.

The phalanges

There are 14 phalanges in each hand, three for each finger and two for the thumb. As they are long bones, each phalanx has a shaft, a large proximal end and a smaller distal end, the head (see Fig. 4.11). The phalanges of the thumb are shorter and broader than those of the fingers.

The proximal phalanx has a concave oval facet on its base for articulation with the head of the metacarpal. The rounded head, which extends further onto the palmar surface, has a wide, pulley-shaped articular surface for the base of the next phalanx. The shaft is curved along its length being convex dorsally. It is convex from side-to-side on its dorsal surface, and is flat on the palmar surface. The middle and distal phalanges are similar to the proximal phalanx. However, the base of the distal phalanx is large, and the head is expanded to support the pulp pad of the digits.

By convention, the digits are described by name rather than by number, and are from lateral to medial, the thumb, index, middle, ring and little fingers. Many of the features described can be seen in Fig. 4.12.

Palpation

By flexing the fingers into a fist, the heads of the proximal and middle phalanges can be palpated. The shafts of the phalanges are also easily followed throughout their length, especially on their dorsal surface.

Ossification

Primary ossification centres appear in the shafts of the phalanges between the eighth and twelfth week *in utero*, with the distal phalanges ossifying first. Secondary centres appear in the bases of the phalanges during the second and third year, fusing with the shaft between 17 and 19 years. Occasionally, a secondary centre may appear in the head as well as in the base.

Anterior view

Lateral view

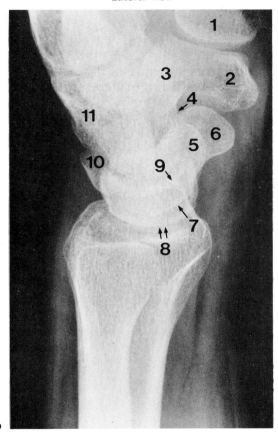

Fig. 4.12   X-rays of the left hand and wrist.

a = Anterior view:
  1 = Styloid process of the radius
  2 = Styloid process of the ulna
  3 = Scaphoid
  4 = Lunate
  5 = Triquetral
  6 = Hamate
  7 = Pisiform
  8 = Capitate
  9 = Trapezoid
  10 = Trapezium
  11 = First metacarpal
  12 = Sesamoid bones
  13 = Proximal phalanx
  14 = Middle phalanx
  15 = Distal phalanx
  16 = Head of metacarpal
  17 = Body of metacarpal
  18 = Base of metacarpal

b = Lateral view:
  1 = Base of first metacarpal
  2 = Trapezium
  3 = Trapezoid and hook of hamate super-
        imposed
  4 = Capitate
  5 = Pisiform
  6 = Tubercle of scaphoid
  7 = Scaphoid
  8 = Lunate
  9 = Styloid process of radius
  10 = Triquetral
  11 = Hamate

Muscles

MUSCLES WHICH MOVE AND STABILIZE THE PECTORAL (SHOULDER) GIRDLE

The pectoral girdle consists of the scapula and the clavicle, articulating with each other at the acromioclavicular joint. It provides the link between the upper limb and the axial skeleton via the shoulder (glenohumeral) joint and the sternoclavicular joint respectively. The flattened triangular scapula provides attachment for many muscles, some of which anchor the pectoral girdle to the thorax and others which control the position of the upper limb. The clavicle, however, acts primarily as a strut holding the upper limb away from the trunk. Because of the connections (both muscular and ligamentous) between the scapula and clavicle, movements of the pectoral girdle, either independently or in association with the upper limb, mean that both bones are always involved. The position and movement of the scapula is determined by the activity of the muscles attached to it. An individual muscle when acting in concert with various combinations of other muscles may be involved in producing several different movements of the pectoral girdle. Consequently, in the following account individual muscles will be described in detail according to their major action. Movements between the scapula and thorax are allowed because the fascia covering adjacent layers of muscles facilitates gliding and sliding movements.

The movements of the shoulder girdle are described as taking place from the anatomical position where the scapula lies obliquely over the second to seventh ribs on the posterior wall of the thorax with the coracoid process pointing anteriorly. The movements described are:

1. *Retraction*—movement of the scapula, whilst maintaining its vertical position, such that its medial border approaches the vertebral column, as in bracing the shoulder. The glenoid fossa thus comes to face more directly lateral.

2. *Protraction*—movement of the scapula forwards around the chest wall, as in rounding the shoulders. There may be some associated lateral rotation in this movement. The glenoid fossa comes to face more directly forwards.

3. *Elevation*—where the pectoral girdle is lifted upwards as in shrugging the shoulders.

4. *Depression*—where the pectoral girdle is pulled downwards.

5. *Lateral (forwards) rotation* of the pectoral girdle is a complex movement whereby the inferior angle of the scapula moves laterally around the chest wall, whereas the strut-like action of the clavicle results in a concomitant upward movement of the scapula, thus causing the glenoid fossa to be turned increasingly upwards.

6. *Medial (backward) rotation* of the pectoral girdle returns the scapula to its resting position.

MUSCLES WHICH RETRACT THE PECTORAL (SHOULDER) GIRDLE

Rhomboid minor
Rhomboid major
Trapezius

Rhomboid minor

Rhomboid minor (Fig. 4.13) is a small quadrilateral muscle whose fibres run obliquely downwards and laterally from the *spinous processes* of *C7* and *T1* and the supraspinous ligament between them and the lower part of the ligamentum nuchae, to attach to a smooth *triangular area* on the *medial border* of the *scapula* at the base of the spine.

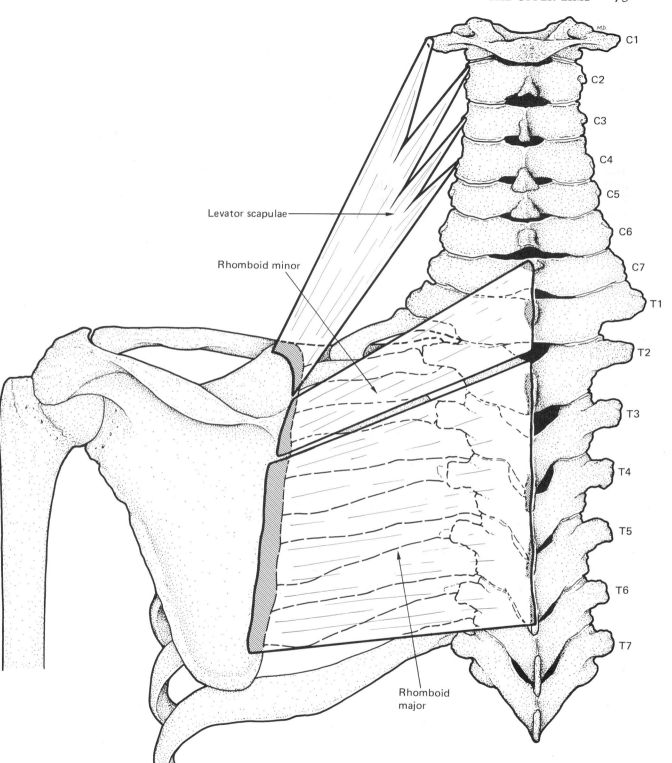

Levator scapulae

Rhomboid minor

Rhomboid
major

C1
C2
C3
C4
C5
C6
C7
T1
T2
T3
T4
T5
T6
T7

Fig. 4.13 The attachments (shaded) of levator scapulae, rhomboid minor and rhomboid major shown on the posterior aspect of the thorax.

Rhomboid major

Rhomboid major (see Fig. 4.13), although larger than rhomboid minor, may be continuous with it. It arises by tendinous slips from the *spinous processes* of *T2* to *T5* inclusive and the intervening supraspinous ligament. The muscle fibres run obliquely downwards and laterally to attach to the *medial border* of the *scapula* between the base of the spine and the inferior angle.

Both rhomboids lie on top of the muscles of the back, being themselves covered by trapezius, except for the lower border of rhomboid major which forms the floor of the 'triangle of auscultation'.

Nerve supply

Both rhomboid muscles are supplied by the *dorsal scapular nerve*, root value C5.

Action

The rhomboids act principally to retract the scapula but are also active, however, in medial rotation of the pectoral girdle. In addition they also act as important stabilizers of the scapula when other muscle groups are active.

Palpation

With the subject's hand placed in the small of his or her back (to relax trapezius), the rhomboids can be palpated through trapezius when the hand is moved backwards. Contraction of the rhomboids can be felt (and occasionally be seen) between the medial border of the scapula and the vertebral column.

Trapezius

Trapezius (Fig. 4.14) is a large, flat triangular sheet of muscle extending from the skull and spine medially to the pectoral girdle laterally. It is the most superficial muscle in the upper back and with its fellow of the opposite side it forms a trapezium, hence its name.

The middle attachment of trapezius runs from the medial third of the *superior nuchal line* and *external occipital protuberance* of the *occipital bone*, the *ligamentum nuchae*, the *spinous processes* of *C7* to *T12* inclusive and

the intervening *supraspinous ligament*. The majority of this attachment is by direct muscular slips, however a triangular aponeurosis exists in trapezius between C6 and T3 which corresponds to a hollow seen in the living subject.

From this extensive central attachment the upper fibres of trapezius run downwards and laterally, the middle fibres almost horizontally, and the lower fibres upwards and laterally to form a continuous line of attachment to the clavicle and scapula. The upper fibres descend to the *posterior border* of the *lateral third* of *clavicle*, while the middle fibres pass to the *medial border* of the *acromion* and *upper border* of the *crest* of the *spine of the scapula*, being separated from the smooth area on the medial part of the spine by a small bursa. The lowermost fibres converge to a tendon which attaches to the tubercle on the inferior edge at the medial end of the spine of the scapula.

The upper free edge of trapezius forms the posterior border of the posterior triangle of the neck, while the lower free border forms the medial boundary of the triangle of auscultation. This latter triangle is an area of the chest wall free of bony obstruction by the scapula and thinly covered by muscle. Its other boundaries are the upper border of latissimus dorsi below and the medial border of the scapula laterally.

Nerve supply

Trapezius receives its motor supply via the spinal part of the *accessory nerve* (XI) which enters it from the posterior triangle. It also receives sensory fibres from the *ventral rami* of C3,4 via the cervical plexus. The skin over trapezius is supplied by the posterior rami of C3–T12.

Action

Trapezius has an important function in stabilizing the scapula as a base for movements of the upper limb. The middle horizontal fibres pull the scapula backwards towards the midline, that is retraction, and may be aided by the upper and lower fibres contracting together to produce a 'resolved' force towards the midline (see Fig. 4.17a). The upper fibres of trapezius elevate the

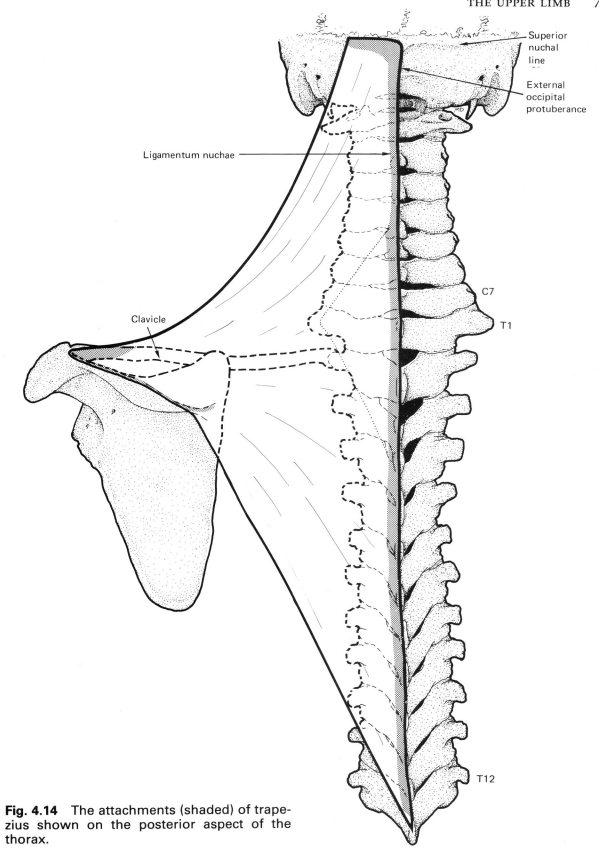

Superior
nuchal
line

External
occipital
protuberance

Ligamentum nuchae

Clavicle

C7

T1

T12

Fig. 4.14 The attachments (shaded) of trapezius shown on the posterior aspect of the thorax.

pectoral girdle and maintain the level of the shoulders against the effect of gravity, or when a weight is being carried in the hand. When both left and right muscles contract they can extend the neck, but when acting singularly the upper fibres produce lateral (side) flexion of the neck. The lower fibres pull down the medial part of the scapula and thus lower the shoulder, especially against resistance, for example when using the arms to get out of a chair. The upper and lower fibres working together produce lateral rotation of the scapula about a point towards the base of the spine. Trapezius is thus important in the overall function of the upper limb as it increases the possible range of movement.

Paralysis of trapezius, particularly its upper part, results in the scapula moving forwards around the chest wall with the inferior angle moving medially. The usually smooth curve of its upper border between the occiput and the acromion process may become markedly angulated.

Palpation

To demonstrate and palpate all three parts of trapezius, the subject should abduct both arms to 90°, flex the elbows to 90° and then rotate them laterally so that the fingers are pointing upwards.

In this position the three sets of fibres can be readily palpated; in a lean subject the contraction of the various parts of the muscle can be seen. For the lower fibres of trapezius the contraction can be further enhanced by asking the subject to clasp his or her hands together above the head and pull hard.

Soft tissue techniques are often applied to the upper muscular fibres of trapezius in the presence of muscle spasm secondary to neck pain, with the aim of inducing relaxation. Deep transverse frictions can also be applied to the tendinous attachment of trapezius on the superior nuchal line when this is the site of a lesion causing pain in the neck or occipital region.

MUSCLES WHICH PROTRACT THE PECTORAL (SHOULDER) GIRDLE

Serratus anterior
Pectoralis minor

Serratus anterior

Serratus anterior (Fig. 4.15) is a large flat muscular sheet covering the side of the thorax, being sandwiched between the ribs and the scapula. Loose fascia exists between the deep surface of the muscle and the ribs or intercostal fascia, and also between its superficial surface and subscapularis in order to facilitate free movement of the scapula. Serratus anterior forms the medial wall of the axilla, and is partly covered by the breast inferolaterally. The upper digitations are behind the clavicle while latissimus dorsi crosses its lower border.

Serratus anterior attaches by fleshy digitations just beyond the midaxillary line to the *outer surfaces* of the *upper eight* or *nine ribs* and the intervening *intercostal fascia*. The upper digitation arises from ribs one and two, whereas each of the remaining digitations arise from a single rib. The lower four digitations interdigitate with the costal attachment of the *external oblique* of the *abdomen*.

From this extensive attachment the muscle fibres run backwards to insert into the *costal surface* of the *medial border* of the *scapula* between the superior and inferior angles. The digitations are not however evenly distributed in their attachment to the scapula. The first passes almost horizontally to the superior angle, while the lower four condense to attach to the inferior angle, with the intervening ones spread along the medial border.

Nerve supply

Serratus anterior is supplied by the *long thoracic nerve*, root value C5,6,7, with the first

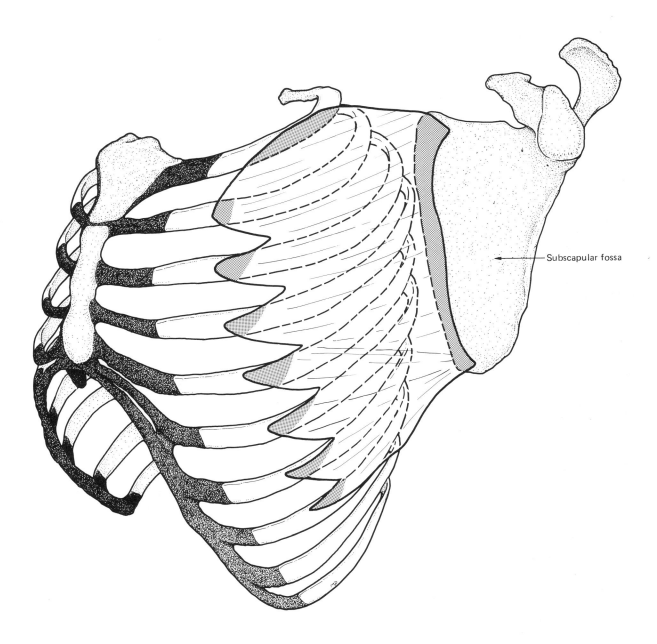

Fig. 4.15 The attachments (shaded) of serratus anterior shown on the lateral thoracic wall with the scapula lifted posteriorly.

Subscapular fossa

two digitations supplied by C5, the next two by C6 and the remaining four by C7. The nerve enters the muscle on its superficial aspect. The skin over the accessible parts of the muscle is supplied by nerves with root values of T3 to T7.

Action

Serratus anterior is a major protractor of the pectoral girdle and as such is involved in all thrusting, pushing and punching movements where the scapula is driven forwards carrying the upper limb with it. Note the massive development of this muscle in boxers.

Serratus anterior plays a vital role in stabilizing the scapula during movements of the upper limb and contracts strongly to hold the medial border of the scapula against the chest wall when the arm is flexed or when a weight is carried in front of the body. Failure to perform this action, as when paralysed, results in 'winging' of the scapula where the medial border stands away from the chest wall, thus severely affecting the function and mobility of the upper limb.

The lower digitations of the muscle work together with trapezius to laterally rotate the scapula, so that the glenoid fossa looks upwards and forwards. When paralysed, the rotating action of serratus anterior means that the upper limb cannot be abducted by more than 90°, thereby seriously limiting the functional capacity of the limb. There is some controversy as to whether serratus anterior acts as an accessory muscle of inspiration during respiratory distress. The line of action of the muscle fibres, except perhaps for the first two digitations and maybe the last, are not directed to cause elevation of the ribs. Indeed, they are more likely to cause depression of the ribs.

Palpation

In a muscular subject the digitations of serratus anterior can be felt and often seen running forwards in the region of the midaxillary line, especially when performing 'press-ups'.

Pectoralis minor

Pectoralis minor (Fig. 4.16) is a thin, flat, triangular muscle situated on the anterior chest wall deep to pectoralis major. Inferiorly it attaches to the *outer surfaces* of the *third, fourth* and *fifth ribs* close to their costal cartilages and the intervening *intercostal fascia*. There may be additional attachments to the second or sixth rib, or more rarely, to both. The fibres converge to a short, flat tendon as they pass upwards to attach to the *upper surface* and *medial border* of the *coracoid process* of the *scapula*.

Nerve supply

Pectoralis minor is supplied by the *medial pectoral nerve* which pierces it. However, within the axilla the medial and lateral pectoral nerves communicate, thereby ensuring that pectoralis minor is supplied by both pectoral nerves. The segmental supply is by C6,7 and 8.

Action

By exerting a strong pull on the coracoid process, the scapula can be pulled forwards and downwards during pushing and punching movements. When leaning on the hands it helps to transfer the weight of the trunk to the upper limb. The nature of its attachment to the coracoid process allows pectoralis minor to help produce medial rotation of the scapula against resistance (see Fig. 4.17b). With the scapula and upper limb fixed, pectoralis minor may be used as an accessory muscle of inspiration during respiratory distress.

Palpation

Contraction of pectoralis minor, lying deep to the great bulk of pectoralis major, is difficult to assess. It is never paralysed alone.

Fig. 4.16 The attachments (shaded) of pectoralis minor shown on the anterior aspect of the thorax.

MUSCLES WHICH ELEVATE THE PECTORAL (SHOULDER) GIRDLE

Trapezius (upper fibres) (see p. 76)
Levator scapulae

Levator scapulae

Levator scapulae (see Fig. 4.13) is situated in the posterior part of the neck, its upper part under cover of sternomastoid and its lower part deep to the trapezius. Its middle portion forms part of the floor of the posterior triangle. It lies superficial to the extensor muscles of the neck. It attaches by tendinous slips to the *transverse processes* of the *upper three* or *four cervical vertebrae*, (attaching to the posterior tubercles of the lower two) behind the attachment of scalenus medius. From here the fibres run downwards and laterally to attach to the *medial margin* of the *scapula* between the superior angle and base of the spine.

Nerve supply

Levator scapulae receives its nerve supply partly from the *dorsal scapular nerve* (C5) and directly from the *anterior primary rami* of C3 and 4.

Action

Working with trapezius, levator scapulae can produce elevation and retraction of the pectoral girdle or resist its downward movement, as when carrying a load in the hand. Again when working with trapezius, contraction of both sides produces extension of the neck, while one side produces lateral flexion of the neck. Levator scapulae also helps to stabilize the scapula and is active in resisted medial rotation of the scapula.

Palpation

Levator scapulae can be palpated when trapezius is not contracting (as for the rhomboids), with the subject upright and the hands in the small of the back. Levator scapulae can be felt anterior to trapezius in the posterolateral part of the neck when the hand is moved backwards with the elbow flexed.

MUSCLES WHICH PRODUCE LATERAL (FORWARD) ROTATION OF THE PECTORAL (SHOULDER) GIRDLE

Trapezius
Serratus anterior

The detailed attachments of these two muscles have already been described (see pp. 76–80).

As can be seen in Figs. 4.14 and 4.15, both muscles are well positioned to cause the inferior angle of the scapula to move laterally around the thoracic wall. The clavicle acting as a strut restricts movement at the acromion process, so that the overall effect of the action of these two muscles is to elevate the acromion process and move the inferior angle laterally, thereby enabling the glenoid fossa to face more directly upwards. This movement of the pectoral girdle is extremely important for increasing the range of movement possible, particularly in terms of abduction and flexion of the upper limb at the shoulder (see p. 166).

Trapezius contributes to the rotation by contraction of its upper fibres which lift the lateral end of the clavicle and acromion process upwards while at the same time its lower fibres pull downwards on the medial end of the spine of the scapula.

Serratus anterior, the more important of the two muscles in this movement, pulls strongly on the inferior angle of the scapula, where the majority of its muscle fibres insert, to pull it laterally around the chest wall. The notional axis about which this rotation takes place is just below the spine of the scapula towards the base. The resultant movements are shown in Fig. 4.17.

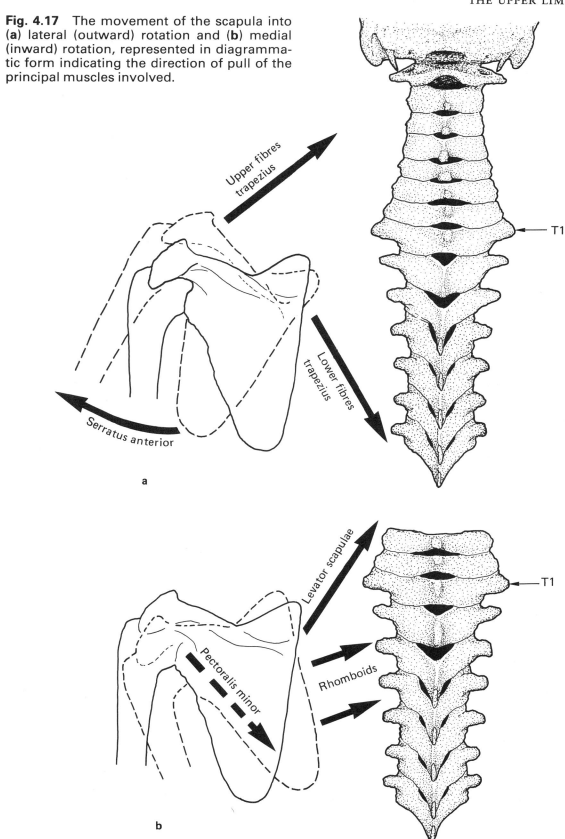

Fig. 4.17 The movement of the scapula into (**a**) lateral (outward) rotation and (**b**) medial (inward) rotation, represented in diagrammatic form indicating the direction of pull of the principal muscles involved.

MUSCLES WHICH MEDIALLY ROTATE THE PECTORAL (SHOULDER) GIRDLE

Rhomboid major
Rhomboid minor
Pectoralis minor
Levator scapulae

The detailed attachments of the above muscles have already been described on pages 74 to 82, as all are active in other movements of the pectoral girdle.

Movement of the inferior angle of the scapula towards the vertebral column is frequently produced by the action of gravity, being controlled by the eccentric activity of the lateral rotators. However, the above muscles contract strongly if the pectoral girdle is to be medially rotated against resistance, as when moving the weight of the body from a position of hanging from a beam to full chin-up. The notional axis of rotation is just below the spine of the scapula, towards the root. Pectoralis minor exerts a downward pull on the lateral side of this axis via its attachment to the coracoid process, while the rhomboids and levator scapulae pull upwards on the medial side. The resultant movements are shown in Fig. 4.17. Details of the movements of the joints of the pectoral girdle can be found in the section on joints (see pp. 158–164).

MUSCLES STABILIZING THE CLAVICLE

Subclavius

Subclavius

Subclavius (see Fig. 4.22) lies entirely beneath the clavicle under cover of pectoralis major. The small, fleshy belly of this muscle attaches to the *floor* of the *subclavian groove* on the under surface of the *clavicle*. The fibres converge and pass medially, becoming tendinous, to attach to the *first* rib near its junction with the costal cartilage.

Nerve supply

Subclavius is supplied by the *nerve to subclavius*, root value C5,6, which arises from the upper trunk of the brachial plexus.

Action

The principal action of subclavius is to steady the clavicle by pulling it towards the disc of the sternoclavicular joint and the sternum during movements of the pectoral girdle. This action tends to depress the lateral end of the clavicle. Paralysis of subclavius has no demonstrable effect.

MOVEMENTS OF THE SHOULDER JOINT

The movements of the shoulder joint will be considered as follows:

Abduction and adduction in the coronal plane
Flexion and extension in the sagittal plane
Medial and lateral rotation about the long axis of the arm.

Reference will be made to functional movements which combine some of the above.

MUSCLES WHICH ABDUCT THE ARM AT THE SHOULDER JOINT

Supraspinatus
Deltoid

Supraspinatus

Supraspinatus (Fig. 4.18) arises from the *medial two-thirds* of the *supraspinous fossa* and the deep surface of the dense fascia which covers the muscle. The muscle and the tendon which forms within it, pass laterally below trapezius, the acromion process and the coracoacromial ligament to cross over the top of the shoulder joint. The tendon of supraspinatus blends on its deep surface with the capsule of the shoulder joint prior to inserting into the upper of the three facets on the *greater tubercle* of the *humerus*.

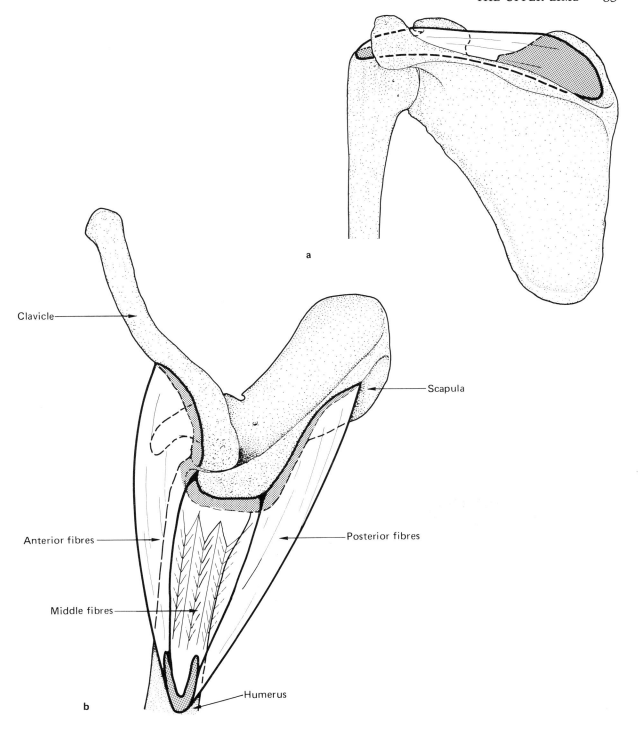

Clavicle

Scapula

Anterior fibres

Posterior fibres

Middle fibres

Humerus

a

b

Fig. 4.18 a = The attachments (shaded) of supraspinatus, posterior view. The broken lines of the muscle indicating its passage below the coracoacromial arch. **b** = The attachments (shaded) of deltoid.

Nerve supply

Supraspinatus is supplied by the *suprascapular nerve*, root value C5,6, a branch from the upper trunk of the brachial plexus. The skin over the muscle is supplied from roots C4 and T2.

Action

Supraspinatus initiates the process of abduction at the shoulder joint, being more important during the early part of the movement than later when deltoid takes over. The role of supraspinatus is probably twofold during this movement. It braces the head of the humerus firmly against the glenoid fossa to prevent an upward shearing of the humeral head, (this has been likened to a 'foot on the ladder' where a small force applied at one end will produce a rotatory rather than a shearing movement) while at the same time producing abduction. After the initial 20° of abduction, when the stronger deltoid takes over, supraspinatus acts to brace the humeral head.

Functional activity

Supraspinatus is one of the four muscles which form a musculotendinous cuff (or rotator cuff) around the head of the humerus. They function to keep the head of the humerus in the glenoid fossa during movements of the shoulder joint.

Palpation

Contraction of supraspinatus can be felt through trapezius if the examiner's fingers are pressed into the medial part of the supraspinous fossa when the subject initiates abduction at the shoulder joint. In the anatomical position, the tendon of supraspinatus is covered by the acromion process but it can be palpated if the subject medially rotates the shoulder with his or her hand resting passively in the small of the back. During this manoeuvre, the greater tubercle moves anteriorly so that the tendon can now be rolled against the bone by a medial to lateral pressure of the examiner's finger against the tubercle. The tendon of supraspinatus is the most frequently damaged soft tissue in the shoulder region and techniques, such as transverse frictions, injection and ultrasound are often applied to this exact location. In severe cases the tendon may be sufficiently eroded to cause its rupture, which then affects the ease with which abduction can occur. In such cases, or when supraspinatus is paralysed, the patient can still initiate abduction by leaning slightly to the side so using gravity. Alternatively, the patient may use the opposite arm to push the affected limb away from the side, or jerk the hips to 'kick' the elbow out. By each of these actions a small yet sufficient degree of abduction occurs to enable the powerful deltoid to take over.

Deltoid

Deltoid (see Fig. 4.18b) is a course, thick, multipennate, triangular muscle which gives the shoulder its rounded contour. Functionally it can be divided into three parts, anterior, posterior and middle, of which only the middle portion is multipennate. It has an extensive attachment to the pectoral girdle. In front, the fibres attach to the *anterior border* of the *lateral third* of the *clavicle*, whilst behind, they come from the *lower lip* of the *crest* of the *spine* of the *scapula*. The most anterior and posterior fibres both run obliquely, in an uninterrupted manner, to the *deltoid tuberosity* on the lateral surface of the shaft of the humerus.

The middle muscle fibres are more complex because of their multipennate arrangement (see Fig. 4.18b). These shorter oblique fibres run from four tendinous slips which are attached to the *lateral margin* of the *acromion process* to join three intersecting tendinous slips which ultimately run to the *deltoid tuberosity*. Consequently, these shorter, more numerous middle fibres of deltoid, working under considerable mechanical disadvantage when active, give this part of the muscle great strength.

Deltoid is separated from the coracoacromial arch and the upper and lateral aspects of the shoulder joint (and the tendons lying on it) by the *subacromial bursa*.

Nerve supply

Deltoid is supplied by the *axillary nerve*, root value C5, 6. The skin covering deltoid is supplied by roots C4 and 5.

Action

Deltoid is the principal abductor of the arm at the shoulder joint, the movement being produced by its middle, multipennate fibres. However, deltoid can only produce this movement efficiently after it has been initiated by supraspinatus.

The true plane of abduction is in line with the blade of the scapula, that is in slight flexion, and for this the anterior and posterior fibres are active in order to maintain the plane of abduction by acting as 'guy ropes'. The tendency for deltoid to produce an upward shearing of the head of the humerus is resisted by the muscles of the rotator cuff, that is by subscapularis anteriorly, teres minor and infraspinatus posteriorly, and supraspinatus from above.

The anterior part of deltoid is a strong flexor and medial rotator of the humerus, while the posterior part is a strong extensor and lateral rotator, and can help in the transfer of the strain of heavy weights carried in the hand to the pectoral girdle. The posterior part of deltoid is also active during adduction of the arm, to counteract the medial rotation produced by pectoralis major and latissimus dorsi.

Functional activity

Deltoid is active in abduction when the middle fibres contract concentrically, but the massive development and multipennate nature of the muscle is probably due to the fact that many activities of the upper limb require that it be maintained or 'held' in this position for long periods of time. Consequently, the middle fibres contract statically when performing activities with the arms in front of the trunk; they then lower the arm back to the side by operating in an eccentric mode.

Palpation

If the seated subject is asked to raise the arm to 60° of abduction in the plane of the scapula, the triangular bulk of deltoid can be felt and seen. Palpating the upper surface of the acromion process and moving the fingers laterally from its edge, the depressions in the muscle caused by the tendinous intersections can be felt if anteroposterior pressure of the fingers is applied.

The anterior and posterior fibres can be made to stand out more clearly if, in the same position as above, the subject is asked to maintain the position against resistance first anteriorly and then posteriorly.

Paralysis of deltoid severely affects the functioning of the shoulder joint and therefore of the upper limb.

MUSCLES WHICH FLEX THE ARM AT THE SHOULDER JOINT

Pectoralis major
Deltoid—anterior fibres (see pp. 86–87)
Biceps brachii—long head (see p. 100)
Coracobrachialis (see p. 94)

Pectoralis major

Pectoralis major (Fig. 4.19) is found on the upper half of the anterior surface of the thoracic wall. It is a thick triangular muscle with clavicular and sternocostal parts, which may be separated by a groove, although they are usually continuous with each other. On their way to the humerus, the twisting fibres of pectoralis major form the rounded anterior fold of the axilla.

The smaller, clavicular attachment of pectoralis major is from the *medial half* of the *anterior surface* of the *clavicle*; the larger, sternocostal attachment comes from the *anterior surface* of the *manubrium* and *body* of the *sternum*, the anterior aspects of the *upper six costal cartilages*, the anterior part of the *sixth rib* as well as the *aponeurosis* of the *external oblique muscle* of the abdomen.

From this large central attachment, the muscle narrows and inserts via a laminated tendon into the *lateral lip* of the *intertubercular sulcus* of the *humerus*. The anterior lamina, which comprises the clavicular part of the muscle, runs to the lower part of the humeral attachment. Fibres from the sternocostal part of the chest wall form the posterior lamina, which passes upwards behind the anterior lamina to the upper part of the attachment of the muscle to the humerus. In this way the tendon comes to resemble a U in cross-section. The posterior part blends with the shoulder joint capsule, while the anterior, clavicular fibres blend with the attachment of deltoid.

As the most superficial of the muscles of the anterior thoracic wall, pectoralis major lies on top of pectoralis minor, the ribs and serratus anterior. In the female, the muscle is covered by the breast, indeed the fibrous septa of the breast are attached to the deep fascia overlying pectoralis major. Pectoralis major is separated from deltoid by the delto-pectoral groove (the infraclavicular fossa) in which lie the cephalic vein and branches from the thoracoacromial artery.

Nerve supply

Pectoralis major is supplied by the *medial* (C8, T1) and the *lateral* (C5, 6, 7) *pectoral nerves*; the clavicular part by roots C5 and 6, and the sternocostal part by C7, 8 and T1. The skin over pectoralis major is supplied by roots T2 to T6.

Action

Pectoralis major as a whole is a powerful adductor and medial rotator of the humerus at the shoulder joint. In addition the clavicular part can flex the humerus to the horizontal, while the sternocostal fibres, because of their direction, can extend the flexed humerus, particularly against resistance. With the humerus fixed, as in gripping a bed table or chair back, pectoralis major pulls on the upper ribs to assist inspiration during respiratory distress.

Functional activity

Pectoralis major is one of the major climbing muscles, so that if the arms are fixed above the head, the massive power of the muscle can be used to pull the trunk upwards. It is assisted in this activity by latissimus dorsi. In pushing, punching and throwing movements, pectoralis major acts to move the humerus forwards forcefully, whilst serratus anterior and pectoralis minor simultaneously protract the pectoral girdle.

In exercises, such as the 'press-up', pectoralis major contracts concentrically on the upward movement and eccentrically on the downward when lowering the body.

Palpation

The clavicular part of pectoralis major can be readily palpated if the arm is flexed to 60° and held against downward pressure. The sternocostal part is best palpated if this same position is maintained against an upward pressure. The integrity of the muscle can be tested by adduction of the arm against resistance.

Fig. 4.19 The attachments (shaded) of pectoralis major, anterior view.

MUSCLES WHICH EXTEND THE ARM AT THE SHOULDER JOINT

Latissimus dorsi
Teres major
Pectoralis major (see p. 88)
Deltoid (posterior fibres) (see pp. 86–87)
Triceps (long head) (see pp. 104–106)

Latissimus dorsi

Latissimus dorsi (Fig. 4.20) is a large flat triangular sheet of muscle running between the trunk, via an extensive attachment, and the humerus by a narrow tendon. Consequently, it acts on both the pectoral girdle and the shoulder joint. The superior surface of the muscle forms the lower border of the triangle of auscultation, while its lateral border forms the medial border of the lumbar triangle.

Latissimus dorsi arises from the posterior layer of the *thoracolumbar fascia*, which attaches to the *spinous processes* of the *lower six thoracic* and *all* of the *lumbar* and *sacral vertebrae*, as well as to the intervening *supraspinous* and *interspinous ligaments*.

That part arising from the lower six thoracic vertebrae is covered by trapezius. In addition to this vertebral attachment, latissimus dorsi arises from the posterior part of the outer lip of the *iliac crest*, most laterally by direct muscular slips. As the muscle fibres sweep upwards and laterally across the lower part of the thorax, they attach to the *outer surfaces* of the *lower three* or *four ribs* and the *inferior angle* of the *scapula*, for which the muscle almost forms a sling. From this widespread origin the fibres converge as they pass to the humerus and form a thin flattened tendon. The tendon winds around and adheres to the lower border of teres major, and inserts into the *floor* of the *intertubercular sulcus* anterior to the tendon of teres major, being separated from it by a bursa. The effect of twisting the muscle through 180° means that the anterior surface of the tendon is continuous with the posterior surface of the rest of the muscle. Consequently, the fibres with the lowest origin on the trunk gain the highest attachment on the humerus.

Nerve supply

Latissimus dorsi is supplied by the *thoracodorsal nerve*, root value C6, 7, 8, which enters the muscle on its deep surface. The skin covering the muscle is supplied by roots T4 to T12 inclusive, by both anterior and posterior primary rami, and L1 to L3 by the posterior rami.

Action

Latissimus dorsi is a strong extensor of the flexed arm, however, if the humerus is fixed relative to the scapula it retracts the pectoral girdle. It is also a strong adductor and medial rotator of the humerus at the shoulder joint.

Functional activity

Functionally, latissimus dorsi is a climbing muscle, and with the arms fixed above the head it can raise the trunk upwards, in conjunction with pectoralis major. Latissimus dorsi has an important function in rowing and during the downstroke in swimming. Attachment of the muscle to the ribs means that it is active in violent expiration, and can be felt pressing forcibly inwards during a cough or sneeze, as it acts to compress the thorax and abdomen.

The attachment to the inferior angle of the scapula allows latissimus dorsi to assist in holding it against the thorax during movements of the upper limb.

If the humerus becomes the fixed point when standing, as for example when using crutches, latissimus dorsi is able to pull the trunk forwards relative to the arms; associated with this is a lifting of the pelvis. In patients with paralysis of the lower half of the body, the fact that latissimus dorsi attaches to the pelvis and is still innervated allows it to be used to produce movement of the pelvis and trunk. Consequently, patients wearing calipers and using crutches can produce a modified gait by fixing the arms and hitching the hips by the alternate contraction of each latissimus dorsi.

Twelfth rib

Fig. 4.20 The attachments (shaded) of latissimus dorsi, posterior view.

Palpation

In a lean subject, latissimus dorsi can be made to stand out relative to the thorax by asking the subject to raise his or her arm to 90° flexion and to hold it steady against an upwardly directed pressure. The muscle can be felt contracting if the posterior axillary fold is held between the finger and thumb while the subject coughs. Adduction of the abducted arm against resistance also enables latissimus dorsi to be seen and felt.

Teres major

In the posterior part of the axilla, teres major (Fig. 4.21) forms the lower boundary of both the upper triangular and quadrangular spaces. It is a thick, chunky muscle, forming, with latissimus dorsi, the posterior fold of the axilla. It arises from an oval area on the *dorsal surface* of the *scapula* near the *inferior angle*, and from the *fascia* between it and adjacent muscles. The muscle fibres, which adhere to those of latissimus dorsi, run upwards and laterally to form a broad, flat tendon which attaches along the *medial lip* of the *intertubercular sulcus*. The tendon is separated from that of latissimus dorsi by a bursa, with the latter muscle virtually covering the whole of teres major.

Nerve supply

Teres major is supplied by the *lower subscapular nerve*, root value C6 and 7.

Action

Teres major adducts and medially rotates the humerus at the shoulder joint. In addition it can help to extend the flexed arm.

Functional activity

Teres major, like latissimus dorsi, is a climbing muscle and works with the latter and pectoralis major to pull the trunk upwards when the arms are fixed. In conjunction with latissimus dorsi and pectoralis major, teres major is important in stabilizing the shoulder joint.

Palpation

Teres major is covered by latissimus dorsi, and as these two muscles have similar actions, considerable care must be exercised when it is tested. The inferior angle of the scapula must first be found, the fingers are then moved upwards and laterally into the posterior wall of the axilla. The subject should then abduct the arm to 90° and keep it there against an upwardly directed resistance. The rounded contour of teres major should now be palpable. During this same manoeuvre the flattened tendon of latissimus dorsi, as it twists around teres major, may also be felt.

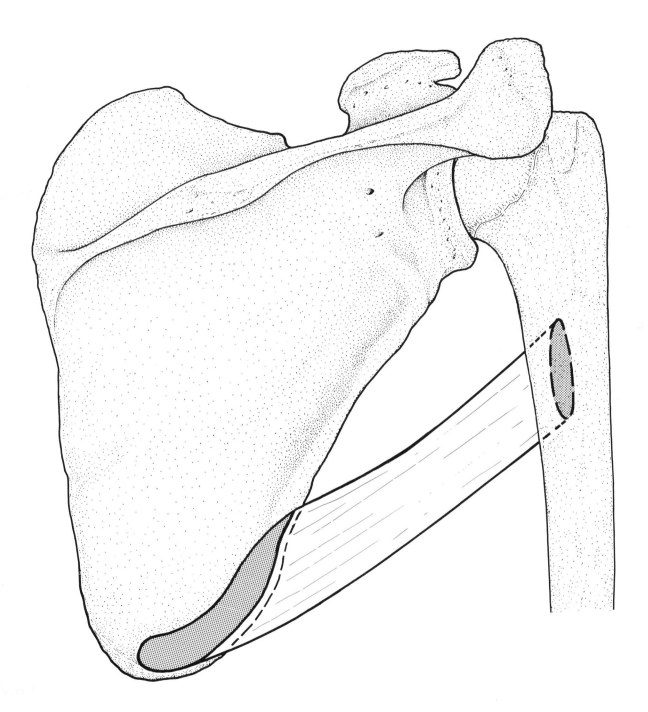

Fig. 4.21   The attachments (shaded) of teres major, posterior view.

MUSCLES WHICH ADDUCT THE ARM AT THE SHOULDER JOINT

Coracobrachialis
Pectoralis major (see p. 88)
Latissimus dorsi (—see p. 90)
Teres major (see p. 92)

Coracobrachialis

Coracobrachialis (Fig. 4.22) is the only true representative in the arm of the adductor group of muscles found on the leg. It arises via a rounded tendon, in conjunction with the short head of biceps brachii, from the *apex* of the *coracoid process* of the *scapula* and attaches by a flat tendon to the *medial side* of the *shaft* of the *humerus* at about its *mid-point*, between triceps and brachialis. Some fibres may continue into the medial inter-muscular septum of the arm.

Nerve supply

Coracobrachialis is usually supplied by the *musculocutaneous nerve* as it pierces the muscle, root value C6, 7. However, the nerve to coracobrachialis may arise directly from the lateral cord of the brachial plexus. The skin over the muscle is supplied by roots T1 and T2.

Action

Coracobrachialis is an adductor and weak flexor of the arm at the shoulder joint.

Palpation

Coracobrachialis can be seen and felt as a rounded muscular ridge on the medial side of the arm when it is fully abducted and held in this position against resistance.

Fig. 4.22 The attachments (shaded) of sub-clavius and coracobrachialis, anterior view.

MUSCLES WHICH MEDIALLY ROTATE THE ARM AT THE SHOULDER JOINT

Subscapularis
Teres major (see p. 92)
Latissimus dorsi (see p. 90)
Pectoralis major (see p. 88)
Deltoid (anterior fibres) (see pp. 86–87)

Subscapularis

Subscapularis (Fig. 4.23) forms the greater part of the posterior wall of the axilla and as such lies in close proximity to teres major and latissimus dorsi. The anterior surface of the muscle lies on serratus anterior. When seen from the front it forms the upper boundary of the upper triangular and quadrangular spaces.

Subscapularis is a multipennate muscle which arises from the *medial two-thirds* of the *subscapular fossa* and from tendinous *septa*, which reinforce the muscle, attached to bony ridges in the fossa. There is also an attachment to the fascia covering the muscle. The muscle fibres narrow and form a broad, thick tendon which attaches to the *lesser tubercle* of the *humerus*, the capsule of the shoulder joint and the front of the humerus below the tuberosity. A bursa, which communicates directly with the shoulder joint, separates the tendon from the neck of the scapula.

Nerve supply

Subscapularis is supplied by the *upper* and *lower subscapular nerves*, root value C5, 6 and 7, from the posterior cord of the brachial plexus.

Action

Subscapularis is a strong medial rotator of the arm at the shoulder joint; it may also assist in adduction of the arm.

Functional activity

As part of the 'rotator cuff', subscapularis plays an important role in maintaining the integrity of the shoulder joint during movement, by keeping the head of the humerus within the glenoid fossa. It also resists upward displacement of the humeral head when deltoid, biceps and the long head of triceps are active.

Palpation

The muscle belly cannot be palpated as it lies deep to the scapula. However, careful deep palpation may allow the tendon to be felt just before its insertion onto the lesser tuberosity.

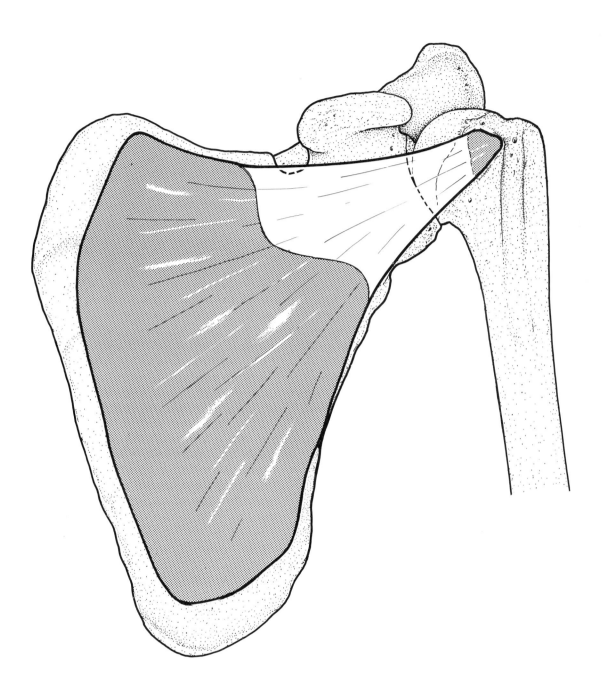

Fig. 4.23 The attachments (shaded) of sub-scapularis, anterior view.

MUSCLES WHICH LATERALLY ROTATE THE ARM AT THE SHOULDER JOINT

Teres minor
Infraspinatus
Deltoid (posterior fibres) (see pp. 86–87)

Teres minor

When seen from the back, teres minor (Fig. 4.24) forms the upper boundary of both the upper triangular and quadrangular spaces. It is a thin muscle which arises by two heads, separated by a groove for the circumflex scapular artery, from the *upper two-thirds* of the *lateral border* of the *scapula*, and the *fascia* between it and teres major (below) and infraspinatus (above). The fibres run upwards and laterally forming a narrow tendon which attaches to the *lowest* of the *facets* on the *greater tubercle* of the *humerus* and to the bone immediately below. The tendon reinforces and blends with the lower posterior part of the capsule of the shoulder joint.

Nerve supply

Teres minor is supplied by the *axillary nerve*, root value C5 and 6. The skin over the muscle is supplied by roots T1, 2 and 3.

Action and palpation

These are considered with infraspinatus.

Infraspinatus

Infraspinatus (Fig. 4.24) is a thick, triangular bipennate muscle which arises from the *medial two-thirds* of the *infraspinous fossa* of the *scapula*, tendinous intersections attached to ridges in this fossa, and the thick fascia covering the muscle. The fibres converge to a narrow tendon which inserts onto the *mid-dle facet* on the *greater tubercle* of the *humerus*, and into the posterior part of the capsule of the shoulder joint. A bursa, which occasionally communicates with the shoulder joint, separates the muscle from the neck of the scapula. The upper part of the muscle lies deep to trapezius, deltoid and the acromion process, however, the lower part is superficial.

Nerve supply

Infraspinatus is supplied by the *suprascapular nerve*, root value C5 and 6. The skin over the muscle is supplied by the posterior rami of T1 to T6.

Action

Infraspinatus and teres minor are both lateral rotators of the arm at the shoulder joint.

Functional activity

Infraspinatus and teres minor are of importance during the sequence of movements which occur when the arm is fully abducted. During the latter part of this movement the humerus is laterally rotated so that the greater tubercle moves clear of the coracoacromial arch thereby enabling the remaining part of the humeral head to come into contact with the glenoid fossa, and full abduction to occur (see p. 186).

Teres minor, infraspinatus, supraspinatus and subscapularis, the musculotendinous 'rotator cuff' of extensible ligaments around the shoulder joint, are all concerned with its stability; the proximity of their tendons to the joint enhances their effect. During movements of the head of the humerus on the glenoid fossa, interplay between these muscles reduces the sliding and shearing movements which tend to occur. When carrying a weight in the hand these same four muscles brace the head of the humerus against the glenoid fossa.

Palpation

When the arm is laterally rotated, contraction of infraspinatus can be felt in the medial part of the infraspinous fossa. Its tendon can be palpated if the greater tuberosity is moved from below the acromion process. To accomplish this the subject lies prone supporting him or herself on the elbows and forearms. The arm is then laterally rotated some 25° and slightly adducted. The tendon can now be palpated just below the acromial angle. It is at this point that soft tissue techniques, such as transverse frictions or electrical treatments are applied if the tendon becomes inflamed.

Teres minor can be felt contracting if the examiner's fingers are placed half way up the lateral border of the scapula and the arm is then actively laterally rotated. The tendon is found just below that of infraspinatus as determined above.

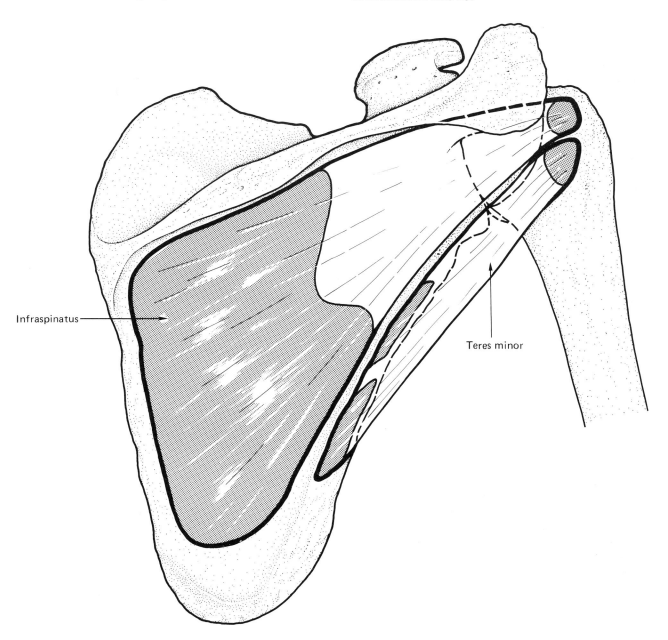

Infraspinatus

Teres minor

Fig. 4.24 The attachments (shaded) of infraspinatus and teres minor, posterior view.

MUSCLES WHICH FLEX THE ELBOW JOINT

Biceps brachii
Brachialis
Brachioradialis
Pronator teres (see p. 108

Biceps brachii

Biceps brachii (Fig. 4.25) is a prominent fusi-form muscle on the anterior aspect of the arm. It arises by two tendinous heads at its upper end, and attaches by two tendinous insertions at its lower end. The upper end is covered by deltoid and pectoralis major, but the main part of the muscle is only covered by skin and subcutaneous fat.

The short head of biceps brachii arises by a flat tendon, shared with coracobrachialis, from the *apex* of the *coracoid process* of the *scapula*. The long head arises from the *supraglenoid tubercle* of the *scapula* and the adjacent *glenoidal labrum* of the shoulder joint. The tendon of the long head runs within the shoulder joint wrapped in a syno-vial sleeve and leaves to enter the intertuber-cular sulcus by passing deep to the transverse humeral ligament. The two fleshy bellies continue towards the elbow with the two heads fusing to form a single muscle just below the middle of the arm. At the elbow, a single flattened tendon is formed which twists through 90° before attaching to the *posterior part* of the *radial tuberosity*. A bursa separates the tendon from the remainder of the radial tuberosity. The prominent *bicipital aponeurosis*, a strong membranous band arising from the lateral side of the main tendon, runs downwards and medially across the cubital fossa, in front of the brachial artery and median nerve, to attach to the deep fascia on the ulnar side of the forearm (Fig. 4.25).

Nerve supply

Biceps brachii is supplied by the *musculocuta-neous nerve*, root value C5, and 6. The skin over biceps is supplied by the roots C5, 6, T2 and T3.

Action

Biceps brachii is not only an important flexor of the elbow joint, but also a powerful supi-nator of the forearm. Often these two actions are performed together with any unwanted actions being cancelled by antag-onists. Maximum power is achieved for both flexion and supination with the elbow at 90°. When the elbow is fully extended the supi-nating action of biceps is lost. Biceps is also a flexor of the shoulder joint, and the fact that the long head crosses the superior part of the joint, means that it has an important stabilizing role.

Functional activity

Biceps may use its supinatory and flexing actions sequentially in an activity, as, for example, in inserting a corkscrew and pull-ing out the cork. During this activity the head of the ulna may move medially due to the force of the biceps contraction trans-mitted to its posterior border via the bicipital aponeurosis.

When deltoid is paralysed, the long head of biceps can be re-educated to abduct the shoulder. This is accomplished by laterally rotating the humerus at the shoulder joint in order to put the long head into a more appropriate position.

Palpation

With the elbow flexed to 90° and the forearm pronated, the muscle can be felt contracting in the middle of the arm when supination against resistance is attempted.

The lower part of the muscle is easily pal-pated through the skin. Proximally, each tendon may be palpated but with some degree of difficulty. The tendon of the long head lies between the two tubercles. Having determined these, firm deep pressure between them is needed to locate the ten-don. This is the point at which deep trans-verse frictions or electrical treatments are applied when the tendon becomes inflamed.

The short head can be found by first pal-pating the apex of the coracoid process, and

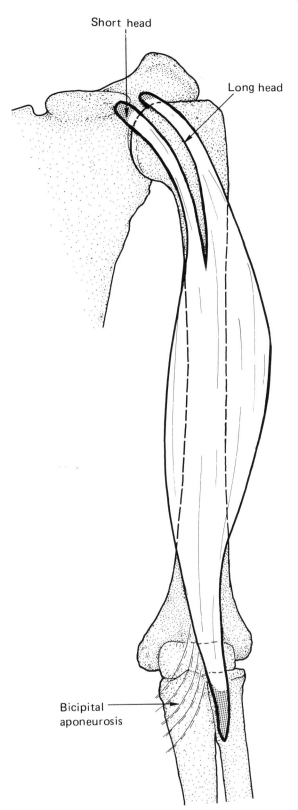

Short head

Long head

Bicipital
aponeurosis

Fig. 4.25 The attachments (shaded) of biceps
brachii, anterior view.

then placing the fingers just below it. As the elbow is flexed, the tendon can be felt to stand out.

At the elbow, the tendon of insertion is best palpated with the elbow flexed to 20°. In this position it can be easily gripped between the index finger and thumb. If, in this same position, the subject is asked to resist a strong downward pressure on the forearm, the upper border of the bicipital aponeurosis can be seen and felt as a crescentic border running downwards and medially from the main tendon.

The tendon of biceps is the point at which the biceps reflex is tested, often by the examiner placing his or her thumb over the tendon and then tapping it with a patella hammer. The resultant reflex contraction can be felt below the thumb and biceps may be seen contracting if the reflex is brisk enough.

Brachialis

Brachialis (Fig. 4.26a) lies under cover of biceps brachii in the lower half of the anterior aspect of the arm. It arises from the *distal two-thirds* of the *anterior surface* of the *shaft* of the *humerus* extending outwards onto the medial and lateral intermuscular septa. The muscle fibres are separated from the lower part of the lateral intermuscular septum by brachioradialis, with which it may be partly fused, and extensor carpi radialis longus. The fibres converge to a thick tendon which forms the floor of the cubital fossa and attaches to the rough *triangular brachialis impression* on the *inferior* part of the *coronoid process* and *tuberosity* of the *ulna*. Some deeper fibres of brachialis insert into the capsule of the elbow joint and serve to pull it away from the moving bones during flexion and prevent them from becoming trapped.

Nerve supply

Brachialis is supplied mainly by the *musculocutaneous nerve*, root value C5 and 6; but also receives a branch from the *radial nerve*, again root value C5 and 6, as it runs along the lateral border of the muscle. However, this latter branch is thought to be almost entirely sensory.

Action

Brachialis is the main flexor of the elbow joint.

Functional activity

Although brachialis flexes the elbow, it is important in controlling extension produced by gravity. In this situation, the flexors of the elbow control the movement by an eccentric contraction.

Palpation

When biceps brachii has been identified (see p. 100), brachialis can be felt extending either side of its belly with the elbow flexed. The tendon can be palpated by applying deep pressure just above the coronoid process of the ulna.

Brachioradialis

Brachioradialis (Fig. 4.26b) is a superficial muscle found on the lateral side of the forearm extending almost as far as the wrist. It forms the lateral border of the cubital fossa, and is covered in its upper part by brachialis, with which it may be partly fused. The proximal attachment of brachioradialis is to the *upper two-thirds* of the *front* of the *lateral supracondylar ridge* of the *humerus* and the adjacent part of the *lateral intermuscular septum*. From here, the fibres run downwards forming a long, narrow, flat tendon in the middle of the forearm. The tendon is crossed by those of abductor pollicis longus and extensor pollicis brevis before it attaches to the *lateral surface* of the *radius* just above the styloid process.

Nerve supply

Brachioradialis is supplied by a branch from the *radial nerve*, root value C5 and 6, which enters its medial side above the elbow. The skin over the muscle is also supplied by roots C5 and 6.

Action

Brachioradialis is a flexor of the elbow joint particularly when the forearm is midway

Fig. 4.26 The attachments (shaded) of (**a**) brachialis and (**b**) brachioradialis, anterior view.

a

b

between pronation and supination. Brachioradialis also helps to return the forearm to this mid position from the extremes of either pronation or supination, and this can be confirmed by palpation.

Functional activity

Brachioradialis acts primarily to maintain the integrity of the elbow joint since its fibres run more or less parallel to the radius. It also works eccentrically as an extensor of the elbow joint in activities such as hammering.

Palpation

With the subject's forearm in a mid-pronated position and the elbow flexed to 90°, the muscle can be seen and felt along the top of the forearm when the position is maintained against resistance. Using firm pressure, the tendon can be palpated proximal to the radial styloid process. In this same position, the brachioradialis reflex can be elicited by firmly tapping its tendon with a patella hammer just above the wrist.

MUSCLES WHICH EXTEND THE ELBOW JOINT

Triceps brachii
Anconeus

Triceps brachii

Triceps brachii (Fig. 4.27a) is situated on the back of the arm and, as suggested by its name, arises by three heads. Two of the heads arise from the humerus, being separated by the spiral groove, and the third comes from the scapula. The three heads are referred to as: the long head, lateral head and medial head. The muscle attaches via a tendon to the ulna.

Long head

The tendinous long head comes from the *infraglenoid tubercle* of the *scapula* and the adjacent *glenoidal labrum*, where it blends with the lower part of the shoulder joint cap-

sule. Named after its length, the long head is also the most medial of the three, the fibres running downwards superficial to the medial head before joining the tendon of insertion. As the long head descends from the infraglenoid tubercle, it passes between teres minor, to which it is anterior, and teres major, to which it is posterior. In its course it forms the medial border of the quadrangular and lower triangular spaces, and the lateral border of the upper triangular space.

Lateral head

The fleshy lateral head arises *above* and *lateral* to the *spiral groove* on the *posterior surface* of the *humerus* between the attachments of teres minor and deltoid. As the fibres pass to join with those of the medial head, they cover the spiral groove.

Medial head

The large, fleshy medial head lies deep to the other two, and arises from the *posterior surface* of the *humerus, below* and *medial* to the *spiral groove* as far distally as the olecranon fossa. It has an additional attachment to the posterior aspect of the medial and lateral intermuscular septa.

The three heads of triceps come together to form a broad, laminated tendon; the superficial part of which covers the posterior aspect of the lower third of the muscle, while the deeper part arises from within the substance of the muscle. Such an arrangement creates a larger surface area for the attachment of the muscle fibres. Both laminae blend to form a single tendon which attaches to the *posterior part* of the *proximal surface* of the *olecranon* of the *ulna*, and to the *deep fascia* of the *forearm* on either side. Some muscle fibres from the medial head attach to the posterior part of the capsule of the elbow joint and serve to pull it clear of the moving bones and prevent it becoming trapped during extension of the joint.

Nerve supply

All three parts of the muscle are supplied separately by branches from the *radial nerve*. The branch to the lateral head is derived

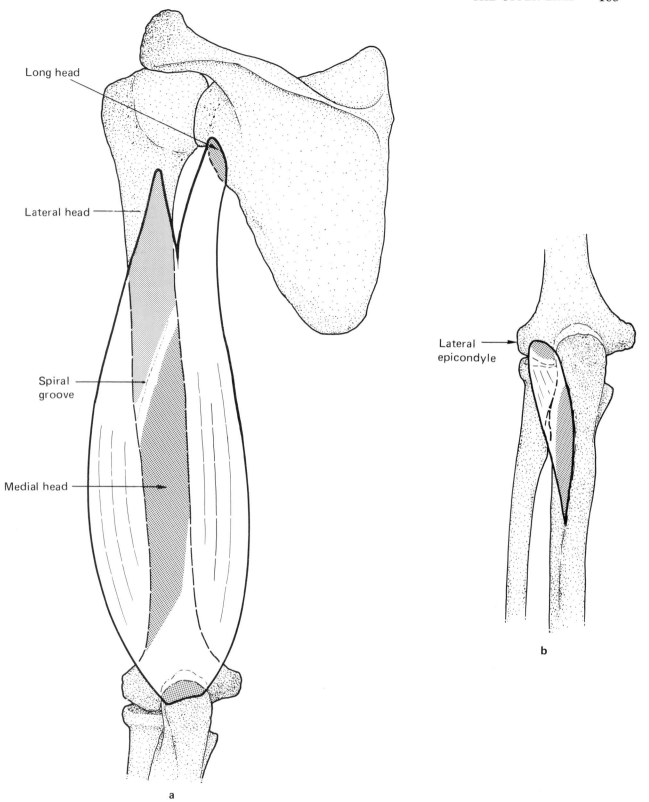

Long head

Lateral head

Spiral
groove

Medial head

a

Lateral
epicondyle

b

Fig. 4.27   The attachments (shaded) of (**a**) triceps and (**b**) anconeus, posterior view.

from C6, 7 and 8, while those to the long and medial heads come from C7 and 8. Of these, the medial head receives two branches, one of which accompanies the ulnar nerve for a considerable distance before entering the distal part of the muscle. The other branch enters more proximally, continuing through the substance of the muscle to end in, and supply, anconeus. The skin over the muscle is supplied by roots C5, 7, T1 and T2.

Action

Triceps brachii is the extensor of the elbow joint. The long head can also adduct the arm and extend it from a flexed position.

Functional activity

Once the elbow has been flexed, gravity often provides the necessary force for extension, with the elbow flexors working eccentrically to control the movement. Triceps only becomes active in this form of extension when the speed of the movement becomes important as in executing a Karate chop. Triceps works strongly in pushing and punching activities, and when performing 'press-ups'. In the latter it is working concentrically in the upward movement, and eccentrically in the downward movement. It works in a similar manner when using the arms to get out of, or to lower oneself into, a chair with arms, or when using crutches or parallel bars to relieve body-weight from the legs during walking. When using a wheelchair, triceps brachii works strongly to push the wheel round and so propel the chair forwards.

Triceps brachii is also an important extensile ligament on the under surface of the shoulder joint capsule during abduction of the arm.

Palpation

The bulk of triceps is easy to see and feel on the posterior aspect of the arm (Fig. 4.28). All three heads can be felt contracting if the subject flexes the elbow to 90° with the hand resting on a table, and then alternately presses downwards and relaxes. The long head can be felt high up on the back of the

arm almost at the axilla; careful palpation enables it to be traced almost to its insertion on the scapula. The lateral head can be felt on the upper lateral part of the arm, extending as far round as the biceps brachii, while the medial head, covered by the other two heads, can be felt contracting just above the olecranon.

The thick tendon of triceps can be easily gripped between the thumb and index finger of the examiner's hand, just above the olecranon of the ulna.

Anconeus

Anconeus (see Fig. 4.27b) is a small triangular muscle situated immediately behind the elbow joint, appearing almost to be part of triceps brachii. It arises from the *posterior surface* of the *lateral epicondyle* of the *humerus* and the adjacent part of the elbow joint capsule. The fibres pass medially and distally to attach to the *lateral surface* of the *olecranon* and *upper quarter* of the *posterior surface* of the *ulna* and to the fascia which covers it.

Nerve supply

Anconeus is supplied by a branch of the *radial nerve* to the medial head of triceps, root value C7 and 8. The skin over anconeus is supplied by root T1.

Action

Anconeus assists in extension of the elbow joint.

Functional activity

By virtue of its long attachment on the ulna, it is thought that anconeus produces lateral movement (abduction of the ulna) and extension of the bone at its distal end. These movements occur during pronation and are essential if a tool, such as a screwdriver, is being used. Movement of the ulna with respect to the radius allows the axis of pronation and supination to be altered so that the forearm rotates about a single axis and so does not describe an arc. This can be seen on an articulated skeleton. This action allows the rotatory movement of the fore-

Fig. 4.28a,b Shoulder muscles of the upper arm:

1 = Trapezius
2 = Teres major
3 = Latissimus dorsi
4 = Pectoralis major
5 = Deltoid
6 = Biceps
  a = Bicipital aponeurosis

7 = Coracobrachialis
8 = Brachialis
9 = Triceps
  a = Long head
  b = Lateral head
  c = Tendon

arm to be transmitted along the screwdriver into the head of the screw.

Palpation

Anconeus can be palpated between the lateral epicondyle of the humerus and the upper part of the ulna during pronation and supination, particularly if the axis of rotation is maintained through the extended index finger. As a practical exercise, it can be demonstrated that anconeus alters the axis of pronation and supination by making each of the fingers, in turn, the axis of rotation.

MUSCLES WHICH PRODUCE PRONATION OF THE FOREARM

Pronator teres
Pronator quadratus
Brachioradialis (see pp. 102–104)

Pronator teres

Pronator teres (Fig. 4.29a) forms the medial border of the cubital fossa at the elbow, and as such is the most lateral of the superficial muscles in the flexor compartment of the forearm. It arises by two heads: the humeral head and the ulnar head. The humeral head arises from the lower part of the *medial supracondylar ridge* and adjacent intermuscular septum. It also comes from the common flexor origin on the *medial epicondyle* and the covering fascia. The ulnar head arises from the *pronator ridge*, which runs downwards from the medial part of the *coronoid process*, to join with the humeral head on its deep surface. Between these two heads passes the median nerve. The muscle fibres pass downwards and laterally to attach via a flattened tendon into a roughened oval area on the middle of the *lateral surface* of the *radius*.

Nerve supply

Pronator teres is supplied by the *median nerve*, root values C6, 7. The overlying skin is supplied by roots C6 and T1.

Action

Pronator teres pronates the forearm by producing an anteromedial swing of the lower end of the radius around the ulna. This movement of the radius carries the hand with it. Pronator teres is also a weak flexor of the elbow.

Palpation

The muscle can be palpated running along the medial border of the cubital fossa between the medial epicondyle of the humerus and the middle of the radius. Pronator teres can be most easily felt, and occasionally seen, when resisting pronation of the forearm.

Pronator quadratus

Pronator quadratus (Fig. 4.29a) is a fleshy, quadrangular muscle lying within the flexor compartment of the forearm. It passes transversely from the lower quarter of the *anterior surface* of the *ulna* to the lower quarter of the *anterior surface* of the *radius*. Some of its deeper fibres attach to the triangular area above the ulnar notch of the radius.

Nerve supply

Pronator quadratus is supplied by the anterior interosseous branch of the *median nerve*, root value C8, T1. The skin overlying the muscle is supplied by roots C6, 7, 8.

Action

Pronator quadratus is the principal pronator of the forearm. The transverse nature of its fibres allows the lower ends of the radius and ulna to be held together when upward pressure is applied, for example when the hand is weight-bearing. It therefore protects the inferior radioulnar joint.

Palpation

Pronator quadratus is difficult to palpate because of its deep position, but if firm pressure is applied between the long flexor tendons in the lower part of the forearm, contraction of the muscle may be felt when it acts against resistance.

Medial epicondyle

Pronator teres

Pronator quadratus

Fig. 4.29a The attachments (shaded) of pronator teres and pronator quadratus of the left arm, anterior view.

MUSCLES WHICH PRODUCE SUPINATION OF THE FOREARM

Supinator
Biceps brachii (see p. 100)
Brachioradialis (see pp. 102–104)

Supinator

Supinator (Fig. 4.29b) lies deep in the upper part of the forearm concealed by the superficial muscles as it surrounds the upper end of the radius. The two heads of the supinator arise in a continuous manner from the *inferior aspect* of the *lateral epicondyle* of the *humerus*, the *radial collateral ligament*, the *annular ligament*, the *supinator crest* and *fossa of ulna*. It is often convenient, however, to think of the supinator as arising by two heads, the humeral and ulnar, between which passes the posterior interosseous nerve to gain access to the extensor compartment of the forearm. From this extensive origin, the muscle fibres pass downwards and laterally to wrap around the upper third of the radius. They insert into the *posterior*, *lateral* and *anterior aspects* of the *radius*, as far forwards as the anterior margin, proximal to the neck and distal to the attachment of pronator teres.

Nerve supply

Supinator is supplied by the posterior interosseous branch of the *radial nerve*, root value C5 and 6. However, the skin overlying the supinator is supplied by roots C5, 6 and T1.

Action

Supinator, as its name suggests, produces supination of the forearm, in which there is an anterolateral swing of the lower end of the radius around the ulna causing the two bones to lie parallel to each other. Unless a particularly powerful supinatory action is required, supinator is probably the prime mover. However, if a powerful movement is required, biceps brachii is recruited to produce the movement. It must be remembered, however, that biceps brachii cannot function as a supinator with the elbow fully extended, and consequently powerful supinatory movements are performed with the elbow flexed to about 120°.

Palpation

With the arm fully extended at the elbow, and the forearm in a mid-pronated position, supinator can be felt contracting over the posterior part of the upper third of the radius when the arm is supinated against resistance.

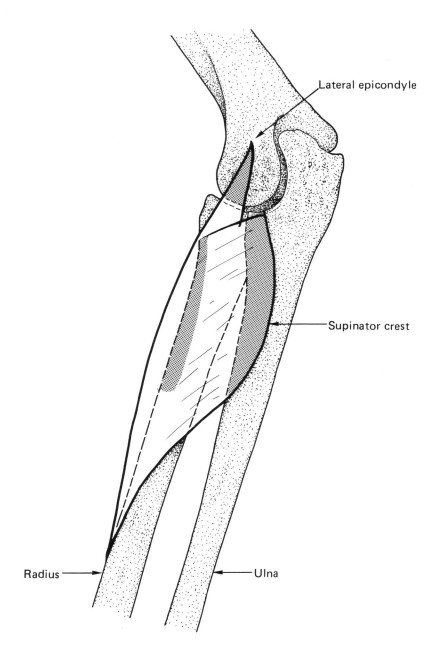

Fig. 4.29b Bony attachments (shaded) of supinator of the left arm, lateral view.

MUSCLES WHICH PRODUCE FLEXION OF THE WRIST

Flexor carpi ulnaris
Flexor carpi radialis
Palmaris longus
Flexor digitorum superficialis (see p. 116)
Flexor digitorum profundus (see p. 118)
Flexor pollicis longus (see p. 120)

Flexor carpi ulnaris

Flexor carpi ulnaris (Fig. 4.30a) lies along the medial border of the forearm, being the most medial of the superficial flexor group. It arises by two heads from the humerus and ulna. The humeral head arises from the *common flexor origin* on the *medial epicondyle* of the *humerus* and the adjacent fascia. The ulnar head arises from the *medial border* of the *olecranon* and, by an aponeurotic attachment, from the upper two-thirds of the *posterior border* of *ulna*. Between these two heads passes the ulnar nerve to gain the medial side of the flexor compartment of the forearm.

The muscle forms a long tendon about halfway down the forearm. This attaches to and invests the *pisiform*. The tendon is prolonged to reach the hook of the hamate and base of the fifth metacarpal by the pisohamate and pisometacarpal ligaments respectively. Occasionally, some fibres may be prolonged into abductor digiti minimi. Lateral to the tendon are the ulnar nerve and vessels.

Nerve supply

Flexor carpi ulnaris is supplied by several branches from the *ulnar nerve*, root value C7,

8. The skin overlying the muscle is supplied by roots C8 and T1.

Action

In conjunction with flexor carpi radialis, and to some extent palmaris longus, flexor carpi ulnaris is a flexor of the hand at the wrist. However, when working with extensor carpi ulnaris, it produces adduction or ulnar deviation of the hand at the wrist. It also plays an important role in stabilizing the pisiform during abduction of the little finger, so that abductor digiti minimi has a firm base from which to work. As with flexor carpi radialis, flexor carpi ulnaris is an important synergist in extension of the fingers.

Palpation

The tendon of flexor carpi ulnaris can easily be identified running proximally from the pisiform where it can be pinched between the thumb and index finger. In the upper medial part of the forearm, the muscle belly can be palpated when flexion of the wrist is performed against resistance.

Palmaris longus

Palmaris longus (Fig. 4.30b) is a small vestigial muscle, being absent in about 10% of the population. Lying centrally among the superficial flexor muscles of the forearm, palmaris longus arises from the front of the *medial epicondyle* of the humerus via the *common flexor origin*. The short muscle fibres soon form a long and slender tendon which passes distally to attach to the superficial surface of the *flexor retinaculum* and inserts into the *apex* of the *palmar aponeurosis*. At the wrist, the tendon lies on top of the median nerve.

Medial epicondyle

Flexor retinaculum

a

b

Fig. 4.30 The attachments (shaded) of (**a**) flexor carpi ulnaris, and (**b**) palmaris longus, anterior view.

Nerve supply

Palmaris longus is supplied by the *median nerve*, root value C8. The skin over the muscle is supplied by roots C7 and T1.

Action

Palmaris longus is a weak flexor of the wrist. However, because of its attachment to the palmar aponeurosis, it may have some slight action in flexing the metacarpophalangeal joints.

Palpation

The tendon of palmaris longus can be identified just proximal to the wrist, where it is the most central structure when flexion of the wrist is resisted. The tendon lies on the medial side of that of flexor carpi radialis.

Flexor carpi radialis

Flexor carpi radialis (Fig. 4.30c) is a fusiform muscle and is the most lateral of the superficial flexor muscles in the lower half of the forearm. It arises from the *medial epicondyle* of the humerus via the *common flexor tendon* and the adjacent fascia. Halfway down the forearm, the muscle fibres condense to form a long tendon which passes below the flexor retinaculum, where it lies in its own lateral compartment within the carpal tunnel. Here the tendon is surrounded by its own syno-vial sheath as it grooves the trapezium. Distally the tendon inserts into the palmar surface of the *bases* of the *second* and *third metacarpals*. Its course in the forearm is oblique, running from medial to lateral and from above downwards. At the wrist, the tendon lies between the radial vessels laterally and median nerve medially.

Nerve supply

Flexor carpi radialis is supplied by the *median nerve*, root value C6, 7. The skin over the muscle is supplied by roots C6 and T1.

Action

Working with palmaris longus and flexor carpi ulnaris, flexor carpi radialis acts as a flexor of the wrist. Abduction or radial deviation of the wrist is produced by the combined action of flexor carpi radialis and extensors carpi radialis longus and brevis. Because of its oblique course in the forearm, flexor carpi radialis may aid pronation. It can also help to flex the elbow.

Palpation

When the joint is flexed and abducted, the tendon of flexor carpi radialis can be palpated as the most lateral of the tendons on the anterior aspect of the wrist, at the level of the radial styloid process.

Fig. 4.30c   Flexor carpi radialis, anterior view.

MUSCLES WHICH PRODUCE FLEXION OF THE FINGERS

Flexor digitorum superficialis
Flexor digitorum profundus
Lumbricals
Flexor digiti minimi brevis

Flexor digitorum superficialis

Flexor digitorum superficialis (Fig. 4.31a) lies in the anterior compartment of the forearm deep to pronator teres, palmaris longus and flexors carpi radialis and ulnaris. It is superficial to flexor digitorum profundus and flexor pollicis longus. This large muscle has a long, linear origin but may be considered to arise by two heads. The medial or humeroulnar head arises from: the *medial epicondyle* via the *common flexor tendon*, the anterior part of the *ulnar collateral ligament* and the *sublime tubercle* at the upper medial part of the *coronoid process* of the *ulna*. The lateral or radial head arises from the upper two-thirds of the *anterior border* of the *radius*, which runs downwards and laterally from the radial tuberosity.

About halfway down the forearm, the muscle narrows to form four separate tendons which pass deep to the flexor retinaculum where they are arranged in two pairs to enter the hand. The superficial pair pass to the middle and ring fingers, while the deep pair pass to the index and little fingers. Within the carpal tunnel the tendons of superficialis are superficial to those of profundus, with which they share a common synovial sheath. In the palm, the tendons separate and pass towards their respective fingers, still lying superficial to the profundus tendons. At the level of the metacarpophalangeal joint, each superficialis tendon splits longitudinally into two parts. The two halves pass around the profundus tendon where they reunite before separating again to attach to either side of the palmar surface of the base of the middle phalanx.

This peculiar arrangement of the superficialis tendons provides a tunnel which allows the profundus tendon to become superficial (Fig. 4.31c). The effect, as far as superficialis is concerned, is to increase the lever arm of the tendon at the proximal interphalangeal joint, thereby enabling a powerful grip of the fingers to be exerted. As well as their main attachment to the *middle phalanx*, the tendons of superficialis also provide attachments for the vincula tendinium which convey blood vessels to the tendon.

Nerve supply

Flexor digitorum superficialis is supplied by the *median nerve*, root value C7, 8, T1. The skin overlying the muscle and its tendons are supplied by roots C6, 7, 8 and T1.

Action

Flexor digitorum superficialis is primarily a flexor of the metacarpophalangeal and proximal interphalangeal joints. Because it crosses the wrist joint, it will also help flexion of the wrist if its action is continued.

Palpation

Contraction of flexor digitorum superficialis can be felt by applying deep pressure through the superficial flexor muscles in the upper part of the forearm whilst the fingers are flexed. The tendons can be palpated in a similar manner proximal to the flexor retinaculum. The muscle can be tested specifically by asking the subject to flex the proximal interphalangeal joint without flexing the distal interphalangeal joint.

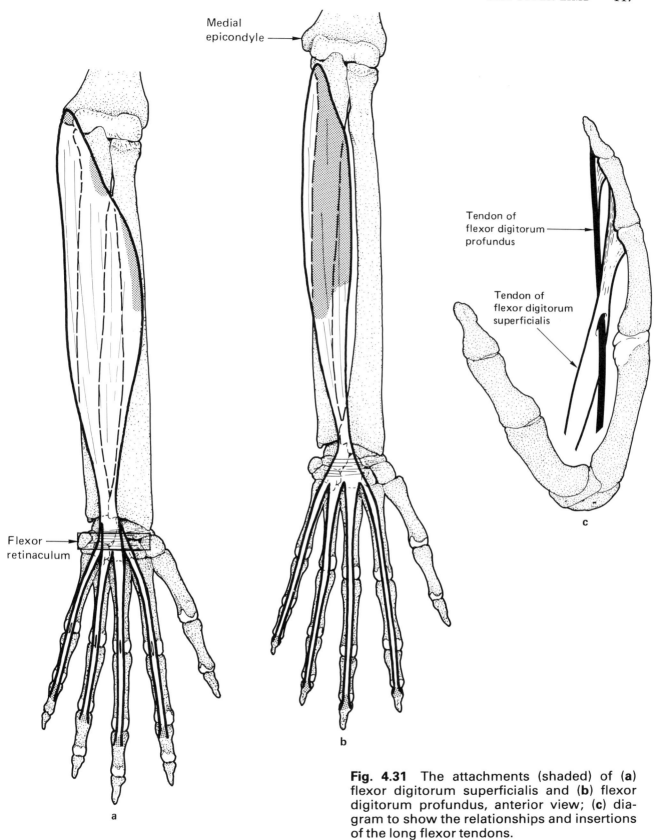

Medial
epicondyle

Tendon of
flexor digitorum
profundus

Tendon of
flexor digitorum
superficialis

Flexor
retinaculum

a

b

c

Fig. 4.31 The attachments (shaded) of (**a**) flexor digitorum superficialis and (**b**) flexor digitorum profundus, anterior view; (**c**) diagram to show the relationships and insertions of the long flexor tendons.

Flexor digitorum profundus

Flexor digitorum profundus (see Fig. 4.31b) lies deep to superficialis on the medial side of the forearm. It arises from the medial side of the *coronoid process* of the *ulna*, the upper three-quarters of the *anterior* and *medial surfaces* of the *ulna*, and from the medial, middle-third of the anterior surface of the adjacent *interosseous membrane*. It also arises from the aponeurosis attaching flexor carpi ulnaris to the *posterior border* of the *ulna*.

The part of the muscle arising from the interosseous membrane forms a separate tendon about halfway down the forearm which passes to the index finger. The remaining tendons are not usually formed until just above the flexor retinaculum. The separate tendons, however, pass below the flexor retinaculum where they lie side-by-side, deep to those of superficialis, but within the same synovial sheath. In the palm, the four tendons pass to their respective fingers. At first, they travel deep to superficialis, but then pass superficially as they go through the tunnel formed by the superficialis tendon at the level of the metacarpophalangeal joint (see Fig. 4.31c).

The tendon of profundus eventually inserts into the *base* of the *palmar surface* of the *distal phalanx*. Like the tendons of flexor digitorum superficialis, the profundus tendons are provided with vincula tendinium.

Nerve supply

Flexor digitorum profundus has a dual nerve supply. The lateral part of the muscle, which gives off tendons to the index and middle fingers, is supplied by the anterior interosseous branch of the *median nerve*, root value C7, 8, T1. The medial part of the muscle, which gives off tendons to the ring and little fingers, is supplied by the *ulnar nerve*, root value C8, T1. The skin over the muscle is supplied by roots C7, 8, T1.

Action

The primary action of flexor digitorum profundus is to produce flexion of the distal interphalangeal joint. However, because it crosses several other joints during its course, it will also aid in flexion of the proximal interphalangeal, metacarpophalangeal and wrist joints.

Palpation

The muscular part of profundus can be palpated immediately medial to the posterior border of the ulna, where its contraction can be felt as the fingers are fully flexed from a position of extension.

Lumbricals

The lumbricals are four small, round muscles found in the palm in association with the deep flexor tendons of the fingers. The lateral two lumbricals are frequently unipennate arising from the *lateral side* of the *flexor digitorum profundus tendons*, passing to the index and middle fingers. The medial two muscles are bipennate, arising from the adjacent sides of the *profundus tendons* of the middle and ring fingers, and the ring and little fingers respectively (Fig. 4.32a).

From this proximal attachment the muscles pass distally, anterior to the deep transverse metacarpal ligament and then obliquely on the lateral side of the metacarpophalangeal joint of the finger concerned. They then attach to the lateral edge of the *dorsal digital expansion* at the side of the proximal phalanx. A few fibres make their way to the bone of the middle phalanx, but the majority can be traced to the base of the distal phalanx.

Nerve supply

The nerve supply varies, but the most common arrangement is for the lateral two lumbricals to be supplied by the *median nerve*, root value T1, and the medial two by the *ulnar nerve* root value T1.

Action

The lumbricals in both hands and feet are unique muscles as they pass between the flexor and extensor tendons. Their anatomical position means that they flex the metacarpophalangeal joint, and extend both interphalangeal joints of the corresponding finger, the 'lumbrical action'. In theory the lumbricals should be able to rotate their respective fingers at the metacarpophalangeal joint. However, this appears to be well marked only in the index finger so that the pad faces medially. The first dorsal interosseous muscle is also involved in producing this movement. Functionally, the lumbricals are involved in the coordination of complex activities of the fingers which involve movements of both flexion and extension, for example as in writing. As a group they have major functional significance in the dexterity of the hand.

Flexor digiti minimi brevis

Flexor digiti minimi brevis is a muscle which is sometimes absent. When present it lies on the lateral side of abductor digiti minimi, arising from the *hook of the hamate* and the adjacent *flexor retinaculum*. It inserts, together with abductor digiti minimi, into the base of the *proximal phalanx* of the little finger on its ulnar side (Fig. 4.32b).

Nerve supply

Flexor digiti minimi brevis is supplied by the deep branch of the *ulnar nerve*, root value T1.

Action

Flexor digiti minimi brevis flexes both the carpometacarpal and metacarpophalangeal joints of the little finger.

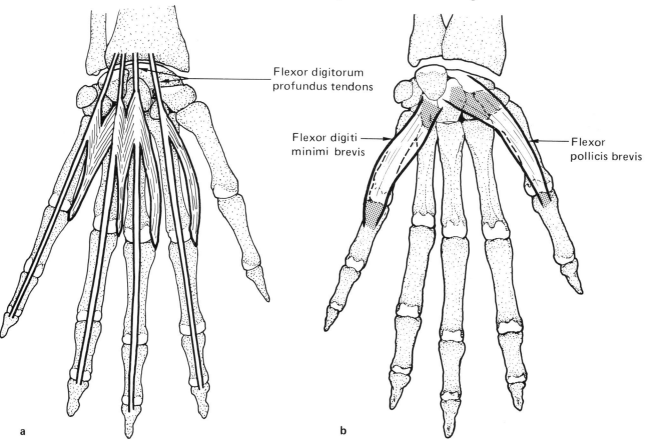

Flexor digitorum profundus tendons

Flexor digiti minimi brevis

Flexor pollicis brevis

a

b

Fig. 4.32 a = The four lumbrical muscles, anterior view. **b** = The attachments (shaded) of flexor digiti minimi brevis, anterior view.

MUSCLES WHICH PRODUCE FLEXION OF THE THUMB

Flexor pollicis longus
Flexor pollicis brevis

Flexor pollicis longus

Flexor pollicis longus (Fig. 4.33a) lies on the lateral side of flexor digitorum profundus. It arises from the *anterior surface* of the *radius* between the radial tuberosity above and pronator quadratus below, and the adjacent anterior surface of the *interosseous membrane*. Occasionally, the muscle also arises by a small slip from the medial border of the coronoid process of the ulna. The fibres pass almost to the wrist before a single tendon is formed.

The tendon of flexor pollicis longus passes below the flexor retinaculum, in its own synovial sheath, to insert into the palmar surface of the distal phalanx of the thumb.

Nerve supply

Flexor pollicis longus is supplied by the anterior interosseous branch of the *median nerve*, root value C8, T1.

Action

Flexor pollicis longus is the only flexor of the interphalangeal joint of the thumb, and is thus vital for all gripping activities of the hand. It also flexes the metacarpophalangeal joint of the thumb and the wrist joint.

Palpation

When only the thumb is flexed, the contraction of flexor pollicis longus can be felt in the lower third of the forearm, immediately lateral to the superficial flexor tendons.

Flexor pollicis brevis

Flexor pollicis brevis (Fig. 4.33b) is the most medial of the three thenar muscles, usually being partly fused with opponens pollicis. It arises from the distal border of the *flexor retinaculum* and *tubercle* of the *trapezium* (the superficial part), with a deeper attachment to the *capitate* and *trapezoid bones*. Both parts form a single tendon containing a sesamoid bone which inserts into the radial side of the base of the *proximal phalanx* of the thumb.

Nerve supply

Flexor pollicis brevis is usually supplied by the *median nerve*, root value T1, but frequently the deep part is supplied by the *ulnar nerve*, root value T1. The skin over the muscle is supplied by root C6.

Action

Flexor pollicis brevis produces flexion of the thumb at the metacarpophalangeal and carpometacarpal joints. Its continued action tends to produce medial rotation of the thumb, since flexion of the carpometacarpal joint automatically involves this movement.

Palpation

Flexor pollicis brevis can be palpated in the medial part of the thenar eminence if flexion of the thumb is resisted.

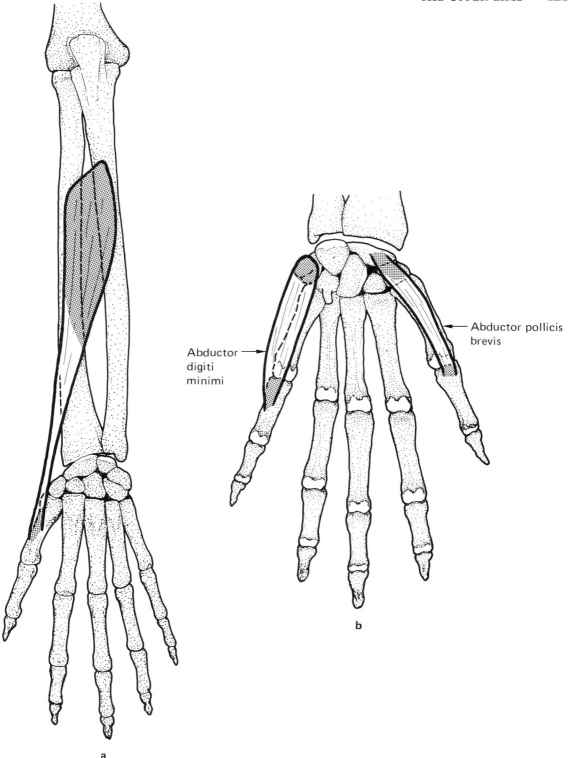

Abductor digiti minimi

Abductor pollicis brevis

a

b

Fig. 4.33 Attachments (shaded) of (**a**) flexor pollicis longus and (**b**) flexor pollicis brevis, anterior view.

MUSCLES WHICH PRODUCE EXTENSION OF THE WRIST

Extensor carpi radialis longus
Extensor carpi radialis brevis
Extensor carpi ulnaris
Extensor digitorum (see p. 126)
Extensor indicis (see p. 128)
Extensor digiti minimi (see p. 128)
Extensor pollicis longus (see p. 130)
Extensor pollicis brevis (see p. 130)

Extensor carpi radialis longus

Extensor carpi radialis longus (Fig. 4.34a) lies on the lateral side of the posterior compartment of the forearm, being partly covered by brachioradialis. It arises from the anterior part of the lower third of the *lateral supracondylar ridge* of the *humerus* and adjacent intermuscular septum. Occasionally, there may be an attachment to the lateral epicondyle by the common extensor tendon. Approximately in the middle of the forearm, the muscle forms a flattened tendon which runs distally over the lateral surface of the radius. In the lower third of the forearm, the tendon, together with that of extensor carpi radialis brevis, is crossed by the tendons of abductor pollicis longus and extensor pollicis brevis. The tendons of extensor carpi radialis longus and brevis pass deep to the extensor retinaculum in a common synovial sheath. Together they groove the posterior surface of the styloid process of the radius. The tendon of extensor carpi radialis longus attaches to the posterior surface of the *base* of the *second metacarpal*.

Nerve supply

Extensor carpi radialis longus is supplied by the *radial nerve*, root value C6, 7, which enters the muscle above the elbow. The skin over the muscle is supplied by roots C5, 6.

Action and palpation

These will be considered with extensor carpi radialis brevis.

Extensor carpi radialis brevis

Extensor carpi radialis brevis (Fig. 4.34b) lies adjacent to and is partly covered by longus, to which it may be partly fused. It arises from the *lateral epicondyle* of the *humerus* via the *common extensor tendon*, the lateral ligament of the elbow and the adjacent fascia. The tendon of brevis forms halfway down the forearm and runs with that of longus deep to abductor pollicis longus and extensor pollicis brevis. It passes below the extensor retinaculum, in a common synovial sheath, to attach to the *posterior surface* of the *base* of the *third metacarpal*.

Nerve supply

Extensor carpi radialis brevis is supplied by the posterior interosseous branch of the *radial nerve*, root value C6 and 7. The skin over the muscle is supplied by roots C5, 6, 7.

Action

Working with extensor carpi ulnaris, extensor carpi radialis longus and brevis produce extension of the wrist. Working with the flexor carpi radialis however, they will produce abduction or radial deviation of the wrist. In addition, extensor carpi radialis longus may help to flex the elbow joint.

Functional activity

Functionally, the wrist extensors work strongly in the action of gripping, where they have a synergic role. The synergy of the two radial extensors and extensor carpi ulnaris is a vital factor in the gripping action. By maintaining the wrist in an extended position, flexion of the wrist under the action of flexor digitorum superficialis and profundus is prevented, with the result that these muscles act on the fingers. If the wrist is then allowed to flex the flexor tendons cannot shorten sufficiently to produce effective movement at the interphalangeal joints. This therefore becomes a state of active insufficiency.

If the radial nerve is damaged the patient is unable to produce an effective grip because of paralysis of the wrist extensors.

Lateral
epicondyle

a

b

Fig. 4.34 The attachments (shaded) of (**a**) extensor carpi radialis longus and, (**b**) extensor carpi radialis brevis, posterior view.

However, if the wrist is splinted in a position of extension, the tendons of superficialis and profundus can act on the fingers and a functional grip can be obtained.

Palpation

When the wrist is extended and abducted against resistance, both extensor carpi radialis longus and brevis can be palpated in the upper lateral aspect of the posterior part of the forearm. The tendons, particularly longus, can be palpated in the floor of the 'anatomical snuff-box' between those passing to the thumb, if the same movement of extension and abduction is carried out.

Extensor carpi ulnaris

Extensor carpi ulnaris (Fig. 4.34c) arises from the *lateral epicondyle* of the *humerus* via the *common extensor tendon* and the adjacent fascia. There is also a strong attachment, via a common *aponeurosis* shared with flexor digitorum profundus and flexor carpi ulnaris, from the *posterior border* of the *ulna*. The muscle forms a tendon near the wrist which passes below the extensor retinaculum in its own synovial sheath and compartment. This is carried in a groove next to the ulnar styloid process. The tendon attaches to a tubercle on the medial side of the *base* of the *fifth metacarpal*.

Nerve supply

Extensor carpi ulnaris is supplied by the posterior interosseous branch of the *radial nerve*, root value C7, 8. The skin over the muscles is supplied by roots C6, 7, 8.

Action

Working with extensors carpi radialis longus and brevis, extensor carpi ulnaris produces extension of the wrist. The functional significance of this has been described in the actions of the two former muscles. Working with flexor carpi ulnaris, extensor carpi ulnaris produces adduction or ulnar deviation at the wrist.

Palpation

The tendon of extensor carpi ulnaris can be identified on the dorsum of the wrist, when the wrist is extended and adducted against resistance. It lies on the lateral side of the ulnar styloid process.

Fig. 4.34c The attachments (shaded) of extensor carpi ulnaris, posterior view.

MUSCLES WHICH PRODUCE EXTENSION OF THE FINGERS

Extensor digitorum
Extensor digiti minimi
Extensor indicis
Interossei (see p. 138)

Extensor digitorum

Extensor digitorum (Fig. 4.35a) is centrally placed within the posterior compartment of the forearm. It arises from the *lateral epicondyle* of the *humerus* via the *common extensor tendon*, the covering fascia and the intermuscular septa at its sides. In the lower part of the forearm the muscle forms four tendons which pass deep to the extensor retinaculum in a synovial sheath which it shares with the tendon of extensor indicis. On the dorsum of the hand the tendons diverge towards the medial four digits, being interconnected by obliquely placed fibrous bands. The arrangement of these bands is variable, however, the tendons for the ring and little fingers are attached usually until they pass just proximal to the metacarpophalangeal joints. The tendon to the index finger may not be attached to that of the middle finger.

The distal attachment of extensor digitorum is complex in that each tendon helps to form an aponeurosis over the dorsum of the fingers. This is called the *dorsal digital expansion* or extensor hood. In its simplest form it is best thought of as a movable triangular hood, the base of which lies proximally over the metacarpophalangeal joint. From here the sides of the hood wrap around the phalanx with the apex pointing distally. The extensor hood forms the dorsal part of the capsule of the metacarpophalangeal joint and extends forwards, either side of the metacarpal head to fuse with the deep transverse metacarpal ligament. As the extensor hood approaches the proximal interphalangeal joint, it narrows and is reinforced on either side by the interosseous and lumbrical muscles for that finger. At the distal end of the proximal phalanx, the extensor hood divides into three parts (Fig. 4.35b). The central part, which is directly continuous with the extensor tendon, inserts into the *base* of the *middle phalanx* on its dorsal aspect. The two collateral parts, which are continuous with the tendons of the interossei and lumbricals, reunite to insert into the base of the *distal phalanx* on its dorsal aspect. There may be an attachment to the base of the proximal phalanx but this is unusual.

The way in which the extensor hood wraps around the phalanges towards the palm facilitates the attachment of the lumbrical and interossei muscles. These enable the complex coordinated movements of the fingers to take place, involving flexion of some joints and extension of others, for example in writing. The overall arrangement of this complex structure is shown in Fig. 4.35b. Detachment or rupture of the dorsal digital expansion from the distal phalanx gives rise to the so called 'mallet finger'.

Nerve supply

Extensor digitorum is supplied by the posterior interosseous branch of the *radial nerve*, root value C7, 8. The skin over the muscle is supplied by roots C6, 7, 8.

Action

The primary action of extensor digitorum is to produce extension of the metacarpophalangeal joint. It also helps to extend both interphalangeal joints, however, the main extensors of these joints are the interossei and lumbricals, which also help to prevent hyperextension of the metacarpophalangeal joint. When these small muscles are paralysed, extensor digitorum hyperextends the metacarpophalangeal joint and is then unable to extend the interphalangeal joints. Extensor digitorum also extends the wrist.

Palpation

The tendons of extensor digitorum can easily be palpated on the dorsum of the hand when the fingers are extended. It may also be possible to identify the fibrous interconnections between some of these tendons. Contraction of the muscle belly can be palpated in the posterior central part of the upper forearm during the same movement.

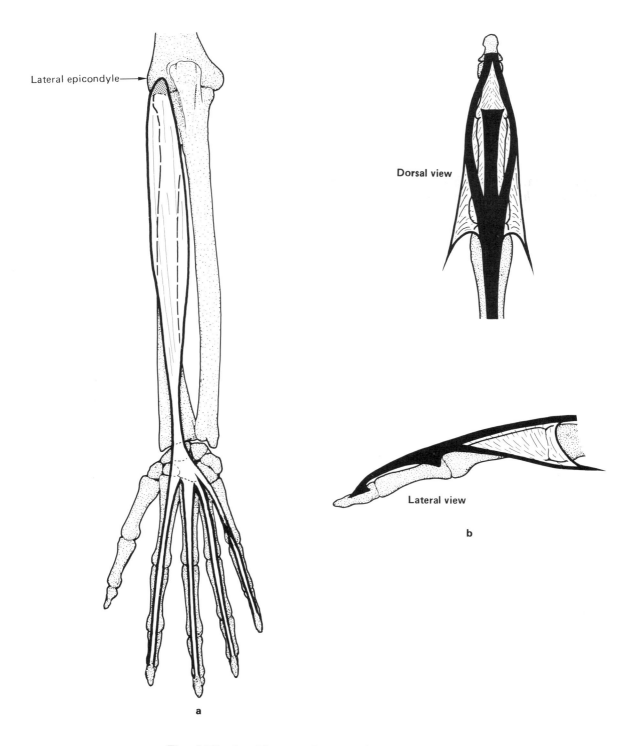

Lateral epicondyle

Dorsal view

Lateral view

b

a

Fig. 4.35a, b   The attachments (shaded) of (**a**) extensor digitorum, posterior view and (**b**) the extensor hood.

Extensor digiti minimi

Extensor digiti minimi (Fig. 4.35c) is a small muscle lying on the medial side of extensor digitorum. It arises from the *lateral epicondyle* of the *humerus* via the *common extensor tendon* and the surrounding fascia. In the lower part of the forearm, extensor digiti minimi forms a single tendon which passes deep to the extensor retinaculum in a separate compartment wrapped in its own synovial sheath. Below the extensor retinaculum it lies immediately behind the inferior radioulnar joint. On the dorsum of the hand, the tendon splits into two with both parts inserting into the *dorsal digital expansion* of the *little finger*. The double tendon of extensor digiti minimi lies medial to that of extensor digitorum.

Nerve supply

Extensor digiti minimi is supplied by the posterior interosseous branch of the *radial nerve*, root value C7, 8. The skin over the muscle is supplied by roots C8, T1.

Action

Extensor digiti minimi assists extensor digitorum in extending the metacarpophalangeal joint of the little finger, and via the extensor hood, the interphalangeal joints. It can also cause ulnar deviation of the little finger. The muscle also acts to aid extension of the wrist.

Palpation

The tendon of extensor digiti minimi can be palpated just distal to the inferior radioulnar joint when the little finger is extended. The muscle belly can be palpated medial to that of extensor digitorum when the same movement is performed.

Extensor indicis

Extensor indicis (Fig. 4.35d) lies deep to extensor digitorum and arises from the lower part of the *posterior surface* of the *ulna* and the adjacent *interosseous membrane*. It forms a single tendon which passes in the same synovial sheath as extensor digitorum below the extensor retinaculum. On the dorsum of the hand the tendon lies on the medial side of the digitorum tendon. It eventually inserts into the *dorsal digital expansion* on the back of the proximal phalanx of the *index finger*.

Nerve supply

Extensor indicis is supplied by the posterior interosseous branch of the *radial nerve*, root value C7, 8. The skin over the muscle is supplied by roots C6, 7.

Action

Extensor indicis assists extensor digitorum in its actions with respect to the joints of the index finger. It does, however, enable the index finger to be used independently, and also aids extension of the wrist.

Palpation

The tendon of extensor indicis, lying medial to that of extensor digitorum, can be palpated on the dorsum of the hand when the index finger is extended. The muscle belly can be palpated by deep pressure over the lower part of the ulna during the same movement.

Fig. 4.35c, d The attachments (shaded) of (**c**) extensor digiti minimi and (**d**) extensor indicis, posterior view.

MUSCLES WHICH PRODUCE EXTENSION OF THE THUMB

Extensor pollicis longus
Extensor pollicis brevis

Extensor pollicis longus

Extensor pollicis longus (Fig. 4.36a) lies deep to extensor digitorum in the posterior compartment of the forearm. Here it arises from the lateral part of the middle third of the *posterior surface* of the *ulna* and the adjacent *interosseous membrane* above extensor indicis. Above the wrist it forms a single tendon which passes in its own synovial sheath deep to the extensor retinaculum, lying in a groove on the back of the radius medial to the dorsal tubercle. Winding around the dorsal tubercle, the tendon changes direction and crosses the tendons of extensor carpi radialis longus and brevis and the radial artery. As the tendon crosses the metacarpophalangeal joint it forms the dorsal part of the joint capsule. It is joined in this region by slips from abductor pollicis brevis laterally and adductor pollicis medially. The whole arrangement forms a triangular expansion, not unlike that of extensor digitorum. The expansion may also be joined by extensor pollicis brevis. The tendon of extensor pollicis longus attaches to the dorsal surface of the *distal phalanx* of the *thumb*. In its course across the back of the hand, the tendon forms the medial boundary of a region known as the 'anatomical snuff-box'.

Nerve supply

Extensor pollicis longus is supplied by the posterior interosseous branch of the *radial nerve*, root value C7, 8. The skin over the muscle is supplied by roots C6 and 7.

Action

Extensor pollicis longus extends all of the joints of the thumb, and assists in extension and abduction of the wrist. Once this has been achieved, the obliquity of the tendon will pull the first metacarpal into a laterally rotated and abducted position. In full abduction or extension of the thumb, extensor pollicis longus can act as an adductor. In addition, it may contribute slightly to supination, due to its oblique course across the lower part of the forearm.

Palpation

The tendon of extensor pollicis longus is easily identified with the thumb extended as the medial border of the 'anatomical snuff-box'. The tendon frequently ruptures in conditions, such as rheumatoid arthritis or post Colles' fracture. As a result, the patient is incapable of extending the interphalangeal joint of the thumb.

Extensor pollicis brevis

Extensor pollicis brevis (Fig. 4.36b) lies on the medial side of and is adjacent to extensor pollicis longus, and distal to abductor pollicis longus to which it closely adheres. It arises from the middle part of the *posterior surface* of the *radius* and adjacent *interosseous membrane*. The tendon is formed above the wrist, and runs with that of abductor pollicis longus deep to the extensor retinaculum in a common synovial sheath, in a groove on the lateral surface of the radial styloid process. Below this point, these two tendons form the lateral boundary of the 'anatomical snuff-box'. The tendon of extensor pollicis brevis partially replaces the dorsal part of the capsule of the metacarpophalangeal joint of the thumb and inserts into the dorsal surface of the *base* of the *proximal phalanx*. Occasionally the tendon may be prolonged, so that it runs with and attaches to the tendon of extensor pollicis longus.

Nerve supply

Extensor pollicis brevis is supplied by the posterior interosseous branch of the *radial nerve*, root value C7 and 8. The skin over the muscle is supplied by roots C6 and 7.

Action

Extensor pollicis brevis extends both the carpometacarpal and metacarpophalangeal joints of the thumb. It may also help in extending and abducting the wrist, particularly against resistance.

Palpation

The tendons of extensor pollicis brevis and abductor pollicis longus run together from the lower lateral aspect of the radius where they form the lateral boundary of the 'anatomical snuff-box'. Both tendons can be palpated when the thumb is extended; that of abductor pollicis longus being the most anteriorly placed.

Application

The synovial sheath of extensor pollicis brevis and abductor pollicis longus frequently becomes inflamed in the region of the radial styloid process (De Quervain's syndrome). Techniques, such as transverse frictions, ultrasound or injection can be usefully applied to this point.

Fig. 4.36 The attachments (shaded) of (**a**) extensor pollicis longus and (**b**) extensor pollicis brevis, posterior view.

a

b

MUSCLES WHICH PRODUCE ABDUCTION/ADDUCTION/ OPPOSITION OF THE THUMB

Abductor pollicis longus
Abductor pollicis brevis
Opponens pollicis
Adductor pollicis
Palmaris brevis

Abductor pollicis longus

Abductor pollicis longus (Fig. 4.37a) lies deep to extensor digitorum in the posterior compartment of the forearm. It arises from: the upper part of the *posterior surface* of the *ulna* below anconeus, the middle third of the *posterior surface* of the *radius* below supinator and the intervening *interosseous membrane*.

As the muscle passes distally, it emerges from its deep position to lie superficially in the lower part of the forearm. The tendon forms above the wrist and passes, with that of extensor pollicis brevis, within the same synovial sheath below the extensor retinaculum, where it lies in a groove on the lateral surface of the radial styloid process. The tendon inserts primarily into the radial side of the *base* of the *first metacarpal*, with a slip which passes to the trapezium, and another which passes to abductor pollicis brevis and the fascia over the thenar eminence.

Nerve supply

Abductor pollicis longus is supplied by the posterior interosseous branch of the *radial nerve*, root value C7, 8. The skin over the muscle is supplied by roots C6, 7.

Action

Working with the extensors of the thumb, abductor pollicis longus helps to extend the thumb at the carpometacarpal joint, while, with abductor pollicis brevis, it abducts the thumb. By itself, the muscle puts the thumb into a mid-extended and abducted position.

Palpation

Palpation of this muscle is described with that of extensor pollicis brevis on p. 131.

Abductor pollicis brevis

Abductor pollicis brevis (Fig. 4.37b) is the most lateral and superficial of the three muscles forming the thenar eminence. It takes its origin mainly from the front of the *flexor retinaculum*, extending onto the *tubercles* of the *scaphoid* and *trapezium* with an occasional contribution from the tendon of abductor pollicis longus. The muscle forms a short tendon which attaches to the radial side of the *base* of the *proximal phalanx* of the *thumb*, with some fibres reaching the expansion of the extensor pollicis longus tendon.

Nerve supply

Abductor pollicis brevis is supplied by the *median nerve*, root value T1. The skin over the muscle is supplied by root C6.

Action

Abductor pollicis brevis abducts the thumb at both the carpometacarpal and metacarpophalangeal joints, causing it to move anteriorly at right angles to the palm. In order to achieve this position there must be some medial rotation at the carpometacarpal joint, the remainder occurring at the metacarpophalangeal joint. This movement is of great significance in terms of the function of the hand as the thumb can be moved towards the fingertips (opposition) where it can carry out precision tasks that require a pincer grip. Because of its partial insertion into the long extensor tendon of the thumb, abductor pollicis brevis can aid in flexion of the metacarpophalangeal joint and extension of the interphalangeal joint.

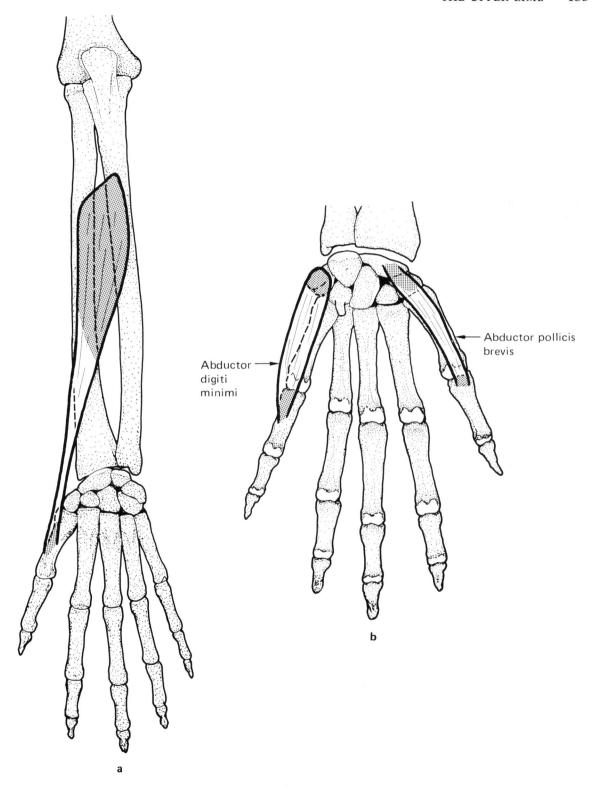

Abductor digiti minimi

Abductor pollicis brevis

a

b

Fig. 4.37a, b The attachments (shaded) of (**a**) abductor pollicis longus, posterior view and (**b**) abductor pollicis brevis, anterior view.

Opponens pollicis

Opponens pollicis (Fig. 4.37c) is covered by abductor pollicis brevis. Arising from the *flexor retinaculum* and *tubercle* of the *trapezium*, it inserts into the whole length of the lateral half of the anterior surface of the *first metacarpal*.

Nerve supply

Opponens pollicis is supplied by the *median nerve*, root value T1. Occasionally, it may be supplied by the ulnar nerve. The skin over the muscle is supplied by root C6.

Action

Opponens pollicis produces the complex movements of the thumb called opposition where the first metacarpal is drawn forwards and medially in an arc towards the fingers. The movement involves, in order of action, abduction, medial rotation, and finally flexion and adduction at the carpometacarpal joint of the thumb. The importance of this action is that the tip of the thumb can be brought into contact with the tip of any finger, thus allowing for very precise action of the hand.

Palpation

The three muscles forming the thenar eminence of the thumb are closely packed together and covered with tough fascia which makes identification of individual muscles difficult. However, if the thenar eminence is carefully palpated during resisted movements, all but opponens pollicis can be identified. If abduction of the thumb is resisted (that is movement away from the palm in a plane at 90° to the palm) abductor pollicis brevis can be identified in the lateral part of the thenar eminence.

Adductor pollicis

Adductor pollicis (Fig. 4.37d) is found in the web space of the thumb on its palmar aspect, and has oblique and transverse heads. The oblique head arises from: the *sheath* of the *tendon* of *flexor carpi radialis*, the *bases* of the *second*, *third* and *fourth metacarpals*, and the *trapezoid* and *capitate* bones. The transverse head arises from the longitudinal ridge on the *anterior surface* of the *shaft* of the *third metacarpal*. Between these two heads, the radial artery passes to gain access to the palmar aspect of the hand. Both heads are inserted into the medial side of the *base* of the *proximal phalanx* of the *thumb* by a tendon containing a sesamoid bone.

Nerve supply

Adductor pollicis is supplied by the deep branch of the *ulnar nerve*, root value C8 and T1. The skin over the muscle is supplied by roots C6 and 7.

Action

Adductor pollicis is a strong muscle that brings the thumb back to the palm from a position of abduction. Also, it is active in the later stages of opposition. Functionally, the strength of this muscle can be demonstrated when the tip of the index finger and thumb are held together in a pincer grip and an attempt is made to pull them apart. Consequently, adductor pollicis is an important muscle in maintaining the precision grip of the hand.

Palpation

Adductor pollicis is found in the web between the thumb and index finger, and can be felt on the palmar aspect when the movement of adduction is resisted.

Palmaris brevis

Palmaris brevis is a superficial muscle found covering the hypothenar eminence of the little finger. It arises from the medial border of the *palmar aponeurosis* and the front of the *flexor retinaculum* and inserts into the *skin* of the medial border of the hand.

Nerve supply

Palmaris brevis is supplied by the superficial branch of the *ulnar nerve*, root value T1. The skin over the muscle is supplied by root C8.

Action

Contraction of the muscle wrinkles the skin on the ulnar side of the hand. This muscle is included in this section as its main function is to assist the thumb in producing a good grip.

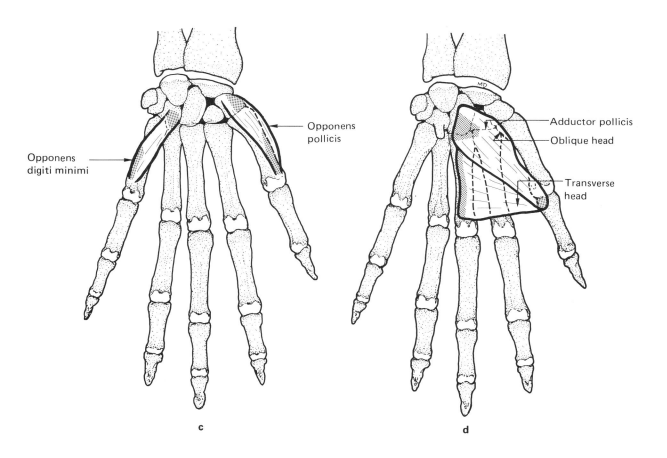

Fig. 4.37c,d The attachments (shaded) of (**c**) opponens pollicis and (**d**) adductor pollicis, anterior view.

MUSCLES WHICH PRODUCE ABDUCTION/ADDUCTION/ OPPOSITION OF THE FINGERS

Abductor digiti minimi
Opponens digiti minimi
Palmar interossei
Dorsal interossei

Abductor digiti minimi

Abductor digiti minimi (Fig. 4.38a) is the most superficial of the hypothenar muscles, lying in series with the dorsal interossei. It arises from the *pisiform*, the *pisohamate* and *pisometacarpal ligaments*, and the tendon of flexor carpi ulnaris, to insert by a tendon into the *ulnar side* of the *proximal phalanx* of the little finger and its *extensor hood*.

Nerve supply

Abductor digiti minimi is supplied by the deep branch of the *ulnar nerve*, root value T1.

Action

Abductor digiti minimi pulls the little finger away from the ring finger into a position of abduction. It also helps to flex the metacarpophalangeal joint. By its attachment to the extensor hood, the muscle may help in extending the interphalangeal joints. Abductor digiti minimi is a powerful muscle playing an important role in grasping a large object with outspread fingers.

Opponens digiti minimi

Opponens digiti minimi (Fig. 4.38b) lies deep to abductor digiti minimi, arising from the *hook* of the *hamate* and adjacent *flexor retinaculum*, to insert into the *medial half* of the *palmar surface* of the *fifth metacarpal*.

Nerve supply

Opponens digiti minimi is supplied by the deep branch of the *ulnar nerve*, root value T1.

Action

Opponens digiti minimi pulls the little finger forwards towards the palm and rotates it laterally at the carpometacarpal joint. This movement deepens the hollow of the hand, and is a necessary part of opposition of the little finger.

Palpation

The hypothenar muscles are closely related to one another, palpation of the individual muscles is therefore difficult. Resistance to abduction of the little finger enables abductor digiti minimi to be palpated on the ulnar border of the hand. For the movements of flexion and opposition of the little finger it is difficult to localize the action of the remaining hypothenar muscles, so accurate palpation is difficult.

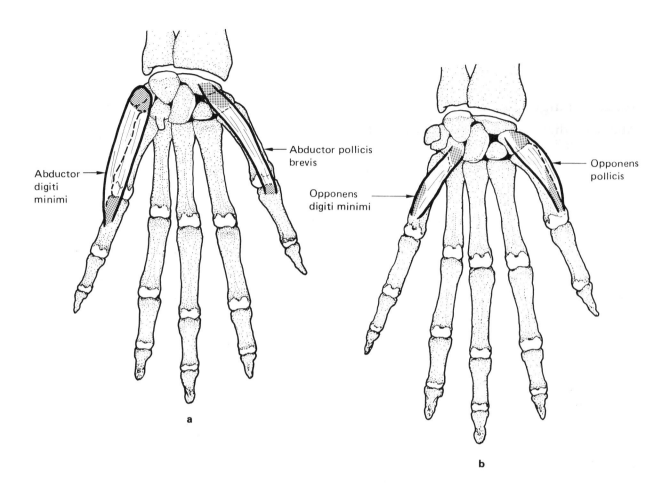

Abductor
digiti
minimi

Abductor pollicis
brevis

Opponens
digiti minimi

Opponens
pollicis

a

b

Fig. 4.38a,b   The attachments (shaded) of (**a**)
abductor digiti minimi and (**b**) opponens digiti
minimi, anterior view.

Palmar interossei

There are four palmar interossei (Fig. 4.38d) situated between the metacarpal bones, with one running to the thumb, index, ring and little fingers. Each muscle arises from the *shaft* of the *metacarpal* of the digit on which it acts, and inserts into the *dorsal digital expansion* and the *base* of the *proximal phalanx* of the same digit.

The first palmar interosseous lies on the medial side of the thumb and passes between the first dorsal interosseous and the oblique head of adductor pollicis to insert into the medial side of the base of its proximal phalanx with adductor pollicis. Of the remaining palmar interossei, the second lies on the medial side of the index finger, while the third and fourth lie on the lateral side of the ring finger and little finger respectively. The tendons of all but the first palmar interosseous pass posterior to the deep transverse metacarpal ligament on their way to the extensor expansion.

Nerve supply

All four palmar interossei are supplied by the deep branch of the *ulnar nerve*, root value T1.

Action

The palmar interossei adduct the thumb, index, ring and little finger towards the middle finger (the midline of the hand). The first palmar interosseous also assists flexor pollicis brevis in flexing the thumb at the metacarpophalangeal joint. The three remaining interossei, by their attachment to the dorsal digital expansion, assist the lumbricals in flexing the metacarpophalangeal joint and extending both interphalangeal joints.

Dorsal interossei

The four dorsal interossei (Fig. 4.38c) lie superficially in the spaces between the metacarpals on the dorsum of the hand. Two attach to the middle finger, and one each to the index and ring fingers. Each is a bipennate muscle arising from the *sides* of *adjacent metacarpals*. The first and second dorsal interossei lie on the lateral side of the index and middle finger respectively, while the third and fourth lie on the medial side of the middle and ring fingers respectively. All of the dorsal interossei insert into the *proximal phalanx* and *dorsal digital expansion* of the appropriate finger, having passed posterior to the deep transverse metacarpal ligament.

Nerve supply

All four dorsal interossei are supplied by the deep branch of the *ulnar nerve*, root value T1. The skin overlying the muscles is supplied by roots C6, 7 and 8.

Action

The dorsal interossei are abductors of the index, middle and ring fingers. In addition, the first dorsal interosseous can rotate the index finger at the metacarpophalangeal joint, and may assist adductor pollicis in adduction of the thumb. Their attachment to the dorsal digital expansion means that, like the palmar interossei, they assist the lumbricals in producing flexion and extension of the metacarpophalangeal and interphalangeal joints respectively.

Palpation

During resisted abduction of the index, middle or ring fingers the dorsal interossei can be palpated on the dorsum of the hand between the metacarpals. The first dorsal interosseous may be seen contracting against resistance in the thumb web. The palmar interossei and lumbricals are too deep to palpate but their actions can be demonstrated by accurate electrical stimulation.

Some of the muscles already described can be seen in Figs. 4.39 (see pp. 140–141).

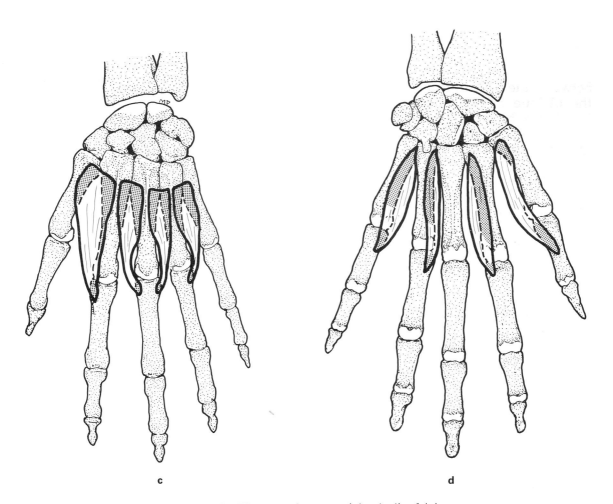

c

d

Fig. 4.38c,d   The attachments (shaded) of (**c**) dorsal interossei, posterior view and (**d**) palmar interossei, anterior view.

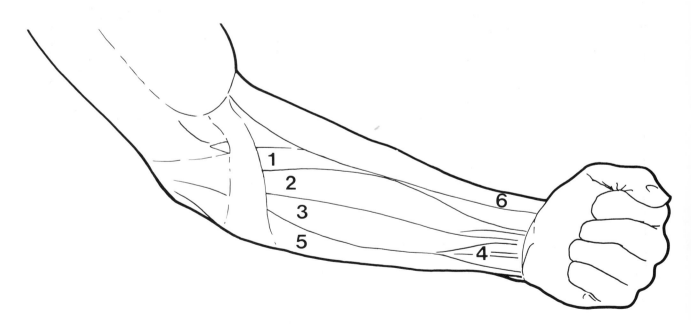

Fig. 4.39a   Flexor surface of the forearm:

  1 = Pronator teres
  2 = Flexor carpi radialis
  3 = Palmaris longus
  4 = Flexor digitorum superficialis
  5 = Flexor carpi ulnaris
  6 = Tendon of brachioradialis

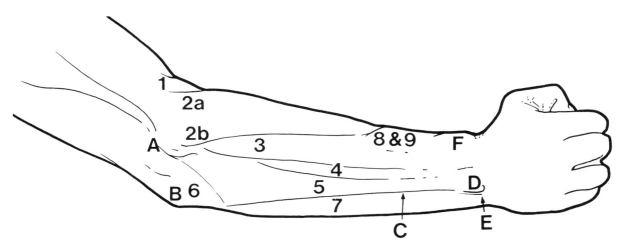

Fig. 4.39b Extensor surface of the forearm and hand:

A = Lateral epicondyle
B = Olecranon
C = Subcutaneous posterior border of ulna
D = Head of ulna
E = Styloid process of ulna
F = Distal end of radius

1 = Brachioradialis
2a = Extensor carpi radialis longus
 b = Extensor carpi radialis brevis
3 = Extensor digitorum
4 = Extensor digiti minimi
5 = Extensor carpi ulnaris
6 = Anconeus
7 = Flexor carpi ulnaris
8 = Extensor pollicis brevis
9 = Abductor pollicis longus

FASCIAE OF THE UPPER LIMB

The superficial fascia

The superficial fascia of the upper limb shows regional differences between, for example, the shoulder region and the hand. In the shoulder region and arm, it contains a variable amount of fat. In the female there is a deposition of fat in this region—a secondary sexual characteristic, the amount of which tends to increase after middle age. At the elbow, a subcutaneous bursa is present between the skin and the olecranon process. This may become enlarged in people who often tend to lean on their elbows, giving rise to a condition known as 'student's elbow'.

There is nothing particularly noteworthy about the superficial fascia in the forearm. However, in the hand there are several specializations, most of which enhance the hand's tactile or prehensile capabilities. On the dorsum of the hand, the fascia is loose and thin, and can be readily lifted away from the underlying tissue. It is in the palm of the hand, as well as the palmar surface of the digits where specializations of the fascia can be seen. In the centre of the palm, strong bands of connective tissue connect the skin to the palmar aponeurosis, which is a thickening of the deep fascia. Overlying the thenar and hypothenar regions the fixation of the skin to the deep fascia is less well marked, but here the superficial fascia is thicker and less fibrous to facilitate the gripping action of the hand. This is because it can adapt to the contours of the object being held. Palmaris brevis lies in the superficial fascia over the hypothenar eminence. By wrinkling the skin, it improves the grip. Similar less fibrous pads of tissue are also found opposite the metacarpophalangeal joints, where the superficial transverse metacarpal ligament (a band of transverse fibres) connects to the palmar surfaces of the fibrous flexor sheath of the fingers.

The pads on the palmar surfaces of the distal phalanges are highly specialized regions which house numerous tactile nerve endings. Here the skin is firmly attached to the latter two-thirds of the distal phalanx.

However, the blood supply to the distal phalanx itself runs through this highly specialized pad. If the pad becomes infected there may be compression of the artery with death of this part of the bone. On the dorsum of the distal phalanx is the nail and there is no superficial fascia deep to it.

The deep fascia

The deep fascia of the upper limb is continuous with that of the upper back, and consequently can be traced superiorly to the superior nuchal line on the occipital bone, to the ligamentum nuchae centrally in the cervical region, and to the supraspinous and interspinous ligaments in the thoracic region. In the shoulder region, the deep fascia is extremely strong over infraspinatus and teres minor, being firmly attached to the medial and lateral borders of the scapula. Superiorly, a sheath is formed for deltoid, which attaches to the clavicle, and the acromion process and spine of the scapula.

The deep fascia covering pectoralis major attaches above to the clavicle, and may be traced, via the clavicle, to the neck. Inferiorly, it is continuous with the fascia of the anterior abdominal wall. Medially, the fascia is firmly attached to the sternum, whereas laterally it becomes thickened as the axillary fascia, which forms the floor of the axilla. Further laterally it becomes continuous with the deep fascia of the arm.

Deep to pectoralis major is the clavipectoral fascia. Medially, this is attached to the first costal cartilage and passes to the coracoid process and coracoclavicular ligament laterally. The clavipectoral fascia splits to surround subclavius superiorly, and thus attaches to the undersurface of the clavicle. It also splits to enclose pectoralis minor inferiorly. An extension of the fascia from the lateral border of pectoralis major passes into the axilla and attaches to the axillary floor. This is often referred to as the suspensory ligament of the axilla. The deep surface of the clavipectoral fascia is connected to the axillary sheath surrounding the axillary vessels and brachial plexus.

In the arm, the deep fascia forms an investing layer around the muscles. It attaches at the elbow to the medial and lateral epicondyles of the humerus and the olecranon process, becoming continuous with the deep fascia of the forearm. Two intermuscular septa arise from the deep surface of this investing layer and pass to attach to the supracondylar ridges of the humerus. Both the medial and lateral intermuscular septa are found only in the lower half of the arm. Besides separating the arm into flexor and extensor compartments they also give attachment to muscles in each compartment. Of the two, the medial intermuscular septum is said to be the stronger.

In the forearm, the deep fascia of the elbow is very strong because many of the muscles arising from either the common flexor or extensor tendons also arise from the overlying fascia. The bicipital aponeurosis helps to strengthen the fascia anteriorly, while the triceps insertion does so posteriorly. The deep fascia is also strong and thick where it attaches to the posterior border of the ulna, because it gives attachment to flexor digitorum profundus, and flexor and extensor carpi ulnaris. However, the fascia becomes thinner as it approaches the wrist, although at the wrist there are two thickenings of the transverse fibres forming the flexor and extensor retinacula. These serve to hold the tendons entering the hand in place and prevent 'bowstringing'.

The flexor retinaculum

The flexor retinaculum (Fig. 4.40a) is found anterior to the carpus where it acts as a strong band for retention of the long flexor tendons, converting the carpal sulcus into a canal. It attaches laterally to the tubercle of the scaphoid and to both lips of the groove on the trapezium, and medially to the pisiform and hook of the hamate. Flexor carpi radialis passes below the flexor retinaculum in its own lateral compartment surrounded by its synovial sheath. Medial to it, the single tendon of flexor pollicis longus is present, lying within its synovial sheath. All eight tendons of flexor digitorum superficialis and profundus run below the retinaculum in a common synovial sheath. The median nerve also enters the hand by passing below the flexor retinaculum, where it lies in front of the superficialis tendons. It is here that it may become compressed if the synovial sheaths become inflamed thus giving rise to the 'carpal tunnel syndrome'.

In the palm of the hand there are two layers of fascia. The deeper layer covers the interossei and encloses adductor pollicis. The more superficial layer is strong in its central part forming the palmar aponeurosis. On each side of this, the fascia thins out to cover the thenar and hypothenar muscles. The palmar aponeurosis strengthens the hand for gripping, yet also protects the underlying vessels and nerves. It is a dense, thick triangular structure bound to the overlying superficial fascia. The apex is at the wrist and its base at the webs of the fingers. From the base four slips pass into the fingers to become continuous with the digital sheaths of the flexor tendons.

Each slip further divides and has attachments to the deep transverse metacarpal ligament, the capsule of the metacarpophalangeal joint and the sides of the proximal phalanx. The slips cross in front of the lumbricals, and the digital vessels and nerves.

Fibro-osseous canals, retinaculae and synovial sheaths of the flexors of the wrist and fingers

The tendons of the digital flexors are held in close proximity to the phalanges by fibrous sheaths. These act to prevent 'bowstringing' of the tendons and ensure that their pull produces immediate movement at the interphalangeal joints. The canals are formed by a shallow groove on the anterior surface of the phalanges and by a fibrous sheath which attaches to the raised lateral and medial edges of the palmar surfaces of the proximal and middle phalanges and the palmar surface of the distal phalanx. The canal is closed distally by attaching to the distal phalanx, but is open proximally deep to the palmar aponeurosis. Most of the fibres of this sheath are arranged transversely, but at the interphalangeal joints they have a criss-cross arrangement to allow flexion to occur (Fig. 4.40b). All five of the fibro-osseous canals are lined with a synovial sheath which surrounds the enclosed tendons. In the fingers, the synovial sheath surrounds the tendons of superficialis and profundus and is connected to them by the vinculae. The sheath of the thumb contains only the tendon of flexor pollicis longus within a synovial covering.

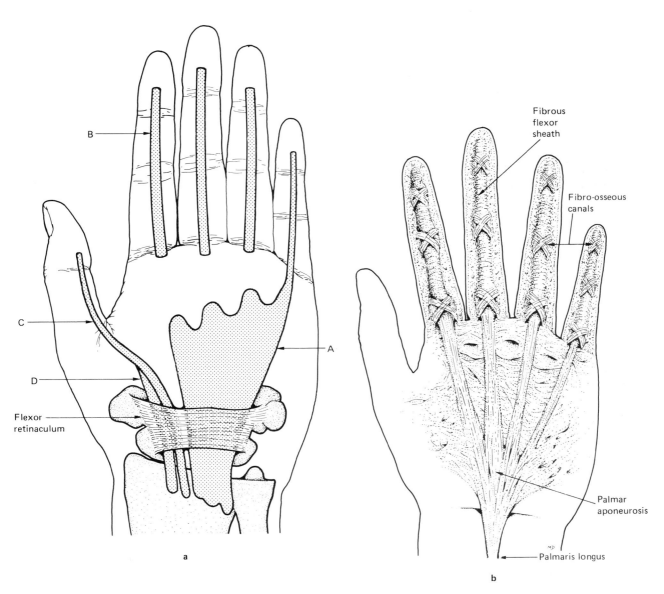

Fibrous
flexor
sheath

Fibro-osseous
canals

Palmar
aponeurosis

Palmaris longus

a

b

Fig. 4.40   **a** = Diagrammatic representation of the synovial sheaths of:

b = The palmar fascia of the hand.

A = Flexors digitorum superficialis and pro-
  fundus
B = Flexor tendons in the fingers
C = Flexor pollicis longus
D = Flexor carpi radialis

Flexor
retinaculum

The extensor retinaculum and synovial sheaths

The extensor retinaculum is a thickening of the deep fascia on the back of the forearm and wrist. It attaches laterally to the distal part of the anterior surface of the radius, and medially to the distal end of the ulna, the pisiform, triquetral and the ulnar collateral ligament of the wrist. Septa run from the deep surface of the extensor retinaculum to the distal ends of the radius and ulna, converting the grooves on the dorsum of the wrist into six separate canals. Each canal is lined by a synovial sheath. From medial to lateral, the compartments transmit extensor carpi ulnaris; extensor digiti minimi; extensor digitorum and extensor indicis; extensor pollicis longus; extensor carpi radialis longus and brevis, and abductor pollicis longus and extensor pollicis brevis. The synovial sheaths extend just above the extensor retinaculum. All except that surrounding extensor pollicis longus, which extends almost as far as the metacarpophalangeal joint of the thumb, end at the middle of the dorsum of the hand (Fig. 4.40c).

The retinaculum functions to retain the extensor tendons in their position and prevent 'bowstringing'.

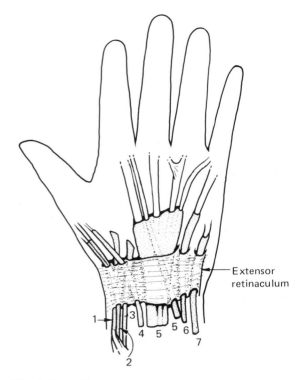

Fig.4.40c   Synovial sheaths of:

1 = Extensor pollicis brevis
2 = Extensor carpi radialis longus
3 = Extensor carpi radialis brevis
4 = Extensor pollicis longus
5 = Extensor digitorum and indicis
6 = Extensor digiti minimi
7 = Extensor carpi ulnaris

Application

In the condition of 'trigger finger', a swelling of the flexor tendons proximal to the fibro-osseous canals means that when the finger (or thumb) is flexed, the swelling moves into the canal and difficulty is thus experienced on attempting extension. In Dupuytren's contracture, the medial portion of the palmar aponeurosis and the fibrous sheaths of the ring and little fingers may become shortened, in which case these fingers are pulled towards the palm. In severe cases, the tips of these fingers may become pressed into the palm. The lateral two fibrous sheaths are less commonly affected.

From the medial and lateral borders of the palmar aponeurosis, septa pass down to fuse with the fascia covering the interossei, thereby dividing the palm into three compartments. Of these, the medial and lateral compartments contain the hypothenar and thenar muscles respectively. The intermediate compartment contains the long flexor tendons and the lumbricals, surrounded by loose connective tissue. A further septum, although often incomplete, runs from the deep aspect of this connective tissue to the shaft of the third metacarpal, further dividing this compartment into two potential spaces—the lateral and medial midpalmar spaces. Proximally they communicate, behind the flexor tendons, with a similar potential space in front of pronator quadratus. Distally, they are prolonged around the lumbrical muscles as the lumbrical canals which pass into the web of the fingers. The web space in turn is in free communication with the subaponeurotic space on the back of the hand deep to the extensor tendons, and with the dorsal subcutaneous space. Accumulations of fluid in the midpalmar spaces, following injury or infection of the hand, can therefore track back in the deep aspect of the flexor compartment, or via the webs of the fingers up the dorsum of the forearm in the loose superficial fascia.

The common synovial sheath for superficialis and profundus tendons extends from 2 cm above the flexor retinaculum and continues downwards through the carpal tunnel to end in the midpalmar region. Only the synovial sheath of the little finger is continuous with the common synovial sheath in the palm; the synovial sheaths lining the fibro-osseous canals of the other three fingers are separated from it (see Fig. 4.40a). The single synovial sheath of flexor pollicis longus has the same upward limit but continues downwards through the carpal tunnel and along the fibro-osseous canal of the thumb (see Fig. 4.40a).

SIMPLE ACTIVITIES OF THE UPPER LIMB

Introduction

The purpose of this short section is to produce a simple analysis of some common activities in order to show how different muscle groups cooperate in producing a desired movement. The analysis will firstly describe the starting position, omitting muscle work, but then go on to describe the sequence of movements involved, naming the joints and the muscles responsible, and ending with a description of how the muscles work with respect to joint movement. These general principles can then be applied to any movement.

Abduction of the arm through to full elevation

Starting position

This movement begins with the subject standing with the arm in the normal anatomical position.

Sequence of movements

Abduction of the humerus   Abduction of the humerus is initiated by *supraspinatus* which raises it by approximately 10°, thereby putting the arm into a position which allows *deltoid* to produce a rotatory force (torque) to continue the movement. Upward shearing of the head of the humerus in the glenoid fossa is prevented by the rotator cuff muscles. These all act isometrically as stabilizers with the exception of supraspinatus which shortens concentrically. Deltoid also works concentrically, the principal force being exerted by its middle multipennate fibres, with the anterior and posterior fibres acting as guides to control the plane of abduction.

Lateral rotation of the scapula Once 30° of abduction has been reached, lateral rotation of the scapula begins, turning the glenoid fossa upwards to increase the total range of movement. For every 15° of abduction from this point onwards, approximately 10° occurs at the shoulder joint and 5° by lateral rotation of the scapula. This lateral rotation of the scapula is produced by a concentric contraction of the upper and lower fibres of *trapezius*, and the lower half of *serratus anterior*. Other muscles assist these two in holding the scapula against the chest wall.

Lateral rotation of the humerus As movement at the glenohumeral articulation approaches 90°, (a position of 120° abduction) there is a lateral rotation of the humerus to prevent it: (1) coming into contact with the coracoacromial arch and (2) stopping any further movement—a locked position. This lateral rotation of the humerus brings the lower part of the articular surface of the head into contact with the glenoid fossa. Lateral rotation of the humerus is brought about by a concentric contraction of *teres minor* and *infraspinatus*.

As the clavicle is firmly attached to the acromion process, lateral rotation of the scapula lifts the lateral end of the clavicle, producing a downward movement of the clavicle at the sternoclavicular joint. There is also a slight rotation of the clavicle about its long axis, which takes place at both the acromioclavicular and sternoclavicular joints.

Pushing or punching

Starting position

The shoulder joint is in 45–90° abduction and fully extended, with the elbow joint fully flexed. The hand is either open, for pushing, or closed, for punching. For this activity the muscle work and joint positions of the hand will not be considered.

Sequence of movements

Abduction and flexion of the shoulder The shoulder is maintained in abduction by isometric contraction of the *middle fibres* of *deltoid*, and is then rapidly flexed by the *anterior fibres* of *deltoid* and *pectoralis*

major, assisted by *coracobrachialis* and the *long head* of *biceps*, all of which work concentrically.

Protraction of the scapula and extension of the forearm To increase the force and range of the movement, the scapula is protracted by a strong concentric contraction of *serratus anterior* and *pectoralis minor*. At the same time there is a forceful contraction of *triceps* to produce rapid extension of the forearm at the elbow joint.

The major difference between pushing and punching is the velocity of the movement, with the latter being a more rapid and explosive movement.

A press-up (movement upwards and then downwards)

Starting position

The subject lies prone with the palmar surfaces of the hands on the ground below the shoulders, which are in 90° abduction and slight extension. The elbows are fully flexed. It will be assumed that static muscle work in the legs and trunk will maintain their neutral position throughout.

Sequence of movements

Upwards movement There is simultaneous extension of the elbows by *triceps* and *anconeus*, and flexion of the shoulders by *pectoralis major* and the *anterior fibres* of *deltoid*, assisted by *coracobrachialis* and the *long head* of *biceps*. The pectoral girdle is strongly protracted by *serratus anterior* and *pectoralis minor*, the arms are straight and the shoulders are protracted. All the muscles work concentrically.

From this position, the downward movement can now be analysed.

Downward movement In the downward phase there is simultaneous movement of both the elbow and shoulder joints under the influence of gravity. The elbows become flexed under the eccentric contraction of *triceps* and *anconeus* working to control the rate of descent. At the shoulder joint, extension is brought about by eccentric contraction of the muscles. Extension is controlled by *pectoralis major* and the *anterior fibres* of *deltoid*, with the *long head* of *biceps* and *coracobrachialis* assisting these muscles. The pectoral girdle retracts under the eccentric control of *serratus anterior* and *pectoralis minor*.

It is worth remembering that the same muscles are involved in producing both movements, upwards by shortening, and then downwards by lengthening.

Pulling

Starting position

The subject stands with the shoulder flexed to 90°, the elbow in full extension and the hand firmly gripping the object to be pulled.

Sequence of movements

The elbow is flexed by concentric contraction of *biceps* and *brachialis*, while the shoulder is extended by the strong concentric action of *teres major*, *latissimus dorsi* and the *posterior fibres* of *deltoid*. The pectoral girdle is retracted by concentric shortening of *trapezius*, *rhomboid major* and *rhomboid minor*.

Gripping

A number of different types of grip can be described depending upon the activity being undertaken.

Power grip

A power grip is the position adopted by the fingers, thumb and wrist when a strong grip on an object, such as a hammer, is required. There is little movement involved and so the joint position and muscle work only will be described.

The distal and proximal interphalangeal joints of the fingers are flexed by *flexor digitorum profundus* and *flexor digitorum superficialis* respectively. The metacarpophalangeal joints are flexed by the *lumbricals* as well as by the long flexors. The thumb is pressed strongly against the flexed fingers by *flexor pollicis longus* and the four *intrinsic* thumb muscles. The wrist is held in extension by the synergic action of *extensor carpi*

radialis longus and *brevis* and *extensor carpi ulnaris*. This position of the wrist prevents the continued contraction of the long flexors pulling the wrist into flexion, and thus prevents a loss of power in the gripping fingers by 'active insufficiency' of the flexor muscles.

Once in the gripping position, all of the muscles named are working isometrically, with the joint positions determined by the size of the object being held. When no object is being gripped, as in a fist, the fully flexed fingers are firmly pressed into the palm.

Precision grip

The position of the wrist and the muscle work involved is the same as for the power grip. Depending upon the activity being undertaken there will be varying degrees of flexion and extension in the joints of the fingers and thumb. In writing, for example, the pen is held between the thumb, index and middle fingers. The muscle work involved is similar to that involved in the power grip, but the strength of contraction is much less. In addition to the long flexors of the fingers and thumb holding the pen, the *lumbricals* and *interossei* produce and control the very fine movements of the fingers, which together with those produced in the thumb, allow the pen to be moved in order to write.

Hand movements are extremely precise and the ability to manipulate small objects and carry out very intricate tasks is one of the characteristics of human development.

Hook grip

In this grip, as in those described earlier, the wrist is maintained in a similar position of extension. The fingers are hooked through some sort of handle to allow carrying, as when holding a suitcase. The distal and proximal interphalangeal joints are flexed by *flexor digitorum profundus* and *flexor digitorum superficialis* respectively. These muscles work isometrically to maintain this grip. The metacarpophalangeal joints are held in a neutral position.

Joints

THE PECTORAL GIRDLE

Introduction

The upper limb has become highly specialized in its functions of prehension and manipulation. Evolutionary forces have produced a limb which is extremely mobile yet without losing the stability required to give the acquired mobility force and precision. The culmination of this evolutionary development is an upper limb which has no locomotor function, except in infants and in those who, of necessity, use walking aids.

All vertebrates possess four limbs of one form or another, these limbs being connected to the axial skeleton by the pectoral and pelvic girdles. The pelvic girdle is firmly anchored to the vertebral column, thereby providing the stability necessary for bipedal locomotion (see p. 300). The pectoral girdle, however, does not articulate with the vertebral column, it articulates only with the thoracic cage (Fig. 4.41), which while providing a mechanism whereby forces generated in the upper limb can be partially transferred to the axial skeleton, it does not unduly restrict movement of the girdle as a whole.

The shoulder blade (scapula) and clavicle are the bones of the pectoral girdle. The shoulder blade is usually referred to as the scapula in descriptive anatomy, morphologically the term has a slightly more restricted meaning (see p. 56). Although movements of the shoulder joint accompany nearly all movements of the joints of the pectoral girdle, it is not part of the pectoral girdle. The shoulder blade is slung in muscle from the thoracic cage, while the clavicle interposes itself between shoulder blade and thorax providing a strut which steadies and braces the pectoral girdle during adduction movements. The clavicle articulates with the thorax by the sternoclavicular joint (Fig. 4.41), and with the shoulder blade by the acromioclavicular joint (Fig. 4.41). The humerus of the upper limb joins the scapula at the shoulder (glenohumeral) joint. It is the summation of the mobility of these three individual, yet mutually interdependent, joints which gives the upper limb its freedom of movement, consequently, the ultimate range of movement of the shoulder complex is much greater than that of the hip. The clavicle moves with respect to the sternum, the scapula with respect to the clavicle and the humerus with respect to the scapula. In addition, the scapula moves with respect to the thoracic wall. This arrangement favours mobility of the shoulder–arm complex, however, it makes stabilization of the upper limb against the axial skeleton much more difficult. Stability is achieved by the powerful musculature which attaches the pectoral girdle to the thorax, vertebral column, head and neck. Furthermore, this musculature acts as a shock absorber when body-weight is received by the upper limbs.

Just as the innominate bone consists of three parts which meet and fuse at the acetabulum, so there are three parts of the shoulder blade (Fig. 4.42). The broad, flat, dorsal part of the shoulder blade is the scapula; the ventral part is the coracoid process, the two joining together in the upper part of the glenoid fossa. (These are the counterparts of the ilium and ischium respectively.) A small piece of bone, the precoracoid, ossifying separately at the tip of the coracoid process is the counterpart of the pubis.

The clavicle has no counterpart in the pelvic girdle. Forces from the upper limb are transmitted by the clavicle to the axial skeleton by the coracoclavicular and costoclavicular ligaments, so that normally neither end of the clavicle transmits much force.

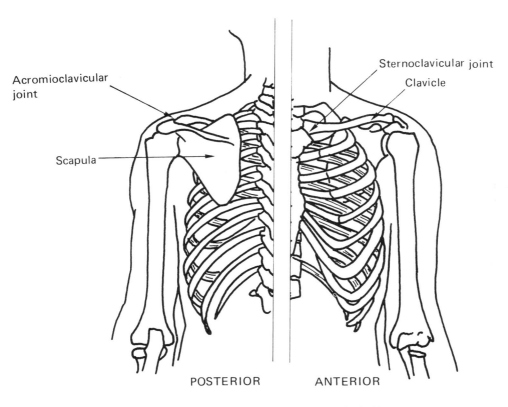

Acromioclavicular joint

Sternoclavicular joint

Clavicle

Scapula

POSTERIOR   ANTERIOR

Fig. 4.41 Relation of the pectoral girdle to the thorax.

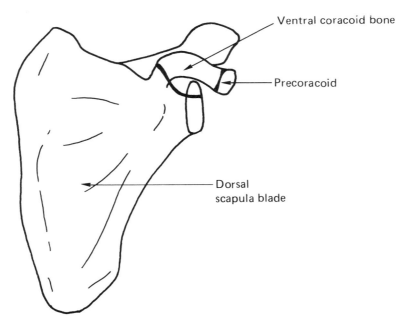

Ventral coracoid bone

Precoracoid

Dorsal scapula blade

Fig. 4.42 The parts of the scapula equivalent to the hip bone.

Sternoclavicular joint

The synovial sternoclavicular joint provides the only point of bony connection between the pectoral girdle and upper limb, and the trunk. Although the joint is functionally a ball and socket joint, it does not have the form of such a joint.

Articular surfaces

The medial end of the clavicle articulates with the clavicular notch at the superolateral angle of the sternum and the adjacent upper medial surface of the first costal cartilage. The clavicular articular surface tends to be larger than that on the sternum. Consequently, the medial end of the clavicle projects above the upper margin of the manubrium sterni.

The articular surfaces are reciprocally concavoconvex (Fig. 4.43a), although they do not usually have similar radii of curvature. The joint, therefore, is not particularly congruent. Congruence is partly provided by an intra-articular fibrocartilaginous disc. The articular surface on the manubrium sterni is set at approximately 45° to the perpendicular. It is markedly concave from above downwards, and convex from behind forwards, being covered with hyaline cartilage. The clavicular articular surface is convex vertically and flattened or slightly concave horizontally (Fig. 4.43a), with the concavity being continued over the inferior surface of the shaft for articulation with the first rib costal cartilage. The greater horizontal articular surface of the clavicle overlaps the sternocostal surface anteriorly and particularly posteriorly, the whole being covered with fibrocartilage rather than hyaline cartilage.

Joint capsule and synovial membrane

A fibrous capsule surrounds the whole joint like a sleeve attaching to the articular margins of both the clavicle and the sternum, with its inferior part passing between the clavicle and the upper surface of the first costal cartilage (Fig. 4.43b). Except for this inferior part, which is weak, the joint capsule is relatively strong, being strengthened anteriorly, posteriorly and superiorly by capsular thickenings known as the anterior and posterior sternoclavicular ligaments and the interclavicular ligament respectively.

Because there are two separate cavities associated with the joint (see below), there are two synovial membranes. A relatively loose lateral membrane lines the capsule, being reflected from the articular margin of the medial end of the clavicle to the margins of the articular disc. Similarly, the medial membrane attaches to the articular margins on the sternum and to the margins of the disc.

Intra-articular structures

A complete, intra-articular, fibrocartilaginous disc separates the joint into two synovial cavities (Fig. 4.43b). The disc is flat and round, being thinner centrally, where it may occasionally be perforated and permit communication between the two cavities, than around the periphery. It is attached at its circumference to the joint capsule, particularly in front and behind. More importantly, however, the disc is firmly attached superiorly and posteriorly to the upper border of the medial end of the clavicle, and inferiorly to the first costal cartilage near its sternal end (Fig. 4.43b). Consequently, as well as providing some cushioning between the articular surfaces, from forces transmitted from the upper limb, and compensating for incongruity of the joint surfaces, the disc also has an important ligamentous action. Although mainly fibrocartilaginous, it is fibrous or ligamentous at its circumference, and holds the medial end of the clavicle against the sternum. It prevents the clavicle moving upwards and medially along the sloping sternochondral surface under the influence of strong, thrusting forces transmitted from the limb, or when the clavicle is depressed as by a heavy weight carried in the hand.

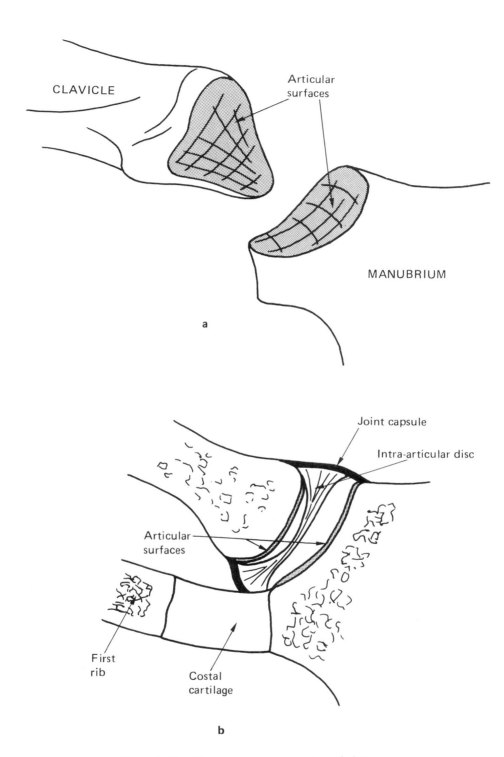

Fig. 4.43 The sternoclavicular joint: **a** = articular surfaces; **b** = joint capsule and intra-articular disc.

Ligaments

The joint capsule is strengthened anteriorly, posteriorly and superiorly by the anterior and posterior sternoclavicular ligaments and the interclavicular ligament respectively. In addition, an accessory ligament, the costoclavicular ligament, binds the clavicle to the first costal cartilage just lateral to the joint.

Anterior sternoclavicular ligament (Fig. 4.44) The anterior sternoclavicular ligament is a strong, broad band of fibres attaching above to the superior and anterior parts of the medial end of the clavicle, passing obliquely downwards and medially to the front of the upper part of the manubrium sterni. It is reinforced by the tendinous origin of sternomastoid.

Posterior sternoclavicular ligament (Fig. 4.44b) The posterior sternoclavicular ligament, although not as strong as the anterior ligament, is also a broad band running obliquely downwards and medially. Laterally it attaches to the superior and posterior parts of the medial end of the clavicle, while medially it is attached to the back of the upper part of the manubrium sterni. The sternal attachment of sternohyoid extends across, and reinforces part of, the posterior ligament.

Interclavicular ligament (Fig. 4.44) The interclavicular ligament strengthens the capsule superiorly, and is formed by fibres attaching to the upper aspect of the sternal end of one clavicle passing across the jugular notch to join similar fibres from the opposite side. Some of these fibres attach to the floor of the jugular notch.

Costoclavicular ligament (Fig. 4.44) The extracapsular costoclavicular ligament is an extremely strong, short, dense band of fibres. It is attached to the upper surface of the first costal cartilage near its lateral end, and to a rough rhomboid impression on the inferior surface of the medial end of the clavicle. The ligament is in two laminae, usually separated by a bursa, which are attached to the anterior and posterior lips of the clavicular rhomboid impression. The anterior fibres run upwards and laterally, while those of the posterior lamina run upwards and medially; thus the fibres have a cruciate arrangement. The direction of fibres in the two laminae is the same as those in the external and internal intercostal muscles respectively.

The costoclavicular ligament essentially limits elevation of the clavicle, however, it is also active in preventing excessive anterior or posterior movements of the medial end of the clavicle. Its position and strength compensate for the weakness of the adjacent inferior part of the joint capsule.

a

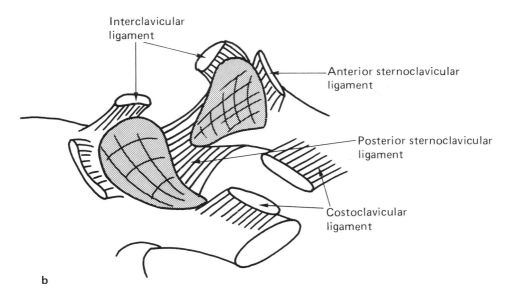

b

Fig. 4.44 Ligaments associated with the sternoclavicular joint: **a** = seen from the front; **b** = with the joint opened out and capsule removed.

Blood and nerve supply

The arterial supply of the sternoclavicular joint is from branches of the internal thoracic artery, the superior thoracic branch of the axillary artery, the clavicular branch of the thoracoacromial trunk, and the suprascapular artery. Venous drainage is to the axillary and external jugular veins. Lymphatics from the joint pass to the lower deep cervical group of nodes, sometimes called the supraclavicular nodes, and thence to the jugular trunk. A few lymphatics may pass to the apical group of axillary nodes.

The nerve supply of the joint is by twigs from the medial supraclavicular nerve (C3, 4) and the nerve to subclavius (C5 and 6).

Relations

Overlying the joint anteriorly is the tendinous attachment of the sternal head of sternomastoid (Fig. 4.45a). Posteriorly, the sternoclavicular joint is separated from the brachiocephalic vein and common carotid artery on the left and the brachiocephalic trunk on the right and by the sternohyoid and sternothyroid muscles (Fig. 4.45b). The superior vena cava is formed on the right hand side, by the union of the two brachiocephalic veins, just below the joint at the lower border of the first costal cartilage (Fig. 4.45c).

On the right hand side, both the phrenic and vagus nerves lie lateral to the sternoclavicular joint as they enter the thorax from the neck. However, on the left hand side, the vagus may pass behind the joint as it descends between the common carotid and subclavian arteries.

Stability

The shape of the articular surfaces and the surrounding musculature provide only a limited amount of security for the joint. The stability of the sternoclavicular joint is primarily dependent on the strength and integrity of its ligaments, particularly the costoclavicular ligament. Unfortunately, when dislocation of the joint takes places it is liable to recur.

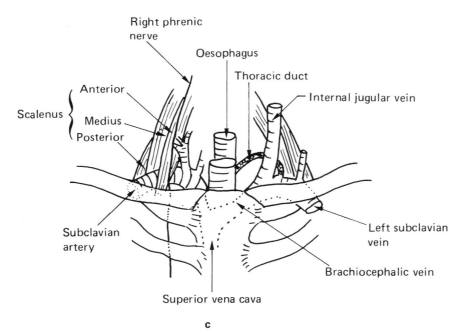

Fig. 4.45 Relations of the sternoclavicular joint: **a** = anterior muscles; **b** = posterior muscles; **c** = vessels.

Movements

Although the articular surfaces do not conform to those of a ball and socket joint, the sternoclavicular joint nevertheless has three degrees of freedom of movement, that is elevation and depression, protraction and retraction, and axial rotation. The fulcrum of these movements, except axial rotation, is not at the joint centre but through the costoclavicular ligament. Consequently, the movements of elevation and depression, and protraction and retraction involve a gliding (1) between the clavicle and the intra-articular disc, and (2) between the disc and the sternum.

Elevation and depression The axis of rotation for elevation and depression runs horizontally and slightly obliquely, anterolaterally through the costoclavicular ligament (Fig. 4.46a). Some authorities have suggested that two axes of rotation can be identified for elevation and depression, one for the gliding of the clavicle with respect to the disc, and the other for gliding of the disc against the sternum. Nevertheless, functionally the combined axis of movement runs through the costoclavicular ligament.

Because the axis of movement is somewhat removed from the joint centre, as the lateral end of the clavicle moves, so its medial end moves in the opposite direction (Fig. 4.46a). Consequently, elevation of the lateral end of the clavicle causes the medial end to move downwards and laterally. The range of movement of the lateral end of the clavicle is approximately 10 cm of elevation and 3 cm of depression, giving a total angular range of movement of some 60°. Elevation is limited by tension in the costoclavicular ligament and by tone in the subclavius muscle. Depression of the clavicle, in which the medial end moves upwards and medially, is limited by tension in the interclavicular ligament and by the intra-articular disc. If these two mechanisms fail, then movement is eventually limited by contact between the clavicle and upper surface of the first rib.

Protraction and retraction The axis of movement for protraction and retraction lies in a vertical plane running obliquely, inferolaterally through the middle part of the costoclavicular ligament (Fig. 4.46b). Again the two ends of the clavicle move in opposite directions because of the position of the fulcrum about which movement takes place (Fig. 4.46b), so that in protraction of the lateral end, the medial end moves back and vice versa. In these movements, the medial end of the clavicle and the intra-articular disc tend to move as one unit against the sternum. The range of movement of the lateral end of the clavicle is approximately 5 cm of protraction (anterior movement) and 2 cm of retraction (posterior movement), giving a total angular range of movement of about 35°. Movement anteriorly is limited by tension in the anterior sternoclavicular and costoclavicular ligaments, while posterior movement is limited by the posterior sternoclavicular and costoclavicular ligaments.

Axial rotation (Fig. 4.46c) Whereas elevation, depression, protraction and retraction of the clavicle are active movements brought about by direct muscle action, axial rotation is entirely passive, being produced by rotation of the scapula and transmitted to the clavicle by the coracoclavicular ligament. Pure axial rotation of the clavicle is not possible in the living subject, it always accompanies movements in other planes. The axis about which rotation occurs passes through the centre of the articular surfaces.

The range of movement is small when the clavicle is in the frontal plane, but increases considerably when the lateral end of the clavicle is carried backwards. The degree of axial rotation possible is between 20° and 40° depending on the position of the clavicle.

That there should be any axial rotation possible at the sternoclavicular joint is due to (1) the relative incongruity of the articular surfaces, (2) the presence of an intra-articular disc and (3) the relative laxness of the capsular thickenings.

Accessory movements

With the subject lying supine, a downward pressure by the thumb on the medial end of the clavicle produces a posterior gliding of the clavicle against the sternum.

Palpation

The line of the sternoclavicular joint can be easily identified through the skin and

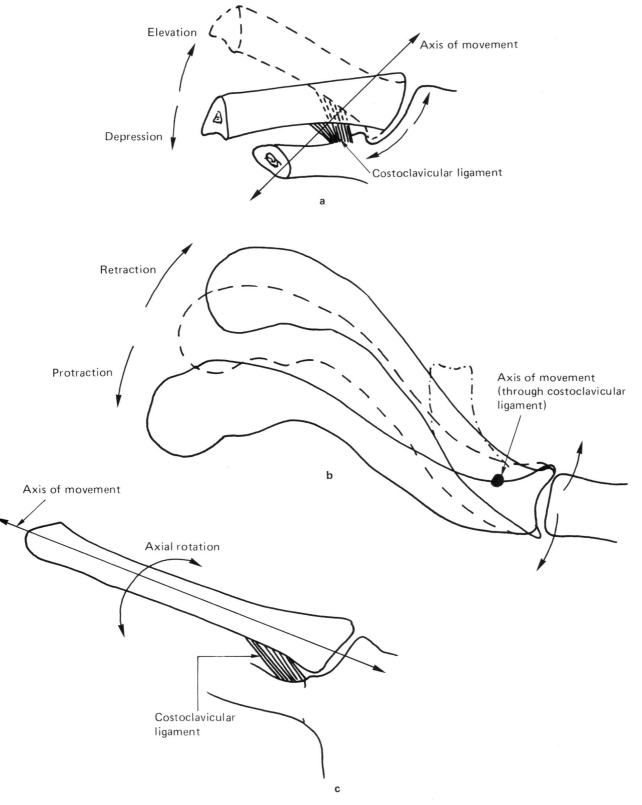

Fig. 4.46 Movements of the clavicle at the sternoclavicular joint: **a** = elevation and depression; **b** = protraction and retraction; **c** = axial rotation.

subcutaneous tissues at the medial end of the clavicle. The projection of the medial end of the clavicle above the sternum can also be palpated.

Acromioclavicular joint

The synovial acromioclavicular joint connects the clavicle with the shoulder blade. The role that this joint plays in the movement of the pectoral girdle is considered by some to be greater than that of the sternoclavicular joint, particularly for movements in or close to the sagittal plane.

Articular surfaces

The articulation is between an oval flat or slightly convex facet on the lateral end of the clavicle, and a similarly shaped flat or slightly concave facet on the anteromedial border of the acromion process (Fig. 4.47a). Both joint surfaces are covered with fibrocartilage. The major axis of both facets runs from anterolateral to posteromedial, so that the clavicular facet faces laterally and posteriorly, and that on the acromion faces medially and anteriorly. Consequently, the lateral end of the clavicle tends to over-ride the acromion, which together with the slope of their articulating surfaces favours displacement of the acromion downwards and under the clavicle in dislocations.

Joint capsule and synovial membrane

A relatively loose fibrous capsule surrounds the joint attaching to the articular margins.

Its strong coarse fibres run in parallel fasciculi from one bone to the other. The capsule is thickest and strongest above where it is reinforced by the fibres of trapezius. Some authorities contend that the joint capsule is reinforced by two strong ligaments, the superior and inferior acromioclavicular ligaments, passing between the adjacent surfaces of the two bones (Fig. 4.47b). In reality these are no more than capsular thickenings, which will show varying degrees of thickening in different individuals.

Synovial membrane lines the inner surface of the capsule attaching to the margins of the articular surfaces.

Intra-articular structures

A wedge-shaped, fibrocartilaginous articular disc partially divides the cavity in most joints (Fig. 4.47b). When present, the disc is attached to the upper part of the capsule and dips down between the two articulating surfaces. Only rarely does the disc form a complete partition within the joint. The presence of the articular disc partially compensates for the small degree of incongruity between the two joint surfaces.

Ligaments

Apart from the capsular thickening alluded to above, the strength of the acromioclavicular joint is provided by an extracapsular accessory ligament, the coracoclavicular ligament.

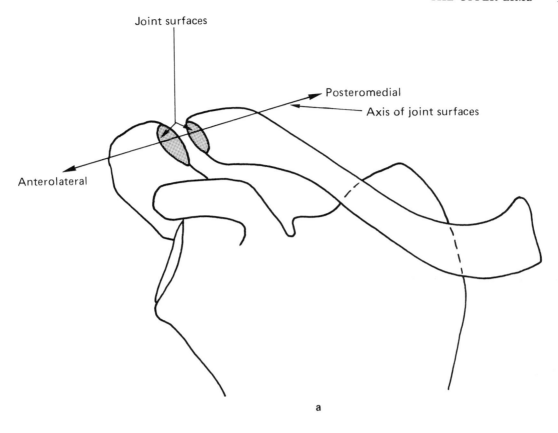

Joint surfaces

Posteromedial

Axis of joint surfaces

Anterolateral

a

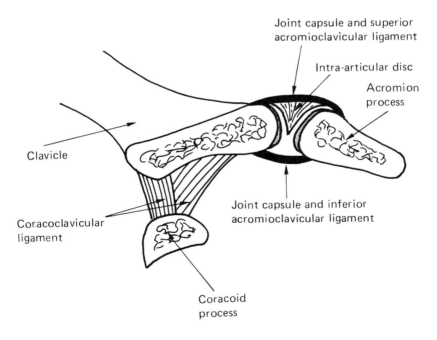

Joint capsule and superior
acromioclavicular ligament

Intra-articular disc

Acromion
process

Clavicle

Joint capsule and inferior
acromioclavicular ligament

Coracoclavicular
ligament

Coracoid
process

b

Fig. 4.47   a = Acromioclavicular joint surfaces; **b** = acromioclavicular joint open, showing intra-articular disc.

Coracoclavicular ligament The coracoclavicular ligament is extremely powerful, anchoring the lateral end of the clavicle to the coracoid process (Fig. 4.48a). The ligament, which is medial to the acromioclavicular joint, stabilizes the clavicle with respect to the acromion. It is in two parts which are named according to their shapes, these being the posteromedial *conoid* and anterolateral *trapezoid* ligaments (Fig. 4.48b). The two parts tend to be continuous with each other posteriorly but are separated anteriorly by a small gap in which is found a synovial bursa.

The apex of the fan-shaped, conoid ligament is attached posteromedially to the 'elbow' of the angulated coracoid process (Fig. 4.48b). From here the ligament broadens as it passes upwards, more or less in the frontal plane, to attach to the conoid tubercle on the under surface of the clavicle.

The stronger and more powerful trapezoid ligament is a flat, quadrilateral band. It is attached inferiorly to a roughened ridge on the upper surface of the coracoid process (Fig. 4.48b). The wider superior surface of the ligament is attached to the trapezoid line on the under surface of the clavicle, which runs anterolaterally from the conoid tubercle. Although the two surfaces of the trapezoid ligament are set obliquely, the ligament lies more or less in the sagittal plane, being more nearly horizontal than vertical.

Because the conoid and trapezoid ligaments lie in different planes, which are more or less at right angles to each other, and because the posterior edge of the trapezoid ligament is usually in contact with the lateral edge of the conoid ligament, a solid angle facing anteromedially is formed between them.

The two parts of the coracoclavicular ligament are set so as to restrain opposite movements of the scapula with respect to the clavicle. The conoid ligament limits forward movement of the scapula, while the trapezoid limits backward movements. The importance of these limiting movements will be discussed more fully in the section on movements of the pectoral girdle (see p. 166). Both ligaments, but especially the trapezoid ligament, prevent the acromion being carried medially under the lateral end of the clavicle when laterally directed forces are applied to the shoulder.

Blood and nerve supply

The arterial supply to the joint is by branches from the suprascapular branch of the subclavian and acromial branch of the thoracoacromial trunk. Venous drainage is to the external jugular and axillary veins. Lymphatic drainage will be to the apical group of axillary nodes.

The nerve supply to the joint is by twigs from the lateral supraclavicular, lateral pectoral, suprascapular and axillary nerves, from roots C4, 5 and 6.

Relations

The attachments of trapezius and deltoid cover the posterosuperior and anterosuperior aspects of the joint respectively. Medial to the coracoclavicular ligament the transverse superior scapular ligament converts the scapula notch into a foramen. The suprascapular vessels pass above the ligament, while beneath it and through the foramen runs the suprascapular nerve. The lateral supraclavicular nerve crosses the clavicle medial to the acromioclavicular joint.

Although not directly associated with the joint, the coracoacromial ligament, as its name suggests, is attached to both the coracoid and acromion processes. Full details of the ligament are given on p. 176.

Stability

The stability of the joint is essentially provided by the coracoclavicular ligament. Trapezius and deltoid by virtue of their crossing the joint will also provide a certain amount of stability during movement of the joint.

Fig. 4.48 The coracoclavicular ligament: **a** = from the front; **b** = sectioned to show its attachments to the coracoid process and clavicle.

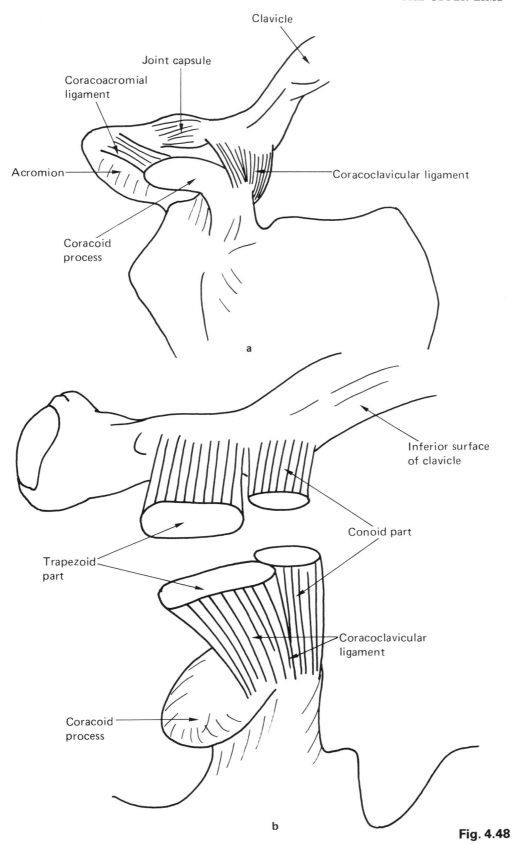

Fig. 4.48

Movement

The movements of the joint are entirely passive as there are no muscles connecting the bones which could cause one to move with respect to the other. Muscles which move the shoulder blade cause it to move on the clavicle. Indeed, all movements of the shoulder blade involve movement at both the acromioclavicular and sternoclavicular joints. All movements at the acromioclavicular joint, except that of axial rotation, are gliding movements with the coracoclavicular ligament acting so as to limit these movements.

The acromioclavicular joint has three degrees of freedom of motion about three axes. These movements are probably best described in terms of their relation to the shoulder blade rather than with respect to the cardinal axes of the body, since the joint constantly changes its relation to the trunk. The most important function of the joint is that it provides an additional range of movement for the pectoral girdle after the range of movement at the sternoclavicular joint has been exhausted.

Movement about a vertical axis This movement is associated with protraction and retraction of the shoulder blade. The axis of movement passes vertically through the lateral end of the clavicle midway between the joint and the coracoclavicular ligament (Fig. 4.49a). As the acromion glides backwards with respect to the clavicle, the angle between the clavicle and shoulder blade decreases: similarly as the acromion glides forwards this angle increases (Fig. 4.49a). Backward movement of the acromion is checked by the anterior joint capsule and actively limited by the trapezoid ligament as it becomes stretched. Forward movement will be checked by the posterior joint capsule and limited by the stretching of the conoid ligament. Towards the end of forward movement of the acromion, the trapezoid ligament may also be put under tension and therefore help to limit the movement. Compensatory movements of the clavicle at the sternoclavicular joint accompany these actions at the acromioclavicular joint.

Movement about a sagittal axis (Fig. 4.49b) Movement about this axis occurs when the shoulder blade is elevated or depressed. It has been estimated that the total range of movement about this axis is no more than 15°. Elevation is limited by tension developed in both parts of the coracoclavicular ligament, with the conoid ligament becoming stretched first; depression is checked by the coracoid process coming into contact with the under surface of the clavicle.

Axial rotation (Fig. 4.49c) Axial rotation at the acromioclavicular joint is associated with medial and lateral rotation of the shoulder blade, that is when the glenoid fossa faces inferiorly or superiorly respectively. The range of rotation of the shoulder blade with respect to the clavicle is of the order of 30°, and occurs about an axis that passes through the conoid ligament and the acromioclavicular joint. The movement allows the flexed arm to be fully elevated. Restraints to rotation are provided by both parts of the coracoclavicular ligament.

Accessory movements

With the subject lying supine, downward pressure applied with the thumb on the lateral end of the clavicle causes it to glide backward against the acromion process.

Palpation

The line of the acromioclavicular joint can be palpated from above by applying a downward pressure to the lateral end of the clavicle.

Fig. 4.49 Movements at the acromioclavicular joint: **a** = about a vertical axis associated with protraction/retraction of scapula; **b** = about a sagittal axis associated with elevation/depression of scapula; **c** = axial rotation of scapula.

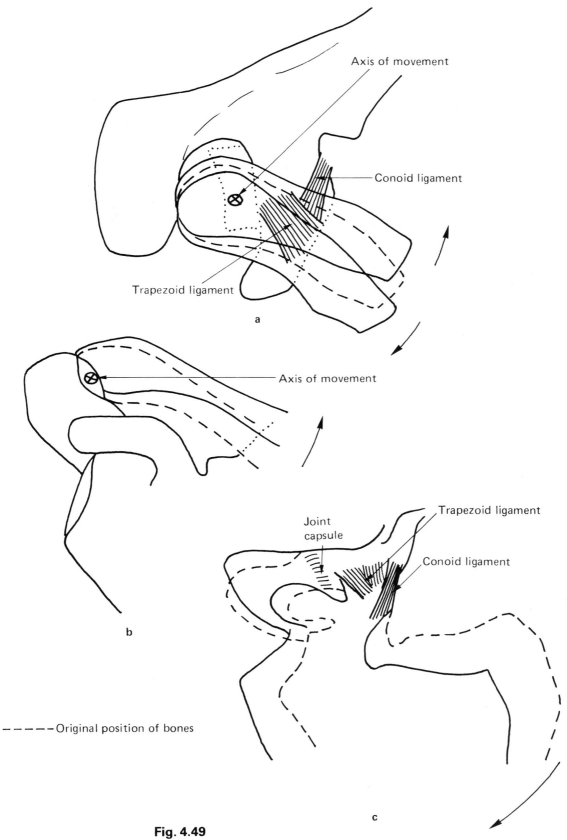

Axis of movement

Conoid ligament

Trapezoid ligament

a

Axis of movement

b

Trapezoid ligament

Joint capsule

Conoid ligament

– – – – –Original position of bones

c

Fig. 4.49

Movements of the pectoral girdle as a whole

Movements of the pectoral girdle serve to increase the range of movement of the shoulder joint, principally by changing the relative position of the glenoid fossa with respect to the chest wall. In all of these movements the clavicle, acting as a strut, holds the shoulder away from the trunk thereby securing greater freedom of movement of the upper limb. It should be remembered that movements of the pectoral girdle accompany virtually all movements of the shoulder joint (see pp. 184–190).

In movements of the pectoral girdle, the glenoid fossa travels in an arc of a circle whose radius is the clavicle, while the medial border of the scapula, held against the chest wall, travels in a curve of shorter radius. Consequently, the relative positions of clavicle and shoulder blade must be capable of changing. This occurs at the acromioclavicular joint. It now becomes obvious that a rigid union between clavicle and shoulder blade would severely limit the mobility of the upper limb.

Lateral movement of the shoulder blade around the chest wall brings it to lie more in a sagittal plane so that the glenoid fossa faces more directly forwards (Fig. 4.50a, b). Medial movement towards the vertebral column brings the shoulder blade to lie more in the frontal plane, with the glenoid fossa facing more directly laterally. These two extreme positions of the scapula form a solid angle of 40° to 45° (Fig. 4.50a). Furthermore, the angle between the clavicle and shoulder blade decreases to approximately 60° on full lateral movement of the shoulder blade, and increases to approximately 70° on full medial movement (Fig. 4.50a). The total range of linear translation of the shoulder blade around the chest wall is about 15 cm.

Elevation and depression of the shoulder blade has a linear range of some 10 to 12 cm (Fig. 4.50c). However, it is usually accompanied by some degree of rotation, so that in elevation the glenoid fossa comes to face increasingly upwards. In depression, the fossa points increasingly downwards. The rotation of the shoulder blade that occurs with respect to the chest wall does so about an axis perpendicular to the plane of the sca-

pula, and is situated a little below the spine close to the superolateral angle. The total range of angular rotation of the scapula amounts to 60° (Fig. 4.50d). This involves a displacement of the inferior angle of the scapula of 10 to 12 cm, and that of the superolateral angle of 5 to 6 cm.

During abduction or flexion of the arm, the clavicle rotates about its long axis so that its anterior surface is increasingly directed upwards. Towards the end of the range of rotation of the scapula against the clavicle, the coracoclavicular ligament becomes taut and transmits the rotating force to the clavicle, whose rotation then accounts for the scapular rotation on the chest wall. Any impairment of the clavicle to rotate at either the sternoclavicular or the acromioclavicular joints will interfere with the free movement of the shoulder blade and upper limb as a whole.

Although movements of medial and lateral translation of the scapula, elevation and depression, and its rotation with respect to the chest wall have been discussed, it is important to remember that they do not occur as pure movements. All movements of the pectoral girdle will involve some degree of each of the above pure movements.

Biomechanics

Stresses on the clavicle

The clavicle is subjected to both pressure and tension stresses, which under normal conditions are absorbed within it. They only become apparent when the integrity of the pectoral girdle is compromised, as by fracture, dislocation or muscular imbalance. Unlike the pelvic girdle, because the pectoral girdle is not a complete bony ring, the intrinsic stresses require the cooperation of muscles attached to it for there to be equilibrium.

A compressive stress along the length of the clavicle directed towards the sternoclavicular joint is produced by the action of trapezius and pectoralis minor as they pull the clavicle towards the sternum. Forces transmitted medially from the upper limb to the glenoid fossa are transmitted from the scapula to the clavicle by the trapezoid liga-

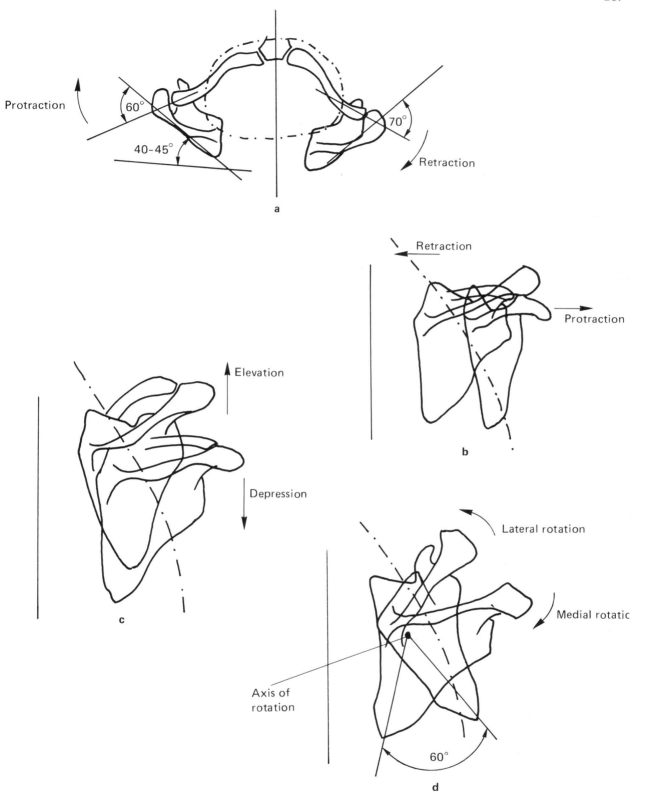

Fig. 4.50 Movements of the pectoral girdle: protraction/retraction seen (**a**) from above and (**b**) from behind; **c** = elevation/depression and **d** = axial rotation.

ment, and from the clavicle to the first rib by the costoclavicular ligament. Consequently, falling on an outstretched hand or elbow puts no strain on either end of the clavicle at the joints. If the clavicle fractures as a result, it does so between these two ligaments. In such fractures, the two fragments tend to over-ride one another. These compressive stresses are increased by lying on one shoulder.

Tension stresses within the clavicle are produced, under the action of deltoid, when the upper limb is abducted. Hanging and swinging forwards by the arms increases these tension stresses. If sufficiently large they may lead to some discontinuity of the pectoral girdle; however, a joint dislocation is much more likely to occur than a fracture.

A rotational force transmitted through the scapula to the clavicle tends to damage the acromioclavicular and/or sternoclavicular joints and their associated ligaments rather than causing a fracture of the bone. Downward forces applied to the lateral end of the clavicle create bending stresses within it, which, if sufficiently large or if the clavicle comes into contact with the coracoid process, may lead to fracture of the bone.

THE SHOULDER JOINT

Introduction

The shoulder (glenohumeral) joint is the articulation between the head of the humerus and the glenoid fossa of the shoulder blade (Fig. 4.51). The intracapsular presence of the epiphyseal line between the ventral coracoid and dorsal scapula in the upper part of the glenoid fossa facilitates adjustments of the joint surfaces during growth of the bone. Similar arrangements are also to be found in the hip and the elbow joints (see pp. 192 and 430 respectively).

It is a synovial joint of the ball and socket variety, with the head of the humerus forming the ball and the glenoid fossa the socket,

in which freedom of movement has been developed at the expense of stability. The mobility of the upper limb is partly due to changes in the shoulder joint which have occurred with the freeing of the upper limbs from locomotor activity, and partly due to mobility of the pectoral girdle linking the limb to the trunk. Comparison of the shoulder and hip joints, equivalent joints in the upper and lower limbs, together with their mode of attachment to the axial skeleton, reveals significant and important differences between them even though the basic features of each are similar.

In the frontal plane, the axis of the head and neck of the humerus form an angle of 135° to 140° with the long axis of the shaft; this is the angle of inclination (Fig. 4.52a). Because of this angulation, the centre of the humeral head lies about 1 cm medial to the long axis. Although the anatomical and mechanical axes of the humerus do not exactly coincide, unlike the femur they both lie inside the bone (Fig. 4.52a). Consequently, the action of muscle groups producing movement at the shoulder joint, especially that of medial and lateral rotation, is more easily understood.

As well as being set at an angle to the shaft of the humerus, the axis of the head and neck is rotated backwards against the shaft some 30° to 40°; this is the angle of retroversion (Fig. 4.52b). The magnitude of the angle of retroversion is said to vary both with age and with race. It is thought that this angle has increased with the attainment of bipedalism, in which there has also been flattening of the thoracic cage anteroposteriorly, and a backward displacement of the scapula. The result being that as the glenoid fossa came to be directed more laterally, the head and neck of the humerus became more twisted in an attempt to maintain maximum joint contact between the two articulating bones. Structurally this adaptation was not entirely successful, which to some extent was fortuitous for in humans the use of the upper limb gradually changed from one of support to one of manipulation.

Fig. 4.51   X-ray of the shoulder joint.

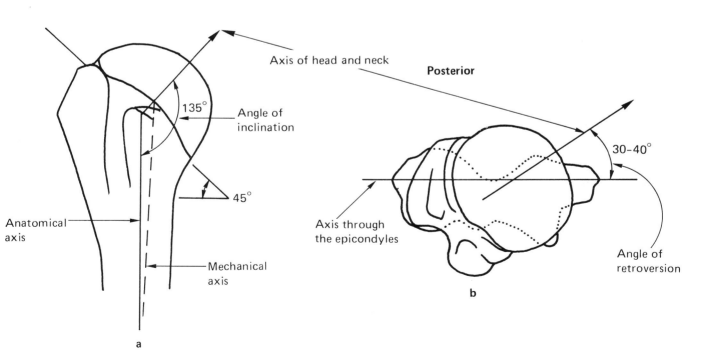

Fig. 4.52   The angle of (**a**) inclination and (**b**) retroversion of the humerus.

Articular surfaces

The articulating surfaces of the joint are the rounded head of the humerus and the rather shallow glenoid fossa. The adaptation of these two surfaces contributes very little, if at all, to the stability and security of the joint. As in the majority of synovial joints, the two articular surfaces are covered by hyaline cartilage.

Glenoid fossa

The glenoid fossa is situated at the supero-lateral angle of the scapula and faces later-ally, anteriorly and slightly superiorly. It is pear-shaped in outline, with a narrower region superiorly, and concave both vertic-ally and transversely (Fig. 4.53a). However, the concavity of the joint is irregular and less deep than the convexity of the head of the humerus. In the plane of the axis of the head and neck of the humerus it has been estimated that the curvature of the glenoid fossa, with its larger radius subtends an angle of some 75°. The articular surface of the fossa is little more than one-third of that of the humeral head. It is deepened to some extent by the presence of the glenoid labrum (see below).

Head of the humerus

The head of the humerus represents two-fifths of a sphere and faces superiorly, medially and anteriorly (Fig. 4.53b,c). With its smaller radius of curvature, the articular surface subtends an angle of approximately 150° in the plane of the axis of the head and neck. Regardless of the position of the joint, only one-third of the humeral head is in con-tact with the glenoid fossa at any time. It is essentially the mismatch in coaptation of the articular surfaces which give the joint its mobility.

Joint capsule and synovial membrane

The fibrous capsule of the joint forms a loose cylindrical sleeve between the two bones (Fig. 4.53d). The majority of the capsular fibres pass horizontally between scapula and humerus, but some oblique and trans-verse fibres are also present. Although it is thick and strong in parts, particularly anter-iorly, because of its laxness the capsule con-veys little stability to the joint. On the scapula, the capsule attaches just outside the glenoid labrum anteriorly and inferiorly, and to the labrum superiorly and poster-iorly. Recesses formed between the anterior capsular attachment and the glenoid labrum may have pathological significance in shoulder joint trauma.

On the humerus, the capsule attaches to the anatomical neck, around the articular margins of the head, medial to the greater and lesser tubercles, except inferiorly where it joins the medial surface of the shaft about 1 cm below the articular margin (Fig. 4.53d). The dipping down of the capsular attach-ment medially causes the medial end of the upper epiphyseal line of the humerus to become intracapsular.

The anterior part of the capsule is thick-ened and strengthened by the presence of the three glenohumeral ligaments, which can only be seen on its inner aspect. The superoposterior part is strengthened near its humeral attachment by the coracohumeral ligament. The tendons of the 'rotator cuff' (see p. 98) muscles spread out over the cap-sule, blending with it near their humeral attachments. These short scapular muscles act as extensible ligaments, and are extre-mely important in maintaining the integrity of the joint.

With the arm hanging in the anatomical position, the lower part of the joint capsule is lax and forms a redundant fold. When the arm is abducted this part of the capsule becomes increasingly taut.

There are two openings in the fibrous cap-sule, occasionally a third may be present. One is at the upper end of the intertubercu-lar groove to allow the long head of biceps to pass into the arm (Fig. 4.53d). This part of the capsule is thickened, forming the transverse humeral ligament, arching over the tendon as it emerges from the capsule. The second opening is in the front of the capsule, between the superior and middle glenohumeral ligaments, and communi-cates with the subscapular bursa deep to the tendon of subscapularis (Fig. 4.53d). A third opening is often present posteriorly allow-ing a communication of the joint cavity with the infraspinatus bursa.

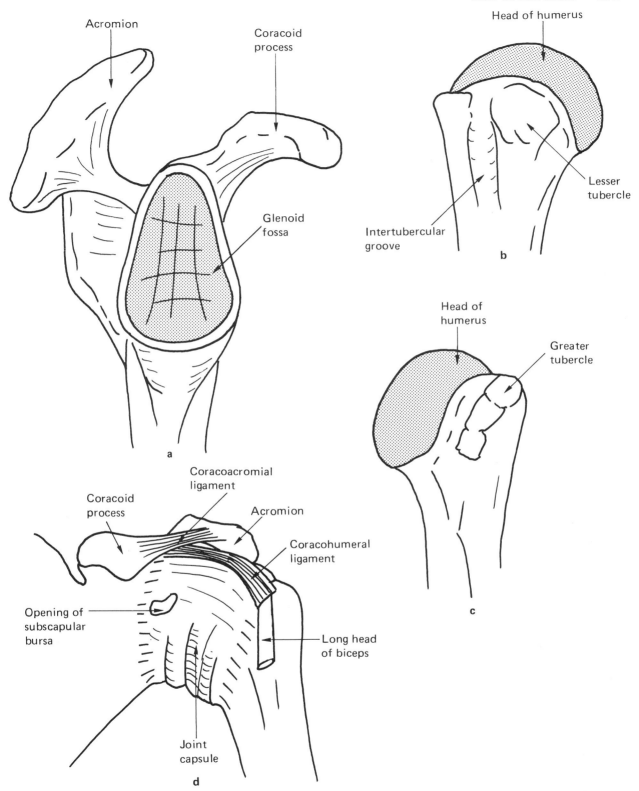

Fig. 4.53 Articular surfaces of the shoulder joint: **a** = glenoid fossa; **b** = head of the humerus viewed anteriorly; **c** = head of the humerus viewed posteriorly; **d** = anterior aspect of the lax joint capsule.

Capsular ligaments

The anterior part of the joint capsule is reinforced by three longitudinal bands of fibres called the glenohumeral ligaments (Fig. 4.54a). They are seldom prominent and when present radiate from the anterior glenoid margin extending downwards from the supraglenoid tubercle.

Superior glenohumeral ligament The slender superior glenohumeral ligament arises from the upper part of the glenoid margin and adjacent labrum immediately anterior to the attachment of the tendon of the long head of biceps. It runs laterally parallel to the biceps tendon to the upper surface of the lesser tubercle.

Middle glenohumeral ligament The middle glenohumeral ligament arises below the superior and attaches to the humerus on the front of the lesser tubercle below the insertion of subscapularis.

Inferior glenohumeral ligament The inferior glenohumeral ligament is usually the best developed of the three ligaments, although it is occasionally absent. It arises from the glenoid margin below the notch in its anterior border and the adjacent anterior border of the glenoid labrum. It descends slightly obliquely to the humerus to attach to the anteroinferior part of the anatomical neck. As it passes from scapula to humerus, the upper part of the inferior ligament may merge with the lower part of the middle.

Although they have no real stabilizing function, certain movements of the shoulder joint will tend to increase the tension in some or all of the glenohumeral ligaments. Lateral rotation of the humerus will put all three ligaments under tension, whereas medial rotation relaxes them. In abduction, only the middle and inferior ligaments become taut, while the superior becomes relaxed.

Transverse humeral ligament At the upper end of the intertubercular groove, the transverse humeral ligament bridges the gap between the greater and lesser tubercles (Fig. 4.54b). It is formed by some of the transverse fibres of the capsule and serves to hold the biceps tendon in the intertubercular groove as it leaves the joint.

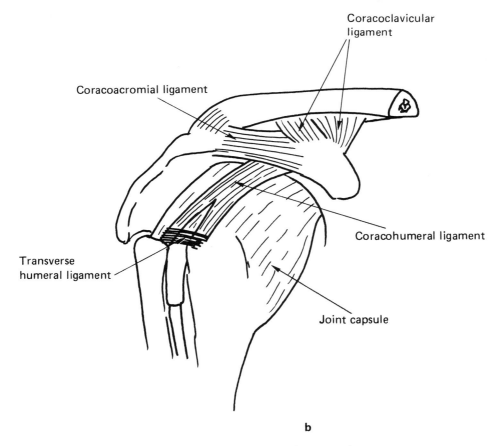

Fig. 4.54 Shoulder joint capsule: **a** = gleno-humeral ligaments; **b** = transverse humeral ligament.

Synovial membrane

The synovial membrane of the joint lines the capsule, and thus also extends downwards as a pouch when the arm is hanging by the side (Fig. 4.55a). It attaches to the articular margins of both bones, and is therefore reflected upwards on the medial side of the humeral shaft to its attachment. Consequently, although the medial part of the epiphyseal line is intracapsular, it is extrasynovial (Fig. 4.55a). The membrane extends through the anterior opening of the capsule forming the subscapularis bursa, which may be limited in its extent to the posterior surface of the tendon of subscapularis. However, it may be sufficiently large to extend above the upper border of the tendon and so come to lie below the coracoid process. This upward extension may be replaced by a separate subcoracoid bursa. The posterior extension of the membrane through the joint capsule forms the infraspinatus bursa.

The intracapsular part of the long head of biceps is enclosed within a double-layered tubular sheath of synovial membrane which is continuous with that of the joint at its glenoid attachment (Fig. 4.55a). This sheath surrounds the biceps tendon as it passes beneath the transverse humeral ligament into the intertubercular groove, and extends some 2 cm into the arm (Fig. 4.55b).

An important, but non-communicating, bursa associated with the shoulder joint is the subacromial bursa (Fig. 4.55). It lies between, and separates, the coracoacromial arch and deltoid from the superolateral part of the shoulder joint. That part of the bursa which extends laterally under deltoid is usually referred to as the subdeltoid bursa.

Some of these bursae are of clinical significance as adhesions may form preventing free gliding movements. This is particularly true for the bicipital sheath and the subdeltoid bursa. Indeed, the subdeltoid bursa may become inflamed (bursitis) and affect the underlying tendon of supraspinatus, leading to its rupture in a small number of cases.

Intra-articular structures

Glenoid labrum

As in the hip joint (see p. 438), the glenoid fossa is deepened by the presence of a fibro-cartilaginous rim, the glenoid labrum (Fig. 4.55c). It is triangular in cross-section, with a thin free edge and is about 4 mm deep. The base of the labrum attaches to the margin of the glenoid fossa; the outer surface gives attachment to the joint capsule posteriorly and superiorly, while the inner (joint) surface is in contact with the head of the humerus and is lined by cartilage continuous with that of the glenoid fossa. The upper part of the labrum may not be completely fixed to the bone so that its inner edge may project into the joint like a meniscus.

The superior outer margin of the labrum gives attachment to the tendon of the long head of biceps, while inferiorly the tendon of the long head of triceps partly arises from it.

Long head of biceps

The tendon of the long head of biceps runs intracapsularly from its attachment to the supraglenoid tubercle and adjacent superior margin of the glenoid labrum until it emerges from the joint deep to the transverse humeral ligament (Fig. 4.55). During its intracapsular course, and for some 2 cm beyond, the tendon is ensheathed in a synovial sleeve.

Fig. 4.55   **a** = Coronal section of the shoulder joint showing the reflection of the synovial membrane around the long head of biceps; **b** = withdrawal of the subacromial bursa, and protrusion of the biceps synovial sheath from the joint capsule when the arm is abducted; **c** = the joint opened out, also showing the blending of some of the rotator cuff muscles to the capsule: **SS** = supraspinatus; **IS** = infraspinatus; **TM** = teres minor.

Synovial membrane

Subacromial bursa

Joint capsule

Joint space

Long head of biceps

Glenoid labrum

Articular surfaces

Epiphyseal line

Synovial sheath for tendon of biceps

Dependent part of joint capsule

a

Subacromial bursa

Long head of biceps and its synovial sheath

Subacromial bursa

b

Acromion

Subacromial bursa

Long head of biceps

SS

IS

TM

Glenohumeral thickenings

Glenoid labrum

SS

IS

TM

c

Fig. 4.55

Ligaments

Apart from the capsular ligaments (see p. 172), there are two further ligaments associated with the shoulder joint. Both are considered to be accessory ligaments, although one, the coracohumeral ligament, blends with the joint capsule. The other, the coracoacromial ligament, completes a fibro-osseous arch above the joint.

Coracohumeral ligament

The coracohumeral ligament is a fairly strong, broad band arising from the lateral border of the coracoid process near its root. It becomes flattened as it passes laterally with its two margins diverging above the intertubercular groove to attach to the upper part of the anatomical neck in the region of the greater and lesser tubercles and to the intervening transverse humeral ligament (Fig. 4.56).

The anterior border of the medial part of the ligament is free, but as it passes laterally it fuses with the tendon of subscapularis as it blends with the capsule prior to its insertion on the lesser tubercle. The posterior part of the ligament blends with the tendon of supraspinatus as it attaches to the superior facet on the greater tubercle.

Coracoacromial ligament

The coracoacromial ligament is not directly associated with the joint but forms, with the coracoid and acromion processes, a fibro-osseous arch above the head of the humerus. It is a strong, triangular ligament, whose anterior and posterior borders tend to be thicker than the intermediate part. Occasionally, the pectoralis minor tendon is prolonged and pierces the base of the liga-ment to become continuous with the coraco-humeral ligament. The coracoacromial ligament is attached by a broad base to the lateral border of the horizontal part of the coracoid process, with the blunt apex fixed to the apex of the acromion in front of the acromioclavicular joint (Fig. 4.56). Superiorly is the clavicle and deltoid, while inferiorly it is separated from the tendon of the supraspinatus and the shoulder joint by the subacromial bursa.

The arch so formed by the ligament and bony processes serves to increase the surface upon which the head of the humerus is supported when force is transmitted upwards along the humerus.

Blood and nerve supply

The arterial supply is from numerous sources as there is an important anastomosis around the scapula involving vessels from the subclavian and axillary arteries and the descending aorta (Fig. 4.57). The supply to the shoulder joint is by branches from the suprascapular branch of the subclavian artery, the acromial branch of the thoraco-acromial artery, and branches from the anterior and posterior circumflex humeral arteries. The latter three are all branches of the axillary artery. The venous drainage is by similarly named veins which drain into the external jugular and axillary veins.

Lymphatic drainage of the joint is to the lymph nodes within the axilla, eventually passing by the apical group of nodes into the subclavian lymph trunk.

The nerve supply to the shoulder joint is by twigs from several nerves which pass close to the joint. The twigs come from the suprascapular, axillary, subscapular, lateral pectoral and musculocutaneous nerves, and have a root value of C5, 6 and 7.

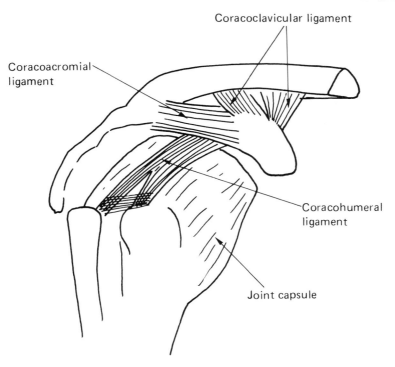

Coracoclavicular ligament

Coracoacromial ligament

Coracohumeral ligament

Joint capsule

Fig. 4.56 The coracohumeral and coracoacromial ligaments.

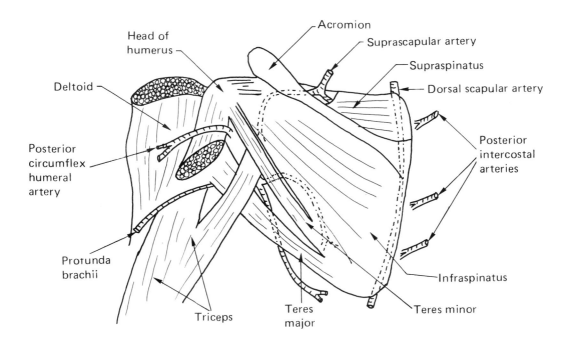

Head of humerus

Acromion

Suprascapular artery

Supraspinatus

Dorsal scapular artery

Deltoid

Posterior circumflex humeral artery

Posterior intercostal arteries

Protunda brachii

Infraspinatus

Triceps

Teres major

Teres minor

Fig. 4.57 Vessels involved in supplying the shoulder region, together with those involved in the scapular collateral anastomosis.

Relations

The shoulder joint is almost completely surrounded by muscles passing between the pectoral girdle and the humerus (Fig. 4.58). They serve to protect the joint by helping to suspend the upper limb from the pectoral girdle and so convey some degree of stability to the joint. Some muscles are more important in this respect than others. The anterior, superior and posterior parts of the joint are directly related to the tendons of subscapularis, supraspinatis, and infraspinatus and teres minor respectively. These tendons all blend with the humeral part of the joint capsule, and because of their action on the shoulder joint (see pp. 84, 96, 98), have become known as the *rotator cuff*. Covering the superolateral part of the joint is deltoid, giving the shoulder its rounded appearance (Fig. 4.58). The greater and lesser tubercles of the humerus can be palpated through deltoid, as can the long head of biceps as it emerges from w.thin the capsule. The tendon of the long head of biceps passes directly above the joint within the capsule. Superiorly, and separated from the joint by the tendon of supraspinatus is the coracoacromial arch. Inferiorly, coming from the infraglenoid tubercle, is the long head of triceps as it passes into the arm almost parallel to the humerus.

Immediately below the shoulder joint is the quadrilateral space, bounded superiorly by teres minor, inferiorly by teres major, medially by the long head of triceps and laterally by the shaft of the humerus (Fig. 4.59). Passing through this space from anterior to posterior are the axillary nerve and posterior circumflex humeral artery. Downward dislocation of the head of the humerus or prolonged upwardly applied pressure, for example as when falling asleep with the arm hanging over the back of a chair, may cause temporary or permanent damage to the nerve and consequent loss of function of deltoid and teres minor. Immediately medial to the quadrilateral space is a triangular space, bounded by teres minor and major and the long head of triceps, through which pass the circumflex scapular vessels (Fig. 4.59). A further triangular space is found below the quadrilateral space. This has the long head of the triceps as its medial border, the shaft of the humerus laterally and the lower border of teres major as its base (Fig. 4.59). It is an important space as the radial nerve and the profunda brachii vessels pass through it to the posterior compartment of the arm. Fractures of the shaft of the humerus, or pressure from the axillary pad of an incorrectly used crutch, may involve the radial nerve, resulting in radial nerve palsy, that is wrist drop, which will affect the functional use of the hand.

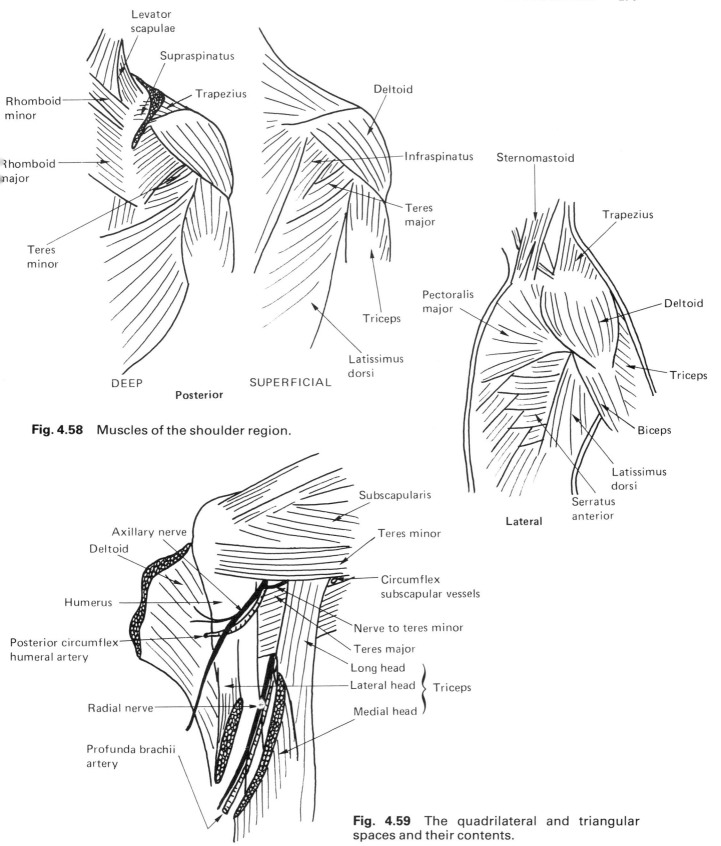

Fig. 4.58 Muscles of the shoulder region.

Fig. 4.59 The quadrilateral and triangular spaces and their contents.

Inferomedial to the shoulder joint is the pyramidal-shaped axilla—the space between the arm and the thorax which enables vessels and nerves to pass between the neck and the upper limb (Fig. 4.60a). The apex of the axilla is formed by the clavicle anteriorly, scapula posteriorly and outer border of the first rib medially. Its concave base or floor is formed by deep fascia extending from the fascia over serratus anterior to the deep fascia of the arm, attached in front and behind to the margins of the axillary folds and supported by the suspensory ligament of the axilla, which is a downward extension of the clavipectoral fascia below pectoralis minor (Fig. 4.60b). The anterior axillary wall is formed by pectoralis major, its lower rounded fold formed by the twisting nature of the muscle fibres as they pass from the chest wall to the humerus (see p. 88). The posterior wall, which extends lower than the anterior, is formed by subscapularis and teres major, with the tendon of latissimus dorsi twisting around teres major (Fig. 4.60b). The medial wall is formed by serratus anterior, and the lateral wall by the floor of the intertubercular groove (Fig. 4.60c). Both the anterior and posterior axillary folds can be readily palpated. A vertical line midway between them, running down the thoracic wall, is the *midaxillary line.*

When the arm is fully abducted the axillary folds virtually disappear as the muscles forming them run almost parallel to the humerus. Indeed, the axillary hollow may be replaced by a bulge.

The principal contents of the axilla are the blood vessels and nerves which pass between the neck and the upper limb (Fig. 4.60b, c). These are the axillary artery and its branches, the corresponding vein and its tributaries, and the branches of the brachial plexus. Together, with the various groups of lymph nodes, they are surrounded by fat and loose areolar tissue. The tendon of long head of biceps runs in the intertubercular groove, and so is just within the axilla. Also within the axilla are the short head of biceps and coracobrachialis. The major vessels and nerve trunks are enclosed within the axillary sheath, a fascial extension of the prevertebral layer of cervical fascia. The axillary sheath is adherent to the clavi-pectoral fascia behind pectoralis minor, and just beyond the second part of the axillary artery blends with the tunica adventitia of the vessels.

The axillary artery runs through the axilla, being posterior and superior to the vein, and can be indicated on the surface of the abducted arm by a straight line running from the middle of the clavicle to the medial prominence of coracobrachialis. With the arm hanging by the side, the artery describes a gentle curve with the concavity facing inferomedially.

The artery is crossed anteriorly by the tendon of pectoralis minor, which serves to divide it into three parts. Above the first part of the artery lie the lateral and posterior cords of the brachial plexus, and behind it is the medial cord—it is crossed by a communicating loop between the medial and lateral pectoral nerves. The second part of the axillary artery, behind pectoralis minor, has the various cords of the brachial plexus in their named positions. The third part of the artery, lying laterally against coracobrachialis, has the musculocutaneous nerve laterally, the median nerve anteriorly, the ulnar and medial cutaneous nerves of the arm and forearm medially, and the axillary and radial nerves posteriorly.

The axillary lymph nodes are widely distributed within the axillary fat, but may be conveniently divided into five groups (Fig. 4.60b, c). The lateral nodes lie along and above the axillary vein and receive the majority of the lymphatic drainage of the upper limb. The subscapular (posterior) nodes lie along the subscapular artery and receive lymph from the scapular region and back above the umbilicus. The pectoral nodes, alongside the lateral thoracic artery, receive lymph from the anterior chest wall including the breast. These groups of nodes drain to a central group, which lie above the axillary floor. From here efferents pass to the apical group of nodes (the only group lying above the tendon of pectoralis minor) and thence to the subclavian lymph trunk (see p. 296).

Because of the involvement of the axillary nodes in the lymphatic drainage of the breast, they may be subjected to radiotherapy treatment in an attempt to limit the secondary spread of cancer from the breast.

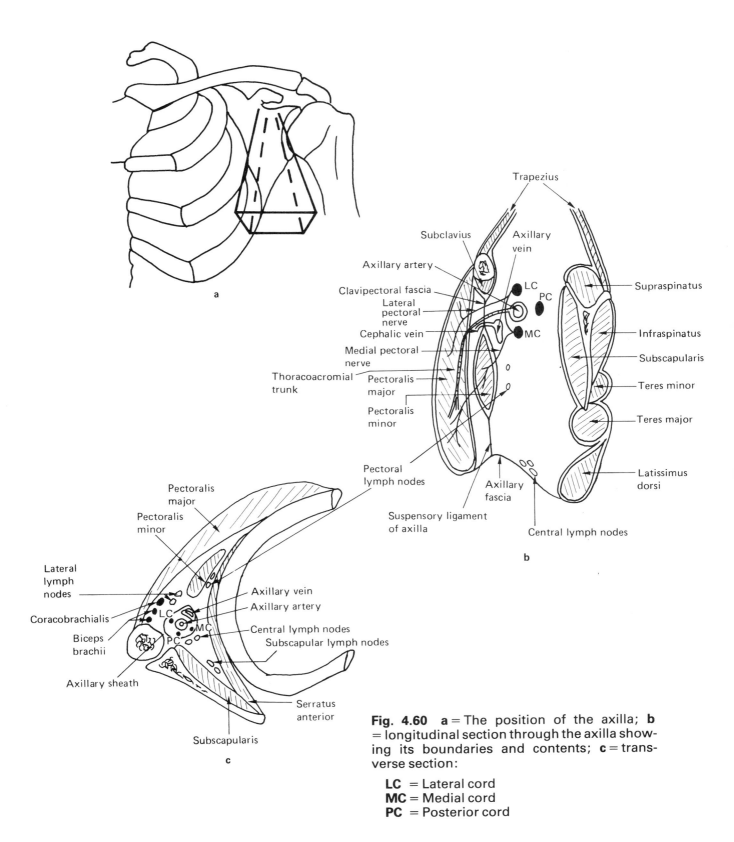

Fig. 4.60 **a** = The position of the axilla; **b** = longitudinal section through the axilla showing its boundaries and contents; **c** = transverse section:

LC = Lateral cord
MC = Medial cord
PC = Posterior cord

It is important to remember that the lateral group of nodes lie above the axillary vein so that they can be excluded from the treatment programmes, otherwise severe problems with the lymphatic drainage of the upper limb may result.

Stability

The incongruity of the articular surfaces, together with the laxness of the joint capsule, suggest that the shoulder joint is not very stable. Although dislocation of the shoulder is rather common it is by no means an everyday occurrence. What factors are responsible for conferring stability on the joint? The glenoid labrum, as well as deepening the fossa, also makes the joint surfaces more congruent, and thus becomes a significant stabilizing factor. Fracture of the glenoid or tearing of the labrum often results in dislocation.

Perhaps the most important factor, however, is the tone in the short scapular (rotator cuff) muscles. Not only do these muscles (supraspinatus, infraspinatus, teres minor and subscapularis) attach very close to the joint, but they fuse with the lateral part of the capsule (Fig. 4.61). In this way they act as ligaments of variable length and tension, and also prevent the lax capsule and its synovial lining from being trapped between the articulating bones. The inferior part of the capsule is the weakest, being relatively unsupported by muscles. However, as the arm is gradually abducted, the long head of triceps and teres major become increasingly applied to this aspect of the joint.

In addition to the rotator cuff muscles, all the muscles passing between the pectoral girdle and the humerus assist in maintaining the stability of the joint (Fig. 4.62). Particularly important are the long heads of biceps and triceps. The tendon of the long head of biceps, being partly intracapsular, acts as a strong support over the superior part of the joint. The long head of triceps gives support below the joint when the arm is abducted.

An upward displacement of the head of the humerus is resisted by the overhanging coracoacromial arch. Although not part of the joint, this arch, separated from the joint by the subacromial bursa, functions mechanically as an articular surface. The arch is so strong that an upward thrust on the humerus will fracture either the clavicle or the humerus first before compromising the arch.

Dislocation of the shoulder is more common than for many joints, being favoured by the need to have the joint as mobile as possible. In addition, the long humerus has great leverage in dislocating forces. In anterior dislocation, which is the more common, the head of the humerus comes to lie under the coracoid process producing a bulge in the region of the clavipectoral groove. At the same time the roundness of the shoulder is lost. In such dislocations, the humeral head usually comes through the joint capsule between the long head of triceps and the inferior glenohumeral ligament.

Because the glenoid fossa faces anterolaterally, it is better situated to resist posteriorly directed forces. The presence of infraspinatus and teres minor also reinforce the capsule posteriorly. Posterior dislocation may result when a large force is applied to the long axis of the humerus when the arm is medially rotated and abducted. The joint capsule tears in the region of teres minor with the head of the humerus coming to lie below the spinous process of the scapula.

Fig. 4.61 The action of the rotator cuff muscles in stabilizing the shoulder joint.

Fig. 4.62 Lateral view of muscles involved in stabilizing the shoulder joint.

Fig. 4.61

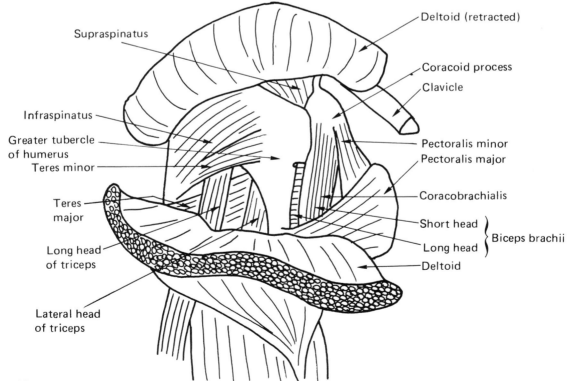

Fig. 4.62

Movements

The architecture of the shoulder joint gives it a greater range of movement than at any other joint within the body. Its ball and socket shape means that movement can take place around an infinite number of axes intersecting at the centre of the head of the humerus. For descriptive purposes, the movements of which the shoulder joint is capable are, flexion and extension, abduction and adduction, and medial and lateral rotation. However, the axes about which they occur have to be carefully defined as the plane of the glenoid fossa does not co-incide with one of the cardinal planes of the body, but is inclined approximately 45° to both the frontal and sagittal planes. It is thus possible to define two sets of axes about which movements occur, one with respect to the cardinal planes of the body (Fig. 4.63a) and the other with respect to the plane of the glenoid fossa (Fig. 4.63b). If the cardinal planes are used, flexion and extension occur about a transverse axis, abduction and adduction occur about an anteroposterior axis, and medial and lateral rotation occur about the longitudinal axis of the humerus, passing between the centre of the head and the centre of the capitulum (Fig. 4.63a). If, however, the plane of the scapula is used to determine these various axes, then flexion and extension take place about an axis perpendicular to the plane of the fossa, abduction and adduction about an axis parallel to the plane of the fossa, with medial and lateral rotation occurring about the same axis as previously (Fig. 4.63b). While the presentation of these two sets of axes may seem initially confusing, the importance of those related to the plane of the glenoid fossa is that in the treatment of certain injuries of the shoulder, the position of the joint which will cause the greatest relief will be when the capsule is not put under tension, that is when the joint is abducted to 90° in the plane of the glenoid fossa.

Irrespective of the orientation of these axes, the incongruity of the joint surfaces means that all movements, except axial rotation, are a combination of gliding and rolling of the articular surfaces against each other. However, unlike the knee, it is not possible to define the extent of each type of motion within each of the various movements. Although the range of movement at the shoulder joint is relatively large, the mobility of the upper limb against the trunk is increased by movements of the pectoral girdle. Indeed, the movements of flexion and extension, and abduction and adduction may be considered to be always accompanied by scapular and clavicular movements, except perhaps for the initial stages. Shoulder joint movement is more concerned with bringing the arm to the horizontal position, while pectoral girdle movements, principally those of the scapula, are more concerned in bringing the arm into a vertical position.

The association of shoulder and pectoral girdle movement also increases the power of the movement. The rotator cuff muscles, being attached close to the axes of movement have a poor mechanical advantage compared with muscles acting on the scapula, which are generally more powerful as well as having considerable leverage. In patients with fused or fixed shoulder joints a large degree of upper limb mobility with respect to the trunk is still possible because of pectoral girdle movements.

In the following account shoulder joint movements are considered initially with respect to the plane of the glenoid fossa. How these are related to movements of the upper limb in the cardinal planes is discussed at the end of this section.

Fig. 4.63 Axes of movement at the shoulder joint: **a** = with respect to the cardinal axes of the body; **b** = with respect to the plane of the glenoid fossa.

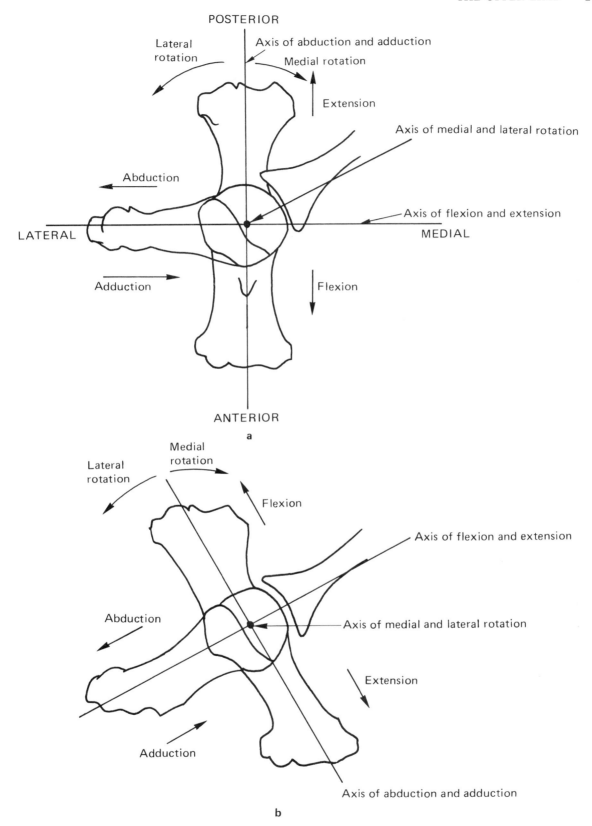

POSTERIOR

Lateral rotation

Axis of abduction and adduction

Medial rotation

Extension

Axis of medial and lateral rotation

Abduction

Axis of flexion and extension

LATERAL   MEDIAL

Adduction

Flexion

ANTERIOR

a

Medial rotation

Lateral rotation

Flexion

Axis of flexion and extension

Abduction

Axis of medial and lateral rotation

Extension

Adduction

Axis of abduction and adduction

b

Fig. 4.63

Flexion and extension

Flexion and extension occur about an axis perpendicular to the plane of the glenoid fossa, so that in flexion the arm moves forwards and medially at an angle of approximately 45° to the sagittal plane (Fig. 4.64). In extension it is carried backwards and laterally (Fig. 4.64). The range of flexion is approximately 110° and that of extension 70°. Both of these ranges may be extended by movements of the pectoral girdle so that flexion of the upper limb with respect to the trunk reaches 180° and extension just exceeds 90°. Extension is limited by the greater tubercle of the humerus coming into contact with the coracoacomial arch.

Flexion is produced by the anterior fibres of deltoid, pectoralis major, coracobrachialis and biceps. Passive extension from the flexion position is essentially due to the eccentric contraction of the above muscles. Beyond the neutral position, however, extension is produced by the posterior fibres of deltoid, teres major and latissimus dorsi, to these may be added the long head of triceps and the sternal fibres of pectoralis major when active extension is performed from a flexed position.

Abduction and adduction

Abduction and adduction occur about an oblique horizontal axis in the same plane as the glenoid fossa. In abduction the arm moves anterolaterally away from the trunk (Fig. 4.65). The total range of movement at the shoulder joint is 120°, however only the first 30° occurs without concomitant rotation of the scapula, so that between 30° and 180° scapula rotation augments shoulder abduction in the ratio of 1:2. The terminal part of the shoulder joint abduction is accompanied by lateral rotation of the humerus. This occurs not to prevent bony interlocking between the greater tubercle and the acromion, but to provide further articular surface on the head of the humerus for the glenoid fossa. Abduction of the medially rotated humerus is limited by tension in the posterior capsule and the lateral rotators.

Adduction beyond the neutral position of the joint is not possible because of the presence of the trunk. Abduction is initiated by supraspinatus which, although nowhere near as strong as deltoid, is better placed to act on the humerus. With the arm hanging at the side the fibres of deltoid, especially the middle fibres, run almost parallel to the humerus, so that on contraction they pull the humerus upwards. Once the arm has been pulled away from the side then deltoid takes over and continues the movement. Supraspinatus is required for the first 20° of abduction. If deltoid is paralysed, supraspinatus is not strong enough to fully abduct the upper limb. If, however, supraspinatus is not functioning, deltoid cannot initiate abduction. A passive abduction of some 20°, or leaning to the affected side so that the limb hangs away from the body, will enable deltoid to continue the movement. In some circumstances biceps may be re-educated to take over the initiating role of a paralysed supraspinatus. As abduction proceeds, teres minor and major hold the head of the humerus down against the pull of the deltoid. Together with subscapularis and infraspinatus, teres minor and major stabilize the humeral head against the glenoid fossa.

Lateral rotation of the scapula accompanying abduction of the humerus is produced by the force-couple of the lower part of serratus anterior, acting on the inferior angle of the scapula, and the upper fibres of trapezius pulling on the acromion process.

Adduction is produced by the eccentric contraction of serratus anterior, trapezius, deltoid and supraspinatus, under the action of gravity. If adduction is resisted then a forceful movement is produced by pectoralis major, teres major, latissimus dorsi and coracobrachialis.

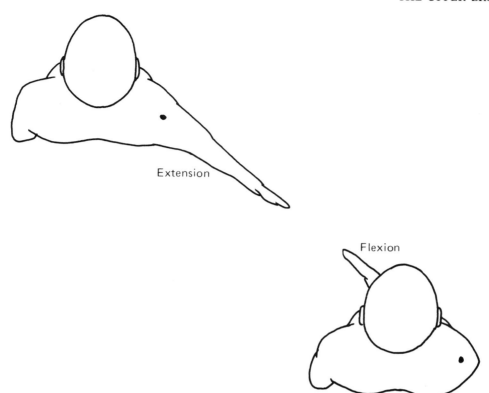

Extension

Flexion

Fig. 4.64 Flexion and extension with respect to the plane of the glenoid fossa.

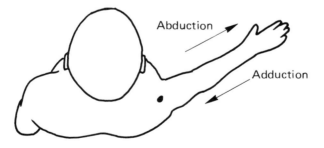

Abduction

Adduction

Fig. 4.65 Adduction and abduction with respect to the plane of the glenoid fossa.

Medial and lateral rotation

Rotation takes place about the longitudinal axis through the humerus as described earlier. In lateral rotation, it is the anterior surface of the humerus which is turned laterally (Fig. 4.66). It is produced by infraspinatus, teres minor and the posterior fibres of deltoid, and has a maximum range of 80°. Medial rotation causes the anterior surface of the humerus to be turned medially (Fig. 4.66). The maximum range of medial rotation is in excess of 90°, however to reach this value the forearm has to be pulled behind the trunk, otherwise contact between the trunk and forearm limits the movements when the elbow is flexed. Medial rotation is produced by subscapularis, pectoralis major, latissimus dorsi, teres major and the anterior fibres of deltoid. The combined range of rotation varies with the position of the arm, being greatest when the arm is by the side, decreasing to 90° with the arm horizontal, and being negligible as the arm approaches the vertical.

Rotation is limited by the extent of the articular surfaces, and tension in the appropriate part of the joint capsule and opposing musculature. Furthermore, it is the movement most commonly affected by pathology or injury to the shoulder joint. When assessing the range of rotation possible at the joint, the elbow must be flexed so as to exclude the possibility of any pronatory or supinatory action of the forearm.

Movements of the shoulder joint with respect to the cardinal planes of the body

Although movements of the shoulder joint have been considered with respect to the plane of the glenoid fossa, it is often more convenient to test the range of movement possible with respect to the cardinal planes of the body.

Movements of the arm about a transverse axis through the humeral head produce what are termed 'flexion' and 'extension' (Fig. 4.67). Strictly speaking these movements are a combination of flexion and abduction, and extension and adduction—the degree of each component depending on the orientation of the scapula on the chest wall. The forward 'flexion' movement has a range of 180°, while the backward 'extension' movement is limited to 50°.

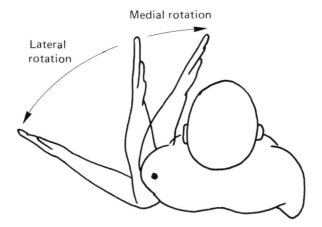

Fig. 4.66   Medial and lateral rotation.

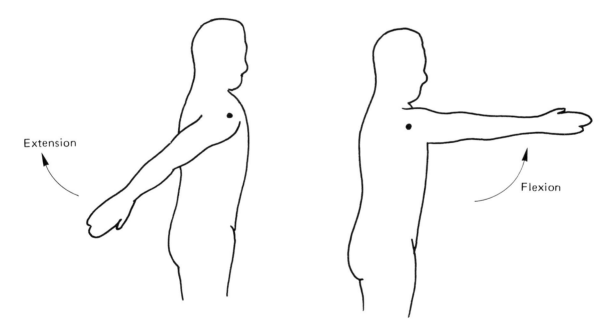

Fig. 4.67   Flexion and extension with respect to the cardinal axes of the body.

In relation to an anteroposterior axis, the movements produced are called 'abduction' and 'adduction' (Fig. 4.68). 'Abduction' is a combination of abduction and extension, and has a range of 180° with scapula rotation. 'Adduction' is the combined movement of adduction and flexion. Once again the movement is limited by the trunk so that adduction beyond the neutral position of the joint is not possible. However, with protraction of the pectoral girdle some 30° of 'adduction' is possible as the arm is brought across the front of the chest. Similarly, retraction of the pectoral girdle allows a minimal amount of 'adduction' to occur behind the back.

Although the terminology used to describe these various movements of the arm at the shoulder joint is of little practical significance, it is nevertheless important to understand the context in which it is being used. It is also important to be fully aware of which movements are being tested when asking individuals to perform certain actions. Two simple activities that demonstrate the mobility of the shoulder joint and pectoral girdle are (1) combing the hair and (2) putting on a coat or jacket.

With respect to the cardinal planes when the arm is flexed at 45° and abducted 60° and neither medially or laterally rotated, it is said to be in the position of function of the shoulder. This corresponds to the position of equilibrium of the short scapular muscles; hence its use when immobilizing fractures of the humeral shaft.

Accessory movements

When the subject is lying supine the muscles around the shoulder are relatively relaxed. In this position the relative laxity of the ligaments and joint capsule allow an appreciable range of accessory movements. By placing the hand high up in the axilla and applying a lateral force to the upper medial aspect of the arm, the head of the humerus can be lifted away from the glenoid fossa by as much as 1 cm.

Proximal and distal gliding movements of the head of the humerus against the glenoid fossa can be produced by forces applied along the shaft of the humerus. Similarly anterior and posterior gliding movements can be produced by applying pressure in an appropriate direction, to the region of the surgical neck.

Palpation

The line of the shoulder joint cannot be directly palpated due to the mass of muscles surrounding it. However, the surface projection of the joint line can be estimated first by identifying the surface projection of the midpoint of the joint. This latter point is approximately 1 cm lateral to the apex of the coracoid process. A vertical line, slightly concave laterally, through this point gives an indication of the joint line.

Biomechanics

The rotator cuff muscles are active during abduction and lateral rotation providing stability at the shoulder joint. However, they are probably also involved in the pathogenesis of dislocation of the shoulder. In any equilibrium analysis of the joint certain assumptions have to be made. The following is based on account given by Morrey and Chao (1981)*. The assumptions these authors made were:

1. that each muscle contributing to the equilibrium acts with a force proportional to its cross-sectional area, this being $6.2 \, kg/cm^2$;
2. that each muscle is equally active;
3. that the active muscle contracts along a straight line connecting the centres of its two areas of attachment.

While none of these assumptions is necessarily true, they do provide a framework within which to work. When the unloaded arm is laterally rotated and abducted to 90° there is a compressive force of approximately 70 kg between the articular surfaces, and anterior and inferior shear forces of 12 kg and 14 kg respectively. These forces are produced by muscles actively resisting the weight of the arm; the resultant force is directed 12° anteriorly with a magnitude of 72 kg.

* Morrey B. F., Chao E. Y. S. (1981). Recurrent anterior dislocation of the shoulder. In: *Clinical Biomechanics: a case history approach.* (Black J., Dumbleton, J. H., eds) pp. 24–46. Edinburgh: Churchill Livingstone.

If, as well as being abducted and laterally rotated, the arm is also extended by 30° and loaded so that the muscles are contracting maximally, then the magnitude of the various forces across the joint increase dramatically. The compressive force across the joint is now of the order of 210 kg, while the anterior and inferior shear forces have increased to 42 kg and 58 kg respectively. The resultant force is now directed 36° anteriorly and has a magnitude of 222 kg. To prevent anterior dislocation occurring, the shearing forces must be balanced by the joint capsule and its associated ligaments, because the glenoid fossa is too shallow to provide much constraint. As the tensile strength of the capsule and ligaments is of the order of 50 kg, an imbalance of forces may occur leading to dislocation at the joint. Once the anterior part of the capsule has been torn then less force is required for subsequent dislocations to occur.

The above force analysis is comparable to the situation when an individual slips when walking on ice and puts out his or her hand and arm to break a backward fall.

Velocity of movement

With the shoulder joint being extremely mobile, some of its movements are performed at fairly high velocities. In many instances, for example when studying natural or artificial joints and their lubrication, a knowledge of the sliding velocities at the articulating surfaces is of importance.

Using cine film techniques and by suitable trigonometric relationships the maximum sliding velocities at the shoulder joint in various common activities have been determined. These are for hanging clothes 100 mm/s, sweeping 34 mm/s, bedmaking 40 mm/s, arm swing during walking 30 mm/s, eating 13 mm/s and dressing 25 mm/s. Obviously in activities requiring a fast and forceful movement at the shoulder, such as the tennis serve, then the sliding velocities will be much greater. The demands made upon the lubricating fluid and articular surfaces in such situations are high. It is not surprising therefore that sometimes the system breaks down and some form of joint trauma results.

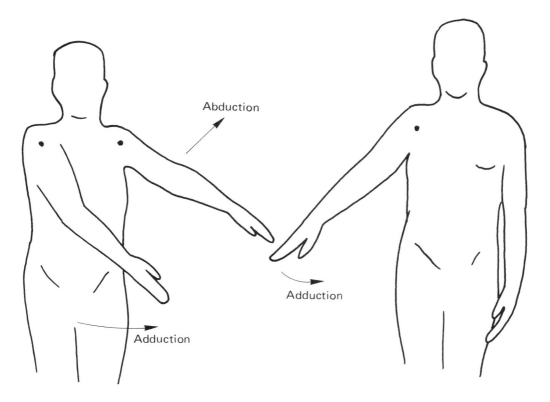

Fig. 4.68 Adduction and abduction with respect to the cardinal planes of the body.

Shoulder joint replacement

Replacement of a damaged or arthritic humeral head offers the immediate relief of pain. However, an intact rotator cuff and a normal glenoid fossa are prerequisites for this type of replacement. The replacement, when used following a severe fracture of the humeral head, should be done as soon as possible, and certainly not later than four weeks following the injury, because of the extensive development of scar tissue and the subsequent limitation of motion.

Total shoulder implants have proved to be more successful than replacement of the humeral head alone. If the rotator cuff is deficient then a restrained shoulder implant will give stability as well as relief of pain. It is not uncommon for the ball and socket of the joint to be reversed, so that the socket is now on the humerus and the ball on the scapula.

THE ELBOW JOINT

Introduction

The elbow joint is the intermediate joint of the upper limb, being between the arm and the forearm. It can be considered to be subservient to the hand in the sense that it enables the hand and fingers to be properly placed in space. The elbow joint is responsible for shortening and lengthening the upper limb: the ability to carry food to the mouth is due to flexion at the elbow. If situations arise in which the hand and forearm are not able to move, then the arm and trunk can move towards the hand.

The elbow joint is a synovial joint of the hinge variety, and shares, with the superior radioulnar joint, the same joint capsule. The superior radioulnar joint is considered in detail on p. 214, but it is important to remember that it plays no part and has no function at the elbow. The elbow joint shows the fundamental characteristics of all hinge joints. The articular surfaces are reciprocally shaped (Fig. 4.69), it has strong collateral ligaments with the forearm muscles grouped at the sides of the joint where they do not interfere with movement.

When viewed laterally, the distal end of the humerus bulges anteriorly and inferiorly at an angle of 45° so that the trochlear lies anterior to the axis of the shaft (Fig. 4.70a). In a similar way the trochlear notch of the ulna projects anteriorly and superiorly at an angle of 45°, and so lies anterior to the axis of the shaft of the ulna (Fig. 4.70a). The projection of these two articular surfaces facilitates and promotes a large range of flexion at the elbow. It delays contact between the two bones, in addition to which there is still a space between them to accommodate the musculature until the bones are almost parallel. Without these two features, particularly the first, flexion beyond 90° would be severely limited.

In spite of the anterior projections of the humerus and ulna the long axes of the two bones coincide when viewed laterally. However, when seen from the front, the ulnar axis deviates laterally from that of the humerus (Fig. 4.70b). This deviation is referred to as the carrying angle, and is said to be approximately 10° to 15° in men and 20° to 25° in women. Normally, the transverse axis of the elbow joint bisects this angle so that when the elbow is acutely flexed the forearm overlies the arm, and the hand covers the shoulder joint. If, however, the bisected parts of the carrying angle are not equal then the hand will be lateral to the shoulder (A < B, Fig. 4.70b) or medial to the shoulder (A > B, Fig. 4.70b) on acute flexion at the joint.

The transverse axis of the elbow joint runs from inferior posteromedially to superior anterolaterally passing approximately through the middle of the trochlear. Because of this slight obliquity there has been some debate as to whether the joint exhibits a pure hinge movement, especially as this axis also oscillates slightly. However, for practical purposes it can be considered as a pure hinge joint.

Fig. 4.69   X-rays of the elbow joint.

Fig. 4.70   a = Relation of the axes of the elbow joint; **b** = the carrying angle.

a   b

Posterior view   Lateral view

Fig. 4.69

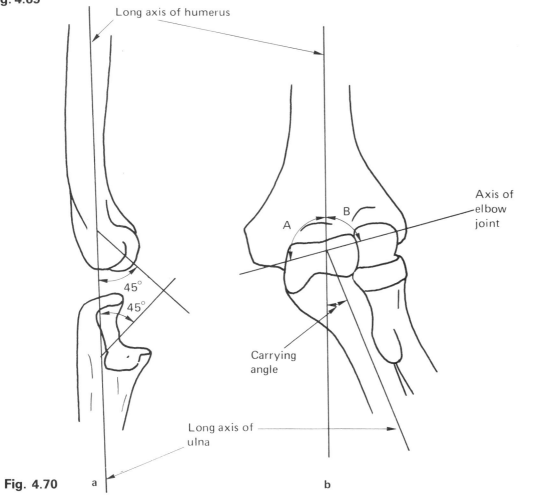

Long axis of humerus

Axis of
elbow
joint

A   B

45°

45°

Carrying
angle

Long axis of
ulna

Fig. 4.70   a   b

Articular surfaces

Three bones are involved in the articulation at the elbow joint; these are the distal end of the humerus, and the proximal ends of the radius and ulna. The distal end of the humerus shows two joined articular regions: the grooved trochlea medially and the rounded capitulum laterally, being separated by a groove of variable depth (Fig. 4.71a). The whole of this composite surface is covered by a continuous layer of hyaline cartilage. The trochlea articulates with the trochlear notch of the ulna, while the capitulum articulates with the cupped head of the radius. Both of these latter surfaces are also covered with hyaline cartilage.

Trochlea of the humerus

The pulley-shaped trochlea with its groove presents a concave surface in the frontal plane and is convex sagittally. It forms almost a complete circle, being separated by a thin wall of bone, which itself may be perforated, so that 320° to 330° of the surface is cartilage covered (Fig. 4.71a, b). The medial free border of the trochlea is not circular but describes part of a helix with a slant directed radially. The groove of the trochlea is limited medially by a sharp and prominent ridge and laterally by a lower and blunter ridge which blends with the articular surface of the capitulum (Fig. 4.71a). The tilt on the trochlea partly accounts for the carrying angle of the elbow.

Although the groove of the trochlea appears to lie in the sagittal plane it does in fact run obliquely. This obliquity shows individual variation, however the most common form is with the anterior part of the groove being vertical and the posterior part running obliquely distally and laterally. As a whole the groove runs in a spiral around the axis of the bone (Fig. 4.71c, i). Occasionally, the groove runs obliquely proximally and laterally at the front and distally and laterally at the back, and so as a whole forms a true spiral around the axis of the bone (Fig. 4.71c, ii). Finally, and rarely, the groove may run obliquely proximally and medially anteriorly, and distally and laterally posteriorly, so that as a whole it forms a circle (Fig. 4.71c, iii). The functional significance of these variations in the angulation of the trochlea is minimal. The only observable differences being in the degree of the carrying angle and the relative positions of the arm and forearm in acute flexion at the elbow.

Immediately above the trochlea anteriorly is the concave coronoid fossa (Fig. 4.71a), which receives the coronoid process of the ulna during flexion. Posteriorly, in a similar position, is the olecranon fossa which receives the olecranon process during extension (Fig. 4.71b). If these two fossae are particularly deep the intervening thin plate of bone may be perforated allowing them to communicate with each other.

Capitulum

The capitulum is not a complete sphere but a hemisphere on the anterior surface of the humerus (Fig. 4.71a). It does not extend posteriorly like the trochlea. Although described as hemispherical, its radius of curvature is not constant, increasing slightly from proximally to distally. The cartilage covering the capitulum is thickest in its central region, and may be as much as 5 mm thick. The medial border of the capitulum is truncated forming the capitulotrochlear groove. Above the capitulum anteriorly is the radial notch which receives the rim of the head of the radius during flexion (Fig. 4.71a).

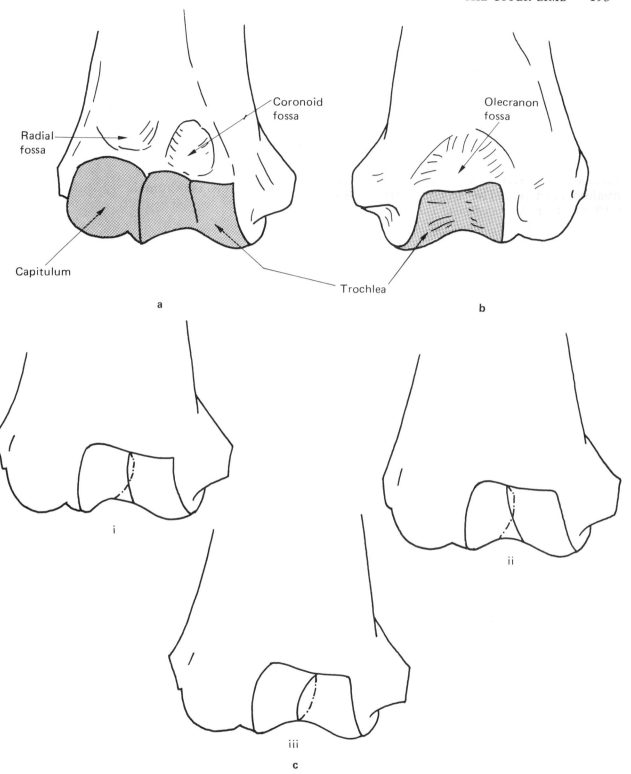

Fig. 4.71 Articular surfaces of the humerus participating in the elbow joint: **a** = anterior view; **b** = posterior view; **c** = the nature of the trochlear groove, anterior view.

Trochlear notch of the ulna

The proximal end of the ulna has the deep trochlear notch which articulates with the trochlea (Fig. 4.72a, b). It has a rounded, curved longitudinal ridge extending from the tip of the olecranon process superiorly to the tip of the coronoid process inferiorly. The ridge snugly fits the groove of the trochlea; on either side of which is a concave surface for the lips of the trochlea. The cartilage of the trochlear notch is interrupted by a transverse line across its deepest part, providing two separate surfaces, one on the olecranon and the other on the coronoid process.

The obliquity of the shaft of the ulna to the ridge accounts for the majority of the carrying angle.

Head of the radius

The superior surface of the head of the radius is concave for articulation with the capitulum, with the raised margin articulating with the capitulotrochlear groove (Fig. 4.72c, d). The cartilage of this surface is continuous with that around the sides of the head: it is thickest in the middle of the concavity.

Because of the articulations between the radius and ulna, their proximal surfaces may be considered as constituting a single articular surface. However, because of the movements between these two bones, they do not maintain the same relative positions with respect to the humerus, nor does the radius always maintain contact with the humerus (see pp. 210–211).

As indicated previously, the articular surface of the trochlea has an angular value of 330°, while that of the capitulum is 180°. The angular values of the articular surfaces of the ulna and radius are much smaller, leaving a large portion of the humeral surfaces exposed at all positions of the joint. The angular value of the trochlear notch is 190°, while that of the head of the radius is only 40°. The difference in angular values between corresponding parts of the elbow is therefore 140°, a value very close to the range of flexion–extension possible at the joint.

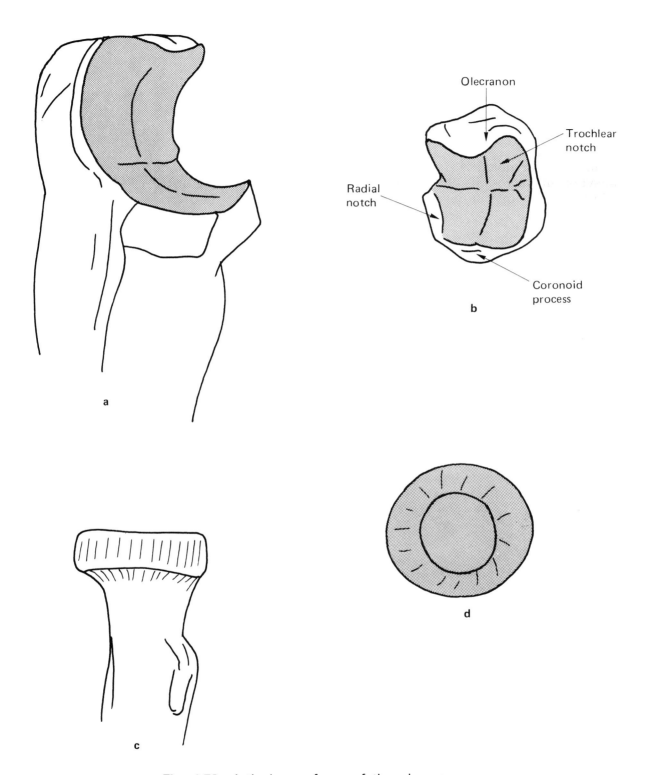

Fig. 4.72 Articular surfaces of the ulna: **a** = lateral view; **b** = from above; **c** = articular surfaces of the radius, anterior view; **d** = from above.

Joint capsule and synovial membrane

A fibrous capsule completely encloses the elbow joint and also surrounds the superior radioulnar joint. It has no openings in it, but slight pouching of the synovial membrane may occur beneath the edge of the capsule in one or two areas.

Anteriorly the capsule arises from the medial epicondyle away from the articular surface of the trochlea. It arches upwards and laterally attaching to the margins of the coronoid and radial fossae, and to the articular margin of the capitulum as it reaches the lateral epicondyle. Posteriorly, the capsule follows the lateral margins of the capitulum and arches upwards around the olecranon fossa, returning to the medial epicondyle some distance from the edge of the trochlear surface (Fig. 4.73).

Distally the capsule attaches to the margins of the trochlear notch around the olecranon and coronoid processes. As the capsule reaches the region of the radial notch it passes on to and attaches to the annular ligament of the radius. Medially and laterally it blends with the collateral ligaments of the joint (Fig. 4.73). It should be remembered that the joint capsule has no direct attachment to the radius. If this were the case, then the movements possible between the radius and ulna would be severely limited.

Because it blends with the collateral ligaments at the sides, the capsule is strengthened in these regions, however, it is relatively weak in front and behind. Anteriorly the capsule consists mainly of longitudinal fibres running from above the coronoid and radial fossae on the humerus to the anterior border of the coronoid process and front of the annular ligament (Fig. 4.73a). Among these longitudinal fibres are some bundles which run obliquely and transversely (Fig. 4.73a). Consequently, this part of the capsule is thicker in its middle region than at the sides; a feature which has led to it being referred to as the capsular ligament. Some of the deep fibres of brachialis insert in the front of the capsule as the muscle passes anteriorly across the joint. This attachment serves to pull the capsule and underlying synovial membrane upwards when the joint is flexed, thereby preventing them becoming trapped between the two moving bones.

The posterior part of the capsule is thin and membranous, being composed mainly of transverse fibres extending loosely between the margins of the olecranon and the edges of the olecranon fossa. A few fibres stretch across the fossa as a transverse band with a free upper border, which does not reach as high as the upper margin of the fossa, without attaching to the olecranon (Fig. 4.73b). Posteriorly the capsule also passes laterally from the lateral epicondyle to the posterior border of the radial notch and the posterior part of the annular ligament. The weakest part of the capsule posteriorly is in the midline of the joint. However, here it is attached to the tendon of triceps which supports it, and performs a similar function to the deep part of brachialis in extension at the joint.

Synovial membrane

The synovial membrane of the joint is extensive attaching to the articular margins of the humerus and ulna. It lines the joint capsule and is reflected onto the humerus to cover the coronoid and radial fossae anteriorly and the olecranon fossa posteriorly. Distally it is prolonged onto the upper part of the deep surface of the annular ligament. The membrane is continued into the superior radioulnar articulation covering the lower part of the annular ligament, and is then reflected onto the neck of the radius. Below the lower border of the annular ligament, the membrane emerges as a redundant fold to give freedom of movement to the head of the radius (Fig. 4.73a). This downward reflection is supported by a few loose fibres which pass from the lower border of the annular ligament to the neck of the radius. The quadrate ligament (see p. 216) supports the synovial membrane as it passes from the medial side of the neck of the radius to the lower border of the radial notch, so preventing its herniation between the anterior and posterior free edges of the annular ligament.

Various synovial folds project into the recesses of the joint between the edges of the articular surfaces. An especially constant fold is one which forms almost a complete ring overlying the periphery of the head of

Fig. 4.73   The joint capsule: **a** = anterior view;
b = posterior view.

the radius, projecting into the crevice between it and the capitulum. Slight pouching of the synovial membrane may occur below the lower borders of the annular ligament and the transverse band of the ulnar collateral ligament; and above the transverse capsular fibres across the upper part of the olecranon fossa (see Fig. 4.73b).

Well-marked extrasynovial fat pads lie adjacent to the articular fossae (see Fig. 4.75). In extension of the joint, they fill the radial and coronoid fossae, and in flexion the olecranon fossa. They are displaced when the appropriate parts of the ulna or radius occupy the fossae.

Ligaments

The collateral ligaments are strong triangular bands which blend with the sides of the joint capsule. They are placed so that they lie across the axis of movement in all positions of the joint. Consequently, they are relatively tense in all positions of flexion and extension, and impose strict limitations on abduction and adduction movements and axial rotation.

Ulnar collateral ligament

The ulnar collateral ligament fans out from the medial epicondyle and has thick anterior and posterior bands united by a thinner intermediate portion (Fig. 4.74a). The anterior band passes from the front of the medial epicondyle to the medial edge of the cor-

onoid process. It is intimately associated with the common tendon of the superficial forearm flexor muscles, giving rise to some of the fibres of flexor digitorum superficialis. The posterior band runs from the back of the medial epicondyle to the medial edge of the olecranon. The apex of the thinner intermediate part of the ligament is attached to the undersurface of the medial epicondyle, while its base is attached to the transverse band stretched between the attachments of the anterior and posterior bands to the coronoid process and olecranon (Fig. 4.74a). The synovial membrane tends to protrude below the free edge of the transverse ligament during movement at the joint. The intermediate grooved part of the ligament is crossed by the ulnar nerve as it passes behind the medial epicondyle to gain access to the forearm.

Radial collateral ligament

The radial collateral ligament is a strong, triangular band attaching above to a depression on the anteroinferior aspect of the lateral epicondyle deep to the overlying common extensor tendon (Fig. 4.74b). Below, the ligament blends with the annular ligament of the radius; the slightly thicker anterior and posterior margins passing forwards and backwards to attach to the margins of the radial notch on the ulna (Fig. 4.74b). The ligament is less distinct than the ulnar collateral.

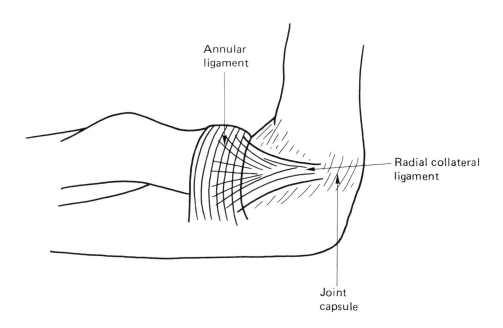

Fig. 4.74   a = The ulnar collateral ligaments of the elbow joint; **b** = the radial collateral ligaments of the elbow joint.

Blood and nerve supply

The arterial blood supply to the joint is derived from an extensive anastomosis around the elbow involving the brachial artery and its terminal branches. Descending from above are the superior and inferior ulnar collateral branches of the brachial artery, and the radial and middle collateral branches of the profunda brachii artery. These vessels anastomose on the surface of the joint capsule with one another, and with the anterior and posterior recurrent branches of the ulnar artery, the radial recurrent branch of the radial artery and the interosseous recurrent branch of the common interosseous artery (Fig. 4.76).

Venous drainage, by vessels accompanying the above arteries, is into the radial, ulnar and brachial veins. Lymphatic drainage of the elbow joint is predominantly to the deep cubital nodes at the bifurcation of the brachial artery, the efferents of which pass to the lateral group of nodes in the axilla. Some of the lymphatics from the joint may pass to small nodules situated along the interosseous, ulnar, radial or brachial arteries and thence to the lateral axillary group.

The nerve supply to the joint is by twigs derived anteriorly from the musculocutaneous, median and radial nerves, and posteriorly from the ulnar nerve and radial nerve by its branch to anconeus. The root value of these nerves is C5, 6, 7 and 8.

Palpation

Palpation of the joint line anteriorly is not possible because of the muscles crossing the joint and its deepness within the cubital fossa. Nevertheless, it can be approximated by drawing a line joining the points 1 cm below the lateral epicondyle and 2 cm below the medial epicondyle. Posteriorly the gap between the head of the radius and the capitulum can be palpated in the large dimple present at the back of the extended elbow.

Fig. 4.75   Sagittal section through elbow joint.

Fig. 4.76   The arterial anastomosis around the elbow joint, anterior view.

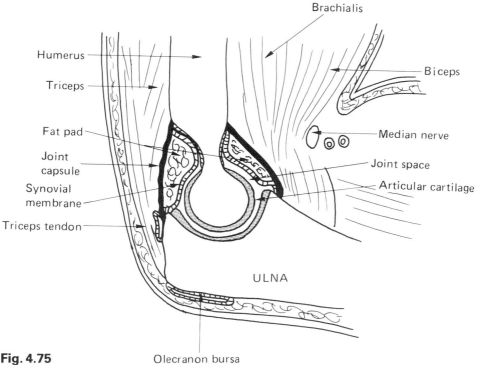

Brachialis

Humerus

Triceps

Biceps

Fat pad

Median nerve

Joint
capsule

Joint space

Synovial
membrane

Articular cartilage

Triceps tendon

ULNA

Fig. 4.75

Olecranon bursa

Brachial
artery

Profunda
brachii

Superior ulnar collateral
artery

Radial
collateral artery

Inferior ulnar collateral
artery

Middle collateral
artery

Interosseous recurrent
artery

Ulnar recurrent arteries

Radial recurrent
artery

Radial artery

Ulnar artery

Common

Posterior } Interosseous arteries

Anterior }

Fig. 4.76

Relations

Posteriorly the olecranon is subcutaneous and can be readily palpated. Either side of the olecranon the medial and lateral epicondyles form easily recognizable bony landmarks. Anteriorly lies brachialis forming the majority of the floor of the cubital fossa, a hollow in front of the elbow through which pass many of the vessels and nerves entering or leaving the forearm.

The cubital fossa is a triangular space bounded above by an imaginary line between the medial and lateral epicondyles, and at the sides by the converging medial borders of brachioradialis laterally and pronator teres medially (Fig. 4.77b). The floor of this region is formed mainly by brachialis with supinator inferolaterally (Fig. 4.77b). It is roofed over by the deep fascia of the forearm, reinforced medially by the bicipital aponeurosis passing from the tendon of biceps downwards and medially to the deep fascia of the forearm (Fig. 4.77a). The deep fascia separates the superficial veins and nerves from the deeper more important structures (Fig. 4.77).

This region is of considerable importance because the large superficial veins are frequently used for venepuncture, while the deeper brachial artery is used for determining blood pressure. The main superficial veins are the cephalic laterally, the basilic medially and the median cubital passing obliquely upwards and medially between them (Fig. 4.77a). It is not unusual for the median cubital vein to lie towards the lateral side of the fossa, or to be joined by the median vein of the forearm. Occasionally, the median cubital vein is absent and the median vein of the forearm divides into lateral and medial branches to join with the cephalic and basilic veins respectively. Lateral to the cephalic vein runs the lateral cutaneous nerve of the forearm, the terminal branch of the musculocutaneous nerve. Crossing the median cubital vein and running with the basilic vein and its tributaries are branches of the medial cutaneous nerve of the forearm (Fig. 4.77a).

Lying within the cubital fossa deep to the deep fascia are several structures passing into the forearm. The most medial of these is the median nerve as it passes downwards through the fossa to emerge between the two heads of pronator teres and thus enter the forearm (Fig. 4.77b). While in the fossa it gives off a branch to pronator teres, and the anterior interosseous branch as it passes through pronator teres. Lateral to the median nerve is the brachial artery, which bifurcates into the ulnar and radial arteries at the neck of the radius in the lower part of the fossa (Fig. 4.77b, see also Fig. 4.75). The ulnar artery passes inferomedially deep to pronator teres, giving off recurrent branches to the elbow joint and the common interosseous artery. The radial artery passes inferolaterally on the tendon of biceps brachii deep to brachioradialis, giving off its recurrent branch to the elbow joint. Running through the central region of the fossa, lateral to both the brachial artery and the median nerve is the tendon of biceps brachii towards its insertion on the radial tuberosity (Fig. 4.77b). As it passes through the fossa the tendon twists on itself so that its anterior surface faces laterally. The most lateral structure passing through the fossa is the radial nerve. In the upper part of the fossa it lies submerged between brachialis and brachioradialis supplying both muscles, and then divides into its terminal branches, the superficial radial and posterior interosseous (deep radial) nerves. The superficial branch continues downwards into the forearm under cover of brachioradialis. The posterior interosseous nerve passes backwards around the lateral side of the radius to enter the forearm between the two heads of supinator.

The ulnar nerve, passing behind the medial epicondyle of the humerus on the intermediate part of the ulnar collateral ligament, lies posteromedial to the elbow joint. It therefore does not pass through the cubital fossa.

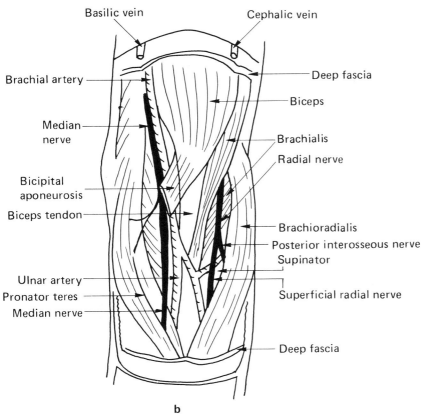

Fig. 4.77 The cubital fossa: **a** = superficial structures; **b** = deep structures.

Stability

Stability of the elbow joint is by virtue of the shape of the articular surfaces of the trochlea and capitulum of the humerus, and the trochlear notch of the ulna and head of the radius. Without strong collateral ligaments and the muscular cuff of triceps, biceps, brachialis, brachioradialis, and the common tendons of the superficial flexors and extensors arising from the medial and lateral epicondyles of the humerus, the elbow joint cannot be considered as an inherently stable joint. The bony surfaces are in closest contact when the forearm is flexed to 90° in a position of mid pronation–supination. This, therefore, is the position of greatest stability of the joint, and is the position naturally assumed when fine manipulation of the hand and fingers is required, as for example when writing.

In spite of ligaments and muscles crossing the joint, dislocations of the elbow can and do occur. In the child, because the head of the radius is small relative to the annular ligament, it is commonly dislocated by traction forces applied to the forearm and hand. In older people, a fall on the hand with the forearm extended may tear the annular ligament with a consequent anterior displacement of the head of the radius (Fig. 4.78a). The head of the radius may also be dislocated by extreme pronation, by tearing the annular ligament. In either case it can be palpated in the cubital fossa.

The majority of elbow dislocations involve a backward movement of the ulna, through the relatively weak posterior capsule, and is often associated with a fracture of the coronoid process (Fig. 4.78b). Both radius and ulna may be displaced together due to their connections at the superior radioulnar joint. This backward displacement can lead to pressure on the brachial artery which may go into spasm and reduce the blood supply to the forearm and hand. Pressure on the brachial artery can also arise in supracondylar fractures as the lower fragment moves forwards. Either of these events can also lead to injury of the median nerve with a consequent loss of pronation and reduced use of the hand. Both dislocations and supracondylar fractures result in considerable swelling in the region of the elbow. The alignment of the epicondyles of the humerus and the olecranon can be used to determine the nature of the trauma in an individual with a swollen elbow. The alignment remains unchanged in supracondylar fractures (Fig. 4.78c), while in dislocations it is changed (Fig. 4.78d). When an apparently dislocated joint cannot be reduced, fracture of the olecranon must be considered, particularly if the joint is extremely unstable.

A forceful abduction applied to the forearm may be sufficient to rupture the ulnar collateral ligament, or more commonly result in avulsion of the medial epicondyle. The ulnar nerve is especially liable to damage at the time of the injury. If the fracture does not unite or the ligament heal, the forearm tends to become more and more abducted with a consequent stretching of the ulnar nerve, leading to sensory disturbances and muscle weakness or paralysis.

Fig. 4.78 **a** = Dislocation of the head of the radius into the cubital fossa; **b** = backward dislocation of the ulna with fracture of coronoid process; **c** = normal alignment of the olecranon and epicondyles of the humerus; **d** = alignment when ulna is dislocated.

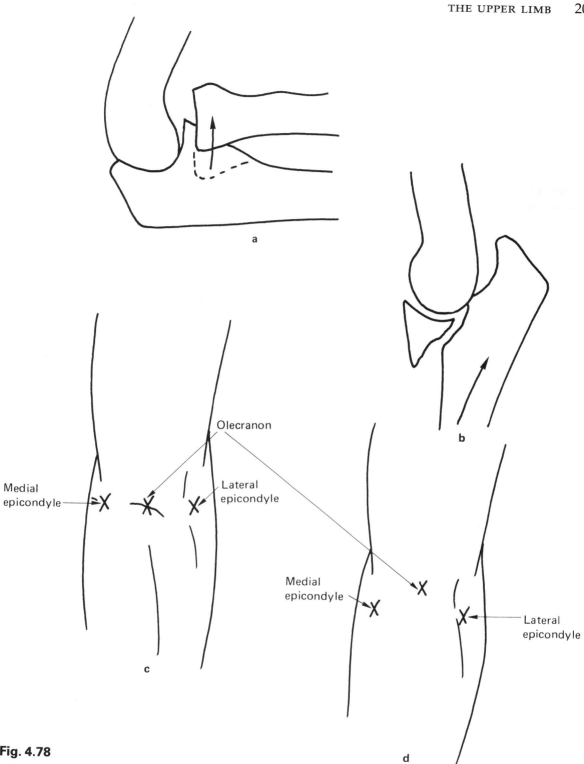

Fig. 4.78

Movements

The movements possible at the elbow joint are flexion and extension, which take place about a transverse axis through the humeral epicondyles (Fig. 4.79). This axis is not at right angles to the long axis of the humerus or of the forearm, as it bisects the carrying angle at the elbow (see Fig. 4.70b). Consequently, its medial end is slightly lower than the lateral. Except at the extremes of flexion and extension, movement between the humerus and the radius and ulna is one of sliding. It is only at the extremes, when the axis of movement changes slightly, that the sliding motion changes to one of rolling between the articular surfaces. The collateral ligaments are tense in all positions of the joint.

Flexion and extension

Flexion is movement of the forearm anteriorly (Fig. 4.79a). It continues until contact between the forearm and arm prevents further movement. The active range of flexion is 145°; passively 160° of flexion can be attained. Because of the obliquity of the axis about which flexion occurs, the hand moves medially to come to lie over the shoulder. Flexion is brought about by brachialis, biceps brachii and brachioradialis. In slow gentle movements, brachialis is the main muscle used, whereas rapid and forceful movements will use all three muscles as well as the superficial forearm flexors arising from the medial epicondyle. Flexion is primarily limited by opposition of the anterior muscles of the arm and forearm, with tension in the posterior part of the capsule and triceps; the impact of bony surfaces being insignificant.

Extension is movement of the forearm posteriorly, and is best defined as returning the forearm to the anatomical position (Fig. 4.79b). Strictly speaking the range of extension possible at the joint is zero since full extension corresponds to the anatomical position. However, relative extension is always possible from any position of the joint. Active extension is brought about by triceps and anconeus, while passive extension is due to the eccentric contraction of the elbow flexors, particularly when a weight is being lowered. Extension is usually limited by tension in the anterior joint capsule and flexor muscles, and to some extent in the anterior parts of the collateral ligaments.

Limitation of movement, either flexion or extension, is rarely due to bony contact, although the presence of small cartilage-covered facets at the bottom of the coronoid fossa and at the sides of the olecranon fossa in some individuals suggests that bony contact occurs during life.

Because the axis of flexion–extension bisects the carrying angle it is only to be expected that there is a linear change in the carrying angle during flexion of the elbow. This occurs irrespective of whether the forearm is fully pronated or supinated or in some mid-position (Fig. 4.79c). The small changes in the position of the axis of movement at the extremes of the range results in a small degree of axial rotation, which is due to the configuration of the ulno-humeral articulation and ligamentous constraints. During initial flexion, the forearm may medially rotate up to 5°, and may laterally rotate up to 5° during terminal flexion. Although not much, the movement nevertheless occurs.

Abduction and adduction

Being a hinge joint, the only movements expected at the elbow have already been described. However, during pronation and supination of the forearm there is a small degree of abduction and adduction respectively, between the trochlear notch of the ulna and the trochlea of the humerus. Full details of these movements are given on p. 220.

Accessory movements

With the elbow almost fully extended a small degree of abduction and adduction at the joint is possible. This can best be demonstrated with the subject lying supine. Holding the lower part of the arm steady and applying alternate medial and lateral pressure to the lower end of the forearm will produce these accessory movements.

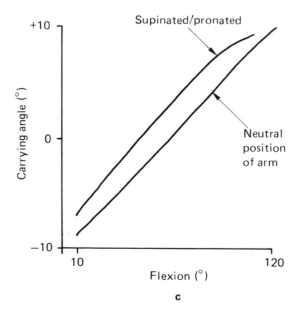

Fig. 4.79 **a** and **b** = Movements at the elbow joint; **c** = changes in the carrying angle with flexion at the joint (adapted from Chao E. Y., Morrey B. F. (1978). Three-dimensional rotation of the elbow. *Journal of Biomechanics,* **11**, 57–74).

Biomechanics

Contact areas

Because of the rounded ridge extending from the tip of the olecranon to the tip of the coronoid process, and the transverse ridge observable on the articular cartilage, the trochlear notch can be conveniently divided into four quadrants (Fig. 4.80a). Direct observation has revealed that the contact area on the humerus changes during flexion and extension. In general, the ulno-humeral contact area increases from full extension to full flexion, and the head of the radius establishes more and more contact with the capitulum. The increasing area of contact supports the view that the stability at the joint increases with flexion. As far as the radius is concerned, it means that it must move proximally during flexion.

In full extension the contact areas of the elbow are in the lower part of the trochlear notch, with concentrations on the medial aspects (Fig. 4.80a); there is no contact between the radius and capitulum. At 90° flexion, the contact area is a diagonal strip running from the lower medial to the upper lateral compartment. Small parts of the superior surface of the coronoid process and of the inferior surface of the olecranon also show contact. There is some contact between the capitulum and the head of the radius (Fig. 4.80b). It is only when the elbow is fully flexed that a definite area of contact between the radius and capitulum can be identified. Trochlear notch contact areas, although of a similar diagonal orientation, are larger and extend into the upper medial quadrant.

This general increase in contact areas across the joint serves to reduce the pressure applied to the cartilage, and so help protect it, particularly when loading is being supported with the elbow flexed, or when fine manipulative movements are being performed in which many muscles crossing the joint may be active.

Muscular action and its efficiency

As a group, the flexor muscles are more powerful than the extensors. Consequently, with the arm hanging loosely by the side, the elbow tends to be slightly flexed. Not only does the power of the muscle groups vary with the position of the shoulder, because of the attachment of biceps and triceps to the supra- and infraglenoid tubercles respectively, but for the flexors the degree of rotation of the forearm is also an important factor. As far as rotation is concerned, the power of the flexors is greater when the forearm is pronated, because biceps is stretched thereby increasing the efficiency of its action. The flexor efficiency ratio of the biceps for pronation and supination is of the order of 5:3.

Biceps work most efficiency between 80° and 90°, brachialis between 90° and 100°, and brachioradialis between 100° and 110°. Consequently, as a whole, the flexor muscles work at their best advantage when the elbow is flexed at 90°. In this position the muscles are at their optimal lengths and their direction of pull (line of action), particularly for biceps and brachialis, is almost at 90° to the forearm. Most of the force of contraction is thus directed towards moving the forearm and not to the maintenance of the integrity of the elbow joint. The reverse is true when the elbow is extended, because in this situation the direction of pull is nearly parallel to the forearm, rather than perpendicular to it. Because the attachment of the flexor muscles, between the fulcrum (elbow joint) and the resistance (weight of the forearm and hand together with any applied loads), conforms to that of a third class lever, it follows that the flexors favour range and speed of movement at the expense of power.

The extensor muscle triceps is most efficient when the elbow is flexed to between 20° and 30°. As flexion increases, the tendon of triceps becomes wound around the superior surface of the olecranon, which thus acts as a pulley. At the same time the muscle fibres become passively stretched. Both of these features help to compensate for the loss of efficiency of the muscle in flexion. Triceps is more powerful when the shoulder is flexed, and also when both the elbow and shoulder are being extended simultaneously from a flexed position, for example when executing a karate chop. On the other hand triceps is weakest when the elbow is extended at the same time as the shoulder is being flexed.

There are, therefore, preferential pos-

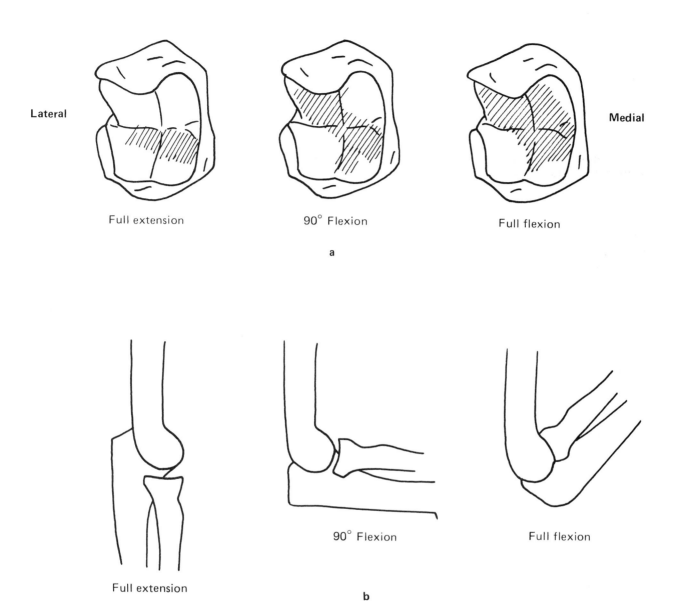

Fig. 4.80 Contact areas at different elbow positions: **a** = of the trochlear notch; **b** = of head of the radius.

itions of the upper limb in which the muscle groups achieve maximum efficiency. For extension this is with the arm and forearm hanging downwards with an angle of 20° to 30° between them. For flexion it is with the arm and forearm stretched above the shoulder. Thus the muscles of the upper limb have retained their adaptation for climbing, developed in the dawn of human evolution.

RADIOULNAR ARTICULATIONS

Introduction

As well as articulating independently with the humerus at the elbow joint, the radius and ulna also articulate with each other. They do so at their proximal and distal ends by synovial joints of the pivot type (Fig. 4.81), and by an interosseous membrane in the manner of a syndesmosis along their shafts (Fig. 4.82). The predominant movement between the two bones is a rotation of the radius around the ulna, so that the two bones cross in space, producing pronation, and the reverse movement to bring the bones into parallel alignment producing supination. In pronation and supination the hand is carried with the rotation of the forearm, thereby giving a further axis of movement of the hand at the wrist. Indeed, in functional terms the combination of pronation and supination of the forearm and the movements possible at the wrist, means that the hand is united to the arm by a universal joint. The fact that the various axes about which movement occurs do not all pass through a common point, and that several joints are involved, gives stability to the hand when performing delicate tasks.

Without freely movable joints between the radius and ulna, perhaps the evolutionary development of the hand as a manipulative tool would not have been so successful. Nor perhaps would there have been so much development and enlargement of the brain, particularly of the cerebral cortex.

a

Posterior view

b

Anterior view in adduction

Fig. 4.81 X-rays of (**a**) the superior and (**b**) the inferior radioulnar joints.

Annular ligament

Oblique cord

Interosseous membrane

Inferior radioulnar joint capsule

Articular disc

Fig. 4.82 The articulation between the radius and the ulna.

Superior radioulnar joint

Articular surfaces

The articulation is between the head of the radius rotating within the fibro-osseous ring formed by the radial notch of the ulna and the annular ligament.

Head of the radius The bevelled circumference of the head of the radius is covered by hyaline cartilage continuous with that on its upper concave surface, so forming a smooth surface for articulation with the ulna and annular ligament (Fig. 4.83a). The anterior, medial and posterior parts of the circumference tend to be wider than the lateral part, for direct articulation with the ulna. The head of the radius tends not to be circular but is slightly oval, with the major axis lying obliquely anteroposteriorly. The major and minor axes have a length ratio of approximately 7:6.

Radial notch The hyaline-covered radial notch is continuous with the trochlear notch of the ulna on its lateral side, being separated from it by a blunt ridge (Fig. 4.83a, c). It forms approximately one-fifth of the articular fibro-osseous ring, and is therefore concave anteroposteriorly but almost flat vertically.

Annular ligament The flexible annular ligament forms the remaining four-fifths of the articular surface which encircles the head and neck of the radius (Fig. 4.83). Its flexibility enables the oval head of the radius to rotate freely in pronation and supination. The ligament is a strong, well-defined band attached to the anterior and posterior margins of the radial notch of the ulna. Posteriorly the ligament widens where it attaches to adjacent areas of the ulna above and below the posterior margin of the notch. The diameter between its lower borders is narrower than that above (Fig. 4.83c), so it cups in under the head of the radius and acts as a restraining ligament preventing downward displacement of the head through the ring.

Superiorly the annular ligament is supported by the firm fusion of the radial collateral ligament and the blending of the lateral part of the fibrous capsule of the elbow joint in front and behind (Fig. 4.84). Inferiorly a few loose fibres attach the ligament to the neck of the radius beyond the epiphyseal line. These fibres are too loose to interfere with movements at the joint, but give some support to a dependent fold of synovial membrane. The upper part of the ligament is lined with fibrocartilage continuous with the hyaline cartilage of the radial notch. The lower part of the ligament is lined with synovial membrane.

Joint capsule and synovial membrane

The superior radioulnar joint is continuous with the elbow joint and consequently shares the same joint capsule (Fig. 4.84). For details of the capsular attachments see p. 198. The synovial membrane associated with the elbow part of the joint space attaches to the upper margin of the fibrocartilage lining of the annular ligament. From the lower border of the fibrocartilage, and lining the lower part of the annular ligament, the synovial membrane extends below the lower border of the ligament to hang as a redundant fold which has a loose attachment to the neck of the radius (Fig. 4.84). The membrane lies on the upper surface of the quadrate ligament, which limits and supports it, and passes medially from the radius to attach to the lower border of the radial notch of the ulna. The redundancy of the synovial membrane below the annular ligament accommodates to the twisting of the membrane that accompanies rotation of the radius.

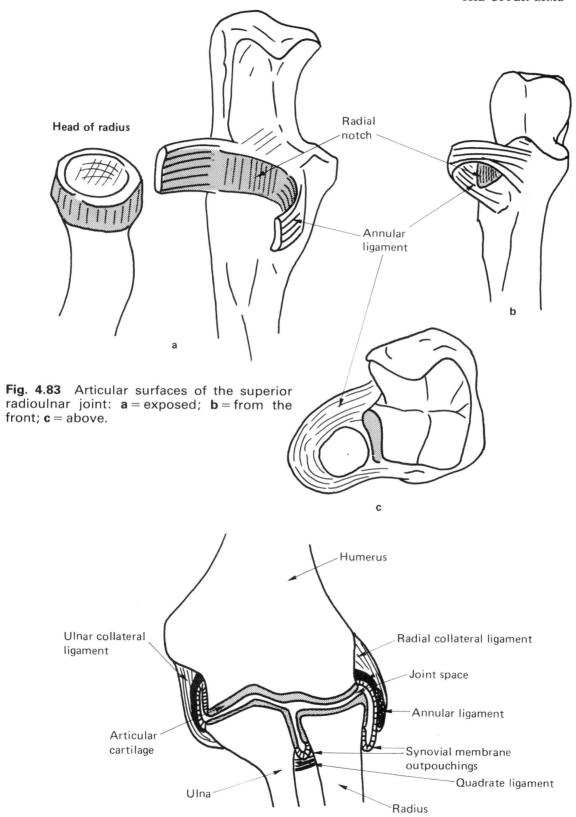

Fig. 4.83 Articular surfaces of the superior radioulnar joint: **a** = exposed; **b** = from the front; **c** = above.

Fig. 4.84 Coronal section through the elbow and superior radioulnar joints.

Ligaments

Although the annular ligament provides an important support for the head of the radius, it is not sufficient by itself to provide the only support to the superior radioulnar joint, because of its need to change shape with rotation of the radius. Indeed, this constant need to accommodate to the changing orientation of the head of the radius may lead to stretching of the ligament. Consequently, there are additional structures which provide support to the joint: the quadrate ligament and the interosseous membrane. (For details of the interosseous membrane see below.)

Quadrate ligament   The quadrate ligament stretches from the lower border of the radial notch of the ulna to the adjacent medial surface of the neck of the radius proximal to the radial tuberosity (Fig. 4.85). Its fibres run in a criss-cross manner between the two bones, so that, irrespective of the relation of the radius to the ulna, some fibres are always under tension. The overall tension within the ligament thus remains constant in all positions of pronation and supination. Its two borders are strengthened by fibres from the lower border of the annular ligament.

Blood and nerve supply

The arterial blood supply to the superior radioulnar joint is by branches from vessels supplying the lateral part of the elbow joint; namely the middle and radial collateral branches of the profunda brachii, and the radial and interosseous recurrent branches from the radial and common interosseous arteries respectively. Venous drainage is by similarly named vessels draining eventually to the brachial vein. Lymphatic drainage is by vessels travelling with the arteries to small nodes associated with the main arteries and then to the lateral group of axillary nodes.

The nerve supply to the joint is by twigs from the posterior interosseous branch of the radial nerve, the musculocutaneous and median nerves, with a root value of C5, 6 and 7.

Surface marking and palpation

The line of the superior radioulnar joint can be palpated posteriorly. Having identified the head of the radius in the depression on the posterolateral aspect of the elbow, a vertical groove between the radius and ulna can be felt medially. This is the position of the joint line. During pronation and supination, the head of the radius can be felt rotating against the ulna.

Relations

Anteriorly the joint is crossed by the tendon of biceps passing to its attachment on the radial tuberosity; posteriorly is the fleshy belly of anconeus. Medial to the tendon of biceps lies the brachial and then the radial artery from above downwards.

Stability

The joint has a reasonable degree of inherent stability. However, in children, the head of the radius may be pulled from the confines of the annular ligament in traction dislocation. Tears of the annular ligament will also result in dislocation at the joint. For further details see p. 206.

Movement

The main movement that occurs at the superior radioulnar joint is rotation of the head of the radius within the fibro-osseous ring of the annular ligament and radial notch of the ulna (Fig. 4.86a). The movement is probably limited by tension developed in the quadrate ligament.

In addition to this principal movement, there are four other movements related to the joint. These are:

1. rotation of the superior concave surface of the radial head in relation to the capitulum of the humerus;
2. the bevelled ridge of the radial head glides in contact with the capitulo-trochlear groove of the humerus;
3. the head of the radius is displaced laterally because the major axis of the oval head comes to lie transversely (Fig. 4.86a);
4. the plane of the radial head becomes tilted laterally and inferiorly during pronation due to the radius moving obliquely around the ulna (Fig. 4.86b).

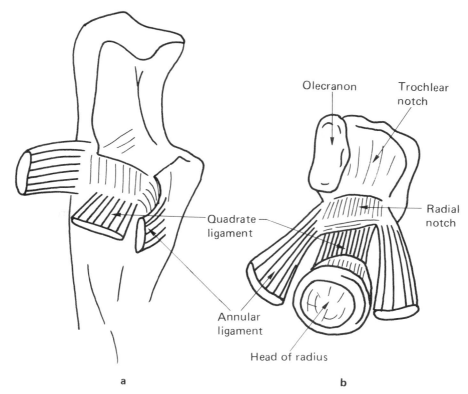

Fig. 4.85   The quadrate ligament: **a** = attachment to the ulna; **b** = seen from above.

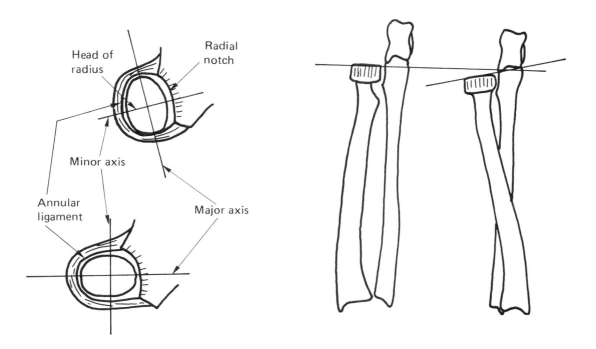

Fig. 4.86   Movements at the superior radioulnar joint during pronation and supination.

Accessory movements

Gripping the head of the radius between the thumb and index finger, it can be moved anteroposteriorly with respect to both the ulna and the capitulum.

Inferior radioulnar joint

Articular surfaces

The articulation is between the head of the ulna and the ulnar notch on the lower end of the radius. The joint is closed inferiorly by an articular disc which passes between the radius and ulna thereby separating the inferior radioulnar joint from the radiocarpal joint of the wrist.

Head of the ulna   The head of the ulna is the slightly expanded lower end of the bone (Fig. 4.87). The crescent-shaped articular surface is situated on its anterior and lateral aspects and is covered with hyaline cartilage, which is continuous with that on the distal end of the ulna over a rounded border. The distal end of the head of the ulna articulates with an intra-articular disc.

Ulnar notch of the radius   The ulnar notch of the radius is situated between the two edges of its interosseous border, and faces medially (Fig. 4.87). It is concave anteroposteriorly and plane or slightly concave vertically. The notch is lined by hyaline cartilage.

Articular disc   A triangular, fibrocartilaginous articular disc is the principal structure uniting the radius and ulna. It attaches by its apex to the lateral side of the root of the ulna styloid process, and by its base to the sharp inferior edge of the ulna notch between the ulnar and carpal surfaces of the radius (Fig. 4.87b). The disc is thicker peripherally than centrally, although it is rarely perforated.

It is an essential part of the total bearing surface of the inferior radioulnar joint by its articulation with the distal surface of the head of the ulna. Inferiorly it participates in the radiocarpal joint. Perforation of its central part would therefore lead to a communication between the inferior radioulnar and radiocarpal joints.

Joint capsule and synovial membrane

The relatively weak and loose fibrous capsule is formed by transverse bands of fibres attaching to the anterior and posterior margins of the ulnar notch of the radius, and to the corresponding regions on the head of the ulna (Fig. 4.88). The inferior margins of these bands blend with the anterior and posterior edges of the articular disc. However, superiorly they remain separated.

The synovial membrane is large in relation to the size of the joint, extending upwards above the margins of the joint capsule between the radius and ulna in front of the interosseous membrane, to form the recessus sacciformis (Fig. 4.88).

Blood and nerve supply

The arterial supply to the joint is by branches from the anterior and posterior interosseous arteries, and from the dorsal and palmar carpal networks, which receive branches from the radial and ulnar arteries. Venous drainage is by similarly named vessels into the deep system of veins. The lymphatic drainage of the joint is by vessels accompanying the deeper blood vessels, some of which pass to nodes in the cubital fossa, but most go directly to the lateral group of axillary nodes.

The nerve supply to the joint is by twigs from the anterior and posterior interosseous nerves, with a root value of C7 and 8.

Relations

Passing directly behind the inferior radioulnar joint is the tendon of extensor digiti minimi, enclosed within its synovial sheath, on its way to the little finger (see Figs. 4.40c, 4.102). Anteriorly lies the lateral part of flexor digitorum profundus enclosed within the common flexor sheath. Proximal to the joint pronator quadratus passes between the radius and ulna holding them together, and thereby protecting the joint.

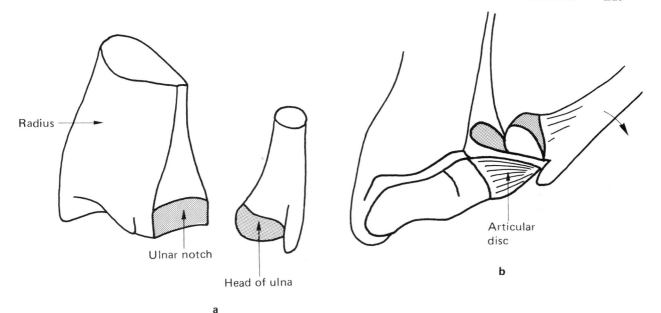

Fig. 4.87 Articular surfaces of the inferior radioulnar joint: **a** = without the articular disc; **b** = with the articular disc.

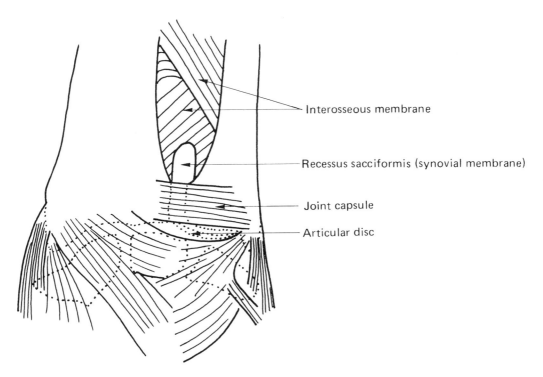

Fig. 4.88 Anterior view of the inferior radio-ulnar joint.

Stability

Although the joint capsule is loose, to allow for movement between the radius and ulna, the inferior radioulnar joint is extremely stable and is rarely dislocated. The stability is due primarily to the articular disc, but also to the interosseous membrane and pronator quadratus.

A fall on the outstretched hand with the wrist extended frequently results in a transverse fracture in the lower 2 or 3 cm of the radius (Colles' fracture), with the fragment being displaced posteriorly. The ulna is usually not involved except that its styloid process may be torn off. In a Colles' fracture the hand is displaced laterally and dorsally. Alternatively, the fall may result in dislocation at the radiocarpal joint, but not at the inferior radioulnar joint.

Movements

The main movement at the inferior radio-ulnar joint is a rotation of the lower end of the radius around the head of the ulna during pronation and supination. However, because during everyday activities the axis of pronation and supination coincides with the axis of the hand along the middle finger, the radial rotation is accompanied by movement of the head of the ulna. So that while the radius rotates about the ulna, the ulna is displaced with respect to the radius (Fig. 4.89). The ulna displacement observed during rotation is merely the result of two elementary movements: slight extension and medial displacement of the ulna at the elbow. The very slight side-to-side movement possible between the trochlea of the humerus and the trochlear notch of the ulna is mechanically amplified at the lower end of the ulna to become a movement of appreciable magnitude. Both the extension and lateral displacement of the ulna are brought about by the action of anconeus, and therefore occur simultaneously during pronation. The arc of the movement described by the head of the ulna does not involve a rotation of the bone, as it remains parallel to itself throughout, that is the ulnar styloid process remains posteromedial (Fig. 4.89).

Accessory movements

Gripping the lower ends of the radius and ulna firmly, the head of the ulna can be moved anteroposteriorly with respect to the radius.

Palpation

The line of the inferior radioulnar joint can be palpated on the posterior aspect of the wrist, running vertically between the two bones.

Interosseous membrane

The interosseous membrane stretching between the interosseous borders of the radius and ulna is a strong, fibrous sheet whose fibres predominantly pass obliquely downwards and medially from the radius to the ulna (Fig. 4.90). Being deficient superiorly, it has a free oblique border which is attached 2 to 3 cm below the radial tuberosity and passes to a slightly lower level on the ulna. Inferiorly the membrane is continuous with the fascia on the posterior surface of pronator quadratus, attaching to the posterior of the two lines into which the radial interosseous border divides. An opening in the lower part of the membrane enables the anterior interosseous vessels to pass into the posterior compartment of the forearm. On the posterior part of the membrane there are a small number of fibrous bands which pass obliquely downwards and laterally (Fig. 4.90). During pronation and supination, tension in the membrane varies, being greatest in the midprone position.

The oblique direction of the fibres of the interosseous membrane serve to transmit forces from the radius to the ulna. The radius is the forearm bone articulating at the radiocarpal joint, receiving impacts and forces from the scaphoid and lunate. At the elbow, however, it has a rather ineffective articulation with the humerus, whereas the ulna has a large and firm articulation. The membrane serves to transmit forces carried from the hand up through the radius to the ulna and thence to the elbow joint and humerus.

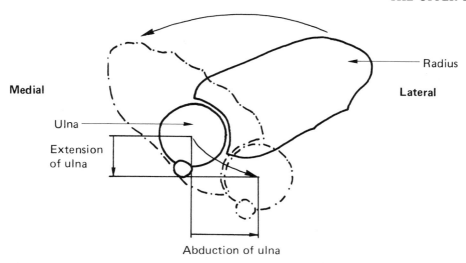

Fig. 4.89 Movements of the radius and ulna at the inferior radioulnar joint.

Fig. 4.90 The interosseous membrane.

As well as providing a firm connection between the radius and ulna the interosseous membrane separates and increases the area of attachment of the deep muscles of the anterior and posterior compartments of the forearm.

Above the upper free border of the interosseous membrane the oblique cord passes upwards and medially from the radius to the ulna (see Fig. 4.90). It is a slender, flattened fibrous band, which is said to represent a degenerated part of flexor pollicis longus or supinator, attached just below the radial tuberosity and to the lateral border of the ulnar tuberosity. In the gap between the oblique cord and the interosseous membrane, the posterior interosseous vessels pass to and from the posterior compartment of the forearm.

Pronation and supination

In the supine position, the bones of the forearm lie parallel to one another (Fig. 4.91); in the anatomical position the palm of the hand therefore faces forwards. In the prone position, the bones of the forearm cross one another (Fig. 4.91), with the radius lying anterior to the ulna; with reference to the anatomical position the palm faces backwards. The movement which causes crossing of the radius and ulna is called pronation, while that causing them to become parallel is called supination. The movements between the radius and ulna occur at the superior and inferior radioulnar joints (see pp. 216, 220 for details of the movements at each joint).

The muscles producing pronation are pronator teres and pronator quadratus, with pronator teres being the more powerful of the two. Flexor carpi radialis, because of its oblique course, can and does assist in pronation. Supination is produced by supinator and biceps brachii, of which biceps is by far the stronger. However, when the elbow is fully extended biceps is unable to act as a supinator because its tendon runs almost parallel to the shaft of the radius, and so cannot produce radial rotation. Of the two movements supination is the more powerful, which is why screws have a right-hand thread because the majority of the population are right-handed. If you are trying to move a particularly stubborn screw from a cabinet or door frame, ask a left-handed friend! Both pronation and supination are most powerful when the elbow is flexed to 90°.

The axis of pronation and supination can vary depending about which finger the movement is occurring. It always passes through the centre of the head of the radius, but at the level of the wrist it can pass through any point between the ulnar and radial styloid processes. Nevertheless, it will tend to lie in the medial half of this region in most instances. Therefore, to state that the axis runs between the centre of the radial head and the base of the ulnar styloid process is not strictly correct. When rotation occurs about a more laterally placed centre at the wrist, ulna movement at the trochlea is insufficient. Consequently, with the elbow flexed the movement is supplemented by rotation of the humerus.

The forearm can be pronated through almost 180°, without medial rotation of the humerus (Fig. 4.92). The constraint to further movement comes predominantly from the passive resistance of the opposing muscles, and not from ligamentous ties. However, if the humerus is allowed to rotate then it becomes possible to turn the hand through almost 360°.

Pronation and supination are frequently used movements in many activities. Consequently loss of the ability to pronate and supinate can be a marked disability. When these movements are lost it is less disabling if the forearm is fixed in a midprone position, so that the palm faces medially.

Supination   **Pronation**

Fig. 4.91   Relation of the radius and ulna in pronation and supination.

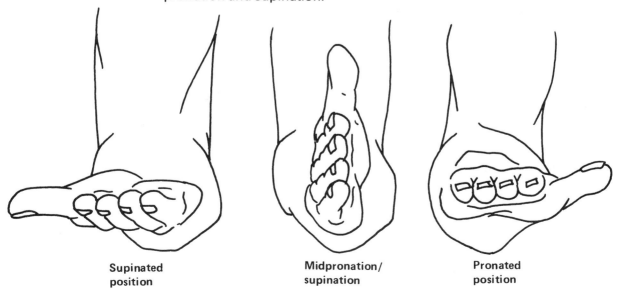

Supinated position   **Midpronation/ supination**   **Pronated position**

Fig. 4.92   Movement of the hand in pronation and supination.

THE WRIST JOINT

Introduction

The wrist joint is not a single joint but comprised of the articulations between the carpal bones (intercarpal joints) and the articulation with the forearm (radiocarpal joint) (Fig. 4.93). Functionally, however, the eight carpal bones are arranged and move as two rows of bones; a proximal row, comprising from lateral to medial: scaphoid, lunate, triquetral and pisiform; and a distal row, again from lateral to medial, formed by the trapezium, trapezoid, capitate and hamate. The two rows articulate with each other at what has become known as the midcarpal joint, a sinuous articular area convex laterally and concave medially (Fig. 4.93). The distal surface of the distal row of bones articulates with the bases of the metacarpals.

Because of the functional interdependence of the wrist and hand, all movements of the hand are accompanied by movements at the radiocarpal and intercarpal joints. The wrist complex is capable of movement in two directions. However, when combined with pronation and supination the hand appears to be connected to the forearm by a ball and socket joint, having great intrinsic stability because of the separation of the three axes about which movement occurs.

Radiocarpal joint

The radiocarpal joint is formed between the distal surfaces of the radius and the articular disc, and the scaphoid, lunate and triquetral of the proximal row of carpal bones. It is a synovial joint of the ellipsoid type allowing movement in two directions.

Articular surfaces

Distal surface of the radius and articular disc The radius and articular disc form a continuous, concave ellipsoid surface, being shallower in its transverse long axis than in its shorter anteroposterior axis (Fig. 4.94a). The articular cartilage on the radius is divided by a low ridge into a lateral triangular and a medial quadrangular area.

Proximal carpal row The proximal row of carpal bones presents an almost continuous convex articular surface (Fig. 4.94b). The three carpal bones are closely united by interosseous ligaments which are continuous with the cartilage on the proximal surfaces of the bones. In the anatomical position, the scaphoid lies opposite the lateral area on the radius, the lunate lies opposite the medial radial area and the articular disc, and the triquetral is in contact with the medial part of the joint capsule (Fig. 4.94b).

Anterior view

Fig. 4.93 X-ray of the wrist showing the carpal bones and their arrangement forming the radiocarpal and midcarpal joints.

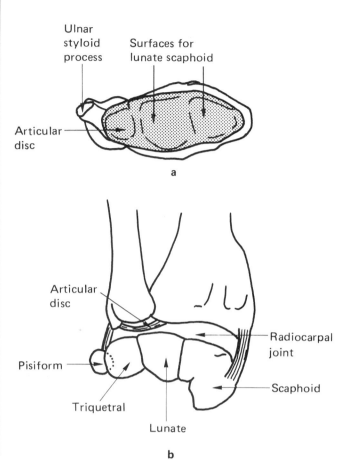

Fig. 4.94 The articular surfaces of (**a**) the radius and articular disc, and (**b**) of the proximal row of carpal bones.

Joint capsule and synovial membrane

A fibrous capsule completely encloses the joint (Fig. 4.95). It is attached to the distal edges of the radius and ulna anteriorly and posteriorly. Laterally and medially it is attached to the radial and ulnar styloid processes respectively. Distally the capsule is firmly attached anteriorly and posteriorly to the margins of the articular surfaces of the proximal row of carpal bones. Medially it passes to the medial side of the triquetral, and laterally to the lateral side of the scaphoid. Both the anterior and posterior parts of the capsule are thickened and hence strengthened, while at the sides it blends with the collateral ligaments.

Capsular ligaments The capsular ligaments are distinct bands of fibres passing between specific bones. As well as strengthening the capsule, their arrangement determines that the hand follows the radius in its movements and displacements.

Dorsal radiocarpal ligament The dorsal radiocarpal ligament extends from the posterior edge of the lower end of the radius to the posterior surface of the scaphoid, lunate and triquetral (Fig. 4.95b). Its fibres run downwards and medially, principally to the triquetral, and are continuous with the dorsal intercarpal ligaments.

Palmar radiocarpal ligament The palmar radiocarpal ligament is a broad band of fibres passing downwards and slightly medially from the anterior edge of the lower end of the radius and its styloid process, to the anterior surfaces of the proximal row of carpal bones (Fig. 4.95a). Some of the fibres are prolonged and extend to attach to the capitate.

Palmar ulnocarpal ligament The palmar ulnocarpal ligament is formed by fibres extending downwards and laterally from the anterior edge of the articular disc and the base of the ulnar styloid process to the

anterior surfaces of the proximal carpal bones (Fig. 4.95a).

These anterior and posterior capsular ligaments become taut in extension and flexion of the radiocarpal joint respectively.

Synovial membrane A relatively lax synovial membrane lines the deep surface of the joint capsule attaching to the margins of all the articular surfaces. It presents numerous folds particularly posteriorly. Because of the presence of the articular disc of the inferior radioulnar joint and the completeness of the interosseous ligaments uniting the proximal surfaces of the proximal carpal row, the synovial cavity is limited to the radiocarpal space. Only occasionally does it communicate with the inferior radioulnar joint by a perforation in the articular disc, or with the intercarpal joint when one of the interosseous ligaments is incomplete.

Ligaments

At the sides of the radiocarpal joint, collateral ligaments reinforce and strengthen the joint capsule. They are active in limiting abduction and adduction at the joint. In adduction, the radial ligament becomes taut while the ulnar relaxes; in abduction the reverse occurs.

Radial collateral carpal ligament The radial collateral carpal ligament passes from the tip of the radial styloid process to the lateral side of the scaphoid immediately adjacent to its proximal articular surface (Fig. 4.95).

Ulnar collateral carpal ligament The ulnar collateral carpal ligament is a rounded cord attached to the ulnar styloid process above and to the base of the pisiform and the medial and posterior non-articular surfaces of the triquetral below (Fig. 4.95). By its attachment to the pisiform the ligament also blends with the medial part of the flexor retinaculum.

a

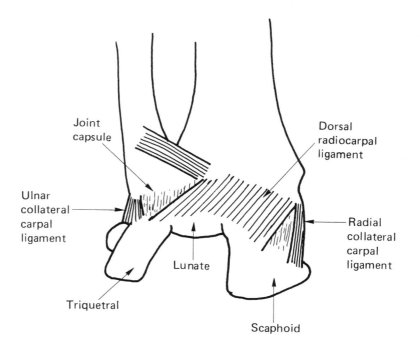

b

Fig. 4.95 The capsular and collateral ligaments of the radiocarpal joint: **a** = anterior; **b** = posterior.

Blood and nerve supply

The arterial supply to the joint is by branches from the dorsal and palmar carpal networks, with venous drainage going to the deep veins of the forearm. Lymphatic drainage of the joint follows the deep vessels.

The nerve supply to the joint is by twigs from the anterior interosseous branch of the median nerve, the posterior interosseous branch of the radial nerve, and the dorsal and deep branches of the ulnar nerve, with root value C7, 8.

Surface marking

The position of the joint is indicated by a line, slightly convex proximally, between the radial styloid process and the head of the ulna, so that the concavity of the radius and articular disc face distally, medially and slightly anteriorly.

Movements

Movements of flexion and extension, and adduction and abduction are possible at the radiocarpal joint. However, each of these is also contributed to by movements between the proximal and distal row of carpal bones at the midcarpal joint.

Flexion and extension   Flexion and extension occur about a transverse axis more or less in the sagittal plane such that the hand moves towards the front of the forearm in flexion and towards the back of the forearm in extension. Flexion is freer than extension and has a maximum range of 50°, whereas extension has a maximum range of 35° (Fig. 4.96). The movements are checked by the margins of the radius, and because the posterior margin extends further distally than the anterior, extension is checked earlier than flexion.

In flexion the scaphoid and lunate move within the concave distal end of the radius so that their proximal surfaces face posterosuperiorly. In addition the scaphoid twists about its long axis so that its tubercle becomes less prominent in full flexion. During extension the twisting of the scaphoid about its long axis makes the tubercle more prominent in full extension.

Adduction and abduction   Adduction and abduction, also referred to as radial and ulnar deviation, are lateral or medial movements respectively of the proximal row of carpal bones in relation to the distal end of the radius (Fig. 4.96). The radial styloid process extends further distally than the ulnar styloid process. Consequently, abduction is more limited at the radiocarpal joint having a range of only 7°, whereas adduction has a range of 30°. In adduction the scaphoid rotates so that its tubercle moves away from the radial styloid process, enabling the lunate to move laterally so that it comes to lie entirely distal to the radius. The triquetral lies distal to the articular disc. In abduction the triquetral moves medially and distally to be clear of the radius, the lunate follows so that its centre lies distal to the inferior radioulnar joint. The movement is limited by impact of the scaphoid tubercle on the radial styloid process.

Accessory movements

An anteroposterior gliding of the proximal row of carpal bones against the radius and articular disc can be produced by firmly gripping the lower end of the radius and ulna with one hand, and the proximal row of carpal bones with the other. Alternate anterior and posterior pressure elicits a palpable gliding movement at the radiocarpal joint. With the same grip, a longitudinally applied force along the line of the forearm pulls the carpal bones away from the radius and articular disc.

Fig. 4.96   Movements at the radiocarpal joint.

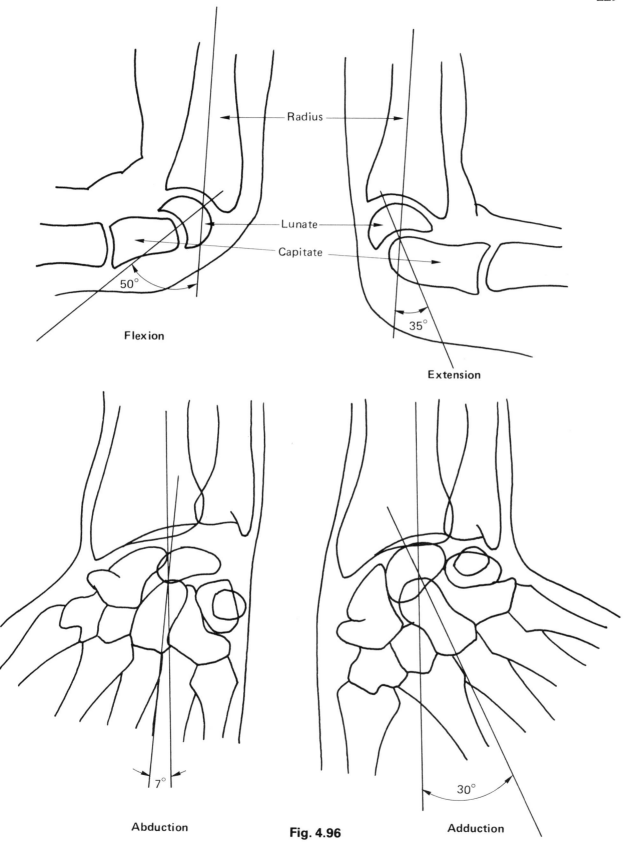

Radius

Lunate

Capitate

50°

Flexion

35°

Extension

7°

Abduction

Fig. 4.96

30°

Adduction

Intercarpal joints

The carpal bones are arranged in two transverse rows between which is the important midcarpal joint (Fig. 4.97). For the majority, the joints between the adjacent individual carpal bones are of the plane synovial type, permitting only slight movement between the bones involved. The only bone which moves appreciably is the capitate.

Joints of the proximal row

Plane synovial joints exist between the distal parts of the adjacent surfaces of the scaphoid, lunate and triquetral (Fig. 4.97). However, because these bones are bound together by interosseous, dorsal and palmar intercarpal ligaments there is minimal movement between them.

The interosseous intercarpal ligaments are short bands attaching to the margins of the joint surfaces involved in the radiocarpal articulation (Fig. 4.97). They unite the bones along their whole anteroposterior length. The palmar and dorsal intercarpal ligaments are transverse bands passing from scaphoid to lunate and from lunate to triquetral on the anterior and posterior aspects of the bones respectively.

The pisiform rests on the palmar surface of the triquetral and has a separate synovial joint with it, which is completely enclosed by a thin but strong fibrous capsule. The pisiform is also anchored to the hook of the hamate by the pisohamate ligament, and to the base of the fifth metacarpal by the pisometacarpal ligament. These two ligaments resist the pull of flexor carpi ulnaris, and transfer its action to the hamate and base of the fifth metacarpal. In this way these ligaments form extensions of the muscle.

Joints of the distal row

As in the proximal row, the four bones of the distal row are united by interosseous, palmar and dorsal intercarpal ligaments, with the joints between the individual bones being of the plane synovial type. Because of these ligaments, movements between adjacent bones is slight.

The interosseous ligaments are not as extensive as in the proximal row, leaving clefts between the bones which communicate with the midcarpal joint proximally, and with the common carpometacarpal joint distally (Fig. 4.97). Occasionally, the midcarpal and carpometacarpal joints communicate with each other between the bones of the distal row. This occurs when one of the interosseous ligaments is incomplete so that communication is around the borders of the ligament, or when one ligament is absent (most commonly that between the trapezium and trapezoid). Dorsal and palmar ligaments generally run transversely across the appropriate surfaces of the bones, uniting trapezium to trapezoid, trapezoid to capitate, and capitate to hamate.

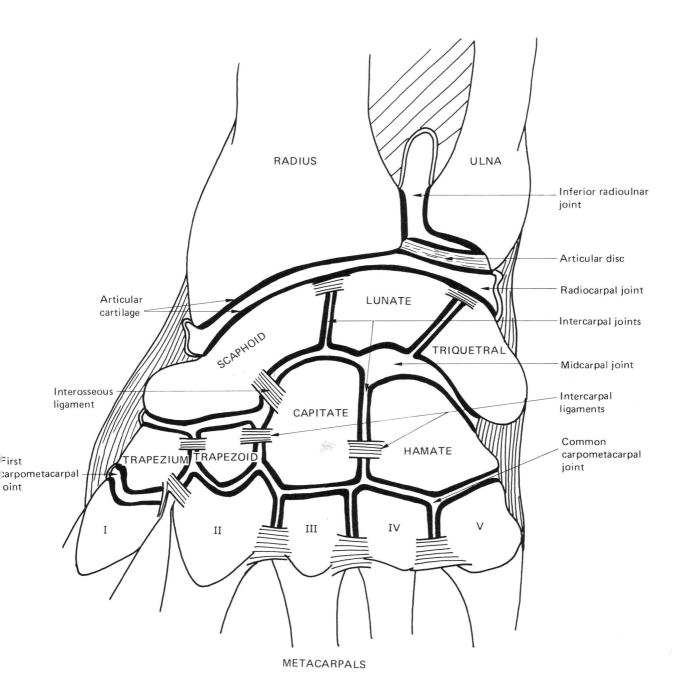

Fig. 4.97 Coronal section through the wrist showing the relationship between the radiocarpal, midcarpal, intercarpal and common carpometacarpal joints.

Midcarpal joint

The midcarpal joint is the articulation between the proximal and distal rows of carpal bones, each of which can be considered to act as a single functional unit (Fig. 4.97). The lateral part of the joint consists of two plane surfaces which are arranged to form a slight convexity directed distally. The larger medial part of the joint is concave distally in all directions.

Articular surfaces (Figs. 4.97, 4.98)

Laterally, plane joint surfaces on the trapezium and trapezoid articulate with the slightly rounded distal surface of the scaphoid. The head of the capitate articulates with the scaphoid and lunate in the central part of the joint. The apex of the hamate also articulates with the lunate, while its ulnar surface articulates with the triquetral.

Joint capsule

The midcarpal joint is surrounded by a fibrous capsule, composed in the main of irregular bands of fibres running between the rows of bones. Anteriorly and posteriorly these bands constitute the palmar and dorsal intercarpal ligaments. At the sides of the midcarpal joint the capsule is strengthened by collateral ligaments.

Intercarpal synovial cavity   The intercarpal joint cavity is large and complex (see Fig. 4.97). It extends from side-to-side between the two rows of carpal bones, however this may be partially or completely interrupted by an interosseous ligament between the scaphoid and capitate. Extensions of the cavity pass proximally between the scaphoid, lunate and triquetral as far as the interosseous ligaments between them (see Fig. 4.97). Rarely is there communication with the radiocarpal joint cavity. Further extensions of the cavity pass distally between the trapezium, trapezoid, capitate and hamate. If the interosseous ligaments connecting these bones do not extend the full depth of the articulation, or one is missing (usually that between trapezium and trapezoid) then the intercarpal joint cavity communicates with the carpometacarpal joint and is prolonged between the bases of the medial four metacarpals (see Fig. 4.97). The intercarpal cavity does not, however, communicate with the first carpometacarpal or the pisiform–triquetral joint spaces.

Synovial membrane lines the capsule and all non-articular surfaces, attaching to the margins of all joint surfaces.

Ligaments

Palmar intercarpal ligament   The palmar intercarpal ligament passes from the bones of the proximal row predominantly to the head of the capitate (Fig. 4.99). This ligament is sometimes referred to as the *radiate capitate ligament*.

Dorsal intercarpal ligament   The dorsal intercarpal ligament merely passes from the bones of one row to those of the other.

Radial collateral ligament   The radial collateral ligament is a strong distinct band passing from the scaphoid to the trapezium (Fig. 4.99). It is a continuation of the radial collateral carpal ligament of the radiocarpal joint.

Ulnar collateral ligament   The ulnar collateral ligament connects the triquetral and the hamate, and is a continuation of the ulnar collateral carpal ligament of the radiocarpal joint (Fig. 4.99).

Interosseous ligament   Occasionally, a slender interosseous ligament passes from the lateral side of the capitate to the scaphoid near its trapezoid articular surface (see Fig. 4.97).

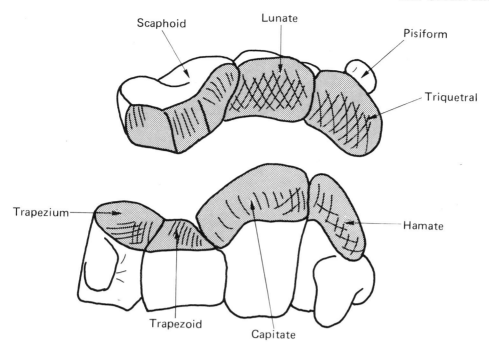

Fig. 4.98 Articular surfaces of the midcarpal joint.

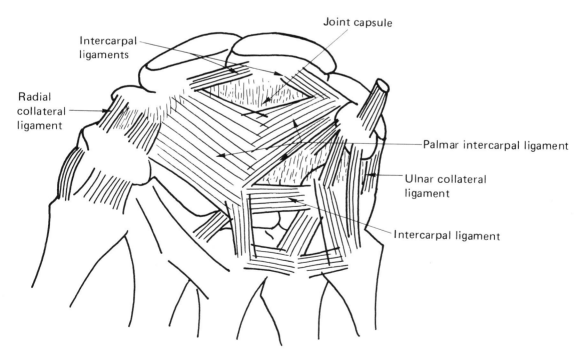

Fig. 4.99 Ligaments associated with the midcarpal joint, palmar aspect.

Blood and nerve supply

The arterial supply to all the intercarpal joints is by branches from the palmar and dorsal carpal networks.

The nerve supply to the joints is by twigs from the anterior and posterior interosseous nerves, and the deep and dorsal branches of the ulnar nerve; root value C7, 8.

Movements

Movements at the intercarpal joints, except the midcarpal joint, are small accompanying and facilitating movements at the radiocarpal and midcarpal joints. Movements possible at the midcarpal joint are flexion and extension, and abduction and adduction. These occur about transverse and anteroposterior axes passing through the head of the capitate.

Flexion and extension In flexion the hand moves towards the front of the forearm, while in extension it moves towards the back of the forearm (Fig. 4.100). Extension is freer than flexion having a range of 50°; flexion has a range of only 35°. In these movements the head of the capitate rotates within the concavity formed by the scaphoid and lunate, while the hamate rotates against the triquetral. Accompanying these movements is a compensatory swing of the scaphoid on the lunate in order to receive the head of the capitate.

Abduction and adduction During adduction the capitate rotates so that its distal part moves medially, the hamate approaches the lunate and separates from the triquetral (Fig. 4.100). In abduction the capitate comes close to the triquetral separating the hamate from the lunate. Accompanying abduction and adduction is a complex movement of torsion between the two rows of carpal bones. During abduction the distal row of carpal bones undergoes a 'rotation' in the direction of supination and extension, while the proximal row 'rotates' in the direction of pronation and flexion. The twisting of the scaphoid delays its impact on the radial styloid process by bringing its tubercle forwards; it also makes the tubercle more easily palpable. In adduction a reverse twisting motion occurs so that the proximal row 'rotates' in the direction of supination and extension, while the distal row moves in the direction of pronation and flexion. It must be emphasized that these movements are of extremely small magnitude. It is debatable whether they contribute much to the normal functioning of the wrist.

The range of abduction and adduction are 8° and 15° respectively. The principal limit to abduction is a closing of the lateral part of the joint space between the scaphoid and the trapezium.

Accessory movements

Anteroposterior gliding movements of any two adjacent carpal bones can be produced if one is stabilized while the other is moved. This can be achieved by gripping each bone between the thumb and index finger.

Anteroposterior movement at the midcarpal joint can be elicited using a similar technique to that described for the radiocarpal joint. A firm circular grip is applied around each carpal row. While the proximal row is stabilized, the distal row can be moved anteroposteriorly. Applying the same grip, a longitudinally applied force separates the two joint surfaces.

Fig. 4.100 Movements at the midcarpal joint.

Flexion

Extension

Abduction

Adduction

Fig. 4.100

Relations

All of the structures entering or leaving the hand have to cross the region of the wrist. Some of these will lie directly against the carpal bones, others will be separated by intervening soft tissues. The nature of the arrangement of the carpal bones, in which they form part of a fibro-osseous canal, makes the anterior aspect of the wrist an extremely important region.

The carpal bones of each row form a transverse arch with a palmar concavity (Fig. 4.101a). The principal structure maintaining the bones in this position is the flexor retinaculum. Consequently, it is considered by some to be an accessory ligament to the intercarpal joints. The flexor retinaculum attaches medially to the pisiform and the hook of the hamate, and laterally to the scaphoid tubercle and to both lips of the groove on the trapezium so forming a small lateral compartment separate from the rest of the canal. Passing through this lateral compartment is the tendon of flexor carpi radialis enclosed within its own synovial sheath (Fig. 4.101b). Through the larger main part of the canal pass:

1. the tendon of flexor pollicis longus most laterally, deep in the concavity of the carpal bones;

2. the four tendons of flexor digitorum profundus lying side-by-side directly over the capitate;

3. the four tendons of flexor digitorum superficialis overlying those of profundus, with the tendons to the third and fourth digits anterior to those for the second and fifth; the tendons of flexors digitorum superficialis and profundus being enclosed within the same synovial sheath;

4. the median nerve lying lateral to the superficialis tendons (Fig. 4.101b).

Inflammation of the synovial sheaths within the so called *carpal tunnel*, may lead to compression of the median nerve, and gives rise to the *carpal tunnel (or median nerve) syndrome*. This leads to paraesthesia and diminution of sensory acuity in the region of the median nerve's sensory distribution, loss of power and limitation of some thumb movements, together with some wasting of the thenar eminence. Passing anterior to and blending with the flexor retinaculum is the tendon of palmaris longus. Also passing superficial to the retinaculum on the medial side is the ulnar nerve with the ulnar artery lateral to it. In addition, the palmar cutaneous branches of the median and ulnar nerves, and the superficial palmar branch of the radial artery enter the hand by crossing the retinaculum.

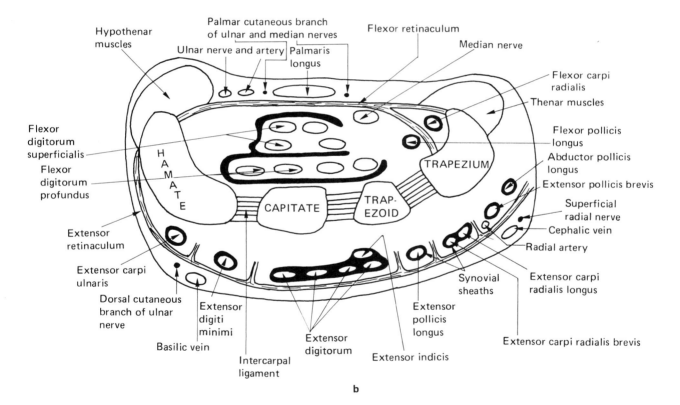

Fig. 4.101 a = Arrangement of the carpal bones and attachment of the flexor retinaculum; **b** = transverse section through the wrist region showing the relationships of the various structures which pass into the hand.

On the posterior aspect of the carpal bones, the extensor tendons pass into the hand. They are bound down by fibrous septa passing from the deep surface of the extensor retinaculum to ridges on the radius, ulna and capsular tissues of the joint (see Fig. 4.101b). The six longitudinal compartments so formed separate and transmit the tendons of nine extensor muscles. Most laterally, over the lateral surface of the radial styloid process and continuing over the scaphoid and trapezium, pass the tendons of abductor pollicis longus and extensor pollicis brevis within the same synovial sheath (Fig. 4.102a). In the adjacent compartment over the radius lateral to the dorsal tubercle, and then over the scaphoid and the most medial part of the trapezium and the trapezoid, run the tendons of extensor carpi radialis longus and brevis (Fig. 4.102a). In the third compartment, in a groove on the medial side of the dorsal tubercle, is the tendon of extensor pollicis longus (Fig. 4.102). However, because this tendon uses the dorsal tubercle as a pulley, it deviates laterally towards the thumb and so crosses the scaphoid and trapezium between the tendons of the two previous compartments. Running over the most medial part of the dorsum of the radius, and then over the adjacent parts of the scaphoid and lunate, and the capitate are the four tendons of extensor digitorum, with the tendon of extensor indicis deep to them (Fig. 4.102b). All five tendons are enclosed with a common synovial sheath. Crossing the posterior surface of the inferior radioulnar joint, the lunate and the adjacent surfaces of the capitate and hamate is the tendon of extensor digiti minimi (Fig. 4.102b). Finally, the tendon of extensor carpi ulnaris passes in a groove on the back of the ulna and onto the triquetral before attaching to the base of the fifth metacarpal (Fig. 4.102b). The dorsal branch of the ulnar nerve and the terminal branches of the superficial radial nerve cross the extensor retinaculum to enter the dorsum of the hand on its medial and lateral sides respectively. The other major structure to enter the hand is the radial artery, and it does so by a convoluted route (Fig. 4.102). In the forearm proximal to the flexor retinaculum, the radial artery can be palpated lateral to the tendon of flexor carpi radialis. It then turns laterally to cross the radial collateral carpal ligament, the scaphoid and trapezium, being crossed by the tendons of abductor pollicis longus and extensors pollicis brevis and longus before passing into the palm of the hand between the two heads of the first dorsal interosseous muscle. The hollowed region between the tendons of abductor pollicis longus and extensor pollicis brevis laterally, and extensor pollicis longus medially when the thumb is extended is known as the 'anatomical snuffbox' (Fig. 4.102a). The radial artery crosses the floor of this hollow, which is formed from proximal to distal by the radial styloid process, scaphoid, trapezium and base of the first metacarpal; its pulsations can be felt readily by applying firm pressure between the tendons.

Fig. 4.102 Principal relations of the wrist region: **a** = lateral; **b** = posterior aspects of wrist region.

Stability

Because of the attachment of the flexor retinaculum and the numerous tendons crossing the joint both anteriorly and posteriorly, the wrist is a relatively stable region (see Figs. 4.101, 4.102). Nevertheless, abnormal stresses applied to it may result in dislocation or fracture.

A fall on the outstretched hand may result in a dislocation at the radiocarpal and/or midcarpal joints, involving anterior dislocation of the lunate. Usually this can be reduced by manipulation. Care must be taken however in not confusing a dislocation with a Colles' fracture. A fall on the hand is more likely to result in the force being transmitted through the trapezium and trapezoid to the scaphoid, which tends to fracture across its waist. Persistent pain on applying pressure in the anatomical snuffbox is characteristic of scaphoid fracture. Care should be taken when setting the fracture that the two fragments are aligned and in contact, otherwise non-union and/or vascular necrosis may result if viable blood vessels reach only one of the fragments. (The blood supply to the scaphoid is from proximal to distal.)

Movements

The movements which occur at the radiocarpal and midcarpal joints take place at the same time. The total range of flexion and extension is therefore 85° in each direction (Fig. 4.103). Flexion is limited by tension in the extensor tendons and is greatly reduced if the fingers are fully flexed. The main muscles providing flexion are the flexors carpi radialis and ulnaris. The main muscles producing extension are the extensors carpi ulnaris and radialis longus and brevis. Radiographic film shows that flexion and extension movements at the wrist occur about a single transverse axis through the head of the capitate (Fig. 4.103).

The total range of abduction and adduction which occurs at the wrist is also the sum of the ranges possible at the radiocarpal and midcarpal joints. Consequently, abduction has a range of 15° and adduction a range of 45° (Fig. 4.103). The movements occur about a single anteroposterior axis passing through the head of the capitate slightly more distal to the axis for flexion and extension (Fig. 4.103). Abduction is more limited than adduction primarily because the radial styloid process projects further distally than the ulnar styloid process. Abduction is brought about by flexor carpi radialis and extensors carpi radialis longus and brevis, while adduction is achieved by flexor and extensor carpi ulnaris.

Fig. 4.103 Movements at the wrist region.

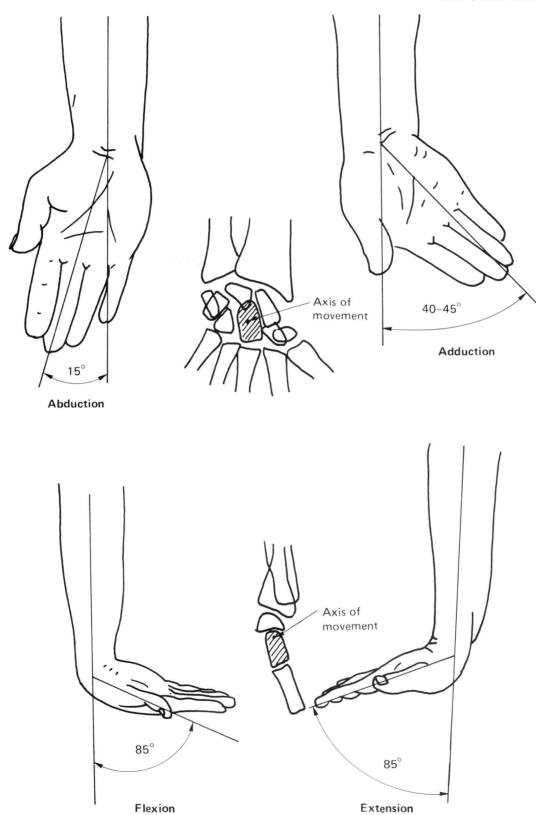

Abduction 15°

Axis of movement

40–45°

Adduction

Axis of movement

85° **Flexion**

85° **Extension**

Fig. 4.103

Biomechanics

The lines of action of the muscles of the wrist are always oblique with respect to the axes of movement (Fig. 4.104). Consequently, by using only one muscle the movement produced would not be a pure movement. For example, contraction of flexor carpi radialis would produce flexion and abduction at the wrist. To produce pure flexion the unwanted abduction movement has to be cancelled out by an adduction move; this is achieved by contracting flexor carpi ulnaris. The importance of this feature is that by combining various forces acting in different directions any desired motion can be produced within the complete range of motion of the joint.

The flexors and extensors of the carpus fix the wrist during extension or flexion of the fingers respectively. In each case they act to prevent the muscles to the fingers from losing power and efficiency, which would occur if they also acted on the radiocarpal and midcarpal joints. When powerful movements of the fingers are required, both the flexors and extensors of the wrist contract simultaneously. The importance of such actions is obvious when attempts are made to grip strongly with the finger flexors when the wrist is already flexed. Extending the wrist stretches the finger flexors so that they can now exert considerable power. Indeed, slight extension of the wrist is the position naturally adopted when the hand is used for gripping. Observe the position of your own wrist when writing or picking up a mug. Therefore, if the wrist is likely to become fixed through disease, it should be secured in a position of slight extension so that a powerful and precise grip can still be achieved.

The extrinsic finger flexors are the major force-producing muscles during exertions of the hand. Deviation of the wrist from the straight position causes these tendons to move against the adjacent walls of the carpal tunnel. When the wrist is flexed the tendons are supported by the flexor retinaculum, and when extended by the carpal bones. It has been suggested that the force between the tendons and the retinaculum compresses the median nerve and may be an important factor in carpal tunnel syndrome. Such compression has been confirmed by direct pressure measurement. As well as the median nerve being compressed, the synovial sheaths of the radial and ulnar bursae surrounding the flexor tendons are also compressed, both in flexion and extension. This may lead to their inflammation and subsequent swelling, which leads to further compression of the median nerve. Taking into account wrist size, the loading of the flexor retinaculum in flexion is 14% greater in females than in males. This may be one of the reasons why carpal tunnel syndrome is between 2 and 10 times more prevalent in women than men.

In some cases of limitation or absence of movement at the wrist, often associated with persistent pain, total wrist arthroplasty can relieve pain and improve mobility. However, the procedure should not be performed in patients who expect to make heavy use of the wrist. In such cases, permanent fixation of the wrist in slight extension usually proves to be a satisfactory procedure.

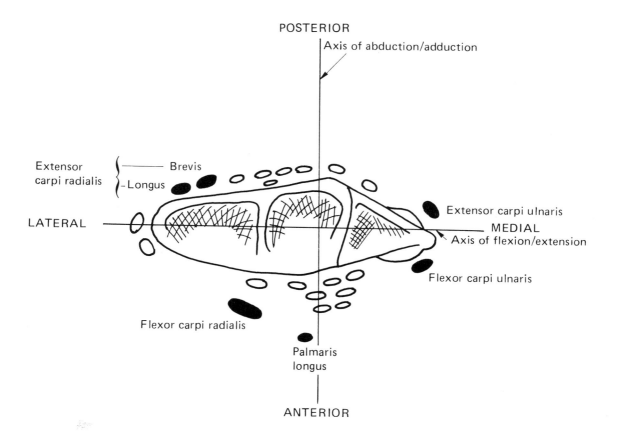

Fig. 4.104 Relationship of the tendons of muscles producing movement at the wrist to the axes of flexion/extension and abduction/adduction.

ARTICULATIONS WITHIN THE HAND

Introduction

Just as the foot has evolved as an organ of support and locomotion so the hand has developed into an instrument of manipulation endowed with fine sensory discrimination. It is often hard to accept that the hand and wrist, and the foot and ankle have similar building blocks in terms of bone and muscular constituents, patterns of innervation and blood supply. Undoubtedly, the refinements that have occurred in the hand followed its release from the burden of supporting and propelling the body. The extent to which the hand is used indicates its importance in everyday life. We use hands to grip and manipulate; they enable us to dress, eat, play instruments and games. The hand has to be capable of applying large gripping forces between the fingers and thumb while performing precision movements. However, its sensory functions must not be overlooked; it relays information regarding texture and surface contour, warns against extremes of hot and cold, and prevents collisions, especially when we cannot use sight. All of these motor and sensory functions require considerable representation in the motor and sensory cortices of the brain. As the hand developed, so the cerebral cortex enlarged to obtain maximum benefit for the new freely mobile, sensitive structure.

Much of the motor functioning of the hand is due to its ability to grip objects. Yet prehension can be observed in many animals from the pincers of the crab to the hand of the great ape. It is the concomitant development of hand and brain forming an interacting functional pair that has led to human dominance in the animal kingdom. Because of the uses to which the hand is put, it is particularly disabling when part or all of it is injured. It is especially vulnerable because it is usually unprotected. As well as diseases of the joints, lesions of the peripheral and central nervous systems and infections, accidental amputations, burns, lacerations and penetrating wounds all serve to disable the hand.

In many respects the arrangement of the bones and their intervening joints are simpler in the hand than the foot, principally because the carpus is limited to the wrist (Fig. 4.105), whereas the tarsus forms the hindfoot. The metacarpals articulate with the wrist region via the carpometacarpal joints, of which the first is different from the remainder, and with each other via the intermetacarpal joints. The head of each metacarpal articulates with a proximal phalanx at the metacarpophalangeal joint (Fig. 4.105a). Adjacent phalanges articulate via interphalangeal joints (Fig. 4.105a). However, because the thumb only has two phalanges it has only one interphalangeal joint, whereas the fingers all have three phalanges and two interphalangeal joints.

Care has to be taken when using the terms *fingers* and *digits* as confusion can often arise. There are four fingers and a thumb, or five digits. If finger and thumb is the preferred terminology then, to avoid confusion, use of an appropriate prefix is advised, that is index, middle, ring and little.

The axis of the hand runs along the middle finger (third digit), and is in line with the long axis of the forearm (Fig. 4.105b). Certain movements of the digits are made with reference to this axis. In describing movements of the thumb, remember that it is rotated through 90° with respect to the remaining digits.

However fine the movements produced in the hand, they must be controlled from a stable base, so that the origins of intrinsic muscles of the hand remain fixed by the musculature of the forearm which is brought into play. The origins of the muscles in the forearm in turn require fixation at the elbow by muscles of the arm, and these in turn require fixation at their origin at the shoulder and pectoral girdle. Even writing therefore involves use of the shoulder muscles as well as those of the fingers and thumb.

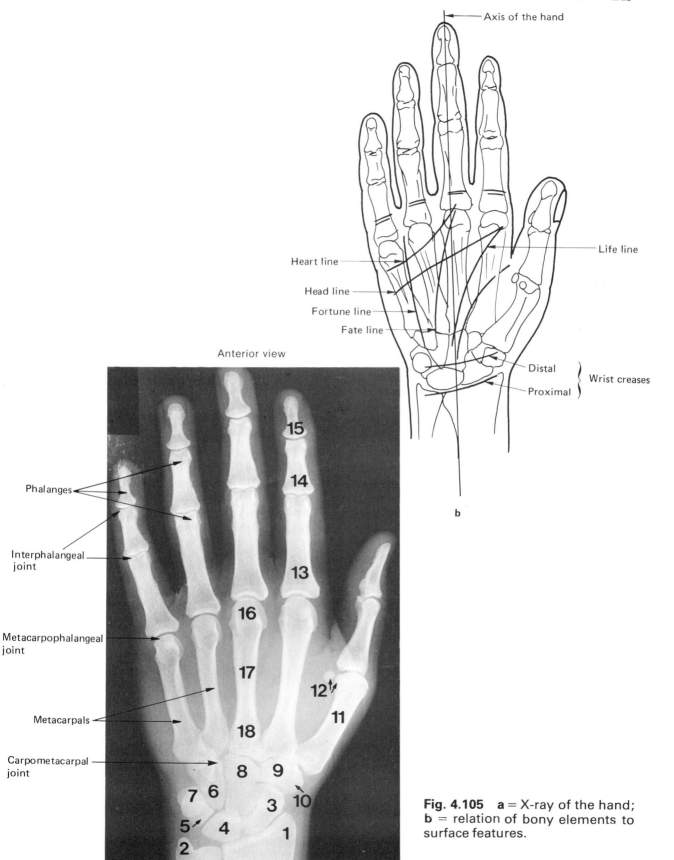

Anterior view

Phalanges

Interphalangeal
joint

Metacarpophalangeal
joint

Metacarpals

Carpometacarpal
joint

Axis of the hand

Heart line

Head line

Fortune line

Fate line

Life line

Distal

Proximal

Wrist creases

Fig. 4.105 **a** = X-ray of the hand;
b = relation of bony elements to
surface features.

Common carpometacarpal joint

The carpometacarpal joints are the sites of articulation between the hand and the wrist. The bases of the medial four metacarpals form, with the distal row of carpal bones, a common carpometacarpal joint, which has an irregular joint line. The joints are, on the whole, plane synovial joints, the only exception being the slightly bevelled joint surfaces between the hamate and the base of the fifth metacarpal.

Articular surfaces

The base of the second metacarpal fits into a recess formed by the medial side of the trapezium, the distal surface of the trapezoid and the anterolateral corner of the capitate. The third metacarpal base articulates only with the distal surface of the capitate. The base of the fourth metacarpal articulates mainly with the anterolateral distal surface of the hamate, but also just catches the anteromedial corner of the capitate. Finally, the base of the fifth metacarpal abuts against the anteromedial part of the distal surface of the hamate (Fig. 4.106, see also Fig. 4.108).

Joint capsule and synovial membrane

A fibrous capsule surrounds the common joint, in which various capsular thickenings can be identified. Synovial membrane lines the capsule and all non-articular surfaces, attaching to the articular margins. The joint cavity extends proximally between the carpal bones, and usually communicates with the midcarpal joint (see p. 232). Distally the joint space extends between the bones of the medial four metacarpals.

Ligaments

The dorsal and palmar carpometacarpal ligaments are really just thickenings of the joint capsule.

Dorsal carpometacarpal ligaments These present as a series of bands of fibres which pass from the distal row of carpal bones to the bases of the metacarpals. In general, each metacarpal receives two bands. Those to the second metacarpal come from the trapezium and trapezoid; those to the third from the trapezoid and capitate, and those to the fourth from the capitate and hamate. The base of the fifth metacarpal receives only a single band arising from the hamate.

Palmar carpometacarpal ligaments The arrangement of the fibrous bands constituting the palmar carpometacarpal ligaments is similar to those for the dorsal ligaments, except that the base of the third metacarpal receives three bands arising from the trapezoid, capitate and hamate (Fig. 4.107).

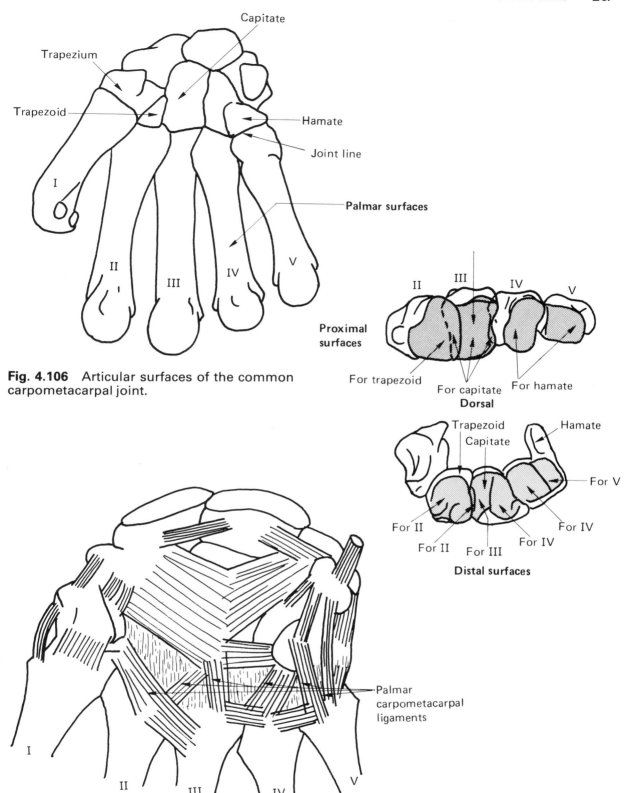

Fig. 4.106 Articular surfaces of the common carpometacarpal joint.

Proximal surfaces

For trapezoid   For capitate   For hamate
Dorsal

Trapezoid   Hamate
Capitate

For II   For V
For II   For IV
For III   For IV

Distal surfaces

Palmar carpometacarpal ligaments

Fig. 4.107 Ligaments of the common carpometacarpal joint, palmar view.

Interosseous ligament A short interosseous ligament is usually present passing from the adjacent inferior angles of the capitate and hamate to the base of the third or fourth metacarpal or both (Fig. 4.108). Occasionally, the ligament divides the joint space into medial and lateral compartments.

Blood and nerve supply

The arterial supply to the joint is from the palmar and dorsal carpal networks, while the nerve supply is by twigs from the anterior and posterior interosseous nerves and the deep and dorsal branches of the ulnar nerve.

Relations

The carpometacarpal joints of the fingers lie deep to the tendons of flexor digitorum superficialis and profundus. Most laterally on the palmar surface, the tendon of flexor carpi radialis crosses the joint to insert into the base of the second metacarpal, while the tendon of flexor carpi ulnaris passes most medially. Also overlying the joint medially are the muscles of the hypothenar eminence.

On the posterior aspect of the joint are the tendons of the extensor muscles as they pass into the hand. From lateral to medial these are: extensor carpi radialis longus and brevis, extensor pollicis longus, extensor indicis, extensor digitorum and digiti minimi, and extensor carpi ulnaris.

Stability

The joint is extremely stable, providing a firm base between the joints of the wrist and the hand.

Movements

There is little movement at the carpometacarpal joints of the fingers. The second and third metacarpals are essentially immobile, while a slight amount of gliding may occur between the fourth metacarpal and the hamate. Only the fifth metacarpal shows any appreciable movement as it glides on the hamate, and this is because of the bevelled joint surfaces. The movement that occurs is flexion, and is seen during a tight grasp and in opposition of the thumb to the little finger. In addition, there is also a slight rotation during opposition due to the action of opponens digiti minimi.

Accessory movements

A slight degree of anteroposterior gliding can be produced between the base of the metacarpal and the adjacent carpal bone if the appropriate pressure is applied.

Intermetacarpal joints

The intermetacarpal joints are plane synovial joints between the adjacent sides of the bones of the second and third, third and fourth, and fourth and fifth metacarpals. The joints are closed anteriorly, posteriorly and distally by palmar and dorsal metacarpal ligaments, and interosseous ligaments respectively, that pass transversely between the adjacent bones (Fig. 4.108). Their joint spaces are continuous with the common carpometacarpal joint distally. The blood and nerve supply to these joints is similar to that for the common carpometacarpal joint. Movements at these joints will accompany movements of the metacarpals against the distal row of carpal bones. In accessory movements, a small amount of anteroposterior gliding can be produced between any two metacarpal bases by appropriately applied pressure.

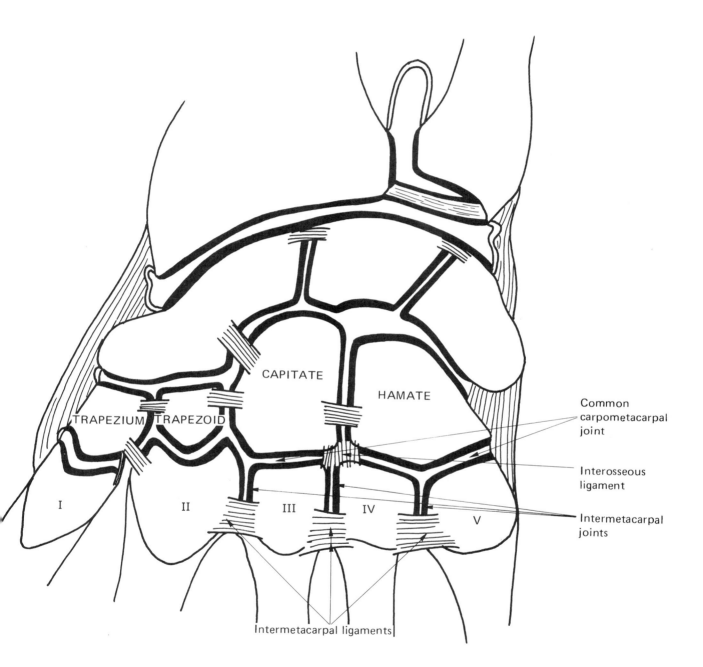

Fig. 4.108 Coronal section through wrist.

Joints of the thumb

The thumb is an extremely mobile and specialized digit, both of which are important prerequisites for the movement of opposition, and for the normal prehensile functioning of the hand.

Carpometacarpal joint

The carpometacarpal joint of the thumb, although extremely mobile, nevertheless provides a stable base from which it can effectively and efficiently work. It plays a vital role in movements of the thumb allowing movement in three dimensions.

Articular surfaces   The joint is between the trapezium and the base of the first metacarpal (Fig. 4.109a). It provides the best example in the body of a synovial saddle joint, with the two surfaces being reciprocally concavoconvex and covered with hyaline cartilage.

The articular surface of the trapezium is concave more or less in an anterposterior direction, and convex perpendicular to this. The base of the first metacarpal has reciprocal curvatures. The concavities and convexities of the surfaces do not lie strictly within the transverse and anteroposterior planes, as will become evident when the axes about which movement occurs are considered.

Joint capsule and synovial membrane   A loose but strong fibrous capsule completely encloses the joint, attaching to the articular margins of both bones (Fig. 4.109b). It is lined with synovial membrane. The capsule is thickened laterally by the radial carpometacarpal ligament, and anteriorly and posteriorly by anterior and posterior oblique ligaments.

Ligaments   The *radial carpometacarpal ligament* passes between the adjacent lateral surfaces of the trapezium and first metacarpal (Fig. 4.109b).

The *anterior and posterior oblique ligaments* pass from their respective surfaces of the trapezium to the medial side of the first metacarpal, converging as they do so (Fig. 4.109b). The posterior oblique ligament becomes taut in flexion of the thumb, while the anterior becomes taut during extension.

Blood and nerve supply   The arterial supply to the joint is by branches from the palmar and dorsal carpal networks, while its nerve supply is by twigs from the anterior and posterior interosseous nerves, root value C7, 8.

Relations   The carpometacarpal joint of the thumb lies deep to the thenar muscles, which cover its anterior aspect. Medially is the tendon of flexor pollicis longus and laterally the tendons of extensor pollicis longus and brevis.

Stability   The joint is principally stabilized and the surfaces kept in opposition by the tone of the muscle whose tendons cross the joint. The shape of the articular surfaces and the looseness of the fibrous capsule allow the joint its large degree of mobility, and hence play only a minor role in its stability.

Movements   Because the thumb is rotated approximately 90° with respect to the plane of the hand, the terminology used to describe its movements appears at first to be confusing. The terms, flexion, extension, abduction and adduction are used as if the thumb were in line with the fingers. That this is not so can be clearly seen when observing your own hand; the thumbnail faces almost laterally while the finger nails face posteriorly. Thus flexion and extension occur in a coronal plane, as does abduction and adduction of the remaining four digits; and abduction and adduction occur in a sagittal plane, as does flexion and extension of the other digits. Due to the nature of the joint surfaces and the looseness of the capsule, a certain amount of rotation is also possible at the joint. Because movements at the joint are brought about in the main by muscles whose tendons lie parallel to the metacarpal, compression across the two opposing sufaces always accompanies the movements. Consequently, the joint surfaces tend to grind against each other, instead of there being simple rolling or gliding.

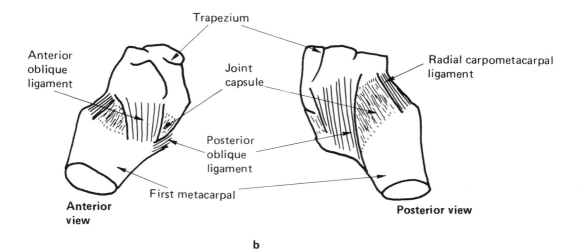

Fig. 4.109 **a** = Articular surfaces of the carpo-metacarpal joint of the thumb; **b** = ligaments of the carpometacarpal joint of the left thumb.

Flexion and extension at the joint occur in the plane of the palm of the hand, so that in flexion the thumb moves medially and in extension it moves laterally (Fig. 4.110). The axis about which the movement occurs passes through the base of the metacarpal at the centres of curvature of the concave trapezium and the convex metacarpal. It does not lie exactly in an anteroposterior plane but is set slightly obliquely from posterior, lateral and proximal to anterior, medial and distal.

The total range of flexion and extension is between 40° and 50°. Towards the end of full flexion, tension developed in the posterior oblique ligament results in a medial rotation of the metacarpal causing the palmar surface of the thumb to face posteriorly. Conversely, towards the end of full extension, lateral rotation of the metacarpal occurs because of tension developed in the anterior oblique ligament. Flexion at the joint occurs as a secondary movement of flexor pollicis longus and brevis acting on the interphalangeal and metacarpophalangeal joints respectively. Similarly extension is due to the actions of extensor pollicis longus and brevis as they act on the interphalangeal and metacarpophalangeal joints respectively.

Abduction and adduction occur at right angles to the palm so that in abduction the thumb is carried forwards away from the palm and in adduction it is moved back towards the palm (Fig. 4.110). The axis about which movement occurs is perpendicular to the axis of flexion and extension. It passes through the trapezium at the centres of curvature of the concave metacarpal and convex trapezium, and runs slightly obliquely from medial, posterior and distal to lateral, anterior and proximal.

The range of abduction and adduction is about 80°, with adduction being brought about by adductor pollicis pulling on the proximal phalanx. Abduction is brought about by the direct action of abductor pollicis longus on the joint, and by the secondary action of abductor pollicis brevis acting on the metacarpophalangeal joint.

Opposition is described as a movement in which the distal pad of the thumb is brought against the distal pad of any of the remaining four digits (Fig. 4.110). It is an essential movement of the hand, and its loss markedly reduces the functional capacity of the hand. The movement is complex involving flexion, abduction and rotation followed by adduction at the carpometacarpal joint, as well as movements at other joints of the thumb.

Essentially, opposition consists of three elementary movements. Initially, flexion and abduction of the thumb occur simultaneously at the carpometacarpal joint due to the action of flexors pollicis longus and brevis and abductor pollicis longus. This produces a certain amount of passive axial rotation of the metacarpal, possible because of the looseness of the joint capsule—the rotation is directed medially due to the posterior oblique ligament becoming taut. At some point during this movement, opponens pollicis contracts to produce an active rotation of the metacarpal—this is the second elementary movement. Finally, adduction occurs at the carpometacarpal joint, produced by adductor pollicis, to bring the metacarpal back towards the plane of the palm of the hand.

Movements of the thumb at the metacarpophalangeal joint contribute significantly to the overall movement of opposition. At the same time as the carpometacarpal joint is being flexed and abducted, so is the metacarpophalangeal joint. Again the simultaneous movements of flexion and abduction of the proximal phalanx bring about a degree of axial rotation at this joint. Consequently, the pad of the thumb comes to face posteromedially.

Returning the thumb to the anatomical position has no specific name. It is brought about mainly by the contraction of the extensor muscles of the thumb. Perhaps it should therefore be referred to as exposition.

Fig. 4.110 Movements of the thumb at the carpometacarpal joint.

Metacarpophalangeal joint

The metacarpophalangeal joint of the thumb is of similar design to those of the fingers, being a synovial condyloid joint between the head of the first metacarpal and the base of the proximal phalanx.

Articular surfaces The articulation is between the rounded head of the metacarpal and the shallow, oval concavity of the base of the proximal phalanx (Fig. 4.111). Both surfaces are covered with hyaline cartilage. The biconvex metacarpal head is wider anteriorly than posteriorly, indeed the articular surface does not extend very far on its posterior surface. In addition, the curvature of the metacarpal head is greater in the transverse plane than in the anteroposterior plane. The base of the proximal phalanx has a much smaller articular area than the metacarpal head. It is increased anteriorly however, by the presence of a fibrocartilaginous plate known as the palmar ligament (Fig. 4.111), which is attached to the anterior surface of the base of the phalanx by a small fibrous band which functions like a hinge.

Joint capsule and synovial membrane A loose fibrous capsule surrounds the joint, being attached closer to the articular margins posteriorly than anteriorly (Fig. 4.111). It is strengthened at the sides by collateral ligaments. Anteriorly the capsule is mainly replaced by the palmar ligament, which has a weak attachment to the neck of the metacarpal. Posteriorly the capsule is strengthened by or may be entirely replaced by the expansion of extensor pollicis longus.

Synovial membrane lines all non-articular surfaces of the joint and presents anterior and posterior recesses when the joint is extended.

Ligaments The *palmar ligament* is a dense fibrocartilaginous pad that increases the phalangeal articular surface anteriorly. It is firmly attached to the anterior surface of the base of the proximal phalanx, and loosely attached to the anterior aspect of the neck of the metacarpal (Fig. 4.111). The collateral ligaments of the joint blend with the sides of the palmar ligament. The ligament contains two small sesamoid bones which are attached to the phalanx and the metacarpal by straight and cruciate fibres. It is grooved on its anterior aspect by the tendon of flexor pollicis longus.

The strong *collateral ligaments* on either side of the joint are attached proximally to the tubercle and adjacent depression on the side of the metacarpal head, and pass to the palmar aspect of the side of the base of the proximal phalanx (Fig. 4.111). Although cord-like in appearance, they do fan out slightly from proximal to distal gaining attachment to the margins of the palmar ligament. The collateral ligaments are relatively lax during extension, becoming increasingly taut with flexion of the joint.

Blood and nerve supply The arterial supply to the joint is by branches from the princeps pollicis artery, while its nerve supply is by twigs from the median nerve, root value C7.

Stability The metacarpophalangeal joint of the thumb is stabilized by the collateral ligaments, as well as the tendons of flexor and extensor pollicis longus as they pass in front of and behind the joint to their insertion on the distal phalanx. Flexor and extensor pollicis brevis and abductor pollicis brevis also cross the joint to insert into the base of the proximal phalanx.

Fig. 4.111 Articular surfaces and ligaments of the metacarpophalangeal joint of the thumb.

Movements Being a condyloid joint, the metacarpophalangeal joint has, according to its shape, two degrees of freedom of movement, these being flexion and extension, abduction and adduction. However, as in the carpometacarpal joint, there is a third movement of axial rotation which occurs passively and is allowed because of a small degree of elasticity of the associated ligaments.

Flexion and extension at the metacarpophalangeal joint occurs about a single, fixed axis which passes transversely through the metacarpal at approximately nine-tenths of its midline length from its base. In passing from flexion to extension, the area of contact shifts from the palmar end of the phalangeal base to its distal end.

Flexion has a range of 45°, while extension is zero under normal circumstances, both actively and passively (Fig. 4.112). It is in full extension that the anterior part of the metacarpal head articulates with the palmar ligament. As flexion proceeds, the palmar ligament gradually loses contact with the metacarpal head. At the same time the synovial recesses progressively become unpleated.

Flexion at the joint is brought about primarily by flexor pollicis brevis, aided by flexor pollicis longus. Similarly, extension from the flexed position is due primarily to extensor pollicis brevis, with some help from extensor pollicis longus.

Abduction and adduction at the joint is limited due to the width of the metacarpal head (Fig. 4.112). The 15° of abduction and negligible adduction occur about an antero-posterior axis through the head of the metacarpal. As well as the bony limitations to the movements, the collateral ligaments also become taut adding to the restriction.

Abduction is caused by contraction of abductor pollicis brevis. Although adductor pollicis attaches to the base of the proximal phalanx, because of the severe limitation of adduction at the metacarpophalangeal joint, its action is seen principally at the carpometacarpal joint.

A certain amount of *axial rotation* is possible at the metacarpophalangeal joint of the thumb, which is of importance during opposition (Fig. 4.112). The movement can be produced actively by the co-contraction of flexor and abductor pollicis brevis, or passively as when pressing the thumb against the index finger. The actively produced rotation is always medially directed, while that produced passively can be in either direction depending which side of the thumb comes into contact with the finger.

Movements at the joint during opposition include a secondary flexion at the metacarpophalangeal joint following that at the carpometacarpal joint during opposition. At the same time there is abduction at the joint, which continues after the metacarpal becomes adducted. The degree of abduction is largest when contact is made with the pad of the little finger. The flexion and abduction movements at the metacarpophalangeal joint cause, initially, an active axial rotation at the joint. After contact has been made the degree of rotation may be augmented passively.

Fig. 4.112 Movements at the metacarpophalangeal joints of the thumb.

Interphalangeal joint

Because the thumb only contains two phalanges, there is only one interphalangeal joint. Like those of the fingers, however, it is a synovial hinge joint permitting movement in one direction only.

Articular surfaces   The articulation is between the pulley-shaped head of the proximal phalanx and the base of the distal phalanx which has a median ridge separating two shallow facets (Fig. 4.113a). As in the metacarpophalangeal joint, a fibrocartilaginous plate (palmar ligament) is attached to the anterior margin of the base of the distal phalanx.

Joint capsule and synovial membrane   A fibrous capsule completely surrounds the joint, being replaced by the palmar ligament anteriorly and strengthened at the sides by the collateral ligaments (Fig. 4.113a).

Ligaments   The *collateral ligaments* are attached to the sides of the head of the proximal phalanx, and pass to the palmar aspect of the base of the distal phalanx. They blend with the lateral margins of the palmar ligament.

As in the metacarpophalangeal joint, the *palmar ligament* is a fibrocartilaginous plate attached to the anterior margin of the base of the distal phalanx. It is loosely attached to the front of the neck of the proximal phalanx via the joint capsule.

Blood and nerve supply   The blood and nerve supply is the same as that for the metacarpophalangeal joint.

Movements   Being a hinge joint supported by strong collateral ligaments, movement is only allowed in one direction (Fig. 4.113b). *Flexion and extension* occur about a transverse axis passing approximately through the neck of the proximal phalanx. The range of flexion is in excess of 90°, while extension is normally no more than 10°. However, passive hyperextension may be marked in some individuals who apply large forces using the thumb, for example butchers.

Accessory movements of joints of the thumb

Carpometacarpal joint   Gripping the trapezium between the thumb and the index finger of one hand, and the base of the first metacarpal with the other, the metacarpal base can be moved in both anteroposterior and mediolateral directions.

Metacarpophalangeal and interphalangeal joints   If the principle of stabilizing the proximal bone and moving the distal one is employed, then anteroposterior gliding movements can be demonstrated at both the metacarpophalangeal and interphalangeal joints. Once again, best results are obtained when each bone is held firmly between the thumb and index finger. A good range of rotation is also possible at the metacarpophalangeal joint.

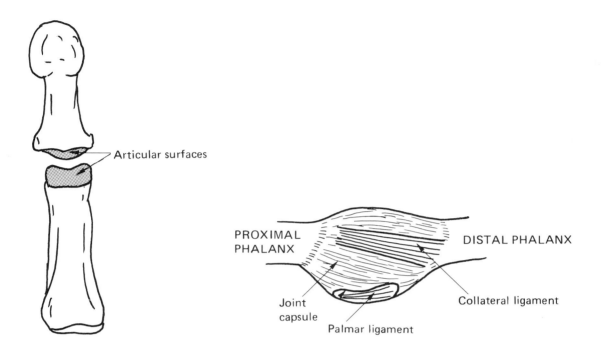

Fig. 4.113   **a** = The articular surfaces and ligaments of the interphalangeal joint of the thumb; **b** = the movements of which it is capable.

Joints of the fingers

In general, the fingers act in one plane to close around an object and so form a pincer action with the opposed thumb. The size of the object being grasped will determine whether, and to what extent, two dimensional movement at the metacarpophalangeal joints occurs.

The articulation of the second to fifth metacarpals with the distal row of carpal bones has already been considered (p. 246), consequently, this section considers the metacarpophalangeal joints and the two interphalangeal joints of each finger.

Metacarpophalangeal joint

The metacarpophalangeal joint of the fingers is structurally and functionally similar to that of the thumb.

Articular surfaces   The articular surface of the metacarpal head is biconvex, with unequal curvatures transversely and anteroposteriorly. It is broader anteriorly than posteriorly, with the hyaline cartilage extending further proximally on its anterior aspect (Fig. 4.114a).

The base of the proximal phalanx is biconcave, but has a smaller articular surface than the metacarpal head (Fig. 4.114a). The surface area is increased by the presence of the palmar ligament attached to the anterior margin of the articular surface.

Joint capsule and synovial membrane   The fibrous capsule surrounding the joint is loose, and is attached closer to the articular margins on the posterior aspects of the bone than anteriorly. The capsule is strengthened on each side by collateral ligaments and replaced anteriorly by the palmar ligament. Posteriorly the extensor expansion of the long extensor tendon replaces the capsule, blending at the sides with the collateral ligaments. The posterior part of the capsule also receives fibres from the distal slips of the palmar aponeurosis (Fig. 4.114a).

The capsule is lined by synovial membrane, which also covers all non-articular surfaces. Synovial-lined anterior and posterior recesses of the capsule permit freedom of movement particularly during flexion.

Ligaments   In addition to the collateral and palmar ligaments associated with each metacarpophalangeal joint, the heads of the second to fifth metacarpals are united by the deep transverse metacarpal ligaments.

The *collateral ligaments* pass from the tubercle and adjacent depression on the side of the head of the metacarpal to the palmar aspect of the side of the base of the proximal phalanx (Fig. 4.114a). They are strong and tend to fan out in passing from metacarpal to phalanx. Anteriorly they blend with the palmar ligament, while posteriorly the extensor expansion joins them.

The *palmar ligament* is a dense fibrocartilaginous plate firmly attached to the anterior margin of the base of the proximal phalanx (Fig.4.114a). Proximally it is loosely attached to the neck of the metacarpal by the joint capsule. On each side it receives some fibres from the collateral ligaments. The palmar ligament acts as a mobile articular surface facilitating flexion at the joint.

The *deep transverse metacarpal ligaments* are a series of short ligaments connecting the palmar ligaments of the four metacarpophalangeal joints of the fingers (Fig. 4.114b). They are continuous with the palmar interosseous fascia and blend with the fibrous flexor tendons. Consequently, they act to bind the heads of the four medial metacarpals together, and so limit their movement apart. (There is no ligament between the first and second metacarpal, hence the independence and freedom of movement of the thumb.) The deep transverse metacarpal ligaments also receive fibres from the distal slips of the palmar aponeurosis, as well as part of the extensor expansion as it passes forwards on each side of the head of the metacarpal.

Passing behind the deep transverse metacarpal ligaments are the tendons of both the dorsal and palmar interossi, while in front of them pass the tendons of the lumbricals.

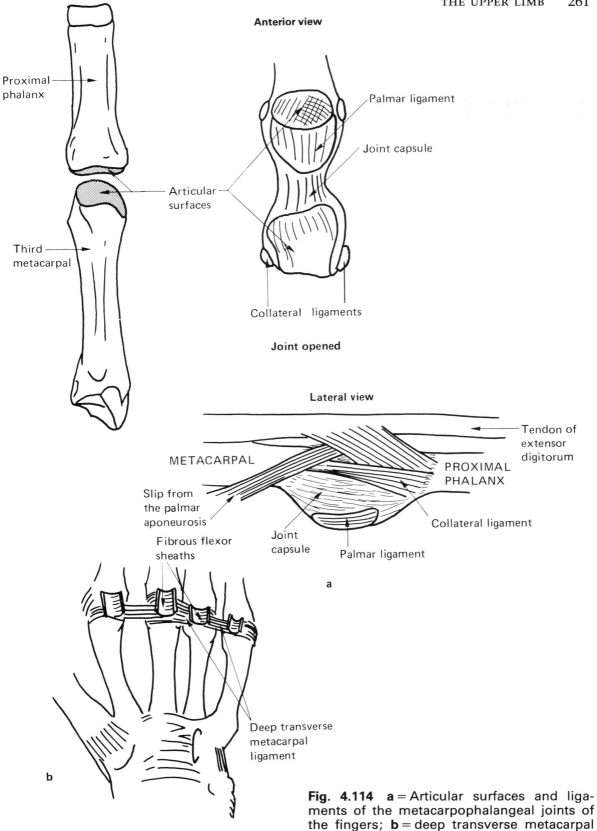

Anterior view

Proximal phalanx

Palmar ligament

Joint capsule

Articular surfaces

Third metacarpal

Collateral ligaments

Joint opened

Lateral view

Tendon of extensor digitorum

METACARPAL

PROXIMAL PHALANX

Slip from the palmar aponeurosis

Collateral ligament

Fibrous flexor sheaths

Joint capsule

Palmar ligament

a

Deep transverse metacarpal ligament

b

Fig. 4.114 **a** = Articular surfaces and ligaments of the metacarpophalangeal joints of the fingers; **b** = deep transverse metacarpal ligament.

Blood and nerve supply   The arterial supply to the joints is by branches from the adjacent digital arteries, while the nerve supply is by twigs from the median, and possibly the radial nerve for the index and middle finger, and the ulnar nerve for the ring and little fingers. Root value of the nerve supply is C7.

Relations   On the posterior aspect of the joint is the expansion of the long extensor tendon (Fig. 4.115a), part of which passes around the sides of the metacarpal head blending with the deep transverse metacarpal ligament. The tendon of the lumbrical muscles passes lateral to the joint (Fig. 4.115a, c), anterior to the deep transverse metacarpal ligament, before attaching to the base of the proximal phalanx and the extensor expansion. Exactly which interosseous tendons pass medial and lateral to each metacarpophalangeal joint depends on which finger is being considered:

1. for the *index finger*, the first dorsal interosseous is lateral and the first palmar interosseous is medial;
2. for the *middle finger*, the second and third dorsal interossei are lateral and medial respectively;

3. for the *ring finger*, the second palmar interosseous is lateral and the fourth dorsal interosseous is medial (Fig. 4.115a);
4. for the *little finger*, the third palmar interosseous is lateral and the tendon of abductor digiti minimi is medial.

Immediately anterior to the joint is the tendon of flexor digitorum profundus, and anterior to that, the tendon of flexor digitorum superficialis, which at the level of the joint splits into two (Fig. 4.115b). Flexor digiti minimi brevis is situated on the anterolateral aspect of the joint of the little finger.

Digital branches from the dorsal and palmar metacarpal arteries, together with digital branches from the median, ulnar and radial nerves, depending on the finger in question, pass either side of the metacarpophalangeal joint.

Stability   The metacarpophalangeal joint is stabilized primarily by the long flexor and extensor tendons crossing the joint, as well as by the lumbricals and interossei. Dislocations of the joint do occur, however they can often be reduced by manipulation.

Fig. 4.115   Relations of the metacarpophalangeal joint of the left ring finger: **a** = posterior; **b** = anterior; **c** = lateral.

a

b

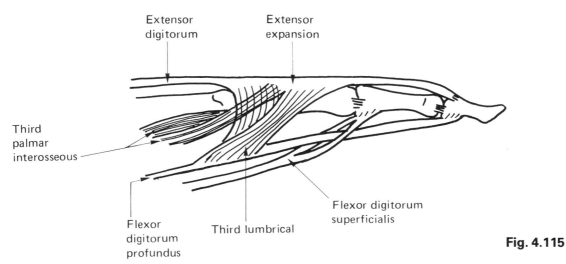

c

Fig. 4.115

Movements   Active movement at the metacarpophalangeal joint takes place about two axes, each of which is located in the metacarpal head approximately nine-tenths of the midline length of the metacarpal from its base. These are the movements of flexion and extension, and abduction and adduction. To these can be added axial rotation, which occurs passively.

Flexion and extension occurs about a transverse axis through the head of the metacarpal (Fig. 4.116). The geometry of the articular surfaces dictates that the intersection of the longitudinal axes of the proximal phalanx and the metacarpal moves distally during flexion. In extension the anterior surface of the metacarpal head articulates with the palmar ligament (Fig. 4.116a). During flexion the ligament moves past the head, turning upon itself to glide along the palmar surface of the shaft of the metacarpal (Fig. 4.116a). As this is occurring, the capsule and its synovial lining is being unfolded so as not to prematurely limit movement. The range of flexion is slightly less than 90° for the index finger, but progressively increases towards the little finger. Flexion of one joint in isolation is limited by tension developed in the deep transverse metacarpal ligaments; flexion is ultimately resisted by tension in the collateral ligaments. The range of active extension is variable between subjects but may reach 50°. Passive extension may reach as much as 90° in individuals with lax ligaments. A study* of over 400 hands gave the following total ranges of active/passive flexion and extension for each of the fingers: index, 148°/155°; middle, 145°/151°; ring, 149°/159° and little, 152°/172°.

Flexion at the metacarpophalangeal joint is brought about primarily by the lumbrical muscles, aided by the tendons of flexor digitorum profundus and superficialis, as well as the interossei. In the little finger, flexor and abductor digiti minimi also contribute to the movement. Extension is achieved at all of the metacarpophalangeal joints by extensor digitorum, with the addition of extensor indicis in the index finger and extensor digiti minimi in the little finger.

Abduction and adduction at the joint occurs about an anteroposterior axis through the metacarpal head; the movement occurs away from or towards the middle finger respectively (Fig. 4.116a). The movement is easier and has a greater range when the finger is extended, being as much as 30° in each direction (Fig. 4.116b). Tension developed in the collateral ligaments in flexion of the joint severely limits the side-to-side movement, so much so that at 90° flexion the total range may be no more than 10°. The total range of active/passive abduction and adduction movements, with the fingers in a neutral position, has been reported* as follows: index, 50°/62°; middle, 40°/53°; ring, 38°/55° and little, 57°/68°.

Abduction at the joint is brought about by the dorsal interossei for the index, middle and ring fingers, and by abductor digiti minimi for the little finger. At the index and middle fingers, the movement may be assisted by the first and second lumbricals respectively via their attachment to the extensor hood. If the joint is hyperextended, then extensor digitorum will also aid abduction. Adduction towards the middle finger is achieved by the palmar interossei and can be assisted by the third and fourth lumbricals for the ring and little fingers. If the joint is being flexed simultaneously, then adduction is assisted by flexor digitorum superficialis and profundus.

Active *rotation* is not possible except in the little finger, however, because of the shape of the joint surfaces and the relative laxity of the associated ligaments, a certain degree of passive rotation can occur (Fig. 4.116a) having a maximum range of 60°. In the index finger, the range of medial rotation is of the order of 45°, while lateral rotation is negligible. Medial and lateral rotation in the remaining fingers have approximately equal ranges of movement.

Fig. 4.116   a = movements at the metacarpophalangeal joints; **b** = the influence of flexion/extension on abduction and adduction at the joint (adapted from Youm Y., Gillespie T. E., Flatt A. E., Sprague B. L. (1978). Kinematic investigation of normal MCP joint. *Journal of Biomechanics*, **11**, 109–18).

*Youm Y., Gillespie T. E., Flatt A. E., Spragne B. L. (1978). Kinematic investigation of normal MCP Joint. *Journal of Biomechanics*, **11**, 109–18.

Flexion

Extension

Metacarpal

Adduction

Abduction

Passive
rotation

a

Abduction/adduction (°)

50

40

30

20

10

90° 60° 30° 0° 30°

Flexion   Extension

b

Fig. 4.116

Interphalangeal joints

Because each finger consists of three phalanges it contains two interphalangeal joints: a proximal joint between the head of the proximal and base of the middle phalanx, and a distal joint between the head of the middle and base of the distal phalanx. All of the joints are hinge joints permitting flexion and extension only, with the articular surfaces covered by hyaline cartilage.

Articular surfaces The articulation is between the pulley-shaped head of the phalanx and two shallow facets separated by a ridge on the base of the immediately distal phalanx (Fig. 4.117). The groove and ridge on the head and base respectively do not lie exactly in an anteroposterior direction, except for the joints of the index finger. In all other joints they run slightly obliquely from posterolateral to anteromedial, with the obliquity increasing from the middle to the little finger.

The articular surface of the phalangeal head is greater than that on the adjacent base, extending further distally on its anterior aspect. The head is also wider anteriorly than posteriorly. A fibrocartilaginous plate, the palmar ligament, similar to that associated with the metacarpophalangeal joint, acts as a mobile articular surface.

Joint capsule and synovial membrane A loose fibrous capsule surrounds the joint, being strengthened at the sides by collateral ligaments, and partly replaced anteriorly and posteriorly by the palmar ligament and extensor expansion respectively. Synovial membrane lines all non-articular surfaces, including the anterior and posterior recesses of the capsule.

Ligaments The *collateral ligaments* attach to the sides of the head of the most proximal phalanx and to the sides of the base of the adjacent more distal phalanx, blending with the margins of the palmar ligament (Fig. 4.117). They tend to be not so obliquely orientated as the collateral ligaments of the metacarpophalangeal joints. The ligaments become increasingly tense with flexion at the joint.

The *palmar ligament* is a mobile fibrocartilaginous plate attached to the anterior margin of the base of the adjacent phalanx. It is loosely attached to the front of the neck of the immediately preceding phalanx by the joint capsule (Fig. 4.117). Also attached to the palmar ligament is the fibrous flexor sheath of the digit.

Blood and nerve supply The arterial supply to the joints is by branches from the digital arteries running along the sides of each finger. Anteriorly the digital arteries arise from the palmar metacarpal arteries, while posteriorly they come from the dorsal metacarpal arteries. Venous drainage is by similarly named vessels, eventually draining into the venae commitantes associated with the radial and ulnar arteries. Posteriorly some venous drainage will pass to the dorsal venous plexus on the dorsum of the hand, and thence into the basilic and cephalic veins. Lymphatic drainage from the joints is by vessels which follow the arteries, with the majority of lymph draining to the lateral group of axillary nodes, although some may pass to cubital or brachial nodes.

The nerve supply to the joint is by twigs from adjacent digital nerves, and have a root value of C7. For the index, middle and lateral side of the ring fingers, the digital nerves are branches of the median nerve anteriorly and the radial nerve posteriorly. For the medial side of the ring and the little fingers the digital nerves all arise from the ulnar nerve.

Relations On the anterior aspect of the proximal interphalangeal joint, enclosed within the fibrous flexor sheath, are the tendons of the flexor digitorum superficialis and profundus (Fig. 4.118), only the tendon of profundus lies in front of the distal interphalangeal joint (Fig. 4.118). The fibrous flexor sheaths are relatively thin and loose over the interphalangeal joints, with a cruciate arrangement of fibres as they pass from the side of one phalanx to the opposite side of the preceding phalanx (Fig. 4.118). Immediately beyond the distal interphalangeal joint, the flexor sheath attaches to the palmar surface of the distal phalanx.

Posterior to the proximal interphalangeal joint is the central slip of the extensor expansion. On the back of the middle phalanx the

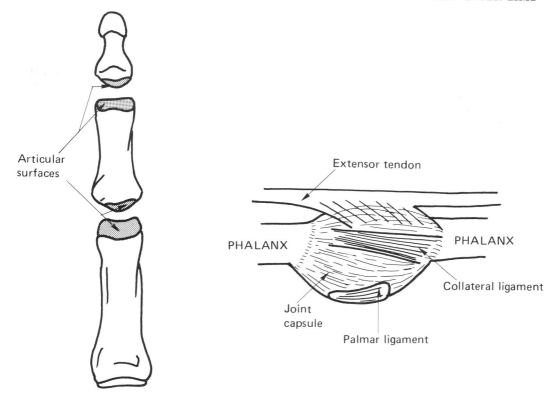

Fig. 4.117 Articular surfaces and ligaments of the interphalangeal joints.

Fig. 4.118 Relations of interphalangeal joints.

two collateral slips of the expansion come together, so that a single tendon crosses the posterior aspect of the distal interphalangeal joint.

Stability   The interphalangeal joints are fairly stable because of the presence of the long flexor and extensor tendons. Nevertheless dislocations can and do occur, they can often be reduced by manipulation.

Movements   Because of the nature of the joint surfaces, the only active movements possible at the interphalangeal joints are flexion and extension (Fig. 4.119a). However, a small degree of passive side-to-side movement is possible, particularly at the distal interphalangeal joint.

Flexion and extension take place about a transverse axis, which for the middle, ring and little fingers runs with increasing obliquity from lateral and distal to medial and proximal (Fig. 4.119b). The axis is approximately perpendicular to the groove on the phalangeal head, so that when the medial fingers are flexed at the interphalangeal joints the movement does not occur in a sagittal plane, but enables these fingers to oppose the thumb more easily. Flexion of the index finger, however, occurs in a sagittal plane.

The range of flexion at the proximal interphalangeal joint is greater than 90° for all fingers, and gradually increases towards the little finger so that this is capable of 135° of flexion. At the distal interphalangeal joint, the range of flexion for the little finger is 90°, and gradually decreases towards the index finger. Active extension at the interphalangeal joints is minimal, being no more than 5° at the distal and only 1° or 2° at the proximal joints. Passive extension may be considerably greater.

Flexion at the proximal interphalangeal joint is primarily due to the action of flexor digitorum superficialis, assisted by flexor digitorum profundus. Only profundus flexes the distal interphalangeal joint. Extension of the interphalangeal joints is produced by contraction of the lumbricals and interossei via their attachments to the extensor expansions. They are assisted in each finger by extensor digitorum, and in the index and little fingers by extensors indicis and digiti minimi respectively.

Simultaneous flexion at one interphalangeal joint and extension at the other is produced by a controlled balance between the activity of the flexor and extensor muscles. Flexion of the wrist facilitates extension of the fingers and opening the fist. The functional position of the wrist (that is in extension) puts the finger flexors beyond their natural length and so enables greater tension to be developed in them facilitating a powerful grip. Similarly, flexing the interphalangeal joints places the extensors of the wrist under increased tension. In stabilizing the wrist, a certain amount of flexor strength and extensor power is sacrificed. Only 70% of the strength of the finger flexors is available from flexion of the interphalangeal joints. Weakness of the wrist extensors, by failing to maintain the position of function, greatly interferes with the strength of the finger flexors and the ability to carry out a forceful closure of the fist.

Accessory movements of the joints of the fingers

Similar accessory movements of anteroposterior *gliding and rotation* are possible at each of the metacarpophalangeal and interphalangeal joints of all four fingers. With the proximal component stabilized between the thumb and index finger, the more distal segment can be made to execute the accessory movements.

Flexion

Extension

Flexion

a

Extension

Fig. 4.119 **a** = Flexion and extension of the interphalangeal joints with and without flexion at the metacarpophalangeal joints; **b** = the obliquity of the joint axes causes the fingers to converge toward the lateral side of the wrist in flexion.

b

Biomechanics

The arrangement of bones, tendons and ligaments within the hand is such that in the so-called position of rest the palm is hollowed, the fingers are flexed and the thumb is slightly opposed (Fig. 4.120a). The flexion of the fingers increases progressively from the index to the little. Underlying the hollowing of the palm and facilitating gripping movements, the bony skeleton can be seen to form a series of arches running in three different directions (Fig. 4.120b). Transversely is the carpal arch maintained by the flexor retinaculum. It continues distally as far as the heads of the metacarpals as the metacarpal arch. The long axis of this 'gutter' crosses the lunate, capitate and third metacarpal. The concavity of this arch at the level of the metacarpal heads is much shallower, and more widespread than at the level of the carpal bones. The shallowness of the arch at the metacarpal heads can be readily seen and appreciated in the relaxed hand. Running longitudinally are the carpometacarpophalangeal arches, which open out from the wrist and are formed for each digit by the corresponding metacarpal and phalanges. These arches are concave on their palmar surface, with the keystone of each being at the level of the metacarpophalangeal joint. Consequently, muscular imbalance at this point interferes with the concavity of the arch. Of these longitudinal arches, the two most important are those of the middle and index fingers. During opposition of the thumb with the fingers, oblique arches are formed running from the thumb into the finger being opposed. The most important oblique arch is that linking the thumb and index finger because of its use in holding objects, such as a pen.

When the palm is hollowed, an oblique gutter, the palmar gutter, runs across the various oblique arches formed with the thumb from the base of the hypothenar eminence, where the pisiform can be palpated, to the head of the second metacarpal. It corresponds approximately to the palmar crease ('life line'), and is the direction taken by the handle of a tool when fully grasped by the hand.

In use, the hand does not always utilize the various arches. When carrying large and heavy flat objects the hand spreads out and becomes flattened, so that contact with the object is made at the thenar and hypothenar eminences, the metacarpal heads and the anterior surfaces of the phalanges. This provides a large area of contact and support, with movement of the object limited by friction between it and the skin.

The digits may be used individually as circumstances dictate. Being functionally separate from the remaining digits, the thumb can be moved and used independently. Although not completely separate, the index finger has a considerable degree of freedom, for example it can be used independently in pointing and gesturing. The relative freedom of the index finger is important in grasping. The remaining fingers cannot be used independently throughout their full range of movement principally because of the linkage between the tendons of extensor digitorum on their dorsal surfaces.

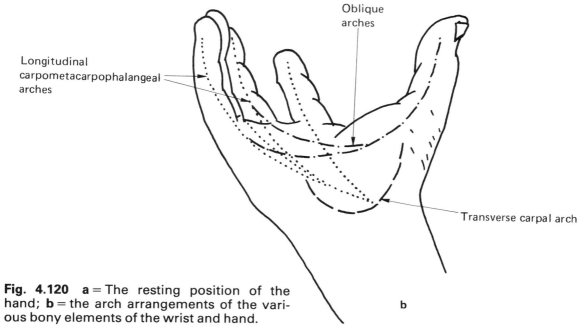

Fig. 4.120 **a** = The resting position of the hand; **b** = the arch arrangements of the various bony elements of the wrist and hand.

Prehension (grip) The way in which the hand is used depends upon several factors, not least of which are the size, shape and weight of the object as well as the use to which it is being put. In general terms, the grip can be classified as being either a 'precision grip' or a 'power grip'. The thumb and the fingers combine in various ways to produce the former, while the hand becomes involved in the latter.

In *precision grips* the object is usually small, and sometimes fragile. It is seized between the pads of the digits, which spread around the object conforming to its shape (Fig. 4.121a). The action involves rotation at the carpometacarpal joint of the thumb, and at the metacarpophalangeal joints of the thumb and finger(s) involved. The muscles involved in precision grips are all the small muscles of the hand, as well as the flexors digitorum profundus and superficialis, and pollicis longus. Within this class of grip, several types can be identified:

1. terminal opposition in which the tips of the pads or sometimes the edges of the nails are used to pick up fine objects, such as a pin—this is the finest and most precise of all precision grips, and consequently is the most easily upset in traumas of the hand;

2. subterminal opposition in which the palmar surfaces of the thumb and index (or other) finger come into contact as when holding a pen—it is the most common form of precision grip, with its efficiency being tested by attempting to pull a sheet of paper from between the thumb and index finger;

3. subtermino-lateral opposition in which the pad of the thumb presses against the side of any of the phalanges of the finger—the grip is less fine but strong and can replace (1) and (2) above when the distal phalanx of the index finger has been lost;

4. adduction between two fingers, usually the index and the middle, with the thumb playing no part in the grip— the grip is weak and generally has little precision, however, with loss of the thumb it can be considerably developed in terms of power.

Fig. 4.121   **a** = Precision grip; **b** = power grip.

In *power grips*, where considerable force may be required, the hand comes into action (see Fig. 4.121b). The long flexors and extensors work strongly partly to fix the wrist and partly to grip the object. Two modes of power grip can be identified:

1. a palmar grip, which is the most powerful, in which the whole hand wraps itself around the object whose long axis lies along the palmar gutter—with the thumb acting as a buttress the fingers close around the object: the volume of the object determines the strength of the grip, which is maximal when the thumb can still touch the index finger, as a result the handles of many tools are sculptured to accommodate the fingers;
2. hook grip in which the object is held firmly between the palm and the flexed fingers, the thumb playing no part at all—the grip is relatively secure but in one direction only, towards the fingers; consequently it is the grip employed in carrying bags and suitcases (Fig. 4.122).

One activity in which both types of grip can be seen, albeit in different hands, is when hammering in a nail. The nail is held precisely between the thumb and index finger, while the hammer is firmly held using a palmar grip.

Joint forces Because of the size and weight of many objects that are carried or manipulated, the forces transmitted across various joints within the hand and digits can reach considerable magnitudes. An indication of the magnitudes of these forces has been required in order to refine finger prostheses. Studies have suggested that the joint reactions at the carpometacarpal, metacarpophalangeal, proximal and distal interphalangeal joints are on average twice, three times, ten times and six times the applied load respectively. The magnitude and direction of action of these forces at various joints have led to predictions of clinical deformities and joint damage.

Fig. 4.122 Hook grip.

Pathology Due to the delicate balance between the soft tissues of the hand, it is highly susceptible to trauma and disability. Well over half of all injuries leading to disability involve the hand and fingers. The various bones may be fractured, or joints dislocated, but the most common injuries are accidental amputation of all or part of the hand and finger(s), burns, tendon lacerations, penetrating wounds and nerve injuries.

The radial nerve may be damaged in the spiral (radial) groove of the humerus thus causing paralysis of all of the extensor muscles of the forearm resulting in 'wrist drop' and an inability to extend the hand or digits (Fig. 4.123a). The interphalangeal joints can still be extended via the lumbricals and interossei. There will also be sensory loss over the cutaneous distribution of the nerve.

Injury to the median nerve can occur just proximal to the wrist or as it passes through the carpal tunnel. The muscles of the thenar eminence become paralysed with a consequent wasting of the area (Fig. 4.123b). Opposition of the thumb is lost, and consequently the majority of precision grips, with the thumb being pulled into an extended and adducted position. Sensory loss occurs over the palmar surfaces of the lateral three and one-half digits and possibly also the lateral half of the palm.

An injury to the ulnar nerve at the wrist produces a 'claw-hand' deformity (Fig. 4.123c). The thumb is abducted and the metacarpophalangeal joints of the fingers are hyperextended; the interphalangeal joints of the index and middle fingers are extended while those of the ring and little finger are partially flexed. Marked wasting of the hypothenar eminence and the thenar web accompany these changes, as well as a sensory loss on both palmar and dorsal surfaces of the medial one and one-half digits and possibly the medial half of the palm.

In some individuals, often the elderly, the medial part of the palmar aponeurosis and the fibrous flexor sheaths of the little and ring fingers may become shortened. There is a progressive flexion of the fingers at the metacarpophalangeal and proximal interphalangeal joints pulling the fingers towards the palm. The distal phalanx is not flexed because the tip of the finger is pressed against the palm. Indeed, in severe cases, the distal interphalangeal joint may become hyperextended. There is an inability to extend the fingers even passively. Treatment usually involves the removal of the offending fibrous tissue, however there is a tendency for it to reform and contract again. The condition is known as *Dupuytren's contracture*.

The most common deformity in rheumatoid arthritis is induced by synovitis of the metacarpophalangeal joint. This allows a narrowing of the articular cartilage and attenuation of the collateral ligaments. Under the influence of these two effects, there is a palmar subluxation of the proximal phalanx on the metacarpal head with laxity of the flexor complex. Under the pull of the flexor tendons there may be further subluxation of the proximal phalanx associated with an ulnar deviation, particularly in the index and middle fingers.

Joint replacement As with all joint replacements the primary object is the relief of pain and restoration of as full a range of movement as possible. However, when considering finger joint replacements the main problem appears to be the maintenance of the cortical bone. Stresses on the endosteal surface of the bone have a tendency to produce gradual deformity, and sometimes erosion so that the prosthesis protrudes into the shaft of the bone. The inserted foreign material may be a contributory factor in this erosion through disruption of the endosteal arterial supply.

In normal bone, the tensile stresses applied to the outer surface of the bone by ligamentous and periosteal attachments make a significant contribution to maintaining the integrity of the cortical bone. When these stresses are replaced by prostheses, that depend on transmission of stress by the endosteal surface, the bone is clearly reacting and remodelling to an entirely different pattern of stresses.

Fig. 4.123 The appearance of the hand in (**a**) radial, (**b**) median and (**c**) ulnar nerve injury.

Nerve supply

THE BRACHIAL PLEXUS

Introduction

The nerves supplying the structures in the arm are all derived from the brachial plexus, a complex of intermingling nerves originating in the neck (see Fig. 4.124).

The brachial plexus is formed by the *anterior primary rami* of the lower four cervical nerves and the first thoracic nerve to give it a root value of C5, 6, 7, 8 and T1. Occasionally, there may be a contribution from C4 or T2 or both.

The *anterior primary rami* are found as the anterior division of the spinal nerve, just outside the intervertebral foramen, lying between scalenus anterior and medius. They are collectively termed the *roots* of the plexus. Each spinal nerve receives an autonomic contribution, C5 and 6 receiving grey rami communicantes from the middle cervical ganglion, while C7, 8, and T1 receive them from the inferior or cervicothoracic ganglion.

Commonly, the upper two roots (C5 and 6) unite to form the *upper trunk*, the lower two roots (C8 and T1) unite to form the *lower trunk*, and the C7 root continues as the *middle trunk*. These three trunks are found running between the scalene muscles and the upper border of the clavicle in the posterior triangle of the neck. The lower trunk may groove the upper surface of the first rib behind the subclavian artery; the T1 root is always in contact with the rib.

Just above the clavicle, each of the three trunks divides into an *anterior* and *posterior division* which supply the flexor and extensor compartments of the arm respectively. The three posterior divisions unite to form the *posterior cord*, while the anterior divisions of the upper and middle trunks unite to form the *lateral cord*, and the anterior division of the lower trunk continues as the *medial cord*. These three trunks pass downwards into the axilla, running firstly posterolateral to the axillary artery, but then in their named positions with respect to the second part of the axillary artery, that is medial, posterior and lateral. The cords and axillary artery are bound together in the axillary sheath—an extension of the prevertebral fascia which protrudes into the axilla.

Applied anatomy

The brachial plexus itself is subject to direct injury, consequently a knowledge of its formation is of help in determining in exactly which parts, and at what levels, the damage has occurred. Traction injuries occur when the roots of the plexus are torn from the spinal cord, or when the constituent parts are partially or completely torn. In extreme cases, the whole plexus may be disrupted to produce a completely denervated arm. If the upper roots are completely torn, an *Erb's paralysis* affecting the musculature of the upper arm is produced; whereas if the lower roots are completely torn, a *Klumpkes' paralysis* affecting the hand and forearm will result.

Nerves arising from the brachial plexus and their distribution

The simplest way in which to describe the nerves of the brachial plexus is to put them into terminological order relating to the part of the plexus from which they originate (and to indicate their root value).

Branches from the roots

1. Nerves to the scalene and longus colli muscles (C5, 6, 7, 8).
2. A branch to the phrenic nerve (C5).
3. The dorsal scapular nerve (C5).
4. The long thoracic nerve (C5, 6, 7).

Branches from the trunks

1. The nerve to subclavius muscle (C(4), 5, 6).
2. Suprascapular nerve (C(4), 5, 6).

There are no nerves arising from the divisions.

Branches from the cords of the plexus

Medial cord:

1. Medial pectoral nerve (C8, T1).
2. Medial cutaneous nerve of the forearm (C8, T1).
3. Medial cutaneous nerve of the arm (T1).
4. Ulnar nerve (C(7), 8, T1).
5. Medial part of the median nerve (C8, T1).

Posterior cord:

1. Upper subscapular nerve (C(4), 5, 6, (7)).
2. Thoracodorsal nerve (C(6), 7, 8).
3. Lower subscapular nerve (C5, 6).
4. Axillary nerve (C5, 6).
5. Radial nerve (C(5), 6, 7, 8, (T1)).

Lateral cord:

1. Lateral pectoral nerve (C5, 6, 7).
2. Musculocutaneous nerve (C5, 6, 7).
3. Lateral part of the median nerve (C(5), 6, 7).

Branches from the roots

The muscular supply to the scalene and longus colli muscles arises by twigs from the upper surface of the anterior primary rami as they emerge from the intervertebral foramen, directly entering the muscles. The C5 contribution to the phrenic nerve arises at the lateral border of scalenus anterior.

The *dorsal scapular nerve* (C5) (Fig. 4.124) passes through scalenus medius to gain the deep surface of the levator scapulae muscle, from which it runs onto the anterior surface of the rhomboid muscles. It supplies both rhomboid major, minor and levator scapulae.

The C5 and 6 roots of the *long thoracic nerve* (Fig. 4.124) unite after piercing scalenus medius and are joined by the C7 root on the anterior surface of the muscle. The nerve passes behind the trunks of the plexus between the first rib and the axillary artery to gain the outer (axillary) surface of serratus anterior which it supplies. The upper two digitations of the muscle are supplied by C5, the next two by C6, and the remaining four by C7.

The long thoracic nerve may be damaged by direct pressure on it from above the shoulder. The resulting paralysis of serratus anterior causes the characteristic 'winged' scapula, with the inability to perform activities, such as abduction of the arm, where the scapula is stabilized or laterally rotated.

Branches from the trunks

The *nerve to subclavius* (C(4), 5, 6) is a small branch from the upper trunk. It descends anterior to the subclavian artery to supply subclavius. It may communicate with the phrenic nerve.

The *suprascapular nerve* (C(4), 5, 6) (Fig. 4.124) is a large branch from the upper trunk. It passes inferolaterally above and parallel to the trunks through the suprascapular notch deep to trapezius to enter the supraspinous fossa of the scapula. It then runs deep to the supraspinatus muscle and enters the infraspinous fossa via the spinoglenoid notch. The suprascapular nerve supplies both supraspinatus and infraspinatus, and also gives articular filaments to the shoulder and acromioclavicular joints.

All of the above branches arise from the plexus above the clavicle, whereas those considered below all arise below the level of the clavicle in the axilla.

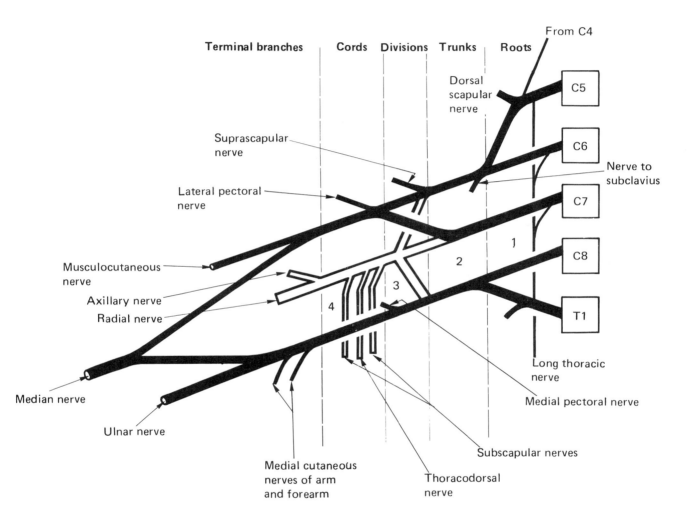

Fig. 4.124   Schematic diagram of the brachial plexus of the right side.

Branches from the cords

The *lateral pectoral nerve* (see Fig. 4.124) arises from the lateral cord of the plexus with a root value of C5, 6, 7. It crosses anteromedially in front of the axillary artery, giving a branch to the medial pectoral nerve before piercing the clavipectoral fascia to gain access to the deep surface of pectoralis major which it supplies.

The *medial pectoral nerve* (see Fig. 4.124) arises from the medial cord with a root value C8, T1. It receives a contribution from the lateral pectoral nerve and passes between the axillary artery and vein to gain access to the deep surface of pectoralis minor which it supplies. It then pierces this muscle to end in pectoralis major which it also supplies.

The *upper* and *lower subscapular nerves* (see Fig. 4.124) both arise from the posterior cord, root values C(4), 5, 6, (7) respectively. From behind the axillary artery they descend towards the subscapular fossa where they both supply the subscapularis muscle. In addition, the lower subscapular nerve enters and supplies teres major.

The *thoracodorsal nerve* (see Fig. 4.124) also arises from the posterior cord (C(6), 7, 8), between the two subscapular nerves. The nerve passes inferomedially along the posterior wall of the axilla, and the anterolateral surface of latissimus dorsi before entering its deep surface to supply it.

The *medial cutaneous nerve of the arm* (see Fig. 4.124) is a small nerve arising from the medial cord (root value T1). It descends through the axilla on the medial side of the axillary vein, and then along the medial side of the brachial artery. It pierces the deep fascia to supply the skin and fascia on the medial side of the proximal half of the arm, extending onto both the anterior and posterior surfaces (Fig. 4.125a). It may be partly or entirely replaced by the intercostobrachial nerve (root value T2,3).

The *medial cutaneous nerve of the forearm* arises directly from the medial cord with a root value of C8, T1. It descends on the medial side of the axillary and brachial arteries. It pierces the deep fascia, together with the basilic vein, in the middle of the arm, and descends with it to the elbow, where it then divides into anterior and ulnar branches. The medial cutaneous nerve of forearm supplies the skin over the lower part of biceps, the medial side of the forearm as far as the wrist, and part of the medial side of the posterior surface of the forearm (Fig. 4.125a).

Fig. 4.125 **a** = Cutaneous nerves of the upper limb:

1 = Supraclavicular nerve
2 = Upper lateral cutaneous nerve of the arm
3 = Lower lateral cutaneous nerve of the arm
4 = Lateral cutaneous nerve of the forearm
5 = Radial nerve
6 = Median nerve
7 = Ulnar nerve
8 = Medial cutaneous nerve of the forearm
9 = Intercostobrachial nerve
10 = Third intercostal nerve
11 = Posterior cutaneous nerve of the arm
12 = Posterior cutaneous nerve of the forearm

b = Dermatomes of the upper limb.

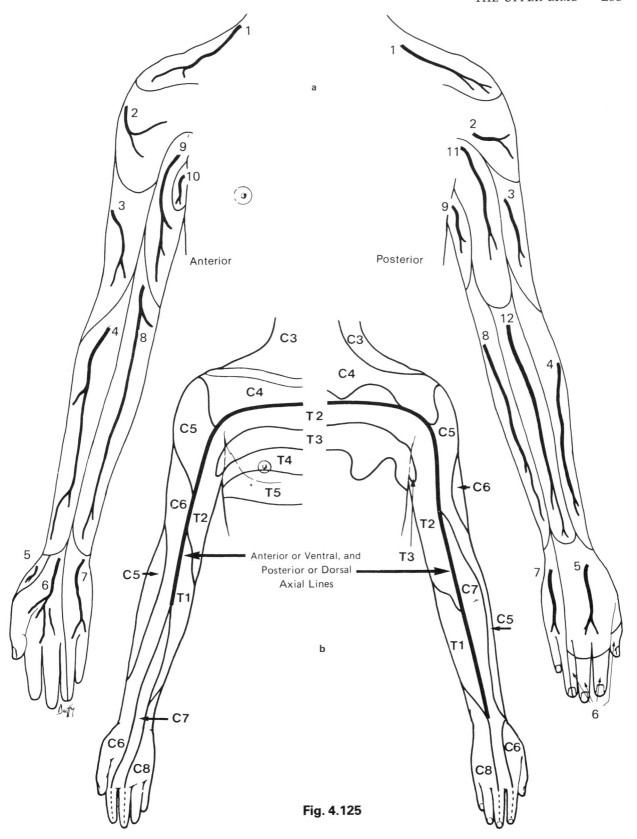

a

Anterior   Posterior

Anterior or Ventral, and
Posterior or Dorsal
Axial Lines

b

Fig. 4.125

The axillary nerve

The axillary nerve (see Fig. 4.128) arises from the posterior cord of the brachial plexus and has a root value of C5, 6. In the axilla it descends behind the axillary artery and in front of subscapularis, at the lower border of which it passes backwards close to the inferior part of the shoulder joint in company with the posterior circumflex humeral vessels. It then passes through the *quadrangular space* (see Fig. 4.128) where it supplies the shoulder joint and divides into anterior and posterior branches. The anterior branch winds around the surgical neck of the humerus, deep to and as far as the anterior part of deltoid, which it supplies. The posterior branch supplies teres minor, and the posterior part of deltoid. It then passes around deltoid as the *upper lateral cutaneous nerve of the arm* which pierces the deep fascia to supply skin over the lower part of deltoid and the lateral head of triceps as far as the middle part of the arm (see Fig. 4.125a).

The axillary nerve is frequently injured when the shoulder is dislocated because of its close proximity to this joint. Paralysis of deltoid and teres minor results, and consequently there is an inability to abduct the arm beyond that possible by the action of supraspinatus. This, in conjunction with an area of anaesthesia over the back of deltoid and lateral head of triceps, allows a clinical diagnosis of nerve injury to be made.

The musculocutaneous nerve

The musculocutaneous nerve (Fig. 4.126) arises from the lateral cord of the brachial plexus and has a root value C5, 6, 7. It lies firstly lateral to the axillary artery and then descends between the artery and coracobrachialis which it supplies and pierces before running distally between biceps and brachialis to reach the lateral side of the arm. At the elbow, the musculocutaneous nerve pierces the deep fascia between biceps and brachioradialis as the *lateral cutaneous nerve of the forearm*.

In the arm the musculocutaneous nerve supplies both heads of biceps brachii and two-thirds of brachialis as well as coracobrachialis.

The *lateral cutaneous nerve of the forearm* (see Fig. 4.125a) divides into anterior and posterior branches. The anterior branch supplies the skin on the lateral half of the forearm as far as the ball of the thumb, while the posterior branch supplies a variable area over the extensor muscles of the forearm, wrist and occasionally the first metacarpal.

Lateral cord of brachial plexus

Coracobrachialis

Musculocutaneous nerve

Lateral cutaneous
nerve of forearm

Fig. 4.126 The musculocutaneous nerve.

The ulnar nerve (Fig. 4.127)

The ulnar nerve is one of the terminal branches of the medial cord of the brachial plexus, having a root value C8 and T1, but frequently contains fibres from C7. It descends on the medial side of the axillary artery behind the medial cutaneous nerve of the forearm, and continues downwards medial to the brachial artery, anterior to triceps. In the distal half of the arm, the ulnar nerve passes backwards and pierces the medial intermuscular septum to enter the posterior compartment of the arm, where it lies on the front of the medial head of triceps. Continuing its descent in the posterior compartment of the arm, the ulnar nerve passes between the medial epicondyle of the humerus and the olecranon of the ulna, lying in the ulnar groove behind the medial epicondyle. The ulnar nerve then enters the anterior compartment of the forearm by passing between the two heads of flexor carpi ulnaris, initially in contact with the ulnar collateral ligament of the elbow. As it descends along the medial side of the forearm, the ulnar nerve lies on flexor digitorum profundus, lateral to the ulnar artery, covered in its upper part by the belly of flexor carpi ulnaris, but in the lower half, only by its tendon. Proximal to the flexor retinaculum it pierces the deep fascia to lie lateral to flexor carpi ulnaris, and passes anterior to the flexor retinaculum lateral to the pisiform where it divides into superficial and deep branches.

During its course, the ulnar nerve gives an articular branch to the elbow joint, and supplies flexor carpi ulnaris, and the medial half of flexor digitorum profundus.

A *palmar cutaneous branch* arises from the ulnar nerve piercing the deep fascia in the distal third of the forearm and descends to supply the skin over the medial part of the palm (see Fig. 4.125a).

The *dorsal branch* of the ulnar nerve, also arises in the distal third of the forearm, passes backwards deep to flexor carpi ulnaris to pierce the deep fascia on the medial side to become superficial. On the medial side of the wrist, it crosses the triquetral, against which it can be palpated, and gives branches to the dorsal surface of the wrist and hand. Here it divides into two or three dorsal digital nerves which supply the skin on the dorsum of the hand and the dorsal surfaces of the medial one and a half or two and a half fingers, excluding the skin over the distal phalanx. The dorsum of the distal phalanges are supplied by branches from the median or ulnar nerves derived from the palm.

The *superficial branch of the ulnar nerve* lies deep to palmaris brevis on the medial side of the hand where it can be compressed against the hook of the hamate. It supplies the palmaris brevis muscle, the skin on the medial side of the palm of the hand, and the skin on the palmar surface of the little and adjacent half of the ring fingers, extending onto the dorsal surface supplying the skin and nail bed of the distal phalanx.

The *deep branch of the ulnar nerve* eventually runs with the deep branch of the ulnar artery and thus loops across the palm from medial to lateral deep to the flexor tendons. It passes initially between abductor digiti minimi and flexor digiti minimi and pierces opponens digiti minimi, supplying all three muscles. As it passes across the deep part of the palm, it supplies the medial two lumbricals, all of the interossei and adductor pollicis. Rarely, the ulnar nerve also supplies the thenar muscles. The deep branch gives articular filaments to the wrist joint.

Applied anatomy The ulnar nerve may be damaged in the groove behind the medial epicondyle either by trauma or entrapment. This leads to a partial or complete loss of muscular and sensory innervation. At the wrist, the nerve can easily be cut or lacerated because of its superficial position. The clinical picture can be complicated if the lesion occurs below the level where the dorsal and palmar cutaneous branches are given off, as a considerable portion of the skin on the ulnar side of the hand still has a sensory supply. The result of an ulnar nerve lesion often gives the typical 'claw-hand' deformity (see Fig. 4.123c). This is due to loss of power in the intrinsic muscles of the hand and the unopposed actions of antagonistic muscle groups. There is 'guttering' between the metacarpals, an inability to abduct the fingers or adduct the thumb. The area of sensory loss usually follows the outline of the sensory map (see Fig. 4.125a).

C8

T1

Medial cord
of brachial plexus

Ulnar nerve

Long head of
triceps

Medial
intermuscular septum

Medial epicondyle

Flexor digitorum
profundus

Dorsal branch
of ulnar
nerve

Palmar cutaneous branch

Flexor retinaculum

Deep branch of ulnar
nerve

Nerve to
hypothenar
muscles

Superficial terminal
branch

Fig. 4.127   The ulnar nerve.

The radial nerve (Fig. 4.128)

The radial nerve is the major nerve from the posterior cord, root value C5, 6, 7, 8 (T1), being one of its terminal branches. In the axilla, the radial nerve lies behind the axillary and upper part of the brachial arteries, passing anterior to the tendons of subscapularis, latissimus dorsi and teres major. The radial nerve, together with the profunda brachii artery, enters the posterior compartment of the arm by passing through the lower triangular space, formed by the humerus laterally, the long head of triceps medially and teres major above (Fig. 4.128). In passing through this space, the nerve enters the spiral (or radial) groove of the humerus, descending obliquely between the lateral and medial heads of triceps, reaching the lateral border of the humerus in the distal third of the arm. The nerve pierces the lateral intermuscular septum to enter the anterior compartment where it lies in a muscular groove between brachialis and brachioradialis. In front of the lateral epicondyle of humerus, the radial nerve divides into its terminal *superficial* and *deep branches* (Fig. 4.128).

In the arm, the radial nerve gives a supply to all three heads of triceps, anconeus, the lateral part of brachialis, brachioradialis and extensor carpi radialis longus. The branches to triceps all arise before the radial nerve enters the spiral groove; anconeus is supplied by a branch to the medial head.

The radial nerve also gives articular branches to the elbow joint and has three cutaneous branches which supply skin on the back of the arm and forearm (see Fig. 4.125a).

The *posterior cutaneous nerve of the arm* arises in the axilla, piercing the deep fascia near the posterior axillary fold. It supplies skin on the posterior surface of the proximal third of the arm.

The *lower lateral cutaneous nerve of the arm* arises before the radial nerve pierces the lateral intermuscular septum, and becomes cutaneous just below deltoid. It supplies the skin over the lower lateral part of the arm and a small area on the forearm.

The *posterior cutaneous nerve of the forearm* arises just below the previous nerve, and supplies a variable area of skin on the dorsum of the forearm as far as the wrist, or occasionally beyond.

The *superficial branch* is the direct continuation of the radial nerve, beginning in front of the lateral epicondyle and descending along the anterolateral side of the forearm. It is entirely sensory. It lies on supinator, pronator teres, flexor digitorum superficialis and flexor pollicis longus covered by brachioradialis with the radial artery medial to it. In the distal third of the forearm, the nerve passes below the tendon of brachioradialis and pierces the deep fascia to become superficial. It supplies the skin on the dorsum of the wrist, the lateral dorsal surface of the hand and dorsum of the thumb, and then divides into four or five digital nerves. The digital nerves supply the skin on the dorsum of the thumb, index, middle and adjacent half of the ring finger as far as the distal interphalangeal joint. The digital branches also give articular branches to the metacarpophalangeal and proximal interphalangeal joints of all five digits.

The *deep branch*, more often called the *posterior interosseous nerve*, is entirely muscular and articular. It begins in front of the lateral epicondyle of the humerus and enters the posterior compartment of the forearm by passing between the two heads of supinator, thereby curving around the lateral and posterior surfaces of the radius. During its course, the nerve supplies both extensor carpi radialis brevis and supinator. It then descends between the deep and superficial groups of extensor muscles, accompanied by the posterior interosseous artery, supplying all the muscles in the extensor compartment of the forearm: extensor digitorum, extensor digiti minimi, extensor carpi ulnaris, extensor pollicis longus, extensor indicis, abductor pollicis longus and extensor pollicis brevis.

In the lower part of the forearm, the posterior interosseous nerve lies on the interosseous membrane and ends in a flattened expansion, which gives articular branches to the intercarpal joints.

Applied anatomy   The radial nerve is often injured as it crosses the humerus, either as the result of a fracture or by pressure from a direct blow or incorrect use of a crutch. Triceps usually escapes denervation as it derives its supply from branches given off high in the arm, but a total paralysis of the extensors of the wrist and digits leads to the deformity of a 'dropped wrist' (see Fig. 4.123a). As a result, any attempt to grip or make a fist leads to increased flexion of the wrist and an inability to carry out effective movement. This is due to the loss of the synergic action of the wrist extensors which usually prevent the unwanted flexion of the wrist produced by the continued action of the finger flexors.

The interphalangeal joints of the fingers can be extended by the lumbricals and interossei which have an attachment to the dorsal digital expansion, but proper use of the hand requires an effective form of 'lively' splint which compensates for the paralysed muscles. Even though the sensory distribution of the radial nerve on the dorsum of the hand appears extensive, overlap by adjacent cutaneous nerves means that the area of exclusive radial nerve supply is a small patch on the dorsum of the thumb web.

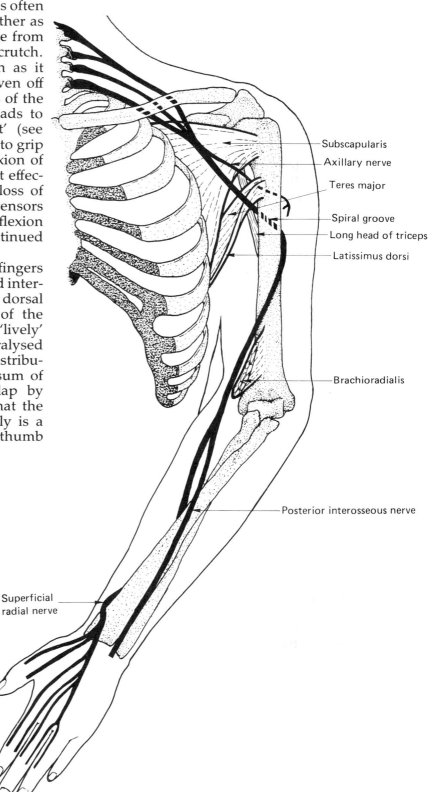

Fig. 4.128   The radial and axillary nerve.

The median nerve (Fig. 4.129)

The median nerve is complex in that it arises partly from the lateral cord (C5, 6, 7) and partly from the medial cord (C8, T1) of the brachial plexus. These two contributing heads of the median nerve unite by embracing the third part of the axillary artery. Once formed, the nerve descends under cover of biceps passing at first laterally to the brachial artery and then medially, having crossed it anteriorly. In the lower part of the arm the median nerve lies on brachialis, and in the cubital fossa is protected by the bicipital aponeurosis which crosses it.

The median nerve enters the forearm by passing between the two heads of pronator teres, and then runs below the tendinous arch connecting the heads of flexor digitorum superficialis to gain access to its deep surface. Closely bound to the deep surface of flexor digitorum superficialis, it descends on flexor digitorum profundus until just above the wrist where it becomes superficial by passing between the tendons of flexor digitorum superficialis and flexor carpi radialis, deep to palmaris longus. The median nerve enters the hand deep to the flexor retinaculum, passing anteriorly to the long flexor tendons. Consequently, it is one of the structures found within the carpal tunnel.

During its course the median nerve gives articular branches to the elbow joint and supplies pronator teres, flexor carpi radialis, palmaris longus and flexor digitorum superficialis.

The *palmar cutaneous nerve* arises in the distal third of the forearm. It pierces the deep fascia and enters the palm by passing superficial to the flexor retinaculum. It supplies a small area of skin on the lateral side of the palm and thenar eminence.

In the cubital fossa, the *anterior interosseous nerve* arises from the median nerve and descends, with the anterior interosseous artery, on the anterior surface of the interosseous membrane between flexor pollicis longus and flexor digitorum profundus. It then runs deep to pronator quadratus to end at the wrist by giving articular branches to the radiocarpal and intercarpal joints. The anterior interosseous nerve supplies flexor pollicis longus, the lateral half of flexor digitorum profundus and pronator quadratus.

Once the median nerve has passed through the carpal tunnel to enter the hand, it divides into lateral and medial terminal branches. The *lateral branch* passes laterally and proximally to enter the thenar eminence and supply abductor pollicis brevis, flexor pollicis brevis, opponens pollicis and the first lumbrical. It gives sensory branches to the adjacent sides of the thumb and index finger.

The *medial branch* of the median nerve divides into a variable number of branches, the palmar digital nerves, the most lateral of which supplies the second lumbrical. These nerves are sensory to the palmar surface of adjacent sides of the index and middle, and middle and ring fingers (Fig. 4.129). Each of these digital nerves produces a dorsal branch which passes backwards to supply the dorsal aspect of the distal phalanx and nail bed, and a variable amount of the middle phalanx of the same digits.

The *digital nerves* lie deep to the palmar aponeurosis and superficial palmar arch, but superficial to the long flexor tendons. As well as the sensory innervation, they also give articular branches to the interphalangeal and metacarpophalangeal joints.

Applied anatomy The median nerve can be injured in the forearm by deep cuts with a resultant loss of flexion at all interphalangeal joints, except the distal ones in the ring and little fingers. The metacarpophalangeal joints of these same fingers can still be flexed by the lumbricals and interossei but the movement of pronation is severely restricted. In the hand, the thumb is held in extension and adduction thus losing its ability to oppose and abduct. This, combined with the sensory loss, proves a major disability. More commonly the nerve is damaged just proximal to the flexor retinaculum by laceration, or deep to it in the carpal tunnel where compression gives rise to the carpal tunnel syndrome. In this instance only the thenar muscles, lateral two lumbricals and sensation in the hand will be affected.

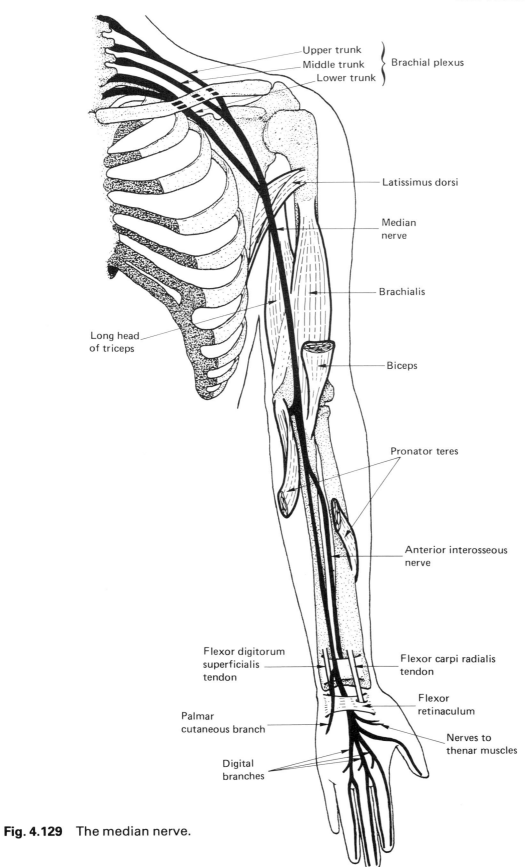

Upper trunk
Middle trunk
Lower trunk
Brachial plexus

Latissimus dorsi

Median
nerve

Brachialis

Long head
of triceps

Biceps

Pronator teres

Anterior interosseous
nerve

Flexor digitorum
superficialis
tendon

Flexor carpi radialis
tendon

Flexor
retinaculum

Palmar
cutaneous branch

Nerves to
thenar muscles

Digital
branches

Fig. 4.129 The median nerve.

Blood supply

THE ARTERIES AND PULSES
(Fig. 4.130)

The main arterial stem of the upper limb passes through the root of the neck, the axilla and the arm before dividing into two in the forearm. It changes its name in each of the regions as it crosses particular bony or muscular landmarks.

The subclavian artery

The right subclavian artery lies entirely within the root of the neck, having arisen from the brachiocephalic trunk. The left subclavian artery arises from the aortic arch in the superior mediastinum to enter the root of the neck. Both arteries pass laterally over the first rib towards the axilla, and end by becoming the axillary artery at its lateral border. The subclavian artery is conveniently divided into three parts by scalenus anterior which crosses it anteriorly.

In the neck, the artery runs from the upper border of the sternoclavicular joint to the middle of the clavicle. The course is convex upwards. The artery can be compressed against the first rib by a downward and backward pressure applied behind the clavicle, lateral to the posterior border of sternomastoid.

Branches from the subclavian artery supply structures within the neck, and the anterior chest wall, and give an important supply to the brain.

The axillary artery

The axillary artery is the continuation of the subclavian artery at the lateral border of the first rib and ends by becoming the brachial artery at the lower border of teres major, at the level of the lateral extremity of the posterior axillary fold. For descriptive purposes, it is divided into three parts by pectoralis minor. However, the length of each part will depend on the position of the arm. The cords of the brachial plexus are named according to their position with respect to the second part of the axillary artery.

The course of the artery is represented by a line drawn from the midpoint of the clavicle and passing immediately below the coracoid process to the medial lip of the intertubercular groove behind coracobrachialis. It thus describes a curve with the concavity facing downwards and medially.

The pulse of the axillary artery is readily palpated in the lateral wall of the axilla in the groove behind the coracobrachialis muscle. This is a useful pressure point to control distal bleeding, although paraesthesia may result from the inevitable pressure on the median, ulnar and radial nerves which are in close relation to the artery at this point.

Branches from the axillary artery supply the shoulder and pectoral regions, as well as the lateral chest wall. They anastomose with branches from the subclavian artery and the posterior intercostal arteries from the descending thoracic aorta. These anastomoses and their vessels may be enlarged in conditions where there is a narrowing of the aorta beyond the origin of the left subclavian artery (coarctation of the aorta), and serve as a collateral system bypassing the restriction.

The brachial artery

This is the continuation of the axillary artery beyond the lower border of teres major and ends in the cubital fossa opposite the neck of the radius. It lies successively on the long and medial heads of the triceps, the coracobrachialis insertion and the brachialis. Anteriorly it is covered by the medial border of the biceps, and is crossed from lateral to medial by the median nerve about halfway down the arm. In the cubital fossa it lies beneath the bicipital aponeurosis, which separates it from the median cubital vein, with the median nerve lying medial to the artery and with the biceps tendon lying lateral. The brachial artery divides into the radial and ulnar arteries.

High division of the brachial artery sometimes occurs proximal to the cubital fossa. Indeed, it may divide at any point between the axilla and the cubital fossa, in which case the two arteries descend side-by-side fol-

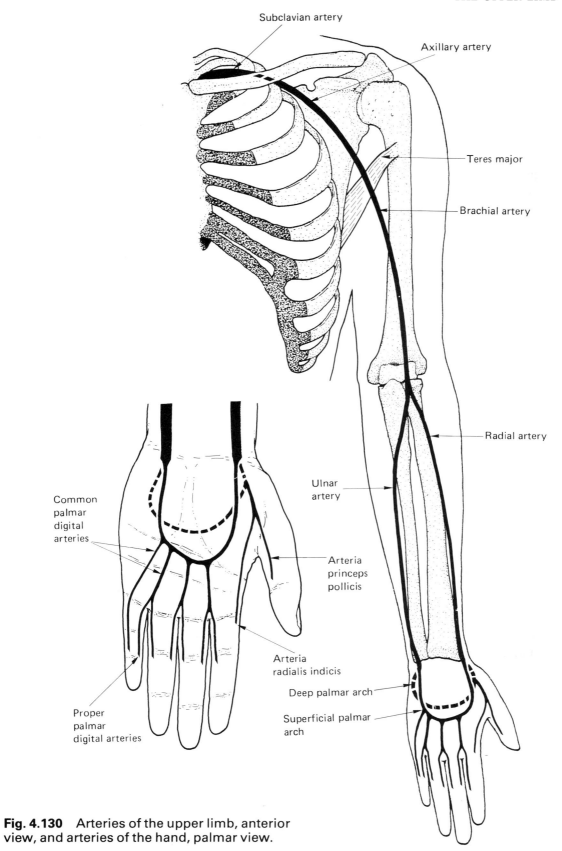

Fig. 4.130 Arteries of the upper limb, anterior view, and arteries of the hand, palmar view.

lowing the normal course of the brachial artery.

The *brachial pulse* may be felt along the whole course of the artery by compressing it against the humerus, directing lateral pressure proximally and dorsolateral pressure distally. It is best felt just medial to the bicipital aponeurosis at the level of the medial epicondyle of the humerus, and it is at this point that one listens for *Korotkoff's sounds* when measuring blood pressure.

A major branch of the brachial artery is the *profunda brachii*, which runs with the radial nerve in the spiral groove between the lateral and medial heads of the triceps to pass into the posterior compartment of the arm. Branches from both the brachial artery and the profunda brachii supply the muscles of the arm and contribute to the anastomosis around the elbow joint.

The radial artery

The radial artery begins in the cubital fossa opposite the neck of the radius and ends by completing the deep palmar arch in the hand. It is usually thought of and described as having three parts. The first part is in the forearm, the second curves laterally around the wrist as far as the first interosseous space, and the third passes through the interosseous space into the palm.

If the arm is placed in a midpronated position and brachioradialis is tensed, then the course of the first part of the radial artery may be indicated by a slightly convex line beginning at the biceps tendon and running down the medial side of brachioradialis to a point just medial to the radial styloid process on the anterior aspect. As it curves around the wrist, the radial artery is within the 'anatomical snuff-box' and lies on the radiocarpal ligament, the scaphoid and trapezium. It is crossed by the tendons of abductor pollicis longus and extensors pollicis brevis and longus from lateral to medial.

The third part of the artery passes between the two heads of the first dorsal interosseous and adductor pollicis before completing the deep palmar arch.

The *radial pulses* may be felt against the distal border of the radius lateral to flexor carpi radialis, and in the 'anatomical snuff-box' against the scaphoid.

Branches from the first part of the artery are involved in the elbow anastomosis and supply the muscles on the radial side of the forearm. From the second part arise branches supplying the wrist and dorsum of the hand and thumb. Before completing the deep palmar arch, the third part of the artery gives off the *princeps pollicis* and *radialis indicis* to the thumb and index fingers respectively.

The ulnar artery

The ulnar artery begins in the cubital fossa as a terminal branch of the brachial artery, and ends at the pisiform by dividing into deep and superficial palmar arteries. It may be represented by a line passing, medially convex, from the tendon of biceps to the pisiform bone and from there to the hook of the hamate. In its course, it lies on brachialis, flexor digitorum profundus and the flexor retinaculum, and is crossed anteriorly, from above downwards by: pronator teres, the median nerve, flexor carpi radialis, palmaris longus and flexor digitorum superficialis, being overlapped lower down by flexor carpi ulnaris. Just below the radial tuberosity, the common interosseous artery is given off, and this divides into anterior and posterior interosseous arteries which run down either side of the interosseous membrane, supplying the deep muscles of both flexor and extensor compartments. Branches from the proximal and distal ends of the artery are involved in the supply to the elbow and wrist joints respectively.

The superficial palmar arch

This is formed mainly by the ulnar artery, with a contribution from the superficial palmar branch of the radial artery. It lies deep to the palmar aponeurosis. The distal convexity of the arch lies level with the flexor surface of the extended thumb.

Four *common palmar digital arteries* arise from the superficial arch with the most medial running along the medial side of the little finger. The other three each divide into two proper digital arteries which supply adjacent sides of the little, ring, middle and index fingers.

The deep palmar arch

This is formed mainly by the radial artery with a contribution from the deep branch of the ulnar artery. It lies deep to the long flexor tendons and their synovial sheaths on the bases of the metacarpals. Its distal convexity is 2 cm distal to the distal crease of the wrist.

THE VEINS (see Fig. 4.131)

The veins of the upper limb are divided into a superficial group which lie in the superficial fascia, and a deep group which accompany the arteries. Both groups of veins have valves which allow proximal drainage (a fact which should be borne in mind when using massage) and drain into the axillary vein.

The deep veins

Apart from the axillary artery, which is accompanied by a single vein, all of the arteries are accompanied by two *venae comitantes*.

The *axillary vein* is the continuation of the basilic vein at the lower border of teres major. It ends by becoming the subclavian vein at the lateral border of the first rib. Its course is identical to that of the axillary artery, which lies lateral to it.

The superficial veins

These are arranged in irregular networks in the superficial fascia. They are connected with the deep veins by inconstant perforating veins which pierce the deep fascia. The blood is drained from the superficial system principally by the basilic and cephalic veins.

The main superficial channels are as follows:

The dorsal venous arch

This would be better named the dorsal venous plexus, for its arch-like nature is seldom apparent. It lies on the back of the hand, its position and pattern being highly variable.

The basilic vein

This arises from the ulnar side of the arch and ascends along the ulnar side of the distal half of the forearm before inclining forwards to pass in front of the medial epicondyle and entering the medial bicipital furrow. Opposite the insertion of the coracobrachialis, it pierces the deep fascia to ascend along the medial side of the brachial vessels to become the axillary vein at the lower border of teres major. In the forearm it can usually be clearly seen, particularly in males. It is joined by tributaries from the forearm and by the median cubital vein in front of the elbow.

The cephalic vein

This arises from the radial end of the dorsal venous arch and receives the dorsal veins of the thumb. Inclining forwards, it ascends on the anterolateral part of the forearm as far as the elbow, and then along the lateral side of the biceps tendon to reach the groove in front of the shoulder between the deltoid and pectoralis major muscles (the deltopectoral groove). It ascends in the groove to the level of the coracoid process where it turns medially between the pectoralis major and pectoralis minor. It pierces the clavipectoral fascia and ends in the axillary vein at a point just below the middle of the clavicle. It receives several tributaries in the forearm, and at the elbow is connected to the basilic vein by the median cubital vein.

The median cubital vein

This is a short, wide vein, useful for venepuncture. It runs upwards and medially across the bicipital aponeurosis. The latter separates it from the underlying brachial artery. It joins the basilic vein just above the medial epicondyle.

The anterior median vein of the forearm

When present, this vein runs up the middle of the front of the forearm and may join the basilic or cephalic vein, or may divide at the cubital fossa into the median cephalic and median basilic veins.

Lymphatics

The lymphatic drainage of the upper limb is by a superficial intermeshing network of vessels just below the skin, and by deep lymphatic channels below the deep fascia. Both groups of vessels drain proximally and end by passing through some of the 25 to 30 lymph nodes in the axilla. This mass of lymph nodes serves to filter the lymph contained in the system and acts as an important defence mechanism in preventing the spread of infection.

The axillary lymph nodes are distributed in the axillary fat throughout the axilla but can be divided into five groups, four of which lie below pectoralis minor and one (the apical group) above pectoralis minor. Ultimately, all lymph from the upper limb passes through the apical group of nodes, from where the efferent lymph channels condense to form the subclavian trunk. On the left hand side, the subclavian trunk joins the thoracic duct, while on the right it drains into the subclavian vein directly or via the right lymphatic duct.

The superficial nodes and lymph vessels

The superficial lymph vessels are found in the skin and drain lymph from the superficial tissues. In the hand a fine meshwork of vessels exists, which drain into progressively larger channels as they pass up the arm. The only superficial lymph vessels which have any consistent course are the larger ones which follow the major superficial veins. These end by passing into the axilla.

In the cubital fossa one or two lymph nodes lie medial to the basilic vein, receiving lymph from the medial fingers and ulnar half of the hand and forearm. There are also one or two lymph nodes in the infraclavicular fossa associated with the cephalic vein. These receive vessels from the shoulder and breast. A single node may be found in the deltopectoral groove.

The deep nodes and lymph vessels

The deep lymph vessels of the upper limb are less numerous than the superficial vessels with which they have many connections. Lying below the deep fascia, they accompany the major arteries in the arm. Most pass directly to the lateral group of axillary nodes.

Small nodes may occur along both the radial and ulnar arteries and deep within the cubital fossa. Efferents from all of these nodes pass to the lateral group of axillary nodes. These latter nodes lie alongside the axillary vein, and from the pectoral and subscapular nodes pass along the lateral thoracic and subscapular arteries respectively. A central group of nodes is formed above the floor of the axilla. Although all the group receives lymph from all areas, the main drainage of the limb is to the lateral group. Drainage of the breast and anterior chest wall is to the pectoral nodes, that of the scapular region and upper back is to the subscapular nodes. Efferents from these groups pass to the central and then the apical group of nodes, the latter also receiving efferents from the superficial infraclavicular nodes.

Application

The larger lymph vessels contain numerous valves which allow lymph to move only in a proximal direction. This fact is important during massage techniques aimed at reducing oedema. The massage strokes are applied from distal to proximal, ending at the axilla, with sufficient depth to compress the lymph vessels and encourage drainage.

Active muscle contraction will also cause compression of the lymph vessels and encourage drainage proximally. This effect can be further enhanced by placing an elastic compressive support or bandage on the upper limb and encouraging active rhythmical contraction of the arm muscles. Elevation of the arm above the level of the axilla will allow gravity to assist the lymphatic drainage.

Pneumatic splints which apply a rhythmically alternating compressive force to the arm, using a small electric compressor pump, can also achieve the effect of increasing lymphatic flow proximally, utilizing the same principles as massage.

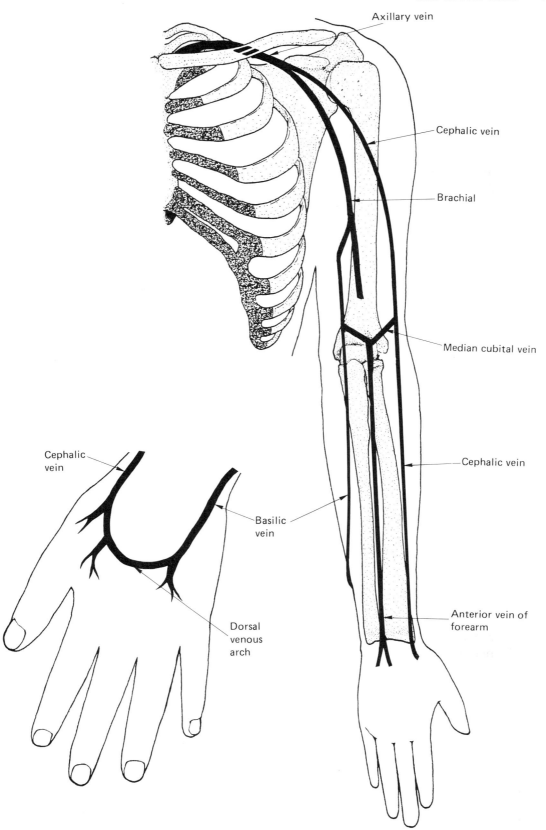

Fig. 4.131 Veins of the upper limb, anterior view, and veins of the hand, dorsal view.

5

The lower limb

The lower limb

INTRODUCTION

The human lower limb is adapted for weight-bearing, locomotion and maintaining the unique, upright, bipedal posture. For all of these functions much more strength and stability are required than in the upper limb. The bones of the lower limb are larger and more robust than their upper limb counterparts, and vary in their characteristics in relation to muscular development and body build. Many bones, particularly the innominate and, to a lesser extent the femur, show sexual differences; variations in the female pelvis for example being an adaptation to child-bearing.

The form and structure of individual bones is adapted to the function of support and resisting mechanical stresses. The internal architecture of the bone is arranged to resist all such stresses and forces. This is particularly marked at the articular regions of the bone. During growth and life continuous modifications are being made in order to maintain the functions of support and resistance to stress as the stresses change. The attainment of an habitual, upright posture and bipedal gait has resulted in a change in both the mechanical and functional requirements of all the bones of the lower limb. Consequently, during evolution, there have been major changes in the lower limb.

The pelvic girdle, formed by the innominate of each side articulating anteriorly at the symphysis pubis, connects the lower limb to the vertebral column via its posterior articulation with the sacrum. This posterior articulation, the sacroiliac joint, provides great strength in the region of weight transference from the trunk to the lower limb at the sacrifice of almost all mobility. The human ilium has developed so that it is no longer blade-like but is shortened and tightly curved backwards and outwards (Fig. 5.1), changing the actions of the gluteal muscles. The changes in the pelvis have resulted in a shift in its positioning from an essentially horizontal to an essentially vertical position. This has enabled the trunk to

be held vertically, but has necessitated a change in the orientation of the sacrum with respect to the ilium with the result that the axis of the pelvic canal lies almost at a right angle to the vertebral column. During evolution there has been a relative approximation of the sacral articular surface to the acetabulum which makes for greater stability in the transmission of the weight of the trunk to the hip joint. The increase in the magnitude of this weight has resulted in an increase in the area of contact between sacrum and ilium relative to the area of the ilium as a whole. For the same reason the acetabulum and femoral head have also increased in relative size during evolution. The shortening of the ischium that has occurred is an adaptation for speed and rapid movements, which is of great importance in bipeds. Thus power of action has been sacrificed for speed.

Changes have also occurred at the knee with the femoral condyles being more parallel in humans as compared with other primates. The major change though has been in bringing the knees inwards towards the body midline, which appears to be part of the overall pattern of centering the body mass, thus reinforcing skeletal rather than muscular equilibrium.

In humans, the tibia and fibula are held tightly together, with the tibia being the weight-bearing component while the fibula is mainly for muscle attachments. There has been a loss of rotation of the fibula with respect to the tibia.

It is the foot, however, which has perhaps undergone the greatest change during evolution (Fig. 5.2). These changes reflect not so much the evolution of a new function as a reduction in the original primate functions, with the foot changing from a grasping, tactile organ to a locomotor prop. Although some non-locomotor function is still possible, the foot has evolved from a generalized to a specialized organ. The joints of the human foot permit much less internal mobility—an adaptation to ground walking. In locomotion, the foot acts as a lever

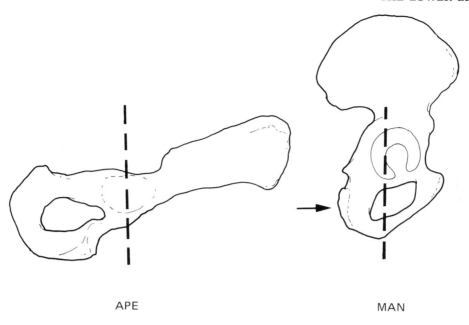

APE   MAN

Fig. 5.1 The evolutionary changes that have occurred to adapt the human pelvis for an erect posture.

CHIMPANZEE   MAN

Fig. 5.2 The evolutionary changes that have occurred within the foot during its adaptation to bipedalism.

adding propulsive force to that of the leg, with the point of pivot being the subtalar joint. The front part of the foot has been shortened relative to the posterior portion, where the main thrust in walking is developed—the power capabilities are thus accentuated.

The arches of the foot are formed by the shape of the bony elements, and are supported by ligaments and tendons. They convert the foot into a complex spring under tension and allow it to transmit the stresses involved in walking, both when body momentum is checked at heel-strike and when the foot is used in propelling the body forward. The lateral arch helps to steady the foot on the ground, while the medial arch transmits the main force of thrust in propulsion. This arched form of the foot is important in providing one of the major determinants of gait, helping to minimize energy expenditure and thus increase the efficiency of walking.

An important consequence of the upright, bipedal posture is that the centre of gravity of the body has been brought towards the vertebral column, so that in humans it lies slightly behind and at about the same level as the hip joint thereby reducing the tendency of gravity to pull the trunk forward. The centre of gravity projection then passes anterior to the knee and ankle joints (see Fig. 5.4). At the knee, the line of weight transmission passes towards the outside. Because of the angulation of the femur, during walking the foot, tibia and knee joint of each leg stay close to the line followed by the centre of gravity, and thus energy expenditure is minimal in maintaining the centre of gravity above the supporting limb. Balance is thus improved and there is more time for the free leg to swing forward enabling an increase in stride length. The alteration in the line of weight transmission is carried into the foot, where it passes to the inner side. However, it must be remem-

bered that weight is also transmitted through the outside of the foot, bringing the entire foot into use as a stabilizing element.

In order to reduce the possibility of collapse or dislocation, due to the forces to which they are subjected, the joints of the lower limb are structurally more stable than those of the upper limb. This stability is either due to the shape of the articular surfaces, the number and strength of the ligaments, or the size of the muscles related to the joint. Commonly, each of these factors contributes to a varying extent.

During the early stages of development the limb buds appear as swellings on the lateral side of the body (Fig. 5.3a), with the upper limb preceding the lower limb in appearance and development. At first, each limb bud projects at right angles to the surface of the body possessing dorsal and ventral surfaces, and cephalic (preaxial) and caudal (postaxial) borders (Fig. 5.3b). As the limb increases in length it becomes differentiated during which time it is folded ventrally so that the ventral surface becomes medial (Fig 5.3c), with the convexities of the elbow and knee directed laterally (Fig. 5.3d). At a later stage, the upper and lower limbs rotate in opposite directions such that the convexity of the elbow is turned towards the caudal end of the body and that of the knee towards the head (Fig. 5.3e). The ventral rami entering a limb bud pass anterior to the myotomes and eventually divide into dorsal and ventral divisions, which unite with the corresponding branches of adjacent ventral rami to form the nerves of the dorsal and ventral aspects of the limb bud. These nerves will supply respectively the sheets of muscle and the overlying skin of the dorsal (extensor) and ventral (flexor) surfaces of the limbs prior to their rotation into the adult pattern. During the foldings and rotations of the limb and the migration of muscle masses, these nerve–muscle connections are maintained.

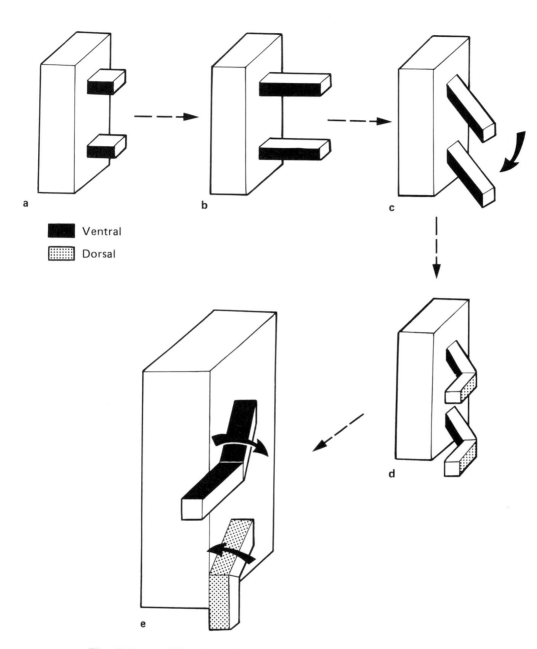

Ventral
Dorsal

Fig. 5.3a–e The development and rotation of the upper and lower limbs.

The rotation of the lower limb in the course of development results in its extensor and flexor surfaces coming to lie anteriorly and posteriorly respectively. This rotation is reflected in the arrangement of the innervation. The muscles on the front of the thigh and leg are supplied by nerves coming from the posterior part of the lumbar and lumbosacral plexus, the femoral and common peroneal nerves, while those at the back of the thigh and leg and in the sole of the foot are from the anterior aspect of the plexus, the tibial nerve.

As in the upper limb, many muscles cross over several joints and exert their actions on each. It is unusual for one joint of the lower limb to be moved in isolation. In standing and walking the joints and muscles form a coordinated mechanism.

The uppermost limits of the lower limb are the iliac crest, the inguinal ligament, the symphysis pubis, the ischiopubic ramus, the ischial tuberosity, the sacrotuberous ligament, and the dorsum of the sacrum and coccyx. The bulge of tissue running between the innominate and the upper part of the femur forms the buttock, but the region is usually named gluteal after the underlying muscles. The free lower limb is divided into the thigh between the hip and knee, the leg between the knee and ankle, and the foot distal to the ankle joint. The foot is divided into foot proper and the toes, and has a superior surface or dorsum and an inferior or plantar surface, which is the sole of the foot (Fig. 5.4).

The bones of the lower limb are those of the pelvic girdle, the femur in the thigh, the medial tibia and lateral fibula in the leg, the seven tarsal bones and five metatarsals in the foot, and the phalanges of the toes—two in the big toe and three in each remaining toe (Fig. 5.4).

REGIONS   BONES   JOINTS

Gluteal

Thigh

Leg

Foot

Dorsum

Plantar
surface

Innominate

Sacrum

Coccyx

Femur

Patella

Tibia

Fibula

Talus

Cuboid

Navicular

Cuneiforms

Meta-
tarsals

Phalanges

Sacroiliac

Hip

Knee

Superior
tibiofibular

Inferior
tibiofibular

Ankle

Fig. 5.4   The regions, bones and joints of the lower limb.

Bones

PELVIC GIRDLE (Fig. 5.5)

Introduction

The pelvic girdle comprises three separate bones, the two *innominate* bones and the *sacrum*, the ring of bone so formed uniting the trunk and the lower limbs. The innominate is a large and irregular bone with two expanded triangular blades twisted 90° with respect to each other in the region of the *acetabulum*. Each triangular blade is also twisted within itself. The innominate bone is formed from three separate bones, the *ilium*, *ischium* and *pubis*, which come together and fuse in the region of the acetabulum so that in the adult the innominate appears as a single bone. The *sacrum* is made made up of five fused vertebrae and is roughly triangular. The *coccyx*, which is the remnant of our tail, consists of four fused coccygeal vertebrae. Each innominate bone articulates with the sacrum posteriorly by synovial joints, which are partly synovial (anteriorly) and partly fibrous (posteriorly). The innominate bones also articulate with each other anteriorly at the pubic symphysis, by a secondary cartilaginous joint.

The pelvis has several functions:

1. it supports the pelvic viscera;
2. it supports the weight of the body transmitted through the vertebrae, thence through the sacrum, across the sacroiliac joints to the innominate bones and then to the femora in the standing position, or to the ischial tuberosities when sitting;
3. during walking the pelvis swings from side-to-side by a rotatory movement at the lumbosacral articulation which occurs together with similar movements of the lumbar intervertebral joints; even if the hip joints are fused, this swing of the pelvis enables a patient to walk reasonably well;
4. as with all but a few small bones in the hand and foot, the pelvis provides attachments for muscles;
5. in the female it provides bony support for the birth canal.

The pelvic girdle transmits the weight from the vertebral column to the lower limbs (see Fig. 5.6), its bony and ligamentous components reflecting this function. There are some differences in the pelvis between females and males. In the female, these are due to adaptation for childbearing and the transmission of the relatively large fetal head during childbirth. The pelvis is essentially a basin, the upper part being known as the greater or false pelvis containing abdominal viscera. That part below the brim or pelvic inlet is the lesser or true pelvis. In the anatomical position, the pelvic inlet forms an angle of about 60° with the horizontal (see Fig. 5.7). The acetabulum is directed outward and downward and the acetabular notch should point directly downward. The *anterior superior iliac spines* and the *pubic tubercles* lie in the same vertical frontal plane. The lowest part of the sacrum lies above the level of the *pubic symphysis*.

The anterior superior iliac spines can be easily palpated in the living subject, particularly in females, where they tend to be further apart than in males. The *iliac crest* can also be palpated about 10 cm above the greater trochanter of the femur. In the sitting position, the ischial tuberosities can be felt, the weight of the body resting on them. The body of the right and left pubic bones can also be palpated; they separate the anterior abdominal wall from the genitalia.

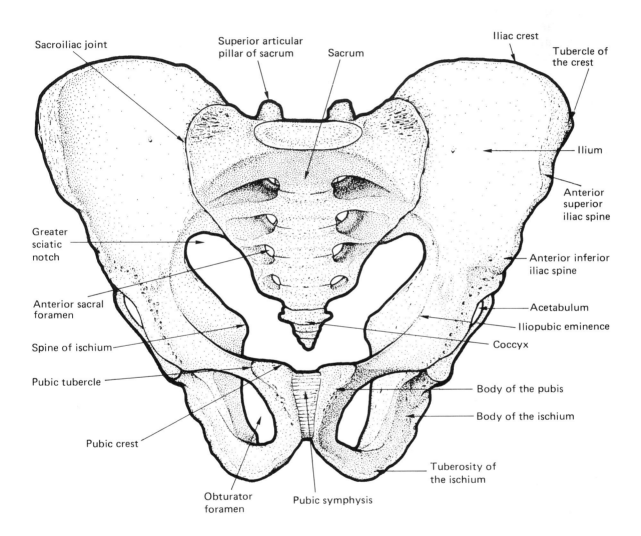

Sacroiliac joint

Superior articular
pillar of sacrum

Sacrum

Iliac crest

Tubercle
of the crest

Ilium

Anterior
superior
iliac spine

Anterior inferior
iliac spine

Greater
sciatic
notch

Anterior sacral
foramen

Spine of ischium

Pubic tubercle

Acetabulum

Iliopubic eminence

Coccyx

Body of the pubis

Body of the ischium

Pubic crest

Obturator
foramen

Pubic symphysis

Tuberosity of
the ischium

Fig. 5.5a   Pelvic girdle, anterior view.

Fig. 5.5b   Radiology of the hip region:

1 = Sacrum
2 = Sacroiliac joint
3 = Ilium
4 = Ischium
5 = Pubis
6 = Pubic symphysis
7 = Anterior superior iliac spine (ASIS)
8 = Anterior inferior iliac spine (AIIS)
9 = Obturator foramen
10 = Coccyx
11 = Head of femur
12 = Acetabulum (cortical bone)
13 = Joint space
14 = Fovea of head of femur
15 = Neck of femur
16 = Shaft of femur
17 = Greater trochanter
18 = Lesser trochanter

Fig. 5.6 Transfer of weight from the vertebral column, through the pelvis to the femur.

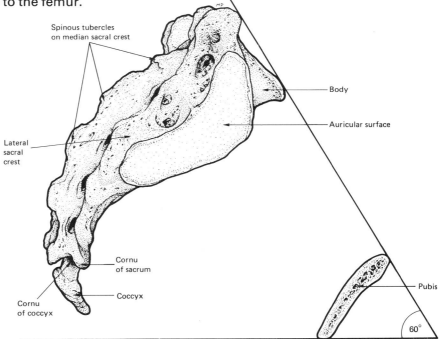

Spinous tubercles
on median sacral crest

Lateral
sacral
crest

Body

Auricular surface

Cornu
of sacrum

Coccyx

Cornu
of coccyx

Pubis

60°

Fig. 5.7 Relative position of the sacrum and pubis in the anatomical position, lateral view.

The innominate (hip) bone
(Figs. 5.8, 5.9)

The irregularly-shaped innominate consists of three bones fused together: the ilium, the pubis and the ischium.

The ilium

The ilium is the upper broad blade for the attachment of ligaments and large muscles. It forms the pelvic brim between the hip joint and the articulation with the sacrum. The anterior two-thirds of the projecting ilium forms the *iliac fossa* medially, which is part of the lateral and posterior abdominal wall, and the gluteal surface laterally, for attachment of the gluteal muscles. The posterior one-third, which is thicker, carries the auricular surface for the sacrum, behind this is a prolonged rough part, the *iliac tuberosity*, for the attachment of the strong sacroiliac ligaments which bear the body weight. The upper border of the ilium is the *iliac crest* which is convex superiorly as well as being curved anteroposteriorly with the anterior part curved outwards. The iliac crest ends anteriorly as the *anterior superior iliac spine* and posteriorly as the *posterior superior iliac spine.* Both spines and the whole of the crest can be palpated. Behind the anterior spine on the outer border is the prominent *tubercle of the crest.* Below the anterior superior spine is the *anterior inferior iliac spine* separated by a shallow notch. Similarly, below the posterior superior spine is the *posterior inferior iliac spine*, again separated by a shallow notch, the two posterior spines being closer together than the two anterior spines. Below the posterior inferior spine is the deep *greater sciatic notch.* The iliac fossa is separated from the pelvic surface of the ilium by the arcuate line which forms part of the pelvic brim. The anterior part of this line has an elevation, the *iliopubic eminence*, marking the junction of the ilium with the pubis. The part of the ilium which participates in the formation of the acetabulum is the *body* of the ilium.

The outer gluteal surface of the ilium follows the curvature of the iliac crest. It shows three curved gluteal lines which demarcate the attachments of the gluteal muscles. The most obvious of these lines is the *posterior gluteal line*, which passes down from the iliac crest to the front of the posterior inferior spine. The *anterior gluteal line* is a series of low tubercles coming from the iliac crest curving upwards and backwards below the iliac tubercle and then down towards the greater sciatic notch. The *inferior gluteal line* is less prominent, curving from below the anterior superior iliac spine towards the apex of the greater sciatic notch. Below the inferior gluteal line is an area of multiple vascular foramina. The fusion of the ilium and the ischium is marked by a rounded elevation between the acetabulum and the greater sciatic notch. Above this the ilium forms the major part of the notch. The gluteal surface is succeeded inferiorly by the acetabular portion of the ilium.

The iliac fossa is the smooth internal concavity of the *ala* of the ilium. It becomes narrower inferiorly ending at the roughened *iliopubic eminence*, the line of junction between the ilium and the pubis. Its deepest part, high in the fossa, is composed of paper-thin translucent bone. The pelvic brim, marked by the *arcuate line* of the ilium, is the posterior–inferior limit of the iliac fossa. Behind and below the iliac fossa and the arcuate line is the sacropelvic surface of the ilium. Posterior to the iliac fossa, this region exhibits the auricular surface for articulation with the first two segments of the sacrum and, behind and above it, the tuberosity. The roughened tuberosity provides attachment for the short posterior sacroiliac ligaments and for fibres of the erector spinae and multifidus muscles. The auricular area extends from the pelvic brim to the posterior inferior iliac spine. Its surface is gently undulating, being convex above to concave below, and roughened by numerous tubercles and depressions. The surface is covered with hyaline cartilage forming a synovial joint, which is immobile, with the ala of the sacrum. In later years, fibrous bands often join the articular surfaces within the joint space.

The pubis

The pubis is an angulated bone. The *body of the pubis* projects laterally and superiorly as the *superior ramus* to join the ilium and

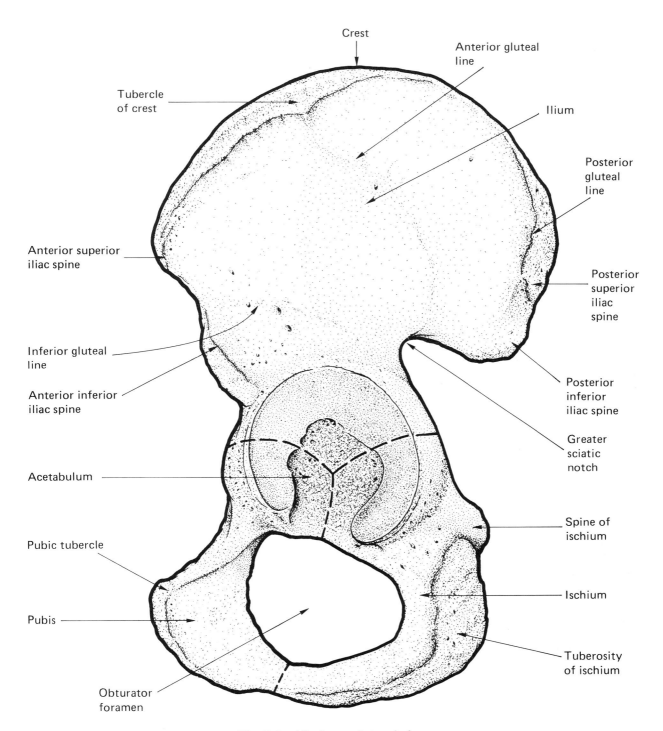

Fig. 5.8 Hip bone, lateral view.

ischium at the acetabulum, forming one-fifth of the acetabulum. A thin and flattened *inferior ramus* extends inferiorly and postero-laterally from the body to fuse with the ischium below the obturator foramen. The body is quadrilateral in shape, with the symphyseal surface being oval; it is crossed by several transverse ridges to which the fibro-cartilage of the symphysis pubis is attached, and coated with hyaline cartilage for the secondary cartilaginous joint that constitutes the symphysis pubis. The upper border of the body is the *pubic crest*, being marked laterally by the *pubic tubercle*. From this tubercle two ridges diverge laterally into the superior ramus. The upper of these two ridges is the *pectineal line*, which is continuous with the arcuate line of the ilium, and forms part of the pelvic brim. The lower, rounded ridge is the obturator crest, passing downwards into the anterior margin of the acetabular notch. Between these two ridges is the *iliopubic eminence*. Below the obturator crest on the superior pubic ramus is the deep *obturator groove*.

The ischium

The ischium is the posterior inferior part of the innominate, being angulated and in the same plane as the pubis. The apex of the angulation is blunt and rounded, forming the *ischial tuberosity*, divided transversely by a low ridge. A smooth oval above this ridge is further subdivided by a vertical ridge into lateral and medial areas. In the sitting position, the weight of the body rests on the two ischial tuberosities. Anteriorly the tuberosity passes upwards as the *ischial ramus*, being continuous with the inferior pubic ramus, forming the *ischiopubic ramus*. The *body* of the ischium forms two-fifths of the acetabulum. The posterior border of the body is continuous above with the ilium, forming the *greater sciatic notch*. Inferiorly this border ends as the blunt medially projecting ischial spine, below which is the groove forming the *lesser sciatic notch*. The pelvic surface of the body is continuous with the pelvic surface of the ilium, forming part of the lateral wall of the pelvis.

The *acetabulum* is formed by the fusion of the three component bones of the innomi-nate; the ilium, ischium and pubis meet at a Y-shaped cartilage which forms their epiphyseal junction. The anterior one-fifth of the acetabulum is formed by the pubis, the superior posterior two-fifths by the body of the ilium, and the inferior posterior two-fifths by the body of the ischium. The acetabulum is a hemispherical hollow on the outer surface of the innominate, facing downwards, forwards and laterally. The prominent rim of the acetabulum is deficient inferiorly forming the *acetabular notch*. The rim gives attachment to the *acetabular labrum* of the hip joint, its uneven internal edge provides an attachment for the synovial membrane of the joint. The *acetabular* labrum continues across the acetabular notch to produce the *transverse ligament*. The transverse ligament and margins of the notch give attachment to the *ligament of the head of the femur*. The heavy wall of the acetabulum consists of a semilunar articular portion covered with hyaline cartilage, open below, and a deep, central non-articular portion, the *acetabular fossa*. The acetabular fossa is formed mainly from the ischium, and its wall is frequently thin.

The *obturator foramen* is a large aperture ringed by the sharp margins of the pubis and ischium, those of the pubis overlapping each other in a spiral forming the obturator groove, which runs obliquely forwards and downwards from the pelvis into the thigh, being converted into a canal by a specialization of the obturator fascia. The obturator membrane is attached to the margins of the foramen, except superiorly at the obturator groove.

Ossification

Each innominate bone ossifies from eight centres: three primary centres, one each for the ilium, ischium and pubis; and five secondary centres, one each for the iliac crest, the anterior inferior iliac spine, the ischial tuberosity, the pubic symphysis and the triradiate cartilage at the centre of the acetabulum. The sequence of ossification has functional significance because of the support given to the pelvic organs and its weight transmission role. The primary ossification centres appear during the third,

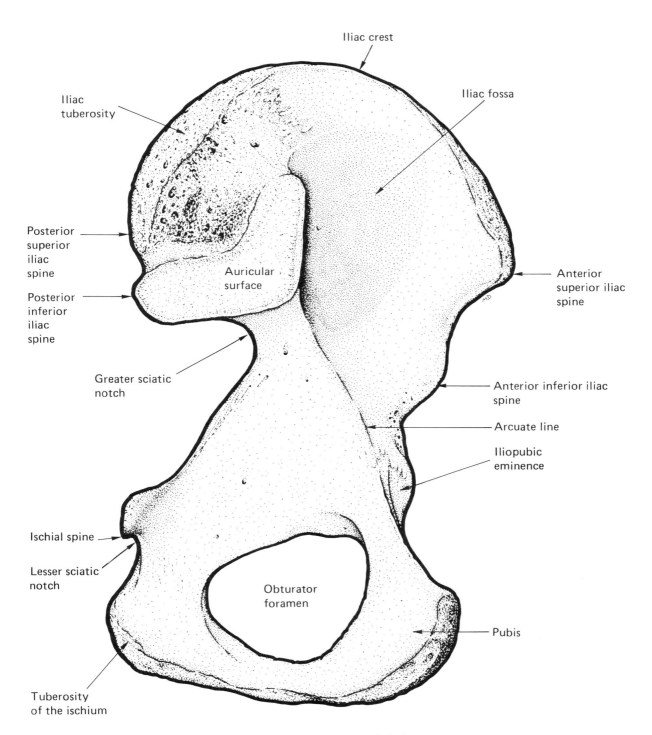

Fig. 5.9 Hip bone, medial view.

fourth and fifth months of development. At birth the ilium, ischium and pubis are quite separate and the secondary ossification centres have not yet appeared. By the age of thirteen or fourteen, the major parts of the ilium, ischium and pubis are completely bony but are still separated by the Y-shaped triradiate cartilage in the acetabulum. At the age of eight or nine, three major centres of ossification appear in the acetabular cartilage. The largest appears in the anterior wall of the acetabulum and fuses with the pubis. Further centres appear in the iliac acetabular cartilage superiorly which fuses with the ilium, and in the ischial acetabular cartilage posteriorly which fuses with the ischium. Fusion of the three bones in the acetabulum occurs between sixteen and eighteen years. The other secondary ossification centres appear at about puberty and unite with the major bones between twenty and twenty two.

Palpation

The anterior superior iliac spines can easily be palpated in the living subject, particularly in females where they tend to be further apart. They are situated at the anterior end of the iliac crest, being found in the upper part of the pocket area. They act as an excellent landmark for many of the surface markings in this region. Tracing backwards from these spines, the iliac crest is easily palpable, having a large tuberosity about 5 cm from its anterior end. If this bony crest is followed as far back as possible, the rather smaller posterior superior iliac spines can be felt. Each is situated in a dimple in the female subject, whereas in the male each spine appears as a small raised tubercle.

About 10 cm below the centre of the crest, the greater tuberosity of the femur can be clearly felt. Hip measurements, when buying trousers or a skirt, are calculated erroneously around these two trochanters. In sitting, the body rests on the ischial tuberosity of each innominate bone; if the hands are placed under this area the tuberosities can be easily felt. This part of the tuberosity is covered with a bursa which often becomes painful and swollen when sitting for too long on a hard surface; this is termed a bursitis.

If the hands are drawn down the front of the abdominal wall, about 5 cm above the genitalia, a bony ring can be felt. This has a central depression where the pubic symphysis is situated with each pubic tubercle about 1 cm lateral and above on either side.

The sacrum

The *sacrum* consists of five fused vertebrae, being broadened by the incorporation of large costal elements and transverse processes into heavy lateral masses. The lateral masses lie lateral to the transverse tubercles on the back of the sacrum and extend between the anterior sacral foramina onto the front of the bone. The *auricular surface* lies entirely on the lateral mass. The sacrum is triangular in shape with the apex inferior. It is wedged between the posterior parts of the innominate with which it articulates at the sacroiliac joints. The *pelvic (anterior) surface* (Fig. 5.10a) is concave and relatively smooth, being marked by four *transverse ridges* separating the original bodies of the five sacral vertebrae. Lateral to each ridge is the *anterior sacral foramen*, which represents the anterior part of the intervertebral foramen. These foramina are directed laterally and anteriorly.

The dorsal surface (Fig. 5.10b) of the sacrum is convex and highly irregular, and presents the dorsal sacral foramina, medial to which the vertebral canal is closed over by the fused laminae. However, usually the spinous processes and laminae of the fourth and fifth sacral vertebrae are absent leaving the sacral canal open. This is the *sacral hiatus*, an inferior entrance to the vertebral canal, which may be used, for example during labour, to introduce an anaesthetic to block the sacral nerves. Dorsally, in the midline, the reduced spinous processes form the *median sacral crest*. Lateral to the dorsal sacral foramina are the prominent lateral sacral crests, representing the transverse processes. These lateral crests provide attachment for the dorsal sacroiliac ligaments, and inferiorly for the sacrotuberous and sacrospinous ligaments. Just medial to the dorsal sacral foramina are the indistinct *intermediate sacral crest*, representing the fused articular processes. The *superior articular processes* of the first sacral vertebra are large and oval,

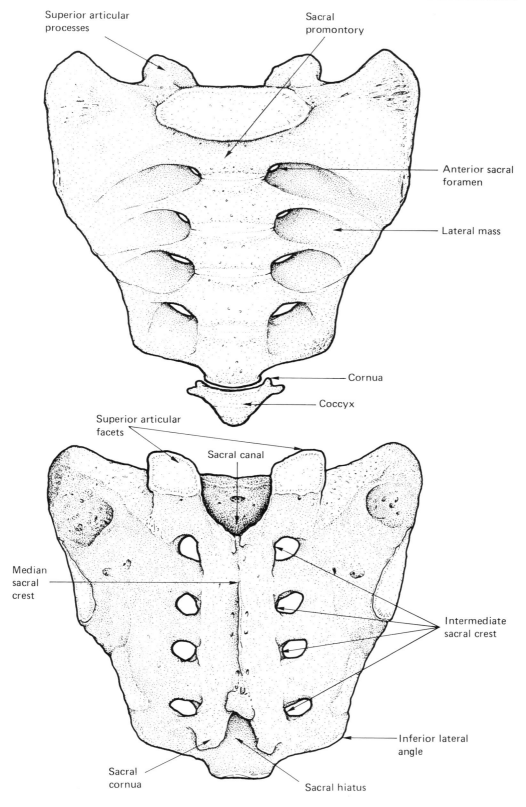

Fig. 5.10   a = Sacrum, anterior view; **b** = sacrum, posterior view.

being supported by short heavy pedicles. Their facets, for articulation with the inferior articular surfaces of the fifth lumbar vertebra, are concave from side-to-side, facing posteriorly and medially. The tubercles of the inferior articular processes of the fifth sacral vertebral form the *sacral horns* and are connected to the horns of the coccyx.

The *lateral surface* of the sacrum (Fig. 5.11a) is triangular, being narrower below. The upper part of this surface is divided into an anterior smoother pitted *auricular surface*, covered in cartilage, for articulation with a similar area on the ilium. The rougher posterior area presents three deep impressions for the attachment of the powerful dorsal sacroiliac ligaments. The *superior surface* (Fig. 5.11b) faces anterosuperiorly having a central oval area which is the upper surface of the first sacral vertebra, being separated from the fifth lumbar vertebra by a thick intervertebral disc. Its anterior projecting border is the *sacral promontory*. On each side of the body of the sacrum is the *ala*, formed by the fusion of the costal and transverse processes of the first sacral vertebra. When articulated with the innominate, the ala of the sacrum is continuous with the ala of the ilium.

Ossification

Primary centres appear in the sacrum between the third and eighth month *in utero*; one for each centra, one for each half of each vertebral arch, and for each costal element in the upper four vertebrae. The costal elements fuse with the arches by the age of 5 years, the arches with the centra slightly later, with the two parts of each arch uniting between the ages of 7 and 10. The segments of the lateral masses fuse together during puberty, with secondary centres appearing for vertebral bodies at about the same time. Bodies and epiphyses fuse between 18 and 25 years. Several secondary centres appear at the ends of the costal and transverse processes from which two epiphyses are formed, one of which covers the auricular surface while the other completes the lower margin of the sacrum.

The coccyx (Fig. 5.11c)

The *coccyx* usually consists of four fused vertebrae forming a single piece or two pieces of bone, which mainly represent the bodies. The pelvic surface is concave and relatively smooth, while on the dorsal surface the rudimentary articular processes present as a row of tubercles. Superiorly the larger pair form the *coccygeal cornua* which articulate with the sacral cornua, and enclose the fifth sacral intervertebral foramen. The posterior wall of the vertebral canal of the coccyx is absent so that the sacral hiatus continues downwards over the back of the coccyx.

Spinous tubercles
on median sacral
crest

Body

Lateral
sacral
crest

Auricular surface

Cornua

Rudimentary
transverse
process

Rudimentary
bodies of
vertebrae

Cornu of sacrum

Coccyx

Cornu
of coccyx

c

a

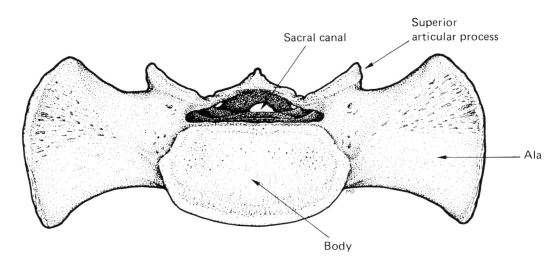

Sacral canal

Superior
articular process

Ala

Body

b

Fig. 5.11   a = Sacrum, lateral view; **b** = sacrum, superior
view; **c** = coccyx, anterior view.

THE FEMUR (Figs. 5.12, 5.13)

The femur transmits the weight from the ilium to the upper end of the tibia. This beautifully-shaped bone is the longest and strongest in the body possessing a shaft and two extremities.

The upper extremity

The upper extremity consists of a *head*, *neck*, and a *greater* and *lesser trochanter*. The head is slightly more than half a sphere being entirely smooth and covered with articular cartilage except for a small hollow just below its centre, the fovea, providing attachment for the ligament of the head of the femur. Connecting the head to the *shaft* is the neck which is approximately 5 cm long and forms an angle with the shaft of 125°. This angle varies a little with age and sex. The neck is flattened on its anterior and posterior surfaces forming an upper and lower border, both being rounded; the upper concave in its long axis, the lower being straight. The anterior surface joins the shaft at the *intertrochanteric line*, the posterior at the *intertrochanteric crest* which is marked at its centre by the large quadrate tubercle.

The greater trochanter

The greater trochanter is situated on the lateral aspect of the upper part of the shaft lateral to the neck. It is a large *quadrilateral process*, having an upper border marked by a *tubercle*, an anterior border marked by a depression and posterior and inferior borders both roughened for muscular attachment. Its lateral surface is crossed by a diagonal roughened line running downwards and forwards having above it a smooth area covered by a bursa. The medial surface, above the neck, is small and presents a deep *trochanteric fossa* at its centre.

The lesser trochanter

The lesser trochanter is conical in shape and situated medially, behind and below the neck, being smaller than the greater trochanter. Its tip is drawn forwards and presents a roughened ridge running downwards and forwards.

The shaft

The shaft is strong, and except for a prominent posterior border, almost cylindrical on cross-section. It is gently convex anteriorly, being narrowest at its centre and growing stouter as it approaches the upper and lower extremities. Its posterior border, the *linea aspera*, is very rough for muscle attachment, presenting a medial and lateral lip with a central flattened area between. In the upper and lower quarters of the shaft the two lips diverge producing a posterior surface. The upper surface is marked centrally by the narrow vertical *pectineal line*, whereas the lateral truncated border is continuous upwards with the posterior border of the greater trochanter to form the *gluteal tuberosity*. The lower surface, between the supracondylar lines above and the condyles below, forms the popliteal surface of the femur. The rest of the shaft is slightly flattened on its anterior, posteromedial and posterolateral aspects.

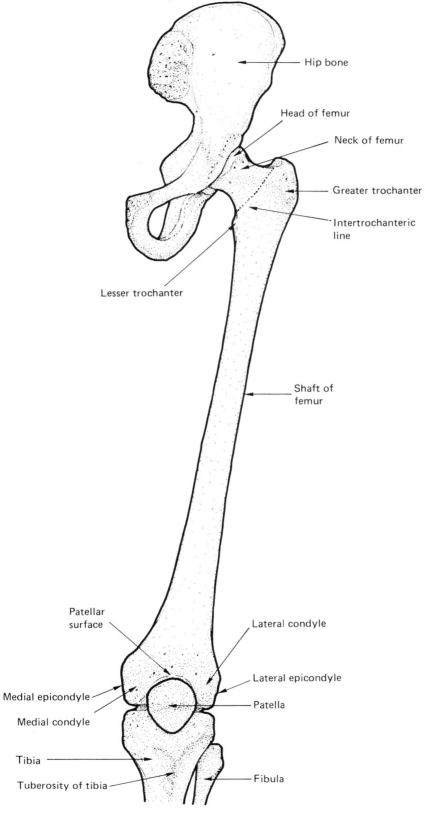

Fig. 5.12 Bones of the lower limb (anterior view, left side).

The lower extremity

The lower extremity (see Fig. 5.16) of the femur consists of two large *condyles*, each of which project backwards beyond the posterior surface of the shaft, the lateral being stouter than the medial. The inferior, posterior and posterosuperior surfaces of the condyles are smooth and continuous anteriorly with the triangularly-shaped patella surface, which is grooved vertically producing a larger lateral and a smaller medial region. The two condyles are separated posteriorly and inferiorly by the intercondylar notch which is marked on its lateral wall posteriorly by the attachment of the anterior cruciate and on its medial wall anteriorly by the posterior cruciate ligament. The separating lips of the linea aspera continue downwards onto the upper aspect of the medial and lateral condyles as the supracondylar lines, the medial presenting at its lower end as the adductor tubercle.

The lateral surface of the lateral condyle is roughened, being marked just below its centre by the *lateral epicondyle* below which is a smooth groove for the passage of the popliteus tendon. The medial surface of the medial condyle is also roughened and again marked just below its centre by the *medial epicondyle*.

Palpation

The femur is almost completely surrounded by muscles and is only palpable in limited areas. At its upper end, the greater trochanter is an obvious landmark, projecting just a little more laterally than the iliac crest, being easily located by running the hands down from the middle of this crest some 7 to 10 cm. The greater trochanter is perhaps easier to feel if the fingers are brought forward from the hollows on the sides of the buttocks in the region of the back pocket. Its posterior border is palpated for about 5 cm, running down towards the shaft, while its upper border is an important landmark to locate the level of the hip joint.

At its lower end, the femur is well covered with muscle until just above the knee joint. As the fingers pass down the medial side of the thigh the medial condyle can be palpated. This is marked just behind its centre by the medial epicondyle, above which the adductor tubercle can be palpated with the tendinous part of the adductor magnus attaching to it. On the lateral side of the knee, the lateral condyle can be palpated with the lateral epicondyle projecting from its outer surface. At the lower edge of each of these condyles, the line of the knee joint can be palpated particularly as it passes forwards.

If the knee is flexed as much as possible, the patella is seen to move downwards revealing on the front of the knee the two femoral condyles, covered by the lower part of the quadriceps femoris muscle and its retinaculae.

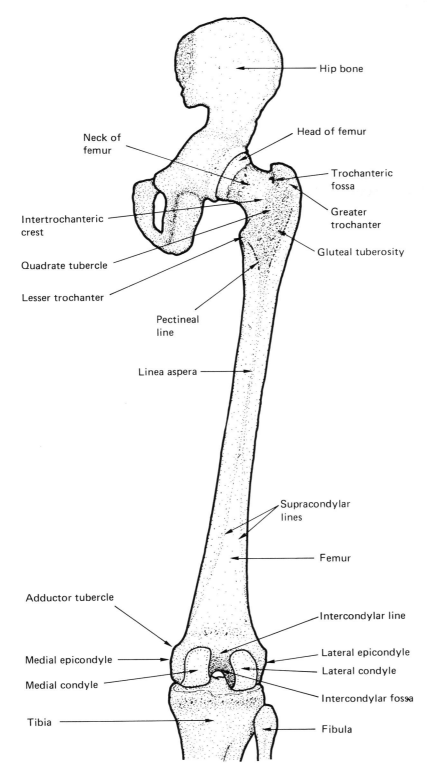

Fig. 5.13 Bones of the lower limb (posterior view, right side).

Ossification (Fig. 5.14)

The primary ossification centre for the shaft appears at 7 weeks *in utero*. At birth, growth plates separate the bony shaft from the upper and lower cartilaginous epiphyses. A secondary ossification centre appears in the lower epiphysis shortly before birth. Secondary ossification centres appear in the upper epiphysis for the head at 1 year and in the greater trochanter at 4 years. The last secondary ossification centre appears in the cartilaginous lesser trochanter at 12 years. The upper epiphysis fuses with the shaft at about the eighteenth year, the last to do so being the head. The lower epiphysis fuses with the shaft at about 20 years. The neck of the femur is ossified as part of the body (shaft) and not from the upper epiphysis.

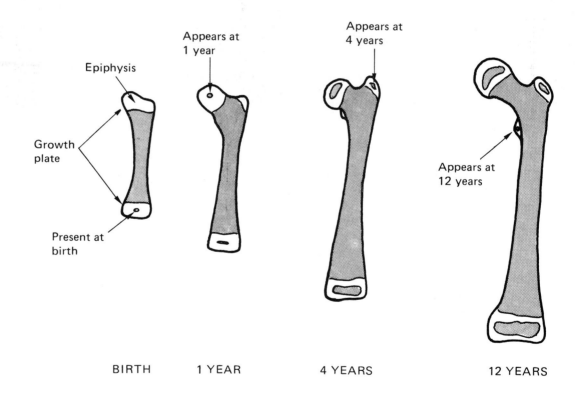

Fig. 5.14a Ossification of the femur.

anteroposterior view

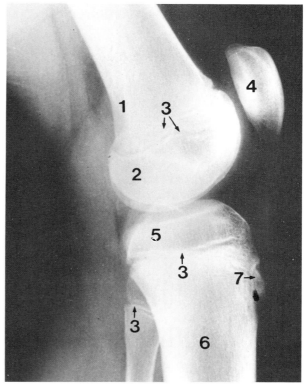

lateral view

Fig. 5.14b   Radiology of the child's knee (aged 12 years):
left = anteroposterior view, **right** = lateral view:

  1 = Flared femoral metaphysis
  2 = Distal femoral epiphysis
  3 = Growth plates
  4 = Patella
  5 = Proximal tibial epiphysis
  6 = Tibial shaft
  7 = Tibial tuberosity

THE PATELLA (Figs. 5.15, 5.16)

The patella is a sesamoid bone formed in the tendon of the quadriceps femoris muscle. It is triangular in shape, with its *apex* pointing downwards and its base uppermost. It is flattened from front-to-back having an anterior and posterior surface and upper, lateral and medial borders.

The anterior surface of the patella is marked by a series of roughened vertical ridges produced by the fibres of the quadriceps which pass over it. It is slightly convex forwards and its shape varies according to the pull of the muscle.

The posterior surface has a large, smooth oval facet covered with hyaline cartilage for articulation with the patellar surface of the femur. It is divided by a broad vertical ridge into a smaller *medial* and larger *lateral facet*. The cartilage on each of these facets is marked by two horizontal lines dividing each surface into an upper, middle and lower section. Below, there is a roughened area on the posterior aspect of the apex for the upper attachment of the ligamentum patellae.

The base of the patella is roughened for the attachment of rectus femoris and vastus intermedius. The medial and lateral borders are rounded but also roughened receiving attachments of vastus medialis and lateralis.

Ossification

At birth the patella is cartilaginous, ossifying from a single centre or several centres between 3 years and puberty. Occasionally the patella may be absent.

Palpation

As the patella lies subcutaneously, the whole margin as well as its anterior surface can be palpated.

Fig. 5.16   Radiology of the adult knee.

a = Anteroposterior view:
  2 = Medial femoral condyle
  3 = Lateral femoral condyle
  4 = Radiological joint space
  5 = Lateral joint space
  6 = Head of fibula
  7 = Neck of fibula
  8 = Intercondylar eminence
  9 = Intercondylar notch

b = Lateral view:
  1 = Patella
  2 = Femoral condyles
  3 = Intercondylar eminences
  4 = Tibial tuberosity
  5 = Lateral tibial condyle

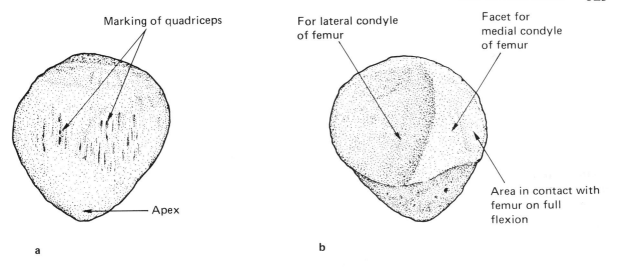

Fig. 5.15   **a** = The patella viewed from the front. **b** = The patella viewed from behind.

a   Adult anteroposterior view

b   Adult lateral view

Fig. 5.16

THE TIBIA (Figs. 5.17, 5.18)

The tibia is a long bone which transmits the body weight from the medial and lateral condyles of the femur to the foot. It is by far the larger of the two bones of the leg, being situated medial to the fibula. It consists of a shaft and two extremities, the upper extremity being much larger than the lower.

The upper extremity

The upper extremity is expanded in all directions, but particularly in its posterior dimension where it projects backwards beyond the line of the shaft. It consists of two *condyles* having between them anteriorly a large, truncated area elongated in its vertical axis, roughened in its upper and smooth in its lower parts. This is the *tuberosity of the tibia*. The lateral condyle projects further laterally than the shaft and has a round articular facet on its posterolateral part for articulation with the head of the fibula. Posteriorly, the space between the condyles is smooth. The two condyles have on their upper surfaces areas for articulation with the condyles of the femur. These superior surfaces are divided by two raised tubercles, the medial and lateral intercondylar tubercles, which are close together and termed the *intercondylar eminence*. In front of and behind the eminence there is an uneven non-articular area which is narrower close to the eminence and which becomes wider as it passes forwards and backwards. This area gives attachment to some important structures of the knee joint. Anterior to the intercondylar eminence three structures are attached: most anteriorly is the anterior horn of the medial meniscus, whilst closest to the eminence is the anterior horn of the lateral meniscus, and between the two the anterior cruciate ligament. The area behind the intercondylar eminence also gives attachment to three structures: most posteriorly is the posterior cruciate ligament, whilst closest to the emi-

nence is the posterior horn of the lateral meniscus, between the two and the posterior horn of the medial meniscus.

The shaft

The shaft of the tibia is triangular in cross-section tapering slightly from the condyles for about two-thirds of its length, widening again at its lower end. It has an anterior border which runs from the lower part of the tuberosity downwards to the anterior part of the *medial malleolus*. The medial border begins just below the back of the medial condyle, and although not always easy to see, can be traced to the posterior part of the medial malleolus. The *interosseous border* begins just below the articular facet on the lateral condyle and runs in a curved line with its concavity forwards, down to the roughened triangular area on the lateral side at the lower end of the bone.

The shaft therefore has three surfaces: medial, posterior and lateral. The smooth medial surface, sloping posteriorly from the anterior border, is subcutaneous in the whole of its extent, from the medial condyle above to the medial malleolus below and is commonly called the shin. The lateral surface between the anterior and interosseous borders is slightly concave, particularly in its upper two-thirds, and gives attachment to tibialis anterior. Inferiorly, it becomes continuous with the anterior surface of the lower end of the bone. The posterior surface between the interosseous and medial borders is crossed by two raised lines, one running obliquely from just below the lateral condyle downwards and medially to join the posterior border about half way down, this is the *soleal line*. The area above it is roughened for the attachment of the popliteus muscle. Below the soleal line is a *vertical line* to which the fascia covering tibialis posterior is attached. It divides the lower part of the posterior surface into two, both being roughened for the attachment of muscle, laterally tibialis posterior and medially flexor digitorum longus.

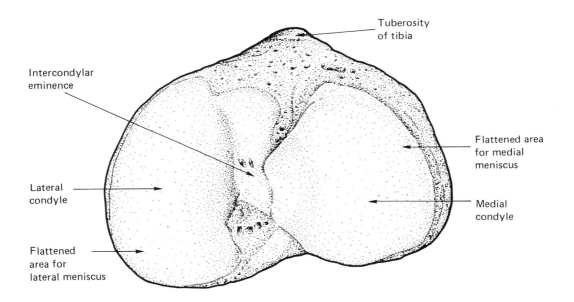

Fig. 5.17a   Left tibia, superior view.

The lower extremity

The lower extremity of the tibia is expanded, but to a lesser extent than the upper. It has a prominent medial malleolus which is continuous with the medial surface of the shaft projecting downwards from its medial side. The inferior surface is smooth for articulation with the superior surface of the body of the talus. Medially it is continuous with the malleolar articular surface. It usually turns upwards on the lateral surface where the fibula articulates with it. The lateral surface is concave anteriorly where the fibula articulates with it and is continued up as a rough triangular area for the attachment of the interosseous ligament. The posterior surface is coarse and grooved by tendons passing into the foot. The anterior surface is smooth and slightly convex.

Ossification

The primary ossification centre for the tibia appears in the shaft during the seventh week *in utero* and spreads so that at birth only the ends are cartilaginous. The secondary centre for the proximal end, which includes the tibial tuberosity, appears at birth, spreading down to the tuberosity after the tenth year. An independent centre for the tuberosity may appear, if it does so, this appears at 11 years. The secondary centre for the distal end appears during the second year. Fusion of the proximal epiphysis with the shaft occurs between 19 and 21 years, and of the distal epiphysis with the shaft a few years earlier between 17 and 19.

Palpation

The tubercle of the tibia is easily recognizable at the upper end of the anterior border of the tibia (the shin), with the ligamentum patellae attaching to its upper portion. The medial and lateral condyles can be palpated about 2 cm higher, as they are subcutaneous as far as the hamstring muscles on either side. The upper edge indicates the line of the knee joint.

Just below and behind the mid point on the lateral side, the head of the fibula stands out clearly. Running down the whole length of the bone from the medial surface of the medial condyle is the inner surface of the shaft, being subcutaneous as far as the medial malleolus. Both anterior and posterior borders are palpable at its edges. The medial malleolus is subcutaneous and its medial surface, borders and tip are easily palpable.

Applied anatomy

Due to the fact that the medial surface of the tibia is subcutaneous, the risks of damage and fracture of this bone are increased. In addition, the likelihood of infection, and delayed non-union of the bone is very high and a common complication in this region. The most common area of damage is at the junction between the upper two-thirds and the lower third of the shaft, this being its thinnest part, and unfortunately the area with the poorest blood supply.

THE FIBULA (Fig. 5.17b, see also Fig. 5.18)

The fibula is a long slender bone being expanded both at its upper and lower ends.

The upper end, or head, is expanded in all directions having on its superomedial side a facet for articulation with the lateral condyle of the tibia. Lateral to this articular facet is the apex of the head which projects upwards. The rest of the upper end is roughened for the attachment of biceps femoris. Just below the head is the neck, around which runs the common peroneal nerve.

The shaft varies considerably in individuals and its features are often difficult to recognize. The fibula actually has three borders and three surfaces. The *anterior border* is more prominent inferiorly where it widens into a smooth, triangular, subcutaneous area continuous with the lateral surface of the malleolus. It runs from below the anterior aspect of the head passing vertically down to the triangular area described above. Medial to the anterior border is the *interosseous border*, again often poorly marked. Extending from the neck, it lies close to the anterior border in its upper third, but then passes backwards and medially to join the

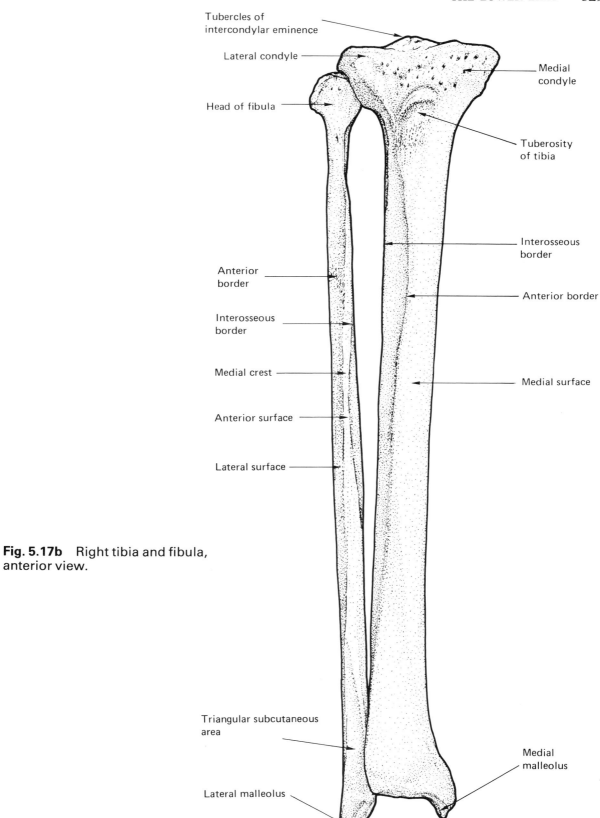

Tubercles of
intercondylar eminence

Lateral condyle

Head of fibula

Medial
condyle

Tuberosity
of tibia

Interosseous
border

Anterior
border

Anterior border

Interosseous
border

Medial crest

Anterior surface

Medial surface

Lateral surface

Triangular subcutaneous
area

Medial
malleolus

Lateral malleolus

Fig. 5.17b Right tibia and fibula,
anterior view.

apex of the roughened triangular area superior to the malleolar articular surface. The *posterior border* begins below the lateral aspect of the head and neck, and passes down to the medial margin of the posterior surface of the lateral malleolus. This border is rounded and more difficult to trace. The *lateral surface* of the fibula is concave and posterolateral to the anterior border. It becomes convex as it winds round posterior to the triangular subcutaneous area to the posterior surface of the malleolus. It is roughened for the attachment of the peroneal muscles. The *anterior surface* is a very narrow strip between the anterior and interosseous borders at its upper end, expanding as it continues downwards. The posterior surface is more expanded than the anterior and lateral surfaces, being divided by a vertical ridge, the crest, into a medial and lateral part similar to the tibia. The region between the crest and the interosseous border is concave and usually divided by an oblique line, whereas the region between the crest and posterior border is flat and roughened in its upper part by the attachment of soleus.

The lower end can be recognized readily, being flattened on its medial and lateral sides and having posteriorly a deep malleolar fossa. On its medial side, just above this fossa, is a triangular area which is smooth for articulation with the lateral surface of the body of the talus. Just above the articular area on the medial side of the lower end is an elongated roughened area for attachment of the interosseous ligament of the inferior tibiofibular joint, and just below this is the malleolar fossa. The fibula varies in shape according to the muscles that are attached to it, and it can be seen that it carries no weight, but contributes to the lateral stability of the ankle joint.

Ossification

The primary centre appears in the shaft during the seventh week *in utero*, again spreading so that at birth only the ends are cartilaginous. The secondary centre for the distal end appears during the second year and fuses with the body between 17 and 19 years. The secondary centre for the proximal end appears slightly later, during the third or fourth years, and also fuses with the body later, between 19 and 21 years.

At birth, the fibula is relatively thick, being about half as thick as the tibia in the third prenatal month. As development and growth continue, the disparity between the thickness of the fibula and tibia increases to give the relative adult proportions. The distal end of the fibula does not reach below the medial malleolus until after its ossification has begun, that is after the second year. It is only after this time that the adult relations of the malleoli can be seen.

Palpation

The head of the fibula can be readily palpated on the posterolateral side below the knee joint. If the hands are placed on the lateral sides of the calves and moved up towards the knees, the bony head can be felt projecting laterally. The head can also be easily palpated if the fingers are placed in the hollow on the lateral side of the knee when it is flexed to 90°. Little of the shaft can be palpated as it is surrounded by muscles, however in its lower third an elongated triangular area can be palpated on the lateral aspect which can be traced down to the lateral malleolus. The lateral malleolus is easily palpated on the lateral side of the ankle projecting down to a point 2.5 cm below the level of the ankle joint.

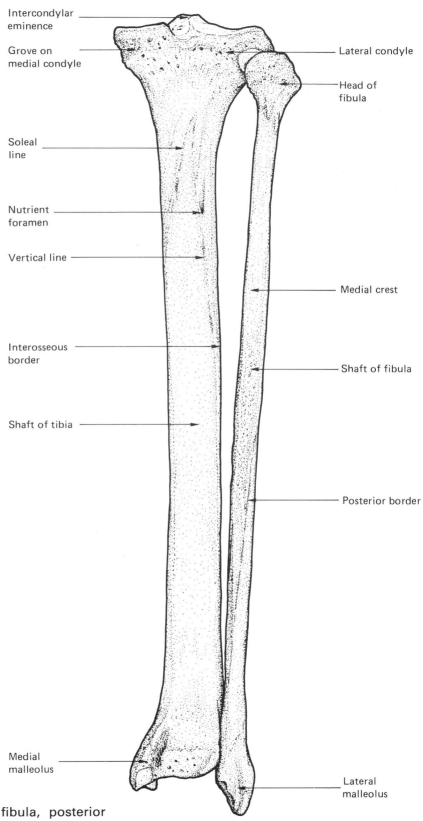

Intercondylar eminence

Grove on medial condyle

Soleal line

Nutrient foramen

Vertical line

Interosseous border

Shaft of tibia

Medial malleolus

Lateral condyle

Head of fibula

Medial crest

Shaft of fibula

Posterior border

Lateral malleolus

Fig. 5.18 Right tibia and fibula, posterior view.

THE BONY STRUCTURE OF THE FOOT
(Fig. 5.19, see also Fig. 5.44a)

The foot consists of many small bones, posteriorly are the *tarsal bones* and anteriorly the *metatarsals* and *phalanges*. The tarsus and metatarsals comprise the foot proper, whereas the phalanges comprise the toes. The largest bone in the foot is the *calcaneus*, while the largest metatarsal is the most medial, having anterior to it the two phalanges of the big toe or hallux. The other metatarsals of the foot each have three phalanges distal to them. Tracing along the bones of the medial longitudinal arch from posterior to anterior, are the calcaneus, the *talus*, (situated more on top of the previous bone) the *navicular*, the three *cuneiform bones*, and the first, second and third metatarsals with their phalanges. Tracing along the lateral longitudinal arch of the foot, again from posterior to anterior, are the calcaneus, the *cuboid*, the fourth and fifth metatarsals with their phalanges.

The calcaneus

The calcaneus lies inferior to the talus and projects backwards to form the prominence of the heel, and is strongly bound to all the tarsal bones by ligaments. It is the largest bone in the foot, being oblong in shape and having six surfaces. The anterior surface faces forwards for articulation with the cuboid, being slightly convex from top-to-bottom and more or less flat from side-to-side. The medial part of this surface extends onto the medial side of the calcaneus to accommodate a backward projection of the cuboid. The posterior surface is rounded presenting three areas. The upper part is smooth where a bursa lies between it and the tendocalcaneus. The middle, which is smooth and convex, except at its lower margin where it ends as a jagged rough edge, receives the attachment of the tendocalcaneus. The lowest part is roughened, being subcutaneous and covered by the strong fibrous tissue and fat of the heel pad. This lowest part of the posterior surface transmits the body weight from the heel to the ground and curves forwards onto the inferior surface.

Here are found the larger medial and smaller lateral tubercles projecting forwards. The inferior surface continues forwards as a rough area terminating as the anterior tubercle. The long plantar ligament attaches to the rough area. The lateral surface of the bone is slightly roughened and nearly flat. It presents two tubercles, one for the attachment of part of the lateral ligament of the ankle joint, and the other, which is slightly lower and more anterior, provides attachments for the inferior peroneal retinaculum. The latter tubercle is elongated, with a groove above and below, and is called the peroneal tubercle. The medial surface is smooth and hollowed being overhung anteriorly by the sustentaculum tali, under which is a groove for the tendon of flexor hallucis longus. On the superior surface of the sustentaculum tali is the middle articular surface for the head of the talus. Behind the middle articular surface is a deep groove, the sulcus calcanei, which continues across the superior surface of the calcaneus in a posteromedial direction. In front of the sinus calcanei is a roughened area for the attachment of muscles and ligaments, while behind it is the posterior articular surface, convex from front-to-back and flat from side-to-side, for articulation with the under surface of the body of the talus. Behind the posterior articular surface is a further roughened area, concave upwards from front-to-back and convex from side-to-side.

The trabeculae of the calcaneus have a particular arrangement due to the weight-bearing nature of the bone. From the posterior articular surface, the supporting trabeculae pass downwards and backwards to the heel and downwards and forwards to the articular area for the cuboid. Running from the heel to the anterior surface are superior and inferior arcuate systems serving to tie the bone together. Between all of these systems there is an area of less dense, and therefore weaker, bone tissue.

The talus

The talus is situated above the calcaneus with the head and neck directed forwards and medially. It transmits the body weight from the tibia to the calcaneus and navicular. The body of the talus is wedge-shaped from front to back being wider anteriorly, and lies between the malleoli of the tibia and fibula. Its upper surface is convex from front-to-back and slightly concave from side-to-side, being pulley-shaped, and articulates with the trochlear surface of the tibia. The lateral surface of the bone is triangular in shape with its apex pointing downwards, and articulates with the medial surface of the lateral malleolus. The medial surface is partly articular, with its upper articular part being comma-shaped. The medial and lateral articular surfaces are continuous with the upper surface of the bone. Below the medial articular surface is a depressed roughened area for attachment of the deep part of the deltoid ligament. The inferior surface of the body is also articular, being concave from front-to-

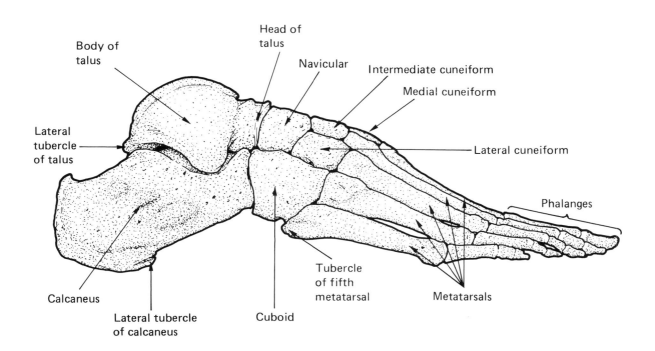

Fig. 5.19a Skeleton of the foot, lateral view.

back and articulates with the posterior facet on the upper surface of the calcaneus.

At the posterior aspect of the bone, there is a groove running downwards and medially for the tendon of flexor hallucis longus. Lateral and medial to this groove are the lateral and medial tubercles of the talus.

From the anterior and medial aspect of the body the neck projects forwards and medially. Its upper, medial and lateral surfaces are roughened, whilst its inferior surface presents an area for articulation with the calcaneus on the upper surface of the sustentaculum tali. Just behind this articular surface there is a deep groove termed the *sulcus tali*, which lies immediately over the *sulcus calcanei* and forms with it the *sinus tarsi*.

The head of the talus is slightly flattened anteriorly and articulates with the posterior surface of the navicular. Below this main articulation there are two smaller articular areas, one for the upper surface of the 'spring' ligament and the other, which continues on to the inferior surface of the neck (see above), for the anterior articular area of the calcaneus.

The navicular

The navicular lies anterior to the head of the talus. On its inferomedial side it presents a large tuberosity. Its posterior surface is concave for articulation with the head of the talus. Its anterior surface is subdivided into three triangular areas by two faint ridges for articulation with the three cuneiform bones. The inferior surface of the bone is narrow and roughened for the attachment of ligaments and muscles. The small lateral and subcutaneous upper surfaces are rough near their edges for the attachment of interosseous ligaments, but together they form a curved surface.

The cuboid

The cuboid has six surfaces, but in reality is a cube that has been flattened from above downwards. It is situated on the outside of the lateral cuneiform bone, in front of the calcaneus and behind the fourth and fifth metatarsal bones. Its posterior surface is

slightly concave from top to bottom but flat from side-to-side, articulating with the anterior surface of the calcaneus. Its medial surface is smooth on its anterior two-thirds for articulation with the lateral cuneiform and sometimes the navicular, whilst the posterior third is usually roughened for the attachment of ligaments. Anteriorly, it is nearly flat, being divided by a slight ridge into two facets for articulation with the bases of the fourth and fifth metatarsal bones.

The lateral surface of the cuboid is by far the smallest due to the convergence of the anterior and the posterior surfaces as they pass laterally. Nearly the entire surface is taken up by a deep groove passing downwards and forwards through which the tendon of the peroneus longus passes. The groove is continued on the under surface of the bone and crosses medially and anteriorly towards the medial cuneiform bone. The groove is very close to the anterior border of the bone and is limited by a prominent ridge posterior to it. The rest of the under surface of the cuboid is rough for the attachment of the long and short plantar ligaments. Its dorsal surface is roughened, and as in the case of the dorsal surfaces of the cuneiform bones and navicular, is subcutaneous.

The cuneiform bones

There are three cuneiform bones: the medial, intermediate and lateral. As their name implies they are wedge-shaped, being triangular at their anterior and posterior ends and having three rectangular surfaces along their length.

The medial cuneiform

The medial cuneiform has its apex projecting upwards and its base downwards. Its anterior and posterior surfaces are smooth for articulation with the first metatarsal bone and the anterior surface of the navicular respectively. Its smooth lateral surface articulates with the intermediate cuneiform bone in its posterior two-thirds, and the base of the second metatarsal on its anterior third. Its superior, medial and inferior surfaces form a continuous surface which forms part of the medial side of the foot. This surface is roughened by ligaments and has a smooth impression at the anteroinferior part of its medial aspect over which the tendon of tibialis anterior runs. This is the largest of the three cuneiforms.

The intermediate cuneiform

The intermediate cuneiform has its base uppermost and its apex projecting downwards. It is shorter than the other two and is only non-articular on its dorsal surface. It articulates medially with the medial cuneiform, laterally with the lateral cuneiform, anteriorly with the second metatarsal and posteriorly with the navicular. Part of the medial surface is rough for the attachment of ligaments.

The lateral cuneiform

The apex of the lateral cuneiform also projects downwards with its base uppermost. The medial surface articulates mainly with the middle cuneiform having a small facet anteriorly for articulation with the second metatarsal. Its lateral surface articulates with the medial surface of the cuboid, its posterior surface with the navicular and its anterior surface with the third metatarsal. The non-articular parts of the medial and lateral surfaces are rough for the attachment of ligaments.

The fact that the medial cuneiform bone has its base projecting downwards, whilst the other two have their bases uppermost contributes to the arch shape across the foot from medial to lateral. With the addition of the cuboid on their lateral side, the cuneiforms make up part of the transverse tarsal arch.

The metatarsal bones

There are five metatarsal bones in each foot, the most medial of which is by far the stoutest, although it is also the shortest. The second metatarsal is the longest, whilst the fifth can be recognized by the large tubercle which projects backwards and laterally from its base. All five metatarsals have certain features in common: a shaft, with a head distally, and a base at the proximal end. The bases articulate with the tarsal bones while the heads articulate with the proximal phalanx of each toe.

The base of the first metatarsal is concave from side-to-side and flat from top-to-bottom, articulating with the anterior surface of the medial cuneiform. Its lateral surface has a facet for articulation with the base of the second metatarsal, whilst its inferior surface projects downwards ending as a tuberosity. The base of the second metatarsal articulates with the intermediate cuneiform posteriorly. Medially it articulates with the medial cuneiform and the first metatarsal, and laterally with the lateral cuneiform and the third metatarsal. The base of the third metatarsal bone is flat and articulates with the lateral cuneiform, and on either side with the adjacent metatarsals. It is roughened on its upper and lower surfaces. The fourth and fifth metatarsal bases articulate with the anterior surface of the cuboid. The fourth has a small facet on either side for articulation with the adjacent metatarsals, whereas the fifth base is more expanded having a large tubercle on its lateral side. The upper and lower surfaces of each are roughened.

All the shafts are more or less cylindrical in form, the first being the thickest and the second usually being the thinnest. All, however, become narrower as they pass forward towards their heads.

The heads are smooth, convex from above downwards as well as from side-to-side. On either side, just behind the head, is a tubercle in front of which is a small depression for attachment of ligaments. The superior non-articular surface is roughened, while the inferior surface is marked by a groove passing forwards, which gives passage to the long and short flexor tendons. The head of the first metatarsal is large and wide forming the ball of the great toe. It articulates with the base of the first phalanx and two sesamoid bones. The plantar surface of this bone is grooved, on each side of a prominent central ridge, by the sesamoid bones in the tendons of the short muscles which pass inferior to it.

The phalanges

There are two phalanges in the great toe and three in each of the other toes. They are miniature long bones having a shaft and two extremities and with certain features in common. Each of the bases of the proximal phalanges has a proximal surface which is smooth and concave for articulation with the head of its metatarsal. The remaining phalanges have a proximal surface divided into two by a vertical ridge. Each bone is flattened on its plantar surface and rounded on it dorsum. The head of each bone, except the terminal phalanges, is divided into two condyles by a vertical groove giving it a pulley shape. The articular surface tends to be more extensive on the plantar surface of the head where it joins the flattened surface of the shaft. The sides of the heads are roughened, being marked by a small tubercle at the centre.

The head of each distal phalanx is flattened on its dorsum and has no articular area. This surface is, of course, the nail-bed.

Ossification of the bones of the foot

Each tarsal bone ossifies from a primary centre which appears in the cartilaginous precursor. The calcaneus is the only bone to have a secondary centre. The primary centres for the calcaneus and talus appear before birth in the sixth and eighth months *in utero* respectively. That for the cuboid appears at nine months *in utero* and may therefore be present at birth, if not, it appears soon afterwards. The centres of ossification for remaining bones appears as follows: at the end of the first year for the lateral cuneiform, during the third year for the medial cuneiform and navicular, and during the fourth year for the intermediate cuneiform. Ossification of these bones is completed shortly after puberty.

The secondary centre for the calcaneus appears at about 9 years in its posterior end and extends to include the medial and lateral processes. Fusion occurs between 15 and 20 years. Occasionally, the lateral tubercle may ossify separately.

Because the ossification centres for the calcaneus, talus and cuboid are usually present before birth, they can be used to assess the skeletal maturity of a new-born child. They may be used in conjunction with the secondary centres in the distal end of the femur and in the proximal end of the tibia.

The metatarsals

A primary centre appears in the body of each metatarsal at 9 weeks *in utero*, so that at birth they are well ossified. Secondary centres appear in the base of the first metatarsal and in the heads of the remaining metatarsals during the second and third years, with the medial ones appearing earlier. Fusion of the epiphyses with the bodies occurs between 15 and 18 years. In the lateral metatarsals, the epiphyses may occasionally be found in the bases instead of the heads.

The phalanges

The primary centres for the distal and proximal phalanges appear during the fourth month *in utero*, with the distal ones appearing first. The centre for the middle phalanx appears between 6 months and birth. Secondary centres for the bases of all phalanges appear during the second and third years and fuse with the bodies between 15 and 20 years.

It is interesting to note that the first metatarsal has an ossification pattern similar to that of the phalanges. It could be argued that instead of the middle phalanx being missing in the great toe it is the metatarsal, so that what we now refer to as the first metatarsal is in fact an enlarged proximal phalanx.

Palpation of the bones of the foot

Posteriorly, the calcaneus can clearly be identified being subcutaneous on its lateral, posterior and medial aspects. The inferior surface is covered with thick plantar fascia, but the medial and lateral tubercles are identifiable on deep palpation posteriorly. Medially, 1 cm below the tip of the medial malleolus, the sustentaculum tali appears as a horizontal ridge, whilst on the lateral aspect, the peroneal trochlea lies approximately 2 cm below and in front of the tip of the lateral malleolus, with the lateral tubercle of the calcaneus (for the attachment of the calcaneofibular ligament) a little behind and above.

The head and neck of the talus can be grasped between the finger and thumb in the two hollows just anteroinferior to the malleoli, the tubercle of the navicular forming a clear landmark anterior to the medial hollow. Midway along the lateral border of the foot, the base of the fifth metatarsal, with its tubercle pointing posteriorly, is prominent. The bases of the fourth to the first metatarsals can be identified crossing the dorsum of the foot, the base of the first being 1 cm anterior to the tubercle of the navicular, the medial cuneiform being interposed.

The shafts and heads of the metatarsal bones can be readily palpated on the dorsum of the foot with bases proximally and heads towards the toes. If the toes are extended, the heads of the metatarsals, especially the first, will become palpable under the forefoot. The heads are a little less obvious on the dorsum of the foot when the metatarsophalangeal joints are flexed.

The proximal phalanx of each toe is easily recognized, being the longest of the three, the rest are hidden to a certain extent by the pulp of the toe.

Dorsiplantar view of foot

Oblique view of foot

Fig. 5.19b   Radiology of the ankle and foot
left = dorsiplantar view of foot, **right** = oblique view of foot:

1 = First metatarsal	**7** = Body of talus
2 = Sesamoid bones	**8** = Cuboid
3 = Lateral cuneiform	**9** = Calcaneus
4 = Medial and intermediate cuneiform	**10** = Medial malleolus
5 = Navicular	**11** = Lateral malleolus
6 = Head of talus	**12** = Fifth metatarsal

Muscles

MUSCLES AROUND THE HIP JOINT

Deep within the gluteal region is situated the hip joint. This is a ball and socket joint capable of movement in many directions.

To produce these movements there is a complex arrangement of muscles around the joint which either act on the thigh with respect to the pelvis or on the pelvis with respect to the thigh. It must be remembered that during many of these movements the hip joint is weight bearing transmitting the weight of the body above it, via the lower limbs, to the ground.

Thus, the muscles surrounding the joint have a dual role. They must be capable of immediate controlled power when needed for sudden powerful activities such as running uphill or upstairs, and yet retain the ability to maintain a set position for long periods of time as in standing, leaning forwards and even sitting.

The hip joint is surrounded on all sides by muscles, which are much thicker and stronger around the posterior and lateral aspects and consequently the joint appears to be situated near the front of the region.

Muscles anterior to the joint tend to be flexors, those posterior tend to be extensors, medially they tend to be adductors and laterally abductors. Both medial and lateral rotation occurs at this joint because of the obliquity of some of the muscle fibres. This is explained more fully under the individual muscles.

Some of the muscles in this region will have their effect on more than one joint. When this is the case, reference is made to the muscle in both regions, but details are only found in one section.

MUSCLES EXTENDING THE HIP JOINT

Gluteus maximus
The hamstrings:
    semitendinosus
    semimembranosus
    biceps femoris

Gluteus maximus

As its name implies this is the largest of the gluteal muscles. It is very powerful and is situated on the posterior aspect of the hip joint, being responsible for the very pleasant shape of this region in humans. In lower primates gluteus maximus is an adductor of the hip; this was also the case in early, primitive humans. However, with the changes that have occurred in the human pelvis to enable the erect posture to be adopted, the muscle has become mainly an extensor of the hip. It is the muscle mainly responsible for the erect position, thereby freeing the forelimbs from a weight-bearing role, and enabling them to become the precision implements that they are today (see Chapter 4).

Gluteus maximus (Fig. 5.20) is quadrilateral in shape consisting of bundles of muscle fibres laid down in the line of pull of the muscle, giving the surface of the muscle a course appearance. The muscle is thick and forms two layers as it passes down to its lower attachment. Above, it attaches to the *gluteal surface* of the *ilium* behind the posterior gluteal line, the posterior border of the ilium and from the adjacent part of the *iliac crest*. It also arises from the side of the *coccyx* and the posterior aspect of the *sacrum*, including the upper part of the *sacrotuberous ligament*. Its upper fibres attach to the aponeurosis of the sacrospinalis while its deep anterior fibres come from the fascia which covers the gluteus medius. Although this appears to be a vast area, it must be remembered that most of these structures can be covered with one hand if it were slipped into the back pocket of a pair of trousers.

The fibres pass downwards and forwards towards the upper end of the femur. The most superficial, about three-quarters, of the fibres form a separate lamina, which narrows down and attaches between the two layers of the *fascia lata* helping to form the iliotibial tract. The deeper remaining one-quarter of the muscle fibres form a broad

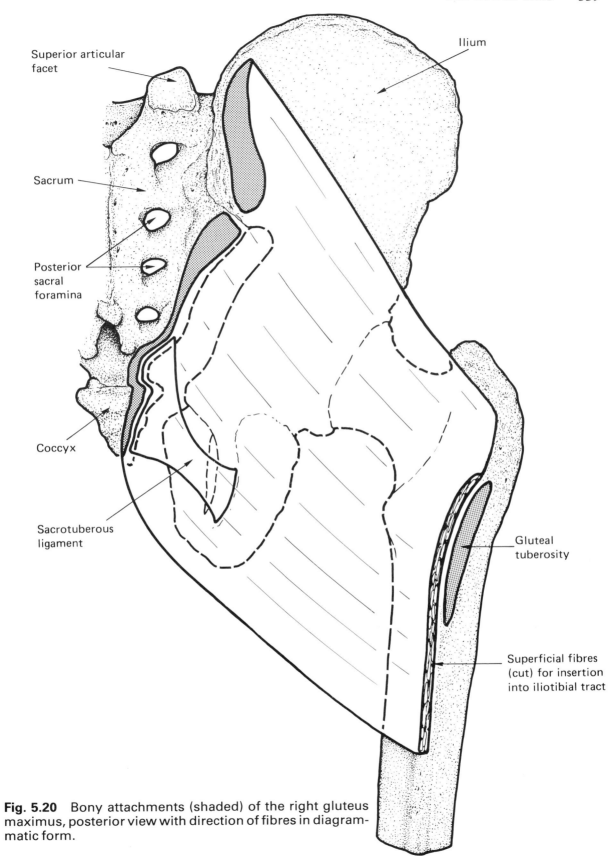

Superior articular facet

Sacrum

Posterior sacral foramina

Coccyx

Sacrotuberous ligament

Ilium

Gluteal tuberosity

Superficial fibres (cut) for insertion into iliotibial tract

Fig. 5.20 Bony attachments (shaded) of the right gluteus maximus, posterior view with direction of fibres in diagrammatic form.

aponeurosis which attaches to the *gluteal tuberosity* of the *femur*, from the posterior aspect of the greater trochanter to half way down the lateral border of the linea aspera.

Nerve supply

Gluteus maximus is supplied by the *inferior gluteal nerve*, root value L5, S1, 2. The skin covering the muscle however, is mainly supplied by branches from L2 and S3.

Action

When acting from above, the muscle pulls the shaft of the femur backwards producing extension of the flexed hip joint. As its lower attachment is nearer to the lateral side of the thigh, the muscle will tend to rotate the thigh laterally during extension. The lower fibres can adduct the thigh, while the upper fibres may help in abduction.

The fibres which attach to the iliotibial tract can produce extension of the knee joint because the lower end of the tract attaches to the lateral tibial condyle anterior to the axis of movement. Through the iliotibial tract, gluteus maximus provides a powerful support on the lateral side of the knee. If the femur is fixed, contraction of gluteus maximus will pull the ilium and pelvis backwards around the hip joint, but this time the pelvis and trunk are the moving parts, and a lifting of the trunk from a flexed position occurs.

Functional activity

Being a powerful extensor of the thigh, especially when the hip has been flexed, means that this muscle is ideally suited for fulfilling its role in such powerful movements as stepping up onto a stool, climbing and running. However, it is not used greatly as an extensor in ordinary walking.

With the hamstrings, it will take part in raising the trunk from a flexed position, as in standing upright from a bent forward position of forward flexion. Indeed, gluteus maximus and the hamstrings provide the main control in forward bending of the body, as the movement primarily occurs at the hip joint.

It plays an important role in balancing the pelvis on the femoral heads thus helping to maintain the upright posture; its ability to aid lateral rotation of the femur when standing assists in raising the medial longitudinal arch of the foot.

The role of the gluteus maximus during sitting should not be dismissed. Although the ischial tuberosities support the majority of the weight of the trunk when sitting, pressure is regularly relieved from these bony points by a static or sometimes dynamic contraction of the muscle which raises the tuberosities of the ischium from the supporting surfaces. The muscle is then relaxed and the weight is then lowered. Sometimes the weight is shifted from side-to-side with the alternate use of the gluteus maximus of each side.

Paralysis of the muscle will lead to a flattening of the buttock with a loss of the beautiful contour, and an inability to climb stairs and run. However it must be kept in mind that there are other muscles which can be brought into action to produce extension of the hip, although it is a much weaker movement. Gluteus maximus can be developed to produce a functional extension of the knee in patients where quadriceps femoris is either very weak or paralysed. This is not a powerful movement, but may be sufficient to enable the patient to extend the knee and enable the lower limb to become weight bearing during walking or standing.

Palpation

On a model or on yourself, first find some bony prominences which will give you the landmarks of the muscle. The crest of the ilium is easily palpated approximately at the belt level, moving your hand backwards along the crest you will come to a small bony process. This is the posterior superior iliac spine. With your fingers running inferiorly and medially let this be the centre of your palm. Your hand will now just about cover the upper attachment of the gluteus maximus; the palm is over the posterior part of the ilium, the sacrum and the back of the sacroiliac joint, while the tips of your fingers are on the edge of the coccyx and the upper end of the sacrotuberous ligament. The bulk of the muscle is now in your palm, follow this path and you will come to the greater trochanter of the femur. Now try the following:

1. Extend the lower limb behind you whilst in the standing position keeping your hand on the muscle; it goes hard and produces a much clearer shape.
2. Place your foot onto a stool and put your hand in the same position as before and step up. Again you will feel the muscle coming into action very strongly.
3. Take up the standing position and place your hands on each gluteus maximus as if they were in your back pocket. Raise the medial borders of your feet as if you were shortening the medial arch of the foot. As the arch is raised you will feel gluteus maximus working quite strongly, with the femur tending to rotate laterally.
4. Finally, take up the sitting position but this time place a hand under each buttock. You will feel the ischial tuberosity resting on your hand. Now move your weight from side-to-side as you would if you were getting tired of sitting. You will find that the gluteus maximus contracts alternately taking the weight off the tuberosity and then lowering it down again.

The hamstrings

This group of muscles is made up of the:

Semitendinosus
Semimembranosus
Biceps femoris

These make up the large mass of muscle which can be palpated on the posterior aspect of the thigh, and are involved with extension of the hip, flexion of the knee and rotation of the flexed knee. When working from above they can either flex the knee as a group, or they can work individually in rotating the flexed knee. If they are working with the lower attachment fixed, they will act as a group extending the hip joint. It is due to this latter very important action that they are included in this section, but the action of the hamstrings is explained in more detail on p. 344.

Semitendinosus (Fig. 5.21)

The upper attachment of this muscle is from the *lower medial* facet of the lateral section of the *ischial tuberosity*. Its tendon of attachment is combined with that of the biceps femoris and the two muscles run together for a short distance. It then forms a fusiform muscle belly which quickly gives way to a long tendon, thus accounting for its name. This tendon passes downwards and medially behind the medial condyle of the femur, being separated from the medial collateral ligament by a small bursa, to attach to a vertical line on the medial surface of the *medial condyle* of the *tibia* just behind the insertion of the sartorius and behind and below the attachment of the gracilis. Near its insertion it is separated from gracilis by a bursa, and with gracilis is separated from sartorius by another bursa.

Nerve supply   Semitendinosus is supplied by the *tibial division of the sciatic nerve*, root value L5, S1, 2. The skin covering the muscle is supplied mainly by S2.

Action   The semitendinosus will, when working from below, help to extend the hip joint when the trunk is bent forward. When working from above it will aid in flexion of the knee joint; if the knee is semiflexed it will produce medial rotation of the knee. If the foot is fixed, semitendinosus will act as a lateral rotator of the femur and pelvis on the tibia.

Semimembranosus

This muscle is situated on the posteromedial side of the thigh in its lower part, deep to the semitendinosus. It attaches by a strong membranous tendon to the upper *lateral facet* on the rough part of the *ischial tuberosity* (see Fig. 5.22) and passes downwards and medially. The muscle becomes fleshy on the medial side of the tendon, being deep to semitendinosus and biceps femoris. From the lower part of the muscle a second aponeurotic tendon arises narrowing down towards its lower attachment, which is a horizontal groove on the posteromedial surface of the *medial tibial condyle*. From here it spreads its fibres in all directions, but particularly upwards and laterally forming the oblique popliteal ligament. Bursae separate the muscle from the medial head of gastrocnemius and from the tibia near its attachment.

Nerve supply   The semimembranosus is supplied from the *tibial division of the sciatic nerve*, root value L5, S1, 2. The skin covering the muscle is the same as that for the semitendinosus, that is mainly from S2.

Action   As for semitendinosus.

Biceps femoris

Biceps femoris (see Fig. 5.23) is situated on the posterolateral aspect of the thigh, arising by two heads as its name implies, these being separated by a considerable distance.

The long head attaches to the *lower medial facet* on the *ischial tuberosity* with the tendon of the semitendinosus, spreading onto the sacrotuberous ligament. These two tendons descend together for a short distance then separate into the two individual muscles, the long head of biceps forming a fusiform muscle running downwards and laterally across the posterior aspect of the thigh superficial to the sciatic nerve. In the lower third of the thigh the long head begins to narrow and is joined on its deep aspect by the short head of biceps.

Fig. 5.21 Right semitendinosus, posterior view.

Fig. 5.22 Right semimembranosus and popliteus, posterior view.

The short head has its upper attachment from the *lower half* of the *lateral* lip of the *linea aspera* reaching almost as far up as the attachment of the gluteus maximus and running down onto the upper half of the lateral supracondylar line of the femur; some fibres arise from the lateral intermuscular septum. The fibres of this short head gradually blend with the narrowing tendon of the long head which lies superficial to it.

On approaching the knee, the tendon can be felt crossing its posterolateral aspect running towards the head of the fibula.

Prior to its attachment to the *head of the fibula* the tendon of biceps femoris is split in two by the fibular collateral ligament. Some fibres of the tendon join the ligament, while a few others attach to the lateral tibial condyle and some to the posterior aspect of the lateral intermuscular septum which lies just in front of it. A bursa separates the tendon from the fibular collateral ligament.

Nerve supply   The long head of biceps femoris is supplied by the *tibial portion of the sciatic nerve*, while the short head is supplied by the *common peroneal portion*; the root value of both is L5, S1, 2. The skin covering the muscle is supplied mainly by S2.

Action   The biceps femoris helps the previous three muscles to extend the hip joint, particularly so when the trunk is bent forwards and is to be raised to the erect position. All three hamstrings will, of course, control the lowering forward of the trunk, however in this case they are working eccentrically, that is working, but its two ends moving apart. The biceps femoris aids the semimembranosus and semitendinosus muscles to flex the knee joint. With the knee in a semiflexed position biceps femoris will rotate the leg laterally on the thigh or if the foot is fixed, medially rotate the thigh and pelvis on the leg.

Functional activity of the hamstrings

It must be remembered that all three muscles cross the posterior aspect of both the hip and the knee joints. Flexion of the knee and their stabilizing effect is no doubt a very important function of these muscles, although for this action a much smaller mus-

cle bulk would have been sufficient. Extension of the hip joint when the thigh is the moving part would also require a far smaller group of muscles, especially when it is remembered that the gluteus maximus is far better situated to do the job. Raising the trunk from a flexed position on the other hand requires a great deal more power as the muscles are working with a very short lever arm: the ischium and its ramus. The weight of the trunk acting on the other side of the hip joint is considerable.

The mode of action of this group of muscles may well be the reason it is injured so frequently during sporting activities. The most common cause of sports injury appears to be in the running section of athletics, being more common in the first 10–20 m of a sprint. This is often blamed on inadequate preparation and warm-up before the start, and to some extent this may be true. It must, however, be remembered that at this stage in a race the hamstrings are contracting strongly and are acting over two joints.

At the start of a race the athlete is in a forward-lean position in order to gain as much forward motion as possible. Starting blocks serve to increase the degree of forward leaning. The hamstrings are therefore working to their maximum, either to raise the trunk to an upright position, or to hold the trunk in such a position that forward collapse of the body as a whole is imminent. At the same time the lower limb is being thrust forward to gain as much ground as possible, with flexion of the knee to prevent the foot touching the ground. The hamstrings must be under immense strain in this position and it is not surprising that the muscle may tear.

The hamstrings play an important part in the fine balancing of the pelvis in the standing position, particularly when the upper trunk is being moved off the vertical axis. Working in conjunction with the abdominal muscles anterosuperiorly and gluteus maximus posteroinferiorly, the anteroposterior tilt of the pelvis can be altered. This will have an effect on the lumbar lordosis.

Finally, the hamstrings have a role in decelerating the forward motion of the tibia when the free swinging leg is extended during walking, and so prevents the knee snapping into extension.

Fig. 5.23 Right biceps femoris, posterior view.

MUSCLES ABDUCTING THE HIP JOINT

Gluteus maximus (see p. 338)
Gluteus minimus
Gluteus medius
Tensor fascia lata (see p. 372)

Gluteus medius

Gluteus medius (Fig. 5.24) is situated on the lateral and upper part of the buttock, just below the iliac crest. It must be considered to be a close companion of the gluteus maximus and is in fact overlapped by this muscle from the back. It is fan-shaped, having its broad part above and its tendon below. It fills the space between the iliac crest and the greater trochanter of the femur.

Its upper attachment is to the *gluteal*, or *lateral surface* of the *ilium* between the posterior and anterior gluteal lines. This area is quite extensive reaching to the crest of the ilium above and almost as far as the sciatic notch below. The muscle is covered with a strong layer of fascia from the deep surface to which it has a firm attachment. It shares the posterior part of this fascia with gluteus maximus.

The posterior fibres pass downwards and forwards, the middle fibres pass straight downwards and the anterior fibres pass downwards and backwards. The fibres come together and form a flattened tendon which attaches to a roughened area, which runs downwards and forwards visible on the *superolateral* side of the *greater trochanter* of the *femur*. The tendon is separated from the trochanter by a bursa, whose position is given by a smooth area on the trochanter in front of the attachment of the tendon.

Nerve supply

The gluteus medius is supplied by the *superior gluteal nerve*, root value L4, 5, S1. The skin covering this muscle is mainly supplied from L1, 2.

Action

With the pelvis fixed, gluteus medius will pull the greater trochanter of the femur upwards. However, as the fulcrum of the movement is at the hip joint, this will cause the femoral shaft to move laterally, this is termed abduction.

If the lower attachment of the muscle is fixed it will pull down the wing of the ilium, producing a downward tilting of the pelvis to the same side and, of course, a raising of the pelvis on the opposite side. In addition, the anterior fibres of gluteus medius acting from a fixed pelvis will help with medial rotation of the femur. Acting with the femur fixed, these fibres rotate the opposite side of the pelvis forward. This is explained in more detail in the section dealing with gluteus minimus (see p. 348).

Functional activity

The gluteus medius plays a vital role in walking, running and when bearing weight on one limb. When the opposite limb is taken off the ground the pelvis on that side would tend to drop through loss of support from below. Gluteus medius on the supporting side works very hard to maintain, or even raise a little, the opposite side of the pelvis, allowing the raised limb to be brought forward for the next step. If the muscle is paralysed the pelvis drops on the opposite side during this manoeuvre.

In walking or running, not only is gluteus medius important for support, but with the help of other muscles, such as gluteus minimus and tensor fascia lata, it produces a rotation of the hip joint. This time with the femur the more fixed point, it controls the pelvic rotation on the same side.

If the muscle is unable to work efficiently due to paralysis or poor mechanics of the hip joint, the pelvis will drop on the opposite side. This is referred to as a *Trendelenburg sign*. Walking in this case is awkward and difficult, and running virtually impossible.

Palpation

Find the middle of the iliac crest, which is directly above the greater trochanter of the femur. About two fingers' breadth below this region is the bulk of the muscle. Now stand alternately on one limb and then the other, you will feel the muscle become hard as the weight is borne on the same limb.

Place the fingers of the other hand on the opposite side, walk slowly down the room. You will feel the two muscles coming into action alternately.

A patient with a Trendelenburg gait, either on one or both sides, compensates for the lack of support of the swing limb by throwing the trunk over the supporting limb so that the weight is balanced over the hip, thus giving time to swing the limb through.

Gluteus minimus

Although this is the smallest of the gluteal muscles it takes the largest attachment from the gluteal surface of the ilium. It is triangular in shape, being wide at the top and narrowing to a tendon below.

Its upper attachment is from the *gluteal surface* of the *ilium* in front of the anterior and above the inferior gluteal lines (see Fig. 5.8), reaching as far forward as the anterior border of the ilium in front and almost to the sciatic notch behind. Its fibres pass downwards, backwards and slightly laterally forming a tendon which attaches to a small depression on the *anterosuperior* aspect of the *greater trochanter* of the *femur*.

Nerve supply

Gluteus minimus is supplied by the *superior gluteal nerve*, root value L4, 5, S1. The skin overlying the muscle is mainly supplied by L1.

Action

If the upper attachment of the muscle is fixed, contraction of its anterior fibres will medially rotate the femur. This is because the femoral attachment lies lateral to the ful-

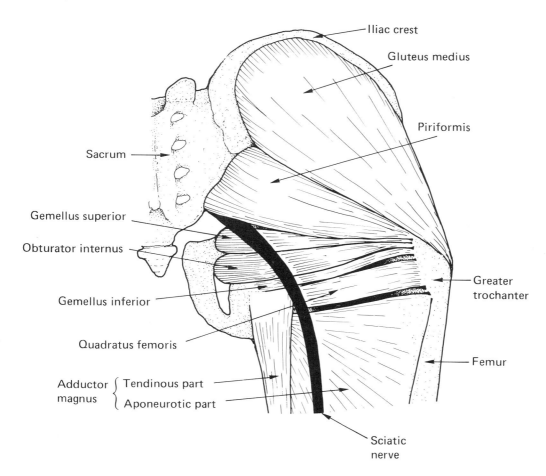

Fig. 5.24 Right gluteal region, posterior view with gluteus maximus removed.

crum of the movement, the hip joint. If the lower attachment is fixed, the muscle will raise the opposite side of the pelvis in a similar way to the gluteus medius (see p. 346). It will also, by pulling the front of the ilium outwards, swing the opposite side of the pelvis forwards.

Functional activity

This muscle appears to play its most important role in the support and control of pelvic movements. It is a well-developed and powerful muscle using its power to a maximum in walking and running when the opposite limb is off the ground. As the limb is swung forward, the pelvis on the same side is also swung forward. This uses the hip of the weight-bearing limb as the fulcrum of the movement, with the gluteus medius and minimus both supporting the pelvis and swinging it forward on the opposite side.

Palpation

Find the anterior superior iliac spine at the front of the iliac crest. Allow the pads of your finger to slip downwards and backwards towards the greater trochanter of the femur. Within two fingers' breadth you will be on the muscle bulk. Now rotate the lower limb medially and you will feel the muscle belly contracting hard. Do the same on the opposite side of the body and then begin to walk forward. You will feel the muscles contracting alternately, as each limb becomes weight bearing.

Tensor fascia lata (see Fig. 5.36b)

This muscle overlies the gluteus minimus and helps in flexion, abduction and medial rotation of the hip joint. It also straightens out the backward pull of gluteus maximus on the iliotibial tract. It is more of a tensor of the fascia lata, as its name implies, and through this is an extensor and lateral rotator of the knee. This muscle is dealt with in more detail on p. 372.

MUSCLES ADDUCTING THE HIP JOINT

Adductor magnus
Adductor longus
Adductor brevis
Gracilis (see p. 364)
Pectineus (see p. 357)

These muscles are situated on the medial side of the hip joint running down the medial side of the thigh.

Adductor magnus

Adductor magnus (Fig. 5.25) is the largest and most posterior of the group, with adductor brevis and adductor longus in front, and semimembranosus and semitendinosus behind. The muscle is really composed of two parts, an adductor part and a hamstring part, forming a large triangular sheet of muscle with a thickened medial margin.

Its upper attachment is from the *femoral surface* of the *ischiopubic ramus* running down to the lateral part of the *inferior surface* of the *ischial tuberosity* (see Fig. 5.30). The part of the muscle which attaches anteriorly to the ischiopubic ramus represents a sheet of muscle which twists before attaching to the femur while the posterior fibres of adductor magnus, from the ischial tuberosity, pass vertically downwards as a thickened cord of muscle fibres.

The ischiopubic fibres fan out and are seen as a large triangular muscular sheet. The most anterior of these fibres pass laterally and slightly backwards to attach to the *upper part* of the *linea aspera* continuing upwards as far as the greater trochanter medial to the attachment of *gluteus maximus*. These upper fibres may be fused with quadratus femoris. Fibres from the posterior part of the ischiopubic ramus attach to the whole length of the linea aspera and medial supracondylar ridge. This attachment to the *femur* is not continuous as there are small fibrous arches close to the bone which allow vessels and nerves to pass from the adductor to the posterior compartment of the thigh. The poster-

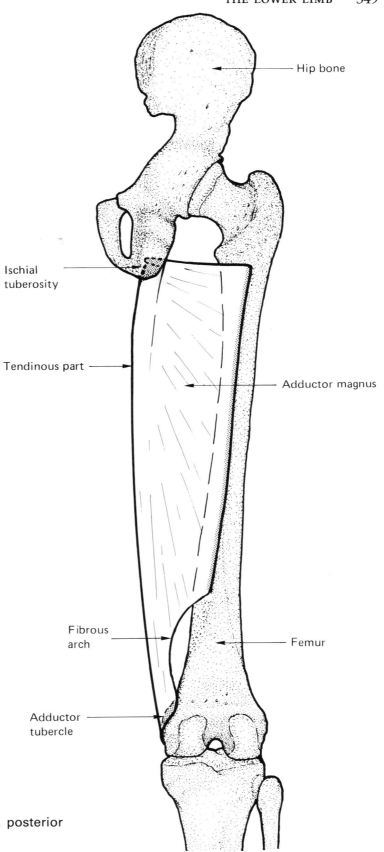

Hip bone

Ischial
tuberosity

Tendinous part

Adductor magnus

Fibrous
arch

Femur

Adductor
tubercle

Fig. 5.25 Right adductor magnus, posterior
view.

ior ischial fibres pass downwards and attach mainly to the *adductor tubercle* situated on top of the medial condyle of the femur at the lower end of the medial supracondylar ridge. Some of these fibres continue downwards to fuse with the medial collateral ligament of the knee.

Nerve supply

Because of its two parts, adductor magnus has a dual nerve supply. The adductor part from the ischiopubic ramus is supplied by the *posterior division of the obturator nerve*, while the hamstring part from the ischial tuberosity is supplied by the *tibial division of the sciatic nerve*. The root value of these nerves is L2, 3, with the skin covering the inner side of the thigh being mainly from L3.

Action

Working as a whole, the muscle is an adductor of the hip joint, although the posterior portion will aid in extension of the hip. Some workers believe that this muscle, along with the adductor longus, medially rotates the hip joint, although it was believed in the past that they also acted as lateral rotators. Whether the muscle acts as a medial or lateral rotator will depend on the position of the thigh, and the line of action of the muscle with respect to the mechanical axis of the femur (see p. 446). All the adductor muscles are important in preventing lateral overbalancing during the support phase of walking.

It is worth noting that the medial ligament of the knee joint appears to be a downwards continuation of the adductor magnus tendon and as such this muscle may very well at some time have crossed the knee joint and therefore have been a flexor of the knee in a similar fashion to gracilis.

Palpation

Adductor magnus is a deep muscle and is therefore difficult to palpate, nevertheless, if the fingers are pushed in just above the medial condyle of the femur, the adductor tubercle can be identified (see p. 319). If the inside of the same foot is now pressed against a stationary obstacle, one can feel the vertical part of the muscle contracting. The muscle can be traced about one-third of the way up the thigh until it becomes hidden by other muscles.

Adductor longus

Adductor longus (Fig. 5.26) is a long, slender, triangular muscle situated on the medial aspect of the thigh, overlying the middle part of adductor magnus. Its upper, narrower attachment comes from a small roughened area just below the medial end of the *obturator crest* on the anterior aspect of the body of the *pubis* (see Fig. 5.30).

Its fibres pass downwards and laterally spreading out as they go to attach to the middle two-fourths of the *linea aspera*, anterior to adductor magnus below and adductor brevis above and posterior to vastus medialis.

Nerve supply

Adductor longus is supplied by the *anterior division* of the *obturator nerve*, root value L2, 3, 4. The skin covering the area of adductor longus is supplied by L3.

Action

Adductor longus is an adductor of the thigh, but as a rotator of the thigh there is some doubt (see also adductor magnus, p. 348). Adductor longus can also flex the extended thigh, and extend the flexed thigh.

Adductor brevis

Adductor brevis (see Fig. 5.27) is again a triangular muscle situated on the medial aspect of the thigh.

Its upper attachment is from the *lateral part* of the front of the body and *inferior ramus* of the *pubis* (see Fig. 5.30). Its fibres pass downwards, laterally and backwards to attach to the upper half of the *linea aspera* anterior to adductor magnus. Its upper part is posterior to pectineus and its lower part is posterior to adductor longus.

Nerve supply

Adductor brevis is supplied by the *anterior*

Fig. 5.26 Right adductor longus, posterior view.

division of the *obturator nerve*, root value L2, 3, 4. The skin covering the area of adductor brevis is supplied by L2.

Action

Adductor brevis is an adductor of the thigh.

Palpation

If the fingers are placed high up on the inside of the thigh and the lower limb is adducted against resistance a mass of muscle can be palpated running down towards to the thigh. These are the adductors; however it is difficult to distinguish between the different muscle masses.

Gracilis

Gracilis (see Fig. 5.31) is the most medial muscle of the adductor group. It is an adductor of the thigh as well as a flexor of the knee (see p. 364).

Pectineus

Pectineus (see Fig. 5.29) is discussed on p. 357.

Functional activity

Although it is quite clear that these muscles are adductors of the thigh, they appear to work most strongly when the hip joint is in the neutral position, that is the anatomical position. They certainly work strongly, synergically, when the knee and hip are being flexed and extended when weight bearing. There is still some confusion over whether these muscles are involved in either medial or lateral rotation of the thigh. They work strongly during walking, particularly when the limb is weight bearing and there is movement at the hip joint. They also contribute to the delicate balancing of the pelvis on the hip joint. The adductors, as a group, are used very strongly when some object is being held between the knees in the sitting position, for example, when sitting on a horse, particularly when the horse is moving.

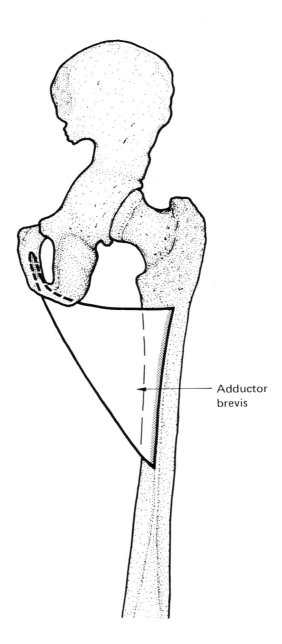

Adductor
brevis

Fig. 5.27   Right adductor brevis, posterior view.

MUSCLES FLEXING THE HIP JOINT

The muscles which flex the thigh on the pelvis are:

Psoas major
Iliacus
Rectus femoris (see p. 368)
Sartorius (see p. 366)
Pectineus

Psoas major

Psoas major (Fig. 5.28) is a large, thick powerful muscle situated mainly in the abdominal cavity. Within its substance the lumbar plexus is found. Psoas major has important relations: at its upper end the diaphragm and medial arcuate ligament are anterior to psoas, whilst lower down, the kidney, psoas minor (when present), the renal vessels and ureter are anterior relations. On the right side, psoas major is overlapped by the inferior vena cava and the ileum. The ascending and descending colon lie lateral to the right and left psoas respectively. Medially is the lumbar part of vertebral column, while directly posterior are the transverse processes of the lumbar vertebrae. The segmental lumbar nerves emerging from the intervertebral foramina are situated directly behind the muscle and pass forward into its substance.

The upper attachment of psoas major is to the *adjacent margins* of the *bodies of the vertebrae*, including the *disc* in between. The uppermost attachment is to the *lower margin* of the *body* of *T12*, while the lowermost attachment is to the *upper margin* of the *body* of *L5*. Psoas major also has an attachment to the front and lateral part of each transverse process, and from *tendinous arches* covering the constricted part of the bodies of the *lumbar vertebrae*.

The fibres of the muscle pass downwards and forwards towards the brim of the pelvis. The individual digitations from the vertebral column join together to form a thick muscle which gradually narrows as it passes under the inguinal ligament over the pelvic brim. At this point the tendon changes direction becoming more vertical, it then passes downwards, backwards and laterally. The muscle is separated from the pubis and the hip joint capsule by a large bursa. Before passing over the pelvic brim psoas is joined, on its lateral side, by fibres from iliacus. Iliacus continues to blend with psoas even after the muscle become tendinous, until it attaches to the *tip* and *posterior aspect* of the *lesser trochanter* of the *femur*. Some fibres of iliacus attach to the femur on a line running downwards and forwards from the lesser trochanter.

Action

Psoas major is a flexor of the hip joint. It also, because of its attachment to the lumbar spine, will use the lower attachment as the fixed point and flex the lumbar spine. There has been much discussion of the role of this muscle in rotation of the hip joint. It was thought at first that as it attached to the posterior and medial aspect of the femur, it must be a lateral rotator of the thigh. However, when the movement of rotation is around an axis drawn through the head of the femur and the lateral condyle of the tibia, it would clearly be seen that it ought to be a medial rotator. Electromyographically, however, it shows little activity during either rotations. The question is still not answered. If the psoas major of one side acts on its own, with reversed origin and insertion, it will produce side flexion of the lumbar spine to that side.

Nerve supply

Psoas major is supplied from the *ventral rami* of L1, 2, 3 and sometimes 4. The muscle only appears near the surface in the area of the groin and this small area of skin is supplied by L1.

Functional activity

The action and functional activity of psoas is included with those of the iliacus as far as flexion of the hip is concerned. However, psoas major does act independently on the lumbar spine when its lower end is fixed. In sitting up from a lying position, the muscle on both sides will help to pull the considerable weight of the trunk up, and this is at a time when the abdominal muscles are working hard to flex the trunk. It is in

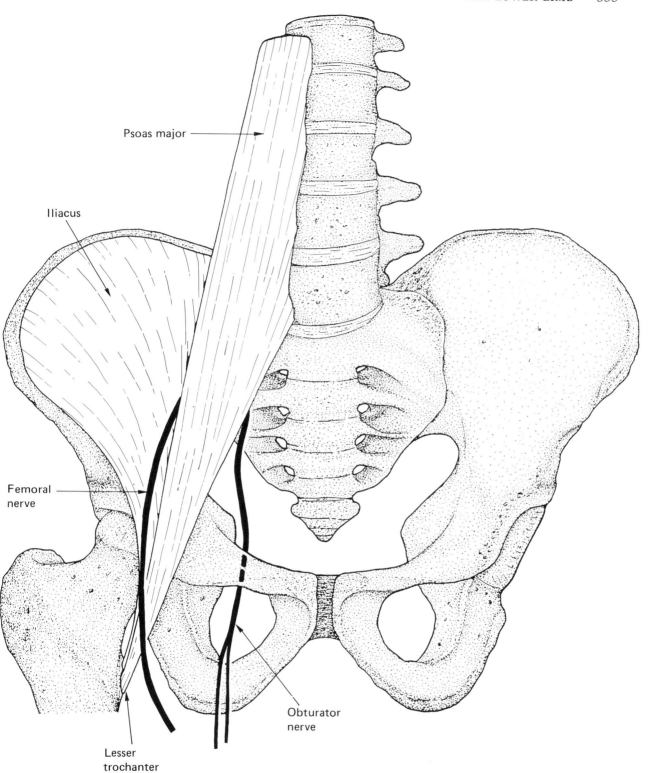

Fig. 5.28   Right psoas major and iliacus, anterior view.

fact very important that the abdominal muscles are brought into action early as this will prevent the lumbar spine being drawn forwards before the trunk begins to rise. Pulling the head up first will prevent this unwanted and potentially damaging movement occurring.

Raising both lower limbs at the same time whilst in the supine position is the cause of much back trouble and, unfortunately, it has recently become a popular exercise with lay teachers. The mechanics of this area must be well-understood before exercising is begun as it is better to prevent back problems rather than try to treat them after they have occurred.

Each lower limb is approximately 15% of the body weight, thus when both legs are raised off the floor the hip flexors will be lifting in the region of 30% of body weight. This initial lift will involve the psoas major, and for about the first 30°, the lumbar spine is pulled upwards due to the muscle working with reversed origin and insertion. This dragging forward of the lumbar spine can cause considerable damage to the area, particularly if some degenerative changes have already occurred. It is believed, erroneously, that this is a good abdominal exercise and will reduce the waistline because the abdominal muscles are working hard.

Palpation

It is almost impossible to palpate this muscle as most of its bulk lies within the abdominal cavity. It appears near the surface in the groin, but it is still quite difficult to feel as it is covered by other structures.

Iliacus

Iliacus (see Fig. 5.28) is a large fleshy triangular muscle situated mainly in the pelvis. Its upper attachment is the larger coming mainly from the upper and posterior two-thirds of the *iliac fossa* with some fibres coming from the *ala* of the *sacrum* and *anterior sacroiliac ligament* (see Fig. 5.50). Its fibres pass downwards, forwards and medially blending with the lateral side of psoas major. This blending of the muscles continues over the pelvic brim where they change direction to pass downwards, backwards and slightly laterally to insert into the lesser trochanter of the femur, some fibres blending with the insertion of the psoas major from the tip of the lesser trochanter. A few fibres are attached to the hip joint capsule.

Nerve supply

The nerve supply to the iliacus is from the *femoral nerve*, root value L2,3. The skin covering the area, where the pendon passes over the brim of the pelvis, is supplied by L1.

Action

Its effect on the hip is similar to that of the psoas. If its upper attachment is the fixed point it will pull the thigh forwards as in flexion of the hip. If the lower attachment is the fixed point it will draw the pelvis forwards, thus tilting it forwards, being again flexion of the hip but this time with the trunk doing the moving.

Functional activity

This muscle will be used with the psoas major in all activities of pulling the lower limb up in front of the trunk as in the drawing of the lower limb forward in walking, running and jumping. It will also, of course, help to draw the trunk forward from a lying supine position to a sitting position. There is the same controversy over rotation of the femur as far the psoas major (see p. 354).

Palpation

It is almost impossible to palpate (see also psoas major, p. 354).

Rectus femoris (see Fig. 5.33)

This muscle is part of the quadriceps femoris group and is discussed on p. 368. Nevertheless, by crossing anterior to the hip joint it is a flexor of the thigh.

Sartorius (see Fig. 5.32)

This muscle is mainly a flexor of the knee (see p. 366) although it does help in flexion of the hip. It is particularly called upon when both flexion of the hip and knee are carried out at the same time.

Pectineus

Pectineus (Fig. 5.29) is a quadrilateral muscle situated at the upper and medial part of the thigh, deep in the groin. It appears to be made up of two layers, superficial and deep, and these are generally supplied by different nerves.

Its upper attachment is to the *superior ramus* (pecten) of the *pubis*, the *iliopubic eminence* and the *pubic tubercle*. It also attaches to the *fascia* which covers it. The fibres pass downwards, backwards and laterally between psoas major and adductor longus to attach to a line which runs from the lesser trochanter to the top of the linea aspera, anterior to the upper part of adductor brevis. This also is often called the *pectineal line*.

Nerve supply

Pectineus is supplied by the *femoral nerve* from its L2, 3 nerve roots and occasionally from the *obturator* or the *accessory obturator* nerve by its L3 root. The skin covering this area of the groin is supplied from the root of L1.

Action

Pectineus flexes and adducts the hip joint. Some authorities also believe the muscle to be a medial rotator of the hip.

Functional activity

It is easy to see how this muscle acts as a flexor and adductor of the hip by looking at the direction of its fibres, which pass downwards backwards and laterally. Contraction of the muscle will therefore draw the thigh inwards and forwards. Most authorities dismiss the rotation element as there is certainly disagreement, although some feel that there must be more to the rotation than has yet been deduced.

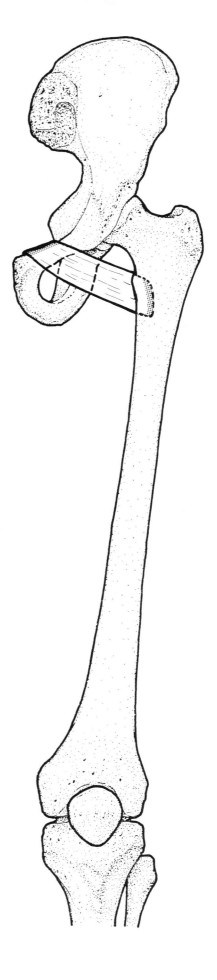

Fig. 5.29   Left pectineus, anterior view.

There is no doubt that the insertion of pectineus is lateral and in front of the axis through the head of the femur and the middle of the lateral condyle of the femur (the line around which rotation would occur in the standing position). Thus the muscle in this case would produce medial rotation (see p. 448). However, when the foot is off the ground, as in the carrying-through phase in walking, the axis would still pass through the hip joint, but now would vary considerably according to the position of the thigh and also that of the pelvis. In fact it would depend very much on the swing of the lower limb.

So far, the functional activity of this muscle has only been considered in the upright, standing or walking position. Much of the time is spent in the sitting position with the hip joint flexed at a right angle. The relationship between the origin and insertion of this muscle are now completely reversed. To make the situation even clearer, the thigh can be raised off the seat until it is at an angle of 45° to the horizontal—as if the legs were going to be crossed. The muscle fibres now pass forwards and upwards, passing well behind the axis of the rotating thigh. The action of the muscle in this position will now be adduction as before, but also extension and lateral rotation, in fact a movement very similar to that of crossing the legs except that the thigh is being pulled down onto the opposite thigh. This movement is comparable with the initial stages of rising from a very low chair, or from the squat position, especially if the movement is being carried out at some speed and under load.

If the argument is taken one stage further, the muscle is obviously a flexor and adductor in the upright position with perhaps medial rotation. The muscle is an extensor and lateral rotator in the fully flexed position, but still performing adduction. Therefore, as in the case of many muscles in the body, pectineus can perform different actions according to its starting position and the relative position of its origin and insertion. It is not surprising, therefore, that it is supplied by nerves from both the flexor and adductor compartment of the thigh.

Remembering the dual nerve supply, the dual action, the closeness of the muscle to the hip joint and its important relations, it is surprising that pectineus only merits a few lines in most anatomy texts. It must have played a vital role in ambulation with a flexed hip, either in climbing or when all four limbs were on the ground. Has its role diminished that much or are we overlooking the true action and worth of pectineus?

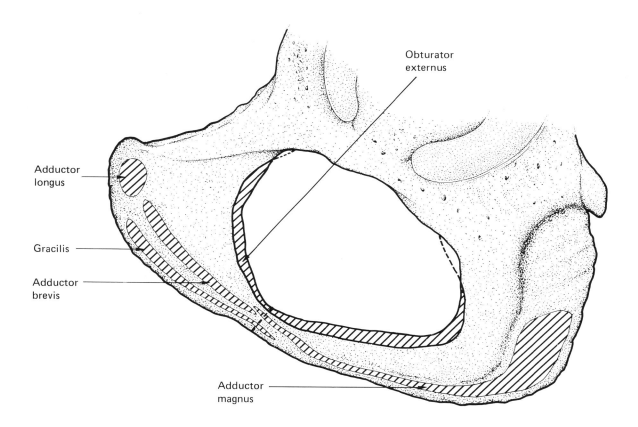

Obturator
externus

Adductor
longus

Gracilis

Adductor
brevis

Adductor
magnus

Fig. 5.30 Figure to show areas of muscle attachment
(shaded) to the outer surface of the pubis and ischium.

MUSCLES WHICH MEDIALLY ROTATE THE HIP JOINT

The muscles which medially rotate the hip joint are:

Anterior part of gluteus medius (see p. 346)

Anterior part of gluteus minimus (see p. 347)

Tensor fascia lata (see p. 372)

Psoas major (see p. 354)

Iliacus (see p. 356)

MUSCLES WHICH LATERALLY ROTATE THE HIP JOINT

The muscles which take part in lateral rotation of the hip joint are:

Gluteus maximus (see p. 338)
Piriformis
Obturator internus
Gemellus superior
Gemellus inferior
Quadratus femoris
Obturator externus

Gluteus maximus

This muscle is mainly an extensor of the hip and can be found on p. 338.

Piriformis

Piriformis (see Fig. 5.24) is found posterior to the hip joint, being in the same plane as the gluteus medius. It is triangular in shape, with its base in the pelvis and the apex in the gluteal region.

Its upper attachment is to the *front* of the *second to fourth sacral segments*, coming between and lateral to the anterior sacral foramina. It has an additional attachment from the *gluteal surface* of the *ilium* and the *pelvic surface* of the *sacrotuberous ligament* as it passes out of the pelvis through the greater sciatic foramen into the gluteal region. Its fibres continue to pass downwards, laterally and forwards, narrowing into a tendon which attaches to the upper border and medial side of the *greater trochanter* of the *femur*. The fibres run in a straight line from the origin to the insertion through the greater sciatic foramen.

Nerve supply

Piriformis is supplied from the *ventral rami of the sacral plexus*, L5, S1, 2; mainly S1. The skin covering this area is supplied by the same nerve roots but it must be remembered that this is a deep muscle and the gluteus maximus intervenes between the two.

Action

In the anatomical position this muscle will certainly be a lateral rotator of the thigh although it is situated a little high. However, in the sitting position this muscle is concerned in the important action of abduction, and in this particular situation is well positioned for this action. It is an important muscle in holding the head of the femur in the acetabulum.

Functional activity

It is well to remember that many times we only consider the action of a muscle in the anatomical position. In the sitting position, the pull of muscles changes and the movement produced may bear little or no relation to the previous action. Piriformis will be particularly concerned in the following activities:

1. abduction when sitting, for example in moving from one chair to another without standing up;
2. moving the legs to the outside of a car in preparation for standing up;
3. stabilizing the pelvis when the trunk is rotated;
4. controlling the balance of the pelvis when standing on a moving bus.

It is not therefore surprising that strain of this muscle is quite common, but unfortunately easily overlooked.

Palpation

This is not easy as piriformis is situated deep inside the buttock. Dig your fingers into the buttock just lateral to the sacrum and then push the outside of the thigh up against the leg of a table or some such resistance, you can then feel the muscle contract, although it must be remembered that a large part of the muscle is in the pelvis.

Obturator internus

Obturator internus (see Fig. 5.24) is again a triangularly shaped muscle, situated partly in the pelvis and partly in the gluteal region posterior to the hip joint. It arises from the internal surface of the obturator membrane and surrounding bony margin, except at the obturator canal. The bony attachment extends backwards as far as the *pelvic surface* of the *ilium.* The muscle fibres pass laterally, but mainly backwards towards the lesser sciatic foramen, through which they pass, narrowing down and becoming tendinous.

As the tendon passes through the lesser sciatic foramen deep to the sacrotuberous ligament it changes direction to pass forwards and laterally to insert into the medial surface of the trochanter of the femur in front of and above the trochanteric fossa. Before attaching to the femur, the tendon is commonly joined by the tendons of the gemellus superior above, and the gemellus inferior below. Occasionally these two tendons will insert into the greater trochanter above and below the tendon of the obturator internus.

The inner (pelvic) surface of obturator internus is covered by the obturator fascia, from which arises part of levator ani. As the tendon of obturator internus turns around the lesser sciatic notch the surface of the bone in this region is grooved and covered with cartilage. A bursa intervenes between tendon and cartilage.

Nerve supply

This muscle is supplied by the *nerve to obturator internus*, root value L5, S1, 2. The skin covering this area is mainly supplied by S3.

Action

In the anatomical position this muscle is a lateral rotator of the thigh pulling the greater trochanter backwards using the hip joint as the fulcrum. However when the hip is flexed to a right angle, it will pull the upper end of the femur medially, and therefore the lower end will move laterally as in abduction.

Functional activity

As in the case of the piriformis (see p. 357), obturator internus will be used when moving sideways in the seated position, in swinging the lower limb sideways, as in placing the limb outside a car, and in balancing and controlling the stability of the trunk when the seated person is being rocked from side-to-side. For the same reasons moving around on the floor or on a platform, either sitting or crawling will require considerable activity in this muscle.

Gemellus superior

As the obturator internus passes out of the pelvis around the lesser sciatic notch it is joined by the gemellus superior and inferior.

Gemellus superior (see Fig. 5.24) arises from the *gluteal surface* of the *ischial spine*. It runs laterally and slightly downwards to blend with the *superior aspect* of the tendon of the *obturator internus*. Sometimes its fibres are prolonged onto the medial surface of the *greater trochanter* of the *femur*.

Nerve supply

The muscle is supplied by the *nerve to obturator internus*, root value L5, S1, 2.

Gemellus inferior

Gemellus inferior (see Fig. 5.24) arises from the *upper part* of the *ischial tuberosity*. It runs laterally and slightly upwards to blend with the *inferior aspect* of the tendon of the *obturator internus*.

Nerve supply

The muscle is supplied by the *nerve to quadratus femoris*, root value L4, 5, S1.

Action

The gemelli aid the obturator internus in its action. As the obturator internus turns around the lesser sciatic notch it will lose some of its power, this will obviously be compensated for by the pull of the gemelli.

Quadratus femoris

This muscle is situated below the gemellus inferior and above the upper margin of adductor magnus (see Fig. 5.24). It is a flat quadrilateral muscle, separated from the hip joint by the obturator externus.

It attaches to the *ischial tuberosity* just below the lower rim of the acetabulum. The fibres pass laterally to attach to the *quadrate tubercle* situated half way down the intertrochanteric crest and the area of bone surrounding it.

Nerve supply

The muscle is supplied by the *nerve to quadratus femoris*, root value L4, 5, S1.

Action

In the anatomical position quadratus femoris is obviously a lateral rotator of the hip joint, but with the hip flexed, it will act as an abductor of the hip.

Obturator externus

This is a triangular muscle having its muscular base attached to the *outer surface* of the *obturator membrane* and the surrounding margins of the *pubis* and *ischium*, excluding the area superiorly around the obturator canal (see Fig. 5.30). The muscle fibres converge onto a tendon which runs in a groove below the acetabulum across the back of the neck of the femur, which it grooves, to insert into the *trochanteric fossa*. The muscle lies deep to the quadratus femoris.

Nerve supply

This muscle is supplied by the *posterior branch of the obturator nerve*, root value L3, 4.

Action

In the anatomical position obturator externus laterally rotates the femur. However, when the hip is flexed it will pull the upper part of the femur medially with the lower part passing laterally, as in abduction.

Functional activity

The functional activities of these muscles must be considered together. The piriformis, gemelli, obturator internus and externus, and the quadratus femoris are always considered in the anatomical position. In this position these muscles will perform an important role in the control of the pelvis, particularly when only one foot is on the ground and even more so in walking. They are responsible together with the gluteus maximus and the posterior part of gluteus medius, in producing lateral rotation of the lower limb in the forward swing-through phase of gait. In sitting, crawling and turning over when lying down they will, however, have a completely different role, producing abduction of the hip and thereby controlling the movements of the pelvis on the flexed thigh (see pp. 360–361).

Palpation

These muscles are situated deep to the thick gluteus maximus and it is almost impossible to distinguish the contraction of these muscles through the overlying muscle tissue, especially as gluteus maximus is usually contracting at the same time. However, overactivity or strain of these muscles may result in acute tenderness deep to the back of the hip joint; the production of this pain with the relevant movement is then obvious.

It is difficult to research the actions of these lateral rotators primarily because of their depth in the gluteal region, but also because much of their action is concerned with the control of the movements of the hip and pelvis. Thus they may be in a state of contraction even when the opposite movement to their primary action is occurring.

To see these muscles, gluteus maximus must be removed—the muscles resembling the rungs of a ladder. Consequently, they are often referred to as the *ladder of muscles*.

MUSCLES PRODUCING MOVEMENT OF THE KNEE JOINT

The main movement of the knee joint is flexion and extension. With the knee in a semi-flexed position and the foot off the ground, there is, in addition, a medial and lateral rotation of the tibia with respect to the femur. If the feet are on the ground when the knees are flexed, the rotation at the knee joint is taken up by the femur, which rotates about a vertical axis, running approximately through the intercondylar eminence. This allows the upper part of the femur to move from side-to-side as in moving along sideways from one seat to another.

The movement between the patella and the patellar surface of the femur must also be taken into account when considering the movements of the knee (see p. 498).

MUSCLES FLEXING THE KNEE JOINT

Muscles producing flexion of the knee joint are:

> Hamstrings, that is:
>> semitendinosus
>> semimembranosus
>> biceps femoris
> Gracilis
> Sartorius (see p. 366)
> Gastrocnemius (see p. 378)

The hamstrings (see p. 342)

It must be emphasized that, with the exception of the short head of the biceps femoris, these three muscles pass over, and act upon both the hip and knee joints. Their action is therefore extremely complex. Although details of their attachments and much of their action is covered on pp. 342–345, the functional activities of these muscles with respect to the knee joint has yet to be considered.

Rotation of the knee joint by the hamstrings is usually considered to take place when the foot is off the ground. However, this is not exactly true. It is certainly easier to describe the rotation that occurs when the foot is off the ground, but in practice the rotation occurs when the feet are firmly on the ground. For example, consider moving sideways from seat to seat. The feet are fixed and body weight is taken onto them, however, the person stays in a sitting position just allowing the buttock to come clear of the seat. The trunk is then moved to one side by a swivelling of the femur on the upper surface of the tibia. This is achieved by the combined action of the medial rotators of one knee and the lateral rotators of the other.

Finally, the simultaneous action of the hamstrings on both the hip and knee joints must be considered. Such a situation arises in the athlete who is accelerating towards a bend. Here the hamstrings are functioning to lift the trunk into a more upright position as well as to flex the knee of the leg that is being swung-through ready for the next stride. As the body is being forced around the bend, the hamstrings will also have to produce a rotation of the knee in order to produce this turning force. It is thought by some that the hamstrings act as a tie between the back of the pelvis and the tibia, which can adjust the relationship between the two bones. This is particularly important when the body is changing posture during active movement as there are additional forces due to the acceleration of body segments. This concept would certainly go some of the way to explain why there are so many injuries of the hamstrings in athletes.

Gracilis

Gracilis (Fig. 5.31), as its name implies, is a long, thin muscle, situated on the medial side of the thigh. It is the most superficial of the adductor group. Its upper attachment is to the *front* of the *body* of the *pubis* and its *inferior ramus*, just encroaching onto the *ramus* of the *ischium* (see Fig. 5.30). The muscle as it descends between semimembranosus posteriorly and sartorius anteriorly, develops a fusiform-shaped belly at about its middle. It becomes tendinous above the knee and crosses the joint before expanding to attach to a short vertical line on the upper part of the *medial surface* of the body of the *tibia*. This attachment is above that of semitendinosus and behind and blending with that of sartorius. Bursae separate the tendon of gracilis from those of sartorius and semitendinosus.

Nerve supply

Gracilis is supplied by the *anterior division of the obturator nerve*, root value L2, 3. The skin covering this area is also through roots L2, 3; the upper part by the obturator nerve and the lower part by the femoral nerve.

Action

Although this muscle is situated in the adductor group of muscles, its action of adduction on the thigh is not so important as its action on the knee. It is mainly a flexor of the knee, but with the knee in a semi-flexed position it will aid medial rotation of the leg on the thigh.

Functional activity

As a flexor of the knee this muscle will help the hamstrings in simple flexion activities, such as the beginning of the swing phase in walking when the knee needs to be flexed. It will also help when strong flexion is required, as when pulling the body forward on the sliding seat of a rowing boat. In horse riding, gracilis is used in all its actions. When the rider is gripping the horse, gracilis will help the adductor muscles, whilst at the same time helping to control the flexed knee.

Palpation

In the sitting position with the medial aspect of the foot against a solid object, such as the leg of a table, or when the toes are inwardly rotated, the tendon can be felt on the posteromedial aspect of the knee joint, being the upper of the two obvious tendons. If traced upwards, the belly of the muscle can be palpated and traced to its attachment on the front of the pubic body.

Fig. 5.31 Left gracilis, anterior view.

Sartorius

Sartorius (Fig. 5.32) is the most superficial muscle in the anterior compartment of the thigh. Its lower part is mainly on the *medial side* anterior to gracilis. It is a long strap-like muscle having flattened tendons at each end. It is renowned as the longest muscle in the body, getting its name from its action, which is to produce most of the actions needed in the lower limb, to produce cross-legged sitting, the position that tailors used to use when making clothes.

Its upper attachment is to the *anterior superior iliac spine* and the area just below. From here the muscle passes medially and inferiorly to attach to a vertical line on the *medial side* of the body of the *tibia*, in front of both semitendinosus and gracilis, partly blending with the latter. A few fibres from the lower tendon go to the medial collateral ligament of the knee joint and to the fascia of the leg. A bursa separates sartorius from gracilis at its lower end. The medial border of the upper third forms the lateral boundary of the femoral triangle whilst the middle third forms the roof of the adductor canal.

Nerve supply

Sartorius is supplied by the *femoral nerve*, root value L2, 3. The area of skin covering this muscle is also supplied by L2, 3.

Action

Sartorius will produce many of the movements which are combined to produce cross-legged sitting, that is flexion of the hip and knee, lateral rotation and abduction of the thigh, and medial rotation of the tibia on the femur. These actions can be summarized by saying that it places the heel on the medial side of the opposite knee.

Functional activity

Going into the cross-legged or the tailor sitting position is a functional activity, however, sartorius will help to produce any activity which involves flexion of the knee and hip together, combined with lateral rotation of the thigh as in drawing up the lower limbs when using the frog-kick in swimming.

Palpation

Sartorius is most easily palpated at its proximal end just below the anterior superior iliac spine. Here its strap-like shape can be easily palpated, particularly when the leg, with the knee slightly flexed, is raised some 15 cm from the floor when lying supine.

Gastrocnemius

Gastrocnemius (see Fig. 5.39a) is mainly a strong plantar flexor of the ankle joint and is dealt with in that section. Nevertheless, it is also a strong flexor of the knee.

The medial and lateral heads of gastrocnemius cross the knee joint on their respective sides. The muscle appears to come into action when the foot is fixed and the body is being pulled forwards on the feet. This is best seen when pulling forwards on the slide of a rowing boat seat, or manoeuvring the fully reclined body. The turning and pulling down of the body when in bed or on a plinth is very important considering that we spend one-third of our lives lying down.

Fig. 5.32 Left sartorius, anterior view.

MUSCLES EXTENDING THE KNEE JOINT

The muscles which extend the knee joint are:

Quadriceps femoris, that is:
    rectus femoris
    vastus lateralis
    vastus intermedius
    vastus medialis
Tensor fascia lata

Quadriceps femoris

The quadriceps femoris is the large muscle bulk on the anterior surface of the thigh. As its name implies, it is composed of four main parts. One part, rectus femoris, has its origin above the hip joint, while the other three parts take origin from the shaft of the femur. All four join together around the patella to form a thick strong tendon called the ligamentum patellae, which inserts into the tibial tuberosity.

Rectus femoris

Rectus femoris (Fig. 5.33) is seen to stand out on the front of the thigh, being a spindle-shaped bipennate muscle. Its upper attachment is by two heads which are continuous with each other, one to the *anterior inferior iliac spine* (this is the straight head) and the other to a rough area immediately above the *acetabulum* (this is the reflected head). It is thought that the straight head is a human acquisition associated with the evolution of an upright posture. From this continuous origin, a single tendon descends from which arises the fleshy belly of the muscle. About two-thirds of the way down the thigh, the muscle begins to narrow to a thick tendon attaching to the *upper border* of the *patella*. From here, some fibres pass around the patella helping to form the ligamentum patellae. The deep surface of the muscle is tendinous and smooth, allowing free movement over a similar surface on vastus intermedius, thus permitting its independent action on the hip joint.

Patella

Ligamentum
patellae

Fig. 5.33 Left rectus femoris, anterior view.

Vastus lateralis

Vastus lateralis (Fig. 5.34) is situated on the anterolateral aspect of the thigh, lateral to rectus femoris. It has an extensive linear attachment from the *upper lateral* part of the *intertrochanteric line*, the *lower border* of the *greater trochanter*, the *lateral side* of the *gluteal tuberosity* and the *upper half* of the *lateral lip* of the *linea aspera*. It also attaches to the *fascia lata* and lateral intermuscular septum. From this origin the muscle fibres run downwards and forwards with those at the top passing almost vertically downwards.

The muscle bulk is mainly situated in the upper half of the lateral side of the thigh, from which a broad tendon arises which narrows down as it approaches the lateral side of the patella. This tendon inserts into the *tendon* of *rectus femoris* and the *base* and *lateral border* of the *patella*. Some fibres pass to the front of the lateral condyle of the tibia blending with the iliotibial tract helping to form the expansion which finally attaches to the line running towards the tibial tuberosity. To a large extent this part of its attachment replaces the knee joint capsule in this region.

Vastus medialis

Vastus medialis (Fig. 5.34) is situated on the anteromedial aspect of the thigh, medial to the rectus femoris, with most of its bulk showing at the lower third just above the patella. It has an extensive linear origin from a line beginning at the *lower medial* end of the *intertrochanteric line*, running downwards around the *medial* aspect of the upper end of the shaft on the *spiral line*, the *medial lip* of the *linea aspera*, continuing onto the upper two-thirds of the *medial supracondylar line*, the *medial intermuscular septum* and the tendon of *adductor magnus*.

Its upper fibres pass mainly downwards, whilst its lower fibres tend to pass almost horizontally forwards. The muscle attaches to the *tendon* of *rectus femoris*, the *medial* border of the *patella*, and the front of the medial condyle of the *tibia*. The expansions which pass across the knee joint to attach to the tibia replace the joint capsule in this region and become fused with the deep fascia. This attachment also runs to the tibial tuberosity (see also p. 466).

Vastus intermedius

Vastus intermedius (Fig. 5.35) is the deepest part of quadriceps femoris lying between vastus lateralis and medialis, and deep to rectus femoris.

It arises by fleshy fibres from the upper two-thirds of the *anterior* and *lateral* surfaces of the *femur*, its fibres pass downwards to form a broad tendon on its more superficial aspect. This attaches to the deep surface of the tendons of *rectus femoris* and the other vastus muscles, and to the *base* of the *patella*. In the middle of the thigh, vastus intermedius is difficult to separate from vastus lateralis, while lower down it is impossible to separate from vastus medialis.

Articularis genus   Some of the deep fibres of vastus intermedius, arising from a small area on the inferior third of the *anterior* surface of the *femur*, pass downwards to attach to the upper part of the *suprapatellar bursa* of the knee joint which lies deep to vastus intermedius. These fibres are the articularis genus. Its main function is to prevent the synovial membrane becoming trapped and interfering with the normal movements of the knee joint.

Vastus lateralis

Vastus medialis

Patella

Ligamentum
patellae

Fig. 5.34 Left vastus lateralis and medialis, anterior view.

Fig. 5.35 Left vastus intermedius, anterior view.

Ligamentum patellae

All four of these tendons contribute to the formation of the ligamentum patellae. It runs from the *apex* of the *patella* to the *upper* part of the *tibial tuberosity* acting as the tendon of insertion of the quadriceps femoris muscle. The patella is really a sesamoid bone in the tendon of rectus femoris and vastus intermedius helping to relay the pull of the quadriceps over the front of the femur.

Nerve supply

Quadriceps femoris, including articularis genus, is supplied by the *femoral nerve*, root value L2, 3, 4. The skin covering the quadriceps is supplied by L2, 3.

Action

Quadriceps femoris is the main extensor of the knee joint. The rectus femoris crosses in front of the hip joint and therefore is also a flexor of that joint. Each muscle appears to have its particular role in extension of the knee and often comes in at different ranges of the movement. For example, vastus medialis is more obviously active in the final stage of extension and is believed to resist the tendency of the patella to move laterally caused by the angulation of the femur.

The rectus femoris works particularly strongly in straight leg raising or in the combined movement of flexion of the hip and extension of the knee.

Functional activity

The quadriceps are used strongly in stepping activities, for example stair climbing and squats. The rectus femoris will perform its function particularly in the swing phase of walking when the lower limb is being carried forward and the knee is being extended. Vastus medialis, in the final stages of extension of the knee, will help in the locking mechanism of the joint when the femur is allowed to rotate medially.

Surprisingly, in the standing position very little or no action is recorded in the quadriceps as in this position the knees are in the closepacked position. It is at these times that if the knees are knocked from behind that forward collapse will almost certainly occur. However, when standing on a moving vehicle the quadriceps will be active. When standing on one leg, all the muscles around the knee will work statically to provide stability at the joint.

The quadriceps is a powerful and an important muscle. It must work strongly throughout its full range. It will lose strength and bulk rapidly if there is any injury to it or to the knee joint. It may take months to regain power, but only days to lose it.

Palpation

When sitting on a chair and straightening the knee joint, particularly against resistance, the separate parts of quadriceps femoris, except vastus intermedius, can easily be palpated. The medialis on the lower medial aspect, the lateralis in the upper half of the lateral side and the rectus running down the centre. Stand with the knees semiflexed, place your hands on the front of each thigh; the three parts of the muscle (as above) can be readily palpated.

In straight leg raising, the muscle should be able to extend the knee into a few degrees of hyperextension, this being the extra range required for the knee to be able to lock. Patients not being able to do this will often complain of their knee giving way during walking.

Tensor fascia lata

Tensor fascia lata (see Fig. 5.36b) is situated anterolateral to the hip joint and superficial to gluteus minimus. It attaches above to the anterior part of the *outer lip* of the *iliac crest*, between and including the tubercle of the crest and the anterior superior iliac spine, the area of *gluteal surface* just below it, the *fascia* between it and gluteus minimus and that covering its superificial surface. Inferiorly, it attaches between the two layers of the *iliotibial tract*, below the level of the greater trochanter.

Nerve supply

Tensor fascia lata is supplied by the *superior gluteal nerve*, root value L4, 5, with the skin overlying the muscle supplied by L1.

Action

Acting with the superficial fibres of gluteus maximus it will tighten the iliotibial tract, and through its attachment to the lateral condyle of the tibia, will extend the knee joint. Acting with the gluteus minimus it will medially rotate the hip joint and its posterior fibres may help in abduction of the thigh.

Functional activity

Due to the fact that this muscle, together with gluteus maximus, links the pelvis with the tibia it will help to steady and control the movements of the pelvis and the femur on the tibia when the limb is weight-bearing. Tensor fascia lata produces strong medial rotation when the hip is in extension and the lower limb, pelvis and trunk are prepared to take the thrust relayed through the lower limb by the calf muscles during the 'toe-off' phase of walking.

When the quadriceps femoris is paralysed, the tensor fascia lata can be developed to produce sufficient extension of the knee to enable the patient to walk, but its action is only weak and limited in range.

Palpation

Place the fingers half way between the anterior superior iliac spine and the greater trochanter of the femur. When the lower limb is medially rotated, the muscle can be felt to contract powerfully. If the weight is taken on the limb and the pelvis is rotated to the same side, a similar contraction of the muscle will be observed.

MUSCLES PRODUCING LATERAL ROTATION OF THE TIBIA AT THE KNEE JOINT

Biceps femoris (see p. 342)

MUSCLES PRODUCING MEDIAL ROTATION OF THE TIBIA AT THE KNEE JOINT

Semitendinosus (see p. 342)
Semimembranosus (see p. 342)
Gracilis (see p. 364)
Sartorius (see p. 366)
Popliteus

Popliteus

Popliteus (see Fig. 5.22) is a triangularly-shaped muscle situated deep in the popliteal fossa, below and lateral to the knee joint. It arises within the joint capsule from a tendinous attachment from the anterior aspect of the groove on the outer surface of the *lateral condyle* of the *femur*, below the lateral epicondyle and the attachment of the fibular collateral ligament. The tendon passes backwards, downwards and medially, crossing the line of the joint over the outer border of the lateral meniscus to which it is attached. This upper part, within the capsule of the knee joint, is enveloped in a double layer of synovial membrane until it leaves the capsule under the arcuate popliteal ligament, from which it has a fleshy origin. Continuing downwards and medially, popliteus attaches by fleshy fibres onto a triangular area on the *posterior surface* of the *tibia* above the soleal line, and into the *fascia* covering the muscle.

Nerve supply

Popliteus is supplied by a branch from the *tibial division of the sciatic nerve*, root value L5, which enters the muscle on its anterior surface after winding around its infero-lateral border. The skin covering the area is supplied mainly by S2.

Action

Popliteus laterally rotates the femur on the tibia when the foot is on the ground, thus releasing the knee from its closepacked or locked position allowing the knee to flex. By exerting a backward pull on the lateral surface of the lateral condyle of the femur, the condyle is rotated laterally about a vertical axis running through the lateral condyle just medial to its centre. This allows the medial condyle of the femur to glide forward releasing the ligaments and muscles involved in its closepacked position (see p. 502).

When strong flexion of the knee is required, popliteus comes into action drawing the tibia backwards on the femoral condyles, and if the foot is off the ground, it will aid the medial hamstrings in medial rotation of the tibia.

Through its attachments to the lateral meniscus, it pulls the meniscus backwards during lateral rotation of the femur preventing it from being trapped between the moving bones. This is believed by some authorities to be the reason for the lateral meniscus being damaged much less frequently than the medial.

Some of the muscles already described can be seen together in Figs. 5.36–5.38.

Fig. 5.36 **a** = Left thigh, posterior view; **b** = left thigh, lateral view.

Iliac crest

Gluteus medius and minimus

Gluteus maximus

Biceps femoris

Semitendinosus

Semimembranosus

a

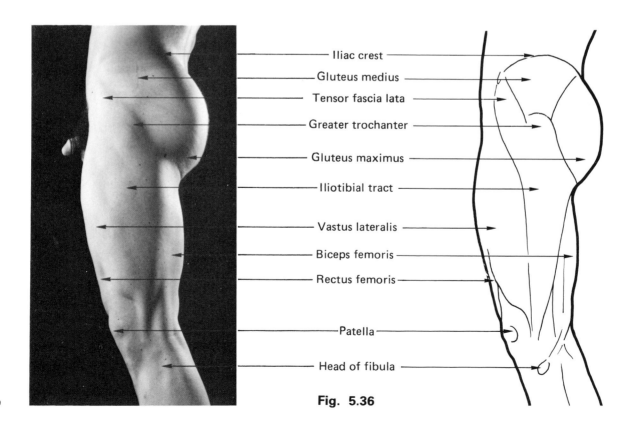

Iliac crest

Gluteus medius

Tensor fascia lata

Greater trochanter

Gluteus maximus

Iliotibial tract

Vastus lateralis

Biceps femoris

Rectus femoris

Patella

Head of fibula

b

Fig. 5.36

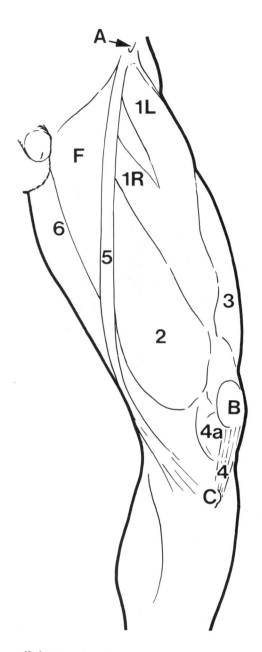

Fig. 5.37 Left thigh, anteromedial aspect:

A = Anterior superior iliac spine
B = Patella
C = Tibial tuberosity
1 = Rectus femoris
1L = Straight head
1R = Reflected head
2 = Vastus medialis

3 = Vastus lateralis
4 = Ligamentum patellae
4a = Infrapatellar fat pad
5 = Sartorius
6 = Medial border of adductor magnus
F = Femoral triangle

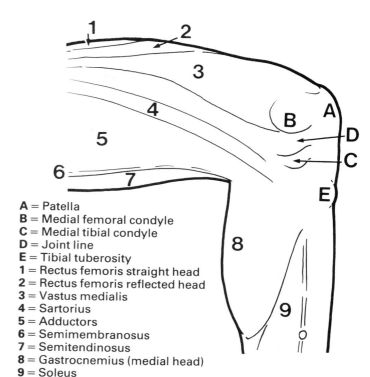

a = Medial aspect

A = Patella
B = Medial femoral condyle
C = Medial tibial condyle
D = Joint line
E = Tibial tuberosity
1 = Rectus femoris straight head
2 = Rectus femoris reflected head
3 = Vastus medialis
4 = Sartorius
5 = Adductors
6 = Semimembranosus
7 = Semitendinosus
8 = Gastrocnemius (medial head)
9 = Soleus

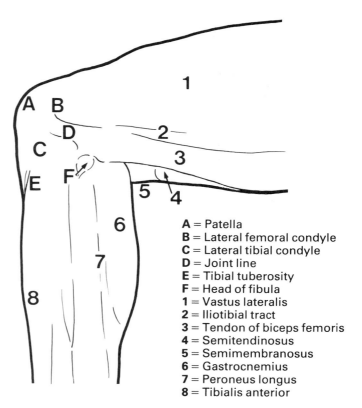

b = Lateral aspect

A = Patella
B = Lateral femoral condyle
C = Lateral tibial condyle
D = Joint line
E = Tibial tuberosity
F = Head of fibula
1 = Vastus lateralis
2 = Iliotibial tract
3 = Tendon of biceps femoris
4 = Semitendinosus
5 = Semimembranosus
6 = Gastrocnemius
7 = Peroneus longus
8 = Tibialis anterior

Fig. 5.38   Left flexed knee.

MUSCLES WHICH PRODUCE PLANTARFLEXION AT THE ANKLE JOINT

Gastrocnemius
Soleus
Plantaris
Peroneus longus (see p. 385)
Tibialis posterior (see p. 384)
Flexor digitorum longus (see p. 392)
Flexor hallucis longus (see p. 396)

Gastrocnemius

The shape of the calf is mainly due to the two fleshy bellies of gastrocnemius (see Fig. 5.39a), being situated on the back of the leg with its muscle bulk mainly in the upper half. Together with soleus and plantaris, gastrocnemius forms a composite muscle referred to as the triceps surae. The two heads of gastrocnemius form the lower boundaries of the popliteal fossa, which can only really be seen when the knee is flexed. The two heads arise from the *medial* and *lateral condyles* of the *femur*. The medial, from behind the medial supracondylar ridge and the adductor tubercle on the popliteal surface of the femur, the lateral head from the outer surface of the lateral condyle of the femur just above and behind the lateral epicondyle. Each head has an additional attachment from the *capsule* of the *knee joint* and from the *oblique popliteal ligament*, below which each head is separated from the capsule by a bursa. The bursa associated with the medial head often communicates with the knee joint. That under the lateral head rarely does. There is often a sesamoid bone, the flabella, in the lateral head as it crosses the lateral condyle of the femur. Less commonly there may be one associated with the medial head.

From each head a fleshy bulk of muscle fibres arise which gradually come together, although not actually blending with each other, to insert into the posterior surface of a broad membranous tendon which fuses with the tendon of soleus to form the upper part of the tendocalcaneus. This broad tendon gradually narrows, becoming more rounded until it reaches about three fingers' breadth above the calcaneus, where it begins to expand again and continues to do so, until its insertion into the middle part of the posterior surface of the calcaneus. A bursa lies between the tendon and the upper part of the calcaneus while a pad of fat lies between the tendon and the posterior aspect of the ankle joint. Inferior to the insertion is the fat pad of the heel.

Nerve supply

Each head of gastrocnemius is supplied by a branch from the *tibial nerve*, root value S1, 2. The area of skin covering the muscle has roots L4, 5, S2.

Action

The gastrocnemius, together with soleus, is the chief plantarflexor of the ankle joint. It provides the propelling force for locomotion. As it crosses the knee joint, gastrocnemius is also a powerful flexor of that joint. However, it is not able to exert its full power on both joints simultaneously. For example, if the knee is flexed gastrocnemius cannot exert maximum power at the ankle joint and vice versa.

Functional activity

In running, walking and jumping gastrocnemius provides a considerable amount of the driving force. When one considers the power needed to throw the body into the air, triceps surae must be one of the most powerful muscle groups in the body.

The habitual wearing of shoes with a high heel can cause considerable shortening of the fibres of gastrocnemius, as the two attachments of the muscle fibres are brought closer together. If shortening has occurred, difficulty in walking in flat shoes or bare feet may be experienced due to limited dorsiflexion at the ankle joint.

Soleus

This muscle is situated deep to gastrocnemius, being a broad flat muscle wider in its middle section and narrower below (see Fig. 5.39b). It arises from the *soleal line* on the posterior surface of the tibia, the posterior surface of the upper third of the *fibula* (including the head) and a *fibrous arch* between these bony attachments. The fibres pass downwards, forming a belly about half way down the calf to the deep surface of a membranous tendon which faces posteriorly. This tendon glides over a similar one on the deep surface of gastrocnemius, thereby enabling independent movement of the two muscles to occur. Inferiorly the two tendons fuse to form the upper part of the tendocalcaneus, which passes behind the ankle joint to insert into the middle part of the *posterior* surface of the *calcaneus*.

Nerve supply

Soleus is supplied by two branches from the *tibial nerve*, root value S1, 2, one of which arises in the popliteal fossa and enters the superficial surface of the muscle, while the other arises in the calf entering the deep surface. The skin over the region of the muscle is predominantly supplied by root S2.

Action

Soleus is one of two main plantarflexors of the ankle joint. It is so placed to prevent the body falling forwards at the ankle joint during standing, and as such is an important postural muscle. Intermittent contraction of the muscle during standing aids venous return (the soleal pump) due to the communicating vessels joining the deep and superficial venous systems which pass through its substance.

Plantaris

Plantaris (see Fig. 5.39c) is a long, slender muscle which is variable in its composition. It may have one muscle belly high up in the calf, or two smaller bellies separated by a tendon. It arises from the lowest part of the *lateral supracondylar ridge*, the adjacent part of the *popliteal surface* of the *femur* and the *knee joint capsule*. The tendon passes obliquely downwards between gastrocnemius and soleus to emerge on the medial side of the tendocalcaneus. It may insert into the *tendocalcaneus* or into the medial side of the *posterior* surface of the *calcaneus*.

Nerve supply

The supply to plantaris is from the *tibial nerve*, root value S1, 2.

Action

Plantaris is a weak flexor of the knee and plantarflexor of the ankle joint.

The tendocalcaneus (Achilles tendon)

This is considered to be the thickest and strongest tendon in the body, being the tendon by which the calf muscles exert their force on the posterior part of the foot during the propulsive phase of many activities, for example, walking, running and jumping. It has been suggested that the tendocalcaneus is able to withstand strains of up to 10 tons. As its fibres pass downwards they spiral through some 90°, with the medial fibres passing posteriorly. This unusual arrangement is thought to explain the apparent elastic qualities of the tendon. For example, when jumping the body will land in an upright position with the foot held in plantarflexion by the active triceps surae. The strain is then taken by the tendocalcaneus which produces a recoil effect.

Functional activity of the calf muscles

The action of the calf muscles as a whole is to plantarflex the foot at the ankle joint. Gastrocnemius acts as the propelling force, working mainly on the ankle but also producing flexion of the knee if working strongly enough. The soleus, on the other hand, is better situated to act more as a postural muscle. This is because its lower attachment is the fixed point and prevents the leg from falling forwards under the influence of body weight, because the vertical projection from the centre of gravity of the body falls in front of the ankle joint.

Gastrocnemius is composed of muscle fibres which give it a pale appearance, consequently it is often referred to as 'white' muscle. Whereas, the soleus has fibres which give it a red appearance and is therefore termed a 'red' muscle.

Plantaris takes very little part in plantarflexion of the ankle and, in fact, sometimes causes pain and disability when it is torn. This condition is referred to as 'tennis leg', occurring during a game of tennis, when the player believes that he or she has been struck on the back of the calf by a tennis ball. The tendon is often completely ruptured and may have to be removed surgically.

Palpation of the calf muscles

When standing, draw your hand down the back of the knee. The two large muscular bellies of gastrocnemius can be felt on either side of the upper part of the calf. The medial head projects slightly higher and lower than the lateral. Both can be felt joining a broad flattened tendon just over half way down the calf. The junction between the muscle fibres and the tendon is very clear and it is along this line that many injuries of the calf occur.

The soleus is not quite so easy to palpate being deep to gastrocnemius, its lateral boundary appearing as a flattened elevation below and lateral to the lateral head of gastrocnemius when the ankle is plantarflexed. When standing on tiptoe, soleus can be seen and felt to the bulge either side of gastrocnemius. Passing the hand further down the calf it will encounter the flattened tendocalcaneus, which is felt to narrow and become rounded at the level of the ankle joint. It then expands slightly to its insertion into the middle section of the posterior surface of the calcaneus.

Fig. 5.39 **a** = Right gastrocnemius, posterior view. **b** = Right soleus, posterior view. **c** = Right plantaris, posterior view.

Fig. 5.39

MUSCLES WHICH PRODUCE DORSIFLEXION OF THE ANKLE JOINT

Tibialis anterior
Extensor digitorum longus (see p. 389)
Extensor hallucis longus (see p. 388)
Peroneus tertius (see p. 386)

Tibialis anterior

Tibialis anterior (Fig. 5.40a) is a long fusiform muscle situated on the front of the leg lateral to the anterior border of the tibia. It is covered by strong fascia and gains its upper attachment from the deep surface of this *fascia*, the upper two-thirds of the *lateral surface* of the *tibia* and the adjoining part of the *interosseous membrane*. The muscle becomes tendinous in its lower third, passing downwards and medially over the distal end of the tibia. The tendon continues under the superior and through the inferior extensor retinaculum to insert into the *medial side* of the *medial cuneiform* bone and *base* of the *first metatarsal*. The insertion reaching the under surface of both bones to blend with that of peroneus longus.

Nerve supply

This muscle is supplied by the *deep peroneal nerve*, root value L4, 5. The skin covering the muscle is also supplied by roots L4, 5.

Action

The tibialis anterior is a dorsiflexor of the foot at the ankle joint. When working with tibialis posterior it acts as an invertor of the foot, in which the sole of the foot is turned to face medially.

Functional activity

As with other muscles in the leg, tibialis anterior is concerned with the balancing of the body on the foot. It works with the surrounding muscles to maintain body balance during activities of the upper part of the body which change the distribution of weight.

Not only is the tibialis anterior responsible for dorsiflexing the foot as the lower limb is carried forward during the swing-through phase of walking, so preventing the toes catching the ground, it also controls the placement of the foot on the ground following initial ground contact by the heel. On close observation, especially in slow motion, it will be seen that the heel does not strike the ground and remain immobile at the initiation of the stance phase, but glides onto the surface and acts as the first braking force of the lower limb's forward movement. Overactivity of tibialis anterior accounts for the wear patterns seen on the posterolateral aspect of the heel, due to the frictional forces between the shoe and the ground. The rest of the foot is then gradually lowered to the ground in a controlled manner taking up the undulations of the surface concerned. The landing of the foot on the ground is similar to the landing of an aeroplane; the main wheels touch down first applying the initial braking force followed by a controlled lowering of the front of the craft as the speed decreases.

The tibialis anterior in association with the other dorsiflexors, therefore, plays an important part in the lowering of the forefoot to the ground in walking or running and will be put under stress in extended activity particularly over rough terrain. The anterior calf muscles are enclosed in particularly tight fascia which allows very little expansion of the tissues. The result is a compression of the muscle during activity and a dragging on the attachments of the surrounding fascia, particularly where it attaches to bone. This leads to a painful condition of this area commonly called 'shin splints'.

Paralysis of tibialis anterior causes footdrop because the remaining dorsiflexors are not strong enough to raise the toes and so prevent them dragging along the ground. The patient may overcome this by flexing the knee more than normal during walking or by fitting a 'toe-raise' spring to the front of the shoe.

Palpation

Both the muscle belly and tendon can be seen and felt when the foot is dorsiflexed against resistance, the tendon being the most medial at the ankle joint.

Medial cuneiform

Fig. 5.40 **a** = Right tibialis anterior, anterior view. **b** = Right tibialis posterior, posterior view.

a

b

MUSCLES WHICH PRODUCE INVERSION OF THE FOOT

Tibialis posterior
Tibialis anterior (see p. 382)

Tibialis posterior

Tibialis posterior (see Fig. 5.40b) is the deepest muscle on the back of the leg. It arises from the upper half of the lateral aspect of the posterior surface of the *tibia* below the soleal line, the *interosseous membrane*, the posterior surface of the *fibula* between the medial crest and interosseous border, and the *fascia* covering it posteriorly. The tendon, enclosed in its own synovial sheath, passes behind the medial malleolus grooving it, being medial to the flexor hallucis longus and flexor digitorum longus. It lies superficial to the deltoid ligament. Lying inferior to the plantar calcaneonavicular ligament, the tendon passes downward to attach principally to the *tubercle* on the *medial side* of the *navicular* and the *plantar surface* of the *medial cuneiform*. Tendinous expansions pass to the plantar surfaces of all the tarsal bones except the talus, although a strip passes back to the tip of the sustentaculum tali, and the bases of the middle three metatarsals.

Nerve supply

Tibialis posterior is supplied by a branch of the *tibial nerve*, root value L4, 5. The skin over the area on the back of the calf is supplied by root S2.

Action

Tibialis posterior is the main invertor of the foot, acting in conjunction with tibialis anterior. By its attachment to the tubercle of the navicular, it pulls upwards and inwards and therefore rotates the forefoot so that the plantar aspect faces medially. It must be noted that inversion and eversion of the foot involves movement at the midtarsal joint, whereby the navicular and cuboid move on the head of the talus and the calcaneus.

The muscle is also a plantarflexor of the foot at the ankle joint, but its contribution is small; gastrocnemius and soleus are better situated and have a more direct line of action. Nevertheless, if the tendocalcaneus is ruptured, then tibialis posterior can produce plantarflexion. Because of its attachments to both the tibia and fibula, contraction of tibialis posterior will tend to bring the two bones closer together. Consequently, during plantarflexion, the malleoli are approximated to maintain their firm grip on the narrower posterior part of the trochlear surface of the talus.

Functional activity

Tibialis posterior will help to maintain the balance of the tibia on the foot, particularly when body weight is tending to move laterally. Being a strong invertor, it controls the forefoot in walking and running by positioning the foot so that the medial arch is not completely flattened. Its many tendinous expansions help to maintain all the various arches of the foot.

Palpation

It is quite impossible to palpate the belly of the muscle due to the other muscles covering it. It is however quite easy to feel the tendon of the muscle as it passes behind the medial malleolus and particularly as it attaches to the tubercle of the navicular. When lying supine, the tendon can be felt and seen behind the medial malleolus when inversion of the plantarflexed foot against resistance is attempted. From just above the flexor retinaculum to its insertion, it is surrounded by a synovial sheath and it is in this area that the tendon can become quite painful if the muscle has been overactive. The pain is sharp and knife-like and is termed tenosynovitis.

MUSCLES WHICH PRODUCE EVERSION OF THE FOOT

Eversion of the foot is the movement whereby the sole of the foot is turned to face laterally. There are three muscles which produce eversion of the foot, all situated on the lateral side of the leg and all arising, in part, from the fibula. These are:

Peroneus longus
Peroneus brevis
Peroneus tertius

Peroneus longus

Peroneus longus (see Fig. 5.41a) is situated on the lateral side of the leg, being a long, thin fusiform muscle with a long belly and an even longer tendon. It is also quite unique in as much as the tendon changes direction three times on its way to its insertion on the medial side of the sole of the foot.

It arises from a small area on the *lateral condyle* of the *tibia* (in conjunction with extensor digitorum longus) and the upper two-thirds of the *lateral surface* of the *fibula*, its lower half lying behind the upper part of the origin of the peroneus brevis. It also takes origin from the *lateral side* of the *head* of the *fibula*, leaving a small area around the neck for the anterior passage of the common peroneal nerve. In front and behind, it attaches to the *intermuscular septa* and to the *fascia* surrounding the muscle.

The tendon forms about a hand's breadth above the lateral malleolus and lies superficial to that of peroneus brevis, sharing the same synovial sheath. It runs in a shallow groove behind the lateral malleolus passing deep to the superior peroneal retinaculum. From here, the tendon passes downwards and slightly forwards to pass below the peroneal tubercle on the calcaneus, being held in position by the inferior band of the peroneal retinaculum. At this point the tendon is enclosed in a separate synovial sheath. As it reaches the inferolateral side of the cuboid, which it grooves, the tendon turns to enter the groove on the inferior aspect of the cuboid. This groove is converted into a tunnel by fibres from the long plantar ligament and tibialis posterior tendon. Whilst in this tunnel the tendon is still surrounded by a synovial sheath. The tunnel conveys the tendon forwards and medially across the foot to its final attachment to the *plantar* and *lateral surfaces* of the *medial cuneiform* and *base* of the *first metatarsal*.

Nerve supply

Peroneus longus is supplied by the superficial branch of the *common peroneal nerve*, root value L5, S1. The skin covering the muscle is supplied by L5, S1.

Action

The muscle is an obvious evertor of the foot because of the fact that it arises from the lateral side of the leg and passes around the lateral side of the foot. In passing from behind the lateral malleolus to the medial cuneiform and first metatarsal, peroneus longus will produce plantarflexion of the foot, with the medial side of the foot being particularly drawn downwards, as in pronation.

It is worth noting that the insertion of this muscle is to the same two bones as the tibialis anterior, although the latter muscle approaches its insertion from the medial side of the foot. This is believed to provide a stirrup for the arches of the foot and help control their height during activity. The attachment of both muscles to the medial cuneiform and base of the first metatarsal bones certainly emphasises the importance of the control of the medial side of the foot in activity, particularly when dealing with uneven terrain.

Functional activity

In standing, peroneus longus, in company with other surrounding muscles, helps to maintain the erect position. It controls sideways sway by pressing the medial side of the foot on to the ground. This function is better seen and appreciated when standing on one leg when peroneus longus works very hard to maintain the leg over the foot and prevent the body falling to the opposite side. Its main functional activity, however, must be during powerful action of the foot as in running, particularly over rough ground. Here, its control, together with tibialis anterior, over the medial side of the foot and the first metatarsal (carrying the great toe), must be vital.

Palpation

When sitting, place the fingers on the lateral side of the knee joint and locate the head of the fibula just below the joint level. The tendon of biceps femoris can be identified coming from the back of the thigh. Run the fingers downwards, keeping the tip of the index finger on the head of the fibula spreading the rest of the finger tips down the lateral side of the fibula. Keeping the fingers in this position, lift up the outer side of the foot. The long vertical belly can be felt contracting. If the fingers are now taken down to the lateral malleolus and placed below and behind it and the same manoeuvre is performed, the two tendons of peroneus longus and brevis can be palpated and can be traced to the peroneal tubercle where they part, the longus passing below and the brevis passing above.

Peroneus brevis

Peroneus brevis (Fig. 5.41b) is also situated on the lateral side of the leg enclosed in the same osteofascial compartment. It arises from the lower two-thirds of the *lateral surface* of the *fibula*, the upper half being anterior to peroneus longus. It also attaches to the *intermuscular septa* at its sides.

The muscle belly is fusiform and short, soon passing into a tendon which accompanies that of the longus to pass behind the lateral malleolus in a common synovial sheath. The tendon then passes forwards and downwards into a groove above the peroneal tubercle of the calcaneus, which is converted into a tunnel by the inferior part of the peroneal retinaculum. It then passess forward to its insertion into the tubercle on the lateral side of the *base* of the *fifth metatarsal* bone. Above the tubercle, the tendon is surrounded by a synovial sheath, which is separated from that of peroneus longus. A slip from the tendon usually joins the long extensor to the little toe. Other separate slips may join peroneus longus, or pass to the calcaneus or cuboid.

Nerve supply

Peroneus brevis is supplied by the *superficial branch of the common peroneal nerve*, root value L5, S1. The skin covering the muscle is innervated by L5, S1, 2.

Action

Peroneus brevis is an evertor of the foot. Because of its course and attachments, the pull of its tendon is in such a direction to produce plantarflexion of the ankle at the same time.

Functional activity

This muscle is also well-positioned to prevent sideways sway in the standing position. In standing on one leg, it will help to prevent the body falling to the opposite side, thus working with a reversed origin and insertion. In walking or running, especially over rough ground, it plays an important part in controlling the position of the foot and should prevent the foot from becoming too inverted. In many cases, however, this mechanism does not always appear to work correctly, and the foot over-inverts causing the weight to come down on the lateral side of the foot forcing the foot into further inversion. This can severely damage or even snap the tendon of the muscle and often the anterior fasciculus of the lateral ligament of the ankle joint.

Palpation

If the fingers are placed on the belly of the peroneus longus and then moved downwards to the lower half of the fibula, (but in the same vertical line), the belly of the brevis can be palpated when the foot is everted and plantarflexed. Its tendon can easily be traced to the groove just above the peroneal tubercle and then forwards to its insertion into the tubercle of the fifth metatarsal.

Peroneus tertius

Peroneus tertius (Fig. 5.41c) is situated on the lower lateral aspect of the leg and appears to have been part of the extensor digitorum longus. It arises from the *front* of the lower quarter of the *fibula* in continuation with the attachment of extensor digitorum longus (with no gap between them),

Peroneus longus

Peroneus brevis

Peroneus
tertius

a

b

c

Fig. 5.41 a,b = Right peroneus longus and brevis, posterior view. **c** = Right peroneus tertius, anterior view.

and from the *intermuscular septum* and adjoining *fascia*. Its fibres pass downwards and laterally into a tendon which passes deep to both the superior and inferior extensor retinacula to insert into the medial aspect of the *base* of the *fifth metatarsal* bone.

Nerve supply

Peroneus tertius is supplied by the *deep branch of the common peroneal nerve*, root value L5, S1. The area of skin covering the muscle is also supplied by roots L5, S1.

Action

The muscle acts as a weak evertor and dorsiflexor of the foot at the ankle joint.

Functional activity

It is difficult to assess the importance of this small muscle as its actions appear to be covered by other muscles which have a much better mechanical leverage. Indeed in some subjects it is absent. It does, however, pass over the anterior fasciculus of the lateral ligament of the ankle joint, and it is well-known that this is very often damaged in inversion injuries. It is therefore well-placed to help prevent too much inversion during sports activities, for example, and may be responsible for keeping down the number of injuries. Unfortunately, the muscle is often torn and may be completely ruptured during violent inversion, which is the cause of considerable pain and swelling. It is possible that with the attainment of bipedalism, peroneus tertius is assuming a more important role because eversion of the foot is a peculiarly human characteristic.

Palpation

Peroneus tertius is very difficult to palpate. However, it can be felt by drawing the fingers downwards from the anterior part of the lateral malleolus into the small hollow found there, the tendon can be felt crossing the lateral part of the hollow to its insertion into the medial side of the base of the fifth metatarsal. Take care not to confuse the tendon of peroneus tertius with that of peroneus brevis, which lies lateral to this point

as it passes forwards to insert into the tubercle on the lateral side of the fifth metatarsal.

MUSCLES WHICH PRODUCE EXTENSION OF THE TOES

Extensor hallucis longus
Extensor digitorum longus
Extensor digitorum brevis
The lumbricals
The interossei (see pp. 399–400)

Extensor hallucis longus

Extensor hallucis longus (see Fig. 5.42a) is situated deep to and between the tibialis anterior and extensor digitorum longus on the front of the leg. Arising from the middle half of the *anterior surface* of the *fibula* and the adjacent *interosseous membrane*, the muscle fibres pass downwards and medially to the tendon which forms on its anterior surface. In this respect it is a unipennate muscle. The tendon passes under the superior extensor retinaculum, through the upper part of the inferior extensor retinaculum in a separate compartment enclosed in its own synovial sheath, and then deep to the lower band of the inferior extensor retinaculum on its way towards the base of the great toe. Generally, the tendon does not form a fully developed extensor hood but passes to attach to the *base* of the *distal phalanx* on its *dorsal* surface. Tendinous slips may be given off to the dorsal aspect of the base of the proximal phalanx and the first metatarsal.

Nerve supply

The extensor hallucis longus is supplied by the *deep branch of the common peroneal nerve*, root value L5, S1. The skin covering this area is supplied by roots L4, 5.

Action

As its name implies, extensor hallucis longus will extend all of the joints of the great toe, but mainly the metatarsophalangeal joint. It is also a powerful dorsiflexor of the foot at the ankle joint.

Functional activity

In running, the great toe is the last part of the foot to leave the ground and therefore the final thrust will come from the long flexors of the toes. After this, the toe must be brought back into the extended position at the same time as the foot is dorsiflexed and slightly inverted, ready for the heel to be placed on the ground for the next weight-bearing phase. By extending the great toe and dorsiflexing the foot, clearance of the surface is also achieved. It should be noted that the great toe does not have a lumbrical muscle or interossei associated with it. Consequently, extension of the interphalangeal joint depends entirely on extensor hallucis longus. Paralysis of the muscle will result in flexion of the joint and buckling of the toe during the last phase of gait, due to the unopposed action of the flexor muscles.

Palpation

If the great toe is extended, the tendon of this muscle is clearly visible as it crosses the first metatarsophalangeal joint to its insertion into the base of the distal phalanx. Trace the fingers up the tendon; it can be felt and seen crossing the anterior aspect of the ankle joint lateral to the tendon of the tibialis anterior. From here the tendon can be felt passing upwards and laterally before passing deep to the surrounding muscles. Continue to move the fingers upwards for another 12 cm and allow them to pass a little laterally; when the great toe is rhythmically extended and flexed, the muscle can just be felt contracting under the fingers.

Extensor digitorum longus

Extensor digitorum longus (see Fig. 5.42b) is again situated on the anterior aspect of the leg, being lateral to tibialis anterior, and overlying extensor hallucis longus. It has a linear origin from the upper two-thirds of the *anterior surface* of the *fibula*, the *deep fascia* and the upper part of the *interosseous membrane* with its upper fibres reaching across to the *lateral condyle* of the *tibia* in conjunction with those of peroneus longus. It is a pennate muscle with the tendon appearing on the medial side; the muscle fibres pass

downwards and medially to reach it. The tendon passes over the front of the ankle joint deep to the superior extensor retinaculum and then through the loop of the inferior extensor retinaculum accompanied by the peroneus tertius. At the level of the inferior extensor retinaculum or immediately distal, it gives rise to four tendons which run to the lateral four toes. The four separate tendons are enclosed in a common synovial sheath at the level of the inferior extensor retinaculum. On the dorsal surface of the proximal phalanx, each tendon forms a triangular membranous expansion, known as the *extensor hood* (dorsal digital expansion). Each hood is joined on its medial side by the tendon of the lumbrical and on the lateral side for the second to fourth toes by the tendon of extensor digitorum brevis. The interossei of the foot do not have an attachment to the extensor hood.

As the hood passes forwards over the proximal phalanx it divides into three parts before reaching the dorsum of the proximal interphalangeal joint. The central portion attaches to the *base* of the *middle phalanx*, while the two outer portions unite before inserting onto the *base* of the *distal phalanx*. An attachment of the extensor hood to the dorsal aspect of the proximal phalanx has also been described.

Nerve supply

This muscle is supplied by the *deep branch of the common peroneal nerve*, root value L5, S1. The skin covering the muscle is supplied by root L5.

Action

As its name implies, extensor digitorum longus is an extensor of the lateral four toes at the metatarsophalangeal joints, and also assists in extension at the interphalangeal joints. However it is unable to perform the latter action unaided, which is primarily performed by the lumbricals. If the lumbricals are paralysed, extensor digitorum longus produces hyperextension of the metatarsophalangeal joint, while the interphalangeal joints become flexed. As the muscle passes across the front of the ankle joint, it also aids in dorsiflexion of the foot.

Functional activity

During walking and running extensor digitorum longus draws the toes upwards after they have been flexed prior to toe-off, and keeps them clear of the ground until the heel and foot make contact with the ground again. Unfortunately, the lateral four toes in most individuals tend to be flexed at the proximal interphalageal joint and extended at the distal interphalangeal joint. Consequently extensor digitorum longus will lift the toes in this adapted position.

Palpation

The muscle belly is easily palpated on the anterolateral aspect of the leg. From the head of the fibula on the lateral side of the leg, just below the knee joint, run the fingers downwards and medially for about 2 cm. When raising the toes off the floor, the muscle can be felt contracting. Now place the fingers over the front of the ankle joint; the tendon can be identified standing out clearly, being lateral to those of the tibialis anterior and extensor hallucis longus. From here the tendon can now either be traced upwards, under the superior part of the extensor retinaculum to join the muscle belly, or downwards where it breaks up into four individual tendons running towards each of the lateral four toes. Each tendon stands clear of the metatarsophalangeal joint as it passes towards the dorsum of the toe.

Extensor digitorum brevis

Extensor digitorum brevis (Fig. 5.42a) is situated on the dorsum of the foot beyond the inferior part of the extensor retinaculum, lateral to and partly covered by the tendons of peroneus tertius and extensor digitorum longus. It is a thin muscle arising from the anterior roughened part of the upper surface of the *calcaneus* and the *deep fascia* covering the muscle, including the stem of the inferior extensor retinaculum. From the small belly, short tendons pass forwards and medially. The most medial of which crosses the dorsalis pedis artery to insert separately onto the dorsal aspect of the *base* of the *proximal phalanx* of the *great toe*. The remaining three tendons join the *lateral* side of the *dorsal hood* of the *second, third* and *fourth toes*. The most medial part of the muscle may develop a separate belly, sometimes referred to as extensor hallucis brevis.

Nerve supply

This muscle is supplied by the *lateral terminal branch of the deep peroneal nerve*, root value L5, S1. The skin covering the muscle is supplied by roots L5, S1.

Action

The medial part of the muscle aids extensor hallucis longus to extend the great toe at the metatarsophalangeal joint, while the other three tendons aid extensor digitorum longus. As with the long extensor tendons, extensor digitorum brevis helps the lumbricals to extend the interphalangeal joints, again, however, it is unable to do this independently.

Functional activity

Extensor digitorum brevis will help extensor digitorum longus and extensor hallucis longus to raise the toes clear of the ground in running and walking.

Palpation

Place the fingers on the tendon of extensor digitorum longus as it splits into its four parts, when the toes are extended extensor digitorum brevis can be felt just lateral and deep to the tendon. The tendons are difficult to trace distally as they become inseparable from those of extensor digitorum longus.

The lumbricals

These are four small muscles associated with the tendons of flexor digitorum longus; they pass from the flexor to the extensor compartment of the foot. The most medial of these muscles arises from the *medial* side of the *tendon* to the *second toe*, adjacent to the attachment of the flexor accessorius (quadratus plantae) to the main longus tendon. The remaining lumbricals arise by two heads from *adjacent sides* of *two tendons*, that is the

Extensor hallucis longus

Extensor digitorum longus

Extensor digitorum brevis

Fig. 5.42 **a** = Right extensor hallucis longus and digitorum brevis, anterior view. **b** = Right extensor digitorum longus, anterior view.

a

b

second from the tendons to the second and third toes, the third from the tendons to the third and fourth toes, and the fourth from the tendons to the fourth and fifth toes. Each muscle then passes forwards below the deep transverse metatarsal ligament on the medial side of the toe, winding obliquely upwards to attach to the medial side of the *extensor hood* and *base* of the *proximal phalanx*.

Nerve supply

The first and most medial lumbrical is supplied by the *medial plantar nerve*, root value S1, 2, while the lateral three are supplied by the *lateral plantar nerve*, root value S2, 3; both being terminal branches of the *tibial nerve*. The skin on the dorsum of the foot at the point of attachment is supplied by roots L5, S1. The skin of the plantar aspect of the foot overlying the muscles is supplied by the medial and lateral plantar nerves, which have the same root values as the supply to the muscles. It should be noted, however, that only the most lateral of the lumbricals has skin over its plantar aspect.

Action

There has been much discussion over the role of these small, almost insignificant muscles. They have a long muscle belly compared with their tendon and they link the flexors of the toes with the extensors. By their attachment to the proximal phalanx, contraction of the lumbricals produces flexion of the toes at the metatarsophalangeal joint. However, because they also insert into the extensor hood, the lumbricals extend the interphalangeal joints. Indeed, this latter action is primarily due to the lumbricals and not the long and short extensor tendons.

Functional activity

The action of the lumbricals prevents clawing of the toes in the propulsive phase of gait. Paralysis of these muscles results in the extensor muscles pulling the toes into hyperextension at the metatarsophalangeal joints. Even at rest the toes become clawed.

The nerves which supply these muscles appear to have many more fibres than would be necessary for such a small muscle and a great number of these are sensory. This leads one to believe that they may have a very important function in the feeding back of information related to the tension developed between the long flexor and extensor muscles. This sort of information is of great importance in locomotion, especially as the point of attachment of the lumbricals is a long way from the muscle bellies of the extensors and flexors.

Palpation

It is not possible to palpate these muscles as they lie deep in the sole of the foot covered by many of the small muscles of the sole and the long flexor tendons.

MUSCLES WHICH PRODUCE FLEXION OF THE TOES

Flexor digitorum longus
Flexor accessorius (quadratus plantae)
Flexor digitorum brevis
Flexor hallucis longus
Flexor hallucis brevis
Flexor digiti minimi brevis
Interossei (see pp. 399–400)
Lumbricals (see p. 390)

Flexor digitorum longus

Flexor digitorum longus (Fig. 5.43a) is situated on the back of the calf deep to soleus for most of its course. It arises from the medial part of the posterior surface of the *tibia* below the soleal line, and from the *deep transverse fascia* surrounding it. The tendon forms about three fingers' breadth above the medial malleolus, lying next to that of tibialis posterior, which has crossed anterior to it to come to lie on its medial side, and medial to the tendon of extensor hallucis longus. Passing deep to the flexor retinaculum the tendon lies in its own synovial sheath along the medial aspect of the sustentaculum tali, sometimes grooving it, to enter the sole of the foot deep to abductor hallucis. Passing forwards and laterally, it crosses the tendon of flexor hallucis longus (on its plantar aspect) and usually receives a slip from that

Flexor digitorum longus

Flexor hallucis longus

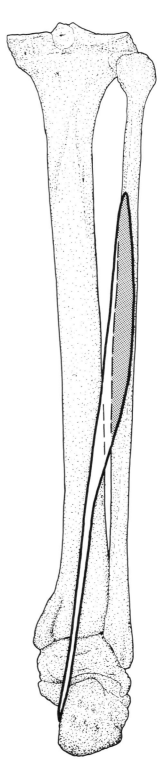

Fig. 5.43 **a** = Right flexor digitorum longus, posterior view. **b** = Right flexor hallucis longus, posterior view.

a

b

tendon which passes into the medial two of its four digitations. About half way along the sole, on its lateral side, the tendon is joined by flexor accessorius (quadratus plantae) and at this point breaks up into its four individual tendons; one for each of the lateral four toes. Just distal to the attachment of flexor accessorius (quadratus plantae) the lumbrical muscles arise.

Just distal to the metatarsophalangeal joint, the tendons enter their respective fibrous sheaths, together with the appropriate tendon of flexor digitorum brevis which lies superficial to it. The tendon of brevis then splits to enable that of longus to pass through and reach the *base* of the *distal phalanx* where it inserts. Both tendons share a common synovial sheath.

Nerve supply

Flexor digitorum longus is supplied by the *tibial nerve*, root value L5, S1, 2. The skin covering this area on the medial and posterior aspect of the calf and the sole is supplied by roots L4, 5, S1.

Action

Flexor digitorum longus flexes the lateral four toes. It flexes the distal interphalangeal joints first, then the proximal interphalangeal joints and finally the metatarsophalangeal joints. Its course behind the medial malleolus means that flexor digitorum longus also helps to plantarflex the foot at the ankle joint. With the ankle plantarflexed, its flexing action on the toes is diminished.

Functional activity

In the propulsive phase of running, jumping or walking, flexor digitorum longus pulls the toes firmly downwards towards the ground to get the maximum grip and thrust during the toe-off phase. When the body is in the standing position, the toes tend to grip the ground to improve the balance.

Palpation

This muscle is very difficult to distinguish as its origin is deep to soleus in the calf, while its tendons in the foot, with the lumbricals, lie deeply. However, with care, the tendon can just be identified as it passes alongside the sustentaculum tali.

Flexor accessorius (quadratus plantae)

Flexor accessorius lies deep to flexor digitorum brevis, arising by two heads from the *medial* and *lateral* surfaces of the *calcaneus* and the adjacent surfaces of the *long plantar ligament*. A flattened muscular band is formed by the merging of the two heads which inserts into the *tendon* of *flexor digitorum longus* in the midpoint of the sole, proximal to the origin of the lumbricals.

Nerve supply

Flexor accessorius is supplied by the *lateral plantar nerve*, root value S2, 3. The skin over the region is supplied by root S1.

Action

It helps long flexor tendons to flex all the joints of the lateral four toes. By pulling on the lateral side of the tendon of flexor digitorum longus, it changes the direction of pull so that the toes flex towards the heel and not towards the medial malleolus.

Functional activity

Flexor accessorius has an important role to play in gait when flexor digitorum longus is already shortened because of plantarflexion of the ankle joint. This muscle exerts its action on the long flexor tendons so that the toes can be flexed to grip the ground giving support and thrust during the propulsive phase. This action essentially means that flexor digitorum longus can be considered to act powerfully across two joints at the same time—an unusual phenomenon.

Palpation

Lying deep in the sole of the foot flexor accessorius cannot be palpated.

Flexor digitorum brevis

Flexor digitorum brevis (Fig. 5.44b) is situated in the sole of the foot lying just deep

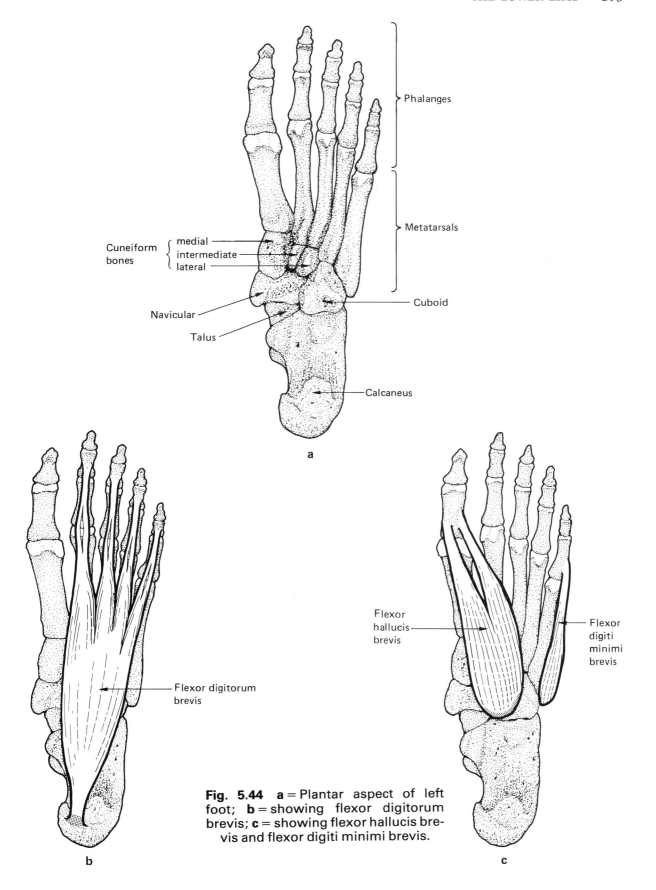

Fig. 5.44 **a** = Plantar aspect of left foot; **b** = showing flexor digitorum brevis; **c** = showing flexor hallucis brevis and flexor digiti minimi brevis.

to the central part of the plantar aponeurosis between abductor hallucis medially and abductor digiti minimi laterally. Arising from the *medial tubercle* of the *calcaneus*, the *deep surface* of the central portion of the *plantar aponeurosis* and the *muscular septa* either side, the fibres pass forwards in the middle of the sole, and separate into four tendons, which pass to the lateral four toes. Just distal to the metatarsophalangeal joint, within their respective fibrous flexor sheaths, each tendon splits into two for the passage of the flexor digitorum longus tendon, which passes from deep to superficial. After rotating through almost 180° the outer margins of the slips of each tendon rejoin, leaving a shallow groove along which the flexor digitorum longus tendon slides. After passing over the proximal interphalangeal joint, the tendon again splits to insert into the sides of the *base* of the *middle phalanx.*

Nerve supply

Flexor digitorum brevis is supplied by the *medial plantar nerve*, root value S2, 3. The skin covering this area is supplied by roots L5, S1.

Action

Flexor digitorum brevis primarily flexes the proximal interphalangeal joint of the lateral four toes, followed by flexion of the metatarsophalangeal joints.

Functional activity

Flexor digitorum brevis is obviously concerned, as is flexor digitorum longus, in producing the thrust from the toes when the demand arises.

Palpation

This muscle is almost impossible to palpate as it is covered with some of the thickest fascia in the body and its tendons lie deep within the foot.

Flexor hallucis longus

Flexor hallucis longus (see Fig. 5.43b) is a powerful pennate muscle situated deep to triceps surae below the deep fascia of the calf. It arises from the lower two-thirds of the posterior surface of the *fibula* and from the *adjacent fascia.*

The muscle fibres pass to a central tendon which lies on its superficial surface, with those on the lateral side extending lower. The tendon passes downwards, deep to the flexor retinaculum in its own synovial sheath, to cross the posterior aspect of the ankle joint lying lateral to flexor digitorum longus. During its course, it grooves the lower end of the tibia, the back of the talus (between the medial and posterior tubercles) and the inferior surface of the sustentaculum tali, where it is held in position by a synovial-lined fibrous sheath which forms a tunnel for it to run through.

In the sole of the foot, the tendon lies superficial to the calcaneonavicular ligament lying lateral to the tendon of the flexor digitorum longus. As it passes forwards, the tendon of flexor hallucis longus crosses deep to that of flexor digitorum longus, and in doing so usually gives a slip to its medial two tendons. It then enters the fibrous digital sheath of the great toe, passing between the two sesamoid bones situated on either side of the base of the proximal phalanx, to insert into the *plantar surface* of the *base* of the *distal phalanx.*

Nerve supply

Flexor hallucis longus is supplied by a branch of the *tibial nerve*, root value S1, 2. The skin covering this area is supplied by root S2.

Action

Flexor hallucis longus flexes all of the joints of the great toe. It first acts on the interphalangeal joint and then the metatarsophalangeal joint. As it crosses the ankle joint, it helps to produce plantarflexion of the foot.

Functional activity

Flexor hallucis longus is of great importance in that it produces much of the final thrust from the foot during walking. At this point in the gait cycle, the calf has already produced its maximum power and the flexors of the lateral four toes are just completing their maximum contraction. Flexion of the great toe is thus the final act before the foot is lifted from the ground ready for the next step. It must also be remembered that the muscle is an important factor in maintaining the medial longitudinal arch.

Palpation

Once again, flexor hallucis longus is almost impossible to palpate as it lies deep to the calf muscles, flexor retinaculum, plantar aponeurosis and the muscles in the foot. Its tendon is set both deep within the calf and the plantar aspect of the foot.

Flexor hallucis brevis

Flexor hallucis brevis (see Fig. 5.44c) is a short muscle situated deep in the sole of the foot, appearing between abductor hallucis medially and flexor digitorum brevis laterally. It arises from the *medial* side of the *plantar surface* of the *cuboid* bone, behind the groove for peroneus longus, and the *adjacent surface* of the *lateral cuneiform* and from the tendon of tibialis posterior.

The muscle fibres run forwards and medially towards the great toe, separating into two fleshy bellies to lie either side and deep to the tendon of flexor hallucis longus. From each belly arises a tendon which inserts onto the appropriate side of the *base* of the *proximal phalanx*. The medial tendon unites with that of abductor hallucis, while the lateral tendon unites with the tendon of adductor hallucis, thereby giving common insertions. A small sesamoid bone, which runs in a shallow groove on the head of the first metatarsal, develops in each tendon.

Nerve supply

Flexor hallucis brevis is supplied by the *medial plantar nerve*, root value S1, 2. The skin covering the area is supplied by root L5.

Action

The action of flexor hallucis brevis is to flex the metatarsophalangeal joint of the great toe.

Functional activity

Flexor hallucis brevis will, of course, aid flexor hallucis longus in the final push off from the ground during activity. Being accompanied at its insertion by abductor and adductor hallucis, suggests that the steadying of the great toe during propulsion must be of great importance, probably to ensure the generation of maximum force. When the great toe is deformed as in hallux valgus, where the tip points laterally and the base medially, this thrust is lost and the patient finds it difficult to run or sometimes walk, even at low speeds.

It is interesting to note that it is not uncommon for injuries to occur to the sesamoid bones particularly in individuals who put considerable strain on the great toe. Such injuries produce an inflamed region where the sesamoid bone slides against the metatarsal. This can cause considerable pain and altered function.

Palpation

This muscle is set so deep in the plantar surface of the foot that it is not possible to palpate. Only the sesamoid bones found within its tendons can be felt, and then only with considerable practice.

Flexor digiti minimi brevis

Flexor digiti minimi brevis (see Fig. 5.44c) is a small muscle situated on the lateral side of the plantar surface of the foot. It arises from the *plantar aspect* of the *base* of the *fifth metatarsal* and the sheath of the tendon of peroneus longus. It is inserted into the *lateral side* of the *plantar surface* of the *proximal phalanx* of the little toe, in conjunction with abductor digiti minimi.

Nerve supply

Flexor digiti minimi brevis is supplied by the *lateral plantar nerve*, root value S2, 3. The skin covering this muscle is supplied by root S1.

Action and functional activity

Flexor digiti minimi brevis is a flexor of the metatarsophalangeal joint, and helps support the lateral longitudinal arch of the foot.

Palpation

Flexor digiti minimi brevis can be palpated contracting, by deep pressure, on the middle part of the plantar aspect, lateral side of the foot when the little toe is flexed.

ABDUCTION AND ADDUCTION OF THE TOES

In the hand, it is the middle finger which is regarded as the central digit when considering abduction and adduction. In the foot, however, the central digit when considering these movements is the second toe. Therefore, if the great toe is drawn medially it is said to abduct, whereas if all the other toes are drawn laterally, i.e. away from the second toe that is also termed abduction. If all the toes are drawn towards the second toe they are said to adduct.

MUSCLES WHICH PRODUCE ABDUCTION OF THE TOES

Abductor hallucis
Abductor digiti minimi
Dorsal interossei

Abductor hallucis

Abductor hallucis (see Fig. 5.45a) is a powerful and important muscle found superficially on the medial side of the plantar aspect of the foot, lying deep to the medial part of the plantar aponeurosis. It arises, in part, from the *plantar aponeurosis*, the *plantar aspect* of the *medial tubercle* of the *calcaneus*, the *flexor retinaculum* and the *intermuscular septum* separating it from *flexor digitorum brevis*.

The fibres pass forwards forming a tendon which passes over the medial side of the metatarsophalangeal joint of the great toe, to insert into the *medial* side of the *base* of the *proximal phalanx* in conjunction with the tendon of the flexor hallucis brevis.

Nerve supply

Abductor hallucis is supplied by the *medial*

plantar nerve, root value S1, 2, with the skin covering the muscle supplied by root L5.

Action

As its name implies, the muscle abducts the great toe at the metatarsophalangeal joint and also helps to flex it at this joint.

Functional activity

Abduction of the great toe is not of importance as such, except perhaps as a party trick and then very few people are able to perform the action easily! However, the muscle is strong and bulky, and it must therefore be assumed that it has an important role to play in some specific activity.

Due to its position along the medial side of the foot, together with the fact that it is attached at the back and front of the medial longitudinal arch, it can act as a bow-string to the arch when the foot is being used for propelling the body forwards. Its attachment to the medial side of the great toe also helps in controlling the central position of this toe when it is being flexed.

It should be noted that when the muscle contracts hard, the great toe does indeed move medially, but more importantly, the foot is positioned laterally, thus improving the relationship between great toe and medial side of foot. Indeed, if this alignment of the foot and toes was encouraged from an early age many deformities of the toes may be prevented.

Palpation

Place the fingers on the medial plantar aspect of the foot, under the medial longitudinal arch. The toes are then flexed and the belly of the muscle can be easily palpated towards the heel. Tracing forwards from the heel, the tendon of the muscle can be felt.

Abductor digiti minimi

Abductor digiti minimi (see Fig. 5.45a) is found on the lateral side of the plantar aspect of the foot, lying deep to the *plantar aponeurosis* from which it gains part of its attachment. It also arises from the *medial* and *lateral tubercles* of the *calcaneus* and from the area between, as well as the *intermuscular septum* separating it from flexor digitorum brevis.

The fibres pass forwards forming a tendon which inserts into the *lateral* side of the *base* of the *proximal phalanx* of the *fifth toe*.

Nerve supply

Abductor digiti minimi is supplied by the *lateral plantar nerve*, root value S2, 3, with the skin covering the muscle being supplied by root S1.

Action

On contraction, abductor digiti minimi abducts the fifth toe at the metatarsophalangeal joint and also help to flex it at this joint.

Functional activity

Because the muscle runs from the posterior to the anterior parts of the lateral longitudinal arch, it acts as a bow-string to this arch in a similar way to abductor hallucis on the medial side of the foot, except of course that the lateral arch can hardly be called a true arch. Nevertheless, the muscle certainly comes into action in running and jumping activities to ensure that this arch is maintained under stress.

Palpation

Unless a subject can abduct their fifth toe easily, the muscle is difficult to palpate.

Dorsal interossei

There are four dorsal interossei (see Fig. 5.45b), being small bipennate muscles situated between the metatarsal bones. Each arises from the *proximal half* of the *sides* of *adjacent metatarsals*, forming a central tendon which passes forwards, deep to the deep transverse metatarsal ligament. It passes between the metatarsal heads to attach to the *side* of the *proximal phalanx* and *capsule* of the *metatarsophalangeal joint*. The tendons do not attach to the extensor hood.

The first, or most medial, arises from the adjacent sides of the first and second meta-

tarsals and attaches to the medial side of the base of the proximal phalanx of the second toe. The second arises from the adjacent sides of the second and third metatarsals and it also attaches to the proximal phalanx of the second toe but to the lateral side. The third and fourth dorsal interossei attach to the lateral side of the proximal phalanx of the third and fourth toes respectively.

Nerve supply

All four dorsal interossei are supplied by the *lateral plantar nerve*, root value S2, 3, those in the fourth interosseous space from the superficial branch, and the rest by the deep branch. The skin covering this area on the dorsum of the foot is supplied by root L5 medially and S1 laterally.

Action

The dorsal interossei abduct the toes at the metatarsophalangeal joint, however this action, as such, is of little importance in the foot. Acting with the plantar interossei, they will produce flexion of the metatarsophalangeal joint.

Functional activity

The dorsal interossei are powerful little muscles and their activity in combination with the plantar interossei controls the direction of the toes during violent activity thus enabling the long and short flexors to perform their appropriate actions.

These muscles, because of their relationship to the metatarsophalangeal joint, can flex these joints and so raise the heads of the second, third and fourth metatarsals, thus helping to maintain the anterior metatarsal arch. They also help, to a limited extent with the maintenance of the medial and lateral longitudinal arches of the foot.

Palpation

Place the finger tips between the proximal parts of the metatarsals on the dorsum of the foot; when the toes are abducted, the muscles can be felt to contract.

MUSCLES WHICH PRODUCE ADDUCTION OF THE TOES

Adductor hallucis
Plantar interossei

Adductor hallucis

Adductor hallucis (Fig. 5.45a) is situated deep within the plantar aspect of the foot. It arises by two heads, oblique and transverse. The oblique head comes from the *plantar surface* of the *bases* of the *second*, *third* and *fourth metatarsals* and the *sheath* of the *tendon* of *peroneus longus*. The transverse head comes from the *plantar surface* of the *lateral three metatarsophalangeal joints* and the *deep transverse metatarsal ligament*.

The muscle fibres of the oblique head pass forwards and medially while those of the transverse head pass medially. The two heads unite and blend with the medial part of the flexor hallucis brevis to insert into the *lateral* side of the *base* of the *proximal phalanx* of the *great toe*.

Nerve supply

Adductor hallucis is supplied by the *lateral plantar nerve*, root value S2, 3, and the skin covering this area is supplied by root S1.

Action

It will adduct the great toe towards the second toe, and flex the first metatarsophalangeal joint.

Functional activity

Working with the abductor hallucis, adductor hallucis helps to control the position of the great toe so that active flexion can be produced and thereby provide the final thrust needed in walking, running or jumping. Due to its transverse position across the forefoot it will also help to maintain the anterior metatarsal arch of the foot.

The pull of the adductor hallucis is almost at right angles to the phalanx and therefore will have a better mechanical advantage than abductor hallucis. If the medial longitudinal arch is allowed to fall, allowing the foot to drift medially and the toes laterally, the pull of the adductor will overcome that of the abductor, thus adding to the deformity often seen in the great toe.

Palpation

This muscle is too deeply situated to be palpated.

Plantar interossei

The plantar interossei (Fig. 5.45c) are smaller than their dorsal counterparts, fusiform in shape and found in the lateral three interosseous spaces. Each arises from the *plantar* and *medial* aspect of the *base* and *proximal end* of the *shaft* of the *metatarsal*. The tendon formed passes forwards and deep to the deep transverse metatarsal ligament to insert into the *medial* side of the *base* of the *proximal phalanx* of the *same toe*.

Nerve supply

All the interossei are supplied by the *lateral plantar nerve*, root value S2, 3, with that in the fourth interosseous space, being supplied by the superficial branch of the nerve. The skin covering the area is supplied on the lateral side by root S1 and medially by root L5.

Action

The plantar interossei adduct the third, fourth and fifth toes towards the second. In conjunction with the dorsal interossei they flex the metatarsophalangeal joints of the lateral three toes.

Functional activity

With the help of the dorsal interossei and the abductor digiti minimi, the plantar interossei help to control the position of the third, fourth and fifth toes during the push-off phase of walking and running. They also help to prevent splaying of the toes when weight is suddenly applied to the forefoot.

Palpation

These muscles are situated too deeply to be palpated.

The position of some of the muscles, tendons and retinacula previously described are shown in Figs. 5.46–5.47.

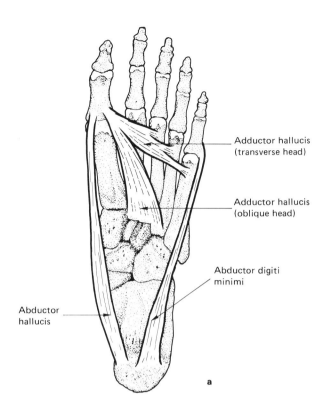

Adductor hallucis
(transverse head)

Adductor hallucis
(oblique head)

Abductor digiti
minimi

Abductor
hallucis

a

Fig. 5.45 **a** = Plantar aspect of left foot showing the abductor and adductor muscles. **b** = Dorsal aspect of left foot showing dorsal interossei. **c** = Plantar aspect of left foot showing plantar interossei.

Dorsal interossei

b

Plantar interossei

c

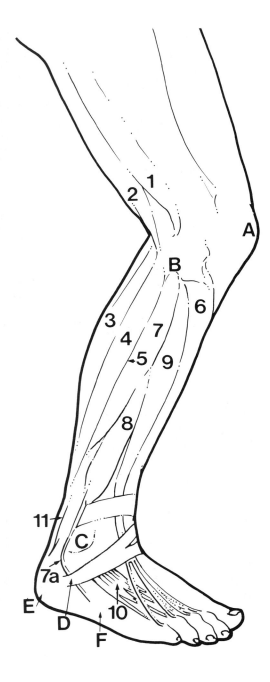

Fig. 5.46 Lateral view of right leg showing ankle and foot:

Bony landmarks
A = Patella
B = Head of fibula
C = Lateral malleolus
D = Peroneal tubercle
E = Calcaneus
F = Tubercle of fifth metatarsal

Soft tissues
1 = Iliotibial tract
2 = Biceps femoris
3 = Gastrocnemius
4 = Soleus
5 = Posterior intermuscular septum
6 = Tibialis anterior
7 = Peroneus longus
7a = Tendon of peroneus longus
8 = Peroneus brevis
9 = Extensor digitorum longus
10 = Extensor digitorum brevis
11 = Tendocalcaneus

a

b

Fig. 5.47 a = Right ankle and foot, dorsal view. **b** = Right ankle and foot, medial view:

Bony landmarks
A = Medial malleolus
B = Lateral malleolus
C = Medial calcaneal tubercle
D = Head of talus

Soft tissues
1 = Superior extensor retinaculum
2 = Inferior extensor retinaculum
3 = Flexor retinaculum
4 = Extensor digitorum longus
5 = Extensor hallucis longus
6 = Tibialis anterior
7 = Tibialis posterior
8 = Flexor digitorum longus
9 = Flexor hallucis longus

FASCIA OF THE LOWER LIMB

Fascial projections from the abdomen into the thigh

The fascial lining of the abdomen and pelvis is a continuous membranous bag being outside the peritoneum. The transversalis fascia is that part lying on the deep surface of transversus abdominis; inferiorly it is thick and strong where it attaches along the inguinal ligament and the iliac crest. From the anterior superior to the posterior superior iliac spines it becomes known as the iliac fascia, being reflected over the surface of iliacus. As the femoral vessels pass from the abdomen, where they are inside the fascia, they drag with them a covering of this fascia which is the femoral sheath. The anterior part of the sheath is derived from the transversalis part of the fascia, while posteriorly it is derived from the iliac part. It is divided into three compartments by septa which pass from the anterior to the posterior walls. About three fingers' breadth below the inguinal ligament, the femoral sheath blends with the adventitia of the femoral vessels.

As the transversalis fascia passes posteriorly, it becomes continuous with the anterior layer of the thoracolumbar fascia covering quadratus lumborum and then with the fascia of the anterior surface of psoas major. At the upper margin of quadratus lumborum and psoas major the fascia is thickened forming the lateral and medial arcuate ligaments respectively. The fascia surrounding psoas major forms a sheath completely enclosing it, from its upper attachments in the abdomen to the lesser trochanter of the femur.

Fascia of the lower limb

Functionally there are two types of fascia in the lower limb. One type merges with and acts as a base for the skin, this is the *superficial fascia* and enables the skin to move freely over the underlying tissue. The other is composed of dense, tough, fibrous tissue and is known as the investing layer of the *deep fascia*. As this investing layer passes over bony projections it usually becomes attached to them. From its deep surface, a sheet of similar tissue passes between groups of muscles forming intermuscular septa. These septa are usually attached to bone and serve to maintain the shape of the body and to exert a compression force on the contents of the osteofascial compartments formed.

Superficial fascia of the lower limb

The superficial fascia is continuous with that of the abdominal wall, the perineum and the back. The two layers present in the lower part of the abdominal wall and perineum continue into the upper part of the anterior thigh. The deeper membranous layer crosses superficial to the inguinal ligament to enter the thigh, fusing with the deep fascia along a line approximately one finger's breadth below and parallel to the inguinal ligament. This attachment limits the spread of fluid into the thigh from the perineum or deep to the superficial abdominal fascia.

The superficial fascia is thick and fatty in the gluteal region, the fat contributing to the shape of the buttock and forms the gluteal fold. There is usually a deposit of fat over the lateral part of the female thigh–a secondary sexual characteristic. Over the ischial tuberosity the fascia has many dense strands of tissue enclosing fat. Such an arrangement helps to distribute high pressures due to the weight of the seated body, and so prevent tissue damage. Similarly on the sole the superficial fascia is characterized by its thickness and the presence of pads of fat under the heel, and balls and pads of the toes. Again they serve to protect underlying structures from high pressures. The heel pad may be as much as 2 cm thick. The fascia covering the rest of the leg and foot shows no particular features.

Deep fascia of the lower limb

The deep fascia is composed of much stronger fibres which tend to be laid down in the same direction to the stress being applied. It covers the limb in a similar way to the superficial fascia, but attaching to the most prominent bony points and all round the groin and buttocks.

Proximally, it attaches to the outer lip of the iliac crest from the anterior superior to the posterior superior iliac spines; the posterior aspect of the ilium and sacrum; the sacrotuberous ligament; the ischial tuberosity; the anterior surface of the ischiopubic ramus; the anterior surface of the body of the pubis and pubic tubercle, and finally onto the inguinal ligament. It can be seen that this forms a complete ring of attachment around the upper end of the thigh.

Below this attachment the deep fascia forms a strong cylinder around the thigh, on the medial side it is thin, but on the lateral side is extremely thick and tough being composed of two distinct layers called the iliotibial tract. The iliotibial tract is attached above to the tubercle of the iliac crest and below to the lateral side of the lateral tibial condyle. The major part of gluteus maximus and all of tensor fascia lata insert between these two layers about one-third of the way down.

In the upper part of the front of the thigh there is an opening in the fascia for the long (great) saphenous vein as it passes to the femoral vein. This saphenous opening (see Fig. 5.165c) is about three fingers' breadth inferior and lateral to the pubic tubercle. Fascia from the inguinal ligament passes downwards and laterally, forming the falciform margin of the saphenous opening, it then passes deep to the great saphenous vein and wraps around the femoral vein to pass superiorly to attach to the superior pubic ramus. Medially the opening has a smooth margin formed from the fascia covering pectineus. The two margins are joined by the cribriform fascia, which is a thin, perforated layer of fibrous and fatty tissue.

In the lower part of the thigh, intermuscular septa pass from the deep surface of the fascia to the femur. The lateral intermuscular septum separates the quadriceps muscles anteriorly from the hamstrings, while the medial septum passes between the adductors anteriorly and the hamstrings posteriorly. Each septum is prolonged downwards onto the medial and lateral supracondylar ridge as far as the medial or lateral condyles of the femur. Higher up in the thigh, a thickening of the fascial septum deep to sartorius forms the roof of the adductor canal.

Around the knee the deep fascia is continuous with that of the leg, and is attached to the medial and lateral condyles of the tibia, the head of the fibula and in front to the patella. The patella is held to the tibial condyle by thickened bands of the deep fascia, the medial and lateral patellar retinacula. Behind the knee, over the popliteal fossa, the fascia is reinforced by transverse fibres.

Below the knee, the deep fascia encompasses the leg attaching mainly to the anterior and medial borders of the tibia and the medial and lateral malleoli. Where the tibia and fibula are subcutaneous, the deep fascia blends with the periosteum of the bone. Intermuscular septa pass to the fibula separating the peroneal muscles from the extensors anteriorly and the flexors posteriorly. A further septum passes across the back of the leg separating the superficial and deep flexor muscles. Around the ankle, the fascia is thickened by numerous transverse fibres forming retaining bands for the tendons of the muscles which pass across the ankle.

The fascia of the foot is continuous with that of the leg. On the dorsum it is thin, wrapping around either side of the foot to become continuous with the plantar aponeurosis, while anteriorly it splits to cover the dorsum of the toes.

The plantar aponeurosis

This comprises some of the thickest fascia in the body being up to 80 layers thick. It is continuous with the fascia over the heel, and on the sides of the foot with the dorsal fascia. It is triangular in shape with the apex at the heel, attaching to the inferior aspect of the calcaneus just behind the medial tubercle, and spreads out anteriorly into five slips which pass forwards and become continuous with the fibrous flexor sheaths of the toes. Most of its fibres run longitudinally, except anteriorly where it splits and then transverse fibres bind the five slips together. As each slip approaches the head of the metatarsal it splits into a superficial and a deep layer. The former attaches to the superficial fascia and produces the deep cleft in the tissue under the base of the toe. The deeper layer splits again into a medial and lateral part which attach to either side of the base of the proximal phalanx of each toe and the deep transverse metatarsal ligament. This is the beginning of the fibro-osseous tunnel which houses the flexor tendons of the toes.

The central part of the aponeurosis gives partial attachment to the muscles lying deep to it. At its edges strong septa pass upwards separating abductor hallucis, flexor digitorum brevis and abductor digiti minimi. Between the five slips, close to the base of the toes, there is a space which gives access to the nerves and vessels supplying the toes.

The plantar aponeurosis is an extremely important structure in the maintenance of the longitudinal arches of the foot. With the toes dorsiflexed, the proximal phalanx winds its slip of the aponeurosis around the metatarsal head, a 'windlass' effect which tightens the aponeurosis and raises the longitudinal arches.

Fibro-osseous tunnels

Where the anterior attachment of the plantar aponeurosis splits to attach to either side of the proximal phalanx it forms the beginning of a fibro-osseous tunnel, which runs under the toe and accommodates the flexor tendons. It is composed of arching fibres passing over the tendons and attaching to the flat plantar surface of each phalanx. At the interphalangeal joints the fibres criss-cross from the medial side of the head of one phalanx to the lateral side of the base of the adjacent phalanx, and vice versa. Each tunnel is lined with a double layer of synovial membrane which facilitates the movement of the tendons in the tunnel.

The retinacula

Around the ankle the deep fascia is thickened by transversely orientated bands forming retinacula. These serve to hold the tendons passing across the ankle joint in position and prevent bowstringing. They are named according to the tendons they serve, that is flexor, extensor and peroneal.

The flexor retinaculum passes between the back of the medial malleolus and the medial tubercle of the calcaneus. From its deep surface septa pass to the tibia and ankle joint capsule forming four tunnels. From medial to lateral these tunnels transmit the tendon of tibialis posterior, the tendon of flexor digitorum longus, the posterior tibial vessels and tibial nerve, and finally the tendon of flexor hallucis longus. Each tendon is enclosed in its own synovial sheath.

The extensor retinacula are the most extensive. The superior extensor retinaculum (Fig. 5.48) runs horizontally across all the extensor tendons between the tibia and fibula just above the ankle joint. The inferior extensor retinaculum is a Y-shaped thickening on the dorsum of the foot (see Figs. 5.47, 5.48). The stem of the Y attaches to the upper surface of the calcaneus anteriorly and also to the floor of the sinus tarsi. The upper part passes to attach to the medial malleolus, while the lower part blends with the deep fascia on the medial side of the foot. This lower band splits into superficial and deep layers, with a septum passing between the two, so forming two tunnels. In the most medial of these tunnels runs the tendon of tibialis anterior, with extensor hallucis longus in the other compartment. Each tendon has its own synovial sheath. Passing under the stem laterally are the tendons of extensor digitorum longus and peroneus tertius in a common synovial sheath. The tendons of tibialis anterior and extensor hallucis usually both pass deep to the upper band of the extensor retinaculum, each in its own synovial sheath, although tibialis anterior may pierce it. The anterior tibial vessels and the deep peroneal nerve pass deep to both extensor retinacula.

The peroneal retinacula are also in two parts. The superior peroneal retinaculum attaches to the lateral side of the calcaneus and passes over the tendons of peroneus longus and brevis to the posterior border of the lateral malleolus. The two tendons are contained within a single synovial sheath. The inferior peroneal retinaculum binds the two peroneal tendons to the lateral side of the calcaneus. A septum passes from its deep surface to the peroneal tubercle to form two separate tunnels, one above the tubercle for the tendon of peroneus brevis and one below for peroneus longus. At this point each tendon is enclosed in a separate synovial sheath.

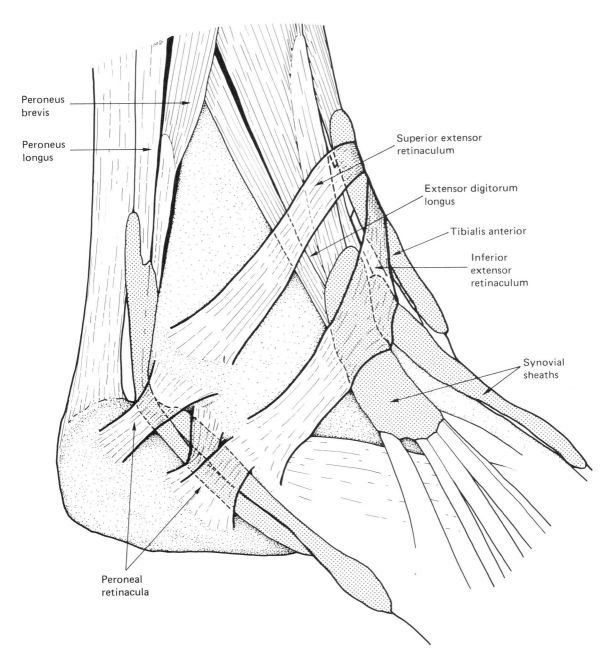

Peroneus brevis

Peroneus longus

Superior extensor retinaculum

Extensor digitorum longus

Tibialis anterior

Inferior extensor retinaculum

Synovial sheaths

Peroneal retinacula

Fig. 5.48 Retinacula and tendons over the anterior and lateral aspect of the left ankle.

Synovial sheaths

As the various tendons pass under the appropriate retinacula around the ankle joint, they are invaginated from the lateral side into a double layer of synovial membrane. This lines the compartments so formed, protruding approximately 1 cm above each of the retinacula. The sheath of tibialis posterior continues down to its insertion, while those of flexor digitorum longus and flexor hallucis longus tendons continue as far as the base of the metatarsals.

Laterally the tendons of peroneus longus and brevis initially share the same sheath, but after passing below the level of the lateral malleolus they occupy separate compartments each lined by separate synovial sheaths which continue as far as the lateral side of the cuboid. The peroneus longus is surrounded by another synovial sheath as it passes through the fibrous tunnel formed on the plantar surface of the cuboid.

Anteriorly both tibialis anterior and extensor hallucis longus are surrounded by separate synovial sheaths. The former reaches down almost to the insertion of the tendon, whereas the latter only passes as far as the mid-metatarsal region. The tendons of the extensor digitorum longus and the peroneus tertius share the same sheath, which is only present as the tendons pass deep to the extensor retinacula (see Fig. 5.48).

The sheaths facilitate the sliding of the tendons under the retinacula and normally are not evident. However, when the sheaths have been damaged in some way, for example by trauma, infection or overactivity, they become inflamed and swollen. They then present a 'sausage-like' swelling along the length of the sheath and around the tendon. This often proves to be acutely painful and quite incapacitating. The condition is referred to as tenosynovitis and can occur around any tendon where it is surrounded by a synovial sheath.

SIMPLE ACTIVITIES OF THE LOWER LIMB

The activities examined here are:

Walking
Standing up from sitting
Climbing steps

It is only possible to give a basic outline of the activities listed above, as it must be remembered that each of them will differ considerably according to the height, weight and build of the individual. There is an additional problem in that everyone has their own characteristic pattern of movement, which may be so clearly individual, that they can be recognized by their movements. Many activities can be influenced by the clothing worn, for example high heels, tight jeans, trousers or skirts. The muscular work involved and joint activity will also vary depending on the speed at which the activity is performed and the surrounding environment. Nevertheless, there are certain factors which tend to be common to most normal individuals and these are dealt with here.

Walking

Walking involves the whole of the body, consequently it must be remembered that a change in the pattern of movement of the upper body will effect the walking pattern. This section will only consider the lower limbs and lower trunk in any detail, with the upper body referred to in outline only.

Each lower limb performs a cycle of events which is similar, but performed half a cycle out of phase with each other. Thus, the left limb will be weight bearing whilst the right is off the ground; as the toes are pushing off in one limb, the heel of the other limb is contacting the ground, and as one limb is being taken forward the other is being drawn backwards.

By examining the cycle of events associated with one limb, an understanding of the composite movement of both limbs will follow. Movements of the *right* lower limb will be presented in the following account;

any reference to the other limb will be clearly distinguished. When considering walking, it is often easier to break up the pattern observed into different phases, however this should not detract from the fact that this is a continuous cycle of events performed smoothly, precisely and efficiently.

Toe-off phase

This account will begin where the foot is being powerfully plantarflexed to push the body forward. At this point the trunk becomes flexed, abducted and rotated at the supporting hip. This rotation is equivalent to medial rotation of the femur. At the hip joint the femur is extended, adducted and medially rotated, the knee is extended and the ankle dorsiflexed. Although the toes are in a neutral position, they are gripping the supporting surface.

Powerful ankle plantarflexion is achieved by the calf muscles gastrocnemius and soleus. As the movement progresses, the toes are forced into extension, but after receiving this initial stretch, the toe flexors also work powerfully, the lateral four toes first, closely followed by the great toe. Because quadriceps femoris is holding the knee almost fully extended, the powerful thrust from the foot is transmitted to the hip, pelvis and trunk, which, because of their forward inclination, will be pushed forwards and upwards.

Carry-through phase

As the great toe leaves the ground the first part of the *carry-through* phase begins. There is extension of the toes, brought about by the extensors hallucis longus and digitorum longus, dorsiflexion of the ankle by tibialis anterior and extensor digitorum longus, flexion of the knee by the hamstrings, flexion of the hip by psoas major, iliacus, rectus femoris, sartorius and pectineus. The hip is laterally rotated by piriformis, the obturators internus and externus, quadratus femoris and the two gemelli. This continues until the foot passes a point immediately below the hip joint. During this phase the unsupported side of the pelvis is also moving forward, firstly because of the thrust it receives at *toe-off*, and secondly because it

is pivoting around the opposite hip joint. The upper trunk, however, tends to rotate in the opposite direction so that the same shoulder, carrying the arm with it, moves backwards. To keep the head facing forwards, the neck rotates towards the opposite side. (For the muscles producing these movements see p. 689).

After the foot passes below the hip joint the limb begins to extend again. The dorsiflexors allow the ankle and toes to assume a neutral position, or even a slightly flexed position, with the foot being slightly inverted by the tibialis anterior and posterior. Contraction of quadriceps femoris extends the knee to just short of full extension. The hip is still being flexed by the same group of muscles and the pelvis is still pivoting forwards under the action of gluteus medius and minimus, and the tensor fascia lata of the supporting limb. The *carry-through* phase terminates when the foot makes contact with the ground again, and the support phase begins once more.

Heel-strike phase

Because the foot is slightly inverted the heel comes into contact with the ground on its lateral side. The frictional forces generated have a dragging effect on the heel which slows the foot allowing it to land and make full contact with the supporting surface. As the foot takes the full weight of the body, the heel is compressed and the intrinsic musculature contracts to support the arches of the foot. The weight is then relayed, via the lateral side of the foot, forwards to the forefoot. The intrinsic muscles of the foot convert it into a semirigid lever, which enables it to absorb the stresses associated with foot contact and yet prepare it for the next propulsive phase preceding *toe-off*.

Support phase

As the weight is taken onto the foot the body is moving forward, the ankle is dorsiflexed, the knee undergoes a small flexion wave and the hip is being extended by the momentum of the body aided, particularly in walking fast, by gluteus maximus and the hamstrings. The pelvis is maintained in a more or less level position by the action of the abductors of the right hip, that is gluteus medius and minimus, allowing the opposite foot to be raised from the ground.

After the foot passes behind the line of the hip joint the calf muscles again contract strongly, thus completing the cycle mentioned earlier. From the point where the weight is borne on the heel to that where the toes push the body forward and upwards, the other limb is being lifted from the ground to perform the same *carry-through* phase as described above.

Standing up from the sitting position

There are many different ways in which one can stand up from a sitting position. As well as the factors listed earlier, the height and type of chair being used may have a profound effect on the pattern of movement. Nevertheless, the fundamentals of rising from a seated position will be outlined, bearing in mind that there are numerous variations.

Sitting

The starting position will, in this case, be sitting upright on a wooden chair which has a firm seat but no arm rests. The feet are both on the floor lying parallel to one another about 10 cm apart. The ankles are at right angles, as are the knees and hips. The arms are by the sides, and in this case will give no assistance to the movement except as a mechanism to aid balance.

The line of gravity through the trunk and upper limbs falls through the seat between, but just anterior to, the ischial tuberosities. During the movement the base is changed from the seat to the feet, consequently some readjustment of the body weight and foot position must be carried out.

Preparation for standing

The first phase in preparation for standing is to move the trunk forward and the feet backwards so that the centre of gravity of the upper body is brought as far forward as possible. The feet are drawn backwards by the hamstrings of both limbs; flexion of the knees and dorsiflexion of the ankles are both increased. However, full contact is still maintained between the feet and the ground. At the same time the trunk is flexed forward by the abdominal muscles, the pectoral girdle is protracted by serratus anterior and pectoralis minor, the neck is flexed by the prevertebral muscles, whilst the head is extended by the rectus capitis posterior major and minor. (Extension of the head is not, however, a natural movement when standing from the seated position.) If leaning forwards does not bring the centre of gravity of the upper body sufficiently over the feet to allow the transfer of weight, then the whole trunk must be shifted forwards.

The next phase is to transfer the weight of the body over the new base, that is the feet. This is brought about by additional contraction of the abdominal muscles to bring forward the upper part of the body. The weight is now taken by the feet and the intrinsic foot muscles contract to maintain the various arches.

Standing

There is now plantarflexion of the ankle to bring it back to just short of a right angle. Plantarflexion is brought about mainly by soleus while the knee is extended by the quadriceps femoris. Extension at the hip is brought about by a combination of hamstrings (which are acting as a tie-mechanism), being drawn down by the tibia which is moving forwards in relation to the femur, and the gluteus maximus, which, in addition to its effect on the hip, pulls on the iliotibial tract to aid in extension of the knee. At the same time as the hip and knee joints are being extended, the back will be extended by the long back muscles, that is sacrospinalis. The pectoral girdle will be retracted by the rhomboids and middle fibres of trapezius, while the neck is extended by the upper fibres of trapezius and splenius cervicis. The head is brought to the neutral position by contraction of longus capitis.

All of these movements occur simultaneously until the erect standing position is achieved.

Climbing steps

Variations in this activity are again so wide that it makes description difficult. There are many combinations of step height and tread which can only but modify the pattern of movement. The example given here is with a step height of 25 cm, the movement being performed fairly slowly.

Toe-off phase

The starting position is with the left foot already up one step and the right about to push off. Each limb again performs a complete cycle of movement, with the limbs being out of phase, such that as the left limb is weight-bearing the right is being carried through. The right foot pushes off with a strong plantarflexion of the ankle brought about by the calf muscles producing a passive extension of the toes, thus stretching the flexors. The latter respond immediately by flexing the toes thereby producing the final thrust from the right foot. It is at this point that the whole body is inclined forward, however, the knee and hip are maintained in an extended position while the trunk flexes to bring body-weight forwards. At the same time the left quadriceps femoris is working maximally to extend the left knee and raise the body to the next step.

Carry-through phase

The right limb now begins its *carry-through* phase. This involves extension of the toes by the extensors digitorum longus and hallucis longus; dorsiflexion of the ankle by tibialis anterior and the long toe extensors; flexion at the knee, by the hamstrings; flex-ion of the hip by psoas major and iliacus, and a raising and forward rotation of the pelvis on the same side by the action of gluteus medius and minimus of the weight-bearing side. This movement continues until the foot has passed the left leg and lies just above the next step.

Foot down and step-up phase

The foot is then lowered onto the step by the eccentric contraction of the hip flexors and weight is transferred to it, thereby beginning the next weight-bearing phase. The intrinsic muscles of the right foot now contract to stabilize the arches while the long flexors pull the toes down towards the supporting surface. The ankle, which was in slight dorsiflexion because of the forwards inclination of the tibia, now comes into a neutral position brought about partly by soleus and partly by extension of the knee. The movement at both ankle and knee contribute to the extension force at the hip which, aided by gluteus maximus and the hamstrings, produces a backward tilting of the pelvis. The back muscles use this firm base to extend the trunk into an upright position.

The *carry-through* phase of the limb is augmented by forward rotation of the pelvis at the hip of the supporting side. This is brought about by the action of gluteus medius and minimus of the weight-bearing limb.

When the hip and knee are fully extended the other foot is placed on to the step above. The ankle of the supporting leg is plantarflexed to throw the body forward onto the left limb and so complete the cycle.

Joints

JOINTS OF THE PELVIS

Introduction

The pelvic girdle is a ring of bone providing articulation for the lower limbs with the trunk, and consists of the two innominate bones and the sacrum (Fig. 5.49a). Each innominate bone articulates with the sacrum posteriorly by a synovial joint, and with each other anteriorly at the symphysis pubis by a secondary cartilaginous joint. The articulation of the pelvis with the lower limb is in the region of the acetabulum (see p. 430), while the articulation with the trunk is via the sacrum. Superiorly, the sacrum articulates with the fifth lumbar vertebra at the lumbosacral joint, and inferiorly with the coccyx at the sacrococcygeal joint. Being part of the vertebral column, these latter two joints are both secondary cartilaginous joints.

The skeletal pelvis is arranged in such a way as to provide great strength for the transference of weight from the trunk to the lower limbs when standing, or to the ischial tuberosities when sitting. This major function of stability has been achieved with loss of mobility at both the sacroiliac joint and the symphysis pubis. However, under certain conditions, namely childbirth, a greater degree of movement at these two joints is possible.

As well as enabling weight transfer from the trunk to the lower limbs, the pelvis also supports the pelvic viscera, provides extensive attachments for muscles of the trunk and lower limb, and in the female gives bony support for the birth canal.

The evolutionary development of the pelvis and of its articulation with the vertebral column via the lumbosacral joint is considered by many to lag behind the adaptations of the remaining skeleton. The anatomical position of the pelvis is neither vertical, as in quadrupeds, nor horizontal (Fig. 5.49b). Consequently, special provision has to be made to prevent the sacrum being pushed downwards and forwards under the superincumbent body weight. The lumbosacral junction represents the transition between the mobile and immobile portions of the vertebral column. It has consequently become the least stable part of the vertebral column, being more exposed to static stresses and less well-equipped to meet them adequately than any other part of the column.

Fig. 5.49 **a** = Anteroposterior radiograph of the pelvis showing the sacroiliac articulations. **b** = Anatomical position of the pelvis.

a

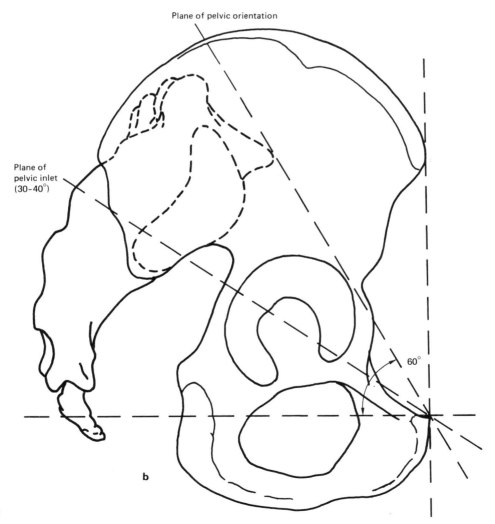

Plane of pelvic orientation

Plane of
pelvic inlet
(30–40°)

60°

b

Fig. 5.49

Sacroiliac joint

Articular surfaces

The sacroiliac joint is a synovial joint formed between the auricular surface of the ilium and that of the ala of the sacrum (Fig. 5.49a). Since the region behind the synovial joint is united by powerful interosseous ligaments, some authorities consider the joint to be both synovial (anterior) and fibrous (posterior). The auricular surfaces are approximately L-shaped, broader above and narrower below, and show marked reciprocal irregularities (Fig. 5.50c). The central part of the sacral auricular surface is concave with raised crests on either side; conversely, the ilial auricular surface has a central crest lying between two furrows. The lower parts of the auricular surfaces are shaped so that the widest part of the sacral surface is on its pelvic side. On the sacrum, the auricular surface occupies the upper two vertebral elements in the female, and usually extends onto the third element in the male. However, the shape and degree of irregularity of the surfaces varies considerably between individuals, and often between the two sides within the same individual. The auricular surface of the sacrum is covered with hyaline cartilage, while the cartilage on the corresponding surface on the ilium is usually a form of fibrocartilage. With increasing age, particularly in males, the joint cavity becomes partially, or occasionally completely, obliterated by fibrous bands or fibrocartilaginous adhesions between the articular surfaces. In very old individuals the joint may show partial bony fusion.

Joint capsule and synovial membrane

A fibrous capsule completely surrounds the joint attaching to the articular margins on both bones. Synovial membrane lines the non-articular surfaces of the joint.

Ligaments

Because of the nature and position of the joint it is richly endowed with ligaments. Extremely strong posterior and slightly weaker anterior ligaments surround the capsule, while accessory ligaments situated some distance from the joint provide additional stability against unwanted movement.

Anterior sacroiliac ligament The anterior sacroiliac ligament is broad and flat, consisting of numerous thin bands, lying on the pelvic side of the joint (Fig. 5.50b). It stretches from the ala and pelvic surface of the sacrum, above and below the pelvic brim, to the adjoining margin of the auricular surface of the ilium. The ligament is stronger in the female, indenting a pre-auricular groove on the ilium just below the pelvic brim.

Posterior sacroiliac ligaments The ligaments lying behind and above the joint are much thicker and stronger than those anteriorly. Several distinct bands can be identified as they fill the impression between the sacrum and the tuberosity of the ilium.

1. *Interosseous sacroiliac ligament*—This is the deepest of all the posterior ligaments, being short, thick and extremely strong. It fills the narrow cleft between the rough areas on the bones immediately behind and above the auricular surfaces (Fig. 5.50c). Small accessory joint cavities, usually no more than one or two, may sometimes be found within the ligament between facets near the posterior superior iliac spine and the transverse tubercles of the sacrum.

2. *Long and short posterior sacroiliac ligaments*—Superficial to the interosseous ligament, the posterior ligament consists of numerous bands passing between the two bones. In general the longer fibres of the posterior ligament run obliquely downwards and medially. However, within this arrangement two sets of fibres can usually be identified. The short posterior sacroiliac ligament is found in the upper part of the cleft between the two bones passing horizontally between the first and second transverse tubercles of the sacrum and the iliac tuberosity (Fig. 5.51a). They are disposed so as to resist forward movement of the sacral promontory. The long posterior sacroiliac ligament has the longest and

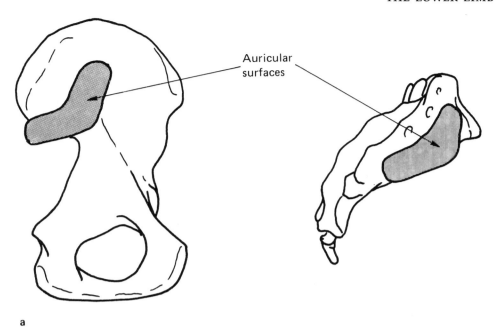

Auricular surfaces

a

Iliolumbar ligaments

Sacrotuberous ligament

Anterior sacroiliac ligament

Sacrospinous ligament

b

Short posterior sacroiliac ligament

Interosseous sacroiliac ligament

Ilium

Sacrum

Anterior sacroiliac ligament

c

Fig. 5.50   a = The articular surfaces of the ilium and sacrum. **b** = Anterior sacroiliac ligaments. **c** = Posterior sacroiliac ligaments.

most superficial fibres of the posterior complex. It runs almost vertically downwards from the posterior superior iliac spine to the third and fourth transverse tubercles of the sacrum (Fig. 5.51a). Its fibres are arranged so as to resist downward movement of the sacrum with respect to the ilium.

Accessory ligaments In addition to the above ligaments accessory ligaments confer added stability to the joint. The most important accessory ligaments are the sacrotuberous and sacrospinous ligaments which help to stabilize the sacrum on the innominate by preventing forward tilting of the sacral promontory. They also convert the greater and lesser sciatic notches of the pelvis into the greater and lesser foramina (Fig. 5.51b), through which several important structures leave the pelvis.

As well as the sacrotuberous and sacrospinous ligaments the iliolumbar ligament assists in strengthening the bond between the ilium and sacrum (for details of this ligament see p. 424).

1. *Sacrotuberous ligament*—The sacrotuberous ligament is a flat, triangular band of great strength (Fig. 5.51b). Superiorly it is attached to the posterior border of the ilium between the posterior superior and posterior inferior iliac spines, to the back and side of the sacrum below the auricular surface, and to the side of the upper part of the coccyx. From this extensive attachment the fibres pass downwards and later-

ally towards the ischial tuberosity, converging as they do so. However, before attaching to the medial surface of the ischial tuberosity, the fibres twist upon themselves and diverge again so that the attachment is prolonged along the lower margin of the ischial ramus. This prolongation is known as the falciform process and lies just below the pudendal canal. The ligament as a whole is narrower in the middle than at either end.

The most superficial fibres of the sacrotuberous ligament attaching to the ischial tuberosity are closely associated with the long head of biceps femoris. Consequently, the ligament is considered to be derived from biceps femoris, being the degenerated tendon of the origin of the long head. The posterior surface of the ligament gives attachment to gluteus maximus.

2. *Sacrospinous ligament*—The triangular sacrospinous ligament lies deep to the sacrotuberous ligament (Fig. 5.51b). Its broad base is attached to the edge of the lower sacral and upper coccygeal segments in front of the sacrotuberous ligament. As the ligament passes laterally it narrows; the apex attaches to the ischial spine. On the pelvic surface of the sacrospinous ligament and closely blended with it is the coccygeus muscle; in fact the ligament can be considered to be a fibrous part of the muscle.

a

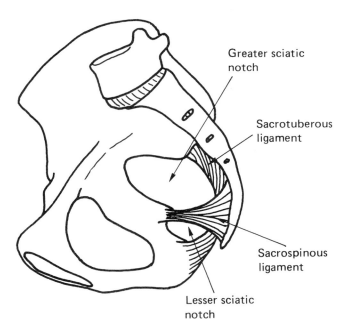

b

Fig. 5.51 **a** = The posterior sacroiliac ligaments. **b** = Sacrotuberous and sacrospinous
ligaments.

Blood and nerve supply

The arterial supply to the joint is by branches of the iliolumbar artery anteriorly and the superior gluteal artery posteriorly (Fig. 5.52). This is reinforced by branches from the lateral sacral arteries both anteriorly and posteriorly. Venous drainage is to correspondingly named veins which drain eventually into the internal iliac vein. The lymphatic drainage of the joint follows the arteries to the internal iliac group of nodes.

The nerve supply to the joint is by twigs directly from the sacral plexus and dorsal rami of the first and second sacral nerves. In addition it also receives branches from the superior gluteal and obturator nerves as they pass close to the joint. The joint is therefore supplied by roots L4 to S2.

Relations

Anterior to the joint, at the level of the lumbosacral intervertebral disc, the common iliac artery divides into its terminal branches: the internal and external iliac arteries (Fig. 5.52). Crossing anterior to this bifurcation, directly in contact with the artery, the ureter enters the lesser pelvis on its way towards the bladder. Posterior to the joint is the erector spinae muscle mass. Indeed, deep to its lateral limb, tendinous fibres of the muscle blend with the posterior sacroiliac, sacrotuberous and sacrococcygeal ligaments.

Medial to the joint running over the ala of the sacrum, are from lateral to medial: the obturator nerve, the iliolumbar artery and the lumbosacral trunk, while laterally in the iliac fossa lies iliacus and its covering fascia.

Surface marking

The line of the sacroiliac joint is far too deep for it to be palpable, however, its surface projection can be estimated as follows. Identify the posterior superior iliac spine; an oblique line at approximately 25°, passing from superolateral to inferomedial and extending 2 cm in each direction represents the joint line.

Stability

The resilient support of the weight of the trunk, head and upper limbs given by curvatures of the vertebral column imposes additional stresses on the sacroiliac joints, because the line of weight passes anterior to them. There is therefore a tendency for the sacral promontory to move downwards into the pelvis, and for the lower part of the sacrum and coccyx to tilt upwards. These tendencies are resisted by a number of factors, all of which are entirely dependent on various ligaments associated with the joint.

Because the line of weight passes anterior to the joint, the bony surfaces are not weight-bearing *per se*. Body weight is suspended by the sacroiliac ligaments, which sling the sacrum below the iliac bones. Providing the sacroiliac joints are intact, then the slight wedging of the auricular surfaces, together with their reciprocal irregularities, are sufficient to help resist rotation and gliding movements of the sacrum with respect to the innominate bones. The strong interosseous and dorsal sacroiliac ligaments usually maintain such opposition. Rotation of the sacrum and coccyx is also resisted by the strong sacrotuberous and sacrospinous ligaments, which hold the lower sacral segments forwards thereby preventing them rotating backwards.

The iliolumbar ligaments, as well as helping to oppose any simple gliding movements of the joint surfaces, also help to prevent the fifth lumbar vertebra from slipping forwards on the surface of the first sacral segment.

Internal iliac vessels

External iliac vessels

Superior gluteal artery

Obturator artery

a

Superior gluteal
vessels and nerve

Inferior gluteal
artery

Sciatic nerve

b

Fig. 5.52a,b Blood vessels and nerves of the
pelvic and gluteal regions.

Movements

The arrangement of the joint surfaces and the ligamentous support given to the joint allow but little movement. There is a slight gliding and rotatory movement between the two bones. Investigations have shown that when standing, compared with lying supine, the sacrum moves downwards some 2 mm, and undergoes forward rotation of some 5°. Obviously any appreciable movement would lead to instability in the erect posture.

During childbirth there is a complex movement of the sacrum which has been likened to nodding of the head. The movement is possible because of the slight softening of the sacroiliac and associated ligaments which occurs during the latter part of pregnancy. The result is that the diameters of the pelvic inlet and outlet increase to facilitate passage of the fetal head. Firstly, the sacral promontory moves superiorly and posteriorly increasing the anteroposterior diameter of the pelvic inlet by between 3 and 13 mm (Fig. 5.53a). After the fetal head has entered the pelvic canal, the sacral promontory moves inferiorly and anteriorly. This increases the anteroposterior diameter of the pelvic outlet by some 15 to 18 mm (Fig. 5.53b). Although the ligaments have become softened, the tension developed in them still limits the degree of movement possible. The extent of the softening, together with the extent of the irregularity of the opposing joint surfaces, accounts for the range of variation reported in pelvic diameter changes.

The sacroiliac joints are important clinically, as a sudden bending forwards can tear the posterior ligaments and possibly even dislocate the adjacent joint surfaces. Either condition is extremely painful in flexion of the trunk and may be disabling. Treatment is in many cases difficult. Manipulation often produces a successful result.

Accessory movements

The ligaments of the sacroiliac joint are so arranged as to allow very little accessory movement. With the subject lying prone, so that the pelvis is supported by the two anterior iliac spines and the pubic region, place the heel of the hand on the apex of the sacrum and apply a downward pressure. A small rotation of the sacrum with respect to the pelvis will be discernible.

Biomechanics

Trabecular systems Two trabecular systems arise in the region of the auricular surface of the innominate, being continuous with those converging towards the auricular surface of the sacrum. Both systems become continuous with trabeculae in the head and neck of the femur as well as uniting with other systems within the pelvis (Fig. 5.54). From the upper part of the auricular surface, trabeculae converge on the posterior border of the greater sciatic notch. Some of the trabeculae fan out laterally towards the inferior aspect of the acetabulum, while the remainder pass downwards into the ischium, intersecting the trabeculae of the acetabular rim as they do so. These trabeculae are compressive, bearing the weight of the body in the sitting position.

Trabeculae arising from the lower part of the auricular surface converge at the level of the pelvic brim. From here some pass laterally towards the superior aspect of the acetabulum, while the remainder pass into the superior pubic ramus towards the body of the pubis, so completing the pelvic ring of the trabeculae.

a

b

Fig. 5.53 **a** = Movement of the sacrum to increase the pelvic inlet. **b** = Movement of the sacrum to increase the pelvic outlet.

Auricular surface

Fig. 5.54 Trabecular systems around the sacroiliac joint.

Symphysis pubis

Articular surfaces

This is a secondary cartilaginous joint between the medial surfaces of the bodies of the two pubic bones. Each oval articular surface is irregularly ridged and grooved, with the irregularities fitting snugly together (Fig. 5.55a). The whole articular surface of each bone is covered with a thin layer of hyaline cartilage, which is joined to the cartilage of the opposite side by a fibrocartilaginous interpubic disc, thicker in females than in males (Fig. 5.55b).

In the upper posterior part of this disc a small fluid-filled cavity appears in early life, but it is never lined with synovial membrane. In females this cavity may eventually extend throughout the greater part of the disc.

Ligaments

Above, below and in front of the joint thickenings of fibrous tissue form ligaments.

Superior pubic ligament This attaches to the pubic crests and tubercles of each side strengthening the anterosuperior aspect of the joint (Fig. 5.55b).

Arcuate pubic ligament The arcuate pubic ligament arches across between the inferior pubic rami, rounding off the subpubic angle and strengthening the joint inferiorly (Fig. 5.55b). Between this rather thick, ligamentous arch and the transverse perineal ligament of the urogenital diaphragm, is a small gap through which passes the dorsal vein of the penis or clitoris to gain entry to the pelvis.

Relations

Overlying the interpubic disc anteriorly are the decussating tendinous fibres of rectus abdominis, external abdominal oblique and adductor longus (Fig. 5.55c). These fibres serve to strengthen the joint and provide additional stability anteriorly. Indeed, some authorities consider this dense feltwork of fibres to constitute a thick anterior pubic ligament. Behind the joint lies the bladder, being separated from it for the most part by the retropubic fat pad (Fig. 5.55d).

Palpation

The line of the symphysis pubis can be palpated anteriorly as a groove between the bodies of the two pubic bones. The alignment of the joint can be checked by placing the hand on the lower abdomen with the finger pointing towards the subject's feet. The index and ring fingers are then placed on the upper surface of the pubis, with the middle finger placed on the intervening disc.

Movements

The nature of the joint is such that there is normally no movement between the bones involved. However, during pregnancy the ligaments associated with the joint, as well as those of other joints, soften and allow a small degree of movement so that there is some separation at the symphysis pubis. The separation is small, being of the order of 2 mm. Nevertheless, it increases the circumference of the pelvic inlet, which probably makes it easier for the fetal head to pass through the pelvic cavity. Occasionally the bone adjacent to the joint is absorbed so facilitating separation at the symphysis.

Pathology

Occasionally there occurs a slipping of one pubic body with respect to the other at the symphysis pubis. This is known as *osteitis pubis*, and seems to affect a few females following childbirth, and surprisingly some professional footballers. The aetiology is essentially unknown although it is thought to be related to abnormal stresses across the symphysis. The unevenness of the pubic arch can clearly be seen on x-ray. Pain associated with the condition is usually referred to the hip joint.

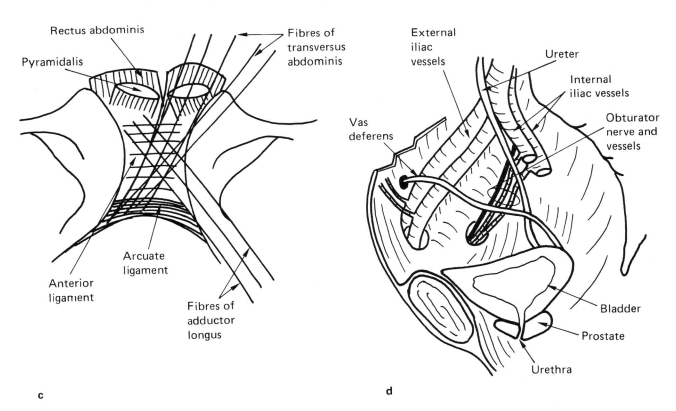

Fig. 5.55 Articular surfaces and principal relations of the symphysis pubis: **a** = medial view; **b** = horizontal section; **c** = anterior view; **d** = medial view.

Lumbosacral joint

The lumbosacral joint is between the last lumbar vertebra, usually the fifth, and the first sacral segment (Fig. 5.56). The superior surface of the sacrum is inclined approximately 30° to the horizontal, while the lumbosacral angle, formed between the axis of L5 and the sacral axis averages 140°. Being part of the vertebral column, the two bones are joined, like all typical vertebrae, by an intervertebral disc, anterior and posterior ligaments, ligamenta flava, interspinous and supraspinous ligaments, and by synovial joints between their adjacent articular processes. Further details of vertebral articulations can be found on p. 728.

Ligaments

In addition to the ligaments mentioned above, the iliolumbar and lateral lumbosacral ligaments help to stabilize the lumbosacral joint.

Iliolumbar ligament   This strong ligament passes inferiorly and laterally from the tip of the transverse process of the fifth lumbar vertebra to the posterior part of the inner lip of the iliac crest (Fig. 5.56b). In reality it is the thickened lower border of the anterior and middle layers of the thoracolumbar fascia. Occasionally an additional smaller ligamentous band passes from the tip of the transverse process of the fourth lumbar vertebra to the iliac crest behind the main iliolumbar ligament (Fig. 5.56b). There are usually some fibrous strands passing between the transverse process of L4 and the iliac crest, only when these strands become condensed can they be considered to constitute a true ligament.

Lateral lumbosacral ligament   The lateral lumbosacral ligament is partially continuous with the lower border of the iliolumbar ligament. It passes obliquely downwards from the lower border of the transverse process of the fifth lumbar vertebra to the ala of the sacrum, intermingling with the anterior sacroiliac ligament (Fig. 5.56b). It consists of bundles of fibres of varying strength.

Blood and nerve supply

The blood supply to the joint is by small branches from the median sacral, and ilio-lumbar arteries. However, it must be remembered that the major component of the joint, the intervertebral disc, is essentially an avascular structure, obtaining its nutrients by diffusion from the adjacent vertebral bodies.

The nerve supply to the joint and associated ligaments is by twigs from both the anterior and posterior rami of L5 and S1.

Stability

Because of the inclination of the superior surface of the sacrum, there is a tendency for the fifth lumbar vertebra to slide inferiorly and anteriorly. Consequently, the lumbosacral junction is the weak link in the vertebral column. The tendency for slippage to occur is prevented by the overlapping of the articular processes of the vertebrae involved. This bony arrangement, together with the spinous and iliolumbar ligaments, are sufficient to prevent any abnormal movements occurring.

Movements

The degree of flexion, extension, and lateral flexion possible at the lumbosacral joint varies from individual to individual and with age. There is no axial rotation at this joint.

Flexion and extension   Between the ages of 2 and 13 the lumbosacral joint is responsible for as much as 75% of the total range of flexion and extension of the lumbar spine. The average range of flexion and extension possible at this joint is of the order of 18°. However, this is greatly reduced from age 35 onwards. The iliolumbar ligaments tend to limit flexion and extension of the joint, with the inferior band limiting extension and the superior band (when present) limiting flexion.

Lateral flexion   The range of lateral flexion at the lumbosacral joint is minimal as it drops from 7° in the child to only 1° in the adult, and zero in the elderly. Again the iliolumbar ligament plays an important role in limiting movement, with the contralateral ligament becoming taut and the ipsilateral ligament slackening. The importance of the presence of the superior band is that it will restrict lateral flexion of L4 with respect to the sacrum.

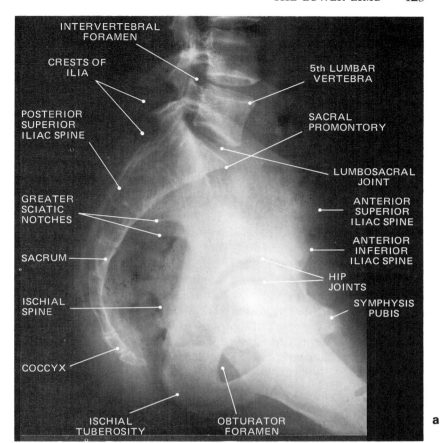

INTERVERTEBRAL FORAMEN

CRESTS OF ILIA

POSTERIOR SUPERIOR ILIAC SPINE

5th LUMBAR VERTEBRA

SACRAL PROMONTORY

LUMBOSACRAL JOINT

GREATER SCIATIC NOTCHES

ANTERIOR SUPERIOR ILIAC SPINE

ANTERIOR INFERIOR ILIAC SPINE

SACRUM

HIP JOINTS

ISCHIAL SPINE

SYMPHYSIS PUBIS

COCCYX

ISCHIAL TUBEROSITY

OBTURATOR FORAMEN

a

Fig. 5.56 **a** = X-ray showing the lumbosacral articulation.
b = The iliolumbar and lateral sacral ligaments.

Iliolumbar ligaments

Lateral lumbosacral ligament

b

Accessory movements

The accessory movements possible at the lumbosacral joint are similar to those between any two lumbar vertebrae.

Pathology

Normally, under the component of body weight acting parallel to the superior sacral surface, the inferior articular process of L5 fits tightly into the superior sacral surface of S1, and binds the lumbar and sacral processes tightly together (Fig. 5.57a). The associated forces act through the pars interarticularis, that part of the vertebral arch between the superior and inferior articular processes. If the pars become fractured or destroyed then the condition of *spondylolysis* exists. Consequently, the buttressing of L5 on S1 no longer occurs, and the body of the fifth lumbar vertebra slips forwards and downwards giving rise to *spondylolisthesis* (Fig. 5.57b). The only structure now providing support to the joint and preventing further slippage is the lumbosacral intervertebral disc, which is put under tension, and the paravertebral muscles, which go into spasm and account for the pain associated with spondylolisthesis. The extent of the anterior movement of L5 relative to S1 can be assessed on oblique radiographs.

It has become apparent recently that spondylolisthesis can arise as a slowly developing fracture of the pars interarticularis, being most common in adolescents who perform contact sports and gymnastics. The mechanism of the injury is probably through impact loading while the L5–S1 interspace is repetitively flexed and extended. The repetitive nature of the loading is important because unless there is some congenital anomaly, the pars interarticularis can withstand the stress induced by a single normal impact. However, with repetitive frequent loading the bending stresses eventually produce a small crack on the tensile side of the pars, which slowly extends across the bone with loading. The bone consequently fatigues and eventually gives way. If the fracture is incomplete when diagnosed, then by avoiding repetitive bending stresses it may heal. However, once the pars has been ruptured the joint becomes relatively unstable. Unfortunately, conservative measures that bring about repair in a stable fracture do not appear to work, and spinal fusion may have to be performed.

Fig. 5.57 **a** = Normal anatomy of the lumbo-sacral junction. **b** = Fracture of the vertebral arch giving rise to spondylolisthesis.

Sacrococcygeal joint

This is the articulation between the last sacral and the first coccygeal segments (Fig. 5.56a, 5.58a) via an intervening interosseous ligament similar to an intervertebral disc. The articular surfaces are elliptical with their long axes lying transversely; that on the sacrum being convex and that on the coccyx concave. The joint is completely surrounded and reinforced by longitudinal fibrous strands collectively called the *sacrococcygeal ligaments* (Fig. 5.58b,c). The lateral part of these strands forms the lateral boundary of the foramen transmitting the anterior ramus of the fifth sacral nerve.

The sacrococcygeal joint frequently becomes partially or completely obliterated in old age.

Flexion and extension are the only movements possible at the joint, and these are essentially passive occurring during defaecation and labour. The increases in the anteroposterior diameter of the pelvic outlet following movement of the sacrum can be further increased by extension of the coccyx.

Palpation

The line of the sacrococcygeal joint can be felt as a horizontal groove between the apex of the sacrum and the coccyx deep within the natal cleft. By moving the palpating finger downwards so that it lies against the back of the coccyx, an applied forward pressure produces a degree of rotation of the coccyx against the sacrum.

a

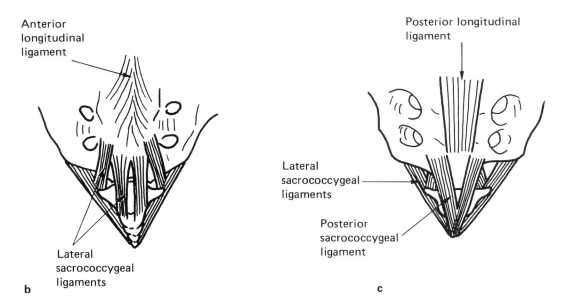

Anterior
longitudinal
ligament

Posterior longitudinal
ligament

Lateral
sacrococcygeal
ligaments

Lateral
sacrococcygeal
ligaments

Posterior
sacrococcygeal
ligament

b

c

Fig. 5.58 The sacrococcygeal joint: **a** = lateral view without ligaments; **b** = anterior view; **c** = posterior view.

THE HIP JOINT

Introduction

The hip joint is the articulation between the *head of the femur* and the *acetabulum* of the innominate bone (Fig. 5.59a). It is a synovial ball and socket joint, and as such permits a wide range of movements compatible with a wide range of locomotor activities. The hip joint connects the lower limb to the trunk, and therefore is involved in the transmission of weight. Indeed, the mechanical requirements of the joint are severe. It must be capable not merely of supporting the entire weight of the body, as in standing on one leg, but of stable transference of the weight, particularly during movement of the trunk on the femur, as occurs during walking and running. The joint must therefore possess great strength and stability, even at the expense of limitation of range of movement. The stability of the joint is determined by the shape of the articular surfaces (a deep socket securely holding the femoral head), the strength of the joint capsule and associated ligaments, and the insertion of muscles crossing the joint, which tend to be at some distance from the centre of movement.

Although the hip is a ball and socket joint, when standing erect the femoral head is not completely covered by the acetabulum, the anterosuperior aspect being exposed. Coincidence of the articular surfaces can be achieved by flexing the hip to 90°, abducting by 5° and laterally rotating by 10°. This position of the thigh corresponds to the quadrupedal position. Thus one of the consequences of attaining the erect position and adopting bipedalism as a means of locomotion is the loss of coincidence of the articular surfaces. This loss of coincidence puts the hip in a potentially vulnerable position regarding its stability.

The acetabulum of the pelvis faces laterally, anteriorly and inferiorly to articulate with the head of the femur, which due to the anteversion of the femoral neck faces medially, anteriorly and superiorly. Consequently, there is an angle of 30° to 40° between the axes of the acetabulum and the femoral neck (Fig. 5.59b), so that the anterior part of the femoral head articulates with the joint capsule. In addition, the lateral inferior inclination of the acetabulum forms an angle of 30 to 40° with the horizontal (Fig. 5.59b), so that the superior part of the acetabulum overhangs the femoral head laterally. An angle of 30° is thus formed between a vertical line through the centre of the femoral head and a line from this centre to the bony margin of the acetabulum. This is the *angle of Wiberg* and can be easily measured on radiographs. Decreases in this angle have implications for stability of the joint.

In a normal individual, a line drawn along the upper margin of the obturator foramen and the inferior margin of the femoral neck to the medial side of the shaft describes a smooth curve. This is *Shenton's line*. The curve is not influenced by small changes in position, however in fractures and dislocations of the femur it may become greatly distorted.

Acetabulum

Head of femur

Shenton's line

a

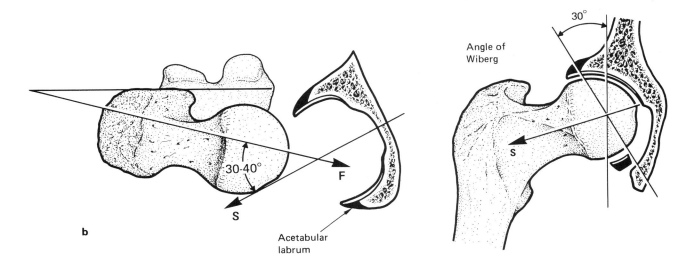

Angle of
Wiberg

30°

F

S

30-40°

S

Acetabular
labrum

b

Fig. 5.59 a = The radiographic appearance of the adult hip.
b = Relation of the femoral head and acetabulum:

F = Axis of femoral neck
S = Axis of acetabulum

Articular surfaces

Acetabulum

The *acetabulum* is a hemispherical hollow on the outer surface of the innominate, formed by the fusion of its three component parts: the ilium, ischium and pubis which meet at a Y-shaped cartilage forming their epiphyseal junction. The anterior one-fifth of the acetabulum is formed by the pubis, the superior posterior two-fifths by the body of the ilium and the inferior posterior two-fifths by the ischium (Fig. 5.60a). The prominent rim of the acetabulum is deficient inferiorly as the *acetabular notch*. The heavy wall of the acetabulum consists of a semilunar articular part, covered with hyaline cartilage, which is open below, and a deep central non-articular part the *acetabular fossa*. The acetabular fossa is formed mainly from the ischium and its wall is frequently thin.

Head of the femur

The *head of the femur* forms approximately two-thirds of a sphere being slightly compressed in an anteroposterior direction. However, the difference between the two principle axes is small. Nevertheless it is best thought of as being an ellipsoid. The head is covered in articular (hyaline) cartilage, except for a small area superolaterally adjacent to the *neck* and at the *fovea capitis*, a pit on the posteromedial part of the head. Anteriorly the cartilage extends on to the femoral neck for a short distance (Fig. 5.60b). This is thought to be a reaction to the pressure from the iliopsoas tendon crossing the joint in this region. Both the femoral head and the acetabulum are composed of cancellous bone covered by a thin layer of compact bone.

Congruence

Although the articular surfaces are reciprocally curved, the hip joint consists of two incongruent shapes. Incongruity implies limited contact between the two surfaces under low loading conditions, with a gradual increase in the area of contact with increasing load. Because of this it is usual to think of the incongruity as a means to distribute load and protect the underlying cartilage from excessive stress. An important factor in the functioning of such a mechanism is the compressibility of the cartilage. The incongruity of the hip joint is determined by an arched acetabulum and a rounded femoral head.

Because of the relationship between the femur and the pelvis, the superior surface of the head of the femur and that of the acetabulum generally sustain the greatest pressures. Consequently, the articular cartilage is thicker in these regions than elsewhere. In the unloaded acetabulum, the cartilage surface is very nearly spherical. The small deviations seen on the cartilage surface (less than 150 μm) reflect the much larger deviations at the cartilage–bone interface (frequently greater than 500 μm). Ultrasonic measurement of the acetabular region has shown that the cartilage and calcified interface surfaces are not concentric, confirming the clinical finding of thinner cartilage in the anteromedial aspect. It is only when weight is taken with the hip joints in extreme flexion, as when squatting, that this anteromedial region of the acetabulum, articulating with the inferior part of the femoral head, becomes involved in weight bearing.

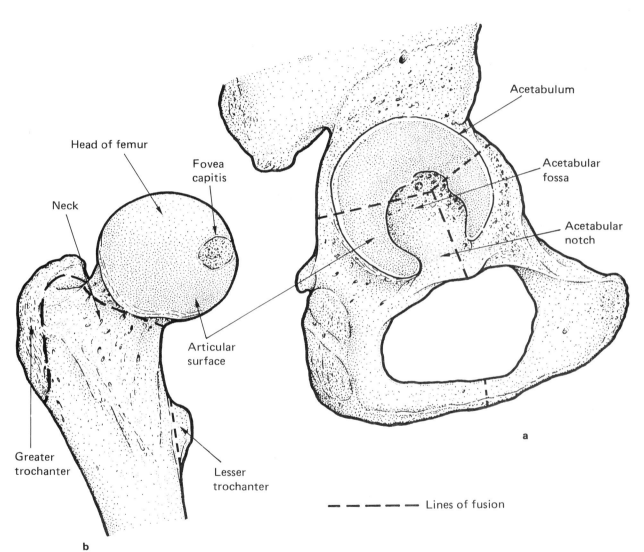

Fig. 5.60   The articular surfaces of the hip joint: **a** = acetabulum; **b** = head of femur.

Joint capsule

Attachments

The fibrous capsule of the hip is very strong, being thicker anteriorly, where the head of the femur articulates, and superiorly enhancing the stability of the joint. Proximally, the capsule surrounds the acetabulum attaching directly to the bone outside the labrum above and behind, and to the bone and outer edge of the labrum in front and below (Fig. 5.61a). Opposite the acetabular notch the capsule attaches to the transverse ligament. On the femur the capsule attaches anteriorly to the intertrochanteric line and to the junction of the neck with the trochanters (Fig. 5.61b). Posteriorly the capsule has an arched free border and covers the medial two-thirds of the neck only (Fig. 5.61c), approximately as far laterally as the groove formed by the tendon of obturator externus. Consequently, part of the femoral neck is intracapsular and part is extracapsular. It is worth noting that the epiphyseal line for the head of the femur is intracapsular, while the trochanteric epiphyseal lines are extracapsular (see Fig. 5.60b). The capsule may be likened to a cylindrical sleeve enclosing the joint and the majority of the femoral neck. Anteromedially the capsule is strengthened by the deep fibres of the reflected head of rectus femoris, while laterally it is strengthened by deep fibres from gluteus minimus.

Direction of fibres

The majority of the fibres of the capsule run from the pelvis to the femur and several distinct sets have been identified (Fig. 5.61d). *Longitudinal fibres*, running parallel to the axis of the cylinder, pass from the acetabular to the femoral attachment of the capsule. They, together with *oblique fibres* which spiral around the cylinder between their attachments, unite the articular surfaces. A series of *arcuate fibres* run in a criss-cross manner from one part of the acetabular rim to another, helping to keep the femoral head within the acetabulum. Deeper fibres run circularly around the capsule and have no bony attachments. They appear to be most marked on the posterior of the capsule and constitute the *zona orbicularis*, where they are reinforced by the deep part of the ischiofemoral ligament. They can be clearly seen on the deep surface of the capsule.

Some of the deeper longitudinal fibres, on reaching the femoral neck, turn upwards towards the articular margin forming the retinacular fibres. These bundles are most marked on the upper and lower surfaces of the neck and convey blood vessels to the head and neck regions. The main longitudinal capsular fibres form named thickened bands which resist the tensile stresses to which the capsule is subjected. The bands are named after their regional attachment around the acetabulum. They may not always be readily identifiable.

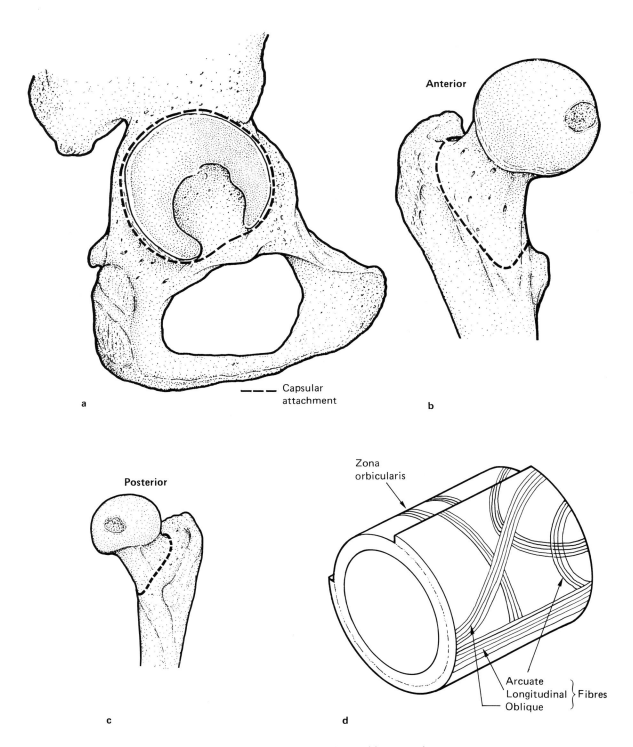

Anterior

Capsular
attachment

Posterior

Zona
orbicularis

Arcuate
Longitudinal } Fibres
Oblique

a

b

c

d

Fig. 5.61a–d The joint capsule and its attachments.

Capsular ligaments

Iliofemoral ligament

The *iliofemoral ligament* is very strong and of considerable thickness, being situated anterior to the joint (Fig. 5.62a). It is a triangular band with the apex attaching to the lower part of the anterior inferior iliac spine and the adjacent part of the acetabular rim, and the base to the intertrochanteric line. However, because the central part is thinner it is often referred to as being Y-shaped, with the stem corresponding to the apex and the two limbs to the base. The outer bands of the ligament attaching to the upper and lower parts of the intertrochanteric line are the strongest parts, with the central area being thinner and weaker.

Pubofemoral ligament

The *pubofemoral ligament* strengthens the inferior and anterior aspects of the joint capsule (Fig. 5.62b). It runs from the iliopubic eminence and superior pubic ramus to the lower part of the intertrochanteric line, blending with the inferior band of the iliofemoral ligament. Between the iliofemoral and pubofemoral ligaments the capsule is at its thinnest. However, it is crossed here by the tendon of iliopsoas. Between the tendon and the capsule is the *psoas bursa*, which usually communicates with the joint cavity through a perforation in this part of the capsule.

Ischiofemoral ligament

The *ischiofemoral ligament* is spiral in shape but less well-defined than either the iliofemoral or pubofemoral ligaments. It arises from the body of the ischium behind and below the acetabulum, the fibres spiralling laterally and upwards to attach to the superior part of the neck and root of the greater trochanter (Fig. 5.62c). Some of the deeper fibres are continuous with the zona orbicularis.

Role of the ligaments

The three ligaments, iliofemoral, pubofemoral and ischiofemoral, have important roles in limiting and controlling the various movements of which the hip is capable. When standing erect, all three ligaments are under moderate tension. On flexing the hip, they all become relaxed. However, on extending the hip they all become taut, with the inferior band of the iliofemoral ligament being under the greatest tension as it runs almost vertically, and is thus responsible for checking the posterior tilt of the pelvis. The concerted action of all three ligaments seen in flexion and extension of the hip is not seen in abduction/adduction or medial/lateral rotation. The attachments of the ligaments demand that during each of these latter movements some will become taut while others relax. During adduction, the superior band of the iliofemoral ligament becomes taut, the inferior band only slightly, while the pubofemoral and ischiofemoral ligaments slacken. The opposite occurs in abduction of the hip. In lateral rotation, both anterior ligaments become taut, that is the iliofemoral and pubofemoral, while the ischiofemoral ligament slackens. In medial rotation of the hip it is the ischiofemoral ligament which becomes taut, the others slackening.

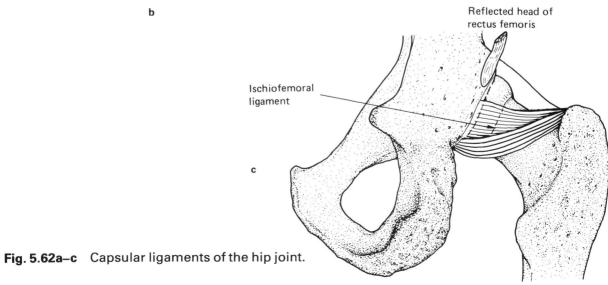

Fig. 5.62a–c Capsular ligaments of the hip joint.

Intracapsular structures

Transverse ligament of the acetabulum

The inferior deficiency in the acetabular rim is completed by the *transverse ligament of the acetabulum* (Fig. 5.63b), creating a foramen with the acetabular notch through which vessels and nerves may enter the joint. The superficial edge of the ligament is flush with the acetabular rim; it consists of strong bands of fibrous tissue.

Acetabular labrum

The acetabulum is deepened all round by the fibrocartilaginous *acetabular labrum* attached to the bony rim and to the transverse ligament (Fig. 5.63b). The labrum is triangular in cross-section with the apex forming the thin free edge (Fig. 5.63c). The diameter of this free edge is smaller than its fixed edge, and is also somewhat less than the maximum diameter of the femoral head. Extending further laterally than the equatorial region of the femoral head, the labrum cups around the head holding it firmly in the acetabular socket (Fig. 5.63d).

Ligamentum teres

Within the hip joint there is a weak, flattened band of connective tissue the *ligamentum teres* (ligament of the head of the femur). It is attached to the adjacent margins of the acetabular notch and the lower border of the transverse ligament (Fig. 5.63b). Narrowing as it passes from these attachments, it inserts into the *fovea capitis* on the head of the femur (Fig. 5.63a). Between its two attachments the ligament is enclosed in a sleeve of synovial membrane, so that although it is intracapsular it is extrasynovial. It lies in the acetabular fossa below the femoral head. The ligament appears to be of little importance in strengthening the hip joint, being variable in size and occasionally absent. Its function in the adult is uncertain. It is stretched when the flexed thigh is adducted or laterally rotated. However, in many cases it is too weak to have any definite ligamentous action. No apparent disability arises from its rupture or absence. A small artery is always found within its substance.

Acetabular fat pad

The *acetabular fat pad* lies within the acetabular fossa; it is really a fibroelastic fat pad. It is said to contain numerous proprioceptive nerve endings, so that when it becomes compressed and partially extruded from the acetabular fossa beneath the transverse ligament, additional proprioceptive information reaches the brain regarding hip joint movements.

Synovial membrane

The synovial membrane lines the internal surface of the fibrous capsule and covers the acetabular labrum. At the acetabular notch it is attached to the medial margin of the transverse ligament, almost completely covering the fatty tissue in the acetabular fossa. It extends like a sleeve around the ligament of the head of the femur, attaching to the margins of the fovea capitis. At the femoral attachment of the joint capsule, the synovial membrane is reflected up towards the head as far as the articular margin. The retinacula raise this reflected part into prominent folds within which blood vessels run towards the head. An extension of the synovial membrane beyond the free margin of the capsule at the back of the femoral neck serves as a bursa for the tendon of obturator externus. The communicating psoas bursa breaches the joint capsule between the inferior limb of the iliofemoral ligament and the pubofemoral ligament.

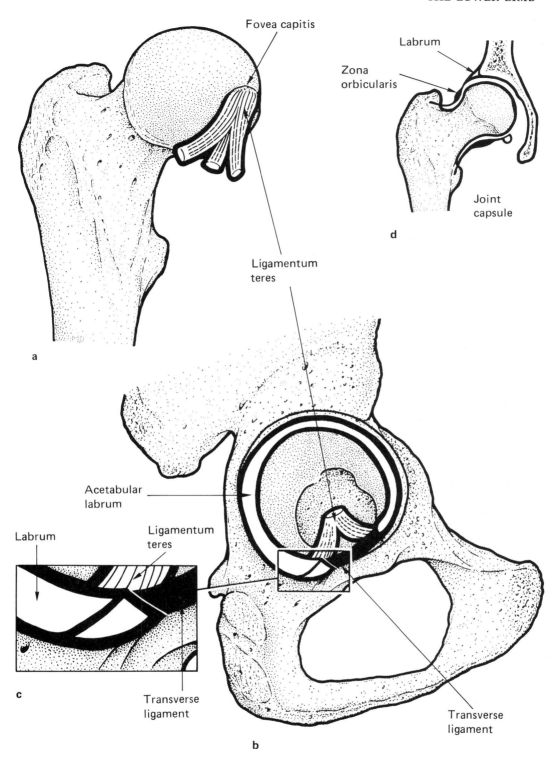

Fig. 5.63a–d The transverse acetabular ligament, acetabular labrum and ligamentum teres.

Blood and nerve supply

Blood supply

The hip joint receives its blood supply from the *medial* and *lateral circumflex femoral arteries*, the *obturator artery* and the *superior* and *inferior gluteal arteries*, which together form a *periarticular anastomosis* (Fig. 5.64a,b). Within the ligamentum teres there is always a small artery derived from the obturator artery, which gains access to the joint by passing below the transverse ligament bridging the acetabular notch. However, this may only be of significance prior to the fusion of the epiphysis of the head with the femoral neck (Fig. 6.64c). The greatest volume of blood reaches the joint via the periarticular anastomosis, the branches piercing the joint capsule at its femoral attachment and passing in the retinacula, between the capsule and synovial membrane, to reach and supply the femoral neck and head.

The adequacy of the periarticular arterial anastomosis is of critical importance for the nutrition of the bone, particularly for the proximal femoral epiphysis until ossification is completed, which is usually between 16 and 20 years. Similarly, following a fracture, healing of the bone requires a good blood supply. Of particular concern is fracture of the femoral neck, occurring frequently in older females. Such fractures tend to be intracapsular and realigning the head and neck fragments can be a problem. Furthermore, the blood vessels serving the head and neck may be ruptured resulting in ischaemic degeneration of the femoral head, the artery of the head of the femur frequently provides an inadequate alternative blood supply. For this reason early prosthetic replacement of the femoral component or of the joint as a whole is often performed in subcapital fractures. In the same way dislocation of the hip and slipping of the femoral epiphysis are both potentially damaging to the retinacular blood vessels.

Lymphatic drainage

The lymphatic drainage of the hip is by vessels accompanying the arteries supplying the joint. The lymph vessels arise primarily from the synovial membrane, and drain to the deep inguinal and iliac lymph nodes, and thence to the common iliac nodes.

Nerve supply

The nerve supply to the hip joint is from the lumbar plexus by twigs from the femoral and obturator nerves, and from the sacral plexus by twigs from the superior gluteal nerve and the nerve to quadratus femoris, with a root value of L2 to S1. This is a typical example of articular innervation, in that the nerve supply to the joint is derived from the same nerves which supply the musculature crossing the joint. The articular supply consists of sensory nerve fibres, transmitting proprioceptive information, and vasomotor fibres.

In posterior dislocation of the hip, the sciatic and other nerves of the posterior hip region may be stretched over the head of the femur or otherwise damaged. Injury to the superior gluteal nerve results in collapse of the pelvis on the opposite side as the leg is raised, from paralysis of the gluteus medius and minimus muscles (positive Trendelenburg sign). Primary disease of the hip joint frequently manifests itself in pain referred to the knee because the same nerves provide branches to that joint.

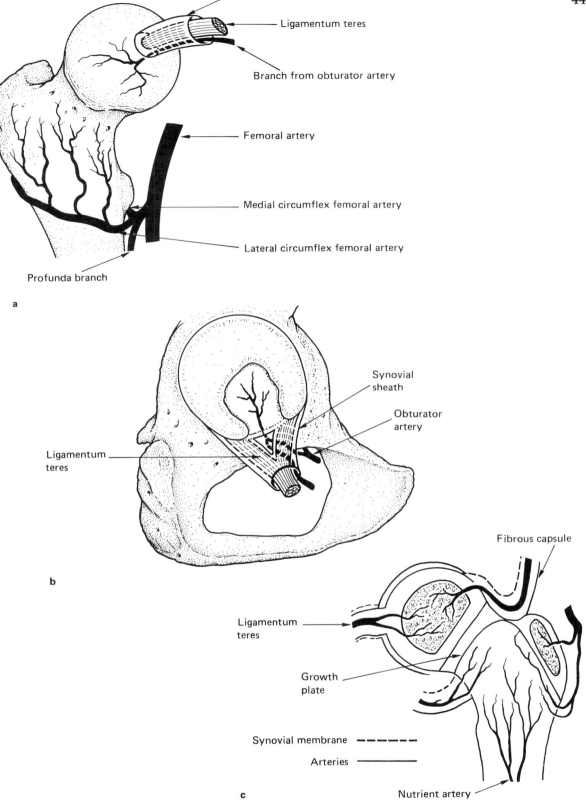

Synovial sheath

Ligamentum teres

Branch from obturator artery

Femoral artery

Medial circumflex femoral artery

Lateral circumflex femoral artery

Profunda branch

a

Synovial sheath

Obturator artery

Ligamentum teres

b

Fibrous capsule

Ligamentum teres

Growth plate

Synovial membrane — — — — —

Arteries ——————

Nutrient artery

c

Fig. 5.64a–c The arterial supply of the hip joint.

Relations

Anteriorly from below upwards the hip joint is related to pectineus, the tendon of psoas major, iliacus and rectus femoris (Fig. 5.65a,c). Indeed, the deep part of the reflected head of rectus femoris is so intimately related to the joint that it strengthens the superior and anterior aspects of the joint capsule. Between the tendons of iliacus and psoas, and separated from the joint capsule by these structures, lies the femoral nerve, while the femoral artery and vein lie on the psoas tendon and pectineus.

Posteriorly, from above downwards, are found piriformis, the tendon of obturator internus with the two gemelli and quadratus femoris (Fig. 5.65b,c). These all lie close to the joint capsule. The nerve to quadratus femoris is deep to obturator internus and therefore lies directly on the joint capsule. The sciatic nerve is separated from the capsule by the obturator internus and gemelli.

In addition to the reflected head of rectus femoris superiorly, gluteus minimus is found more laterally, part of which may blend with the joint capsule. Inferiorly, the obturator externus winds backwards below the capsule lying between the capsule and quadratus femoris.

The deep fascia of the thigh, of which the fascia lata is the uppermost subdivision, invests the soft tissue of the lower limb. The fascia lata is a strong membranous fascia, thicker where it is reinforced by tendinous contributions and thinner in the gluteal region. It has a continuous bony and ligamentous attachment superiorly. Between the iliac crest and the superior border of gluteus maximus the fascia is thickened by vertical tendinous fibres, the gluteal aponeurosis. The remaining gluteal portion and adductor part of the fascia lata are thin except for a lateral band, the iliotibial tract, which is especially strong.

An opening in the front of the fascia lata, the saphenous opening, provides passage for the long (great) saphenous vein to its termination in the femoral vein. The efferent vessels from the superficial inguinal nodes also pass through this opening, mainly to travel within the femoral sheath to the external iliac nodes.

Outside the fascia lata, the subcutaneous connective tissue contains a considerable amount of fat over the hip and thigh, although it varies in different regions. In the gluteal region the fat is deposited in a thick layer which contributes to the contour of the buttock and the formation of the gluteal fold. At the fold of the groin the subcutaneous tissue is separable into a superficial fatty layer and a deeper membranous layer, between which are found the subcutaneous blood vessels and nerves.

Palpation

Because it is completely surrounded by muscles the hip joint cannot be directly palpated. However the approximate position of the joint centre, in relation to the anterior surface of the body, can be determined in the living body. The joint centre lies in a horizontal plane passing through the top of the greater trochanters; these can be palpated. This plane passes 1 cm below the middle third of the inguinal ligament. This is the position of the joint centre. Passive movement of the thigh on the pelvis and palpation in this area will improve the estimation of the centre of movement for the hip joint.

Stability

The stability of the hip is determined by the shape of the bones, the strong reinforced capsule, the acetabular labrum and the muscles crossing the joint. Although the articular surfaces of the femur and pelvis fit well together and provide a good degree of support for the joint, the periarticular muscles are essential for the continued stability of the joint, particularly those muscles that cross the joint transversely.

Fig. 5.65 Muscular relations around the hip joint:
a = anterior; **b** = posterior; **c** = lateral.

Muscular factors

Muscles whose fibres run parallel to the femoral neck will tend to keep the femoral head in firm contact with the acetabulum. Muscles in this category are psoas, iliacus and pectineus anteriorly, gluteus minimus superiorly, and gluteus medius, obturator internus and externus, the gemelli, quadratus femoris and piriformis posteriorly. On the other hand, muscles whose fibres run parallel to the femoral shaft, that is longitudinally, may have a tendency to cause dislocation of the joint superiorly, particularly if the roof of the acetabulum is everted. The adductor muscles run longitudinally, and in some positions of the joint, for example attempting adduction of the extended and laterally rotated thigh, their action is such that without the synergistic activity of other muscles around the hip, there would be a tendency for anteromedial dislocation of the joint. It should not be inferred from this that the hip joint is continually liable to dislocation; in the normal joint it is not. However, if there is some malformation of the acetabular socket, such as eversion of the roof, then the probability of dislocation occurring is increased. Eversion of the roof is an acetabular malformation present in congenital dislocation of the hip (CDH). In the presence of this malformation the adductors can cause dislocation, especially when the limb is adducted. However, when the limb is abducted the dislocating influence of the adductors decreases until in full abduction the adductors eventually favour apposition of the joint surfaces.

Bony factors

Normally the angle between a horizontal line running through the cartilages (at A in Fig. 5.66; see also Fig. 5.59) and a line tangential to the acetabular roof is 25° in the neonate and 15° after the first year; when this angle exceeds 30° congenital malformation is present.

The direction of the femoral neck in both frontal and horizontal planes is of considerable importance in the stability of the hip (see Fig. 5.67). During embryonic development, and even after birth, the femoral shaft becomes adducted and medially rotated, as a result of which the head and neck become angulated against the shaft in both the frontal and horizontal planes. In the frontal plane the angle between the neck and shaft indicates the adaptation of the femur to the parallel position of the legs assumed in bipedalism. This is the *angle of inclination* (see Fig. 5.67a), which in the newborn is about 150° decreasing in the early years to the adult value of 125°. In the horizontal plane the angle between the neck and shaft is also due to the assumption of an upright stance. The neck and head are outwardly rotated against the shaft. This *angle of anteversion* is about 10° in the adult (see Fig. 5.67b), having decreased from about 25° in infants and young children.

In some pathological conditions, such as CDH, the angle of inclination can be as much as 140° producing a *coxa valga*, and the angle of anteversion may be as large as 40°, thereby increasing the risk of anterior dislocation of the joint. In other conditions the angle of inclination may be reduced, for example in acquired dislocation of the hip, and there may be a reduced or even reversed angle of anteversion, that is the head and neck are retroverted with respect to the femoral shaft.

The values for the angles of inclination and anteversion given above are mean values. Within a normal population there will be considerable racial and individual variation in these angles, which will have important consequences as far as joint stability is concerned. If the angle of inclination and/or the angle of anteversion are greater than 130° and 15° respectively, the coincidence and thus the stability of the two joint surfaces is decreased.

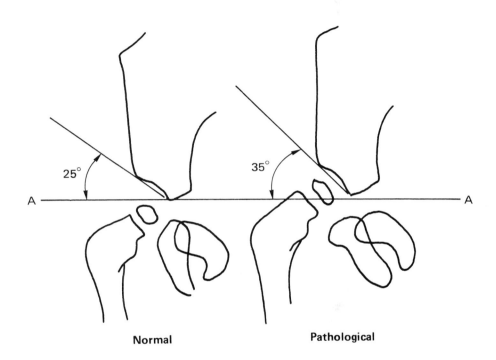

Normal   **Pathological**

Fig. 5.66a,b   Eversion of the developing ace-
tatulum as a factor in stability of the hip joint.

Because of the length of the femoral neck and its angulation with respect to the shaft, in both the horizontal and frontal planes, a line joining the centre of the femoral head to the centre of the knee joint, that is to the middle of the intercondylar notch, passes mainly outside the bone on its medial side. This is the *mechanical axis* of the femur about which medial and lateral rotation occurs. The *anatomical axis* of the femur deviates by some 6° in the frontal plane from the mechanical axis. In turn, the mechanical axis deviates some 3° from the vertical, so that its upper end is lateral to its lower end.

Dislocations and fractures

Traumatic dislocation of the hip is not common except as the sequel of a car accident. Posterior dislocation is more common, being favoured by the usual direction of the dislocating force in such accidents. The joint capsule will be ruptured, the head of the femur will be in the posterior iliac fossa and the limb will be shortened, adducted and medially rotated, the knee on the affected side tending to overlie the normal knee. The position is almost diagnostic, being contrasted with the position in fracture of the femoral neck, in which the limb is shortened but laterally rotated.

Fracture of the upper third of the femoral shaft exemplifes the effects of muscle pull. The proximal fragment has the attachment of iliopsoas to the lesser trochanter, and the gluteal and other muscles of the posterior femoral group to the greater trochanter. This fragment is therefore strongly flexed, abducted and laterally rotated, while the distal fragment is displaced upwards and medially by the adductors and hamstrings. Realignment requires some form of traction with surgical intervention often necessary in the adult.

Movement

The movements possible are those of a typical ball and socket joint, being flexion and extension around a transverse axis, adduction and abduction around an anteroposterior axis and medial and lateral rotation around a vertical axis. Circumduction is also allowed. The three axes intersect at the centre of the femoral head. Since the head is at an angle to the shaft, all movements involve conjoint rotation of the head.

Fig. 5.67 Angulation of the femur; **a** = anterior view;
b = medial view; **c** = superior view.

Flexion and extension (Fig. 5.68a)

Flexion of the hip joint is free, being limited by contact of the thigh with the anterior abdominal wall when the knee is flexed. With the knee extended, flexion of the hip is limited by tension in the hamstring muscles. Extension of the hip beyond the vertical is limited partly because of the tension in associated ligaments and partly because of the shape of the articular surfaces. Extension beyond 30° is not normally possible. In going from a position of flexion to one of full extension, the capsular ligaments become increasingly tense pulling the femoral head more tightly against the acetabulum. Because ligaments are slightly extensible and articular cartilage deforms slightly under compressive loads, the point at which no further extension is possible will vary slightly with the magnitude of the extending force. During extension of the hip joint, part of the acetabular fat pad is extruded from the acetabular fossa below the transverse ligament. Flexing the joint draws the fat pad back in again to fill the potential space created by the lateral movement of the femoral head, which occurs with flexion.

Abduction and adduction (see Fig. 5.68b)

Abduction and adduction of the hip joint, some 45° each, are free in all positions of the lower limb, except of course for adduction in the anatomical position. Abduction is greatest when the hip is also partly flexed. It is limited by the tension in the adductor muscles and the pubofemoral ligament. Adduction is easier with the hip flexed than when extended, it is limited by the opposite limb, tension in the abductor muscles and the lateral part of the iliofemoral ligament.

Rotation (see Fig. 5.68c)

Rotation at the hip joint is about the mechanical axis of the femur and does *not* take place about the long axis of the shaft of the femur. Consequently, in medial rotation the shaft of the femur moves anteriorly around the mechanical axis, carrying with it the calf and foot so that the toes point towards the midline. In lateral rotation, the shaft of the femur moves posteriorly, with the result that the toes point away from the midline. Rotation in both directions is freer when combined with flexion of the hip rather than when the hip is extended. Of the two, lateral rotation is freer than medial rotation, and is also the more powerful movement. Lateral rotation is limited by tension in the medial rotators of the thigh and the iliofemoral and pubofemoral ligaments; medial rotation is limited by tension in the lateral rotators and the ischiofemoral ligament. A small amount of rotation of the hip joint occurs automatically in association with terminal extension and the beginning of flexion at the knee, particularly with the foot fixed. The total range of medial and lateral rotation is some 90°.

Because the axis about which rotation occurs is mainly outside the femur, there has been some confusion as to the role of certain muscles in producing medial or lateral rotation at the hip joint. In general terms, any muscle whose line of action passes anterior to the mechanical axis will produce medial rotation, while those whose line of action passes posterior to this axis will produce lateral rotation. However, it should be remembered that the position of the line of action of a muscle with respect to the mechanical axis can change depending on the degree of flexion or extension of the joint. Consequently, in some positions of the joint a muscle may be a medial rotator, while in another it may be a lateral rotator. Similarly, in large muscles crossing the hip joint it may be more convenient to consider more than one line of action for the muscle, in which case one part of the muscle may medially rotate and another laterally rotate the hip joint.

Fig. 5.68a Movements of the hip joint.

Flexion

Fig. 5.68a

Extension

When assessing the range of movement at the hip joint it is important to determine that there is no movement of the pelvis or vertebral column. An apparent increase in flexion or extension may be due to flexion or extension of the vertebral column, especially in the lumbar region. Similarly, an apparent increase in abduction or adduction may be produced by a lateral bending of the trunk to the opposite or same side respectively.

Hip joint axis

The greater trochanters can normally be palpated, and in the erect standing position a horizontal line through the tips of the greater trochanters represents the common hip joint axis in the frontal plane. The position of the greater trochanter with respect to the hip joint varies little with flexion and extension. However, with respect to the centre of the hip joint, it moves upwards in abduction and downwards in adduction.

Limits to mobility

In conditions other than those involving the hip there may be some loss of hip mobility. For example, in *osteitis pubis* there may be some loss of hip mobility, particularly medial rotation and in some cases lateral rotation, a finding typically associated with *upper femoral epiphysiolysis*. In situations requiring free medial rotation of the hip joint in both flexion and extension, when movement is restricted stress will be applied across the hip joint to the pelvis. The stress will be specifically a shearing stress causing anteroposterior movement of one half of the pelvis with respect to the other in extension, or proximodistal movement in flexion. Such forces are perhaps less liable to be applied in other instances of pathological restriction of hip joint movement, as in *degenerative joint disease*, where soft tissue tension rather than abnormal joint shape is the restricting factor.

Abduction

Adduction

90°

30°

b

Medial rotation

30°

Lateral rotation

60°

c

Fig. 5.68b,c

Developmental features of the hip joint

For normal acetabular development to occur as the pelvis enlarges, a delicate balance must be maintained between the growth of the acetabular and triradiate cartilages and that of the adjacent bone. As all the secondary centres of ossification for the acetabulum appear (at 8 to 9 years) more bone is formed at the periphery than at the inner part of the acetabulum, thus increasing depth and contributing to the cup-like shape of the cavity.

The acetabular cartilage complex is composed of epiphyseal growth-plate cartilage adjacent to the bones, of articular cartilage around the acetabular cavity, and, for the most part, of hyaline cartilage. Interstitial growth within the triradiate part of the cartilage complex causes the acetabular socket to expand during growth. The concavity of the acetabulum develops in response to the presence of the femoral head (Fig. 5.69a). The depth of the acetabulum increases during development as a result of interstitial growth in the acetabular cartilage, of appositional growth at the periphery of this cartilage, and of periosteal new-bone formation at the acetabular margin.

Congenital dislocation of the hip is thought to be due to faulty development of the acetabulum, especially of its upper rim, in addition to which the femoral head may also be poorly developed. In such hips, a cartilaginous ridge is present in the acetabulum dividing the socket into two sections. This ridge may be formed exclusively by a bulge of acetabular cartilage or by a bulge of acetabular cartilage covered by an inverted acetabular labrum. The acetabular cartilage usually shows signs of degeneration, whereas the triradiate cartilage is normal. The condition is much more common in young females.

From radiographs of the developing hip, a growth quotient, the *acetabular index*, can be determined. The index shows periods of limited intensive growth of the hip. These periods occur in both sexes between the ages of 5 and 8 and again between the ages of 9 and 12 in females and 11 and 14 in males. In pathological hip joints, the triradiate cartilage closes earlier. The development of the acetabular roof and the closure of the triradiate are closely related.

During growth, ossification of the femoral head occurs at a faster rate in breadth than in height (Fig. 5.69b). The growth rate in breadth also exceeds that of the proximal metaphysis. The radiographic appearance of these two regions is therefore characteristic of the individual's age. Fortunately, the osseous acetabulum also grows at a faster rate in breadth than in depth (Fig. 5.69b). Up to the age of 15 the width of the articular space gradually decreases and approaches adult values. However, in the region of the acetabular fossa the width of the articular space does not decrease in a parallel manner, the result is the appearance of the double-arched pattern of the acetabulum.

Bone

Cartilage

Direction
of growth

a

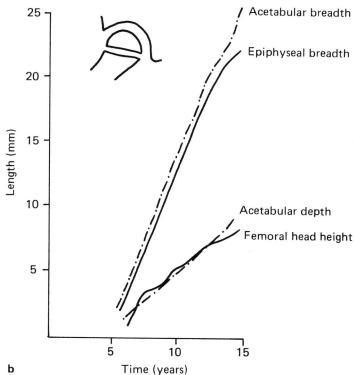

b

Fig. 5.69 **a** = Directions of growth in the acetabulum and
the proximal end of the femur. **b** = Growth in height of the
osseous femoral head and depth of the acetabulum, and
breadth of the epiphysis and acetabulum. (Adapted from
Meszaros T., Kery L. (1980). Quantitative analysis of growth
of the hip. A radiological study. *Acta Orthopaedica Scandinavica*, **51**, 275–84.)

Biomechanics

Joint forces

The estimation of hip joint forces during simple activities, such as walking, has a long history. Such estimates are continually being refined with the use of sophisticated measuring techniques and the advent of powerful microcomputers. The use of such estimates has been invaluable in the design of replacement joints. The majority of studies, however, are still limited to determining joint forces during walking. In one-legged stance, hip joint forces of between 1.8 and 3 times body weight have been reported. In the stance phase of walking, hip joint forces increase to between 3.3 and 5.5 times body weight. In running higher forces would be expected. The pattern of these forces during walking is shown in Fig. 5.70 from which it can be seen that the resultant joint forces reach a maximum shortly after heel-strike and just prior to toe-off. The major component of this resultant is the vertical joint force. However, the anteroposterior force (Y in Fig. 5.70) exceeds body weight at both heel-strike and toe-off, indicating that there is considerable stress on the joint in this direction at these times. Even during straight leg raises, when the heels are lifted 5 cm off the surface, the resultant hip joint force is of the order of two times body weight.

With estimates of hip joint forces in normal subjects ranging up to nearly six times body weight, the trabeculae within the acetabulum and the head and neck of the femur must be arranged to minimize bending and shearing stresses within the bone.

Trabecular systems

The trabecular systems which arise in the pelvis and run towards the acetabulum become continuous with those in the femoral head and neck (Fig. 5.71). Two trabecular systems arise in the region of the auricular surface of the innominate. From the upper part of this surface the trabeculae converge onto the posterior surface of the greater sciatic notch, from here they are reflected towards the inferior aspect of the acetabulum. This system lines up with one in the femur that arises from the cortical layer of the lateral aspect of the shaft to the inferior aspect of the cortical layer of the neck and inferior part of the femoral head. A second system arising from the lower part of the pelvic auricular surface converges at the level of the superior gluteal line, from here it is reflected laterally towards the upper aspect of the acetabulum. This system lines up with one that arises from the cortical layer of the medial aspect of the femoral shaft running to the superior aspect of the femoral head. This latter system develops in response to the compressive forces transmitted across the joint. If the pattern of stresses applied to the hip changes, as for example in acquired dislocation of the hip, the two trabecular systems will remodel to realign with the new stress patterns. The outward appearance is a change in the relation of the head and neck of the femur with respect to the shaft (Fig. 5.72).

There are within the upper end of the femur two accessory trabecular systems; a trochanteric bundle arising from the cortical layer of the medial aspect of the shaft, this system develops in response to the tension forces applied to the greater trochanter with muscular contraction. The second trabecular system is entirely within the greater trochanter.

The hip joint is the pivot upon which the human body is balanced particularly in gait. The acetabulum and femoral head being cancellous bone provides some elasticity to the joint, that is it has the ability to be deformed without sustaining structural damage. The presence of large quantities of relatively deformable bone suggests spreading under load and, indeed, spreading occurs and is essential if the stress (force per unit area) on the articular cartilage is to be kept within tolerable limits. Since the bony portions of the hip deform under load, maximum contact area and congruence must occur in the deformed position. This congruity should occur only under full load. A congruous fit under no load would lead to an incongruous fit under load when the femoral head tends to flatten.

Fig. 5.70 Hip joint reaction forces; resultant and components.

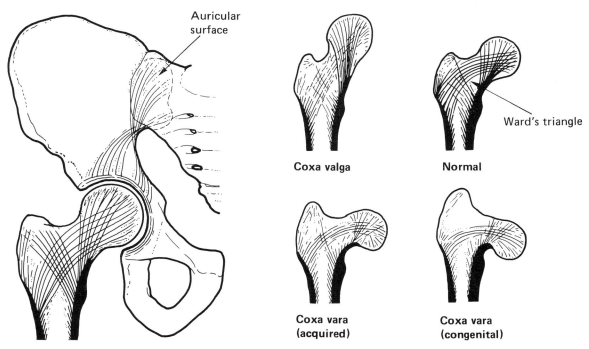

Fig. 5.71 The arrangement of the bony trabecular system in the innominate and upper part of the femur.

Fig. 5.72 Changes in the angle of inclination in coxa valga and coxa vara showing the internal remodelling that has occurred as a result.

Deformation of the bone under load has a significant effect on protecting the overlying articular cartilage from impulsive loads. The true sparing effect of trabecular bone on the overlying cartilage involves an increase in the available potential contact area. However, excessive deformation of trabecular bone, particular when sustained repetitively, can lead to microfracture with subsequent remodelling and stiffening of the underlying trabecular network. It has been suggested that stiffening and loss of congruence can lead to deterioration of the articular surfaces and to osteoarthrosis.

Contact area

The area of contact between the femoral head and acetabulum increases with increasing load. Under light loads there are two distinct areas on the anterior and posterior aspects of the head, which merge superiorly as the load increases (Fig. 5.73a). With loads applied across the hip joint ranging from 150–3200 N, the contact area increases from 2470–2830 mm². Dividing the applied load by contact area gives the mean contact stress. It appears that during walking the mean contact stress in the hip is in the range 2–3 MN/m². It is interesting to note that the measured contact areas coincide closely with regions of stiff cartilage. The stiffest cartilage being located in bands of variable size extending over the superior surface of the femoral head round to the anterior and posterior facets; there being a very soft area of cartilage near the margin of the fovea capitis (Fig. 5.73b). These observations suggest a direct link between the load or normal stress distribution and the pattern of cartilage stiffness.

In situations where the load bearing area of the femoral head is diminished, perhaps because of deformity, the stress on the remaining load-bearing cartilage is concentrated and degenerative changes frequently follow.

Both abnormally large joint incongruities and abnormally low cartilage compliance cause the load to shift away from the superior weight-bearing area of the hip toward the periphery of the contact area. As a consequence transverse compressive stresses, which may be of appreciable magnitude but make no contribution to weight-bearing, are built up through much of the superior and central portions of the femoral head. Most small changes in the overall cartilage thickness or in its thickness distribution, when considered in isolation from hip compliance changes, have only minor effects on the internal stress distribution. However, an important exception is cartilage thinning at the superior margin, which can result in abrupt longitudinal compressive stress concentrations. Such aberrations of the normal patterns of stress transmission may contribute to sclerosis or the formation of osteophytes or cysts in the osteoarthritic hip.

Joint space

There is still a joint space in the loaded hip although it is variable in size between individuals, and changes in shape with different joint positions in the same individual under comparable loads. The intra-articular joint space in the hip is to allow synovial fluid to have access to the joint for lubrication and nutrition, with the acetabular fossa acting as a fluid reservoir. Under high loading of the joint there is an egress of synovial fluid from the joint space to the reservoir; when the pressure in the joint space falls below that in the reservoir the flow is reversed, thus lubricating and nourishing the joint.

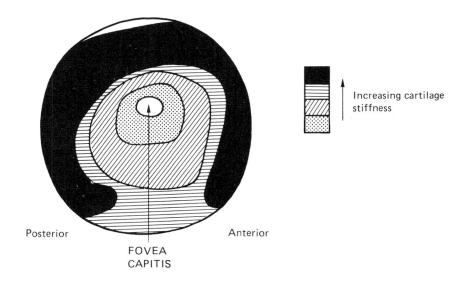

Fig. 5.73   a = The contact area of the acetabulum. **b** = The distribution of cartilage stiffness over the femoral head.

Pathology

If the blood supply to the femoral head is severely disrupted infarct of part of the femoral head may result. The intact viable bone surrounding a weakened infarct preferentially takes up additional load, with the degree of stress relief being dependent upon both the degree of necrotic stiffness deficit and the geometry of the infarct. Infarcted bone in the superior weight-bearing area must continue to carry high stresses even though load is progressively transferred out through the periphery of the lesion. Vulnerability to mechanical overload would appear to be more pronounced superiorly than inferiorly, and may partially explain the clinically observed collapse sequence which usually begins just beneath the subchondral bone. The elastic instabilities found to occur at the peripheral aspects of the viable, weight-bearing subchondral region suggest that fracture of the subchondral bone is caused by excessive compressive hoop stress. The increased functional demand placed upon viable bone bordering on an infarct tends to enhance the sclerosing effects of hypervascularity.

Male/female considerations

Although the radii of the right and left femoral heads are practically identical for any individual, the femoral head is significantly smaller in females than in males in relation to pelvic dimensions (Fig. 5.74). This may result in an increased stress level in the hip joints of females. Because of the greater breadth of the female lesser pelvis, due to the adaptation for childbearing, the weight of the individual acting through the body's centre of gravity lies at a greater distance from the centre of the hip joint (Fig. 5.75). This longer resistance arm, coupled with the shorter lever arm of gluteus medius reduces the mechanical advantage of the abductor muscles. Consequently, greater abductor force is required to control pelvic tilt. Moreover, the greater force requirement acts over a smaller femoral head, resulting in greater femoral head pressures in females. It would appear, therefore, that the adaptation to childbearing, and its effects on the female pelvis, is a major contributing factor to mechanical dimorphism of the human hip.

Fig. 5.74 Male/female distribution of the ratio of femoral head radius to distance between the hip joints. (Adapted from Brinckman P., Hoefert H., Jongen H. Th. (1981). Sex differences in the skeletal geometry of the human pelvis and hip joint. *Journal of Biomechanics*, **14**, 427–30.)

Radius of femoral head
Distance of hip joints

Fig. 5.75 The lever and resistance arms acting about the hip joint in males and females.

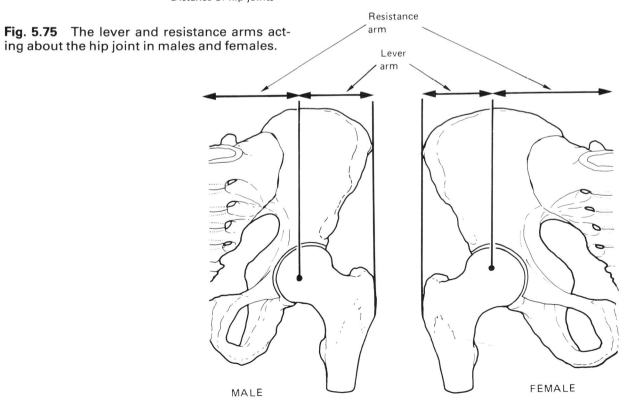

THE KNEE JOINT

Introduction

The knee joint is the largest and one of the most complex joints of the body. It is a synovial bicondylar hinge joint between the condyles of the femur and those of the tibia with the patella anteriorly (Fig. 5.76a). Three separate articulations may be identified: the two femorotibial joints and the femoropatellar articulation. The arrangement of the synovial membrane suggests that these three articulations were completely separate at some stage in human evolution. However, in *Homo sapiens* the three joint cavities are not separate being connected by restricted openings thus forming a large single joint cavity.

The knee joint satisfies the requirements of a weight-bearing joint by allowing free movement in one plane only combined with considerable stability, particularly in extension. Usually stability and mobility are incompatible functions of a joint, with the majority of joints sacrificing one for the other. However, at the knee both functions are secured by the interaction of ligaments and muscles, and complex gliding and rolling movements at the articular surfaces. Nevertheless, the relatively poor degree of interlocking of the articular surfaces, which is essential for great mobility, renders it liable to strains and dislocations. Although functionally the knee joint is a hinge joint, allowing flexion and extension in the sagittal plane, it also permits a small amount of rotation of the leg, particularly when the knee is flexed and the foot is off the ground.

The support of the weight of the body on the vertically opposed ends of the two largest bones in the body is obviously an unstable arrangement. However, security at the knee is ensured by a number of compensating mechanisms. Among these are an expansion of the weight-bearing surfaces of both the femur and the tibia, the presence of strong collateral and intracapsular ligaments, a strong capsule and the reinforcing effects of aponeuroses and tendons.

The knee joint plays an important role in locomotion, being the shortener and lengthener of the lower limb. It can also be considered to work by axial compression under the action of gravity. Being endowed with powerful muscles it acts with the ankle joint as a strong forward propeller of the body. It receives and absorbs vigorous stresses which the lateral movements of the body in the frontal plane and axial rotations in the transverse plane impart to it.

Because the femoral neck overhangs the shaft, the anatomical axes of the femur and tibia do not coincide, but form an outward opening angle between 170–175° (the *femorotibial angle*). However, the joint centres of the hip, knee and ankle all lie on a straight line, which is the mechanical axis of the lower limb (Fig. 5.76b). In the leg, this axis coincides with the anatomical axis of the tibia, while in the thigh it forms an angle of some 6° with the axis of the femoral shaft. Because the hip joints are further apart than the ankles, the mechanical axis of the lower limb runs obliquely inferiorly and medially, and forms an angle of 3° with the vertical. This latter angle is larger the wider the pelvis, as in females. In some pathological conditions, the femorotibial angle may be increased or decreased giving the appearance of 'bowlegs' or 'knock-knees', genu varus and genu valgus, respectively. Genu valgus is not uncommon in the toddler, generally disappearing with growth.

The transverse axis of the knee joint is horizontal, with the common axis of both knee joints lying in a frontal plane. This axis does not bisect the femorotibial angle, so that the angle between it and the tibia is larger (about 93°) than that with the femur (about 81°) (Fig. 5.76b). Comparing the axes of the hip, knee and ankle joints in upright standing, the knee maintains a position of inwards rotation with respect to both the head and neck of the femur, and the lower end of the tibia.

b

Fig. 5.76 **a** = Anteroposterior and lateral radiograph of the knee. **b** = The anatomical and mechanical axes of the femur and tibia.

a

Articular surfaces

Femur

The articular surfaces of the femur are the two condylar areas which rest on the tibia, and the patellar surface which unites the condyles in front and is opposed to the deep surface of the patella (Fig. 5.77a). At the junction of the condylar and patellar surfaces are two faint grooves. Laterally this groove is almost transverse, being emphasized at each end, while on the medial condyle the medial end of the groove begins further forwards passing obliquely backwards and disappears before reaching the lateral edge. In this region there is a narrow crescentic area marked off where the patella articulates in acute flexion. The medial condylar area can be divided into two parts, a posterior part parallel to the lateral condyle and equal in extent, and an anterior triangular extension which passes obliquely and laterally. The patellar surface is divided by a well-marked groove into a smaller medial part and a larger and more prominent lateral part.

When viewed from below the femoral condyles form two prominences convex in both planes, being longer anteroposteriorly than transversely. They are not identical since the medial condyle juts out more than the lateral and is also narrower. In addition, their long axes are not parallel but diverge posteriorly (Fig. 5.77b). The intercondylar notch, however, continues the line of the groove of the patellar surface. In the transverse plane the convexity of the femoral condyles corresponds more or less to the concavity of the tibial condyles, whereas in the sagittal plane the radius of curvature of the condyles is not uniform but varies as a spiral. The manner in which the condyles become increasingly flatter from before backwards is particularly significant in the mechanics of the joint.

The spirals of the femoral condyle are not simple spirals, even though their radii of curvature increase regularly, because they do not have a single centre of rotation but a series of centres which themselves lie on a spiral. Thus the curve of the condyles represents a spiral of a spiral (Fig. 5.77c). On each condyle can be identified the groove separating the condylar and patellar surface areas. Both anterior and posterior to this point the radius of curvature decreases. However, it must be remembered that the two condyles do not show the same curvature, thus their radii of curvature will differ. The internal architecture of the femoral condyles will reflect their geometry as well as the stresses to which they are subjected (see Fig. 5.105, p. 507).

Fig. 5.77 The articular surfaces of the right femur. **a** = From in front and behind. **b** = From below. **c** = The spiral of the femoral articular condyles (paramedian section).

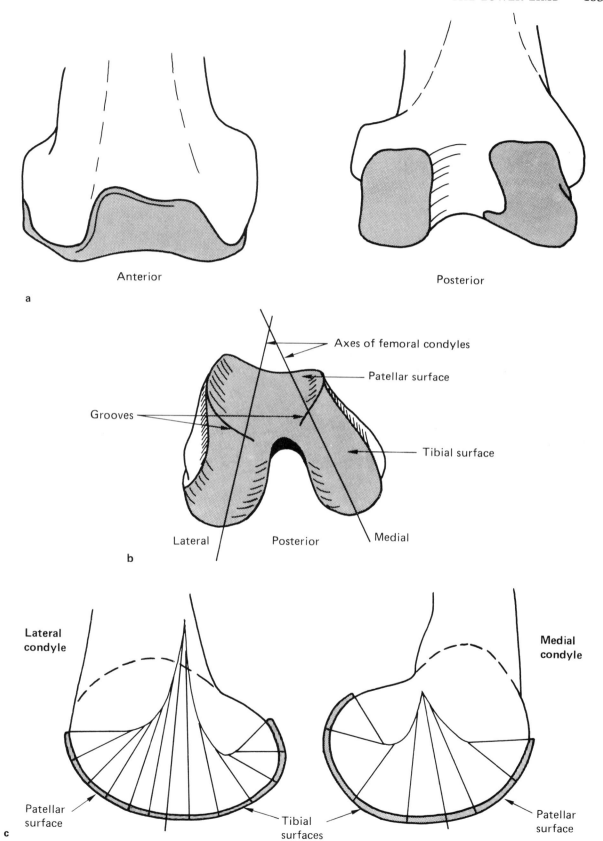

Anterior

Posterior

a

Axes of femoral condyles

Patellar surface

Grooves

Tibial surface

Lateral   Posterior   Medial

b

Lateral condyle

Medial condyle

Patellar surface

Tibial surfaces

Patellar surface

c

Fig. 5.77

Tibia

The articular surfaces of the tibia are carti-lage-covered areas on the upper surface of each tibial condyle, being separated from each other by the intercondylar eminence and triangular intercondylar areas in front and behind (Fig. 5.78a). The articular areas are comparatively flat following the slight (3–5°) posteroinferior inclination of the tibial condyles with respect to the horizontal. The medial articular surface is larger, oval and slightly concave. The lateral articular surface is smaller, rounded and concave from side-to-side, but concavoconvex from front-to-back (Fig. 5.78b). Posteriorly, the lateral surface extends downwards over the condyle in relation to the tendon of popliteus. The fossae of the articular surfaces of the tibia are deepened by the menisci, intervening between the femur and tibia. The menisci rest on a flattened strip at the periphery of each tibial condyle. Again the internal archi-tecture reflects the shape of the upper end of the tibia and the stresses to which it is subjected (see Fig. 5.105, p.507).

The basic shapes of the articular surfaces of the tibia and femur essentially only allow movement in one plane, that is flexion and extension. Axial rotation involves the twist-ing of the femur against the tibia, or vice versa, during which the intercondylar emi-nence of the tibia, lodging in the intercondy-lar notch of the femur, acts as a pivot. The pivot consists of the intercondylar tubercles which form the lateral border of the medial condyle and the medial border of the lateral condyle. Through this latter point runs the vertical axis about which axial rotation occurs.

Patella

The articular surface of the patella is oval and can be divided into a larger lateral and a smaller medial area by a vertical ridge, for corresponding areas on the femur. Two faint transverse ridges separate three facets on each side, and a further faint vertical ridge separates a medial perpendicular facet from the main medial area (Fig. 5.78c). In acute flexion, this medial facet articulates with the crescentic facet of the medial femoral con-dyle. The remaining facets articulate in suc-cession from above downwards with the patellar surface of the femur as the joint moves from flexion to full extension. Because of the stresses to which the patella is subjected, particularly during locomotion, the cartilage on its deep surface is extremely thick, and may be the thickest of anywhere in the body.

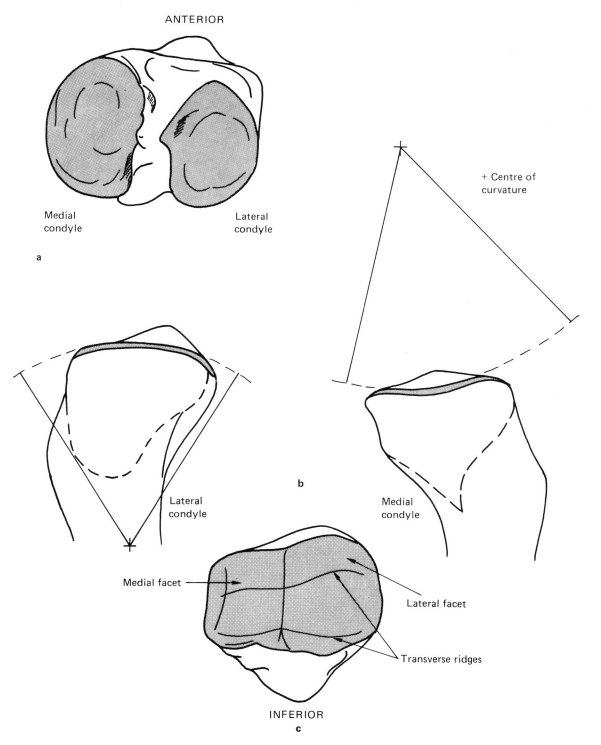

ANTERIOR

Medial
condyle

Lateral
condyle

a

+ Centre of
curvature

Lateral
condyle

b

Medial
condyle

Medial facet

Lateral facet

Transverse ridges

INFERIOR
c

Fig. 5.78 The articular surfaces of the right tibia: **a** = from above; **b** = schematic representation of the anteroposterior condylar curvatures; **c** = the articular surface of the right patella.

Joint capsule

The knee joint is surrounded by a thick ligamentous sheath composed mainly of muscle tendons and their expansions (Fig. 5.79). There is no complete, independent fibrous capsule uniting the two bones; only occasionally are there true capsular fibres running between them. The capsular attachment to the femur is deficient anteriorly, where it blends with the fused tendons of the quadriceps muscles. Its attachment to the tibia is more complete, being deficient only in the region of the tibial tuberosity, which gives attachment to the ligamentum patellae. In spite of its composite nature, it is nevertheless convenient to think of the joint capsule as a cylindrical sleeve passing between femur and tibia, with a deficiency anteriorly which lodges the patella.

Posteriorly the true capsular fibres arise from the femoral condyles, just above the articular surfaces, and the intercondylar line, and pass vertically downwards to attach to the posterior border of the upper end of the tibia. At the side of the joint, capsular fibres descend from the femoral to the tibial condyles. They blend posteriorly with a ligamentous network, and anteriorly with the various tendinous expansions of the quadriceps.

Capsular strengthening

The majority of what is seen and taken for as the knee joint capsule is in fact the ligamentous feltwork associated with the joint. This feltwork is extremely important as it provides the capsule with its strength, as well as providing the necessary control and restriction to movement that is required at the knee.

Oblique popliteal ligament (Fig. 5.79a)

The central region of the posterior part of the capsule is strengthened by the *oblique popliteal ligament*, an expansion of the semimembranosus tendon. It passes upwards and laterally to attach to the intercondylar line of the femur. It has large foramina for the vessels and nerves which perforate it.

Arcuate popliteal ligament (Fig. 5.79a)

The lower lateral part of the capsule is strengthened by the *arcuate popliteal ligament*, as it passes from the back of the head of the fibula arching upwards and medially over the popliteus tendon to spread out over the posterior surface. The most medial part of the arcuate ligament arches downwards onto the posterior part of the intercondylar area of the tibia, while the most lateral of the fibres appear as a separate band that runs to the back of the lateral femoral condyle.

On the lateral side of the joint the true capsular fibres are short and weak, only bridging the interval between the femoral and tibial condyles. Indeed, some of them are separated from the lateral meniscus by the passage of the popliteal tendon.

Because the points of attachment of both collateral ligaments lie behind the vertical axis of the bones, they are most tightly stretched in extension and so prevent hyperextension. They will also prevent any abduction or adduction of the femur and tibia. In extension, the fibular collateral ligament is directed downwards, while the tibial collateral ligament runs downwards and forwards. This relationship prevents rotation of the femur medially or the tibia laterally. With the knee flexed the ligaments are relaxed and rotation can occur relatively easily.

At the front of the joint the ligamentous sheath is mainly composed of the fused tendons of the various quadriceps muscles (see Fig. 5.79b). The fibres of these tendons descend from above and each side to attach to the margins of the patella as far as the attachment of the ligamentum patellae. Superficial tendinous fibres pass downwards over the patella into the ligamentum patellae. The aponeurotic tendons of vastus medialis and vastus lateralis expand over the sides of the joint capsule as the medial and lateral patellar retinacula respectively, to insert into the front of the tibial condyles and oblique lines of the condyles as far to the sides as the collateral ligaments. Medially the retinaculum blends with the periosteum of the tibial shaft; while laterally it blends with the overlying iliotibial tract.

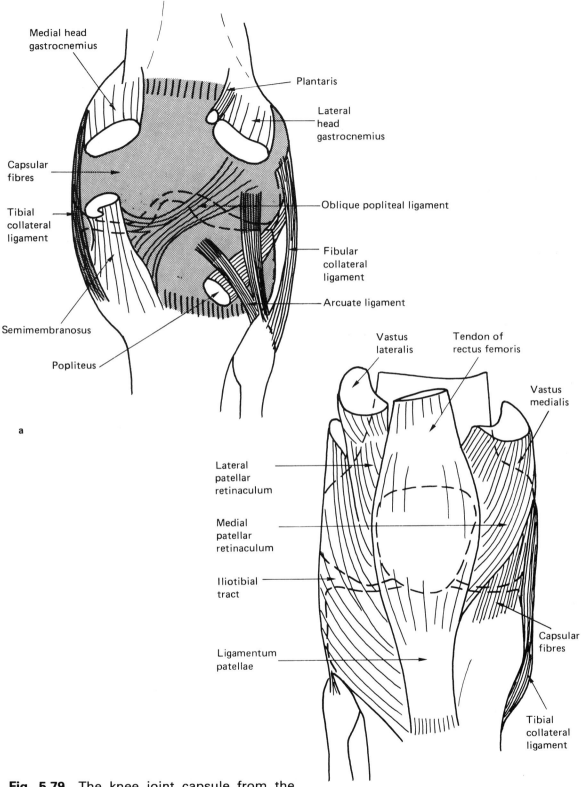

Fig. 5.79 The knee joint capsule from the front and back showing the contributions from the various muscles and ligaments crossing the joint: **a** = posterior; **b** = anterior.

Some tendinous fibres of the vastus muscles pass obliquely downwards across the patella into the opposite retinaculum. Other deeper fibres from each side of the patella pass across to the front of each femoral epicondyle.

Ligamentum patellae (see Fig. 7.79b)

The ligamentum patellae is the continuation of the tendon of the quadriceps femoris muscle. It is a strong, flat band attaching around the apex of the patella, being continuous over the front of the patella with fibres of the quadriceps tendon. It extends to the tibial tuberosity, ending somewhat obliquely as it is prolonged downwards further on the lateral than on the medial side. Between the ligament and the bone, immediately above its insertion, a deep infrapatellar bursa intervenes, while in the subcutaneous tissue over the ligament is the large subcutaneous infrapatellar bursa.

Superficial to the fibrous bands associated with the quadriceps complex are strong expansions of the fascia lata covering the front and sides of the joint. As it descends to attach to the tibial tuberosity and oblique lines of the condyles, it overlies and blends with the patellar retinacula. The thickened and strong iliotibial tract descends across the anterolateral part of the joint to insert into the lateral tibial condyle after blending with the joint capsule (see Fig. 5.79b). A strong band passes forwards from the tract to attach to the upper part of the lateral edge of the patella; this is the superior patellar retinaculum. On the thinner medial side of the patella, the fascia lata sends a few fibres inferiorly to blend with the expansion of sartorius.

The whole of the anterior covering of the knee joint, together with the patella, is kept tense by the tone of the extensor muscles, being tightly braced when these muscles are active in extension. This appears to contradict the philosophy of hinge joints in that the extensor portion of joint capsules should be loose in the extended position in order to permit free flexion to occur. At the knee, the extensor part of the capsule is in reality continued into the extensor muscles above rather than being attached directly to bone. Consequently, it may be kept relatively taut in all positions of the joint.

Ligaments

As is characteristic of all hinge joints, collateral ligaments are found at the sides of the knee joint, although the form of the medial and lateral ligaments differs greatly.

Tibial collateral ligament (Fig. 5.80a,b)

The tibial (medial) collateral ligament is a strong flat band extending from the medial epicondyle of the femur passing downwards and slightly forwards to attach to the medial condyle of the tibia and the medial side of its shaft. A few fibres at the femoral attachment can usually be traced upwards into adductor magnus. Consequently, the tibial collateral ligament has been regarded as having been formed, in part at least, from an original tibial insertion of adductor magnus. The most superficial fibres of the ligament descend below the level of the tibial tuberosity; deeper fibres have a shorter course from femur to tibia, with the deepest fibres spreading triangularly to attach to the medial meniscus. The tibial collateral ligament is 8–9 cm long, being well-defined anteriorly where it blends with the medial patellar retinaculum; however, bursae may partially separate them. Under cover of the posterior border of the ligament a downward expansion from semimembranosus reaches the tibial shaft, adding considerable strength to this aspect of the joint capsule. Between this expansion and the ligament the inferior medial genicular vessels and nerve run.

Fibular collateral ligament (Fig. 5.80a,c)

In contrast the fibular (lateral) collateral ligament is a rounded cord some 5 cm long which stands clear of the thin lateral part of the fibrous capsule. It is attached to the lateral epicondyle of the femur above and behind the groove for popliteus, and passes down to attach to the lateral surface of the head of the fibula in front of the apex, splitting the tendon of biceps femoris as it does so. Occasionally the fibular collateral ligament continues into the upper part of peroneus longus, and can be thought of as a femoral origin of the muscle. Passing deep to the ligament is the tendon of popliteus, together with the inferior lateral genicular vessels and nerve as they run forwards.

Fibular collateral ligament   Tibial collateral ligament

a

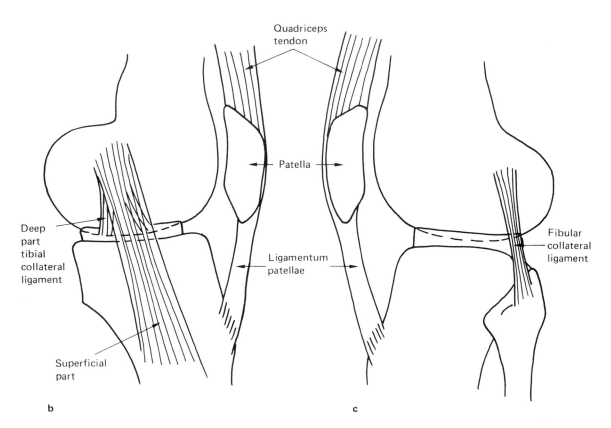

Quadriceps
tendon

Patella

Deep
part
tibial
collateral
ligament

Ligamentum
patellae

Fibular
collateral
ligament

Superficial
part

b   c

Fig. 5.80a–c The tibial (medial) and fibular (lateral) collateral ligaments of the knee joint.

Synovial membrane and bursae

The synovial (joint) cavity of the knee is the largest joint space within the body, having an irregular shape with identifiable regions in free communication with each other. The synovial membrane lines the joint capsule and is reflected onto the bone as far as the margins of the articular cartilage. The central part of the joint space lies between the deep surface of the patella anteriorly and the patellar surface of the femur and the cruciate ligaments posteriorly. It extends outwards to pass between the femoral and tibial condyles and also above and below the menisci. From the articular margins of the patella, the synovial membrane passes in all directions onto the deep surface of the anterior joint capsule. Below the patella, however, the synovial membrane is pushed backwards into the joint space by the infrapatellar fat pad, lying on the deep surface of the ligamentum patellae and extending towards the intercondylar notch. The synovial reflections over this fat pad are thrown into a series of folds (Fig. 5.81a). A vertical crescentic fold, the infrapatellar fold, passes in the medial plane towards the cruciate ligaments, attaching to the intercondylar fossa in front of the anterior cruciate ligament and lateral to the posterior cruciate ligament. From the edges of the patella horizontal double folds of synovial membrane, the alar folds, project into the interior of the joint. They also cover collections of fat.

Several recesses extend from the central part of the joint cavity. The suprapatellar bursa extends three fingers' breadth above the patella between the femoral shaft and the quadriceps femoris muscle. Initially it develops as a separate bursa, but soon communicates freely with the joint space. To the upper part of the suprapatellar bursa is attached to the articularis genus (see Fig. 5.82a), bundles of muscle fibres from the deep surface of vastus intermedius, which serve to maintain the bursa during extension of the knee. There are also recesses behind the posterior part of each femoral condyle. In this region the two heads of gastrocnemius overlie the joint capsule, and there is usually a bursa between each muscle head and the capsule (see Fig. 5.82). The bursa under the medial head of gastrocnemius occasionally communicates with the joint cavity; it may also enlarge and present as a cyst behind the knee joint. The recesses behind the femoral condyles are separated by the interposition of the cruciate ligaments, which are intracapsular but extrasynovial. A vertical fold of synovial membrane covers the cruciate ligaments on their fronts and sides, but not posteriorly where the posterior cruciate ligament blends with the joint capsule (Fig. 5.81b).

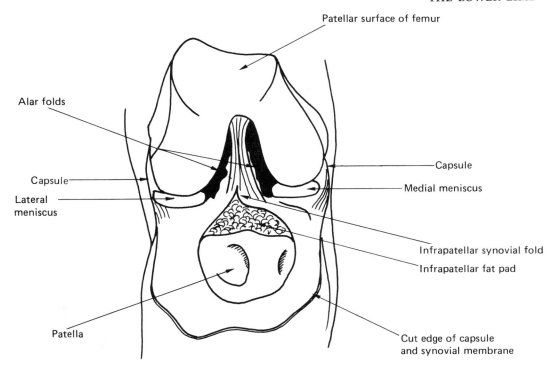

Patellar surface of femur

Alar folds

Capsule

Capsule

Medial meniscus

Lateral meniscus

Infrapatellar synovial fold

Infrapatellar fat pad

Patella

Cut edge of capsule and synovial membrane

a

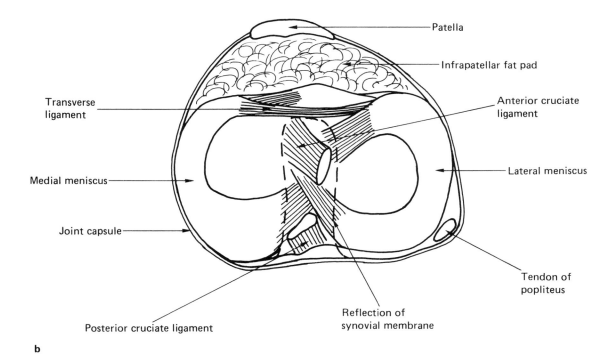

Patella

Infrapatellar fat pad

Transverse ligament

Anterior cruciate ligament

Medial meniscus

Lateral meniscus

Joint capsule

Tendon of popliteus

Posterior cruciate ligament

Reflection of synovial membrane

b

Fig. 5.81   a = The right knee joint opened from the front showing the infrapatellar fat pad and synovial folds. **b** = Intracapsular reflections of the synovial membrane on the tibia.

The remaining recess of the joint cavity is associated with the tendon of popliteus (Fig. 5.82b). As the tendon passes from its intracapsular femoral attachment, the synovial membrane invests its medial side thereby separating it from the lateral meniscus, except where the tendon attaches to the meniscus. As the popliteal tendon emerges through the back of the joint capsule, it takes with it a synovial extension associated with its deep surface which lies between the tendon and the superior tibiofibular joint. Occasionally the cavity of the superior tibiofibular joint communicates with the subpopliteal bursa, and hence with the knee joint itself.

Since all of the tendons and muscles which cross the knee run parallel to the bones, and thus pull lengthwise across the joint, there are numerous other bursae associated with it: the subcutaneous prepatellar bursa (Fig. 5.82a) lies between the skin and the lower part of the patella while the subcutaneous infrapatellar bursa overlies the patellar ligament; the subfascial prepatellar bursa lies between the tendinous and fascial expansions that pass over the patella, while the subtendinous prepatellar bursa separates the deep and superficial tendinous fibres; finally there is the deep infrapatellar bursa which lies between the patellar ligament and the upper part of the tibia, being separated from the knee joint by the infrapatellar fat pad (Fig. 5.82a). On the lateral side of the joint is the subtendinous bursa of biceps femoris between the fibular collateral ligament and the tendon. As well as the subpopliteal bursa an additional bursa may intervene between the popliteus tendon and the fibular collateral ligament. Medially the bursa anserina separates the tendons of sartorius, gracilis and semitendinosus from the tibial collateral ligament. There may be, in addition, bursae intervening between the individual tendons. The semimembranosus bursa (Fig. 5.82) lies between the muscle and the tibia and tibial collateral ligament.

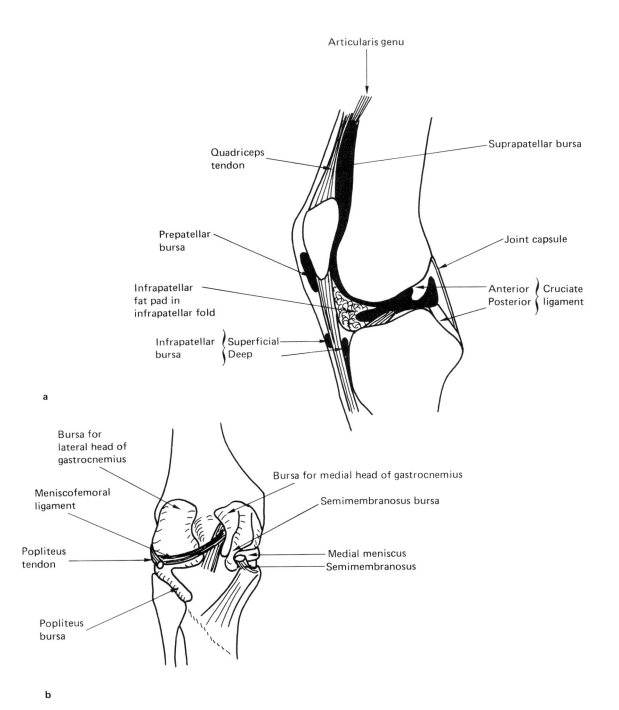

Fig. 5.82 Synovial membrane and bursae of the knee:
a = paramedian section; **b** = from behind.

Intra-articular structures

Within the capsule of the knee joint are found two sets of structures which play an important part in the functioning of the knee from both anatomical and mechanical viewpoints. These structures are the cruciate ligaments, anterior and posterior, and the menisci, medial and lateral. Of these, the cruciate ligaments are extrasynovial.

Cruciate ligaments

The cruciate ligaments are so called because of the way they cross each other between their attachments, the anterior and posterior ligaments being named according to their tibial attachments.

Anterior cruciate ligament (Fig. 5.83, see also Fig. 5.81b).   The anterior cruciate ligament (ACL) is attached to the tibia immediately anterolateral to the anterior tibial spine. It passes beneath the transverse ligament, blending somewhat with the anterior horn of the lateral meniscus, and runs posteriorly, laterally and proximally to attach to the posterior part of the medial surface of the lateral femoral condyle. The femoral attachment is not as strong as that to the tibia and takes the form of a segment of a circle. During its passage from tibia to femur it undergoes a medial spiral of some 110°. The ACL can be divided anatomically into two parts: an anteromedial band attaching to the anteromedial region of the tibial attachment, and the posterolateral bulk which constitutes the remainder of the ligament. The posterolateral bulk of the ligament is said to be taut in extension, with the anteromedial band lax (and vice versa in flexion). Functionally the ligament should be considered as a continuum with part of it being taut throughout the whole range of knee movement, thereby having a restraining influence in all positions of the joint.

Posterior cruciate ligament (Fig. 5.83, see also Fig. 5.81b).   The posterior cruciate ligament (PCL) attaches to a depression in the posterior intercondylar area of the tibia. It runs anteriorly, medially and proximally, passing on the medial side of the ACL to attach to the anterior part of the lateral surface of the medial femoral condyle. The PCL is shorter and less oblique in its course, as well as being almost twice as strong in tension, than the ACL. It is closely aligned to the centre of rotation of the knee joint and, as such, may be its principal stabilizer. Like the ACL, the PCL can be divided into two parts, an anterolateral band and a posteromedial band. The more superficial posteromedial fibres also have an attachment to the posterior horn of the lateral meniscus, and constitute the meniscofemoral ligament. Functionally, however, it is best considered as a continuum.

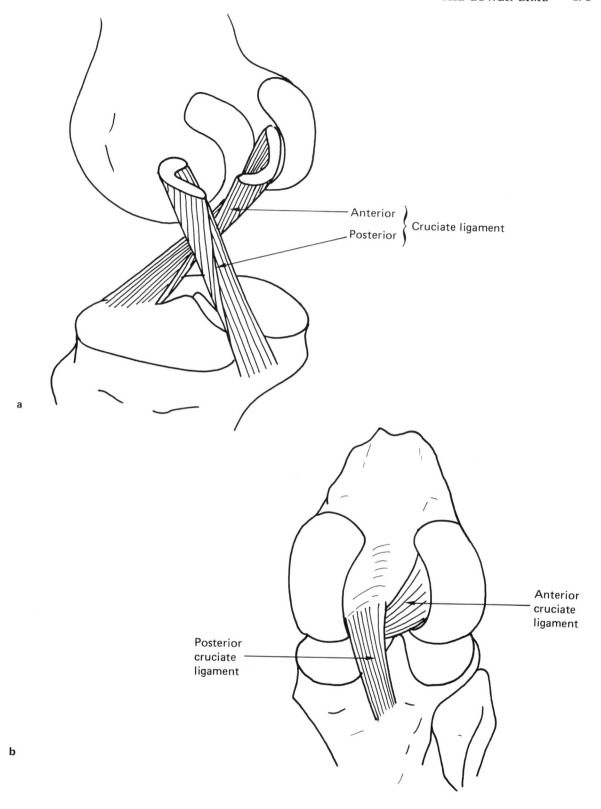

Fig. 5.83 The anterior and posterior cruciate ligaments:
a = oblique view showing twisting of fibres; **b** = posterior
view showing them crossing in space.

The crossing and twisting of the cruciate ligaments as they pass from their tibial to their femoral attachments arises because on the tibia the attachments are more or less in a sagittal plane, while on the femur they are almost in a frontal plane. The cruciate ligaments are said to have a constant length ratio of 5:3 (ACL:PCL), and that this ratio together with their sites of attachment are the primary factors which control the type of movement seen at the knee joint (Fig. 5.84). They provide, almost exclusively, the resistance to anterior and posterior displacements of the tibia with respect to the femur. The ACL provides approximately 86% of the restraint to anterior displacement, and the PCL about 94% of the restraint to posterior displacement of the tibia on the femur. Rupture of the ACL results in very little increase in the anterior draw (anterior tibial displacement at 90° flexion), while rupture of the PCL results in a posterior draw of up to 25 mm. The latter is probably due to lack of collateral resistance to posterior displacement and a lax capsule posteriorly. In addition to their role in an anteroposterior direction, the cruciate ligaments also provide some mediolateral stability. The PCL provides 36% of the resistance to lateral displacement, with the ACL providing 30% of the resistance to medial displacement.

Microscopically, the cruciate ligaments are composed mainly of collagen fibres, with a small proportion of elastic fibres (10%), thereby giving the ligaments high tensile strength. These fibres are arranged to form fasciculi a few millimetres in diameter. In the ACL two types of fasciculi can be identified: those that run directly between the tibial and femoral attachments, and those that spiral around the longitudinal axis of the ligament, with a helical axis of 25°. This helical arrangement of many of the fibres has important consequences. When loaded lightly only a few fibres are under tension, but as the load increases the ligament unwinds bringing more fibres into play and effectively increasing its strength. Two phases of loading of the cruciate ligaments can be identified; prior to the yield point the deformation is elastic due to the stretching and unwinding of the ligament. Further

loading, however, causes disruption of the crosslinks between fibres and permanent deformation occurs. Although gross damage may not be apparent until this later phase, microfailure can occur at stresses below the yield point. The strength of the ligaments can be influenced by several factors:

1. tensile strength, but not stiffness, decreases significantly with age;
2. cyclical loading, as in gait, softens the ligaments causing a decrease in yield point, however, recovery occurs within a few hours;
3. immobilization may cause a decrease in tensile strength of up to 60%, even in otherwise healthy ligaments; this is probably due to disuse atrophy, recovery does occur but it may take many months;
4. internal rotation reduces tensile strength by as much as 6%, consequently torsional forces are potentially much more damaging;
5. exercise may increase strength slightly.

The bony attachments of the ligaments show a complex interdigitation of the collagen fibres from the bone and the ligament, between which is interposed a transitional zone of fibrocartilage. This allows a gradual change in stiffness and prevents stress concentrations in this region.

The cruciate ligaments possess a fairly good blood supply, derived mainly from the middle genicular artery, with a small contribution from the inferior lateral genicular artery. The blood vessels form a periligamentous sheath around the ligaments from which small penetrating vessels arise.

Mechanoreceptors, resembling Golgi tendon organs, are situated near the femoral attachments of the ligaments, located around the periphery where maximum bending occurs, and running parallel to the long axis of the ligament. They probably convey information regarding angular acceleration, and may be involved in reflexes to protect the knee from potential injury. The nerve supply enters and leaves via the femoral attachment of each ligament.

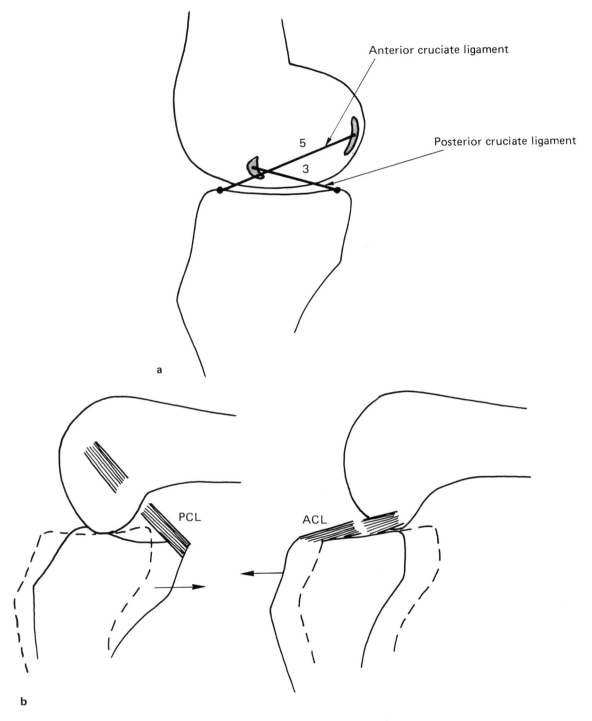

Fig. 5.84   a = The length ratio of the two cruciate ligaments.
b = Tibial displacements with ACL or PCL rupture.

The menisci

The menisci are so called because of their 'half-moon' or 'meniscal' configuration; they may also be referred to as semilunar cartilages. Intra-articular discs are found where three conditions exist: (1) in joints with a large degree of rotation about an axis perpendicular to the articular surface; (2) in joints with flat articular surfaces, and (3) where the forces across a joint tend to bring the two surfaces together in a rotatory movement. The menisci in the knee are slightly inclined to the tibial surface, thus enabling a viscous lubricating film to be set up in the region of the loadline of the joint. Joints without menisci (surgically removed) show an increased mechanical curvature. The function of the menisci is four-fold:

1. to increase the congruence between the articular surfaces of the femur and tibia;
2. to participate in weight bearing across the joint;
3. to act as shock absorbers;
4. to aid lubrication.

The menisci are first recognisable as a region of closely packed cells with a long axis transverse to that of the limb at about 8 weeks *in utero*. By week 19, both menisci are well-developed with well-defined collagen arrangements. During the next 4 weeks, extensive collagenous rearrangement occurs so that at week 23 the collagen bundles lie parallel to one another and show the adult meniscal morphology even though there is no fibrocartilage present. However, the fetal meniscus has a high cellular content and is well vascularized. Postnatal changes in the menisci are:

1. a gradual decrease in cellularity;
2. decrease in vascularity from centrally outwards;
3. growth to match the femoral and tibial enlargements;
4. a configurational change which accommodates the changing contact areas, with growth of the menisci being linearly related to that of the tibial condyles;
5. an increase in collagen content.

The higher vascularity of the young meniscus results in an increased efficiency of repair and a reduced tendency to injury. As age increases, the ratio of collagenous to non-collagenous proteins increases leading to a lower tensile strength. This changing biochemical balance is an important determinant of collagen fibre arrangement. The histological arrangement being accounted for by the adaptation of the menisci to weight bearing, with the collagen fibres becoming more circumferentially arranged. This latter refinement occurs at about 3 years, following the attainment of an upright posture and gait in the infant. The change in fibrillar arrangement is an important factor confirming the role of the menisci in weight bearing.

The menisci are crescentic-shaped structures of triangular cross-section, being composed normally of fibrocartilage, interposed between the femoral and tibial condyles (Fig. 5.85). Their thick peripheral border is convex and attached to the deep surface of the joint capsule. These capsular fibres attach the menisci to the tibial condyles and constitute the medial and lateral coronary ligaments. By its capsular attachment, the medial meniscus is anchored to the tibial collateral ligament, whereas the lateral meniscus is attached only to the weak fibres of the lateral side of the capsule and not at all to the fibular collateral ligament. In addition where the lateral meniscus is crossed by the popliteal tendon, the periphery of the meniscus is not attached to the joint capsule. Consequently, the lateral meniscus is much more mobile than the medial. The inner border of each meniscus is thin and concave forming the free inner edge. Superiorly the meniscal surface is smooth and concave articulating with the femoral condyles. The horns of the menisci are the sites of attachment of the meniscus to the tibia, being regions where fibrocartilage gives way to bands of fibrous tissue.

ANTERIOR

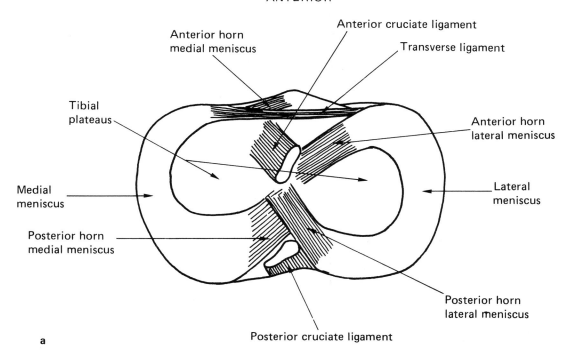

Anterior horn
medial meniscus

Anterior cruciate ligament

Transverse ligament

Tibial
plateaus

Anterior horn
lateral meniscus

Medial
meniscus

Lateral
meniscus

Posterior horn
medial meniscus

Posterior horn
lateral meniscus

Posterior cruciate ligament

a

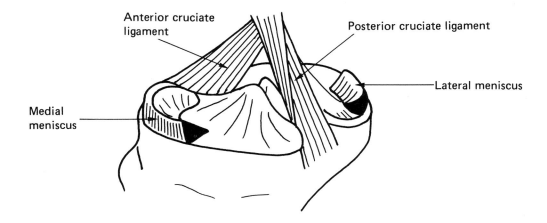

Anterior cruciate
ligament

Posterior cruciate ligament

Medial
meniscus

Lateral meniscus

b

Fig. 5.85 **a** = The menisci seen from above. **b** = The menisci, oblique view showing their triangular cross-section.

Medial meniscus (see Fig. 5.85) The medial meniscus is the larger of the two, being semicircular in shape, with its posterior part being broader than that anteriorly. The anterior horn is attached to the anterior part of the intercondylar area on the tibia immediately in front of the ACL. The most posterior of these fibres are continuous with the transverse ligament of the knee. The posterior horn attaches to the posterior intercondylar area between the PCL posteriorly and the posterior horn of the lateral meniscus anteriorly. Its entire periphery attaches to the joint capsule.

Lateral meniscus (see Fig. 5.85) The lateral meniscus forms about four-fifths of a circle and is of uniform breadth throughout. The two horns of the lateral meniscus are attached close together, the anterior horn attaching in front of the intercondylar eminence posterolateral to the ACL with which it partially blends. In this region it is twisted upwards and backwards as it rests on the sloping bone of the tibial condyle. The posterior horn attaches behind the intercondylar eminence anterior to the posterior horn of the medial meniscus. Posterolaterally the lateral meniscus is grooved by the tendon of popliteus, from which it receives a few fibres.

Meniscal attachments (Fig. 5.86) Besides their capsular attachments the two menisci are attached anteriorly by a fibrous band of variable thickness, the transverse ligament of the knee. A posterior transverse ligament is present in about 20% of knees. The posterior part of the lateral meniscus usually contributes a ligamentous slip to the PCL; this slip splits on the lateral side of the cruciate ligament to run both in front of and behind the ligament. That part which runs anteriorly is the anterior meniscofemoral ligament, while the other is the posterior meniscofemoral ligament. Of the two, the posterior is the more constant, however, when present, both end on the medial femoral condyle in association with the PCL. A few fibres from the anterior horn of the medial meniscus may run with the ACL.

The connection between the lateral meniscus and the PCL is in keeping with the typical lower mammalian situation, in which the lateral meniscus is attached posteriorly to the medial femoral condyle behind the PCL rather than to the tibia.

Posteriorly the lateral meniscus gives rise to some of the fibres of popliteus, while the medial meniscus is attached via the joint capsule to the oblique popliteal ligament, the expansion of semimembranosus.

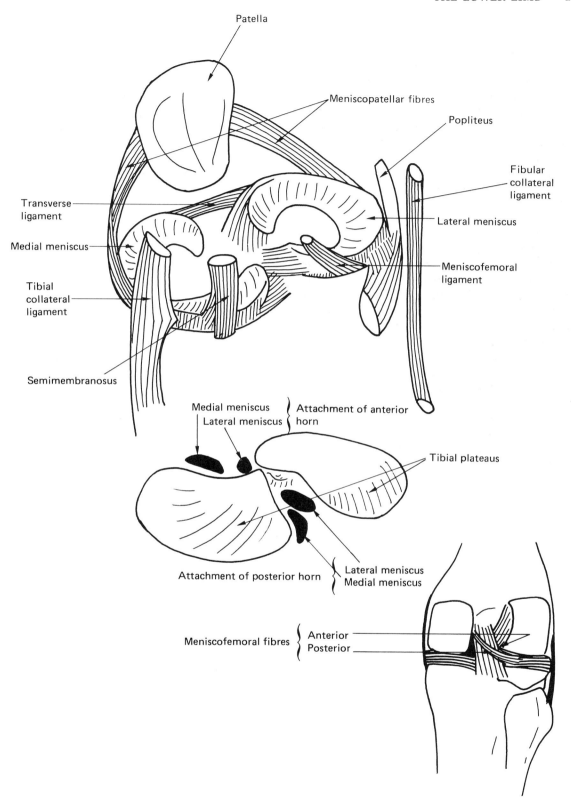

Fig. 5.86 Attachments of the menisci.

Structure Histologically, the fibrocartilaginous menisci are described as being composed of a substance that is between dense fibrous cartilage and hyaline cartilage, containing large collagen bundles embedded in a matrix. The fibrocartilage does, however, retain the ability to change into either hyaline or fibrous cartilage, as is seen in regenerating menisci where the hypertrophic cells form a purely fibrous structure.

Microscopically, the collagen fibres arrange themselves into circumferential (spanning between the tibial attachments) and radial patterns, which are determined by meniscal age and functional requirements (Fig. 5.87). The radially arranged fibres are primarily found at the femoral and tibial surfaces, many of them curving to come to travel perpendicular to the meniscal surface. The orientation of the collagen fibres is closely related to the direction of stresses during weight bearing. Under compression, the major force is outwards and is resisted by the circumferential fibres. The radial fibres probably act as ties to prevent longitudinal splitting.

Severe strain on a meniscus, usually involving rotation, can result in a longitudinal and sometimes a transverse splitting of the fibrocartilage (Fig. 5.88). Because of its attachment to the tibial collateral ligament, the medial meniscus is more frequently injured, with the inner thinner portion separating from the thicker outer part (bucket-handle rupture). The detached part may move into the centre of the joint thereby preventing full extension of the knee.

The menisci receive a blood supply from the middle, medial and lateral inferior genicular arteries. There is a peripheral perimeniscal plexus which gives rise to small penetrating branches which reach the menisci via the coronary ligaments. In the fetus and young child, the entire meniscus is vascularized, but with increasing age the central regions become avascular. By age 11 the adult pattern is seen, whereby only the peripheral 20% and the horns are vascular. The vessels themselves are located mainly within the deep part of the meniscus, with the various surfaces receiving only a limited blood supply. The main source of nutrition of the menisci is via diffusion from the synovial fluid. The outer third of the menisci may be innervated by a few myelinated and non-myelinated fibres. However, no specialized nerve endings have been found so their precise role is not understood, although some will undoubtedly be vasomotor.

Tangential fibres

Thickness of meniscus

Radial fibres on tibial surface

Collagen bundles from radial fibres entering substance of meniscus

Well-orientated circumferential fibres

Fig. 5.87 The arrangement of the collagen bundles within the meniscus.

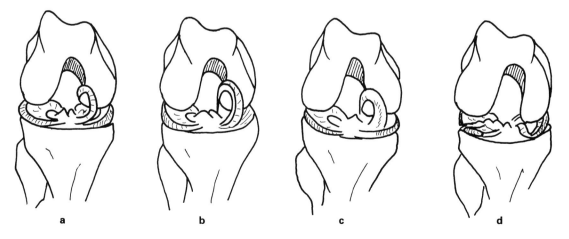

a   b   c   d

Fig. 5.88 Meniscal lesions: **a** = longitudinal splitting; **b** = complete detachment; **c** = complex tear; **d** = transverse tear and detachment of anterior horn.

Blood supply

At the knee there is an important genicular anastomosis which consists of a superficial plexus above and below the patella, and a deep plexus on the joint capsule and the adjacent condylar surfaces of the femur and tibia. Some ten vessels are involved in the anastomosis: two descending from above (the *descending branch* of the *lateral circumflex femoral artery* and the *descending genicular branch* of the femoral artery), three ascending from below (the *circumflex fibular artery* from the posterior tibial artery, and the *anterior* and *posterior tibial recurrent branches* from the anterior tibial artery), and the remainder being branches of the *popliteal artery* (Fig. 5.89). The popliteal artery lies deep within the popliteal fossa, lying on (from above downwards) the fat covering the popliteal surface of the femur, the back of the knee joint, and the fascia covering popliteus. The five branches of the popliteal artery involved in the anastomosis are the *lateral superior* and *inferior*, the *medial superior* and *inferior*, and the *middle genicular* (Fig. 5.89).

Venous drainage of the joint is by corresponding veins accompanying the arteries. However, venostasis is a major contributory factor in degenerative changes of the knee joint.

The lymphatics of the joint drain to the popliteal and inguinal node groups.

Nerve supply

The nerve supply to the joint is from many sources. However, it must be remembered that the articular cartilage has no direct nerve supply. Proprioceptive information is via nerve endings located in the bone, periosteum and cruciate ligaments, while pain and pressure sensitivity comes from endings in the collateral ligaments and joint capsule. The root values of the branches supplying the knee joint are L2 to S3. From the femoral nerve, articular branches reach the joint via the nerves to vastus medialis and through the saphenous nerve. The posterior division of the obturator nerve, after supplying adductor magnus, ends in the knee joint. Both the tibial and common peroneal nerves send articular branches to the joint. Those from the tibial nerve follow the two medial genicular arteries and the middle genicular artery, while those from the common peroneal nerve follow the lateral genicular arteries and the anterior tibial recurrent artery.

Fig. 5.89 Blood supply to the knee joint, together with a schematic representation of the vessels involved in the genicular anastomosis:

P = Popliteal
MSG = Medial superior genicular
LSG = Lateral superior genicular
MIG = Medial inferior genicular
LIG = Lateral inferior genicular
MG = Middle genicular
DG = Descending genicular
LCF = Lateral circumflex femoral
CF = Circumflex fibular
PR = Posterior recurrent
AR = Anterior recurrent
AT = Anterior tibial
PT = Posterior tibial

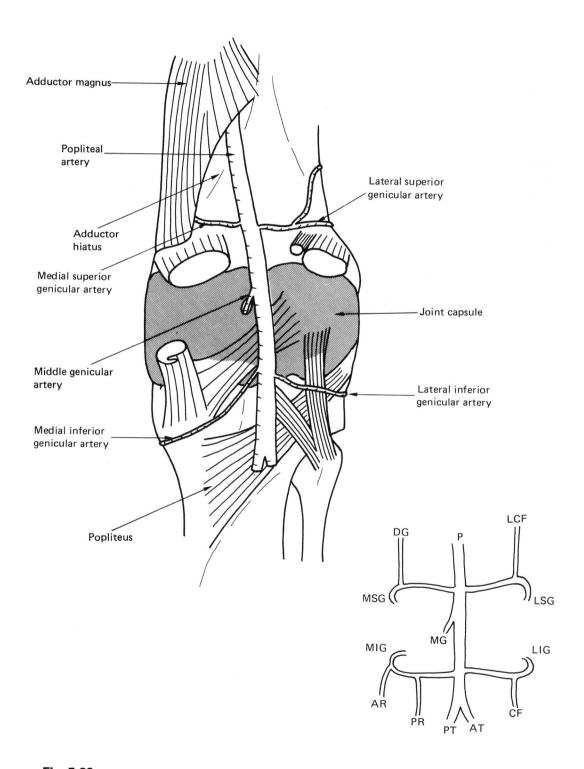

Adductor magnus

Popliteal artery

Adductor hiatus

Medial superior genicular artery

Middle genicular artery

Medial inferior genicular artery

Popliteus

Lateral superior genicular artery

Joint capsule

Lateral inferior genicular artery

DG   P   LCF

MSG   LSG

MIG   MG   LIG

AR   CF

PR   PT   AT

Fig. 5.89

Palpation

Several parts of the knee joint can be readily palpated, particularly at the sides and front, thus confirming the superficial position of the joint within the lower limb. Although many musculotendinous structures cross the joint, they tend to do so posteriorly, together with the major blood vessels and nerves. The following parts of the joint can be easily palpated:

1. the whole of the circumference of the patella, particularly its medial border;
2. the articular margin of each femoral condyle;
3. the anterior articular margin of each tibial condyle;
4. the joint line medially, anteriorly and laterally;
5. the tibial tuberosity together with the ligamentum patellae attaching to it;
6. the adductor tubercle, and the medial and lateral epicondyles of the femur.

No part of the joint can be identified posteriorly. However, the tendons of semitendinosus and semimembranosus medially, and that of biceps femoris laterally stand out and can be identified in the knee flexed against resistance (Fig. 5.90).

The tibial collateral ligament can be palpated on the medial side of the knee, and can be tested for laxity by applying a laterally directed force to the inside of the ankle with the knee held in extension. The fibular collateral ligament can be palpated as a rounded cord above the head of the fibula on the lateral side of the knee, and can be tested for laxity by applying a medially directed force to the outside of the ankle. The ligamentum patellae can be palpated running between the apex of the patella and tibial tuberosity.

The cruciate ligaments are placed deep within the joint, and so cannot be palpated. However, they can be tested for laxity by placing the knee of the supine subject at 90° with the foot flat on the bed, and applying alternative anterior and posterior pressure on the upper end of the tibia. Pressure directed backwards tests the posterior cruciate, while the forwards pressure tests the anterior cruciate.

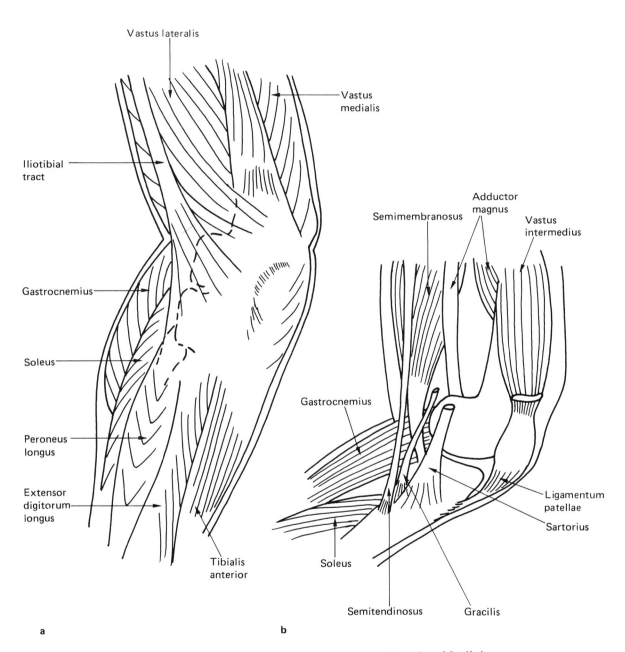

Fig. 5.90 **a** = Lateral relations of the knee joint. **b** = Medial relations of the knee joint.

Relations

On the posterior aspect of the joint is a region known as the popliteal fossa, which contains from superficial to deep the major nerves, veins and arteries passing between the thigh and leg. The fossa is diamond-shaped, being bound below by the medial and lateral heads of gastrocnemius and above by the diverging hamstring tendons. Laterally the tendon of biceps femoris crosses the lateral head of gastrocnemius, while medially the superimposed tendons of semitendinosus and semimembranosus cross the medial head of gastrocnemius. The floor of the popliteal fossa is formed from above downwards by the popliteal surface of the femur, the posterior part of the knee joint capsule, reinforced by the oblique popliteal ligament, and the popliteus with its covering fascia.

The whole of the fossa is covered by dense popliteal fascia, which is continuous with both the fascia of the thigh and that of the leg, being strengthened in this region by transverse fibres as well as by expansions from the tendons of sartorius, gracilis, semitendinosus and biceps femoris (Fig. 5.91). Directly under the fascia are found the tibial and common peroneal divisions of the sciatic nerve, together with the posterior cutaneous nerve of the thigh. Within the fossa, the tibial nerve emerges from under cover of semimembranosus to pass obliquely across the back of the popliteal vessels to lie medial to them on popliteus, deep to gastrocnemius and plantaris. It gives muscular branches to gastrocnemius, plantaris and popliteus, and genicular branches to the knee joint, and the cutaneous sural nerve which eventually pierces the deep fascia in the middle third of the posterior surface of the leg. The common peroneal nerve passes under cover of biceps femoris and its tendon coursing downwards and along the lateral margin of the fossa to reach the back of the head of the fibula. It passes subfascially into the leg by curving around the neck of the fibula where it can be readily palpated. Within the popliteal fossa the common peroneal nerve gives genicular branches to the knee joint, and two cutaneous branches: the lateral cutaneous nerve of the leg, and the peroneal communicating branch which joins the sural nerve.

Just above the popliteal fossa, the femoral vessels lie opposite the posterior border of the femur and the lower end of the adductor canal, against the tendon of adductor magnus. Continuing their backward inclination, they pass through the adductor hiatus into the popliteal fossa, and so become the popliteal vessels. The popliteal artery is the deepest of the major structures within the popliteal fossa lying next to the bone where it is well protected from external trauma but is vulnerable to supracondylar fractures of the femur. It ends by dividing into anterior and posterior tibial arteries at the distal border of popliteus, level with the distal part of the tibial tuberosity. With the knee flexed the popliteal pulse can be felt. Within the fossa the artery gives off the five genicular branches supplying the knee joint and participating in the genicular anastomosis.

The popliteal vein is formed by the anterior and posterior tibial veins at the lower border of popliteus. Ascending through the fossa it crosses from medial to lateral behind the artery, being bound to it by a dense fascial sheath. As well as receiving the genicular veins, the popliteal vein also receives the small (lesser) saphenous vein, which pierces the fascial roof of the fossa.

Both the popliteal artery and vein are embedded in a considerable amount of fat and areolar connective tissue, which also lodges the popliteal lymph nodes.

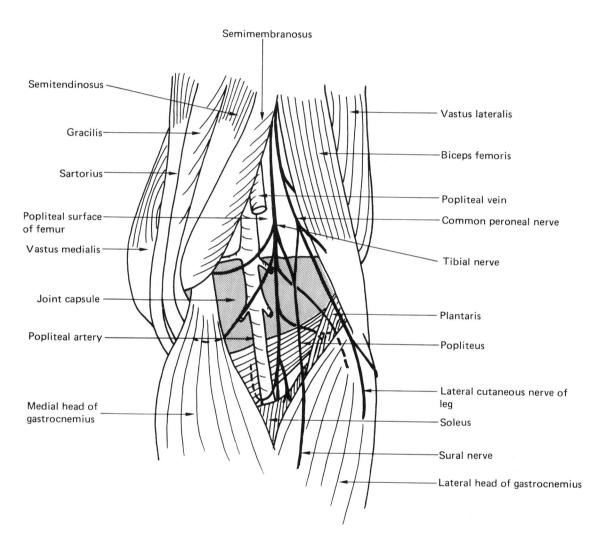

Semimembranosus

Semitendinosus

Gracilis

Sartorius

Popliteal surface
of femur

Vastus medialis

Joint capsule

Popliteal artery

Medial head of
gastrocnemius

Vastus lateralis

Biceps femoris

Popliteal vein

Common peroneal nerve

Tibial nerve

Plantaris

Popliteus

Lateral cutaneous nerve of
leg

Soleus

Sural nerve

Lateral head of gastrocnemius

Fig. 5.91 Posterior relations of the knee joint—the popliteal fossa.

Stability

The stability of the knee joint is primarily maintained by the ligaments associated with the joint, notably the collateral and cruciate ligaments, being reinforced by the musculotendinous ties that cross the joint. In fact it is the interaction between the two sets of ligaments which provides the all round stability of the joint.

Since the anatomical axis of the femur runs inferiorly and medially, the force applied to the tibia (F) can be resolved into vertical (V) and horizontal (T) components. The horizontal component will tend to tilt the joint laterally so widening the medial joint interspace. This potential disruption of the joint is normally resisted by the tibial collateral ligament. The greater the degree of genu valgus, then the greater the demand made upon the medial ligaments (Fig. 5.92a).

During walking and running, the knee is continually subjected to side-to-side stresses. There is no danger of tearing the collateral ligaments during such activities unless accompanied by the application of a violent transverse force. However, when the knee is severely sprained, abnormal side-to-side movements can be demonstrated about an anteroposterior axis. Such movements are best seen with the knee fully extended or hyperextended. In such a position, if the leg can be displaced laterally this indicates disruption of the tibial collateral ligament (Fig. 5.92d). Similarly, medial displacement of the leg indicates disruption of the fibular collateral ligament (Fig. 5.92e).

As well as the collateral and cruciate ligaments, musculotendinous ties are also important in securing the stability of the joint. Laterally the fibular collateral ligament is aided by the iliotibial tract, which can be tightened by tensor fascia lata and/or gluteus maximus. While medially the tibial collateral ligament is assisted by sartorius, semitendinosus and gracilis. In addition the collateral ligaments are aided by the retinacular fibres of quadriceps femoris. Those fibres which do not cross the midline will prevent opening out of the joint space on the same side, while those which cross the midline will prevent it opening out on the other side. Consequently, each vastus muscle influences the stability of the joint on both the medial and lateral aspects. It is therefore not surprising that atrophy of the quadriceps muscles may weaken the stability of the knee so that it tends to 'give way'.

The structures involved in maintaining the anteroposterior stability of the knee are dependent on its position. If the knee is flexed, even slightly, the projection of the line of gravity falls behind the knee joint axis and so acts to cause further flexion. This is resisted by quadriceps femoris. If on the other hand, the knee is hyperextended, the centre of gravity projection falls in front of the joint axis, there is then a natural tendency for the hyperextension to increase. In this latter position of the knee the cruciate ligaments have both become taut, which, together with the posteriorly placed arcuate and oblique popliteal ligaments and the collateral ligaments, act to limit further hyperextension. Although the ligaments are sufficiently strong to limit hyperextension, their action is reinforced by the flexor muscles crossing the joint. Without this active component the ligaments would become lax through stretching, eventually leading to a decreased stability at the joint.

Fig. 5.92 **a** = Components of the forces transmitted to the tibia. **b** = Impact-dislocation of lateral tibial condyle. **c** = Fracture-dislocation of medial tibial condyle. **d,e** = Ruptures of the collateral ligaments.

In patients with paralysis of the quadriceps femoris, an exaggerated hyperextension of the knee (genu recurvatum) is often seen. This allows the patient to stand erect and even to walk. However, it has to be remembered that when the knee is hyperextended the mechanical axis of the femur runs obliquely inferiorly and posteriorly. The resultant force vector can be resolved into vertical and horizontal components. The posteriorly directed horizontal component acts to accentuate hyperextension. Thus if the genu recurvatum is too severe, the cruciate, collateral and posterior ligaments of the joint become stretched and a vicious circle is set up which results in a further accentuation of hyperextension.

Rotational stability at the knee is also provided by the collateral and cruciate ligaments. Axial rotation can only occur with the knee flexed. In the extended knee it is prevented by tension in both the cruciate and collateral ligaments. In the flexed knee lateral rotation of the tibia with respect to the femur causes the cruciate ligaments to become more vertical and separate, so that they become relaxed. However, at the same time the collateral ligaments are becoming more oblique with a corresponding increase in their tension. Lateral rotation of the tibia with respect to the femur is therefore resisted by the collateral ligaments, especially the lateral (Fig. 5.93a).

When the tibia medially rotates with respect to the femur, the collateral ligaments become more vertical and relaxed, particularly the lateral collateral ligament, while the cruciate ligaments become coiled around each other and are effectively shortened and tightened. The most effective element in resisting tibial rotation is the posterior cruciate ligament as it wraps around the anterior, and the medial collateral ligament (Fig. 5.93b).

It is clear then that the cruciate and collateral ligaments work in concert to provide three-dimensional stability of the knee joint. However, it must also be remembered that the menisci, by their movements which accompany those of the femur and tibia, interact with the ligaments in providing stability at the joint. Disruption of the ACL will obviously lead to a decreased stability, and subsequent increased movement, in all actions in which this ligament is put under tension, as well as in those movements limited by the PCL as it wraps around the ACL. Experiments have shown that isolated section of the ACL significantly increases the anterior displacement of the tibia (Fig. 5.94), with a loss of the coupled tibial rotation accompanying this displacement. By itself, medial meniscectomy has no influence on anterior displacement at the joint, but when associated with ACL section, the anterior displacement observed is significantly greater than that in isolated ACL section, thus highlighting the fact that while it is possible to assign specific roles to individual stabilizing structures in the knee joint, there is considerable interaction between them which may not always be fully appreciated.

a   b

Fig. 5.93 The action of the cruciate and collateral ligaments in limiting axial rotation either (**a**) laterally, or (**b**)
medially, in the knee.

Fig. 5.94 The influence of anterior cruciate ligament (ACL)
division and medial meniscectomy on the anterior displacement of the tibia. (Adapted from Levy I. M., Torzilli P. A.,
Warren R. F. (1982). The effect of medial meniscectomy on
anterior-posterior motion of the knee. *Journal of Bone and
Joint Surgery*, **64A**, 883–7.)

Movements

Concerning movements of the knee, two separate articulations have to be considered: that between the femur and tibia, which is the most important as it controls the lengthening and shortening of the lower limb, and that between the patella and the femur, with the patella acting as a pulley for the quadriceps tendon, changing its line of action.

The main movements that occur at the knee joint are flexion and extension, together with a limited amount of active rotation when the joint is flexed. Consequently, it is termed a modified hinge joint. It differs from a typical hinge joint, for example the interphalangeal joints, not only because of the rotation that occurs but also because the axis about which movement occurs, together with the contact area between the articular surfaces, moves during extension and flexion forwards and backwards respectively. The change in the position of the axis of rotation is due to the constantly changing radius of curvature of the femoral condyles. There is, in addition, an accompanying passive rotation of the joint towards the end of extension.

Flexion and extension (Fig. 5.95)

Flexion is movement of the leg so that the posterior aspect of the calf moves towards the posterior aspect of the thigh, extension being the opposite movement. Some movement, usually passive, of the tibia beyond the position of alignment of the long axis of the leg and thigh may be possible. This movement is usually referred to as hyperextension.

The range of flexion achieved is dependent on the position of the hip, and also according to whether the movement is performed actively or passively. Maximum flexion is attained when the movement is carried out passively.

Active flexion of the knee can reach 140° if the hip is already flexed (Fig. 5.95a), but only 120° if the hip is extended (Fig. 5.95b). This is because the hamstrings lose some of their efficiency with hip extension. If the hamstrings contract abruptly and powerfully, however, some measure of passive flexion follows the active movement so that the range may be increased. Passive movement of the knee joint allows the heel to touch the buttock, giving a range of flexion of 160° (Fig. 5.95c). Normally knee flexion is only limited by contact of the thigh and calf muscles. If, however, the movement is arrested before this occurs it may be due to retraction of the quadriceps muscles or by shortening of the capsular ligaments. In such circumstances, the effectiveness of intervention procedures can be assessed in terms of the distance between the heel and the buttock.

Because the hamstrings are both extensors of the hip and flexors of the knee, their action on the knee depends on the position of the hip. As the hip is flexed, the distance between the hamstring attachments progressively increases as they wrap around the ischial tuberosity (Fig. 5.96). Thus the more the hip is flexed, the greater the degree of relative shortening of the muscles and the more stretched they become. With hip flexion greater than 90° it becomes increasingly more difficult to keep the knee fully extended because of the stretching of the hamstrings (Fig. 5.96c). However, when the hamstrings are stretched by hip flexion their efficiency as knee flexors increases. Therefore during climbing, when one limb moves forwards, flexion of the hip increases the efficiency of hamstring action at the knee. It should also be remembered that extension of the knee will increase the efficiency of the hamstrings as extensors of the hip.

Fig. 5.95a–c Range of flexion of the knee joint.

120°

140°

a

160°

c

b

b₃

s₂

*

a

b₂

s₁

Arc of constant hamstring length

Arc of hamstring attachment to tibial condyles with knee fully extended

d

c

b₁

b

b

a

Fig. 5.96 Influence of limb position on the effectiveness of the hamstrings as flexors of the knee: **a,b** = hamstring attachments to ischium and tibia; **s** = degree of lengthening.

From the foregoing, it might seem that the efficiency of knee flexion is subject to modification according to the position of the hip. This is not necessarily the case as both the short head of biceps and popliteus, crossing only the knee joint, have the same efficiency irrespective of hip position.

The movement of the femoral condyles is achieved by a combination of rolling and gliding actions, with the ratio of rolling to sliding changing during flexion and extension (Fig. 5.97). Beginning with full extension, the femoral condyles begin to roll without sliding, and then the sliding movement becomes progressively more important so that towards the end of flexion the condyles slide without rolling. There are, however, differences between the condyles in the extent of their rolling action. For the medial condyle, pure rolling occurs only during the initial 10–15° of flexion, while for the lateral condyle it continues until 20° flexion. This initial 15–20° of pure rolling corresponds to the normal range of movement during the support phase of gait, when stability is the prime requirement.

The change from rolling to sliding is very significant for the functioning of the knee joint in which both stability and mobility are required. Beyond 20° flexion the knee becomes looser as the radius of the femoral condyles becomes smaller. The tibia moves closer to the axis of movement in the femur, consequently the ligaments passing between the two bones become relaxed. This loosening up prepares the joint for a wider range of axial rotation.

Not only do the relative positions of the femur and tibia change during flexion and extension of the knee joint, with the contact area moving anteriorly and also increasing with extension thereby promoting greater stability of the joint, but the two menisci interposed between them also move (Fig. 5.98). If this were not so then the range of movements possible at the joint would be severely impaired. However, as well as following the movement of the femur with respect to the tibia, the menisci also undergo considerable distortion during their movement. In going from extension to flexion both menisci move posteriorly, with the lateral receding twice as far as the medial, approximately 12 mm and 6 mm respectively. During this movement the lateral meniscus undergoes greater distortion than the medial; primarily because its anterior and posterior horns are situated closer together.

Only one passive element is involved in displacement of the menisci; the femoral condyles push them anteriorly during extension. In contrast, there are many active elements involved in meniscal movements. During extension both menisci are pulled forwards by the meniscopatellar fibres, which are stretched and these pull the transverse ligament forwards. In addition, the posterior horn of the lateral meniscus is pulled anteriorly by the meniscofemoral ligament as the posterior cruciate ligament becomes taut.

During flexion, the lateral meniscus is pulled posteriorly by the attachment of popliteus to it. The medial meniscus is drawn posteriorly by the semimembranosus expansion attached to its posterior edge; the anterior horn is pulled posterosuperiorly by fibres of the anterior cruciate ligament attached to it.

Fig. 5.97 The extent of the rolling and gliding action of the femoral and tibial condyles during flexion and extension: ––– fully extended; –·–·– fully flexed, —— limit of pure rolling action.

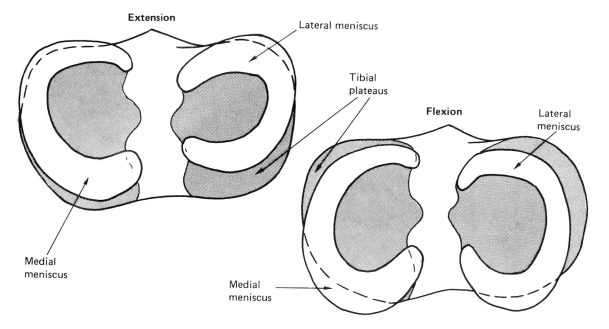

Fig. 5.98 Meniscal movements during flexion and extension.

While these various movements of the femur, tibia and menisci are occurring, it is clear that the patella is changing its relationship to the femur. This must be so given the fact that the meniscopatellar fibres attaching to the margins of the patella, become stretched and pull the menisci forwards during extension. Movement of the patella during flexion is along the groove of the patellar surface of the femur as far as the intercondylar notch. This almost vertical displacement, over a distance of twice its length, is accompanied by a turning movement of the patella about a transverse axis (Fig. 5.99a). Considering the tibia as the moving bone, and going from extension to flexion, the deep surface of the patella goes from facing posteriorly to facing superiorly. However, if the tibia is considered fixed so that the femur moves, then the patella tilts on itself some 35° in such a way that its deep surface which faced posteriorly to begin with looks posteroinferiorly in full flexion (Fig. 5.99b).

It is the capsular recesses in relation to the patella which allow these movements to occur, that is the suprapatellar bursa superiorly and the parapatellar recesses on either side. Inflammatory adhesions developed in these recesses cause their cavities to become obliterated, resulting in the patella being held firmly against the femur so that it cannot move down to the intercondylar notch. This is one of the causes of post-traumatic or postinfective 'stiff knee'.

Normally there is no transverse movement of the patella, it being held against the femur by the quadriceps tendon, increasingly more firmly as flexion increases. In full extension the appositional force is diminished; there may even be separation of the femur and patella in hyperextension. If this occurs there is a tendency for the patella to be drawn laterally due to the pull of the quadriceps femoris. Lateral displacement is prevented by the lateral lip of the patellar surface of the femur, which is further forwards than the medial lip, and the horizontally placed fibres of vastus medialis attaching to the medial border of the patella. If, however, this lateral lip is underdeveloped or there is weakness of vastus medialis, the patella is no longer held and will dislocate laterally in extension. A severely underdeveloped lateral lip may lead to lateral patellar dislocation during flexion movements. This is the mechanism underlying recurrent dislocation of the patella.

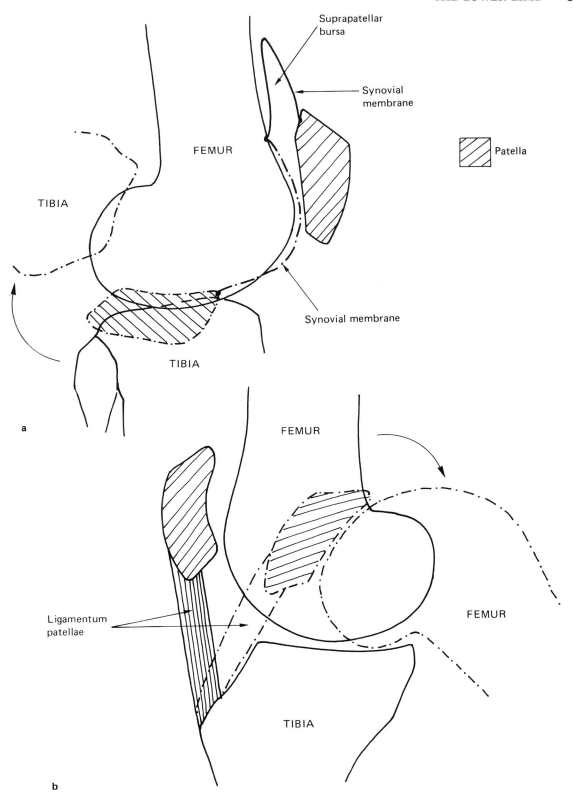

Fig. 5.99   Movements of the patella: **a** = with femur fixed;
b = with tibia fixed.

Axial rotation (Fig. 5.100)

Rotation of the leg about its long axis can only be performed with the knee flexed. Medial rotation brings the toes to face medially conversely, lateral rotation brings the toes to face laterally. The ranges of rotation are influenced slightly by the degree of knee flexion, and hence the efficiency of the appropriate part of the hamstrings. With the knee at right-angles, active medial and lateral rotation are 30° and 40° respectively. These ranges may be increased to 35° and 50° if the movement is performed passively.

In lateral rotation of the tibia on the femur, the lateral femoral condyle moves forwards over the lateral tibial condyle while the medial femoral condyle moves backwards over the medial tibial condyle. In medial rotation the reverse occurs. The extent of this anteroposterior movement differs for the medial and lateral condyles. The medial condyle moves hardly at all, while the lateral moves an appreciable amount and in so doing comes to lie slightly higher than the medial condyle. Although small, this height difference is nevertheless real. The shape difference between the two tibial condyles is reflected in the configuration of the intercondylar tubercles. The medial tubercle acts as a shoulder against which the medial femoral condyle abuts, while the lateral femoral condyle moves easily past its respective tubercle. Consequently, the axis of rotation passes through the medial tubercle and not between the two tubercles.

As might be expected the two menisci follow the displacements of the femoral condyles during axial rotation (see Fig. 5.101). Therefore, during lateral femoral rotation, the medial meniscus is pulled forwards over the tibia while the lateral meniscus is drawn posteriorly. The reverse occurs in medial femoral rotation. Again, during their movements both menisci undergo distortion. The meniscal displacements during axial rotation are mainly passive, by the femoral condyles. However, the meniscopatellar fibres become taught as a result of movement of the patella with respect to the tibia; this tension draws one of the menisci anteriorly. Failure of the menisci to follow the movements of the femoral condyles can lead to transverse tears, longitudinal splitting, detachment of the anterior horn, or complete detachment of the meniscus from the capsule. As soon as a meniscus is damaged, the injured part fails to follow the normal movements and may become wedged between the femoral and tibial condyles. Consequently, the knee 'locks' in a position of flexion, with the locking more marked the more posterior the damage; full extension becomes impossible.

Fig. 5.100 The ranges of axial rotation determined
(**a**) actively and (**b**) passively.

During axial rotation the patella moves in a frontal plane with respect to the tibia. In medial rotation of the tibia with respect to the femur, the patella is dragged laterally, so that the ligamentum patellae runs obliquely inferiorly and medially. The opposite occurs in lateral tibial rotation (Fig. 5.102).

There is also an automatic, involuntary rotation of the knee associated with the terminal part of extension and the beginning of flexion. The movement can be described with respect to either the femur or the tibia, depending on which of the two limb segments, thigh or leg, is fixed. With the tibia fixed, the femur undergoes a medial rotation in the terminal stages of extension. Consequently, during the initial part of flexion the femur is laterally rotated by popliteus. When the knee is in the fully extended, rotated position it is said to be *close-packed*, denoting the maximum contact between the femoral and tibial articular surfaces, with all the ligaments under tension. Hence the joint is at its most stable. The rotation that occurs is due to three independent mechanisms:

1. the unequal length of the articular profiles of the femoral condyles, with the lateral condyle rolling over a greater distance than the medial;
2. the shape of the tibial condyles whereby the medial femoral condyle is more or less contained within the concave medial tibial condyle, while the lateral femoral condyle glides more freely over the convex lateral tibial condyle;
3. the direction of the collateral ligaments, which means that the medial collateral ligament becomes stretched more rapidly than the lateral.

In addition to the above mechanisms, there are two force couples acting to produce rotation. At the beginning of flexion lateral femoral rotation with respect to the tibia is brought about by the action of the flexors gracilis, sartorius and semitendinosus, and by popliteus. Towards the end of extension, it is the tension developed in the anterior cruciate ligament which produces medial femoral rotation, again with respect to the tibia.

Accessory movements

The amount of accessory movement available at the knee joint is controlled to a great extent by its position, and hence the degree of tension in the ligaments. In the close-packed position no accessory movement is possible. However, if the knee is flexed to 25° a number of accessory movements can be demonstrated. The tibia can be moved anteriorly and posteriorly on the femur by applying the appropriate forces. Also in this position rotation of the tibia on the femur can be taken further than the available range by applying a firm rotatory force to the tibia. In this position the tibia can also be rocked medially and latterally. Lastly, it is possible to distract the tibia away from the femur if a longitudinal pulling force is applied.

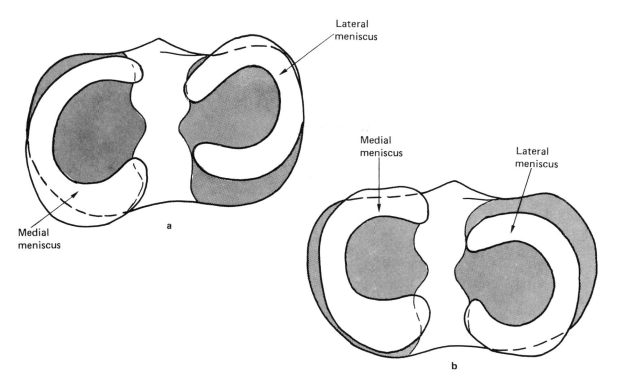

Fig. 5.101 a = Meniscal movements during medial rotation of the femur with respect to the tibia. **b.** = Meniscal movements during lateral rotation of the femur with respect to the tibia.

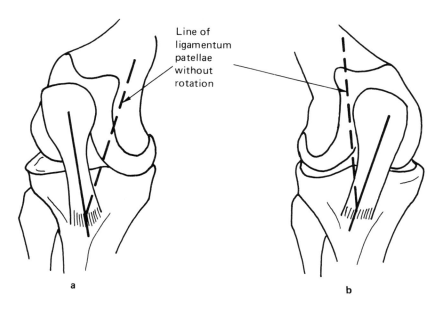

Fig. 5.102 Patella movements during axial rotation of the tibia **(a)** medially and **(b)** laterally, with respect to the femur.

Biomechanics

Joint forces

When considering knee joint forces, those acting on both compartments of the joint, that is the femorotibial and femoropatellar, must be taken into account. During level walking the force across the femorotibial joint can reach five times body weight, although for most of the gait cycle it is usually between two and four times body weight. The force across the femoropatellar joint in similar circumstances is of the order of half body weight. The precise level of loading will depend on internal factors, such as alignment between the femur and tibia and any residual deformity, and external factors, such as the speed of walking and environmental conditions. Ascending or descending ramps and stairs appear to have little influence on femorotibial forces. In contrast, femoropatellar forces increase significantly to between one-and-a-half and two times body weight when ascending, and to between two-and-a-half and three times body weight when descending ramps and stairs. However, the greatest forces across the femoropatellar joint, in everyday as opposed to vigorous activities, are found when getting out of a chair unaided by arms. In such an activity, femoropatellar forces reach three and one-half times body weight, while the corresponding femorotibial forces are four times body weight. Activities such as running and jumping will significantly increase the magnitude of these forces.

In jumping, for example, femorotibial joint forces may reach 24 times body weight, and femoropatellar joint forces 20 times body weight. The articular cartilage of the two joints is therefore subjected to extremely high stresses. It is not too surprising that gymnasts present with articular cartilage degeneration of the knee, accompanied by significant bone buttressing of the femoral and tibial condyles. The pattern and magnitude of the forces in level walking is shown in Fig. 5.103a. Joint force increases rapidly following heel-strike, reaching its peak value as the foot makes full contact with the ground. The magnitude of this peak is dependent on two factors, one being the acceptance of full body weight onto the supporting limb and the other being the result of muscle activity across the joint to prevent collapse of the knee. The second joint force peak is associated with the propulsive part of the stance phase. Its magnitude is primarily determined by the level of muscle activity across the joint; quadriceps femoris acting to extend the knee and gastrocnemius to plantarflex the foot, thus propelling the body forwards. When walking up and down stairs, the increased activity of quadriceps femoris is responsible for the three-to six-fold increase in femoropatellar joint forces.

In contrast to the high vertical forces across the joint, mediolateral joint forces are low, being of the order of one-quarter of body weight.

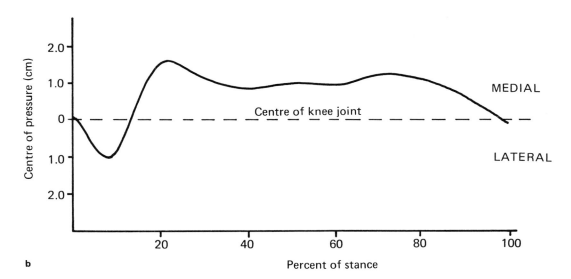

Fig. 5.103   a = Loading profiles of normal knees. The peaks *a, b* and *c* correspond to hamstring, quadriceps and gastrocnemius contraction. **b** = The centre of joint pressure during level walking for normal individuals.

Because of the angulation between the femur and tibia, the two parts of the femorotibial joint, that is medial and lateral, are not equally loaded. Indeed, the degree of angulation, varus or valgus, has a profound influence on the loading pattern. During gait for a normal subject, the centre of force is located just medial to the midline of the joint for the majority of the stance phase (see Fig. 5.103b). This does not necessarily mean that the contact stresses are greater on the medial side. Indeed, because of the shape of the femoral and tibial condyles it is likely that the contact stresses on the lateral side of the joint are greater. In varus deformities the medial contact forces will increase dramatically. In 2.5° varus, for example, these medial forces increase by 70%, and in 5° varus by 95%. Consequently, the centre of force location throughout the stance phase lies medial to the midline of the joint (Fig. 5.104, line a). Similarly, in valgus deformities there is an increase in the contact forces on the lateral side of the joint. In 2.5° valgus the lateral forces increase by 50%, and in 5° valgus by 75%. In such conditions, the centre of force location is now on the lateral side of the joint midline (Fig. 5.104, line b). However, when the valgus deformity is of the order of 15° the centre of force location fluctuates about the midline of the joint (Fig. 5.104, line c). This is achieved by the patient compensating for the valgus load in order to reduce the lateral compartment loading. One compensatory mechanism the patient could adopt would be to use the hip abductors during the stance phase to produce a large lateral horizontal force at the foot. This would necessitate an abduction movement on the tibia thus loading the knee medially. Alternatively, and perhaps more commonly, the hip may be abducted during the swing phase, placing the foot medially at heel-strike. This would also require a similarly large lateral force at the foot during stance in order to maintain equilibrium, resulting in increased loading of the medial compartment of the knee.

It would appear then that individuals can modify force transmission by adopting compensatory mechanisms that result in unloading a particular compartment of the knee. Studies suggest that it is easier to compensate for a valgus than a varus deformity. Whether femoropatellar joint forces increase with a valgus or varus deformity is not known, however, it is likely that the pattern of loading at this joint changes.

Trabecular arrangement (Fig. 5.105)

As well as being subject to high contact forces during activity, the knee is also subjected to considerable side-to-side stresses. This is reflected in the internal architecture of the articulating bones, where the trabeculae are arranged along the lines of mechanical stress, either tension or compression.

The distal end of the femur shows two main sets of trabeculae emanating from the cortex of the shaft, and a transverse set uniting the two condyles. From the cortical region of the shaft medially and laterally, trabeculae fan out into both condyles. The system running to the ipsilateral condyle resists compression forces, while that which runs to the contralateral condyle resists traction forces. The proximal end of the tibia has similarly arranged trabecular systems. From the cortex of the shaft, trabeculae radiate into both tibial condyles. Ipsilaterally they again resist compression forces while contralaterally they resist traction forces. A transverse system unites the two tibial condyles. As in the femur, the trabecular systems arising from the medial and lateral sides of the tibial shaft cross each other approximately at right angles. An important set of trabeculae run into the tibial tuberosity from the anterior aspect of the shaft. This system has developed in response to the tensile stresses to which the tuberosity is subject by the pull of the ligamentum patellae.

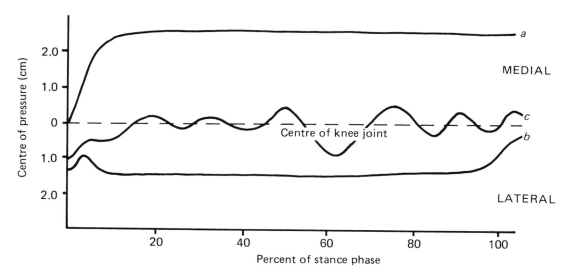

Fig. 5.104   The centre of joint pressure during level walking. *a* = With a varus deformity. *b,c* = With a valgus deformity.

Fig. 5.105   The trabecular arrangement in the femur and tibia around the knee joint.

Contact areas

Femorotibial joint Because the radius of curvature of the femoral condyles increases anteriorly, then the greatest area of contact between the femur and tibia will be in the fully extended position. However, not only is the contact area position-dependent, it is also load-dependent. At low loading levels, up to 500 N, the joint, including the menisci, is not congruous, but with loads greater than 1500 N it becomes markedly congruous. The menisci play a very important role in load transmission across the joint, as can be seen from Fig. 5.106a, which shows that the total contact area is doubled with the menisci present. With the knee fully extended and with an applied load of 1000 N the contact area is of the order of $11.5 \times 10^2 \, mm^2$ with the menisci present, and only $5.2 \times 10^2 \, mm^2$ with the menisci removed. This indicates that with the menisci removed the average stress across the joint doubles compared with that of the intact knee. Peak pressure at 1000 N loading on the intact knee is of the order of 3 MPa, while with the menisci removed it is of the order of 6 MPa. The highest pressure areas are on the lateral meniscus as well as the uncovered part of the articular cartilage of the lateral compartment.

The menisci actually account for about 70% of the total contact area at the 1000 N loading level. At lower loads they account for a greater proportion of the total contact area (Fig. 5.106b). It can also be seen from Fig. 5.106b that the two menisci do not account for the same percentage contact areas in the medial and lateral compartments. This is because of the different shapes of the medial and lateral menisci, as well as the relative positions of their sites of attachment to the intercondylar eminence. Rather surprisingly, reported contact areas in osteoarthritic knees were significantly larger than in normal knees, both with and without the menisci present (Fig. 5.106a), suggesting that the menisci play a less significant role in osteoarthritic knees.

From the foregoing, it is clear that the menisci give elastic stability to the joint, having both load-bearing and load-spreading functions. They provide surface compliance and serve to transmit stresses across a wider area to the periphery of the joint. The menisci, therefore, help to avoid stress concentrations both in the articular cartilage and in the subchondral bone.

Femoropatellar joint The femoropatellar joint has two complex mechanisms for ameliorating the forces transmitted across it. With increasing flexion, the extensor lever arm is lengthened by virtue of the fact that the axis of rotation of the knee joint moves posteriorly, particularly in the range 30–70° flexion. In addition, there is an increasing area of contact between the patella and the femur. Within the 30–70° range of flexion the patella is solely responsible for transmitting the quadriceps force to the femur. The deep surface of the patella is covered by the thickest cartilage in the body, and perhaps not surprisingly is the most frequent site of

Fig. 5.106 **a** = The contact area of the femorotibial joint with and without menisci:
  C = Control
  M = Mild osteoarthritis
  S = Severe osteoarthritis
b = The percent contact area of the menisci compared with total contact area. (Adapted from Fukubayashi T., Kurosawa H. (1980). The contact area and pressure distribution pattern of the knee. A study of normal and osteoarthritic knee joints. *Acta Orthopaedica Scandinavica*, **51**, 871–80.)

a

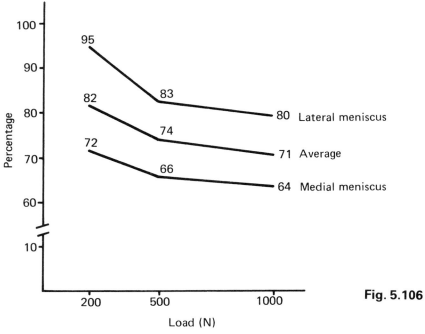

b

Fig. 5.106

cartilage degeneration. Stresses applied to the cartilage of the order of 2–4 MN/m^2 have been calculated for level walking and ascending/descending steps.

Between 30° and 90° of flexion, the contact area almost triples (Fig. 5.107a). This is achieved by an increasingly larger proportion of the patella coming into contact with the femur (Fig. 5.107b). However, by 135° flexion, the contact area has decreased (Fig. 5.107c), being limited to the upper part of the lateral facet and the odd facet.

The Q-angle and valgus vector explain the predominance of pathological lesion on the lateral side of the joint as well as the associated dislocations, subluxations, lateral pressure syndromes and patellofemoral arthrosis.

Mechanical role of the menisci

The average pressure in the articular cartilage of the femorotibial joints is much less with load-bearing menisci than without (see p. 508). With loads distributed over a larger contact area, not only is the average pressure lower, but the pressure gradients are also lower. Consequently, the cartilage deformation is small. Following meniscectomy the pressure distribution becomes non-uniform with a high average pressure, higher stress gradients and large cartilage deformations. As articular cartilage contains 65–85% water, then the less uniform the pressure distribution the more rapid will be the loss of fluid from high pressure zones, and therefore the greater the rate of increase in cartilage deformation. With several thousand stress reversals within the course of a single day cartilage degeneration often ensues.

Therefore, failure or removal of a meniscus usually has detrimental effects on the adjacent articular cartilage. The area of cartilage most regularly affected after meniscec-

tomy is that on the tibial condyle (originally enclosed by the meniscus) because it is unavoidably subjected to increased pressure every time the joint is loaded. There may also be a modification in the shapes of the femoral and tibial condyles; a response of the bone to the change in pressure distribution. The articular cartilage on the tibial condyle within the embrace of the meniscus constitutes an area of non-habitual contact, and is said to be functionally different from the cartilage in other areas of the joint. Age-dependent surface degeneration is commonly encountered at these sites. Consequently, it is generally accepted that the menisci should be regarded as an important and integral part of the articular surfaces of the tibia, with their function being to distribute load over a large area of the articular surfaces at a pressure which the cartilage can tolerate.

The importance of the menisci in lubricating, and hence providing nutrients for, the articular surfaces must not be underestimated. A particular pattern of articular destruction can be seen in many knees. The pattern is in the form of a triangle of erosion or osteophyte formation on the medial femoral condyle, sometimes with associated strips on the lateral condyle (Fig. 5.108). The base of the triangle on the medial condyle is where rotation occurs with full extension. The regions of destruction are those which are normally in contact with the anterior horns of the menisci in full extension, and are only found in association with a flexion contracture. In other words, the lesion arises in those areas which have no opposing articular surface because of the inability to fully extend the joint.

As if the above functions were not sufficient, the menisci also play an important role in absorbing shock transmitted across the knee joint. Meniscectomy reduces the knee's shock absorbing capacity by some 20%.

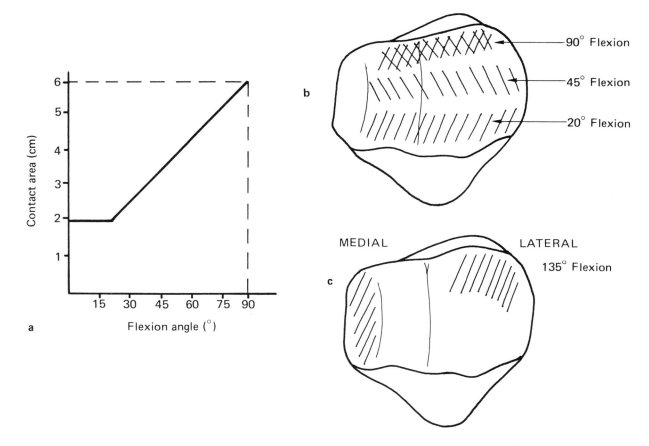

Fig. 5.107 The area of contact between the patella and femur increases up to 90° flexion (**a,b**) after which it decreases again (**c**).

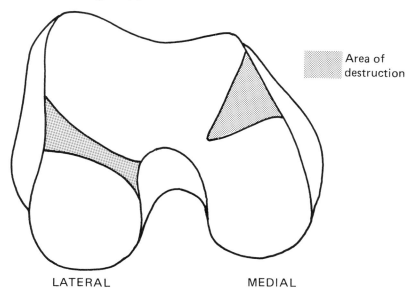

Fig. 5.108 The commonly observed pattern of articular cartilage destruction over the lower end of the femur.

Patella pathology

Stress analysis of the normal patella suggests that areas of high tensile stress on its medial aspect may exist during knee flexion. The high tensile stress being a function of Q-angle, reduction of which dramatically reduces the values of combined stress within the cartilage, thereby reducing the possibility of fatigue failure of the cartilage collagen.

Vertical tensile stresses can occur over the medial side of the lateral facet. If this tensile stress is combined with high contact stresses applied normal to the surface, a situation exists of very high shear stresses which may fatigue the deeper layers of articular cartilage (Fig. 5.109). If this combination of stresses persists it may lead to a closed type of chondromalacic lesion centred on the medial region and commonly extending onto the lateral surface.

Chondrosclerotic lesions, which are rare, are caused by an extreme compression phenomenon, which is the result of high bending stresses combined with high contact stresses over the lateral facet.

To some extent the high stresses within the patella articular cartilage may be relieved by a forward or forward-and-medial displacement of the tibial tuberosity. Such a remedy has been found to provide a satisfactory method of treatment, certainly for relieving unevenly distributed or high femoropatellar pressures.

Cruciate ligament replacement

Injuries to the knee joint are rarely isolated, other damage is frequently obscured at the time of injury due to swelling and becomes apparent later. Secondary injury may develop as a result of abnormal forces acting across the joint. The cruciate ligaments, because of their blood supply, are capable of a certain amount of repair, however severe ruptures have to be dealt with surgically. The primary aim of knee joint repair is restoration of static and dynamic stability in the flexed knee since this is the usual position of function. It is vital that any reparative measures restore normal biomechanical functioning of the joint. If this fails to happen then the altered pattern of forces transmitted across the joint may well lead to secondary changes both at the knee and other joints in a similar manner to that which would occur in the absence of surgical intervention.

The complexity of the cruciate ligaments, with their spiralling fibres and intracapsular position, makes repair or replacement difficult. Surgical repair with sutures have in general not been very successful; treatment usually requires immobilization and rest. Replacement of the ligaments are now becoming more common and successful as new surgical techniques and materials are being developed. There are three broad categories of cruciate ligament replacement: synthetic prostheses, autologous tendon grafts and carbon fibre prostheses.

Synthetic prostheses, such as teflon, are largely untested. Their use has two major disadvantages: they cannot withstand the forces generated in the joint and often break, and they often induce foreign body changes, such as fibrosis, within the joint. The latter, of course, can lead to compromised joint function.

One way of avoiding rejection of the implant is to use the patient's own tendons as the graft. By preserving the graft's original blood supply, the success of the procedure is enhanced, since the tendon is capable of repair and remodelling. Although greater than synthetic prostheses, the strength of tendon grafts is still less than that of the cruciates, so rupture may occasionally occur. Tendon grafts are essentially of two types: static or dynamic stabilizers. Static stabilizers attempt to mimic the course of the original ligament, with the ends of the graft secured to the tibia and femur, often in specially prepared tunnels. Although initially quite effective, the grafts often stretch, with the original problems returning. In addition, the fixation sites are prone to rarification and become loose. Both of these problems may be partially overcome by fixing the knee between 45° and 90° of flexion for 1–2 months postoperatively to allow the graft to mature and undergo some remodelling. This may reduce stretching. If bony plugs can be preserved at each end of the graft, fixation is by bony union thereby overcoming the problem of loosening. In

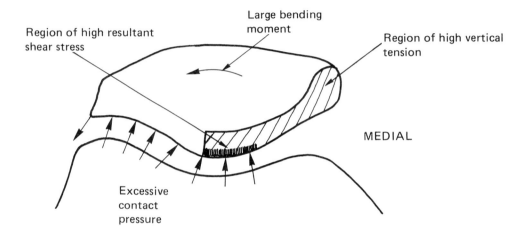

Fig. 5.109 The pattern of patellar stresses which may lead to the formation of a closed chrondromalacic lesion of the patella.

practice, however, there may be considerable difficulty in assessing the length of tendon to use.

In contrast to static tendon grafts, dynamic tendon grafts preserve the muscular attachment of the tendon. In such situations, the insertion of the tendon is detached and passed through the joint capsule and a tunnel in one bone and tied to the other by staples or a bony plug. The course of the tendon is such that it mimics that of the original ligament. The posterior cruciate ligament is commonly replaced using this method, with either the tendon of semitendinosus or the medial head of gastrocnemius. The anterior cruciate ligament may be replaced by the iliotibial tract, semitendinosus, gracilis, sartorius or by a middle patellar tendon graft. Dynamic tendon grafts give little passive resistance to movement, and the drawer sign usually persists, although it may be slightly decreased. During use, however, subluxing forces are resisted by the active contraction of the muscle. Such grafts may also provide protection to excessive movements by initiating muscle stretch reflexes to oppose the movement. Very often the joint kinetics and gait on the operated side are indistinguishable from the normal side.

Carbon fibre prostheses are a recent development, but may soon become the preferred choice of treatment. In these prostheses, the ligament is replaced with high strength carbon fibres, situated within the joint to mimic the course of the original ligament. The implant does not provoke a significant foreign body reaction, although at the sites of insertion some fibrosis may occur. Instead it appears to induce the formation of new ligamentous tissue, and orientates the newly laid down collagen. With use, the carbon fibre gradually breaks down causing increased loading of the collagen, which stimulates the formation of additional collagen. In the knee, this process is slow, probably because being an intracapsular implant there is little mesenchymal tissue present to form collagen. Usually, however, a new ligament is formed, which bears a close morphological resemblance to the original; it is often larger.

Carbon fibre implants significantly reduce the drawer sign, but there may be some loss of flexion at the joint. Breakage of the implant prior to adequate ligament formation is a frequent problem. This could be prevented by externally fixing the joint postoperatively, but this seems to prevent the induction process involved in ligament formation. Partial immobilization of the joint for a short period postoperatively may be sufficient to protect the new implant yet induce new ligament formation.

Replacement of the menisci

The treatment of meniscal injuries includes complete or partial meniscectomy, repair and prosthetic replacement. Complete meniscectomy can cause instability and osteoarthritic changes at the knee and other joints. Loss of the shock-absorbing capacity of the meniscus may lead to back pain and headaches. Partial meniscectomy, with a peripheral rim being preserved, has two functional consequences. It maintains some stability and prevents high stress concentrations, and because the periphery is vascular it allows meniscal regeneration. The new meniscus is formed from the synovial membrane and resembles the original except that its attachments are usually thicker and it projects less into the centre of the joint cavity. The success of regeneration is age-dependent, being more successful in younger patients.

Meniscal repair is an important consideration for the competitive athlete, who wants to return to training as soon as possible. Repair of the meniscus is by suturing followed by immobilization at 45° flexion. Full knee motion is usually regained within 3 months.

If a meniscal tear is so large or involves twisting and buckling then complete meniscectomy may be the only course of action. However, recently attempts have been made to replace the menisci. In some instances, synovial flaps can be created and positioned to act as menisci. Such procedures produce good repair and appear to slow the usual postmeniscectomy degenerative changes. Replacement with a teflon net has also been attempted. After several months bony changes are minimal, as are degenerative changes of the cartilage. The net is invaded by synovial and fibrous material which comes to resemble a meniscus. However, there is often a long-term low grade inflammatory response, in addition to which the net may become adherent to the popliteus tendon and reduce mobility.

Carbon fibre nets have also been used, with the aim of inducing a replacement meniscus. They have, however, proved to have serious disadvantages. They often dislocate and therefore require removal; they can cause fibrosis; there is an inflammatory response, and surprisingly they show poor infiltration with reparative tissue. This is in marked contrast to the use of carbon fibre in cruciate ligament prostheses. The unsatisfactory response with respect to meniscal replacement may be due to their intrasynovial position, with virtually no mesenchymal tissue available to induce collagen formation.

Knee joint replacement

Because of the complex nature of the knee, it presents many problems in designing a suitable prosthesis. Early designs were simple hinge devices, which had a high rate of loosening because they did not allow the normal rotatory movements of the knee to occur. However, hinge replacements are still used in patients with badly deformed or unstable knees. In reality they are only suitable for sedentary patients who will not make great demands on the prosthesis.

There are now available a large range of so called semiconstrained and unconstrained prostheses, which all attempt to mimic, to a greater or lesser extent, the movement of the knee. Obviously, correct alignment of the implant is of crucial importance in the transmission of forces across the joint and the possibility of loosening. Loosening is a fairly common problem, particularly of the tibial component. As the knee goes into extension the anterior part of the tibial implant is pushed downwards, which tends to raise the posterior part. The bone resection required at operation greatly reduces the amount of bony buttress at the back of the tibia, this coupled with the cement's inability to resist tensile stresses promotes loosening of the prosthesis.

To give the implant some shock-absorbing features, and so reduce the transmission of high frequency, high magnitude forces across the joint, the tibial component is of plastic. A few prostheses have attempted to insert artificial menisci between the two replacement joint surfaces in an attempt to (1) improve stability, (2) increase the area of contact and so spread the load more evenly, and (3) improve the shock-absorbing capacity of the joint.

Even if the replacement has been successful clinically, in that there has been a reduction or complete loss of pain on movement, and a more or less full range of movement has been achieved, there may still be abnormalities of gait and difficulty in negotiating stairs.

TIBIOFIBULAR ARTICULATIONS

Introduction

The tibia and fibula articulate together in such a way that there is no active movement between them. However, there is some slight movement between the two bones which appears to be mechanically linked to movement at the ankle joint. The two bones are united by a synovial joint at their proximal ends and by a fibrous joint at their distal ends, with an interosseous membrane connecting the shafts of the two bones.

Superior tibiofibular joint (Fig 5.110)

This is a plane synovial joint between the circular or oval facet on the head of the fibula and a similar facet on the posterolateral aspect of the undersurface of the lateral tibial condyle. The fibular articular facet faces anteriorly, superiorly and medially, while that on the tibia faces posteriorly, inferiorly and laterally. A fibrous capsule attaches to the margins of the facets on both tibia and fibula, and is strengthened by accessory ligaments anteriorly and posteriorly.

The fibrous bands of the short, thick *anterior ligament of the head of the fibula* pass obliquely upwards and medially from the front of the head of the fibula to the front of the lateral tibial condyle. Posteriorly a single band, the *posterior ligament of the head of the fibula*, runs in a similar direction between the head of the fibula and the back of the lateral tibial condyle. The tendon of popliteus is intimately related to the posterosuperior aspect of the joint as it crosses the posterior ligament. The popliteal bursa, prolonged under the tendon from the knee joint, occasionally communicates with the synovial cavity of the tibiofibular joint through an opening in the upper part of the capsule.

The blood supply to the joint is from the lateral inferior genicular and anterior tibial recurrent arteries. Its lymphatic drainage is to the popliteal nodes. The nerve supply to the joint is by twigs from the recurrent branch of the common peroneal nerve and the branch to popliteus from the tibial nerve. The root value of this supply is L5.

The joint is overhung by the apex of the head of the fibula, to which attaches part of the tendon of biceps femoris: the remainder going to the lateral aspect of the head below the apex. The fibular collateral ligament attaches between the biceps insertion and the joint.

There is slight movement at the superior tibiofibular joint, which gives a small degree of flexibility to the relationship between the tibia and fibula during movements of the ankle joint, and also in response to the pull of the muscles attached to the fibula.

a

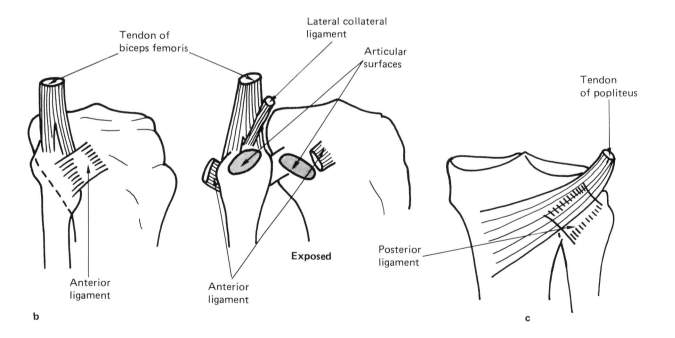

Tendon of
biceps femoris

Lateral collateral
ligament

Articular
surfaces

Tendon
of popliteus

Anterior
ligament

Anterior
ligament

Exposed

Posterior
ligament

b

c

Fig. 5.110 X-ray of the superior tibiofibular joint. **b** = The
superior tibiofibular joint, anterior view. **c** = The superior
tibiofibular joint, posterior view.

Inferior tibiofibular joint (Fig. 5.111)

This is a fibrous joint between the rough, triangular convex surface of the medial aspect of the lower end of the fibula above the articular facet, and a corresponding rough, triangular concave surface, the fibular notch, on the lateral side of the tibia. Uniting the two bones is the strong interosseous ligament, continuous with the interosseous membrane above, and consisting of short fibrous bands. It forms the principal connection between the two bones, and is supplemented by anterior, posterior and transverse tibiofibular ligaments.

The *anterior* and *posterior tibiofibular ligaments* are longer and more superficial bands stretching from the borders of the fibular notch of the tibia to the anterior and posterior surfaces of the lateral malleolus of the fibula. Of the two, the posterior ligament is thicker and broader. The inferior edges of both ligaments cover the lateral ridge of the trochlear surface of the talus; the anterior during flexion of the ankle joint, and the posterior during extension. Both ligaments run downwards and laterally. Under cover of the posterior ligament is the *transverse tibiofibular ligament*. It attaches along the whole length of the inferior border of the posterior surface of the tibia and the upper part of the malleolar fossa of the fibula. This strong, thick ligament projects below the margin of the bones, so closing the posterior angle between the tibia and fibula, and in doing so forms part of the articular surface for the posterior part of the trochlear surface of the talus.

A synovial-lined recess of the ankle joint cavity usually extends upwards between the tibia and fibula (about 1 cm or less), being blocked above by the distal end of the interosseous membrane. Occasionally the articular cartilage on the lower ends of the tibia and fibula extends upwards for a short distance on the walls of the recess.

The blood supply to the joint is from the peroneal and anterior tibial arteries. The nerve supply is by twigs from the deep peroneal and tibial nerves, with roots L4 to S2.

Anterior to the inferior tibiofibular joint runs the tendon of peroneus tertius, with that of extensor digitorum lying medially together with the anterior tibial artery and deep peroneal nerve. Posteriorly the tendons of peroneus longus and brevis lie lateral to the joint, with brevis perhaps overlying it slightly.

The inferior tibiofibular joint provides a firm union between the tibia and fibula, and makes a significant contribution to the integrity of the malleolar mortise of the ankle joint. The fibrous tissue of the joint allows a slight yielding of the bones for the accommodation of the talus in movements of the ankle joint. In radiographs centred on the ankle, the fibula shadow encroaches upon the anterior border of the fibular notch. If the distance yz is greater than xy then diastasis of the ankle joint is said to be present (Fig. 5.111a).

a

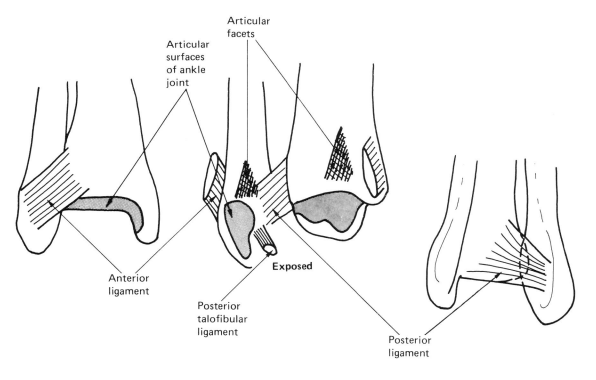

Articular
facets

Articular
surfaces
of ankle
joint

Anterior
ligament

Exposed

Posterior
talofibular
ligament

Posterior
ligament

b

c

Fig. 5.111 a = X-ray of the inferior tibiofibular joint.
b,c = The inferior tibiofibular joint.

Interosseous membrane (Fig. 5.112a)

The interosseous membrane may be regarded as a form of fibrous joint uniting the tibia and fibula. It is tightly stretched between the interosseous borders of the two bones, and consists predominantly of fibres passing laterally and downwards from the tibia to the fibula. The upper margin of the membrane does not reach as far as the superior tibiofibular joint, to allow the anterior tibial vessels to gain access to the anterior compartment of the leg. The membrane is, however, continuous below with the interosseous ligament of the inferior tibiofibular joint. At its end there is a small opening for the passage of a branch from the peroneal artery.

The interosseous membrane separates the muscles of the anterior and posterior compartments of the leg, as well as giving attachment to some of the muscles of each group (see Fig. 5.112b).

Movement of the fibula (see Fig. 5.113)

Plantarflexion and dorsiflexion at the ankle joint will automatically cause passive movements at both tibiofibular joints. Although the magnitude of these movements is small, they are nevertheless real.

In dorsiflexion the broader, anterior part of the trochlear surface of the talus is forced into the narrower posterior part of the tibiofibular socket. This causes a separation of the tibia and fibula, with increased tension in the interosseous and transverse tibiofibular ligaments. Consequently, the talus is held securely between the malleoli. In plantarflexion the narrower part of the talus moves into the broader part of the socket. The malleoli come together again to retain their grip on the talus, however, in full plantarflexion some side-to-side movement can be demonstrated. The grip of the malleoli upon the talus is a function of the inferior tibiofibular joint, the strong ligaments of which provide the spring mechanism involved.

This moving apart and coming together of the two malleoli during ankle movements imparts a complex movement to the fibula, which is partly guided by the shape and orientation of the lateral surface of the talus, and partly by the tension developed in various ligaments associated with the inferior tibiofibular joint. When the malleoli are separated, as in ankle dorsiflexion, both the anterior and posterior tibiofibular ligaments are put under tension. As the fibres in each of these ligaments run downwards and laterally, there is a tendency for the fibula to be lifted superiorly in an attempt to maintain the integrity of the ligaments. There are no bony constraints to this movement as the lateral articular surface of the talus is convex anteroposteriorly and concave superoinferiorly. At the same time as the lateral malleolus is moving laterally and superiorly, the fibula itself is undergoing some axial rotation. The direction of this rotation depends upon the shape of the lateral talar surface, which if convex anteroposteriorly, would result in a slight medial rotation. If, however, the lateral talar surface is plane then a slight lateral rotation of the fibula will occur.

When plantarflexion at the ankle joint occurs the two malleoli come together again, partly under the tension developed in the anterior, posterior and interosseous tibiofibular ligaments but also under the action of tibialis posterior, particularly in full plantarflexion. As the lateral malleolus moves medially, it also moves inferiorly with the fibula undergoing axial rotation in the opposite direction to that experienced in dorsiflexion.

These movements of the fibula at the inferior tibiofibular joint are transmitted to the synovial superior tibiofibular joint, which has plane articular surfaces and offers no resistance to the movements.

Accessory movements

Superior tibiofibular joint

Accessory movements of the superior tibiofibular joint are an anteroposterior glide of the fibula on the tibia. The movements can be produced by pressure in the appropriate direction when the head of the fibula is gripped between the thumb and index finger.

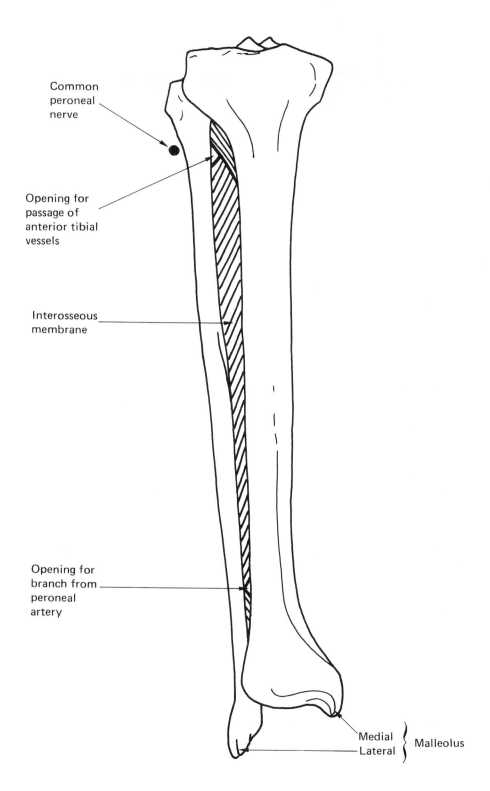

Common
peroneal
nerve

Opening for
passage of
anterior tibial
vessels

Interosseous
membrane

Opening for
branch from
peroneal
artery

Medial
Lateral } Malleolus

Fig. 5.112a The interosseous membrane,
anterior view.

Inferior tibiofibular joint

Accessory movements are difficult to produce in the inferior tibiofibular joint, but a slight anteroposterior movement can be felt if the lateral malleolus is gripped between thumb and index finger, and pressed anteriorly then posteriorly.

Palpation

The head of the fibula can be palpated below the posterior part of the lateral condyle of the tibia, on approximately the same horizontal level as the tibial tuberosity. The tendon of biceps femoris can be felt and seen passing to its insertion on the head. Immediately below the head is the narrower neck, around which passes, on the lateral side, the common peroneal nerve (see Fig. 5.112a).

In the region of the ankle both malleoli can be palpated. The lateral malleolus extending further distally, and lying in a more posterior plane than the medial malleolus. Various tendons pass behind both malleoli on their way to attach in the foot. Passing in front of the ankle joint are the extensor tendons to the dorsum of the foot. All of the tendons are bound down by thickenings of the deep fascia—the retinacula.

Fig. 5.112b Transverse section at middle of leg.

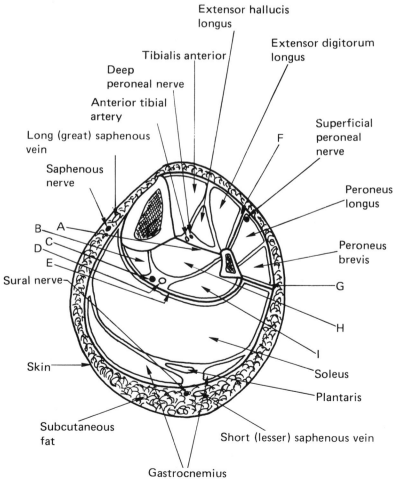

A = Interosseous membrane
B = Flexor digitorum longus
C = Tibial nerve
D = Posterior tibial artery
E = Transverse intermuscular septum
F = Anterior intermuscular septum
G = Posterior intermuscular septum
H = Tibialis posterior
I = Flexor hallucis longus

Talus

a

Talus

b

Fig. 5.113 **a** = Movements of the fibula during dorsiflexion. **b** = Movements of the fibula during plantarflexion. (Large arrows indicate movement of fibula; – · – · – direction of fibres in the tibiofibular and interosseous ligaments in the neutral position; —— new direction of these same fibres in either full dorsiflexion (aa) or full plantarflexion (bb)).

THE ANKLE JOINT

Introduction

The ankle joint is a synovial hinge joint with one degree of freedom of movement, that is it allows only plantarflexion and dorsiflexion (flexion and extension respectively). The forward and backward fluctuation of the line of gravity, which in normal standing falls in front of the joint, is regulated at the ankle so that it is kept within the limits of the supporting surface. The joint has the appearance of a mortise and tenon, with the box-like mortise being constructed by the distal ends of the tibia and fibula, and the body of the talus forming the tenon (Fig. 5.114).

In the anatomical position the axis of the ankle joint is horizontal but set obliquely to the frontal plane some 20–25°, so that as it passes laterally it also runs posteriorly (Fig. 5.115). This obliquity is due to the outward rotation of the lower end of the tibia, and means that in dorsiflexion the foot moves upwards and medially while in plantarflexion it moves downwards and laterally. Although both the knee and the ankle joint axes lie in a horizontal plane, simultaneous movements at both joints can only be achieved if movement is allowed at other joints to compensate for the obliquity of the ankle joint axis. This compensation is essentially provided by the subtalar joint. Indeed, movement of the foot at the ankle joint is rarely performed alone, it is invariably combined with subtalar and midtarsal joint motion, so that plantarflexion is associated with adduction and supination of the foot, and dorsiflexion with abduction and pronation of the foot. These combined movements are usually referred to as inversion and eversion of the foot respectively.

The ankle and foot are the structures which provide restraint and propulsion at each step so that equilibrium can be maintained while the body is in motion. To accomplish this there have been changes in certain of the tarsal bones, and the establishment of interrelated articulations. A single joint, the ankle joint, has been established between the leg and the foot which controls the foot in the sagittal plane. It takes care of adjusting the line of gravity in standing and in providing the propulsion and restraint required during gait. A second articulation has been established between the talus and the calcaneus. This is the subtalar joint (see p. 552). Lastly a joint has been established which interrupts the structure of the foot in the middle of the tarsus, this is the midtarsal joint (see p. 560).

This series of joints, assisted by axial rotation of the knee, is equivalent to a single joint with three degrees of freedom of movement; they allow the foot to take up any position in space and to adapt to any irregularities in the ground during walking. However, unlike a single joint, these three separate articulations provide a high degree of stability without the usual sacrifice to mobility.

Fig. 5.114   Radiographic appearance of the ankle joint.

Fig. 5.115   The relation of the ankle joint axis
to the knee joint and femoral neck axes.

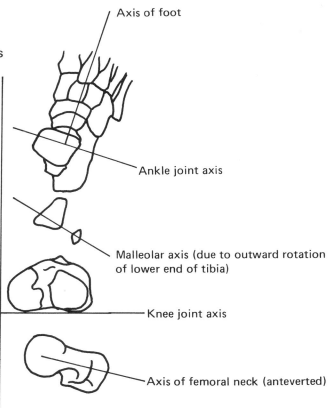

Axis of foot

Ankle joint axis

Malleolar axis (due to outward rotation
of lower end of tibia)

Knee joint axis

Axis of femoral neck (anteverted)

Articular surfaces

The joint involves the distal ends of the tibia and fibula proximally and the body of the talus distally. The weight-bearing surfaces are the trochlear surfaces of the tibia and talus. Stabilizing surfaces are those of the medial and lateral malleoli, which grip the body of the talus.

Tibia (Fig. 5.116)

The distal end of the tibia provides a continuous articular surface which receives the trochlear surface and medial edge of the body of the talus. The trochlear surface is concave anteroposteriorly, and slightly convex transversely with a blunt sagittal ridge which fits into a corresponding groove on the talus, being slightly wider in front than behind. On either side of the ridge is a medial and lateral gutter which receive the corresponding lips of the talar trochlear surface. The posterior part of this surface projects slightly downwards, and is sometimes known as the posterior malleolus.

The cartilage on the trochlear surface of the tibia is continuous medially with that on the lateral surface of the medial malleolus, the junction being a rounded angle.

Fibula (Fig. 5.116)

The medial surface of the lateral malleolus of the fibula forms the lateral surface of the mortise of the joint. The articular surface is approximately triangular with the inferior apex being slightly convex. The base of the triangle extends up as far as the tibial articular surface, with the joint cavity usually extending between the two bones. In the angle between the lateral malleolus and the trochlear surface of the tibia is a narrow cleft distal to the interosseous ligament. This cleft disappears posteriorly as it is filled by the transverse tibiofibular ligament.

Talus (Fig. 5.116)

The body of the talus forms the whole of the distal surface of the ankle joint, articulating superiorly and medially with the tibia and laterally with the fibula. The trochlear surface is convex anteroposteriorly with a central longitudinal groove bound by medial and lateral lips, and is slightly broader in front than behind. The groove and lips make the trochlear surface slightly concave transversely. The cartilage covering the trochlear surface is continuous with that on the sides of the body of the talus.

The medial surface is nearly plane, except anteriorly where it is inclined medially, and can be likened to a comma placed on its side with the tail pointing backwards. It lies in a sagittal plane and articulates with the lateral surface of the medial malleolus. The lateral articular surface runs obliquely anteriorly and laterally, being concave superoinferiorly as well as anteroposteriorly. The surface is triangular and much larger than that medially, curving inferiorly to a laterally projecting apex. It articulates with the medial surface of the lateral malleolus, and with the deep surface of the transverse tibiofibular ligament posterosuperiorly at the angle between the trochlear and lateral surfaces. The interval between the tibia, fibula and the transverse tibiofibular ligament posteriorly is padded by a synovial fold.

Fig. 5.116 The articular surfaces of the ankle joint: **a** = trochlear surfaces of the tibia and talus; **b** = medial anterior oblique view; **c** = lateral anterior oblique view; **d** = coronal section.

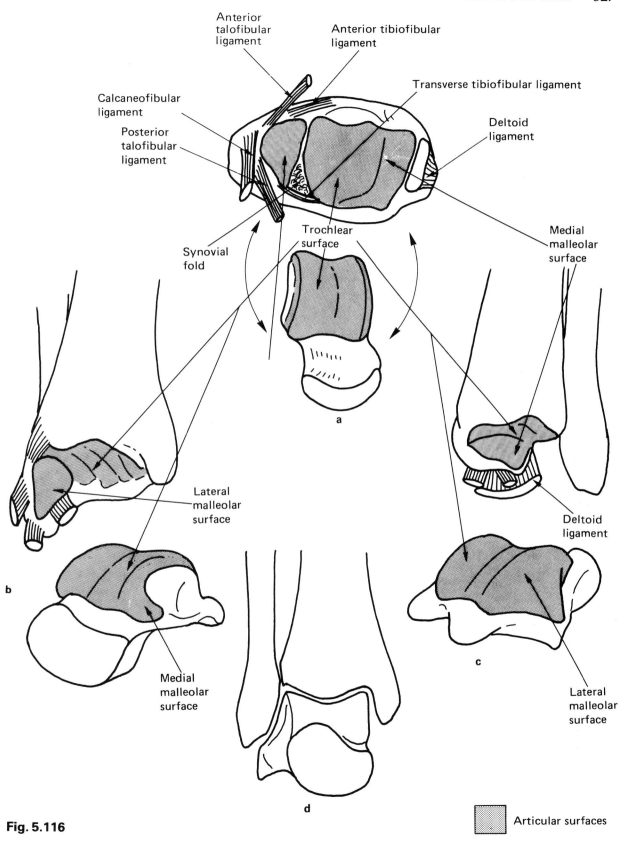

Anterior talofibular ligament

Anterior tibiofibular ligament

Transverse tibiofibular ligament

Calcaneofibular ligament

Posterior talofibular ligament

Deltoid ligament

Synovial fold

Trochlear surface

Medial malleolar surface

Lateral malleolar surface

Deltoid ligament

Medial malleolar surface

Lateral malleolar surface

a

b

c

d

Articular surfaces

Fig. 5.116

Joint capsule

A fibrous capsule completely surrounds the joint, attaching above to the articular margins of the tibia and fibula, and below to just outside the edges of the corresponding articular areas of the talus, except anteriorly where it attaches to the neck of the talus. The capsule is thin and weak in front and behind to accommodate the movements of flexion and extension, but is strengthened laterally and medially by collateral ligaments. Posteriorly the capsule is attached to the posterior tibiofibular ligament.

Synovial membrane

The synovial membrane of the ankle joint is loose and capacious. It lines the joint capsule and is reflected anteriorly onto the neck of the talus before attaching to the articular margins. It covers well-marked fatty pads that lie in relation to its anterior and posterior parts. The synovial membrane extends upwards between the tibia and fibula as far as the interosseous ligament of the inferior tibiofibular joint and may be covered in part by an extension of the articular cartilage on the tibia and fibula.

Ligaments

As with all hinge joints, there is, associated with the ankle, an extremely strong set of collateral ligaments. Medially is the deltoid ligament while laterally there are three separate ligaments. Both sets of ligaments radiate downwards from the malleoli and both have a middle band to the calcaneus and anterior and posterior bands to the talus. The deltoid and anterior and posterior lateral ligaments blend with the joint capsule.

Deltoid ligament (Fig. 5.117a)

The deltoid ligament is a strong, roughly triangular ligament composed of several bands of fibres fused together; the various bands only being differentiated by their distal attachments. It can be considered to have deep and superficial parts, attaching by its apex to the anterior and posterior borders and to the fossa at the tip of the medial malleolus. The thick base forms a continuous attachment from the navicular anteriorly to the body of the talus posteriorly.

The deeper parts of the ligament are the *anterior* and *posterior tibiotalar* bands. The anterior tibiotalar band is the most anterior and runs obliquely forwards and downwards to attach to the medial part of the neck of the talus. The posterior tibiotalar band is the most posterior and thickest part of the deltoid ligament. Its fibres run laterally and backwards to the medial side of the talus under the tail of the comma-shaped articular facet and to the medial tubercle of its posterior process.

The more superficial parts of the deltoid ligament partly overlie the anterior tibiotalar band, and have a continuous attachment from the navicular to the sustentaculum tali of the calcaneus. The *tibionavicular* band runs forwards and downwards towards the tuberosity on the navicular bone attaching to its upper and medial parts. Continued backwards this band blends below with the upper medial border of the plantar calcaneonavicular (spring) ligament. It is succeeded by the *tibiocalcaneal* band whose fibres descend almost vertically to attach to the whole of the length of the sustentaculum tali.

Lateral ligaments (Fig. 5.117b)

The lateral collateral ligament is composed of three separate parts, the *anterior* and *posterior talofibular* ligaments and the *calcaneofibular* ligament. These separate ligaments do not constitute as strong a ligamentous structure as the deltoid ligament, as evidenced by the fact that most ankle sprains involve the lateral ligaments. The anterior talofibular ligament is a flat band stretching

Fig. 5.117 a = The deltoid ligament. **b** = The lateral ligaments.

between the anterior border and tip of the lateral malleolus to the neck of the talus. Its fibres run anteromedially. The posterior talofibular ligament is a strong, thick ligament running almost horizontally. It arises from the bottom of the malleolar fossa of the lateral malleolus and passes posteromedially to the lateral tubercle of the posterior process of the talus. Above it lies the posterior tibiofibular ligament. In plantarflexion these two ligaments lie edge-to-edge, while in dorsiflexion they diverge medially.

Between the two talofibular ligaments lies the calcaneofibular ligament, a narrow rounded cord which is free from the fibrous capsule, but has the two talofibular ligaments fused with its upper part. It arises from the front and tip of the lateral malleolus and passes downwards and slightly backwards to attach to above and behind the peroneal tubercle on the middle of the lateral surface of the calcaneus.

Anterior and posterior ligaments (Fig. 5.118)

The anterior and posterior ligaments of the joint are localized thickenings of the joint capsule. The anterior ligament runs obliquely from the anterior margin of the lower end of the tibia to the upper surface of the anterior part of the neck of the talus. The posterior ligament has fibres arising from both the tibia and fibula, which converge to attach to the medial tubercle of the posterior surface of the talus.

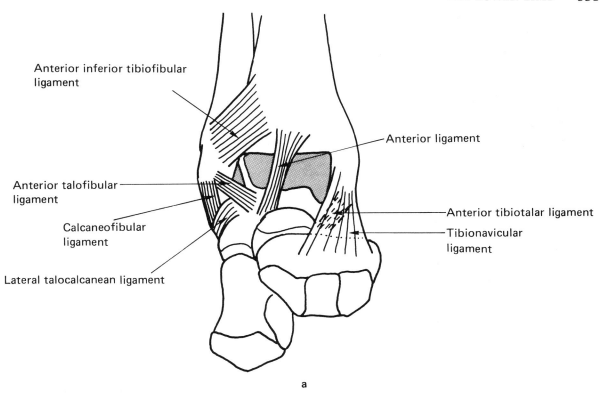

Anterior inferior tibiofibular ligament

Anterior ligament

Anterior talofibular ligament

Calcaneofibular ligament

Lateral talocalcanean ligament

Anterior tibiotalar ligament

Tibionavicular ligament

a

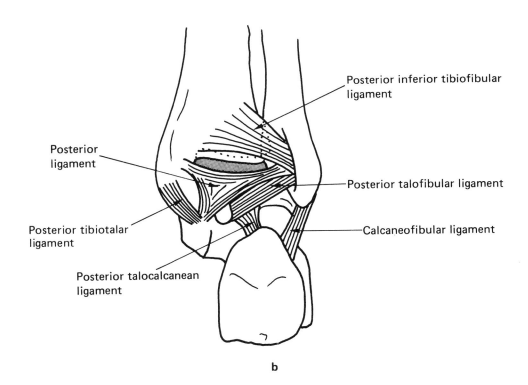

Posterior inferior tibiofibular ligament

Posterior ligament

Posterior talofibular ligament

Posterior tibiotalar ligament

Calcaneofibular ligament

Posterior talocalcanean ligament

b

Fig. 5.118   The anterior and posterior capsular thickenings (joint capsule removed): **a** = anterior; **b** = posterior.

Role of the collateral ligaments
(Fig. 5.119)

Laxity of the ankle joint is dependent on its position; full dorsiflexion being the position of least laxity, reflecting talar geometry and the inferior tibiofibular syndesmosis. The ligaments of the joint are primarily responsible for maintaining its stability and controlling the movements of which it is capable. Damage to some or all of the collateral ligaments will seriously impair the integrity of the joint.

In experimental studies, sectioning of the lateral ligaments is associated with an increase in the range of dorsiflexion, but not plantarflexion, and an increase in internal rotation of the talus, particularly when the ankle is plantarflexed. Only when all the collateral ligaments had been severed was an increase in external talar rotation observed, which was more marked in dorsiflexion. Talar tilt was also increased with gradually increasing injury. Prior to complete severing of all collateral ligaments talar tilt was maximum in plantarflexion, but after total disruption of the ligaments talar tilt was most marked in dorsiflexion.

The role of the various parts of the collateral ligaments in maintaining stability can be summed up as follows. The tibiocalcaneal and tibionavicular bands control abduction of the talus, while adduction is controlled by the calcaneofibular ligament. The anterior tibiotalar band and the anterior talofibular ligament control plantarflexion, while dorsiflexion is resisted by the posterior tibio-talar band and the posterior talofibular ligament. In combination, both the anterior and tibionavicular bands control external rotation, and, together with the anterior talofibular ligament, internal rotation of the talus. In isolation, neither the anterior nor the posterior tibiotalar ligaments appear to play any major role in ankle stability. In contrast, the anterior talofibular ligament appears to be an extremely important structure, and can probably be considered as the primary stabilizer of the ankle. It provides significant resistance to varus tilt of the talus in all positions of flexion.

Apart from the pain involved in a sprain of the ankle, the accompanying instability is probably due to involvement of the anterior talofibular ligament, as most sprains are due to a turning of the ankle outwards (foot inwards) and a consequent straining of the lateral ligaments (inversion stress).

Blood and nerve supply

The blood supply of the joint is from the *malleolar branches* of the *anterior tibial*, *peroneal* and *posterior tibial arteries*, which form an anastomosis around the malleoli. Venous drainage is by the corresponding venae commitantes accompanying the arteries. The lymphatics drain into the deep system of vessels, which again accompany the arteries.

The nerve supply to the joint is from roots L4 to S2 by articular branches from the tibial nerve and lateral branch of the deep peroneal nerve.

Fig. 5.119 The role of lateral (**a**) and medial (**b**) collateral ligaments in rotational stability of the ankle joint. (Adapted from McCullough C. J., Burge P. D. (1980). Rotatory stability of the load-bearing ankle—an experimental study. *Journal of Bone and Joint Surgery*, **62B**, 460–4.)

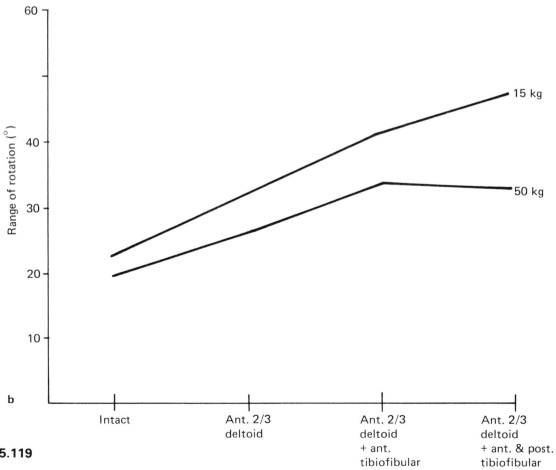

Fig. 5.119

Relations

All of the muscles, vessels and nerves entering the foot do so by crossing the ankle joint. Anteriorly are, from medial to lateral, the tendons of tibialis anterior, extensor hallucis longus, extensor digitorum longus and peroneus tertius as they pass through the inferior extensor retinaculum (Fig. 5.120a). The first two tendons lie within separate compartments surrounded by their own synovial sheaths, while the last two share a compartment and synovial sheath. Deep to the extensor retinaculum, behind the middle compartment pass the anterior tibial artery, which becomes the dorsalis pedis artery at the inferior border of the retinaculum, and the deep peroneal nerve. Anterior to the extensor retinaculum is the superficial peroneal nerve, and in front of the medial malleolus the long (great) saphenous vein draining from the dorsal venous plexus, and the saphenous branch of the femoral nerve (Fig. 5.120a).

Behind the medial malleolus and bound down by the flexor retinaculum are, from anteromedial to posterolateral, the tendons of tibialis posterior, flexor digitorum longus, the posterior tibial artery, the tibial nerve and the tendon of flexor hallucis longus (Fig. 5.120a). The latter tendon passes in a groove on the posterior part of the talus between the medial and lateral tubercles, and enters the foot by passing below the sustentaculum tali. As they pass behind the medial malleolus, both the posterior tibial artery and the tibial nerve divide into their terminal medial and lateral plantar branches. All of the tendons are surrounded by individual synovial sheaths.

The tendons of peroneus longus (anterolateral) and peroneus brevis (posteromedial) pass in a common synovial sheath behind the lateral malleolus bound down by the superior peroneal retinaculum (Fig. 5.120a). Below the level of the joint these two tendons diverge to pass either side of the peroneal tubercle of the calcaneus: longus below, brevis above. At this point each tendon has its own synovial sheath. Behind these two tendons as they pass posterolateral to the ankle joint are the sural nerve and short (lesser) saphenous vein.

Posterior to the joint, but separated from it by an extensive fat pad, is the tendocalcaneus (Achilles tendon) passing to its attachment on the posterior tubercle of the calcaneus.

Palpation

Both the medial and lateral malleoli can be readily palpated on their anterior and posterior borders, as well as at their tips. The two malleoli are however basically different. The lateral malleolus is bigger than the medial, it extends further distally and lies more posteriorly. The peroneal tendons can be palpated behind the lateral malleolus (Fig. 5.120b), and those of tibialis posterior and flexor digitorum longus behind the medial malleolus (Fig. 5.120b). All of the tendons crossing anterior to the joint can be identified and palpated.

The pulsations of the anterior tibial artery can be felt between the tendons of extensor hallucis longus and extensor digitorum, while those of the posterior tibial artery can be felt behind the medial malleolus posterior to the tendon of flexor digitorum longus.

The line of the ankle joint can be palpated on the dorsal surface. Starting medially, the joint can be identified by applying firm pressure along the inner border of the medial malleolus. If the extensor tendons are moved aside the lower end of the tibia can be palpated, as well as the medial edge of the lateral malleolus.

Fig. 5.120   a = Transverse section across the ankle showing the various structures related to it. **b** = Medial and lateral relations of the ankle joint.

Stability

The anteroposterior stability of the ankle joint and the coaptation of its articular surfaces depend upon the effect of gravity to keep the tibia pressed against the superior surface of the talus. In addition, the anterior and posterior margins of the tibial surface form bony spurs, due to its concave shape, which help prevent the talus from escaping posteriorly or anteriorly respectively. The collateral ligaments are passively responsible for the coaptation of the articular surfaces and are assisted by the muscles crossing the joint, provided that the joint is intact. In a subluxed or dislocated joint the ligaments and muscles may act to cause further joint distraction.

The ankle joint, by virtue of its structure, should not be able to exhibit movements other than flexion and extension. Transverse stability depends on the interlocking of its articular surfaces (Fig. 5.121a). Provided that the distance between the malleoli remains relatively unchanged, they grip the talus on each side. This can only be accomplished when the malleoli and the ligaments of the inferior tibiofibular joint are intact. Furthermore, the collateral ligaments prevent any rolling movements of the talus about its long axis.

When the foot is forcibly moved laterally, as in a violent movement of abduction, the lateral surface of the talus knocks against the lateral malleolus. The sequence of events which follow depends on the severity of the movement, the state of the bone and the integrity of the various ligaments of the joint. If there is rupture of the inferior tibiofibular ligaments the grip of the malleoli is disrupted, leading to a widening of the mortise (diastasis of the ankle). The talus is no longer held tightly and can move from side-to-side (rattling of the talus) (Fig. 5.121b).

It is also able to rotate about its long axis (tilting of the talus), which is made all the more easier if the deltoid ligament is sprained (Fig. 5.121c), and turn around its vertical axis so that the posterior part of the body of the talus abuts against the posterior margin of the tibia, possibly fracturing it. If the abduction movement continues both medial and lateral malleoli may become fractured, the lateral above the inferior tibiofibular joint (Fig. 5.121e). This is one form of *Pott's fracture*. Occasionally the lateral malleolus does not fracture and the fibular fracture occurs at the level of the neck.

Both inferior tibiofibular ligaments do not always rupture, very often the anterior tibiofibular ligament resists tearing. There is still fracture of both malleoli, but with the lateral malleolus fracturing through the inferior tibiofibular joint (Fig. 5.121f). This is another form of Pott's fracture. Instead of the medial malleolus fracturing, the deltoid ligament may be ruptured, but again the lateral malleolus fractures through the inferior tibiofibular joint (Fig. 5.121g).

In all of these fractures, a chip of bone is often broken off the posterior margin of the tibia: this can present as a separate fragment of bone or form a single unit with the malleolar fragment.

In violent adduction movements of the foot, the talus is forced to rotate about its vertical axis fracturing both malleoli, the lateral below the inferior tibiofibular joint. In these bimalleolar adduction fractures, the inferior tibiofibular and both collateral ligaments remain intact (Fig. 5.121h).

Obviously these lesions require proper treatment if full structural and functional integrity of the joint is to be restored. If the bony and soft tissue damage is excessive then a fusion of the joint may be the only practical way of restoring stability.

Fig. 5.121   Disruption of the transverse stability of the ankle joint.

Movement

Movement at the ankle joint takes place about a transverse axis level with the tip of the lateral malleolus and slightly below the level of the medial malleolus. Strictly speaking the axis is not horizontal, but slopes slightly downwards and laterally, passing through the lateral surface of the talus just below the apex of the articular triangle, and through the medial surface at a higher level, just below the concavity of the comma-shaped articular area. The axis also changes slightly during movement because the upper surface of the talus is elliptical rather than the arc of a circle. This change, however, is of no practical importance. Because of the obliquity of the joint axis there is a slight movement resembling inversion on full plantarflexion, and eversion on full dorsiflexion. These 'inversion/eversion' movements are not true inversion and eversion.

The movements possible at the ankle joint are dorsiflexion and plantarflexion of the foot through a maximum range approaching 90°. In the normal standing position the foot makes a right angle with the leg, this is the neutral position of the joint (Fig. 5.122a). In dorsiflexion the foot is drawn upwards towards the leg; plantarflexion is movement in the opposite direction from the neutral position. The ranges of dorsiflexion and plantarflexion are essentially determined by the profiles of the articular surfaces: dorsiflexion having a range of 30°, and plantarflexion a range of 50°. There is, however, considerable individual variation in the extent of these movements (Fig. 5.122b).

In dorsiflexion the broader, anterior part of the trochlear surface of the talus is forced between the narrower posterior part of the tibiofibular mortise, causing a slight separation of the tibia and fibula and increased tension in the interosseous and transverse tibiofibular ligaments. It is in this close-packed position that the stability of the ankle joint is greatest. The movement of the fibula away from the tibia during dorsiflexion causes it to rotate about its long axis and to move upwards (see tibiofibular joints, p. 520). Dorsiflexion is produced by tibialis anterior, extensor hallucis longus, extensor digitorum and peroneus tertius crossing the joint anteriorly. It is limited by tension in gastrocnemius and soleus, the posterior part of the deltoid ligament, the calcaneofibular ligament and the posterior joint capsule, and the wedging of the talus between the malleoli. Should dorsiflexion continue, the anterior margin of the tibia can come into contact with the upper surface of the neck of the talus. If sufficient force is behind the movement, the neck of the talus or the anterior tibial margin or both can be fractured. The anterior part of the joint capsule is prevented from being nipped between the tibia and talus by being pulled up by the extensor muscles, whose sheaths are attached to the capsule (see Fig. 5.123a).

Shortening of the gastrocnemius and soleus muscles may check dorsiflexion prematurely. If the shortening is severe the ankle may be permanently fixed in plantarflexion (talipes equinus); lengthening of the tendocalcaneus by surgical intervention is required to restore full function.

In plantarflexion the narrower, posterior part of the trochlear of the talus moves forward into the broader part of the tibiofibular mortise. The malleoli tend to come together again to retain their grip upon the talus. In full plantarflexion some rotation, abduction and adduction, and side-to-side movement of the talus is possible. This is the position of least stability of the ankle joint. The approximation of the medial and lateral malleoli during plantarflexion is partly passive (recoil of the stretched interosseous and transverse tibiofibular ligaments) and partly active under the action of tibialis posterior, which attaches to both tibia and fibula. The accessory movements of the fibula are the reverse of those seen during dorsiflexion (see p. 522).

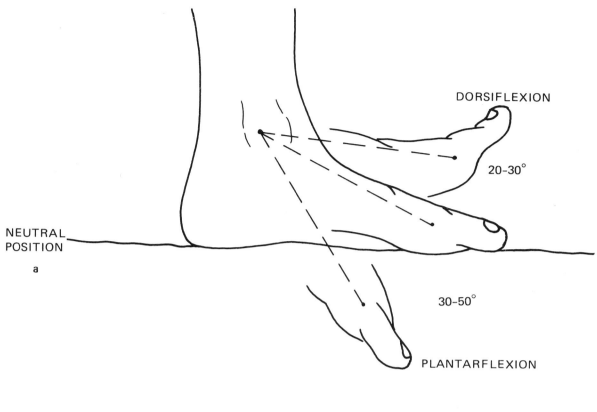

NEUTRAL
POSITION

DORSIFLEXION

20-30°

30-50°

PLANTARFLEXION

a

70°

DORSIFLEXION

20-30°

PLANTARFLEXION

30-50°

140-150°

ANTERIOR

b

Fig. 5.122   a = Movements of the foot in dorsiflexion and plantarflexion. **b** = The range of dorsiflexion and plantarflexion at the ankle joint determined by the profiles of the articular surfaces.

Plantarflexion is brought about mainly by soleus and gastrocnemius. However, all of the muscles which enter the foot behind the malleoli produce plantarflexion at the ankle, i.e. tibialis posterior, flexor digitorum longus, flexor hallucis longus, peroneus longus and peroneus brevis. The movement is checked by tension in the anterior muscles, the anterior part of the deltoid ligament, the anterior talofibular ligament and the anterior joint capsule. If these structures fail to arrest a forceful plantarflexion movement, then the posterior margin of the tibia may come into contact with the tubercles on the posterior surface of the talus, particularly the lateral. Rarely does this latter tubercle become fractured. The posterior joint capsule avoids becoming trapped between the bones by the presence of the posterior talofibular ligament and by its attachment to the sheath of flexor hallucis longus medially and the peronei laterally (Fig. 5.123b).

The wedge-shaped form of the joint surfaces helps to prevent backward displacement of the foot on the leg when coming to a sudden stop in jumping or running. The maintenance of this positive grip upon the talus is the function of the inferior tibiofibular joint.

When the body is erect, muscular effort, mainly by soleus and gastrocnemius, is necessary to prevent forward collapse. This destabilizing effect of gravity can be, and usually is, minimized by turning the feet out a little laterally, so that the inclination between the two ankle joint axes is increased.

Accessory movements

Two accessory movements are possible at the ankle joint. The first is a longitudinal distraction in which the talus is pulled away from the tibia and malleoli. It is performed with the subject lying supine. The calcaneus at the heel and the head of the talus on the dorsum of the foot are gripped and a longitudinal pull is exerted along the line of the tibia.

The second of these movements is in an anteroposterior direction. Again it is performed with the subject lying supine. The knee is flexed to 90° keeping the sole of the foot firmly pressed against the table. In this position the ankle joint is partly plantarflexed. Gripping the lower ends of the tibia and fibula they can be moved anteriorly and posteriorly by applying pressure in the appropriate direction.

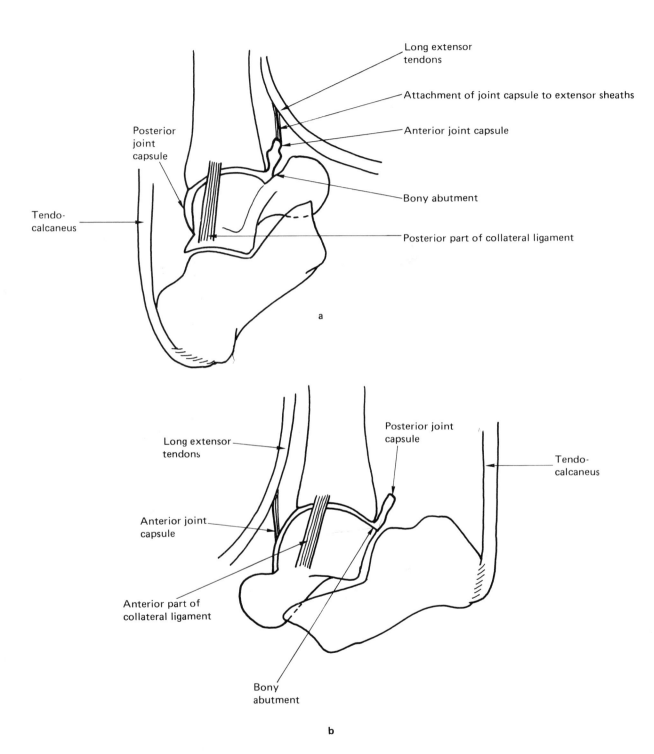

Fig. 5.123 Factors involved in limiting dorsiflexion (**a**) and plantarflexion (**b**).

Biomechanics

Although the total range of ankle joint motion approaches 90°, a much smaller range than this is used during gait. However, it must be remembered that with increasing speed of walking, ankle joint motion decreases, being mainly a decrease in plantarflexion (Fig. 5.124).

At heel-strike the ankle is slightly plantarflexed, immediately after which plantarflexion increases and then begins to decrease when full foot contact is made. As the body moves over the supporting foot, the ankle goes into dorsiflexion, which reaches a maximum just prior to the heel leaving the ground, after which it decreases. Just prior to toe-off the ankle once again becomes plantarflexed. During the swing phase there is a second wave of dorsiflexion, which together with a second wave of knee flexion ensures clearance between the toes and ground. Towards the end of the swing phase, the ankle becomes plantarflexed prior to heel-strike. Not only does an increase in cadence decrease the range of motion seen during the stance phase, it also brings forward the peak dorsiflexion wave well before the heel leaves the ground (Fig. 5.124).

Joint forces

During the gait cycle there are both tangential shear forces and compressive forces acting across the ankle joint. The tangential shear forces are in the anteroposterior direction and are the result of a combination of internal musculotendinous forces and external forces as the body moves over the foot. The force is biphasic and mainly directed posteriorly during the stance phase, reaching 80% of body weight as the heel leaves the ground (Fig. 5.125). During the last 15% of the stance phase, as the ankle goes into plantarflexion again, the shear force is directed anteriorly reaching 20% of body weight prior to toe-off.

Compressive forces across the ankle joint rise to three times body weight between heel-strike and full foot contact. Following heel-lift these forces rise to five times body

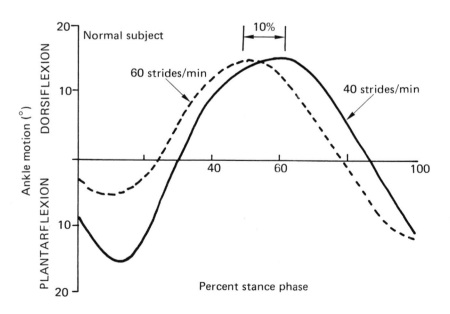

Fig. 5.124 The effect of walking speed on ankle joint motion. (Adapted from Stauffer R. N., Chao E. Y. S., Brewster R. C. (1977). Force and motion analysis of the normal, diseased, and prosthetic ankle joint. *Clinical Orthopaedics and Related Research*, **127**, 189–96.)

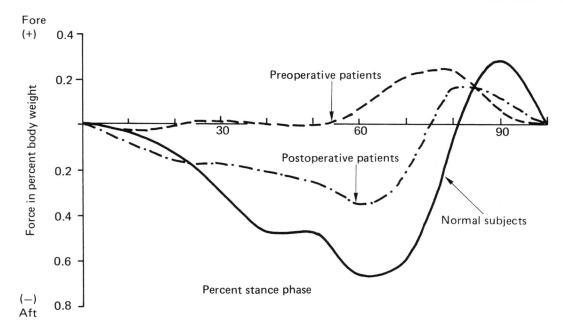

Fig. 5.125 The pattern of tangential ankle force during the stance phase of gait. (Adapted from Stauffer R. N., Chao E. Y. S., Brewster R. C. (1977). Force and motion analysis of the normal, diseased, and prosthetic ankle joint. *Clinical Orthopaedics and Related Research*, **127**, 189–96.)

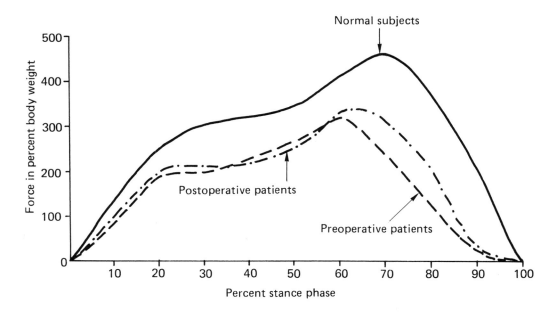

Fig. 5.126 The pattern of compressive ankle forces during the stance phase of gait. (Adapted from Stauffer R. N., Chao E. Y. S., Brewster R. C. (1977). Force and motion analysis of the normal, diseased, and prosthetic ankle joint. *Clinical Orthopaedics and Related Research*, **127**, 189–96.)

weight and then decrease to toe-off (see Fig. 5.126). With increasing speed, the relatively smooth pattern of compressive forces becomes markedly biphasic. Although the absolute magnitudes of these forces following heel-strike and prior to toe-off are not much greater than at lower speeds, the relative unloading of the cartilage between the two peaks effectively means that the articular cartilage undergoes two loading cycles per gait cycle. This rapid and alternating pattern of loading of the articular cartilage during fast walking may over a long period of time be responsible for some cartilage degeneration.

It would appear that patients with ankle joint disease have a poor tolerance to both compressive and shear forces across the joint (see the dashed line on Figs. 5.125, 5.126). Consequently, they modify their gait patterns in an attempt to reduce the magnitude of these forces.

Contact area and contact stresses

The occurrence of osteoarthrosis of the ankle joint is small in comparison with the other joints of the lower limb. If degenerative disease is the result of a fatigue process, it becomes important to know the magnitude of the contact stresses as well as the loading cycle. To calculate contact stresses the contact area of the joint needs to be known. Studies have suggested that the mean contact area at the ankle joint is between 1000 and 1500 mm^2. Bearing in mind that compressive forces across the joint are between three and five times body weight for the majority of the stance phase, this gives compressive contact stresses of between 1.4 MN/m^2 and 3.5 MN/m^2. These values are very similar to those calculated for the hip joint, which shows a much higher incidence of osteoarthrosis. This difference in the incidence of pathology under seemingly similar magnitudes of contact stresses can probably be accounted for by the much more complex loading patterns at the hip.

Trabecular arrangement (Fig. 5.127)

The transmission of mechanical forces across the joint is reflected in the arrangement and direction of the trabeculae within the associated bones. Two sets of trabeculae can be seen crossing the joint. One arises from the cortex on the anterior surface of the tibia and passes posteroinferiorly through the talus to the calcaneus. The other begins in the cortex on the posterior surface of the tibia and passes forwards and inferiorly through the talus. Medially, this system can be traced to the head of the first metatarsal, while laterally it can be traced to the head of the fifth metatarsal. The trabecular systems within the bones of the foot are considered in the section dealing with biomechanics of the foot (see p. 584).

Joint replacement/fusion

With total replacement of the joint the range of motion of the ankle joint during gait is generally within normal limits. However, the patterns are often abnormal. Normally in gait initial foot contact is with the heel, with the ankle slightly plantarflexed. In contrast, in patients with total replacement, initial foot–floor contact is with the entire foot with the ankle in maximum available passive plantarflexion. At the end of the stance phase the normal change from dorsiflexion to plantarflexion is not seen. Such alterations in the pattern of motion do not appear to be related to ligament instability, stiffness or pain in the ankle or foot.

Consequently, ankle fusion remains the procedure of choice for most painful ankle conditions, particularly if the subtalar and midtarsal joints are not involved and if the patient is going to subject the extremity to high levels of activity. Arthrodesis should be performed in a neutral position. An equinus position is unfavourable as it prevents an effective heel-strike occurring at the beginning of the stance phase of gait.

Fig. 5.127 The trabecular arrangement around the ankle joint: **a** = lateral view; **b** = medial view.

JOINTS OF THE FOOT

Introduction

It is widely believed that the human foot has evolved from the mobile, prehensile organ seen in many primates to the specialized, supporting structure necessary for bipedal locomotion. In contrast to the anthropoid foot the human foot is characterized by a reduction in the ability to oppose the great toe (Fig. 5.128a). This ability is not completely lost, however, as the requisite musculature is still present. Under certain circumstances, for example congenital absence of upper limbs, opposition of the great toe can become remarkably well developed, to the extent of holding a pen or fork. However, with this general reduction in opposability the metatarsal heads are no longer rotated towards each other as the gripping function of the toe requires, but are directed anteroposteriorly (Fig. 5.128b). With this, the axis of leverage of the foot has shifted to come to lie from between the second and third to between the first and second metatarsals. Correspondingly the axis of abduction/adduction of the toes is through the second digit, compared with the third in the hand (see Fig. 4.116, p. 265).

With the assumption of bipedal locomotion important changes have occurred within the calcaneus. The sustentaculum tali has become more massive, as has the calcaneus as a whole, and has assumed a more horizontal position (Fig. 5.128c), in order to be able to support the body of the talus and the superincumbent body weight. The calcaneus as a whole has changed its relative position within the foot from a downward to an upward position.

In primates adduction of the great toe gives the forefoot a medial direction. In the human foot this angulation disappears so that the axis of the foot follows a straight line (Fig. 5.128d). Consequently, the first and second metatarsals run more parallel to each other. With the medial shift of the axis of leverage, the medial border of the foot becomes flattened and depressed, and a transverse arch develops so that the supporting ball occupies the entire width of the foot (Fig. 5.128e).

The developmental changes which have occurred within the foot are essentially based upon the requirements to adjust the centre and line of gravity to a small supporting surface area. Having achieved this and adjusted the gravitational stresses to the area of support for a bipedal gait, further changes enabling a bipedal gait to be adopted had to be undertaken. An alternating bipedal gait has been the stimulus for the development of certain articulations to provide for static balance during standing and dynamic propulsion during walking and running.

The ankle and foot are the structures which provide propulsion and restraint at each step. A single joint, the ankle joint, has been established between the leg and the foot, which controls the foot in the sagittal plane (see p. 538). A second articulation, which allows side-to-side adjustment of the line of gravity in standing, as well as participating in restraint and propulsion, has been established between the talus and the calcaneus. This is the subtalar joint. Lastly a composite, functional joint has been established which interrupts the structure of the foot in the middle of the tarsus, the transverse (mid) tarsal joint. This joint plays an important part in putting the spring into the propulsive phase of gait, by allowing the anterior part of the foot to adjust itself

---

Fig. 5.128 **a** = The transition from an anthropoid to a human foot. **b** = Loss of rotation of the metatarsals during evolution of the human foot. **c** = Changes in the obliquity of the sustentaculum tali. **d** = Reduction in the angulation of the great toe. **e** = Anterior support of the foot, showing that all of the metatarsals participate.

Fig. 5.128

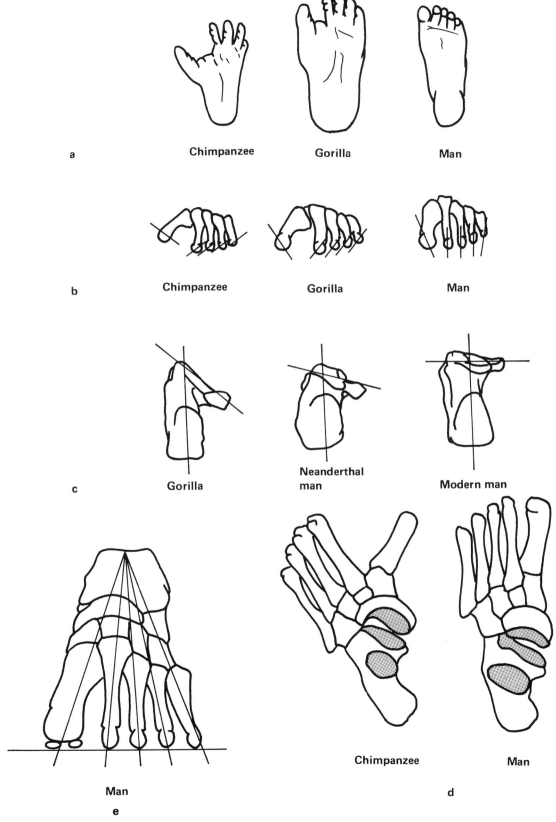

a   Chimpanzee   Gorilla   Man

b   Chimpanzee   Gorilla   Man

c   Gorilla   Neanderthal man   Modern man

d   Chimpanzee   Man

e   Man

against the posterior. By so doing the anterior footplate is able to maintain full contact with the supporting surface independent of the posterior part.

Besides forcing the foot into a right-angled posture with respect to the leg, bipedal gait has also produced some changes in the arrangement of the musculature around the ankle and within the foot. In humans, tibialis anterior has lost its insertion into the great toe. Both extensor digitorum longus and extensor hallucis longus split off from the primitive extensor plate as separate units, and a new unit, peroneus tertius, is formed. Peroneus tertius is an important muscle which aids in the pronation of the formerly supinated foot. Peroneus longus and brevis run behind the human ankle joint axis and are consequently now plantarflexors, as opposed to their previous role of dorsiflexors. In addition, because of the increased stress put on the anterior part of the foot in bipedal locomotion, the insertion of peroneus longus has migrated across the sole of the foot. Consequently, it now acts as a tie which helps to maintain the arches of the foot against depression. Finally, tibialis posterior has developed a fan-shaped insertion to all of the tarsal bones except the talus, thereby providing one of the principal supports of the longitudinal arches of the foot.

The human foot is strong to support the weight of the body, but also flexible and resilient to absorb the shocks transmitted to it and to provide spring and lift during activity. These properties are achieved by the presence of a series of arches, convex above, composed of a number of bones and their interconnecting joints. The joints and ligaments, together with muscle action, provide for spring for they yield when weight is applied and recoil when the weight is removed.

The bones of the foot are arranged in longitudinal and transverse arches (Fig. 5.129). The longitudinal arch, sometimes regarded as having two parts, lateral and medial, is supported posteriorly on the tuberosity of the calcaneus, and anteriorly on the metatarsal heads. The talus is at the summit of this arch, being primarily related to the navicular, the three cuneiforms and the medial three metatarsals (this is the medial longitudinal arch). The calcaneus is more directly related to the cuboid and lateral two metatarsals (the lateral longitudinal arch). These differences appear in the function of the foot, for the medial longitudinal arch has a greater curvature and is more elastic than the lateral. The flatter, more rigid lateral arch makes contact with the ground and provides a firm base for support. The transverse arch results from (1) the shape of the tarsal bones in the distal row, and (2) the bases of the metatarsals. Being broader dorsally, the bones articulate in a domed curve, thus forming a transverse arch.

The maintenance of these arches depends on the integrity of the tarsal, tarsometatarsal and intermetatarsal joints, because it is here that the bones are held in their proper relationships as segments of the arches. Some ligaments are consequently more important than others, being extremely strong to resist undue yielding of the joints and collapse of the arches. They are found on the plantar aspect of the joints and are themselves supported by the plantar aponeurosis and by the intervening musculature.

Fig. 5.129 **a** = Oblique X-ray of foot. **b** = Lateral X-ray of the tarsal bones. **c** = The medial longitudinal arch. **d** = The lateral longitudinal arch.

a

b

Talus

Calcaneus

Navicular

Cuneiforms

c

Talus

Metatarsals

Phalanges

Calcaneus

Cuboid

Fig. 5.129

d

As well as the movements of plantarflexion and dorsiflexion of the foot, both of which occur at the ankle, the foot can also be adducted or abducted about the long axis of the leg (Fig. 5.130a), and pronated or supinated about its own longitudinal axis (Fig. 5.130b). The movements of adduction (toes pointing towards the midline) and abduction take place in a transverse plane, and are only possible when the knee is flexed, when axial rotation of the tibia at the knee is possible. The adduction/abduction which occurs when the knee is extended is the result of medial and lateral rotation of the femur at the hip joint. The total range of abduction and adduction when they occur exclusively in the foot is 35°–45°. However, contributions from the leg (with the knee flexed) or whole limb (at hip joint) can increase this range to 90° in each direction, as seen in ballerinas. Movement of the foot about its own long axis causes the sole to face medially (supination) or laterally (pronation). The range of supination is about 50°, while that of pronation is only 25°–30°.

Because of the arrangement of the joints of the foot, neither adduction and abduction nor supination and pronation can occur as pure movements. Adduction of the foot is always accompanied by supination, while abduction is always accompanied by pronation. If plantarflexion and dorsiflexion are added to each of the above combinations of movements respectively then these movements are now known as inversion and eversion. An apparently pure movement of supination can be achieved by laterally rotating the leg at the knee to compensate for the accompanying adduction. Similarly, medial rotation of the leg at the knee can compensate for the linked abduction of the foot to produce an apparently pure movement of pronation. When balancing on one leg, a lateral rotation of the leg (i.e. relative adduction of the foot) is accompanied by pronation of the forefoot in an attempt to maintain full foot contact with the supporting surface. Supination of the forefoot accompanies medial rotation of the leg under similar circumstances.

The joints of the foot can be divided into four groups:

1. Intertarsal
2. Tarsometatarsal and intermetatarsal
3. Metatarsophalangeal
4. Interphalangeal

Intertarsal joints

The intertarsal joints are the subtalar, the talocalcaneonavicular, the calcaneocuboid, the transverse (mid) tarsal, the cuneonavicular, the intercuneiform and the cuneocuboid joints. The transverse tarsal joint is a functional description and comprises the separate talocalcaneonavicular joint medially and the calcaneocuboid joint laterally. The most important of these joints are those between the talus, calcaneus and navicular, and between the calcaneus and the cuboid. All of the joints are characterized by interosseous, dorsal and plantar ligaments, of which the plantar ligaments are much stronger than the dorsal. The bones and ligaments receive their blood supply from branches of the dorsalis pedis, medial plantar and lateral plantar arteries. They are supplied on the dorsal aspect by the deep peroneal nerve, and on their plantar aspect by the medial and lateral plantar nerves.

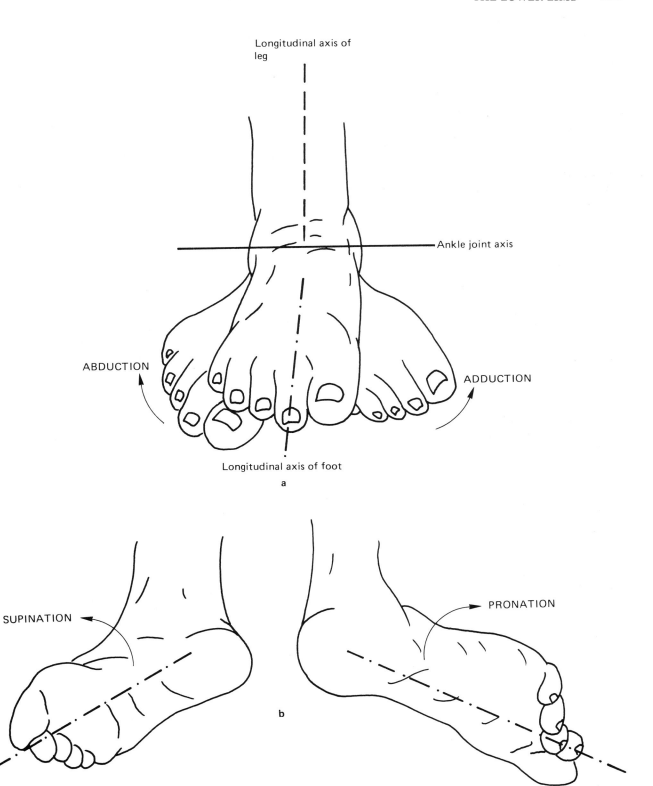

Longitudinal axis of
leg

Ankle joint axis

ABDUCTION

ADDUCTION

Longitudinal axis of foot

a

SUPINATION

PRONATION

b

Fig. 5.130 Abduction and adduction of the foot about the
longitudinal axis of the leg (**a**), and pronation and supination about the longitudinal axis of the foot (**b**).

Subtalar joint

Articular surfaces

The subtalar joint is a synovial joint formed between the concave facet on the undersurface of the body of the talus and the convex posterior facet on the upper surface of the calcaneus (Fig. 5.131). The articular facet on the calcaneus is roughly oval, with the long axis running anterolaterally; it is about this axis that the facet is convex, being plane or concave about the other axis. Consequently, the joint surface can be considered to be cylindrical, with the axis of the cylinder running obliquely from anterior, lateral and superior to posterior, medial and inferior.

The corresponding surface of the talus also has this cylindrical shape with a similar radius and a similar axis.

Joint capsule

A thin, loose, fibrous capsule surrounds the joint and attaches close to the margins of the articular surfaces. It is thickened medially, posteriorly and laterally forming the medial, posterior and lateral talocalcanean ligaments. The capsule is lined with synovial membrane; the joint cavity does not communicate with that of any other joint.

The anterior part of the capsule is thin and attaches to the floor and roof of the sinus tarsi. (The sinus tarsi is a narrow tunnel running obliquely forwards and laterally between the talus and calcaneus, in front of the subtalar joint. Its anterolateral end opens onto the dorsum of the foot.) Also attaching within the sinus tarsi is the posterior part of the talocalcaneonavicular joint capsule. Where the two capsules are adjacent to each other they are thickened and form the interosseous (talocalcanean) ligament.

Ligaments

Interosseous (talocalcanean) ligament This is a strong band composed of several laminae of fibres with fatty tissue between them. The interosseous ligament can best be thought of as two thick quadrilateral bands, an anterior and a posterior band (Fig. 5.132). The dense fibres of the anterior band pass obliquely superiorly, anteriorly and laterally from the floor of the sinus tarsi to the inferior surface of the neck of the talus just behind the articular surface of the head. The thick fibres of the posterior band run from the floor of the sinus tarsi obliquely superiorly, posteriorly and laterally to just in front of the posterior articular facet of the talus.

Between the two parts of the interosseous ligament lies the deep extension of the lateral limb of the inferior extensor retinaculum, which attaches to the floor of the sinus tarsi (Fig. 5.131).

Medial talocalcanean ligament The medial talocalcanean ligament runs from the medial tubercle of the posterior process of the talus to the posterior border of the sustentaculum tali (Fig. 5.132a).

Posterior talocalcanean ligament The posterior talocalcanean ligament is a short band whose fibres radiate out from a narrow attachment on the lateral tubercle of the talus to the upper and medial surfaces of the calcaneus (Fig. 5.132b)

Lateral talocalcanean ligament The lateral talocalcanean ligament is parallel to and deep to the calcaneofibular ligament. It runs obliquely inferiorly and posteriorly from the lateral tubercle of the talus to the lateral surface of the calcaneus (Fig. 5.132b).

Ligamentum cervicis At the lateral end of the sinus tarsi is the ligamentum cervicis (see Fig. 5.131), a strong discrete band attaching to the neck of the talus above and to the calcaneus below. It forms a strong ligamentous connection between the two bones, becoming taut in inversion.

The calcaneofibular ligament and talocalcaneal part of the deltoid ligament of the ankle joint act as accessory ligaments for the subtalar joint and provide additional support.

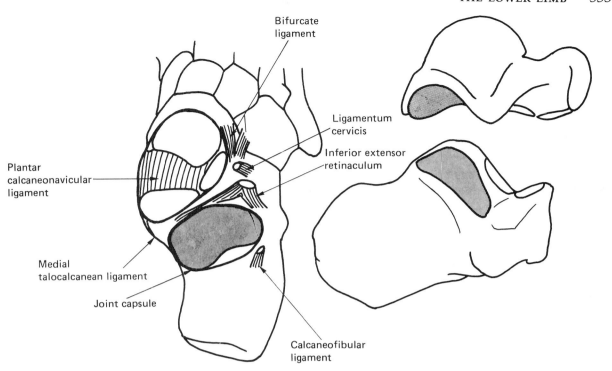

Fig. 5.131   The articular surfaces of the subtalar joint.

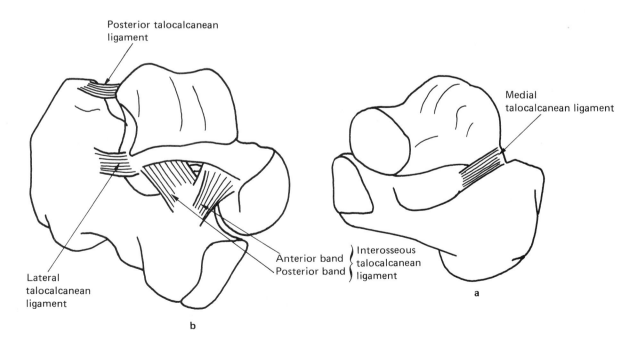

Fig. 5.132   The medial talocalcanean ligament (**a**) and the lateral, posterior and interosseous talocalcanean ligaments (**b**) associated with the subtalar joint.

Stability

The interosseous talocalcanean ligament plays an essential part in maintaining the stability of the subtalar joint, both at rest and during activity. It occupies a central position between the subtalar and talocalcaneonavicular joints, lying directly below the long axis of the leg (Fig. 5.133). Acting as the fulcrum around which movements of the leg and foot occur, it is continually being subjected to twisting and stretching strains.

The calcaneal parts of the medial and lateral ligaments of the ankle joint confer a considerable degree of stability at the subtalar joint by holding the talus between the leg and the calcaneus. In addition, the peroneal muscles laterally and flexor hallucis longus medially reinforce the ligamentous support. Indeed, without active muscle support the ligaments around the joint as well as the capsule would stretch under continuous strain.

Surface marking and palpation

The depth and complex articulations involved at this joint make surface marking and palpation impractical.

Accessory movements

With the subject lying prone with the foot overhanging the end of the bed, the talus can be gripped and stabilized by hooking one hand in front of its anterior surface. Firm pressure applied to the back of the heel with the other hand causes the calcaneus to slide forwards on the talus.

Talocalcaneonavicular joint

Articular surfaces

This is a synovial joint of the ball and socket variety. The ball is formed by a large continuous facet on the head and lower surface of the neck of the talus (Fig. 5.134a). The articular surface conforms in shape to the socket and is marked by faint ridges into a facet for the navicular anteriorly, for the sustentaculum tali posteroinferiorly with an anterolateral facet for the anterior part of the calcaneus, and a facet inferomedially for the plantar calcaneonavicular ligament.

The deep and extensive socket is formed partly by bone and partly by ligaments (Fig. 5.134b). Anteriorly, the socket is formed by the concave articular surface of the navicular, and posteriorly by the concave upper part of the sustentaculum tali and a concave facet on the anterior end of the upper surface of the calcaneus. These latter two facets may be fused into a single concavity. Between the articular surfaces on the calcaneus and navicular the head of the talus articulates with the deep surfaces of two ligaments, medially the plantar calcaneonavicular ligament and laterally the calcaneonavicular fibres of the bifurcate ligament.

Joint capsule and synovial membrane

The joint capsule is thin and encloses the common articular cavity. However, because of the nature of the bony and ligamentous socket, a true fibrous capsule is only present on the posterior and dorsal aspects of the joint. One end of the capsular sleeve attaches to the neck of the talus around the articular margin of the head. It extends forwards so that the other end of the sleeve attaches to the upper margin of the navicular, medially with the anterior fibres of the deltoid ligament that go to the navicular, the upper medial edge of the plantar calcaneonavicular ligament, the floor of the sinus tarsi, the medial limb of the bifurcate ligament and back to the upper surface of the navicular. The posterior part within the sinus tarsi blends with the anterior part of the subtalar joint capsule to form the interosseous (talocalcanean) ligament (see p. 552).

Synovial membrane lines all non-articular surfaces, including the fat pad that lies between the bifurcate and plantar calcaneonavicular ligaments on the plantar aspect of the joint. It is thought that this fat pad helps to spread synovial fluid over the moving head of the talus.

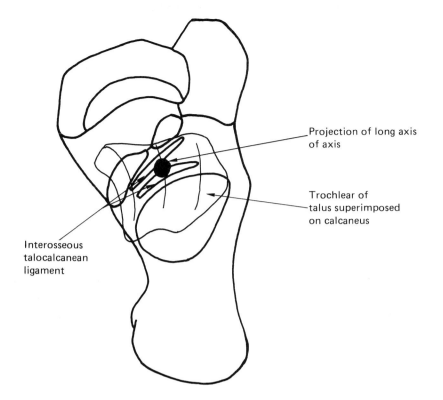

Fig. 5.133 The long axis of the leg projected into the foot showing its relationship to the interosseous talocalcanean ligament.

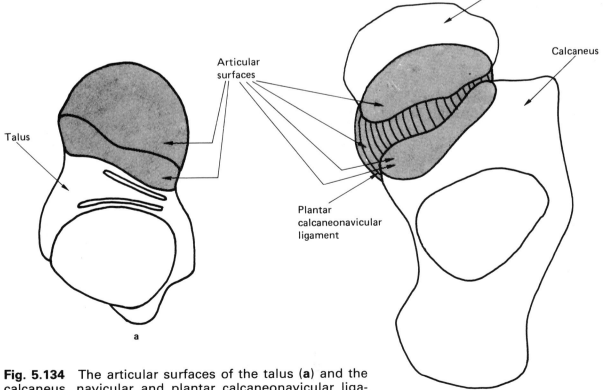

Fig. 5.134 The articular surfaces of the talus (**a**) and the calcaneus, navicular and plantar calcaneonavicular ligament (**b**) forming the talocalaneonavicular joint.

Ligaments

Two ligaments are intimately associated with the joint, their deep parts participating in the formation of the articular surfaces.

Plantar calcaneonavicular ligament The plantar calcaneonavicular ligament is a thick, dense fibroelastic ligament of considerable strength. It extends from the anterior end and medial border of the sustentaculum tali posteriorly, spreading out to attach to the entire width of the inferior surface of the navicular and to its medial surface behind the tuberosity (Fig. 5.135). The lower fibres of the ligament lie almost transversely across the foot. The ligament blends with, and is supported by, the deltoid ligament medially. The upper surface of the ligament is smooth and faceted and contains a fibrocartilaginous plate, for articulation with the head of the talus (see Fig. 5.134b). Because of its elasticity under the head of the talus, the ligament is also known and referred to as the 'spring ligament'.

Bifurcate ligament The calcaneonavicular part of the bifurcate ligament, which completes the socket laterally, is composed of short fibres that pass from the upper surface of the anterior end of the calcaneus to the adjacent lateral surface of the navicular bone (Fig. 5.135) (see also p. 558).

Dorsal talonavicular ligament The dorsal talonavicular ligament, which runs from the neck of the talus to the dorsal surface of the navicular (Fig. 5.135), reinforces the joint capsule dorsally between the bifurcate and the plantar calcaneonavicular ligaments.

Stability

The major elements contributing to the stability of the joint are the plantar calcaneonavicular and bifurcate ligaments described above, together with the tendon of tibialis posterior. The latter turning into the sole of the foot under the plantar calcaneonavicular ligament and therefore acting as a sling, both for the ligament and the head of the talus. Tension within the plantar calcaneonavicular ligament, supported by tibialis posterior, resists the tendency of body weight to push the head of the talus downwards between the two bones with which it articulates.

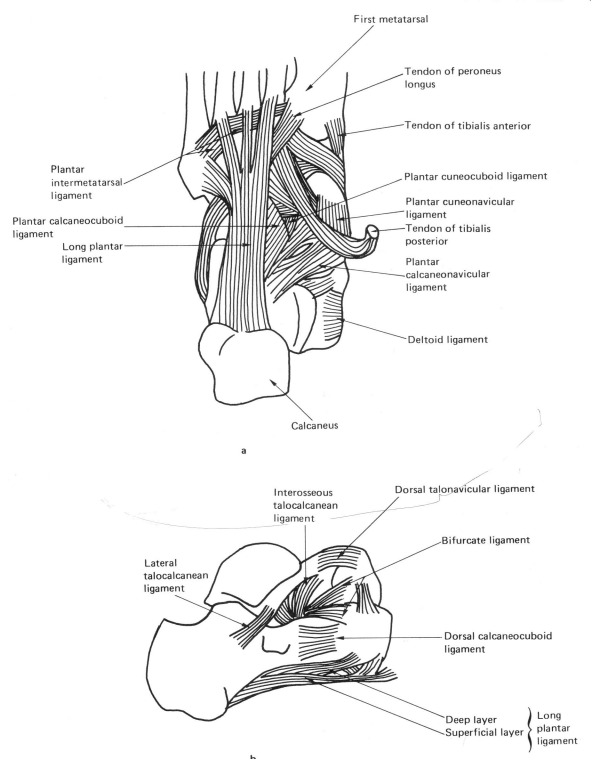

First metatarsal

Tendon of peroneus longus

Tendon of tibialis anterior

Plantar cuneocuboid ligament

Plantar cuneonavicular ligament

Tendon of tibialis posterior

Plantar calcaneonavicular ligament

Deltoid ligament

Plantar intermetatarsal ligament

Plantar calcaneocuboid ligament

Long plantar ligament

Calcaneus

a

Interosseous talocalcanean ligament

Dorsal talonavicular ligament

Bifurcate ligament

Lateral talocalcanean ligament

Dorsal calcaneocuboid ligament

Deep layer
Superficial layer } Long plantar ligament

b

Fig. 5.135 Ligaments associated with the talocalcaneonavicular joint seen from below (**a**) and laterally (**b**).

Calcaneocuboid joint

Articular surfaces

The calcaneocuboid joint is the articulation between the facets on the anterior surface of the calcaneus and the posterior surface of the cuboid (Fig. 5.136a). The articular surfaces of the two bones are gently undulating and quadrilateral in shape. The upper part of the facet on the calcaneus is concave transversely and vertically, while the lower part is convex both transversely and vertically. The articular surface of the cuboid is reciprocally concavoconvex, however there may be a medial extension of the facet which articulates with the navicular (Fig. 5.136b). If present, this extension is in the form of a plane surface.

Joint capsule and synovial membrane

A simple capsule completely surrounds the joint, separating the joint cavity from adjacent ones. It is thickened above and below by the dorsal and plantar calcaneocuboid ligaments respectively (see below). Synovial membrane lines the inside of the fibrous capsule and attaches to the margins of the articular surfaces.

Ligaments

Dorsal calcaneocuboid ligament The dorsal calcaneocuboid ligament is a relatively thin broad band which strengthens the dorsal aspect of the capsule (Fig. 5.136c).

Bifurcate ligament On the dorsomedial aspect of the joint is the calcaneocuboid part of the bifurcate ligament (Fig. 5.136c). It arises, in common with the calcaneonavicular part of the ligament, from the deep hollow on the upper surface of the calcaneus lateral to the anterior articular surface in front of the sinus tarsi undercover of extensor digitorum brevis, and attaches to the adjacent dorsomedial angle of the cuboid. This part of the bifurcate ligament is one of the main connections between the first and second row of tarsal bones.

Plantar calcaneocuboid ligament On the plantar aspect of the joint are two special ligaments separated by areolar tissue. The deeper plantar calcaneocuboid ligament (Fig. 5.136c) blends with and reinforces the joint capsule. It is a strong, broad band of short fibres which pass forwards from a rounded eminence at the anterior end of the inferior surface of the calcaneus, to the plantar surface of the cuboid behind the ridge that bounds the peroneal groove. The plantar calcaneocuboid ligament is sometimes known as the short plantar ligament.

Long plantar ligament Superficial to the plantar calcaneocuboid ligament is the long plantar ligament, which covers the plantar surface of the calcaneus (Fig. 5.136c). Posteriorly, it is attached between the posterior and anterior tubercles of the calcaneus. As it passes forwards the deeper fibres attach to the ridge on the cuboid, while the intermediate fibres bridge the groove on the cuboid to attach to its tuberosity, so forming a fibrous roof over the tendon of peroneus longus. The most superficial of the fibres passes forwards to attach to the bases of the lateral four metatarsals. Most of the ligament is covered by flexor accessorius (quadratus plantae), so that only its posterior part may be visible in the gap between the medial fleshy and lateral tendinous parts of the muscle. The long plantar ligament thus stretches under nearly the whole length of the lateral part of the foot, strengthening the plantar aspect of all of the joints in this region.

Stability

The calcaneocuboid joint receives the weight of the body as it is transmitted to the lateral part of the longitudinal arch of the foot. The essential stability required at this joint is provided by the plantar calcaneocuboid and long plantar ligaments. The tendon of peroneus longus passing anteromedially across the cuboid is an important tie reinforcing the ligaments.

Fig. 5.136 **a** = Articular surfaces of the calcaneocuboid joint. **b** = Medial view of the cuboid showing the occasional articular surface for the navicular. **c** = Ligaments associated with the calcaneocuboid joint.

Surface marking and palpation

The line of the calcaneocuboid joint can be determined by applying pressure to the dorsal surface of the lateral border of the foot just proximal to the tubercle of the fifth metatarsal.

Accessory movements

With the joint line identified, grip the calcaneus firmly between the thumb and index finger of one hand, and the cuboid with the other. Holding the calcaneus still the cuboid can slide up and down against it.

Transverse (mid) tarsal joint

The transverse tarsal joint is the name given to the combined talocalcaneonavicular and calcaneocuboid joints. It provides an irregular plane extending from side-to-side across the foot, with the talus and calcaneus behind and the navicular and cuboid in front (Fig. 5.137). Although the joints do not communicate they combine in a distinctive movement pattern which is an important contribution to the action of the foot. A small joint cavity frequently exists between the posteromedial angle of the cuboid and the lateral margin of the navicular. When present, the articulation is continuous in front with the cuneonavicular joint.

Ligaments

In addition to the ligaments associated with the component parts of the joint, additional ligaments unite the cuboid and navicular.

The *dorsal* and *plantar cuboideonavicular* ligaments pass between the adjacent parts of the corresponding surfaces of the two bones. A strong *interosseous cuboideonavicular* ligament connects the rough non-articular portions of their adjacent surfaces.

Movements of the subtalar and transverse tarsal joints

In dorsiflexion and plantarflexion the talus rotates in the tibiofibular mortice, so that the foot moves as a single unit. In other movements of the foot the calcaneus and navicular move on the talus, and in so doing carry with them the distal tarsal bones and the metatarsals. The movements which occur at the subtalar and transverse tarsal joints produce inversion and eversion of the foot. These movements allow the foot to be placed firmly on slanting or irregular surfaces and yet still provide a firm base of support. In walking across sloping surfaces, for example, the upper foot has to be everted and the lower inverted. Furthermore, when turning at speed the movements of inversion and eversion are essential in order to lean sideways on a foot whose sole is flat on the ground. Most inversion/eversion movements are consequently performed on a foot anchored to the ground, with the leg and body inverting and everting above it.

In inversion, the foot is twisted so that the medial border is raised and the lateral border depressed until the sole faces medially. Inversion is a combined movement of adduction and supination of the foot, accompanied by plantarflexion at the ankle; indeed, adduction and supination cannot occur as pure movements, one always accompanies the other. Eversion is the opposite of inversion so that the lateral border of the foot is raised and the medial lowered so that the sole is turned laterally. Similarly, eversion is the combined movement of abduction and pronation of the foot, usually being accompanied by dorsiflexion at the ankle. As before, abduction and pronation cannot occur as pure movements, one is always accompanied by the other.

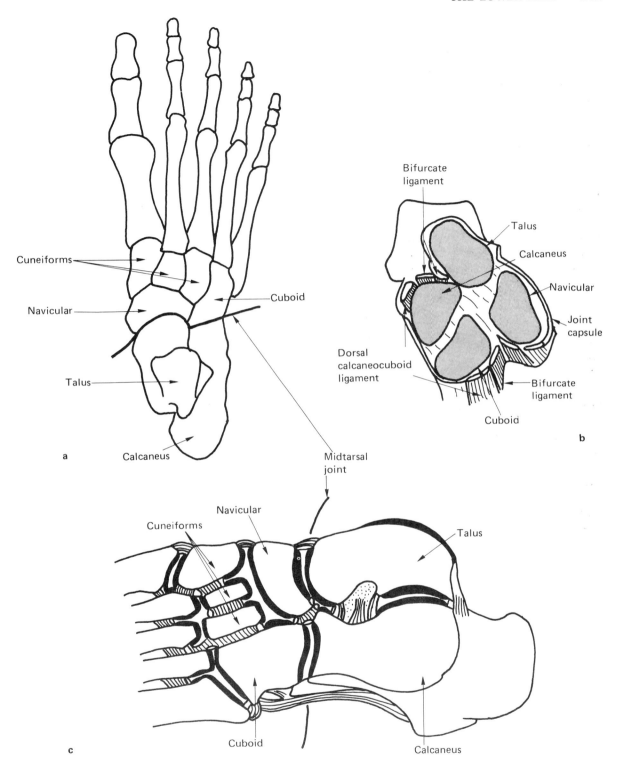

Fig. 5.137 **a** = Line of the midtarsal joint seen on dorsal
view of foot. **b** = Articular surfaces of the midtarsal joint.
c = Oblique section of left foot showing the line of the midtarsal joint.

Inversion and eversion occur principally at the subtalar and transverse tarsal joints, although movement does occur at other tarsal and the tarsometatarsal joints, with the amount diminishing the further distal the joint. The composite movements of the calcaneus, navicular and cuboid with respect to the fixed talus are of necessity complex, nevertheless inversion and eversion can be considered to occur around a single axis. This axis runs obliquely upwards, forwards and medially beginning at the posterolateral tubercle of the calcaneus, through the sinus tarsi in the region of the ligamentum cervicis to emerge at the superomedial aspect of the neck of the talus. The subtalar and transverse tarsal joints are thus mechanically linked.

Inversion is produced by tibialis anterior and tibialis posterior, assisted occasionally by extensor and flexor hallucis longus. The dorsiflexion and plantarflexion effects of the tibialis muscles cancel out to produce inversion. Under the action of tibialis posterior the navicular (and with it the cuboid) is pulled medially (adducted) so that the forefoot moves anteriorly and medially (Fig. 5.138a). This movement is checked by tension in the dorsal talonavicular ligament. At the same time these two bones rotate about an anteroposterior axis passing through the bifurcate ligament, which actively resists torsion and traction stresses. This rotation produces supination because the navicular

is raised while the cuboid is lowered (Fig. 5.138a). The elevation and depression of the medial and lateral longitudinal arches respectively causes the sole to face medially.

Eversion is produced by the peroneal muscles longus, brevis and tertius. The plantarflexing actions of peroneus longus and brevis are offset by the dorsiflexing action of peroneus tertius and extensor digitorum longus. Under the action of the peroneal muscles the navicular and cuboid are pulled laterally (abducted) so that the forefoot moves anteriorly and laterally (Fig. 5.138b). Rotation of the two bones about the same anteroposterior axis as before produces pronation by raising the cuboid and lowering the navicular (Fig. 5.138b). The effect on the lateral and medial longitudinal arches is to turn the sole to face laterally. Eversion is checked by impact of the talus on the floor of the sinus tarsi, which consequently closes down. In addition, the upward movement of the cuboid on the calcaneus is limited by the anterior process of the calcaneus and tension developed in the powerful plantar calcaneocuboid ligament, which rapidly stops the joint interspace opening out inferiorly.

During inversion/eversion movements the calcaneus does not remain immobile below the talus. In inversion it is pulled anteriorly by the cuboid, while during eversion it moves posteriorly.

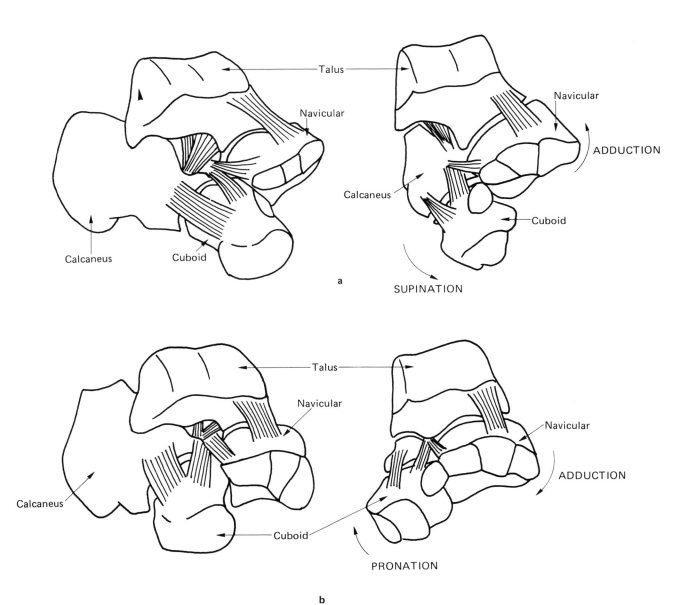

Fig. 5.138 Relationship of the talus, calcaneus, cuboid and navicular during inversion (**a**) and eversion (**b**) of the foot.

Cuneonavicular joint

Articular surfaces

The anterior surface of the navicular is generally convex but shows three distinct articular facets (Fig. 5.139a), separated by more or less vertical ridges, for the concave posterior ends of the three cuneiform bones. The articular surfaces glide against each other and move apart so that the interspace of the joint gapes slightly.

Joint capsule and cavity

A fibrous capsule surrounds the joint, which is distinct on all sides except laterally where it may communicate with the cuneocuboid joint, and always with the cuboideonavicular joint when present. Anteriorly the joint cavity forms recesses between the cuneiforms (Fig. 5.139b), which may communicate with the tarsometatarsal joint between the intermediate cuneiform and the second and third metatarsals, and with the intermetatarsal joints between the second and third, and third and fourth metatarsals.

Ligaments

Dorsal cuneonavicular ligaments The dorsal cuneonavicular ligaments are relatively weak short bands in the upper and medial parts of the capsule (Fig. 5.139c). They pass from the navicular to each cuneiform.

Plantar cuneonavicular ligaments The plantar cuneonavicular ligaments are much stronger bands, on the plantar surface of the joint. They blend with and are inseparable from the slips of insertion of the tibialis posterior tendon.

Intercuneiform joints

The cuneiforms articulate by plane synovial joints on the posterior aspect of their adjacent surfaces (Fig. 5.139b). The three cuneiforms are bound together by the relatively weak, transverse dorsal intercuneiform ligaments, and the much stronger interosseous and plantar intercuneiform ligaments. The

latter two ligaments usually form the anterior boundary of the joint cavities.

Cuneocuboid joint

Articular surfaces

The articulation is between a round facet on the posterosuperior surface of the cuboid and a large round articular surface on the posterolateral aspect of the lateral cuneiform (Fig. 5.139d).

Ligaments

Dorsal cuneocuboid ligament The dorsal cuneocuboid ligament is a weak band, blending with the capsule, passing between the dorsal surfaces of the two bones (Fig. 5.139c).

Plantar cuneocuboid ligament The plantar cuneocuboid ligament is also weak, and attaches to the adjacent surfaces of the bones, again blending with the joint capsule.

Interosseous cuneocuboid ligament The interosseous cuneocuboid ligament is stronger than the dorsal and plantar ligaments and unites the adjacent surfaces of the bones. It limits the joint cavity anteriorly.

Stability

The cuboid and the three cuneiform bones, being placed side-by-side across the foot form the tarsal part of the transverse arch. Stability and integrity of the joints is maintained by the strong interosseous and plantar intercuneiform and cuneocuboid ligaments. The tendon of peroneus longus passing transversely across the foot provides additional support.

Movements

The cuneonavicular, intercuneiform and cuneocuboid joints permit a slight gliding movement between the adjacent bones, which contributes to the flexibility and adaptability of the foot.

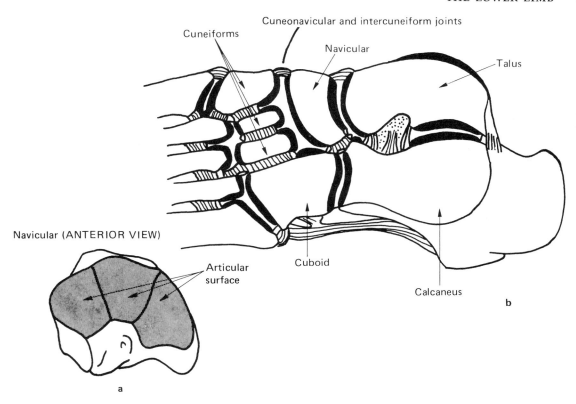

Cuneiforms

Cuneonavicular and intercuneiform joints

Navicular

Talus

Navicular (ANTERIOR VIEW)

Articular surface

Cuboid

Calcaneus

b

a

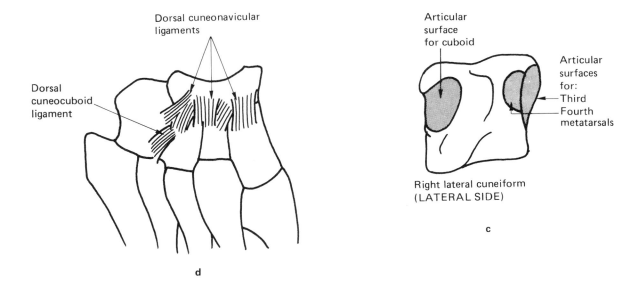

Dorsal cuneonavicular ligaments

Dorsal cuneocuboid ligament

Articular surface for cuboid

Articular surfaces for:
— Third
— Fourth metatarsals

Right lateral cuneiform (LATERAL SIDE)

c

d

Fig. 5.139 **a** = Articular surface of the navicular for the cuneiforms. **b** = Oblique view of the foot showing the cuneonavicular and intercuneiform joints. **c** = Articular surface on the lateral cuneiform for the cuboid. **d** = Dorsal cuneonavicular and cuneocuboid ligaments.

Accessory movements

The basic principle of demonstrating accessory movements at the cuneonavicular, intercuneiform and cuneocuboid joints is the same; one of the bones is held steady while the other is moved against it. This is achieved by gripping the two bones between the thumb and index finger, one in each hand. A gliding of one bone against the other is produced by holding one steady and applying pressure to the other. For example, if the navicular is held steady the medial cuneiform can be felt to move up and down against it.

Surface markings and palpation

The tuberosity of the navicular can be readily palpated distal to the head of the talus on the medial border of the foot. With careful and fairly deep palpation the transverse running joint lines of the cuneonavicular joints and the anteroposterior joint lines of the intercuneiform joints can be identified on the dorsum of the foot.

Tarsometatarsal joints

These joints are between the four anterior tarsal bones (cuboid and the three cuneiforms) and the bases of all five metatarsals (Fig. 5.140a). The 'line of the joint' is irregular and arched, yet it is fairly mobile.

Articular surfaces

The tarsometatarsal joints are all plane synovial joints which overlap one another. The first metatarsal articulates only with the medial cuneiform. The base of the second metatarsal is held in a mortise formed by the three cuneiforms and therefore articulates with all of them; the lateral side of the medial, the distal end of the intermediate, and the medial side of the lateral cuneiform (Fig. 5.140a). Because of this deep mortise, the second metatarsal is the least mobile of the metatarsals. The third metatarsal articulates with the lateral cuneiform only. The fourth metatarsal articulates mainly with the cuboid, but also to a small extent with the

lateral cuneiform, while the fifth metatarsal articulates only with the cuboid.

Joint cavities, capsule and synovial membrane

The presence of two strong interosseous tarsometatarsal ligaments (see below) divides the joint cavity into three separate parts (Fig. 5.140a). The medial cavity is confined to the articulation between the first metatarsal and the medial cuneiform. The intermediate cavity includes the articulations between the second and third metatarsals and the intermediate and lateral cuneiforms respectively. This cavity is usually prolonged forwards between the bases of the two metatarsals. In addition it may communicate behind with the cuneonavicular joint between the intermediate and medial cuneiforms. The lateral cavity is the articulation between the fourth and fifth metatarsals and the cuboid. This cavity extends forwards between the bases of the two metatarsals.

The joint capsules surrounding the tarsometatarsal joints attach to the articular margins of the various bones. In practice there are very few true capsular fibres as the interosseous, plantar and dorsal tarsometatarsal ligaments close the joints.

Synovial membrane lines the non-articular joint surfaces, attaching to the articular margins.

Ligaments

Dorsal tarsometatarsal ligaments These are weak, short slips that pass between the adjacent dorsal surfaces of the tarsal and metatarsal bones, each metatarsal receiving a slip from the tarsal bones that it articulates with (Fig. 5.140b).

Fig. 5.140 **a** = Dorsal aspect of foot showing the line of the tarsometatarsal joint. **b** = The dorsal tarsometatarsal ligaments. **c** = The plantar tarsometatarsal ligaments. **d** = Oblique view of foot showing the tarsometatarsal and intertarsal joints.

Dorsal tarsometatarsal ligaments

Plantar tarsometatarsal ligaments

Tarsometatarsal joint line

Navicular

Cuneiforms

Metatarsals

Talus

Calcaneus

Cuboid

Fig. 5.140

a

b

c

d

Plantar tarsometatarsal ligaments These are similar bands on the plantar surface of joints but are generally less well organized, consisting of both longitudinal and oblique fibres (Fig. 5.140c). Those ligaments associated with the medial two metatarsals are the strongest, with the remaining tarsometatarsal joints being strengthened by fibres from the long plantar ligament.

Interosseous tarsometatarsal ligaments Two interosseous tarsometatarsal ligaments are always present; there may occasionally be a third. The first interosseous ligament passes from the anterolateral surface of the medial cuneiform to the medial side of the base of the second metatarsal. The second interosseous ligament passes from the anterolateral angle of the lateral cuneiform to the medial surface of the base of the fourth metatarsal. Between these two ligaments is found the third, inconstant interosseous ligament. When present it passes from the lateral side of the second metatarsal to the lateral cuneiform.

Stability

The various ligaments associated with the joints convey a certain degree of stability, particularly medially. Stability is further reinforced on the plantar surface medially by the insertion of muscles. Slips from the tibialis posterior tendon reinforce the plantar aspects of the joints of the medial three metatarsals. The insertion of tibialis anterior to the medial sides of the first metatarsal and medial cuneiform, and of peroneus longus laterally further strengthen and stabilize the tarsometatarsal joint of the great toe.

Intermetatarsal joints

The bases of the lateral four metatarsals articulate by small synovial joints between facets on their adjacent sides (see Fig. 5.140d). There is no joint between the bases of the first and second metatarsals as they are joined together by interosseous fibres only. The joint spaces between the second and third, and third and fourth metatarsals are forward extensions of the intermediate tarsometatarsal joint cavity, while that between the fourth and fifth metatarsals is continuous with the lateral tarsometatarsal joint cavity.

The various joint spaces are closed on their dorsal and plantar aspects by transverse running dorsal and plantar ligaments passing between the adjacent surfaces of the bases of the metatarsals. Anteriorly the joint spaces are limited by the strong interosseous metatarsal ligaments.

Stability

The stability of these joints is due to the dorsal, plantar and interosseous metatarsal ligaments. In particular the strong bands of the interosseous ligaments help to maintain the transverse arch of the foot by holding together the bases of the metatarsals as segments of that arch.

Surface markings and palpation

The transverse joint line between the base of the first metatarsal and the medial cuneiform is readily palpable on the medial side of the foot. Similarly, on the lateral side the joint line between the base of the fifth metatarsal and the cuboid is easily recognized. However, the joint lines of the second, third and fourth tarsometatarsal joints are not so easy to determine. The lines of the metatarsal joints between the first and second, and fourth and fifth metatarsals can be identified running anteroposteriorly between the bones. Once again, the intervening joint lines are difficult to determine.

Accessory movements

Accessory movements between adjacent bones can be demonstrated by holding one bone steady and moving the other. Perhaps the most impressive of these movements that can be demonstrated in this region is that between the base of the fifth metatarsal and the cuboid.

Blood and nerve supply

The blood supply to the tarsometatarsal and intertarsal joints is from branches of the dorsalis pedis on their dorsal aspects and the medial and lateral plantar arteries of their plantar aspect.

Similarly, the nerve supply is by twigs from the deep peroneal nerve dorsally and the medial and lateral plantar nerves on their plantar aspect.

Movements

The interlocking of the bones at the tarso-metatarsal joints and the strong intermetatarsal ligaments allows, except at the first tarsometatarsal joint, only a small degree of movement. In spite of this small amount of movement, the joints contribute to the flexibility of the foot, particularly to inversion and eversion.

As a whole, the line of the tarsometatarsal joints runs obliquely from medial, superior and anterior to lateral, inferior and posterior, so that its medial end lies approximately 2 cm anterior to the lateral end (Fig. 5.141a). Although the line of the joint is oblique, the two ends have opposite obliquity, with the medial joint space running anterolaterally while the lateral joint space runs anteromedially. The obliquity of the axis, which essentially only allows flexion and extension movements to occur, is a contributory factor to inversion and eversion. Consequently, the axis of flexion and extension of the lateral tarsometatarsal joints is oblique to the long axis of the metatarsals, so that during plantarflexion the metatarsals move towards the axis of the foot. In other words, flexion of the metatarsals is accompanied by adduction. Similarly, because of the obliquity of the first tarsometatarsal joint, plantarflexion of the first metatarsal is accompanied by about 15° adduction (Fig. 5.141b).

This plantarflexion and adduction of the first metatarsal is accompanied by a slight degree of rotation. The adduction movements of the metatarsals is assisted by the shapes of the articular surfaces of the cuboid and cuneiforms.

As the heads of the metatarsals move inferiorly and towards the axis of the foot in plantarflexion, this increases the curvature of the transverse arch with a hollowing of the anterior part of the foot (Fig. 5.141b). Conversely, dorsiflexion at the tarsometatarsal joint, in which the metatarsals move superiorly and away from the axis of the foot, causes a flattening of the transverse arch.

The mobility of the first metatarsal in comparison to the remaining metatarsals is necessary during adaptation of the foot to the ground in inversion and eversion, as when walking over rough terrain. In contrast, the immobility of the second metatarsal, wedged between the medial and lateral cuneiforms, together with the slenderness of its shaft are contributory factors in 'spontaneous' fracture of the bone.

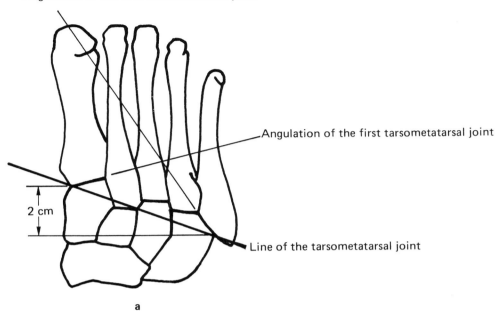

Angulation of the fifth tarsometatarsal joint

Angulation of the first tarsometatarsal joint

2 cm

Line of the tarsometatarsal joint

a

M5 M4 M3 M2 M1

Weightbearing

Non-weightbearing

b

Fig. 5.141 **a** = The general obliquity of the tarsometatarsal joint axis, showing that the medial end of the joint line is some 2 cm anterior to the lateral end. **b** = Change in the height of the transverse metatarsal arch upon weight-bearing.

Metatarsophalangeal joints

These are synovial condyloid joints between the rounded head of the metatarsal and the cupped base of the proximal phalanx (Fig. 5.142). The convex articular surfaces of the metatarsals cover the dorsal, distal and plantar surfaces, with the plantar surface being more extensive to facilitate plantarflexion at the joint.

Joint capsule and capsular thickenings

The joint capsule is loose and attaches close to the articular margins of the bones (Fig. 5.143a). It is lined by synovial membrane which also attaches to the articular margins. The capsule is reinforced laterally by strong collateral ligaments, on its plantar surface by the plantar ligament, and dorsally by fibres from the extensor tendons.

Ligaments

Collateral ligaments   The strong collateral ligaments of each joint pass from the tubercles on each side of the head of the metatarsal, fanning out to attach to the sides of the proximal end of the phalanx as well as to the sides of the plantar ligament (Fig. 5.143a). Passing obliquely downwards and forwards they become tense during flexion of the joint, and therefore serve to restrict this movement.

Plantar ligament   The plantar ligament is a dense fibrocartilaginous plate firmly attached to the proximal plantar border of the proximal phalanx, forming part of the articular surface for the metatarsal head, attaching at the sides to the collateral and deep transverse metatarsal ligaments. In the great toe, the sesamoid bones and their interconnecting ligamentous band almost completely replace the plantar ligament. The sesamoid bones are cartilage-covered on their upper surface and articulate with grooves on the undersurface of the head of the first metatarsal. The plantar ligaments are grooved by the long flexor tendons passing to the toes.

Deep transverse metatarsal ligament   The plantar ligaments of all the joints are interconnected by the deep transverse metatarsal ligament, which connects the heads and joint capsules of all the metatarsals (Fig. 5.143b). The ligament is crossed on its plantar surface by the tendons of the lumbrical muscles, and on its dorsal surface by the interosseous tendons.

Stability

The metatarsophalangeal joints have the long extensor and flexor tendons crossing on their dorsal and plantar surfaces respectively. In the lateral four toes these tendons provide some stability for the joints. However, the great toe has no extensor expansion or flexor sheath, the long tendons being held in place by strands of deep fascia. If the phalanges of the great toe become displaced laterally and the fibrous sheaths give way, then the pull of extensor hallucis longus, like that of extensor hallucis brevis, becomes oblique to the long axis of the toe, tending to increase the hallux valgus deformity.

In rheumatoid arthritis, the metatarsophalangeal joints often assume a dorsiflexed position due to the imbalance in muscle tension across the joint. There may be dislocation of the sesamoid bones with them becoming repositioned in the first web space. In association with the dorsiflexed position of the joint, the metatarsal heads become depressed and subcutaneous. If the depression is severe it produces a plantarward convex arch.

a
b

Fig. 5.142 Dorsiplantar (**a**) and oblique (**b**) views of the foot showing the metatarsophalangeal and interphalangeal joints.

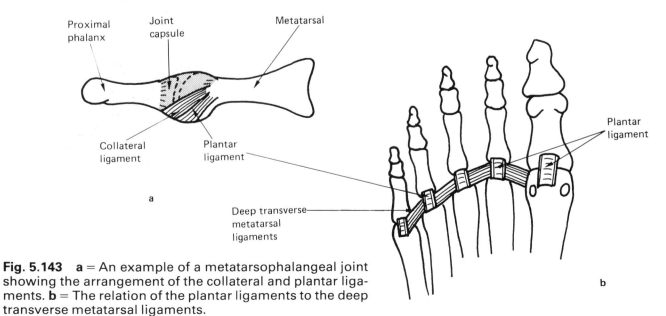

Proximal phalanx   Joint capsule   Metatarsal

Collateral ligament   Plantar ligament

a

Deep transverse metatarsal ligaments

Plantar ligament

b

Fig. 5.143   a = An example of a metatarsophalangeal joint showing the arrangement of the collateral and plantar ligaments. **b** = The relation of the plantar ligaments to the deep transverse metatarsal ligaments.

Movements

The metatarsophalangeal joints permit dorsiflexion, plantarflexion, abduction, adduction and circumduction.

Dorsiflexion is carried out by the extensors, and is such that the proximal phalanx can be carried beyond the line of the metatarsal (Fig. 5.144a). During dorsiflexion the toes tend to be spread apart and become slightly inclined laterally.

Plantarflexion is performed by the flexor tendons passing to the digits (Fig. 5.144a). During this movement the toes tend to be pulled together.

Because of the arrangement of the interosseous muscles and the immobility of the second metatarsal, abduction and adduction take place about the second toe. Abduction being the province of the dorsal interossei and the abductors hallucis and digiti minimi. Adduction is carried out by the plantar interossei and adductor hallucis.

Accessory movements

With the head of the metatarsal gripped and stabilized between the thumb and index finger of one hand, and the adjacent phalanx held with the other, the phalanx can be slid up and down as well as rotated with respect to the metatarsal.

Surface markings and palpation

With the metatarsophalangeal joints flexed, the heads of the metatarsals stand out and can be easily palpated on the dorsal surface of the foot. Moving the toes slowly back to the neutral position the line of each of the metatarsophalangeal joints can be identified on palpation of the dorsal aspect of the foot.

Interphalangeal joints

Articular surfaces

The head of the more proximal phalanx articulates with the base of the next distal phalanx in the series (see Fig. 5.142). The heads of the phalanges have a pulley-shaped articular surface, which appears as a double convexity, and articulate with a double concavity on the base of the more distal phalanx (Fig. 5.144b).

Joint capsule and capsular thickenings

As with the metatarsophalangeal joints, the joint capsule attaches close to the articular margins, being reinforced or indeed replaced by collateral ligaments at the sides, the thick plantar ligament, and the expansion of the extensor tendon, where appropriate dorsally (see Fig. 5.143a). The joint capsule is lined by synovial membrane which attaches to the articular margins. The distal interphalangeal joint of the little toe is often obliterated.

Ligaments

Collateral ligaments The strong collateral ligaments of each joint pass downwards and forwards from the sides of the head of each phalanx, adjacent to the articular surface, to the base of the more distal phalanx, again attaching adjacent to the articular surface (see Fig. 5.143a). The ligaments also pass to the sides of the plantar ligaments.

Plantar ligaments The plantar ligament, like that of the metatarsophalangeal joint, is a pad of fibrocartilage forming part of the articular surface for the phalangeal head.

Movements

Because of the shape of the articular surfaces the interphalangeal joints are hinge joints permitting dorsiflexion and plantarflexion only (Fig. 5.144a). Plantarflexion towards the sole of the foot is produced by the flexor digitorum longus and brevis muscles at the distal and proximal interphalangeal joints respectively. Dorsiflexion away from the sole is produced by the extensor muscles, as well as the lumbricals and the interossei.

Accessory movements

These are the same as for the metatarsophalangeal joints except that there is little rotation.

Surface markings and palpation

The larger interphalangeal joints can be palpated on the dorsal surface of the toes, the joint lines running transversely between the bones.

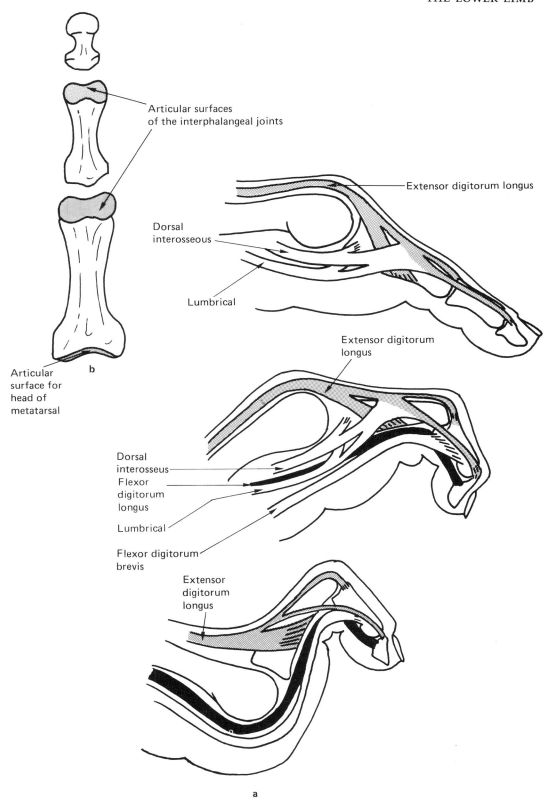

Fig. 5.144 **a** = Medial view of second toe showing movements of the interphalangeal and metatarsophalangeal joints. **b** = Articular surfaces of the interphalangeal joints seen from the plantar aspect.

Blood and nerve supply

The blood and nerve supply to both meta-tarsophalangeal and interphalangeal joints are from branches of the dorsal and plantar digital vessels and nerves.

Palpation of the foot

The medial and lateral malleoli are readily palpable (see pp. 329–330). Behind each malleolus is a hollow behind which the tendocalcaneus is easily palpated. It can be traced onto the prominent projection of the calcaneus at the heel.

Below the lateral malleolus and slightly anterior to its tip is the peroneal tubercle on the lateral side of the calcaneus. In front of the lateral malleolus the talus is palpable for a short distance. If the foot is inverted the head of the talus forms a marked projection on the superolateral aspect of the foot approximately 4 cm anterior to the lateral malleolus. In a slender foot the distal end of the calcaneus can be felt leading to a hollow over the cuboid to the projection of the base of the fifth metatarsal.

Medially below the malleolus the talus can be felt, especially if the foot is everted, with the sustentaculum tali of the calcaneus below it. Below the sustentaculum tali is the prominence of the heel. Anterior to the medial malleolus the tubercle of the navicular can be palpated, and anterior to that the medial cuneiform, then the base of the first metatarsal. Moving laterally from the medial cuneiform, the remaining cuneiforms and then the cuboid can be identified.

Along the borders of the foot the shafts leading to the heads of the first and fifth metatarsals can be palpated, as can the shafts of all the metatarsals on the dorsum of the foot.

On the sole of the foot, the heads of the metatarsals can be readily palpated, particularly with the toes dorsiflexed. The phalanges may be palpated at their sides along their length.

With care and practice each of the tarsal and metatarsal bones can be identified and palpated. Consequently, in a relaxed position, the integrity and mobility of any of the joints of the foot can be tested by applying firm pressure to the appropriate bones in the direction of movement.

On the dorsum of the foot the tendons of tibialis anterior, the extensors hallucis and digitorum longus, and peroneus tertius can be seen and traced from their relative positions in front of the ankle joint to their insertions (Fig. 5.145a). The fleshy belly of extensor digitorum brevis can be seen as a swelling lateral to the digitorum longus tendons, on the dorsal surface of the calcaneus beyond the ankle joint, from which the individual tendons can be traced to the medial four toes.

Running behind the lateral malleolus, the tendons of peroneus longus and brevis can be palpated, separating to pass below and above the peroneal tubercle respectively (Fig. 5.145b), peroneus brevis can be traced to its insertion while peroneus longus disappears deep to the plantar aponeurosis.

The tendons of tibialis posterior and flexor digitorum longus can be identified behind the medial malleolus but soon pass into the sole of the foot (Fig. 5.145b). In a slender foot the tendon of flexor hallucis longus may occasionally be felt in the hollow between the flexor digitorum longus tendon and the tendocalcaneus.

The dorsalis pedis artery, a continuation of the anterior tibial artery, passes into the foot lateral to the tendon of extensor hallucis longus (Fig. 5.145a). Its pulsations can be felt over the medial cuneiform before it passes through the space between the first and second metatarsals. The posterior tibial artery passes behind the medial malleolus midway between the malleolus and the tendocalcaneus (see Fig. 5.120a, p. 535). Its pulsations can be felt by applying light pressure against the lower part of the tibia; it is at this point that the artery can be compressed to stem arterial bleeding.

The dorsal venous arch can usually be seen on the dorsum of the foot, and arising from its medial and lateral ends the long (great) and short (lesser) saphenous veins respectively. The long (great) saphenous vein passes into the leg in front of the medial malleolus, while the short (lesser) saphenous vein passes behind the lateral malleolus (Fig. 5.120a, p. 535).

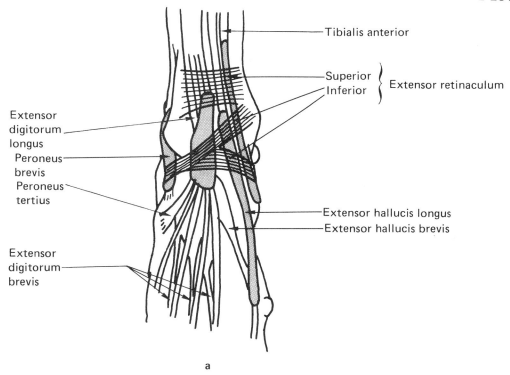

Tibialis anterior

Superior ⎫
Inferior ⎬ Extensor retinaculum
          ⎭

Extensor digitorum longus

Peroneus brevis

Peroneus tertius

Extensor digitorum brevis

Extensor hallucis longus
Extensor hallucis brevis

a

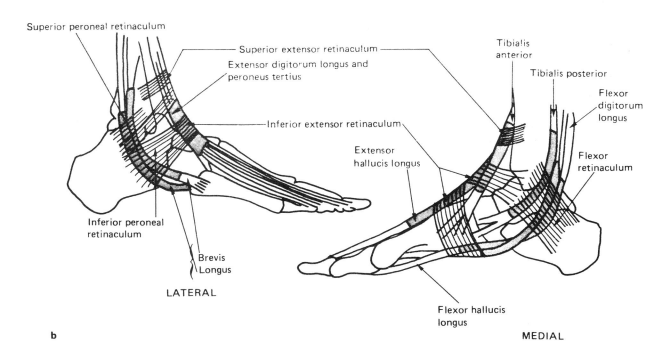

Superior peroneal retinaculum

Superior extensor retinaculum
Extensor digitorum longus and peroneus tertius

Inferior extensor retinaculum

Inferior peroneal retinaculum

Brevis
Longus

LATERAL

Tibialis anterior

Tibialis posterior

Flexor digitorum longus

Extensor hallucis longus

Flexor retinaculum

Flexor hallucis longus

MEDIAL

b

Fig. 5.145   **a** = Relationship of the tendons on the dorsum of the foot, showing also the extent of their associated synovial sheaths. **b** = Medial and lateral view showing the long tendons of the calf muscles entering the foot, together with the extent of their synovial sheaths.

Biomechanics

Owing to its wide variety of functions the foot may be considered as one of the most dynamic structures within the body. It provides physical contact with the environment, being strong to support the weight of the body, yet is also flexible and resilient to absorb shocks transmitted to it and to provide the spring and lift for many activities. Any changes in its structure and/or flexibility will modify its function, resulting in changes in the way the foot is used during activity.

The arched structure of the foot involving a number of bones and their interconnecting joints, together with numerous ligaments and muscle action, give it the stability and flexibility necessary for function. Of the longitudinal arches, the medial has a greater curvature and is characterised by its remarkable elasticity. The more rigid and flatter lateral longitudinal arch makes contact with the ground and thereby provides a firm base for support in the upright position. The factors maintaining the integrity of the arches of the foot are the same as those in any joint of the body, i.e. ligaments and muscles. However, their relative importance is different in each of the three arches of the foot.

In the medial longitudinal arch, ligaments are important, but by themselves are not capable of maintaining the arch. The plantar aponeurosis is the most important ligament stretched between the supporting pillars of the arch (Fig. 5.146). Extension of the toes shortens the aponeurosis bringing the two pillars together and increases the concavity of the arch. The plantar calcaneonavicular (spring) ligament supports the head of the talus preventing it sinking between the navicular and calcaneus (Fig. 5.146). When this ligament is stretched the medial arch decreases in height. As well as these two major ligamentous components, all the interosseous ligaments assist in maintaining the medial arch. However, muscles are indispensable in the maintenance of this arch, for if they are paralysed or weakened the ligaments alone cannot cope.

In a living foot, the medial arch cannot be flattened because the ligaments are too strong. In static standing the ligaments are the primary support, indeed the muscles are relaxed in this condition. Muscular support of the foot only becomes significant in the larger movements of shifting the weight in the erect posture and in more extensive body movements. If the muscles become weakened the ligaments become progressively stretched and flat foot results. (Flat foot is usually accompanied by eversion and adduction of the forefoot.)

Fig. 5.146 The medial longitudinal arch of the foot and the muscles associated with its maintenance.

The most important and efficient muscular supports are those that run longitudinally beneath the medial arch (see Fig. 5.146). Of these, flexor hallucis longus is the most efficient, being the largest of the deep calf muscles. As well as running to the great toe it also gives a slip to the tendons of flexor digitorum longus which pass to the second and third toes. During short periods of standing, flexor hallucis longus is not active because body weight is supported towards the back of the foot with the toe pads off the ground. If standing is prolonged, flexor hallucis longus contracts to press the toe pads against the ground so relieving the ligaments. It is during the toe-off phase of gait, and when landing on the feet, that flexor hallucis longus contracts strongly to take the greater strain placed on the medial arch. Abductor hallucis and the medial part of flexor digitorum brevis also assist in maintaining this arch.

Both tibialis anterior and posterior significantly influence the medial arch (see Fig. 5.146), but in a different way to the muscles already mentioned because they have no direct action on the pillars of the arch. Their action of inverting and adducting the foot raises the medial border from the ground. Although of functional importance, these two muscles are less important factors in maintaining the integrity of the arch.

Finally, peroneus longus may accentuate the medial arch as it pulls it towards the ground during eversion (see Fig. 5.146). Peroneal spasm in young children, however, is usually seen as an everted flat foot.

In the lateral longitudinal arch, ligaments play a relatively more important role than they do medially. The lateral part of the plantar aponeurosis as well as the various plantar ligaments are significant in their action. The thicker short plantar ligament joins the calcaneus and cuboid, while the thinner long plantar ligament helps to maintain the concavity of this arch (Fig. 5.147). Several muscles provide support for the lateral arch. Peroneus longus pulls upwards on the lateral arch as its tendon passes under the foot, and in addition provides elastic support for the calcaneus as it passes below the peroneal tubercle (Fig. 5.147). It is perhaps the single most important factor maintaining the integrity of the lateral arch. Peroneus brevis and tertius prevent the arch opening out inferiorly. The tendons of flexor digitorum longus to the fourth and fifth toes, assisted by flexor accessorius (quadratus plantae), together with the lateral half of flexor digitorum brevis and abductor digiti minimi help to maintain the lateral arch by preventing separation of the supporting pillars.

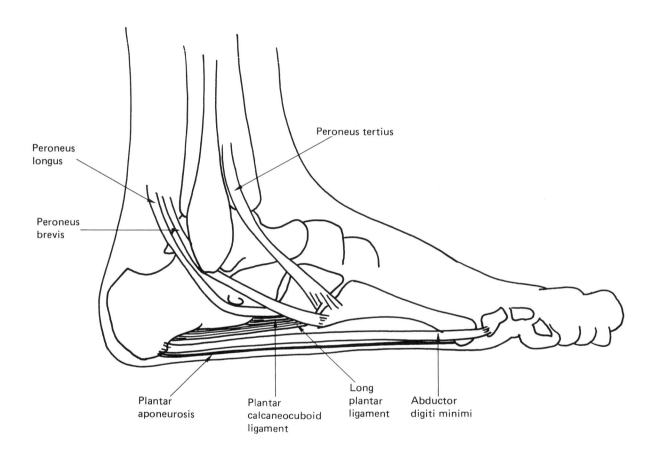

Fig. 5.147   The lateral longitudinal arch of the foot and the muscles associated with its maintenance.

Although the wedge-shape of the cuneiforms, and to some extent the cuboid, suggest that the integrity of the transverse arch is maintained by bony factors, because of the shape of the medial cuneiform, it is clear that bony factors in fact play only a small part. Ligaments binding together the cuneiforms and the bases of the metatarsals are more important. However, the most important factor appears to be peroneus longus, as it pulls the medial and lateral borders of the foot together (Fig. 5.148). At the level of the metatarsal heads, a shallow arch is maintained by the deep transverse ligament of the metatarsal heads, by the transverse fibres binding together the digital slips of the plantar aponeurosis, and by the transverse head of adductor hallucis, which is relatively weak (Fig. 5.148). This shallow arch rests on the ground via soft tissues. The head of the second metatarsal, being the highest above the ground, is the keystone of this arch. The second and third metatarsal heads occupy intermediate positions above the ground, while the first and fifth lie approximately at the same level on the ground. The arch of the metatarsal heads is the area of culmination of the metatarsal rays of the foot. Because of the nature of the arch involving the cuneiforms and the cuboid, each metatarsal forms a different angle with the ground as it runs forwards (Fig. 5.149). The first (medial) ray is the highest forming an angle between 18° and 25° with the ground. Passing laterally, the angle gradually decreases, being approximately 15° for the second ray, 10° for the third, 8° for the fourth, and only 5° for the fifth (lateral) ray.

Having considered the various factors which contribute to the integrity of the foot and its arched structure, it is now possible to see how these mechanisms work to enable the foot to act in propulsion of the body and as a shock absorber. A rigid foot could act as a propulsive mechanism because the chief factor responsible for propulsion during walking, running and jumping is contraction of gastrocnemius and soleus, with plantarflexion of the foot at the ankle joint. This mechanism is, however, greatly enhanced and made more efficient by having a flexible foot.

During walking, the weight of the body is taken successively on the heel, the lateral border and then the ball of the foot, with the anterior pillar of the medial longitudinal arch being the last part to leave the ground. In contrast, in sprinting the heel remains clear of the ground, but the anterior pillar is still the last to leave the ground. As the heel leaves the ground during walking the medial toes are extended. Extension of the great toe pulls the plantar aponeurosis around the head of the first metatarsal, and in this way increases the height of the medial longitudinal arch. In addition the flexors hallucis longus and digitorum longus are stretched, thereby increasing the force of their subsequent contraction. Contraction of the long and short toe flexors press the toes against the ground increasing the force of toe-off. By far the most powerful muscle acting this way is flexor hallucis longus. The toes are prevented from buckling under by the action of the lumbricals.

When landing from a jump, the toes and then the forefoot take the strain before the heel touches the ground. In this way much of the damaging high energy and high frequency components associated with ground impact are dissipated. Muscles and ligaments are put under tension and stretched, absorbing as much as 50% of the energy. Even in quiet walking the muscles and ligaments play an essential role in absorbing the shock of landing. Indeed, by stretching the ligaments and muscles the energy stored is released again towards the end of the stance phase of gait thereby contributing to propulsion and reducing the overall energy cost of walking.

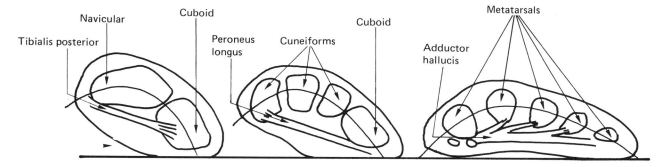

Fig. 5.148 The transverse arches of the foot at different levels, together with important muscles involved in their maintenance at each level.

Fig. 5.149 Angulation of each metatarsal with respect to the horizontal, showing how it decreases from medial to lateral.

Trabecular arrangement within the foot

The transmission of mechanical forces within and through the foot is reflected, as in other regions, in the arrangement of the bony trabeculae. On the medial side of the foot, following the medial longitudinal arch, trabeculae in the lower end of the tibia can be traced posteriorly and anteriorly (Fig. 5.150a). Those trabeculae arising from the cortex of the anterior surface of the tibia pass obliquely inferiorly and posteriorly through the body of the talus to the calcaneus, where they spread out, eventually reaching the posterior support of the arch, the posterior tubercle of the calcaneus. From the cortex of the posterior surface of the tibia, the trabeculae run inferiorly and anteriorly through the neck and head of the talus, the navicular and medial cuneiform to the first metatarsal.

On the lateral side of the foot, transmission of mechanical forces occurs through the talus and the underlying calcaneus. Two sets of trabeculae can be readily identified (Fig. 5.150b). Arising from the cortex of the anterior surface of the tibia, trabeculae again pass inferiorly through the posterior part of the body of the talus and fan out in the calcaneus. Trabeculae from the posterior tibial shaft pass initially through the neck of the talus where it rests on the sustentaculum tali, and then run forwards through the navicular and fifth metatarsal to the anterior part of the lateral longitudinal arch.

Because of the stresses imparted to the calcaneus two additional trabecular systems are seen within it (Fig. 5.150c). A superior arcuate system, concave inferiorly, converges into a dense lamella at the floor of the sinus tarsi. These trabeculae resist compressive stresses. The second system, the inferior arcuate system concave superiorly, converges towards the cortical bone of the inferior surface of the calcaneus. This second system resists tension forces. Between these two systems, however, lies an area with relatively few trabeculae, and hence a point of weakness. If a sufficiently violent stress is applied vertically through the talus, injury involving this weak region may result. The long plantar ligament may be able to resist the shock, but the lateral arch gives way at the level of the anterior process of the calcaneus (the keystone of the arch), with the sustentaculum tali being broken off along a vertical line passing through the weak area. The medial tubercle of the calcaneus may also be detached along a line running sagittally. Such fractures of the calcaneus may prove difficult to reduce, as not only has the superior articular surface of the calcaneus to be restored but also the sustentaculum tali, otherwise the medial arch remains collapsed.

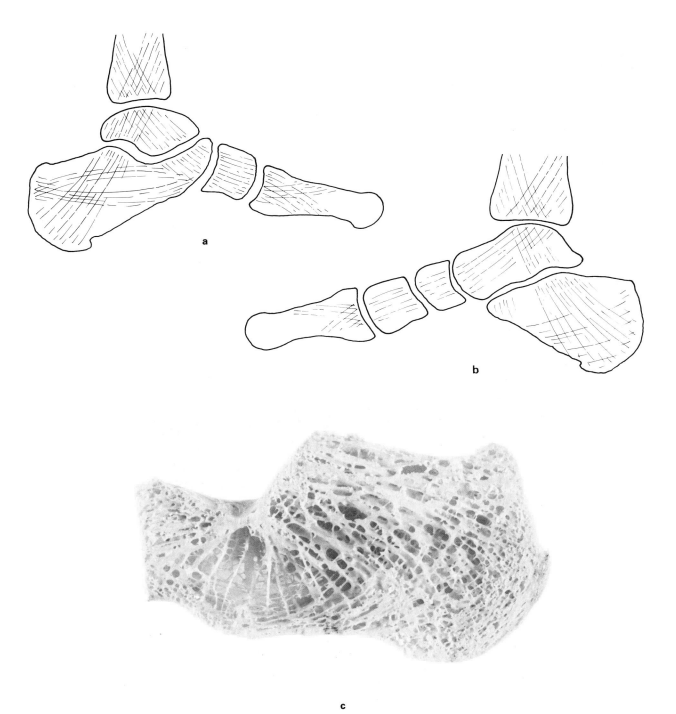

Fig. 5.150 The trabecular arrangement within the tarsal and metatarsal bones. **a** = Lateral view. **b** = Medial view. **c** = Photograph of the trabecular arrangement in the calcaneus (sagittal section).

Distribution of stresses during static loading

Upon weight-bearing, the forces are distributed in three directions towards the supports of the plantar vault, with the result that each of the arches of the foot is flattened and lengthened.

In the medial arch, the soft tissue under the posterior tubercle of the calcaneus becomes compressed and comes to lie closer to the ground. The sustentaculum tali is lowered, and as a result the talus moves backwards on the calcaneus. As the talus is moving closer to the ground, the navicular rises on the talar head. Both the cuneonavicular and the medial tarsometatarsal joints gape inferiorly, while the angle that the first metatarsal makes with the ground reduces. The arch is lengthened by a posterior displacement of the heel and a slight anterior displacement of the sesamoid bones under the head of the first metatarsal (Fig. 5.151a).

In the lateral arch movements of the calcaneus are the same. Both the cuboid and the lateral tubercle of the fifth metatarsal are lowered by similar amounts. The calcaneocuboid and the lateral tarsometatarsal joints gape inferiorly, so that the head of the fifth metatarsal is displaced anteriorly, which together with recession of the calcaneus, lengthens the lateral arch (Fig. 5.151b).

The anterior arch of the foot is flattened so that the foot becomes splayed out either side of the second metatarsal (Fig. 5.151c). The transverse arch involving the cuneiforms and cuboid is also flattened (Fig. 5.151d).

The result of the flattening of these various arches is that the head of the talus and the lateral tubercle of the calcaneus become displaced medially, leading to a twisting of the foot at the midtarsal joint. The hindfoot becomes slightly adducted, pronated and extended, while the forefoot undergoes a relative movement of flexion, abduction and supination.

Because the heels receive about half the body's weight when standing erect, and more momentarily when walking, the wearing of shoes with a small heel area results in indentations being made on floors with a plastic covering.

Fig. 5.151 The effects of weight-bearing on the medial (**a**) and lateral (**b**) longitudinal arches, and the anterior (**c**) and midfoot (**d**) transverse arches. The solid line represents the relationship between segments on weight-bearing; the dotted lines show the non-weight-bearing relationships.

Foot pathology

The curvature of the various arches of the foot and the orientation of their various components depends upon a very delicate balance between the muscles and ligaments involved. An insufficiency or contracture of even a single muscle will disrupt the overall equilibrium of the foot and lead to some form of deformity. The process may be gradual with progressively more muscles becoming involved until the foot assumes an unnatural shape and position. The simple footprint may provide a useful aid to diagnosis. For example, when compared with a normal footprint the various stages in the development of clawfoot (*pes cavus*) can be identified (Fig. 5.152a). In the first stage, the footprint shows a lateral projection on its lateral border, with a deepening of the concavity medially. The next stage shows a divided footprint, and finally the toe prints disappear due to a secondary clawtoe deformity.

In a similar manner, the progression of flat foot (*pes planus*) can be seen when compared with a normal footprint (Fig. 5.152b). In this case the medial border of the foot gradually becomes filled in, and may even become convex in long-standing cases.

The muscle imbalance associated with pes cavus may also result in a secondary imbalance involving the anterior arch. The imbalance may be an overloading of the medial or lateral or both supports of the anterior arch, with callosities forming under the appropriate metatarsal heads. Occasionally the anterior arch may become flattened and splayed, with the formation of callosities under each metatarsal head.

If a widely splayed foot is confined within a pointed shoe the great toe becomes displaced laterally (Fig. 5.152c). With time the imbalance soon becomes permanent due to the shortening of the capsular ligaments of the joints, lateral dislocation of the sesamoid bones and the tendon, and formation of an exostosis on the medial side of the first metatarsal head. The result is *hallux valgus*. The intermediate metatarsals are displaced by the great toe exaggerating the deformity. The fifth toe may undergo a converse deformity, which further enhances the deformity of the intermediate toes (Fig. 5.152c). If the deformity is severe the anterior arch may become convex.

Both normal and pathologic foot function may be assessed clinically by observation of the subject's gait and of the pattern of wear on the soles of shoes. As suggested previously, callosities on the sole of the foot can indicate areas of excessive loading. The magnitude and duration of such loading can be assessed using suitable forms of instrumentation. From such techniques, both minor and major changes in foot function can be determined and evaluated.

Fig. 5.152 The progressive change in the footprint seen in pes cavus (**a**) and pes planus (**b**). **c** = Relationship of the skeletal elements of the toes and outward appearance of the foot in hallux valgus with an associated varus of the little toe.

NORMAL

a   PES CAVUS

NORMAL

b   PES PLANUS

HALLUX
VALGUS

Varus
deformity
of little
toe

c

Nerve supply

INTRODUCTION

The nerve supply to the lower limb is derived from the ventral rami of the first lumbar to the fourth sacral spinal nerves. Before emerging from their appropriate intervertebral foramina, the roots of these spinal nerves have travelled for some distance in the vertebral canal. The first lumbar nerve roots separate from the spinal cord about two vertebrae above their exit, while those of the fourth sacral nerve separate from the cord at its termination, between the first and second lumbar vertebrae.

As each nerve passes out of the intervertebral foramen it receives a grey ramus communicans connecting it to the sympathetic trunk. The first and second lumbar roots are also connected to the trunk by a white ramus communicans.

The ventral rami of the first three and the upper part of the fourth lumbar nerves form the lumbar plexus in the substance of the psoas major. The remainder of the fourth lumbar and that from the fifth lumbar nerve form the lumbosacral trunk which passes over the ala of the sacrum to join the ventral rami of the first, second, third and upper part of the fourth sacral nerves to form the lumbosacral plexus. The fourth and fifth sacral nerves form the sacral plexus.

THE LUMBAR PLEXUS

The lumbar plexus is formed by the ventral rami of the first, second, third and part of the fourth lumbar nerves. Occasionally there is a contribution from the subcostal nerve (T12). The plexus is formed within the substance of psoas major with the rami entering the muscle between its attachments to the body and transverse process of each vertebra.

The most common arrangement of the plexus is that the first lumbar nerve, with the communication from T12, if present, divides into an upper and a lower branch. The upper branch again divides into the *iliohypogastric* and the *ilioinguinal* nerves. The lower part of the first lumbar nerve joins the upper part of the second to form the *genitofemoral* nerve (Fig. 5.153).

The lower part of the second, the third and upper part of the fourth nerves all divide into smaller anterior and larger posterior divisions. The anterior divisions join to form the *obturator* nerve, branches from the third and fourth divisions may occasionally unite to form an *accessory obturator* nerve.

The posterior divisions of all three nerves join to form the *femoral* nerve, with branches from the second and third only forming the *lateral cutaneous nerve of the thigh* (Fig. 5.153).

Direct muscular branches to psoas major (L1, 2, 3) and quadratus lumborum (L1–4) arise separately from the ventral rami.

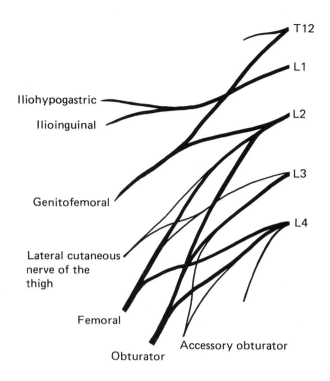

Fig. 5.153 Diagram to show the formation of the lumbar plexus.

The iliohypogastric nerve (Fig. 5.154)

This derives its fibres from L1 and occasionally T12. It emerges from the upper lateral border of *psoas major* passing in front of quadratus lumborum and behind the kidney. At about the midaxillary line, it pierces the deep surface of the transversus abdominis, giving off a lateral cutaneous branch, and continues forwards in the neurovascular plane between transversus abdominis and the internal oblique muscle, which it pierces 2 cm medial to the anterior superior iliac spine. It passes medially deep to the external oblique aponeurosis, the nerve becoming cutaneous about 4 cm above the superficial inguinal ring. The iliohypogastric nerve supplies the muscles of the lateral abdominal wall, and a strip of skin running from the upper lateral gluteal region to just above the pubis.

The ilioinguinal nerve (Fig. 5.154)

This derives its fibres from L1 and again occasionally from T12. It emerges from the lateral border of the *psoas major* just below the iliohypogastric nerve and passes obliquely downwards around the inside of the abdomen, lying deep to quadratus lumborum. It pierces the internal oblique passing deep to the external oblique aponeurosis and enters the inguinal canal, reaching the skin through the superficial inguinal ring and external spermatic fascia. The ilioinguinal nerve gives branches to the *internal* and *external oblique* muscles as it passes between them and is sensory to the skin over the pubic symphysis and upper medial part of the femoral triangle, as well as to part of the genitalia.

The lateral cutaneous nerve of the thigh (Figs. 5.154, 5.155)

This is formed from the posterior divisions of the second and third lumbar nerves, emerging from the lateral border of *psoas major*. Passing downwards and forwards onto the pelvic surface of *iliacus*, it leaves the pelvis just medial to the anterior superior iliac spine, either below or through the inguinal ligament. It passes laterally through, or deep to, sartorius and then the fascia lata to become superficial. The nerve then divides into two branches which pass down the lateral surface of the thigh. The anterior branch supplies the anterolateral surface of the thigh as far as the knee, with the posterior branch supplying the lateral proximal two-thirds of the thigh below the greater trochanter.

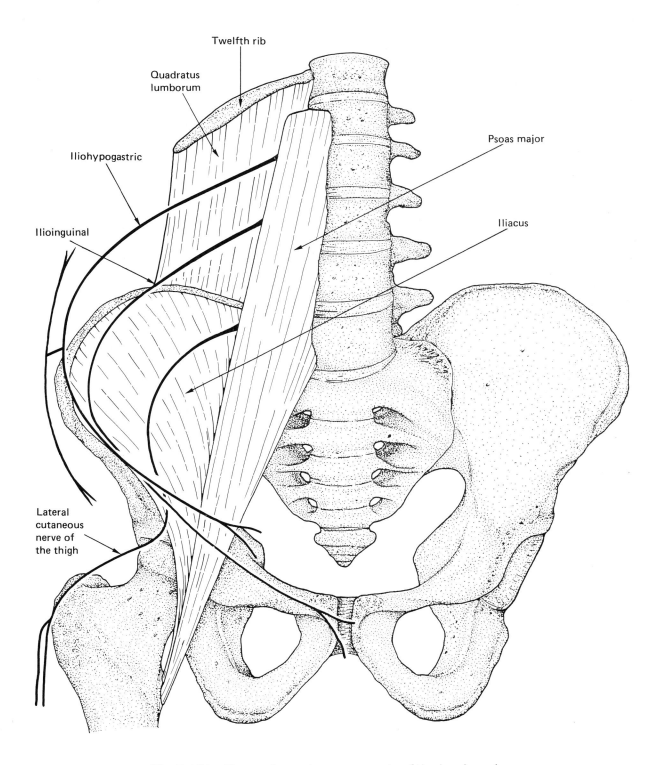

Fig. 5.154 Nerves from the upper roots of the lumbar plexus.

The genitofemoral nerve (Fig. 5.155)

This is formed within the substance of *psoas major* from L1 and L2. It emerges from the anterior surface of the muscle close to its medial border, piercing the fascia as it does so. It descends downwards and forwards on the fascia, passing behind the ureter towards the inguinal ligament where it divides into two, the *genital* and *femoral* branches.

The genital branch enters the deep inguinal ring to pass into the inguinal canal where it supplies the *cremaster* muscle, and is then sensory to the skin of the scrotum (or labia major) and the adjacent part of the thigh.

The femoral branch passes under the inguinal ligament lying lateral to the femoral artery. It becomes superficial by passing through the saphenous opening and supplies the skin over the upper part of the femoral triangle.

The obturator nerve (Figs. 5.155, 5.157)

This is formed by the anterior divisions of the second, third and fourth lumbar nerves, which unite within the substance of *psoas major*, emerging from the medial border of the muscle on the lateral part of the sacrum. The obturator nerve crosses the sacroiliac joint and obturator internus to enter the obturator canal, below the superior ramus of the pubis above the obturator membrane. On leaving the canal, the nerve lies above obturator externus and divides into *anterior* and *posterior* branches. The anterior branch descends into the thigh anterior to obturator externus and adductor brevis, and posterior to pectineus and adductor longus, with its terminal twigs lying between adductor magnus and the medial intermuscular septum.

The anterior branch sends branches to *adductor longus*, *gracilis*, *adductor brevis* (usually) and *pectineus* (occasionally), and is sensory to the skin on the medial side of the thigh, the distal third of which passes via the subsartorial plexus. In addition, an articular branch reaches the hip joint via the acetabular notch.

The posterior branch pierces obturator externus and descends between the adductor brevis anteriorly and magnus posteriorly. It passes obliquely through adductor magnus and enters the popliteal fossa. The nerve ends by piercing the oblique popliteal ligament to supply the posterior part of the knee joint including the cruciate ligaments.

The posterior branch supplies *obturator externus* and *adductor magnus*.

The accessory obturator nerve

When present, this arises from the anterior divisions of the third and fourth lumbar nerves between the obturator and femoral nerves. It emerges from the medial border of the *psoas major* and descends between the pelvic brim and the external iliac vessels to enter the thigh between the pubic bone and the femoral vessels. Here it usually splits into three branches: one to *pectineus*, one to the hip joint and one which communicates with the anterior branch of the obturator nerve.

The femoral nerve (Fig. 5.155)

This is formed from the posterior divisions of the second, third and fourth lumbar nerves, emerging from the lateral border of *psoas major* to run down in the groove between psoas and iliacus deep to the iliac fascia. It passes into the thigh below the inguinal ligament lateral to the femoral sheath to enter the femoral triangle, where it almost immediately divides into a number of branches which can be loosely grouped into *anterior* and *posterior* divisions. The anterior division supplies *sartorius* and gives the medial and lateral branches of the anterior cutaneous nerve of the thigh. The posterior division supplies *quadriceps femoris* and sends articular branches to the hip and knee joints as well as giving off the saphenous nerve. While still in the abdomen, the main nerve supplies *iliacus*.

The nerves to sartorius

These arise from the anterior division of the femoral nerve and enter the deep surface of the muscle by long and short fibres.

The anterior cutaneous nerves of the thigh

These arise as lateral and medial branches from the lateral side of the femoral nerve in the upper part of the femoral triangle. After entering the subsartorial canal and

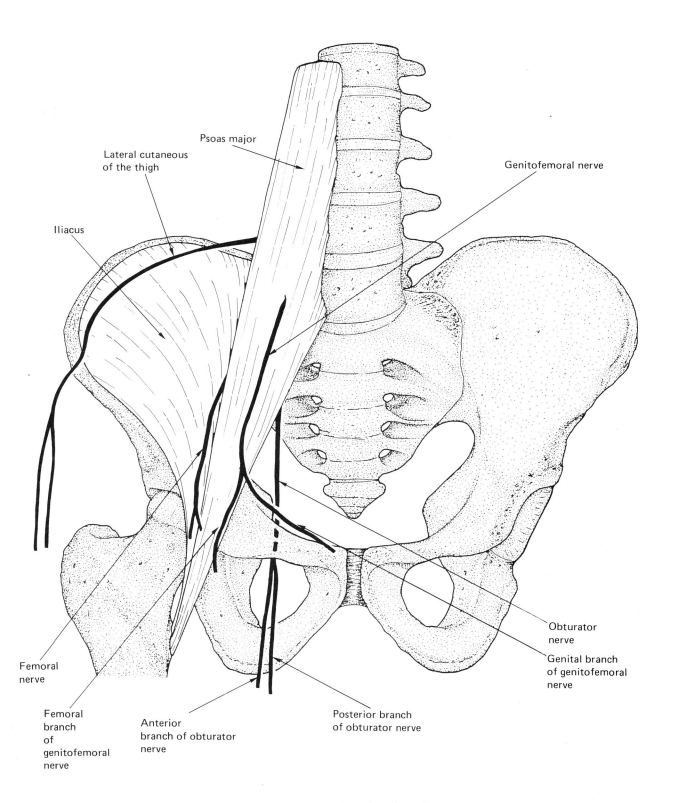

Psoas major

Lateral cutaneous
of the thigh

Genitofemoral nerve

Iliacus

Femoral
nerve

Femoral
branch
of
genitofemoral
nerve

Anterior
branch of obturator
nerve

Posterior branch
of obturator nerve

Obturator
nerve

Genital branch
of genitofemoral
nerve

Fig. 5.155   Nerves of the lumbar plexus.

crossing to the medial side of the artery, the lateral branch divides into anterior and posterior parts, becoming subcutaneous in front and behind sartorius to supply an area of skin over the lower part of the medial side of the thigh, knee and upper leg. The two lateral branches pass directly down the thigh becoming superficial by piercing the fascia over sartorius to supply the skin on the anterior aspect of the thigh as far down as the knee joint.

The nerves to quadriceps femoris

These pass to all four parts of the muscle. The nerves to the *rectus femoris* and *vastus lateralis* pass with branches of the lateral circumflex femoral artery to enter the deep surfaces of the muscles. *Vastus medialis* is supplied by two branches, one of which enters proximally and also supplies *vastus intermedius*. The other branch accompanies the saphenous nerve in the adductor canal to about half way down the thigh where it enters the medial surface of the muscle. The nerve to vastus intermedius enters the more superficial surface of the muscle, passing through it to supply *articularis genus*. All these branches to the vastus muscles give a supply to the knee joint, while the nerve to rectus femoris sends a branch to the hip joint.

The saphenous nerve (see Fig. 1.157)

This is the longest of the branches of the femoral nerve. Beginning about 3 cm below the inguinal ligament, it passes through the femoral triangle to enter the adductor canal on the lateral side of the femoral vessels, giving a branch to the subsartorial plexus. The saphenous nerve pierces the roof of the adductor canal and becomes cutaneous between sartorius and gracilis posteromedial to the knee joint, to which it sends a branch. Passing behind the medial condyles of the femur and tibia, it descends along the medial side of the leg with the long (great) saphenous vein to lie anterior to the medial malleolus. It then passes to the medial side of the foot as far as the head of the first metatarsal. Branches of the nerve supply skin and fascia on the front and side of the knee, leg and foot as far as the base of the great toe.

THE LUMBOSACRAL PLEXUS (Fig. 5.156)

The lumbosacral plexus lies on the posterior wall of the pelvis between piriformis and its fascia, and is formed from the ventral rami of the fourth lumbar to fourth sacral nerves. The fifth lumbar and the lower part of the fourth form the lumbosacral trunk, which passes over the ala of the sacrum to join the laterally running ventral rami of the first to fourth sacral nerves. A grey ramus communicans joins each of the rami, while from the second, third and fourth sacral ventral rami, preganglionic parasympathetic fibres (the pelvic splanchnic nerves) pass to join the autonomic plexuses of the pelvis to supply the urogenital organs and lower third of the gastrointestinal tract.

Each ventral ramus divides into an anterior and a posterior division which all converge on the greater sciatic foramen. The following nerves are formed by the union of various of the anterior divisions: *nerve to quadratus femoris, nerve to obturator internus, pelvic splanchnic* nerves, *posterior femoral cutaneous* nerve and the *pudendal* nerve. Similarly, from posterior divisions arise the following: branches to *piriformis, coccygeus* and *levator ani* the *superior and inferior gluteal* nerves, *posterior femoral cutaneous* nerve, *perforating cutaneous* nerve and the *perineal branch of S4*. The *sciatic nerve* consists of the medially-placed *tibial nerve* (anterior divisions L4 to S3), and the laterally-placed *common peroneal* nerve (posterior divisions L4 to S2) bound together in a common sheath.

Nerves to piriformis, coccygeus and levator ani

The nerve to *piriformis* arises from the posterior division of S2, with an occasional contribution from S1. It passes directly backwards to enter the anterior surface of the muscle. Twigs from the S3,4 descend to supply *coccygeus* and *levator ani*. The perineal branch of S4 also supplies *coccygeus* and *levator ani*, as well as the *external anal sphincter*, and the overlying skin and fascia.

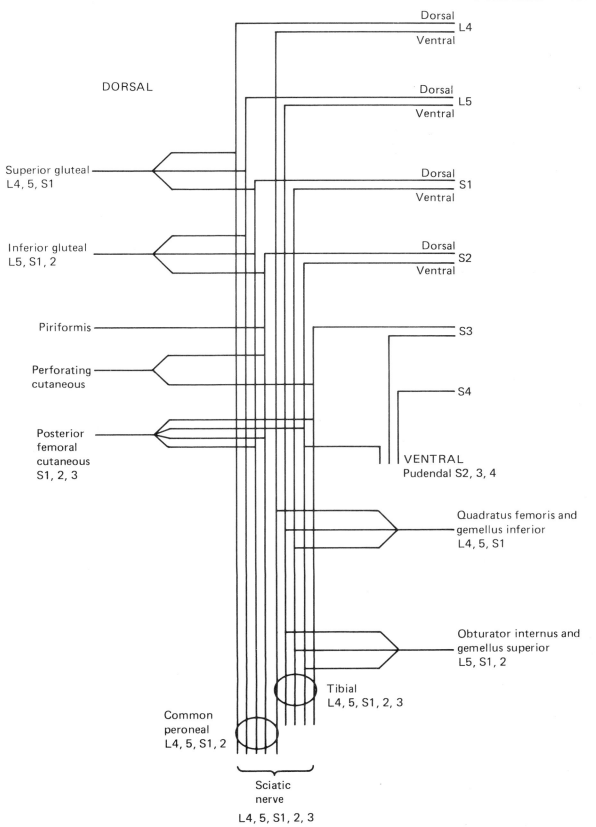

Fig. 5.156 Simplified diagram to show nerves of the lumbo sacral plexus.

The superior gluteal nerve

This is formed by the union of the posterior divisions of L4,5,S1 and passes postero-laterally to leave the pelvis above the piriformis muscle with the superior gluteal vessels. It divides into superior and inferior branches, which pass forwards between gluteus medius and minimus. The superior branch supplies *gluteus medius* while the inferior supplies *gluteus medius* and *minimus* and *tensor fascia lata*.

The inferior gluteal nerve

This arises from the posterior divisions of L5,S1,2. It leaves the pelvis below the piriformis muscle superficial to the sciatic nerve, and passes directly into the deep surface of *gluteus maximus*.

The posterior cutaneous nerve of the thigh (Fig. 5.157)

This is formed from the anterior divisions of S2,3 and the posterior divisions of S1,2. It leaves the pelvis through the greater sciatic foramen on the posterior surface of the sciatic nerve below piriformis, and descends down the posterior aspect of the thigh as far as the back of the knee joint deep to the fascia lata, which it then pierces. Branches are given off which supply the skin over the lower part of the buttock, the posterior aspect of the thigh, the popliteal fossa and the upper part of the calf.

The perforating cutaneous nerve (Fig. 5.157)

This arises from the dorsal divisions of S2,3. It leaves the pelvis by piercing the sacro-tuberous ligament, or by passing directly backwards through the medial side of the gluteus maximus to become cutaneous. It supplies the skin covering the lower part of the buttock and medial part of the gluteal fold.

The nerve to quadratus femoris

This arises from the anterior divisions of L4,5,S1, entering the gluteal region through the lower part of the greater sciatic foramen, lying anterior to the sciatic nerve on the posterior surface of the ischium. It supplies *quadratus femoris*, *inferior gemellus* and gives an articular branch to the hip joint.

The nerve to obturator internus

This arises from the anterior divisions of L5,S1,2, passing around the ischial spine, between the sciatic nerve and the pudendal vessels, leaving the greater sciatic foramen and entering the lesser. It supplies *superior gemellus* and *obturator internus*, the latter from its deep medial surface.

The pudendal nerve

This is the principal nerve of the perineum, usually being formed from the anterior divisions of S2,3,4. It leaves the pelvis through the inferomedial part of the greater sciatic foramen, with the pudendal vessels and nerve to obturator internus. It passes over the sacrospinous ligament to gain the lesser sciatic foramen and enter the pudendal canal on the obturator fascia. As well as supplying the genitalia, the pudendal nerve also supplies *levator ani* and is cutaneous to the skin around the anus.

Cutaneous nerves

Fig. 5.157   Nerves and dermatomes of the lower limb:

a = Anterior aspect:
  1 = Lateral cutaneous nerve of the thigh
  2 = Lateral anterior cutaneous nerve of the thigh (a branch of the femoral nerve)
  3 = Medial anterior cutaneous nerve of the thigh (a branch of the femoral nerve)
  4 = Lateral cutaneous nerve of the calf
  5 = Infrapatellar branch of the saphenous nerve
  6 = Superficial peroneal nerve
  7 = Sural nerve (a branch of the tibial nerve)
  8 = Deep peroneal nerve
  9 = Saphenous nerve (a branch of the femoral nerve)
  10 = Obturator nerve
  11 = Ilioinguinal nerve

b = Posterior aspect:
  1 = Iliohypogastric
  2 = Dorsal rami of L1,2,3
  3 = Dorsal rami of S1,2,3
  4 = Perforating cutaneous nerve
  5 = Posterior cutaneous nerve of the thigh
  6 = Medial cutaneous nerve of the thigh
  7 = Obturator nerve
  8 = Saphenous nerve
  9 = Sural nerve
  10 = Medial calcaneal branches of the tibial nerve
  11 = Medial plantar nerve (a branch of the tibial nerve)
  12 = Lateral plantar nerve (a branch of the tibial nerve)
  13 = Superficial peroneal nerve
  14 = Lateral cutaneous nerve of the calf
  15 = Lateral cutaneous nerve of the thigh

The sciatic nerve (Fig. 5.158)

This is formed by the ventral rami of L4,5,S1,2,3 and leaves the pelvis to enter the gluteal region through the greater sciatic foramen, below piriformis. It passes down the back of the thigh deep to biceps femoris lying on, from above downwards, superior gemellus, obturator internus, inferior gemellus, quadratus femoris and adductor magnus. At a point, usually about two-thirds of the way down the thigh, it divides into its terminal branches: the *common peroneal* and *tibial* nerves. However, division of the nerve may occur at a higher level in the thigh, or the two components of the nerve may be separate as they leave the pelvis. In the latter case, the tibial nerve leaves below piriformis, while the common peroneal may leave above piriformis or pierce the muscle. The nerve can be marked on the surface by a line drawn from a point midway between the ischial tuberosity and the greater trochanter of the femur to a point two-thirds of the way down the back of the thigh where the medial and lateral hamstrings part.

The *sciatic* nerve gives articular branches to the knee joint and muscular branches to *semitendinosus, semimembranosus, biceps femoris* and the *hamstring part* of *adductor magnus*. The short head of biceps femoris is supplied by the common peroneal part of the nerve, while the others are all supplied by the tibial part.

The tibial nerve (Fig. 5.158)

This is the medial terminal branch of the *sciatic* nerve, being formed by the anterior divisions of the ventral rami of L4,5,S1,2,3. It continues the course of the sciatic nerve through the popliteal fossa, lying at first lateral to the popliteal vessels then crossing superficially to the medial side to enter the leg under the tendinous arch of soleus. The nerve descends obliquely inferomedially between flexor digitorum longus and flexor hallucis longus to pass behind the medial malleolus deep to the flexor retinaculum between the tendons of these same muscles. As it enters the plantar aspect of the foot the tibial nerve divides into the *medial* and *lateral plantar* nerves.

In the popliteal fossa the tibial nerve gives muscular branches to both heads of *gastrocnemius, soleus, plantaris, popliteus* and *tibialis posterior*. Gastrocnemius is supplied from its deep surface while soleus and plantaris are supplied from their superficial surfaces. The nerve to popliteus descends over the superficial surface of the muscle, bends around its inferior border to enter its deep surface. Articular branches are given off to the ankle, knee and superior tibiofibular joints, and cutaneous branches through the *sural* nerve. The sural nerve (see Fig. 5.157) descends between the two heads of gastrocnemius, to pierce the deep fascia in the middle of the calf. It is joined by the *peroneal communicating* nerve and passes behind the lateral malleolus and runs forward along the lateral side of the foot. The sural nerve is sensory to the skin over the posterior and lateral sides of the lower third of the leg, the lateral border of the foot and fifth toe except over the distal phalanx.

In the leg, the tibial nerve gives muscular branches to the deep surface of *soleus, flexor digitorum longus, flexor hallucis longus* and *tibialis posterior*. It also gives articular branches to the ankle joint and a cutaneous branch to the heel and posterior part of the foot.

The medial plantar nerve (Figs. 5.158, 5.163a)

This passes forwards deep to abductor hallucis, accompanied on its medial side by the medial plantar artery, to the interval between the muscle and flexor digitorum brevis. It supplies *abductor hallucis, flexor digitorum brevis, flexor hallucis brevis* and *the first lumbrical*. At the base of the metatarsals, the nerve passes transversely across the foot giving cutaneous branches to the medial side of the sole and great toe and the adjacent sides of the great, second, third and fourth toes, to include the dorsal surface of the distal phalanx and nailbed. Articular branches are given to the tarsal and tarsometatarsal joints.

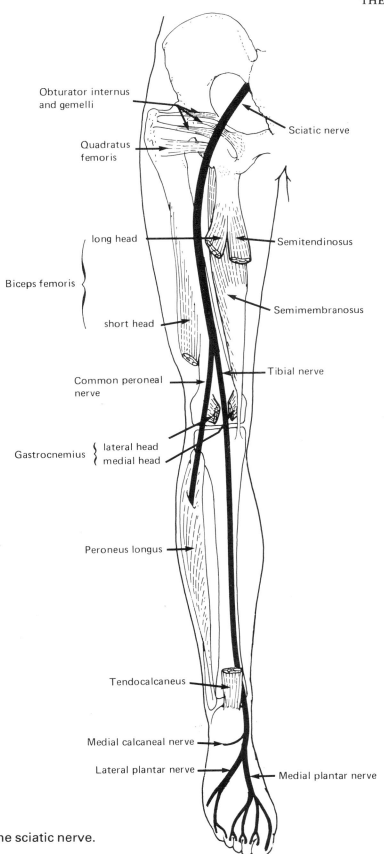

Obturator internus
and gemelli

Quadratus
femoris

Sciatic nerve

long head

Semitendinosus

Biceps femoris

Semimembranosus

short head

Common peroneal
nerve

Tibial nerve

Gastrocnemius { lateral head
medial head

Peroneus longus

Tendocalcaneus

Medial calcaneal nerve

Lateral plantar nerve

Medial plantar nerve

Fig. 5.158   The sciatic nerve.

The lateral plantar nerve (see Figs. 5.157, 5.163a)

This passes anterolaterally towards the base of the fifth metatarsal between flexor digitorum brevis and flexor accessorius (quadratus plantae). It then divides into superficial and deep branches. The superficial branch runs forwards between flexor digitorum brevis and abductor digiti minimi, while the deep branch passes medially with the plantar arch on the plantar surface of the metatarsal bases. The lateral plantar nerve gives muscular branches to *flexor accessorius (quadratus plantae)*, *flexor digiti minimi brevis, abductor digiti minimi, adductor hallucis,* the *lateral three lumbricals* and all the *interossei*. It also gives cutaneous branches to the lateral side of the sole and fifth toe and to the adjacent sides of the fourth and fifth toes, including the nailbeds and dorsum of the distal phalanx. Articular branches pass to the tarsal and tarsometatarsal joints.

It is worth noting the similarity in the distribution of the lateral plantar nerve in the foot with the ulnar nerve in the hand, and also of the medial plantar nerve with the median nerve in the hand.

The common peroneal nerve
(see Figs. 5.158, 5.159)

This is the lateral terminal branch of the *sciatic* nerve being composed of the posterior divisions of L4,5,S1,2. It passes along the upper lateral side of the popliteal fossa lying deep to biceps femoris and its tendon until it reaches the posterior part of the head of the fibula. It passes forwards around the neck of the fibula within the substance of peroneus longus, where it ends by dividing into the *superficial* and *deep peroneal* nerves. The nerve can be palpated behind the head of the fibula and as it winds around the neck of the fibula. The common peroneal nerve gives articular branches to the knee and superior tibiofibular joint. The *lateral cutaneous* nerve of the calf (see Fig. 5.157) supplies the posterolateral side of the proximal two-thirds of the leg. It usually arises in common with the *peroneal communicating* branch which joins the sural nerve in the middle third of the leg.

The superficial peroneal nerve
(see Figs. 5.157, 5.159)

This descends almost vertically between extensor digitorum longus and peroneus longus anterior to the fibula. About halfway down the leg it becomes superficial by piercing the deep fascia on the anterior surface and divides into its terminal branches, the medial and intermediate dorsal cutaneous nerves which pass over the anterolateral aspect of the ankle joint to enter the foot.

The superficial peroneal nerve gives muscular branches to *peroneus longus* and *brevis*, and cutaneous branches to the anterolateral aspect of the leg and around the lateral malleolus. The medial dorsal cutaneous branch supplies the medial side of the dorsum of the foot, the great toe, and the adjacent sides of the second and third toes. The intermediate dorsal branch supplies the dorsum of the foot and the adjacent sides of the third, fourth and fifth toes. However, the skin over the distal phalanx is supplied by branches from the plantar nerves.

The deep peroneal nerve (Fig. 5.159)

This passes inferomedially into the anterior compartment of the leg deep to extensor digitorum longus to join the anterior tibial vessels on the anterior surface of the interosseous membrane. It descends on the interosseous membrane deep to extensor hallucis longus and the superior extensor retinaculum. At the ankle joint, the nerve lies deep to the inferior extensor retinaculum and the tendon of extensor hallucis longus which crosses it. As it enters the dorsum of the foot the nerve lies superficially between the tendons of extensor hallucis and digitorum longus, and divides into *medial* and *lateral* branches. The medial branch passes to the cleft between the great and second toes, supplying the skin on the adjacent sides as far as the distal interphalangeal joint. The lateral branch supplies the *extensor digitorum brevis* and many of the small joints of the foot, particularly on the lateral side.

In the leg, the nerve gives muscular branches to *extensor digitorum longus, tibialis anterior, extensor hallucis longus* and *peroneus tertius*, and sends articular branches to the inferior tibiofibular and ankle joints.

Fig. 5.159 **a** = Nerves of the leg viewed from anterior and lateral aspects. **b** = Skin supplied by the common peroneal nerve.

THE SACRAL PLEXUS

This is formed from the ventral rami of S4 and 5. Muscular branches pass to both *coccygeus* and *levator ani*. The plexus is cutaneous to the region next to the coccyx and posterior to the anus.

THE CUTANEOUS NERVE SUPPLY AND DERMATOMES OF THE LOWER LIMB
(Fig. 5.160)

Throughout the above account of both the lumbar and lumbosacral plexuses, cutaneous nerves have been given off to supply particular areas of the limb. Gradually the whole of the skin surface is supplied. The various nerves derive their fibres from the rami from which their parent nerves arise. Described in this way they appear to have no particular pattern to them.

A *dermatome* is an area of skin supplied by one spinal nerve through both its rami. The overlap of these areas, however, is considerable, particularly with the nerves immediately above and below. In some areas the main supply of the nerves is located some distance away from those above and below, and in these situations the overlap is minimal (see Fig. 5.157). If these regions are now traced on the surface of the limb, paying little regard to the actual nerve through which the fibres reach the surface, a much clearer pattern of supply emerges. In the development of the lower limb, it should be noted that the section from the knee downwards has completely reversed so that which was the anterior surface of the leg becomes medial and then posterior, and that which was posterior becomes lateral and anterior. Consequently, the tibial nerve, which derives its fibres from the anterior divisions of the ventral rami, lies at the back of the limb supplying this area and the plantar aspect of the foot, while the common peroneal nerve, which derives its fibres from the posterior divisions of the ventral rami, passes anterolaterally supplying the areas on the anterior and lateral aspects of the limb.

The dermatomes, therefore, form bands which run from posterior to anterior around the lateral side of the limb displaying a much simpler distribution than is at first imagined. As the cutaneous supply of the posterior primary rami are included in this description, it can be seen that most roots supply a strip of skin, varying in width, from the spinal region to the lower limb. Some strips are so narrow in their upper region that they are merely a line, their main distribution being further down the limb.

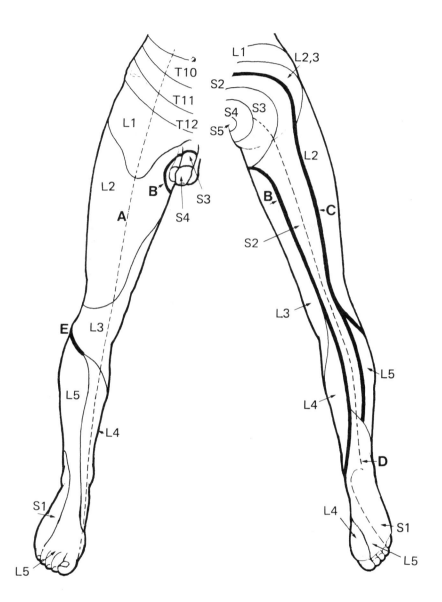

Fig. 5.160 Dermatomes of the lower limb:

A = Preaxial border
B = Ventral axial line
C = Dorsal axial line
D = Postaxial border
E = Extension from dorsal axial line

Blood supply

THE ARTERIES

The main arterial supply to the lower limb is through the *femoral* artery, although there is sufficient collateral circulation to maintain the tissues of the resting limb for a period of several hours. This collateral circulation is an invaluable asset when there is blockage of the femoral artery if surgery needs to be performed on the major vessels.

The femoral artery (Fig. 5.161)

This is a continuation of the external iliac artery, which in turn arises from the abdominal aorta via the common iliac artery. It enters the thigh under the inguinal ligament, being contained in a funnel-shaped prolongation of the abdominal fascia, termed the *femoral sheath*, (see p. 404). The femoral vein lies medially within a separate compartment of the sheath, while the femoral nerve is lateral, but outside the sheath. Psoas major lies deep to the artery which can easily be palpated just below the fold of the groin, half way between the anterior superior iliac spine and the pubic tubercle (the femoral pulse). Within the femoral triangle it passes medially across the femoral vein to enter the subsartorial canal which continues from the apex of the femoral triangle. It leaves the anterior compartment of the thigh through a fibrous arch in the adductor magnus, the adductor hiatus, to enter the popliteal fossa and become the *popliteal* artery.

The femoral artery gives off branches to the lateral iliac and gluteal region through the *superficial circumflex iliac* artery. It supplies the genital region through the *superficial* and *deep external pudendal* arteries; a *descending genicular* branch which participates in the anastomosis around the knee; muscular branches to the surrounding muscles, and through the *profunda femoris* to most of the deep structures in the thigh.

The profunda femoris (Fig. 5.161b)

This is the largest branch of the *femoral* artery, having approximately the same diameter. It arises from its lateral side about 5 cm below the inguinal ligament, passing behind the femoral artery to leave the femoral triangle between pectineus and adductor longus to gain access to the anterior surface of adductor brevis and magnus. In the lower part of the thigh, it passes through adductor magnus as the fourth perforating artery contributing to the anastomosis around the knee joint. The profunda femoris gives off several branches soon after its commencement: the *lateral circumflex femoral* artery, which gives ascending, transverse and descending branches which supply the gluteal region and hip joint, the quadriceps and the knee joint respectively; the *medial circumflex femoral* which anastomose with the lateral circumflex femoral, giving branches which supply similar areas.

As well as giving numerous muscular branches, the profunda femoris also gives off the *perforating* arteries which pass either above or through small openings in adductor magnus to link with the descending branch of the lateral circumflex femoral artery (Fig. 5.161b).

Fig. 5.161   a = Vessels in the femoral triangle.
b = Arteries of the thigh.

The popliteal artery (Fig. 5.162)

This is a continuation of the *femoral* artery as it emerges through the adductor hiatus. Within the popliteal fossa it runs vertically from the upper medial border and ends by dividing into the *anterior* and *posterior tibial* arteries at the level of the tibial tuberosity. The popliteal artery is the deepest of the structures within the popliteal fossa.

In the popliteal fossa it supplies cutaneous branches to the back of the leg, muscular branches to adductor magnus and the hamstrings, and articular branches to anastomose around the knee joint. The latter are given off in three groups. The upper being the *medial* and *lateral superior genicular* arteries which encircle the lower part of the femur just above the condyles. The *middle genicular* being smaller, and piercing the posterior part of the capsule and supplying the cruciate ligaments, and the lower group formed by the *medial* and *lateral inferior genicular* arteries which encircle the upper part of the tibial condyles just below the line of the knee joint. The superior and inferior arteries communicate with each other via vertical arteries which pass down either side of the patella (Fig. 5.162b). Further details of the blood supply to the knee joint are given on pages 488 and 489.

The anterior tibial artery (Fig. 5.162b)

This begins at the distal border of popliteus and ends in front of the ankle by becoming the *dorsalis pedis* artery. It passes forwards through an opening above the interosseous membrane between the tibia and fibula. As the artery passes above the membrane, *recurrent* arteries are given off which pass upwards to join the anastomosis around the knee joint. Running down the anterior surface of the interosseous membrane it becomes superficial and crosses the ankle joint under the extensor retinaculum and between the tendons of extensor hallucis longus and extensor digitorum longus, where it can be easily palpated as the anterior tibial pulse. It enters the dorsum of the foot as the dorsalis pedis artery and runs towards the first interosseous space through which it passes to the plantar aspect of the foot (see Fig. 5.163b). In this region the pulse may again be palpated as the dorsalis pedis pulse.

Before leaving the dorsum of the foot the dorsalis pedis gives a large branch, the *arcuate* artery (see Fig. 5.163b), which passes across the bases of the metatarsal bones, and becomes continuous laterally with the *peroneal* artery. From the arcuate artery arise the *dorsal metatarsal* arteries, which when reaching the cleft of the toe divide, each into two *dorsal digital* arteries to supply the adjacent sides of the toes. The medial side of the great toe and the lateral side of the little toe are usually supplied by separate branches from the arcuate artery.

Fig. 5.162   **a** = Arteries of the posterior aspect of knee and
leg. **b** = Arteries around knee joint, anterior view.

The posterior tibial artery

This is the larger of the two terminal branches of the *popliteal* artery, beginning at the distal border of popliteus (see Fig. 5.162a). It passes down the back of the leg under cover of the soleus and gastrocnemius lying on the flexor digitorum longus and flexor hallucis longus. About two-thirds of the way down the leg it is only covered by deep fascia and skin, crossing the ankle joint behind the medial malleolus deep to the flexor retinaculum, with the tendon of the flexor digitorum longus anterolaterally and the tibial nerve posteromedially. It immediately divides into *medial* and *lateral plantar* arteries. In this region the posterior tibial pulse may be readily palpated.

As the posterior tibial artery passes down the posterior aspect of the leg, it gives off the large *peroneal* branch (see Fig. 5.162a), which descends between tibialis posterior and flexor hallucis longus. During its course, it gives *malleolar* branches and a *perforating* branch which cross the ankle joint to anastomose with branches of the anterior tibial and dorsalis pedis arteries.

The medial and lateral plantar arteries
(Fig. 5.163a)

The smaller medial plantar artery passes forwards along the inner side of the foot, medial to its plantar nerve, between abductor hallucis and flexor digitorum brevis. The artery gives three digital branches, which pass forwards to join the *medial plantar metatarsal* arteries.

The *lateral plantar* artery passes forwards and laterally between flexor digitorum brevis and flexor accessorius (quadratus plantae), on the lateral side of its plantar nerve. At the base of the fifth metatarsal it passes medially and deep to arch across the foot on the metatarsals as the *plantar arch* to become continuous with the dorsalis pedis artery on the lateral side of the first metatarsal. The arch gives off the *plantar metatarsal* arteries, which each divide when they reach the cleft of the toes, after being joined by the *digital* arteries from the medial plantar artery.

The arteries on the dorsum of the foot communicate with those on the plantar aspect by *perforating* arteries which pass between the metatarsals.

Fig. 5.163a Arteries and nerves of the foot, plantar view.

Plantar digital nerve

Plantar metatarsal artery

Plantar arch

Superficial terminal branch of lateral plantar nerve

Deep terminal branch of lateral plantar artery

Medial plantar artery

Medial plantar nerve

Lateral plantar nerve

Lateral plantar artery

Medial calcaneal branch of tibial nerve

Superior extensor retinaculum

Inferior extensor retinaculum

Extensor digitorum brevis

Extensor digitorum longus

Peroneus tertius

Arcuate artery

Dorsal metatarsal arteries

Digital arteries

Anterior tibial artery

Tibialis anterior

Dorsalis pedis

Extensor hallucis longus

Fig. 5.163b Arteries of the dorsum of the foot, dorsal view.

THE VEINS

The venous drainage of the lower limb varies considerably in its arrangement from subject to subject and even from limb to limb. The following description, therefore, is considered to be the most commonly found. The veins are usually described as being superficial and deep, the superficial veins being larger with fewer valves and situated in the superficial fascia, whereas the deep veins are normally two small vessels accompanying the arteries, these are called the *venae commitantes*. They are situated deep in the limb and possess many valves.

The superficial veins (Fig. 5.164)

On the dorsum of the foot these veins are easily seen. They form a network which receives venous blood from the dorsal and plantar aspects of the toes, from either side of the foot, and from the deep plantar areas via the *perforating* veins which pass between the metatarsals. The *dorsal venous network* is drained on either side by the *medial* and *lateral marginal* veins, the medial continue as the *long (great) saphenous* vein, the lateral as the *short (lesser) saphenous* vein.

The long (great) saphenous vein (Fig. 5.164a)

The long (great) saphenous vein passes in front of the medial malleolus, and ascends obliquely up the posteromedial aspect of the calf towards the knee. It lies posteromedial to the femoral and tibial condyles, and continues upwards, forwards and laterally in the thigh. It then passes through the cribriform fascia of the saphenous opening, situated just below the centre of the inguinal ligament, to join the *femoral* vein deep in the groin (see p. 615). During its course, the long saphenous vein has between 8 and 20 bicuspid valves.

The long saphenous vein receives many tributaries as it passes up the limb, mainly draining the medial side of the leg and thigh. In the leg, it communicates freely with the *short (lesser) saphenous* vein, and through the deep fascia with the *deep intermuscular* veins, particularly near the knee and ankle joints.

Before passing through the saphenous opening, it receives drainage laterally from the iliac region through the *circumflex iliac* vein, from the genital area through the *superficial external pudendal* vein, and from the lower abdominal area through the *superficial epigastric* vein.

The short (lesser) saphenous vein (Fig. 5.164b)

The short (lesser) saphenous vein passes behind the lateral malleolus, along the lateral side of the tendocalcaneus to the posterior aspect of the calf. It enters the popliteal fossa between the two heads of the gastrocnemius by piercing the deep fascia which forms the roof of the fossa, and drains into the *popliteal* vein behind the knee joint. In its course it contains between 6 and 12 bicuspid valves, and is accompanied by the sural nerve. The short saphenous vein receives tributaries from the lateral side of the ankle and leg.

The deep veins

Two veins, the venae commitantes, accompany the smaller arteries of the lower limb and are similarly named. Only the *popliteal*, *femoral* and *profunda femoris* veins are single vessels. The veins possess numerous valves.

The popliteal vein

The popliteal vein is formed at the lower border of popliteus by the union of the *anterior* and *posterior tibial* veins, and receives the *genicular* and *short saphenous* veins. In its course through the popliteal fossa, it passes from medial to lateral across the artery. It passes through the adductor hiatus to become the *femoral* vein.

The femoral vein

The femoral vein ascends in the adductor canal to enter the femoral triangle, where it ends by becoming the *external iliac* vein as it passes deep to the medial part of the inguinal ligament within the femoral sheath. In its course from the adductor hiatus to the inguinal ligament, the vein passes behind the femoral artery from lateral to medial. During its course it receives the *profunda femoris* and *long saphenous* veins. The long saphenous enters some 3 cm below the inguinal ligament just prior to the femoral vein entering the femoral sheath.

Application

There is abundant communication between the superficial and deep venous systems. The veins under and deep within the foot tend to drain into the *dorsal venous network*, while in the calf the drainage is from the superficial to the deep via *perforating* veins. Contraction of the calf muscles compresses the local veins within the surrounding fascial compartments, pumping the blood into the deep system because of the arrangement and direction of the valves within the perforating vessels.

Commonly, the valves in the perforating veins become incompetent and allow blood to flow back into the superficial system, the veins of which then become engorged, swollen and tortuous. In such situations the veins appear as large, ugly and often blue swellings on the posteromedial side of the calf and the medial side of the thigh. These are termed 'varicose veins'.

Fig. 5.164a,b Superficial veins of the lower limb.

  1 = Dorsal venous arch
  2 = Lateral marginal vein
  3 = Short saphenous vein
  4 = Long saphenous vein
  5 = Lateral accessory vein
  6 = Superficial circumflex iliac vein
  7 = Superficial epigastric vein
  8 = Superficial external pudendal vein
  9 = Popliteal vein
  A = Saphenous opening

Lymphatics

The lymphatic vessels begin in the tissues as a series of blind-ended tubules being composed of a single cell layer. They exist between most tissues, gradually becoming larger in diameter as they pass proximally. In their course, *lymph vessels* are interrupted by *lymph nodes*, which serve partly as filters and partly as a source of lymphocytes. The *superficial vessels* lie in the skin and subcutaneous tissues and frequently accompany the superficial veins. They join the *deep vessels* at constant sites in the limbs. The deep vessels, draining areas deep to the fascia, accompany blood vessels of the region.

Superficial drainage

The superficial drainage of the lower limb follows the long saphenous vein on the medial and the short saphenous vein on the lateral side. The vessels on the medial side of the limb converge to the *vertical group* of the *superficial inguinal* nodes (Fig. 5.165a,c) around the long saphenous vein near the saphenous opening (Fig. 5.165c). The *horizontal group* of *superficial inguinal* nodes (Fig. 5.165a,c) receives lymph from the skin below the level of the umbilicus, as well as from the lower part of the anal canal and external genitalia (excluding the testes in males). The efferent vessels from both groups of superficial nodes pass through the cribriform fascia of the saphenous opening to end in mainly the *external iliac* nodes with some passing to *deep inguinal* nodes.

The superficial vessels associated with the short saphenous vein pierce the deep fascial roof of the popliteal fossa and drain into the *popliteal* nodes (Fig. 5.165c).

Deep drainage

The deep lymph vessels accompany the arteries and venae commitantes, following the same route back to the femoral triangle as the deep veins, gradually growing larger in diameter as they progress up the limb. The few nodes associated with the deep vessels are usually small. An *anterior tibial* node is situated on the upper part of the interosseous membrane. The *popliteal* nodes receive the *anterior* and *posterior* tibial vessels and the lymphatic drainage from the knee as well as the vessels accompanying the short saphenous vein. Efferents from the popliteal nodes pass to the *deep inguinal* nodes which lie on the medial side of the femoral vein. They receive some vessels from the *superficial inguinal* nodes, and all the *deep* vessels from the territory of the femoral artery.

From the deep and superficial inguinal nodes the lymphatics leave the lower limb by passing under the inguinal ligament through the femoral canal, the most medial compartment of the femoral sheath, to reach the *external iliac* nodes. One of the deep inguinal nodes may be situated within the femoral canal.

Fig. 5.165a–c   Lymphatics of the lower limb:

1 = Inguinal lymph nodes
 1a = Vertical group
 1b = Lateral group
 1c = Medial group
2 = Popliteal nodes
3 = Anterior tibial nodes
A = Saphenous opening

6

The head, neck and trunk

The head, neck and trunk

INTRODUCTION

One of the major features which distinguishes human beings from other animals is their bipedal posture and gait. As the hindlimbs progressively took over the locomotor function the vertebral column assumed a new role. No longer is it held horizontally (Fig. 6.1a), where it is under compression, but it has become a vertical weight-bearing rod, held erect by ligaments and muscles (Fig. 6.1b). The change in function of the vertebral column has been accompanied by changes in its form, as well as by changes in its relationship to the skull and pelvic girdle.

Major differences in the form of the vertebral column are evident among quadrupeds, where it depends mainly on the distribution of mass in the animal. The so-called centre of gravity moves forward or backwards along the vertebral column in relation to there being more weight in the head and shoulder region or hindlimbs and tail respectively. In the evolution of the primates, the centre of gravity moved backwards towards the hindlimbs. It did so because both the length and musculature of the hindlimbs increased, and because of the enlargement of the tail. The first of these changes gave additional power to leaping and grasping, while the latter provided balance when jumping. An important factor in locomotion is that the forward propelling force should pass through the centre of gravity, otherwise the body will rotate about the centre of gravity.

The early changes in body form during primate evolution made possible the sitting position, thereby freeing the forelimbs for manipulative activities. It also made possible the later stages of human evolution with the adoption of a bipedal gait. Although the human tail has been lost, the low position of the body's centre of gravity has been maintained because of further development of the hindlimbs, a slightly reduced muscle mass in the forelimbs, and changes in the form and position of the trunk and abdomen.

A prerequisite for efficient arboreal locomotion was the evolution of an extremely flexible vertebral column. The increased range of flexion of the vertebral column, together with that of the lower limbs, gave additional propulsion in jumping as well as the ability to absorb the shock of impact on landing. However, in brachiating primates some of the flexibility of the vertebral column is lost because it does not have such an important role in locomotion. It seems that human beings could have evolved from a brachiating primate because of the relative stiffness of the vertebral column as well as other morphological features. In addition, four other fundamental changes have occurred in both the vertebral column and the thorax during human evolution, which are adaptations to a fully erect posture.

Firstly, the vertebral bodies increase in size towards the lumbar region (Fig. 6.1b) because the compression forces along the trunk are no longer constant but increase progressively from above downwards. The proportions of the vertebral bodies also change from above downwards. Secondly, the spinous processes are more or less equally developed along the length of the vertebral column because the tendency to bend is no longer restricted to the limb girdles (the points of support), but is more evenly distributed. This is perhaps most clearly seen in the cervical region because the human head is more or less balanced on the vertebral column. Thirdly, the stiffening effect of the sternum and abdominal muscles on the vertebral column has become less important. The sternum has come to lie nearer the vertebral column so that the thorax is wider and less deep (Fig. 6.1c). This has resulted in a reduction in the angulation of the ribs between the 'neck' and the 'body'. Finally, the increased weight transmission through the pelvis and legs has brought about an enlargement of the sacrum, so that the human sacrum is usually composed of five fused segments. It is also relatively wide and more convex on its pelvic surface.

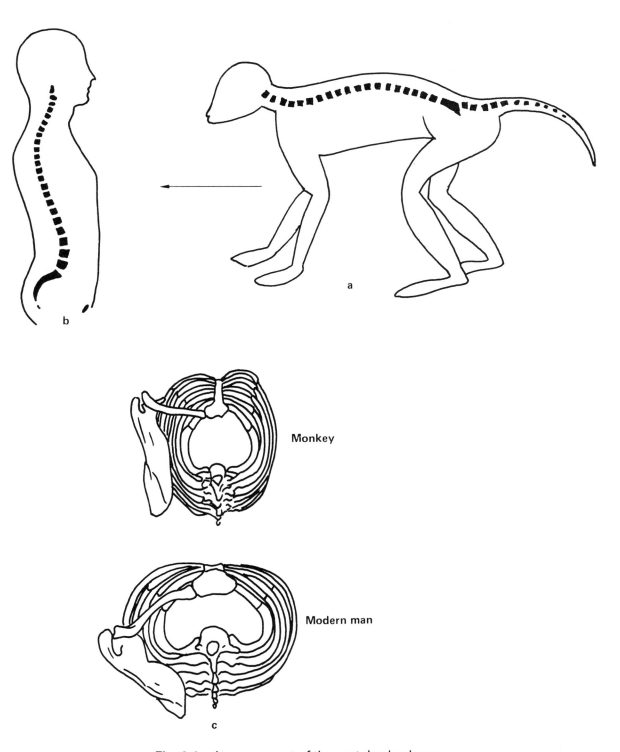

Fig. 6.1 Arrangement of the vertebral column in a quadrupedal monkey (**a**) and modern human (**b**). The changes in the anteroposterior dimensions of the thoracic cage are shown in (**c**).

Concomitant with the changes in the vertebral column and trunk, the relation and form of the skull and its associated musculature have also changed dramatically. In quadrupedal animals, the head is supported by the postvertebral (nuchal) muscles and ligaments (these being under tension), which produce compression of the cervical vertebrae. As a more erect posture evolved the strength required in the postvertebral muscles was reduced because more of the weight of the head was carried directly by the vertebrae. This was accompanied by a reduction in the muzzle and an enlargement of the brain (Fig. 6.2a) causing the centre of gravity of the head to move more nearly over the point of support (the occipital condyles). It would be undesirable to have the head perfectly balanced on the occipital condyles because humans possess no powerful prevertebral muscles to support the skull from the front. Consequently, the centre of gravity projection falls just anterior to the occipital condyles, being balanced by the postvertebral muscles (Fig. 6.2b). That the postvertebral muscles have been reduced in importance is evident by the relatively small area of their attachment to the skull in humans compared with primates (Fig. 6.2c).

In human beings the tail is reduced to between three and five fused coccygeal vertebrae, which curve ventrally and help form the pelvic cavity. Ligaments running from the coccyx to the ischium play an important role in maintaining this relationship, and in so doing contribute to the function of support of the abdominal and pelvic viscera. The abdominal viscera are carried in a sack-like cavity supported behind by the vertebral column, below by the pelvis and anterolaterally by the abdominal muscles (rectus abdominis, the external and internal abdominal obliques and transversus abdominis).

Although the vertebral column has changed in form and orientation during human evolution, it still has to fulfill essentially the same functional requirements as in quadrupedal animals:

1. It carries and supports the thoracic cage, maintaining the balance between it and the abdominal cavity.
2. It gives attachment to many muscles of the pectoral and pelvic girdles.
3. It provides anchorage for many powerful muscles which move the vertebral column, these same muscles maintain the balance and erectness of the human trunk.
4. It surrounds and protects the spinal cord against mechanical injury.
5. It acts as a shock absorber, by virtue of its curvatures and the intervertebral discs, receiving and distributing the impacts associated with the dynamic functioning of the body.
6. It is able, by virtue of its flexibility, to produce and accumulate moments of force as well as to concentrate and transmit forces received from other parts of the body.

The upright posture and independent functioning of the human upper limbs have greatly increased the dynamic demands made on the vertebral column. Nevertheless, the adaptation has been reasonably, although not altogether, successful such that the vertebral column has become a complicated and delicate mechanical unit. That the transition from quadrupedal to bipedal has not been entirely successful is witnessed by the fact that low back pain and its associated problems take a heavy toll.

Fig. 6.2 **a** = Reduction in the size of the muzzle and increase in brain size from lower primates (Hylobates) to modern human. **b** = Relation of the centre of gravity of the head to the occipital condyles. **c** = Reduction in area of attachment for the postvertebral muscles.

The vertebral column comprises a series of mobile segments held together by ligaments and muscles, each separated from adjacent segments by an intervertebral disc. There are usually 33 bony segments, of which only 24 present as separate bones: the lower nine are fused, five forming the sacrum and four the coccyx. The 24 presacral vertebrae are designated either cervical, thoracic or lumbar according to their features and position within the trunk: there are seven cervical, twelve thoracic and five lumbar vertebrae (Fig. 6.3). The length of the vertebral column is between 72 and 75 cm for the majority of individuals, of which approximately one-quarter is accounted for by the intervertebral discs. About 40% of an individual's height is due to the length of the vertebral column. Variations in total height between individuals reflects differences in the length of the lower limbs rather than differences in the length of the vertebral column. However, diurnal variations in height, up to 2 cm between early morning and late evening, are due to compression and loss of thickness of the individual intervertebral discs. (It is as well to remember this when charting the change in height of an individual.) Loss of height in elderly individuals is also associated with thinning of the discs as a result of age-related changes within them.

The adult vertebral column has four curvatures (Fig. 6.3), an anterior convexity in the cervical and lumbar regions, and an anterior concavity in the thoracic and sacro-coccygeal regions. Both the cervical and lumbar curvatures are acquired, in the sense that they are not present in early fetal development. Until late in fetal development, the vertebral column shows a single curvature concave anteriorly (see Fig. 6.4a). Late in fetal life the secondary cervical curvature (see Fig. 6.4b) begins to appear, becoming more accentuated between 6 and 12 weeks after birth as the infant begins to hold up its head to enlarge its visual environment. The secondary lumbar curvature (see Fig. 6.4c) appears when the child begins to sit up at around 6 months, becoming more marked with standing and the onset of walking. It is the extension of the hip which accompanies standing and walking which tilts the pelvis forwards so that the axis of the pelvic cavity is no longer in line with that of the abdominal cavity. The lumbar curvature develops in order to keep the trunk erect when standing. The lumbar curvature is not fully developed until after the age of 2, when a more or less adult pattern of walking is established. Sadly, in old age the vertebral column tends to assume a gentle C-shaped curve (see Fig. 6.4d) which is reminiscent of the early fetal curve. The reason for this is because the shape of the vertebral column is largely determined by the intervertebral discs, and to a much lesser extent by the vertebrae themselves. Consequently, as the discs degenerate and thin with increasing age the secondary curvatures gradually disappear.

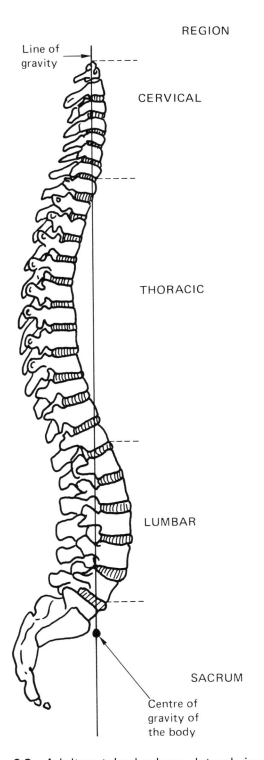

REGION

CERVICAL

THORACIC

LUMBAR

SACRUM

Line of gravity

Centre of gravity of the body

Fig. 6.3 Adult vertebral column, lateral view.

The relatively shallow cervical curvature begins in the dens of the axis and ends at the level of the second thoracic vertebra. It can be reduced or obliterated by bending the head forwards. The permanent thoracic curve is due in part to the shape of the thoracic vertebral bodies; the posterior height being greater than that anteriorly. This curvature ends at the twelfth thoracic vertebra. An increase in the thoracic curvature is known as *kyphosis*. The lumbar curvature, which tends to be deeper and more prominent in women, ends at the lumbosacral junction. Changes in the orientation of the pelvis (pelvic tilt) will be accompanied by changes in the lumbar curvature in an attempt to keep the trunk upright. The wearing of high-heeled shoes throws the pelvis forwards resulting in an increase in the lumbar curvature. A similar situation arises during pregnancy in an attempt to move the centre of gravity backwards and so prevent overbalancing. An increase in lumbar curvature is known as a *lordosis*, although the normal lumbar curve is often referred to as a *lumbar lordosis*. The curvature of the sacrum is permanent because of its fused constituent parts. It should be remembered that the lumbosacral angle is not a part of the vertebral curvatures. However, because it is the region where the mobile and immobile parts of the vertebral column meet, the structures associated with it, e.g. the intervening intervertebral disc and ligaments, are put under considerable stress.

The normal curvatures of the vertebral column make it a flexible support, and give it a resilience to axial compressive forces which are absorbed by the giving way and recovery of the various curves.

Seen from the front, the vertebral column appears almost straight and symmetrical with perhaps a very slight right thoracic curve, probably due to the presence of the arch of the aorta. A large lateral curvature is abnormal and is known as a *scoliosis*. Scoliosis also involves rotation of the vertebral column so that the spinous processes of the vertebrae turn towards the concavity of the curvature. Compensatory curves in the reverse direction occur in order to keep the head facing forwards and over the feet. The condition is extremely complex, often appearing during childhood at periods of increased growth (i.e. 6 to 8 years, and during early puberty).

The vertebral curves pass in front of and behind the line of gravity along which the weight of the head, upper limbs and trunk is projected to the lower limbs. This line is said to pass progressively through the dens, the bodies of the second and twelfth thoracic vertebrae and the promontory of the sacrum (see Fig. 6.3), with the centre of gravity of the body located just in front of the sacral promontory. However, it must be remembered that the line of gravity is not constant, it is continually changing, both as the body moves and also when standing still. Nevertheless, it is a useful concept in reminding us of the natural balance and beauty of the body. By visualizing changes in the projection of this line, it may be possible to determine the structures put under increased strain in certain postures and pathologies.

Fig. 6.4 The changing curvatures of the human vertebral column: **a** = at birth; **b** = at 6 months; **c** = adult; **d** = old age.

Bones

THE SKULL

This awesome looking structure, commonly used to portray death and instill terror, is in reality a complex arrangement of many individual bones, and is one of the most interesting bony structures in the vertebrate skeleton. The skull is the skeleton of the head and face, and consists of two main elements: the large, hollow cranial cavity (the walls of which enclose the brain) and the bones of the face which lie anteroinferiorly, completing the walls of the orbits and nasal cavity, and also forming the roof of the mouth. The mandible, although a separate bone, completes the bony framework of the face.

The discovery of many fossilized vertebrate remains, particularly of skull fragments and teeth, has led to a detailed study of the skull revealing a fascinating history of the evolutionary development of the human skeleton. The size and shape of the cranial, orbital and nasal cavities, the jaw and the teeth have all provided a detailed catalogue of the probable evolutionary history of vertebrates. Estimates of relative brain size from the size and shape of the cranial cavity reveals information regarding possible intelligence. The size and shape of the jaw and teeth give clues as to the type of food eaten, and indirectly provide information regarding changes in body posture with respect to adaptation for the gathering and provision of food (e.g. running and hunting). The size and direction of the orbits, together with changes in the upper cervical spine, indicate the increasing importance of the power and range of vision. This, together with the bipedal posture adopted during the same period, gives an insight into the defence, protection and manipulation of tools necessary for survival.

The cranial cavity (Fig. 6.5a)

The cranial cavity of the human skull is relatively large, and projects anteriorly over the facial skeleton. Its walls are composed of plates of bone arranged as two outer layers of compact bone enclosing a central layer of cancellous bone. These bones ossify in membrane (*intramembranous ossification*) and are joined edge-to-edge by fibrous interlocking joints known as *sutures* (see p. 24).

The top and most of the sides of the skull are formed by the two large *parietal bones*, joined together along their medial borders at the *sagittal suture* (see Fig. 6.7a). Anteriorly the skull is formed by the frontal bone, which joins the two parietal bones at the *coronal suture*. The point where the coronal and sagittal sutures meet is termed the *bregma*. At birth, the region of the bregma is not ossified and appears as an easily felt diamond-shaped area of connective tissue known as the *anterior fontanelle*. This gap gradually decreases in size and closes at about 18 months after birth.

The frontal bone forms the forehead and separates the orbital cavities from the anterior cranial fossa. It therefore forms the roof of each orbital cavity and the floor of the anterior fossa.

The remaining part of each side of the cranial cavity is formed by the squamous part of the temporal bone and part of the greater wing of the sphenoid. The region where the frontal, parietal, temporal and sphenoid bones almost meet is termed the *pterion*. The pterion has a small sphenoidal fontanelle which is present at birth but which closes within 3 months of birth. Passing medially and slightly forwards from the squamous part of the temporal bone is the petrosal part of the temporal bone, forming most of the floor of the middle cranial fossa; it contains and protects the organs of hearing and balance.

The most posterior section of the cranial cavity is formed by the occipital bone, which meets the posterior border of each parietal bone at the *lambdoid suture*. The meeting point of the lambdoid and sagittal sutures is termed the *lambda*. Again, at birth, this region is not ossified and appears as a triangular area of connective tissue known as the *posterior fontanelle*. This gap rapidly

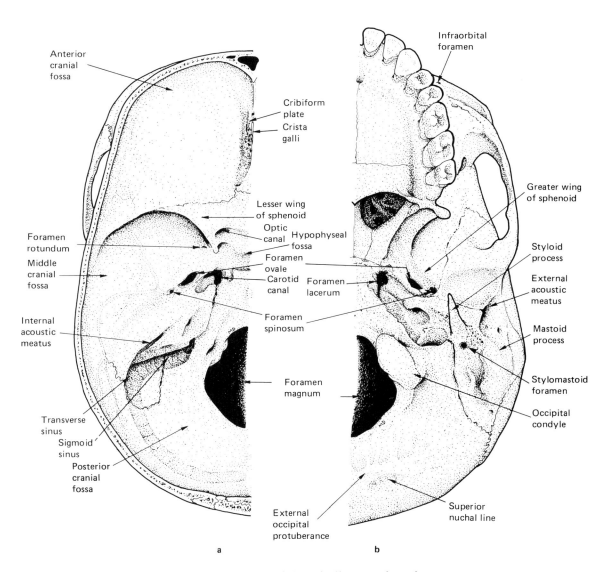

Fig. 6.5   a = Base of the skull, superior view;
b = base of the skull, inferior view.

decreases in size and closes between the third and sixth month. The occipital bone curves forwards to surround the foramen magnum and project anteriorly, as the basilar part of the occipital bone, which joins the body of the sphenoid.

The outside of the top of the skull needs little description as the parietal bones and the parts of the frontal and occipital bones concerned show few bony landmarks except for the sutures where they join. It is, however, worth noting that the skull is widest towards the back. Its roundness means that the effects of a blow to the head can be distributed and minimized. On the inner aspect of the skull, in the region of the sagittal suture, is a faint groove formed by the superior sagittal sinus as it passes posteriorly between the two layers of the dura mater as far as the internal occipital protuberance. On either side of this groove deeply pitted areas can usually be seen. They are formed by the underlying arachnoid granulations, which themselves are involved in the regulation of the flow of cerebrospinal fluid into the systemic circulation. The base of the skull, however, shows many features and openings which allow blood vessels and nerves to enter and leave the cranial cavity.

The floor of the cranial cavity (see Fig. 6.5a)

This is formed by the base of the skull, with both the right and left sides having similar features. The two halves are divided in the sagittal plane by the crista galli anteriorly, the body of the sphenoid centrally, and the foramen magnum and internal occipital protuberance posteriorly. The floor is further divided into anterior, middle and posterior fossae by prominent ridges of bone, so that each fossa lies at a different level; the posterior being at the lowest level and the anterior the highest.

Anterior cranial fossa (see Fig. 6.5a) The anterior cranial fossa lies above and in front of the middle cranial fossa, being separated from it by the posterior concave edge of the lesser wings of the sphenoid. It contains the lower part of the frontal lobes of the brain. The walls and most of the floor of the fossa are formed by the frontal bone, with the posterior part of the floor being formed by the

lesser wings of the sphenoid. Between the two sides is a sagittally directed elongated hollow. Running centrally in this hollow is a crest known as the crista galli on either side of which is a perforated horizontal plate. It is through this that the olfactory nerves from the upper part of the nasal cavity pass to the olfactory bulb sitting on the horizontal (cribriform) plate.

Middle cranial fossa (see Fig. 6.5a) The middle cranial fossa lies behind and below the anterior cranial fossa, being formed by the temporal and sphenoid bones. It consists of a median and two lateral parts. The lateral parts contain the temporal lobes of the brain, while the raised median part is formed by the body of the sphenoid. Passing laterally from the body of the sphenoid are the greater wings of the sphenoid, which, together with the squamous part of the temporal bone, turn upwards forming the lateral wall of the skull in the temporal region. The floor of the middle cranial fossa is formed by part of the greater wings of the sphenoid anteriorly and the gently sloping superior surface of the petrous part of the temporal bone. Anteriorly each greater wing of the sphenoid turns upwards forming the anterior wall of the fossa. The superior part of this anterior wall is overlapped by the posterior edge of the anterior cranial fossa, i.e. the lesser wings of the sphenoid.

The body of the sphenoid has a smooth, hollowed depression superiorly, called the *hypophyseal fossa*, in which sits the pituitary gland. Small horn-like (clinoid) processes project on either side from the front and back of the hollow. They give attachment anteriorly to a horizontal fold of dura mater (the *tentorium cerebelli*) which passes between the cerebral and cerebellar hemispheres. The cavernous sinuses (see p. 854), part of the intracranial venous sinus system, are formed between the two layers of the dura mater either side of the body of the sphenoid. Within the walls, or through these sinuses, pass many of the nerves destined for the orbital cavity, as well as the internal carotid artery. The internal carotid artery emerges from the sinus anterolateral to the anterior clinoid process. Anterior to this region, between the two roots of the lesser wing of the sphenoid, is the optic canal running forwards and laterally conveying the optic nerve and ophthalmic artery to the orbit. Passing transversely between the two optic canals is a groove called the *sulcus chiasmatis*; it does *not* lodge the optic chiasma. Between the greater and lesser wings of the sphenoid is a gap which becomes narrower as it passes laterally. This is the superior orbital fissure and opens directly into the back of the orbit. Consequently, it transmits many structures to and from the orbital cavity, these being the third, fourth, the ophthalmic division of the fifth, and sixth cranial nerves, and the ophthalmic veins. Below the superior orbital fissure in the anterior wall of the middle cranial fossa close to the body of the sphenoid is the rounded *foramen rotundum*, through which passes the maxillary division of the fifth (trigeminal) cranial nerve into a region known as the *pterygopalatine fossa*.

In the floor of the middle cranial fossa between the greater wing of the sphenoid and the petrous temporal bone is an irregular fissure known as the *foramen lacerum.* In life, the edges of the foramen lacerum are connected by fibrous tissue, which supports the internal carotid artery as it passes medially from the carotid canal to the side of the body of the sphenoid. Lateral to the foramen lacerum are two openings in the greater wing of the sphenoid. The larger, medial one is the *foramen ovale*, which transmits the mandibular division of the trigeminal nerve as well as the lesser petrosal nerve and small blood vessels. The more lateral opening is the *foramen spinosum*, through which passes the middle meningeal artery to supply the meningeal coverings of the brain.

Posterior cranial fossa (Fig. 6.5a) The posterior cranial fossa is the largest and deepest of all three fossae, and in it lodges the cerebellum. The temporal bone is seen as a hard ridge passing backwards and laterally from the body of the sphenoid. Along its superior border runs a longitudinal groove for the superior petrosal sinus.

The floor and most of the posterior wall of the fossa are formed by the concave surface of the occipital bone; a small part of the posterior wall being formed by the parietal bones. The anterolateral wall is formed by the posterior surface of the petrous part of the temporal bone, with the body of the sphenoid, and the basilar part of the occipital bone forming the anterior wall.

The most obvious feature of the posterior fossa is the large oval opening (foramen magnum) slightly narrower from side-to-side than from front-to-back. It transmits the spinal cord, being at the junction of spinal cord and brainstem, as well as a number of blood vessels and the spinal part of the eleventh cranial nerve. Passing upwards from the posterior margin of the foramen magnum is the internal occipital crest ending at the internal occipital protuberance. Running down towards this protuberance is the continuation of the groove of the superior sagittal sinus. As it approaches the protuberance, the groove passes to the right to run transversely around the posterolateral wall of the fossa as the groove for the transverse sinus. On reaching the petrous part of the temporal bone, the groove turns downwards and continues in an S-shaped manner towards the jugular foramen. This latter groove is known as the groove of the sigmoid sinus. A similar arrangement of transverse and sigmoid grooves can be observed in the left hand side of the posterior fossa. The sigmoid sinus passes through the jugular foramen to become the internal jugular vein. As it does so it is joined by the inferior petrosal sinus, which runs in the groove between the petrous temporal and basioccipital bones towards the jugular foramen. As well as these two venous channels passing through the jugular foramen, it also transmits the ninth, ten and eleventh cranial nerves.

Anterior to the jugular foramen is the carotid canal through which passes the internal carotid artery and its associated plexus of sympathetic nerves. In the posterior surface of the petrous part of the temporal bone is the opening of the internal auditory meatus, and both the seventh and eighth cranial nerves enter this canal.

Running forwards and upwards from the anterior margin of the foramen magnum is the clivus, which has the basilar artery separating it from the brainstem. On the lateral part of the clivus, medial to the groove for the inferior petrosal sinus, runs the sixth cranial nerve before piercing the dura to run in the sinus. Above the lateral margin of the foramen magnum is the hypoglossal canal, which runs anterolaterally and transmits the twelfth cranial nerve.

The skull viewed inferiorly
(see Fig. 6.5b)

The skeleton of the face attaches to the under surface of the anterior half of the cranial cavity. Consequently, a view from below reveals the mandible, maxilla and palatine bones. With the mandible removed the maxilla and palatine bones can be clearly seen.

The anterior and lateral margins of the maxilla are marked by the sockets for the teeth, being somewhat smaller at the front, increasing in size as they pass around the alveolar margin. The area between these bony margins is formed by the palatine part of the maxilla anteriorly and the horizontal plate of the palatine bone posteriorly. Projecting backwards in the midline from the posterior border of the palatine bones is the nasal spine, while laterally are the medial and lateral pterygoid plates of the sphenoid directed inferiorly, the medial with the hook-like pterygoid hamulus. At the lateral edges of the palatine bones are the greater and lesser palatine foramina transmitting the corresponding vessels and nerves. At the front of the hard palate is the incisive canal, through which pass terminal branches of the greater palatine and spheno-palatine vessels, and the nasopalatine nerves.

The central section of the under surface of the skull is formed mainly by the sphenoid bone with its many bony processes and foramina. Laterally lies the temporal bone marked by the mandibular fossa which receives the condyle of the mandible. Posterolaterally is the external acoustic meatus, while posteromedially is the styloid process of the temporal bone—a long and slender projection passing downwards and anteromedially. Medial to the styloid process anteriorly is the carotid canal and posteriorly the jugular foramen. In front of the carotid canal is the foramen spinosum, separated from it by the spine of the sphenoid. Behind the external acoustic meatus is the large breast-shaped mastoid process of the temporal bone, with the stylomastoid foramen lying medially between it and the styloid

process. It is here that the seventh cranial nerve emerges from the skull. Centrally the large foramen magnum is unmistakable with the occipital condyles on its antero-lateral borders. The hypogossal canal lies anterior to the condyle, while posterior is the condylar canal. Posterior to the foramen magnum, and being joined to it by the external occipital crest, is the external occipital protuberance. Passing laterally towards the mastoid process is the superior nuchal line, between this line and the foramen magnum are less distinct lines, the inferior nuchal lines, which also curve laterally. The area between the two nuchal lines and the foramen magnum give attachment to the post-vertebral muscles.

The skull viewed anteriorly (Fig. 6.6)

When viewed from the front the upper third of the skull consists of the cranial cavity and is formed by the frontal bone; this is the forehead. Parts of the parietal, sphenoid and temporal bones can also be seen in this region. Below the forehead are the two large orbital cavities, whose margins are formed by the frontal bone above, the zygoma inferolaterally and the maxilla inferomedially. The walls of the orbital cavity are formed by the maxilla inferiorly, the zygoma and greater wing of sphenoid laterally, the frontal bone and lesser wing of sphenoid superiorly, and the ethmoid and lacrimal bones medially. Deep within the cavity can be seen the superior and inferior orbital fissures and the optic canal. Along the medial part of the superior margin is the supraorbital notch, transmitting the corresponding vessels and nerves. Towards the front of the medial wall is the opening for the nasolacrimal duct, which conveys secretions from the eye (i.e. tears) to the nose for eventual swallowing. Below the inferior orbital margin on the front of the face is the large infraorbital foramen, through which pass the infraorbital nerve and vessels onto the face.

Below and medial to the orbits is the pear-shaped nasal aperture, bound almost entirely by the maxillae, with only the superior part being bound by the two nasal bones. Within the nasal cavity a more-or-less midline septum can be seen; this is formed by the *vomer* and the perpendicular plate of the

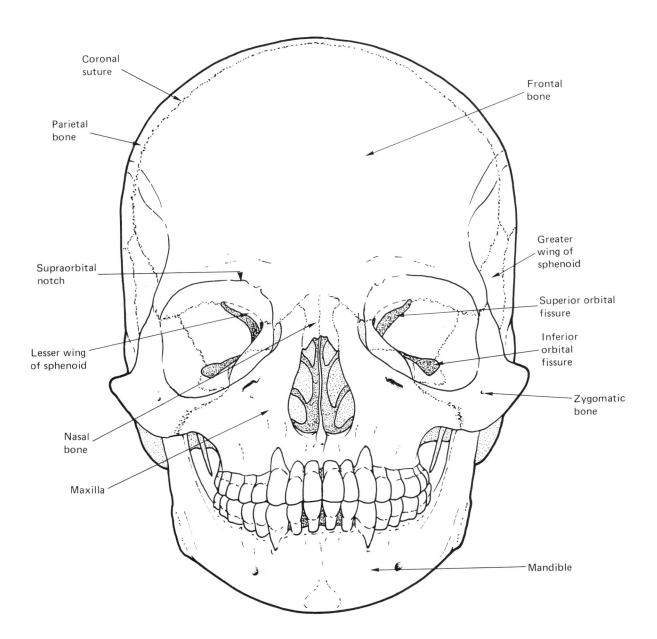

Fig. 6.6   Skull, anterior view.

ethmoid. Projecting medially into the cavity from its lateral walls can be seen the *inferior* and *middle conchae* (the two superior conchae lie deeply behind the nasal bones). The inferior alveolar margin of the maxilla, supporting the teeth, forms an almost horizontal convex arch, which fits snugly with the corresponding arch of the mandible.

The skull viewed from the lateral side
(Fig. 6.7b)

The temporal bone is central to the lateral aspect of the skull. Above it joins the parietal bone posteriorly and the greater wing of the sphenoid anteriorly, while posteroinferiorly it is joined by the occipital bone. It is marked just behind and below its centre by the external acoustic meatus, above which is a bony ramus passing forwards to meet a similar backwardly projecting process from the zygomatic bone to form the zygomatic arch. Just below the posterior part of this arch the mandibular fossa can be seen. The styloid process is seen projecting downwards from deep to the external acoustic meatus.

The mandible (Fig. 6.7b)

The mandible or jaw completes the skull. It consists of a horizontal convex body, with two upwardly projecting rami from the posterior ends of the body. The rami and body all present an outer and an inner surface, with the body having superior and inferior borders, while the rami have anterior and posterior borders. The outer surface of the body is slightly concave from top-to-bottom and markedly convex from side-to-side, and may show a vertical line in the midline where the two halves have fused. Towards the front of the body on each side is the *mental foramen* transmitting the mental nerve and vessels. The inner surface of the body is divided by a slightly raised ridge of bone, the *mylohyoid line*, into an upper and lower area. Behind the front of the mandible, above this line, is the *sublingual fossa* in which lodges the sublingual salivary gland, while below this line, in the middle third of the body, is the *submandibular fossa* for the submandibular gland. On the inner surface of the anterior midline region are two pairs of bony projections called the *mental spines.* The upper pair lie above the mylohyoid line and give rise to part of the tongue (genioglossus), while the lower pair lie below the line and give attachment to geniohyoid. The superior border of the body consists of a series of sockets for the teeth. The bone behind the third molar is thickened as it joins the anterior border of the ramus. The lower border of the body is thick and rounded, but shows two fossae anteriorly one each side of the midline. These are the *digastric fossae*, each giving attachment to the anterior belly of digastric. Posteriorly the body meets the lower posterior part of the ramus at the angle which tends to be everted in the male and inverted in the female. Just in front of the angle the lower border is notched where the facial artery crosses it to enter the face.

Each ramus is continuous with the body, but is flatter. The inner surface is marked by the *mandibular foramen*, which is partially covered by the lingula. The inferior alveolar nerve and vessels enter the mandible at the mandibular foramen giving off mylohyoid branches before they do so. These pass in the downward and forward running mylohyoid groove, also seen on the inner surface of the ramus. The area behind the mylohyoid groove towards the angle of the mandible is roughened for the attachment of the medial pterygoid muscle. The sphenomandibular ligament attaches to the lingula. The outer surface of the ramus is roughed for the attachment of masseter. The posterior border is thick and rounded, particularly at its lower end, and may show a shallow fossa for part of the parotid gland. The anterior border is also thick inferiorly but becomes a thin pointed projection superiorly; this is known as the *coronoid process.* The concave superior border passes between the coronoid process anteriorly and the condylar process (head) posteriorly. The head, which articulates with the mandibular fossa of the temporal bone, is much broader from side-to-side than from front-to-back, and is marked at its lateral and medial ends by prominent tubercles.

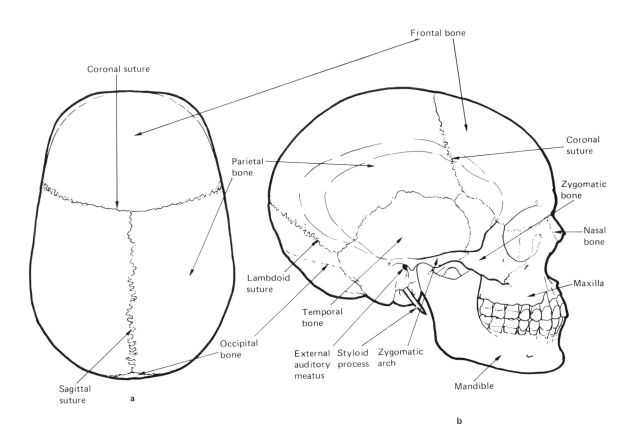

Fig. 6.7 **a** = Skull, superior view; **b** = skull, lateral view.

Growth of the skull (Fig. 6.8)

At birth the cranial cavity is relatively large but the face is small, being approximately one-eighth of the whole skull compared with one-third in the adult. The teeth are not fully formed and the paranasal sinuses are rudimentary, so that both the jaws and nasal cavities are small. The individual bones are joined by cartilage; ossification progressing with age. There is no mastoid process so the styloid process and stylomastoid foramen are near the side of the head. Undue pressure applied during a forceps delivery in the region of the developing mastoid may therefore damage the facial nerve. The maxilla is shallow because it has no sinus, and consists mainly of alveolar processes and developing teeth. The nasal bones are flat, so that the infant has no bridge to the nose, which together with the absence of superciliary arches, gives the forehead its prominent appearance. The orbits are relatively large and have the nasal cavity lying almost completely between them.

After birth the skull grows rapidly until the seventh year, with the greatest increase in the size of the cranial cavity occurring during the first year. During the second year, the styloid process and stylomastoid foramen recede as the mastoid process begins to grow. By the seventh year the orbits are almost adult-sized; however the petrous part of the temporal bone, body of the sphenoid and foramen magnum have reached full-size. The jaws have enlarged in preparation for the eruption of the permanent teeth. Growth of the skull after the age of 7 years is slower than it was before, except for during puberty when a rapid growth in all directions occurs, particularly in the frontal and facial regions accompanying the increasing size of the paranasal sinuses.

From the early twenties to middle age there is gradual fusion of the various sutures between the individual bones of the skull, beginning with the sagittal suture.

Palpation

Virtually the whole of the outer surface of the cranial cavity is palpable, being either subcutaneous or lying just below a thin sheet of muscle. The top of the skull, composed of parietal and frontal bones, can be taken between the examiner's hands as in giving a blessing. On the upper part of the occipital bone, the external occipital protuberance can be readily determined by the finger tips. On the temporal bone, to the side of the skull, the external acoustic meatus is visible, and behind the pinna of the ear the mastoid process can be identified becoming pointed at the level of and behind the lobe of the ear. From just above the external acoustic meatus the posterior part of the zygomatic arch can be identified running forwards to join the zygomatic bone, which presents as the point of the cheek and is thus easily palpable.

Anterosuperior to the cheek the margins of the orbit can be palpated, being particularly marked deep to the eyebrow.

The entire length and depth of the mandible is palpable with the angle posteriorly, being prominent, particularly in the male, even though the posterior border and lateral surface of the ramus is mainly covered by muscle and part of the parotid gland. The lateral tubercle on the condyle can be palpated anterior to the tragus of the ear below the posterior part of the zygomatic arch. Identification is easier with the subject opening and closing the mouth, when the condyle can be felt gliding forwards on the articular surface of the temporal bone.

The hyoid bone (Fig. 6.8c)

The hyoid bone is a U-shaped piece of bone, deficient posteriorly, and suspended in the neck by muscle attachments below the tongue and above the larynx (Fig. 6.10b, c). Being attached to the tongue, it moves up and down with the tongue during swallowing. Because the hyoid is also firmly attached to the larynx by the thyrohyoid membrane, when the hyoid moves upwards it carries the larynx with it. The hyoid consists of a body anteriorly, a pair of greater horns which project upwards and backwards from the body, and a pair of lesser horns which project upwards and backwards from the junction of the body with the greater horns. The lesser horns and upper part of the body of the hyoid are derived from the second pharyngeal arch,

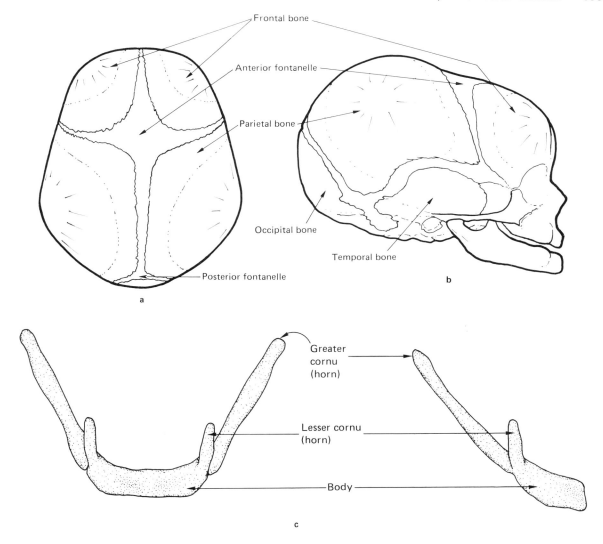

Fig. 6.8 **a** = Fetal skull, superior view; **b** = fetal skull, lateral view; **c** = hyoid bone, superior and lateral views.

while the greater horns and lower part of the body are from the third arch. The stylohyoid ligament, also from the second arch, attaches to the lesser horn. A pair of ossification centres, which soon unite, appear in the body shortly before birth, as well as a single centre for each greater horn. During the first year centres appear for the lesser horns. Not until middle age do the body and greater horns fuse, and only in old age do the lesser horns fuse with the remainder.

The hyoid is connected by muscles and ligaments to the tongue, the mandible, base of the skull (styloid process), thyroid cartilage and sternum.

Palpation

The two greater horns can be felt through the skin below the mandible if firm pressure is applied between finger and thumb above the thyroid cartilage of the larynx. In this position the bone can be moved from side-to-side. The body can be palpated in the front of the neck about 2 cm above the laryngeal prominence with the chin elevated.

Muscles

MUSCLES WHICH CHANGE THE SHAPE OF THE FACE

The muscles which change the shape of the face are commonly known as the muscles of facial expression (Fig. 6.9a). Although with the contraction of individual or groups of muscles, human beings can smile, frown, look happy or sad, and generally convey many emotions, it must be borne in mind that the primary action of the majority of these muscles is to dilate (open) or constrict (close) the eyes, nose and mouth. In addition, one of these muscles, buccinator, plays an important role in mastication (see p. 639), while others are involved in forming and shaping the sounds produced by the larynx into recognizable words.

To be able to perform these many complex actions it is not surprising that the majority of the muscles have only one attachment to bone, the other being to the superficial fascia and skin. Consequently, when the facial muscles contract to dilate or constrict the eyes, nose or mouth, their secondary action has a profound effect on facial expression, through which an individual can convey his or her emotions to the world at large, and recognize the feelings of others.

All of the muscles of facial expression are derived from the second pharyngeal arch, and consequently they are all supplied by branches of the *facial* (seventh cranial) *nerve*. Damage to the branches of the facial nerve will result in a loss of tone in the muscles supplied by that branch, with a consequent sagging of that part of the face. The skin of the face is supplied by the ophthalmic, maxillary and mandibular branches of the *trigeminal* (fifth cranial) *nerve*.

These muscles are best considered in groups in relation to whether they act upon the eyes, nose or mouth. Those muscles which do not adhere to this plan are considered individually.

MOVEMENTS OF THE EYEBROWS

Occipitofrontalis
Corrugator supercilii
Procerus

Occipitofrontalis

The movement of raising the eyebrows, as in an expression of surprise, is produced by occipitofrontalis which is a muscle in two parts united by the strong aponeurosis of the scalp. The posterior part arises from the outer part of the superior nuchal line and the mastoid part of the temporal bone from where it passes to attach to the aponeurosis. The larger anterior part of the muscle runs from the aponeurosis to the superficial fascia of the forehead and eyebrow, interlacing with orbicularis oculi (see p. 638).

Action

Contraction of the posterior or anterior bellies of occipitofrontalis pulls the scalp backwards or forwards respectively. The anterior bellies acting from the aponeurosis raise the eyebrows either together in surprise, or individually as in a quizzical expression. This action produces the deep transverse lines on the forehead.

Corrugator supercilii

This is a small muscle arising from the medial end of the superciliary arch (eyebrow), blending with orbicularis oculi. Its fibres run upwards and laterally to attach to the skin of the eyebrows. On contraction they pull the two eyebrows together medially and downwards as in a frown, so producing the deep vertical wrinkles between the eyebrows.

Fig. 6.9 **a** = The muscles of facial expression; **b** = the superficial part; **c** = the left temporalis muscle; **d** = the left pterygoid muscles shown with the zygomatic arch and part of the mandible removed.

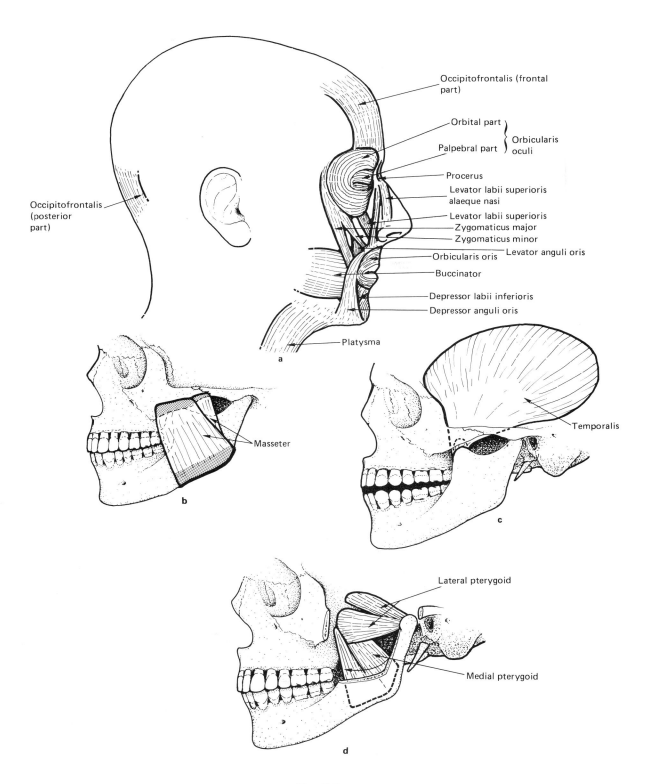

Occipitofrontalis (frontal part)

Orbital part

Palpebral part

Orbicularis oculi

Procerus

Levator labii superioris alaeque nasi

Levator labii superioris

Zygomaticus major

Zygomaticus minor

Levator anguli oris

Orbicularis oris

Buccinator

Depressor labii inferioris

Depressor anguli oris

Platysma

Occipitofrontalis (posterior part)

a

Masseter

b

Temporalis

c

Lateral pterygoid

Medial pterygoid

d

Fig. 6.9

Procerus

These are small muscles being continuous with each other across the midline. They run from the lower part of the nasal bone to the skin over the lower part of the forehead, intermingling with the anterior belly of occipitofrontalis. On contraction they pull down the medial part of the eyebrow producing transverse wrinkles at the root of the nose.

MUSCLES AROUND THE EYE

Orbicularis oculi

Orbicularis oculi

One of the most complex muscles of the face, and by far the most important around the eye, is orbicularis oculi. It consists of three parts: an orbital part, a palpebral part and a lacrimal part. The orbital part surrounds the orbit, spreading onto the forehead, temple and cheek, taking its origin from the medial margin of the orbit and the medial palpebral ligament. The fibres arising from above the ligament run elliptically around the orbit to attach again below the ligament.

The palpebral part of the muscle is much thinner and lies within the eyelids. Again the fibres arise from the medial palpebral ligament, running outwards within the eyelids to unite at the lateral palpebral raphe.

The lacrimal part of orbicularis oculi arises from fascia behind the lacrimal sac and crest of the lacrimal bone, passing laterally to attach to the tarsal plates of each eyelid.

Action

This muscle plays an important part in protecting the eye by washing the eyeball with tears and by firmly closing the eye against insult and injury. The orbital part of the muscle, which can act independently or with other parts, draws the skin of the forehead and cheek towards the medial angle of the orbit, so that the eye is screwed up tightly as when a bright light is shone into the eyes or when dust blows towards them. This action produces the characteristic 'crow's feet' at the lateral corner of the eye.

The palpebral part of the muscle exerts much finer control over the individual eyelids, and by reflex or voluntary contraction pulls down the upper and raises the lower eyelid to close the eye. By pulling the eyelids medially during regular blinking, tears produced by the lacrimal gland are wiped over the surface of the eyeball to keep it moist and wash particles towards the lacrimal puncta. The small movements of the eyelids are very important in non-verbal communication between humans.

The lacrimal part of the muscle dilates the lacrimal sac.

Application

When orbicularis oculi is paralysed there is an inability to close the eye. The resultant failure of this mechanism for blinking and washing the eyeball means that the eyeball tends to become red and inflamed.

MUSCLES AROUND THE NOSE

Nasalis
Levator labii superioris alaeque nasi
Depressor septi

The small muscles around the nose act to dilate or constrict the nasal apertures. These actions are rudimentary in humans, but are of obvious importance in some animals, for example, camels. The dilators are nasalis and levator labii superioris alaeque nasi, which also acts on the upper lip, while the constrictor is depressor septi.

MUSCLES AROUND THE MOUTH

Orbicularis oris
Buccinator
Levator labii superioris alaeque nasi
Levator labii superioris
Zygomaticus major and minor
Levator anguli oris
Depressor anguli oris and depressor labii inferioris
Risorius and mentalis

Orbicularis oris

Surrounding the mouth is orbicularis oris a composite sphincter muscle having deep and superficial parts. Vertically it extends from the nasal septum to midway between the chin and lower lip. The deep fibres are continuous with buccinator, while the superficial fibres are in reality all derived from other muscles. The deep fibres attach to both the maxilla and mandible near the lateral incisor. Between the deep and superficial layers of the muscle, the intrinsic fibres of orbicularis oris run elliptically around the mouth, having no bony attachment. Some of the superficial fibres decussate like those of buccinator.

Action

Orbicularis oris produces movements of the lips as in 'puckering' or whistling. It has an important role in speech by changing the shape of the mouth and lips to help form recognizable sounds. It is also important in mastication as its contraction against the teeth helps to push food back between the teeth when chewing. Contraction of the various muscles which insert into orbicularis oris, thereby changing its shape.

Buccinator

Buccinator is continuous with the deep part of orbicularis oris, and forms the substance of the cheek. It arises from both the maxilla and the mandible opposite the molar teeth, and from the pterygomandibular raphe, which stretches from the pterygoid hamulus to the posterior end of the mylohyoid line. The fibres run forwards to blend with those of orbicularis oris. The medial fibres decussate posterolateral to the angle of the mouth, so that the lower fibres run to the upper lip, while the upper ones run to the lower lip. The interlacing of the deep buccinator fibres, with some of the superficial fibres of orbicularis oris, forms an easily felt nodule at the angle of the mouth known as the *modiolus*.

Action

Buccinator presses the cheek in against the teeth or resists outward pressure against the cheek. The former action is important in mastication as it prevents the accumulation of food in the cheek—a common problem when buccinator is paralysed. When blowing up a balloon, buccinator can be felt resisting the outward pressure of air against the cheek. When the lips are protruded by orbicularis oris, buccinator causes the cheek to 'cave in', thereby producing a sucking action. Buccinator can also be used to pull orbicularis oris back against the teeth, or to retract the angle of the mouth to expose the premolar and molar teeth.

Palpation

If a finger is placed between the cheek and teeth, buccinator can be felt contracting as it presses the finger against the teeth.

Levator labii superioris alaeque nasi

This muscle arises from the maxilla and attaches to the ala of the nose and skin, and the muscle of the upper lip.

Levator labii superioris

This muscle arises from the maxilla above the infraorbital foramen and attaches to the upper lip towards its lateral end.

Zygomaticus major and minor

These both arise from the zygomatic bone and attach to the upper lip near its angle.

Levator anguli oris

This muscle arises from the maxilla below the infraorbital foramen, inserting into skin and muscle at the angle of the mouth. A few of its fibres may pass to the lower lip.

Action

All of these muscles when contracting on both sides raise the upper lip as in smiling. Contraction of one side produces a sneer. The tone of these muscles is important in maintaining the normal horizontal position of the mouth. When paralysed, there is a gradual drooping of the angle of the mouth on the affected side which leads to leakage of saliva with a constant dribble from the corner of the mouth. Zygomaticus major, assisted by levator anguli oris, raises and pulls the angle of the mouth laterally, as in laughing.

The following facial muscles have their effect on the lower lip:

Depressor anguli oris and depressor labii inferioris

Depressor anguli oris arises from the front of the mandible below the mental foramen and blends with the muscles of the lower lip at the angle of the mouth, as well as inserting into skin. Some of its fibres may pass into the upper lip. The muscle is continuous with platysma and overlaps depressor labii inferioris which also arises from the mandible below the mental foramen. Its fibres attach to the skin and muscle of the lower lip, the fibres from each side blending together.

Risorius and mentalis

The remaining two muscles, although considered as part of the lower lip musculature, usually only have connections to the skin of the lower lip. Risorius arises from the fascial covering of the parotid gland and inserts into skin at the angle of the mouth. Mentalis comes from the mandible below the incisors and passes to the skin of the chin. Platysma, with which risorius may be completely fused, is considered later (see p. 644).

Action

Depressor anguli oris and depressor labii inferioris pull the mouth downwards and laterally giving an expression of sadness. By itself depressor labii inferioris curls the lower lip downwards. Mentalis, on the other hand, pulls the skin of the chin upwards, causing a protrusion of the lower lip as in pouting. Risorius merely pulls the angle of the mouth laterally.

Application

If the muscles on one side of the face are paralysed, as in Bell's palsy, the typical problems encountered are: an inability to close the eye; a tendency for food to accumulate between the cheek, lips and teeth of the paralysed side; the corner of the mouth droops downwards on the affected side, and on smiling, the mouth is pulled towards the sound side by the unopposed action of the intact musculature.

MUSCLES WHICH MOVE THE MANDIBLE

The movements of the mandible are complex involving the coordinated action of the muscles attached to it. Because of the nature of the temporomandibular joint (see p. 648), four basic movements of the mandible can be identified, these being:

1. *protraction*—pulling the mandible forwards so that the head articulates indirectly with the articular tubercle of the temporal bone;
2. *retraction*—pulling the mandible backwards so that the head moves back into the mandibular fossa;
3. *elevation*—closing the mouth;
4. *depression*—opening the mouth.

Combinations of these basic movements occur in chewing and grinding. Opening the mouth, particularly against resistance, as when eating sticky foods, will involve the infrahyoid group of muscles in order to stabilize the hyoid bone and provide a firm base against which mandibular movements can be made.

MUSCLES WHICH ELEVATE THE MANDIBLE

Masseter
Medial pterygoid
Temporalis (see p. 641)

Masseter

Masseter (see Fig. 6.9b) is a flat quadrilateral muscle with deep and superficial parts. The superficial part arises from the *zygomatic process* of the *maxilla* and the *anterior two-thirds* of the *zygomatic arch*. The muscle fibres running downwards and backwards to attach to the outer surface of the *angle* of the *mandible*, extending onto the lower half of the *outer surface* of the *ramus*. The deeper part arises from the deep surface of the *zygomatic* arch, the fibres of which run downwards and backwards to attach to the *ramus* and *coronoid process* of the *mandible* (see Fig. 6.9b).

Nerve supply

Masseter is supplied by the anterior division of the *mandibular division* of the *trigeminal* (fifth cranial) *nerve*. The skin over the muscle is supplied mainly by the anterior rami of C2 and 3, but partly by the mandibular branch of the trigeminal nerve.

Action

Masseter elevates the mandible so approximating the upper and lower teeth. The superficial fibres help pull the mandible forwards during the movement of protraction.

Palpation

Masseter can be easily palpated by applying pressure through the cheek below the zygomatic arch when the teeth are clenched together.

Medial pterygoid

The medial pterygoid (see Figs. 6.9b, 6.15) is a thick quadrilateral muscle arising from the medial side of the *lateral pterygoid plate* and from the pyramidal process of the *palatine bone*. A smaller head arises from the *maxillary tubercle*. From these two origins, which surround the lower fibres of lateral pterygoid, the muscle fibres run downwards, backwards and laterally to attach to a rough *triangular impression* on the inner surface of the *mandible* between the angle and the mylohyoid line (see Fig. 6.9b).

Nerve supply

The medial pterygoid is supplied by the *mandibular division* of the *trigeminal* (fifth cranial) *nerve*.

Action

The medial pterygoid elevates the mandible and so closes the mouth. Because of the direction of the muscle fibres, it also pulls the mandible forwards. When the medial and

lateral pterygoid muscles of one side contract together, the chin swings to the opposite side. Such movements are important in chewing.

MUSCLES WHICH RETRACT THE MANDIBLE

Temporalis
Digastric (see p. 642)
Geniohyoid (see p. 644)

Temporalis

Temporalis (see Fig. 6.9b) is large, flat, fan-shaped muscle which arises from the *temporal fossa* of the *temporal bone* and the fascia covering it. The muscle fibres in the anterior part of the muscle run almost vertically, while those in the most posterior part are almost horizontal. All of the muscle fibres, however, converge to a thick tendon which passes deep to the zygomatic arch to insert into the *apex* and *deep surface* of the *coronoid process* and the *anterior border* of the *ramus* of the *mandible*. A few fibres may become continuous with buccinator, while other more superficial fibres may fuse with masseter.

Nerve supply

Temporalis is supplied by the *mandibular division* of the *trigeminal* (fifth cranial) *nerve*. The skin over the muscle is supplied mainly by the mandibular branch of the trigeminal nerve and the anterior rami of C2 and 3.

Action

The posterior fibres retract the mandible after it has been protruded. The anterior vertical fibres of temporalis elevate the mandible and close the mouth; they are constantly active to counteract the effects of gravity.

Palpation

Temporalis can be palpated by applying firm pressure above the zygomatic arch through the temporal fascia over the temporal fossa, particularly when the teeth are firmly clenched together.

MUSCLES WHICH PROTRACT THE MANDIBLE

Lateral pterygoid
Medial pterygoid (see p. 641)
Masseter (see pp. 640–641)

Lateral pterygoid

The lateral pterygoid (see Figs. 6.9b, 6.15) has two heads, an upper one which arises from the inferior surface of the *greater wing* of the *sphenoid*, and a lower one which arises from the *lateral surface* of the *lateral pterygoid plate*. From this extensive double origin, the muscle fibres pass backwards and slightly laterally to insert into the front of the *neck* of the *mandible* and into the *capsule* and *intra-articular disc* of the temporomandibular joint.

Nerve supply

The lateral pterygoid is supplied by the *mandibular division* of the *trigeminal* (fifth cranial) *nerve*.

Action

Contraction of lateral pterygoid pulls the head of the mandible, the intra-articular disc and the joint capsule forwards onto the articular eminence; a movement which occurs during protraction of the mandible and opening the mouth. Working with the medial pterygoid of the same side, the lateral pterygoid produces a slight rotation of the jaw so that the chin swings to the opposite side. When all four pterygoid muscles contract, the mandible is protruded so that the lower incisors are carried in front of the upper ones (see Fig. 6.18b). When only both lateral pterygoids are working, the head of the mandible is carried forwards and there is slight rotation of the head against the intra-articular disc so that the mouth opens. This is essentially what happens when sleeping with the mouth open. The lateral pterygoid is the main antagonist to retraction, its eccentric contraction therefore helps to control this movement.

MUSCLES WHICH DEPRESS THE MANDIBLE

Digastric
Mylohyoid
Geniohyoid
Platysma

Digastric

Digastric (Fig. 6.10a), as its name suggests, is a muscle with two bellies, anterior and posterior, united by an intermediate tendon. The posterior belly passes downwards and forwards from the *medial surface* of the *mastoid process* in close association with stylohyoid, to an intermediate tendon which passes through the insertion of stylohyoid and is held by an *aponeurotic sling* to the *upper surface* of the *hyoid bone*. The anterior belly of the muscle runs upwards and forwards to attach to the *digastric fossa* on the lower border of the *mandible* close to the symphysis menti.

Nerve supply

The posterior belly of digastric is supplied by the *facial* (seventh cranial) *nerve*, and the anterior belly by the *nerve to mylohyoid* from the inferior alveolar branch of the mandibular division of the *trigeminal* (fifth cranial) *nerve*.

Action

If the hyoid is fixed, digastric can depress the mandible thereby opening the mouth, an action required when acting against resistance. With the mandible elevated, digastric also helps in retraction of the mandible. With the mandible fixed, digastric raises the hyoid bone and with it the larynx, an important action in swallowing.

Mylohyoid

Mylohyoid (Fig. 6.10a) arises from the *mylohyoid line* on the inner surface of the body of the mandible. Its fibres run downwards and medially towards the midline to insert

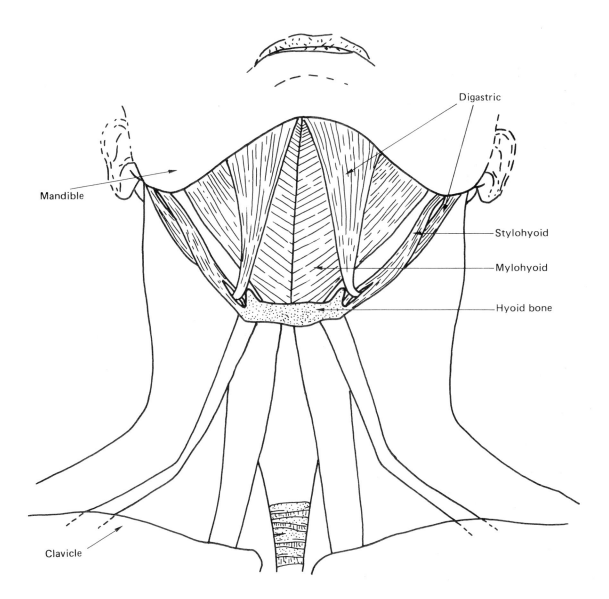

Fig. 6.10a The suprahyoid muscles, anterior view.

into a *median fibrous raphe* which extends from the symphysis menti to the upper surface of the body of the hyoid bone. The two mylohyoid muscles thus give rise to a muscular sheet which forms the floor of the mouth.

Nerve supply

Mylohyoid is supplied by the *nerve to mylohyoid* from the inferior alveolar branch of the mandibular division of the *trigeminal* (fifth cranial) *nerve.*

Action

Mylohyoid can depress the mandible against resistance, elevate the hyoid, and also raise the floor of the mouth. In elevating and fixing the hyoid, it helps to press the tongue against the roof of the mouth and so is important in swallowing.

Geniohyoid

Geniohyoid is a small muscle found deep to mylohyoid. It runs from the *inferior mental spine* on the posterior surface of the symphysis menti to the front of the *body* of the *hyoid bone.*

Nerve supply

Geniohyoid is supplied by *fibres from C1,* which reach the muscle by travelling with the hypoglossal nerve.

Action

Depending upon which end of the muscle is fixed, geniohyoid can elevate the hyoid bone or depress the mandible. When the hyoid is pulled upwards and forwards, the floor of the mouth is shortened and the pharynx is widened ready to receive food.

Platysma

Platysma is a broad, flat sheet of muscle lying in the superficial fascia covering the front of the neck. It is variably developed in different people, arising from the *skin* and *superficial part* of the *chest* and *shoulder.* The fibres cross the clavicle running upwards over the front and sides of the neck to attach to the *lower border* of the *body* of the *mandible* and *fascia* of the lower part of the face. In the neck the two platysma muscles are separated by a gap in the midline, but just below the chin the most medial fibres decussate with those of the opposite side.

Nerve supply

Platysma is supplied by the *facial* (seventh cranial) *nerve.*

Action

Platysma can depress the mandible and therefore help to open the mouth. However, as a muscle of facial expression, it can produce expressions of horror by depressing the angle of the mouth and lower lip. When a supreme effort is being made, as in weight lifting, platysma can be seen standing out in the neck. Similarly, platysma can be seen to stand out in runners after strenuous exertions. In these circumstances platysma may be acting as an accessory muscle of respiration by pulling on the chest wall. However, it is more probable that the muscle acts to prevent compression of the great veins and the sucking in of the soft tissues of the neck due to the violent respiratory efforts being made. Paralysis of the muscle causes the skin of the neck to fall away in slack folds.

MUSCLES WHICH ELEVATE THE HYOID BONE

Stylohyoid
Digastric (see p. 642)
Mylohyoid (see pp. 642–644)
Geniohyoid

Stylohyoid

Stylohyoid (see Fig. 6.10a) is a small, thin muscle arising from the posterior part of the *styloid process* of the *temporal bone* near its root. It runs downwards above the posterior belly of digastric, splitting into two slips enclosing the intermediate tendon of digastric. These slips unite before attaching to the *root* of the *greater horn* of the *hyoid bone.*

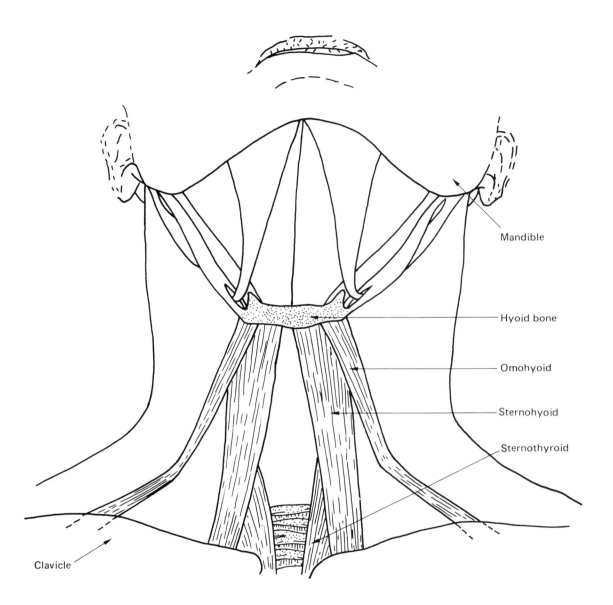

Mandible

Hyoid bone

Omohyoid

Sternohyoid

Sternothyroid

Clavicle

Fig. 6.10b The infrahyoid muscles, anterior view.

Nerve supply

Stylohyoid is supplied by the *facial* (seventh cranial) *nerve*.

Action

Stylohyoid elevates and retracts the hyoid bone, taking with it the tongue and lengthening the floor of the mouth.

MUSCLES WHICH DEPRESS THE HYOID BONE

Sternohyoid
Sternothyroid
Thyrohyoid
Omohyoid

Sternohyoid

Sternohyoid is a strap muscle which arises from the *medial end* of the *clavicle*, the posterior sternoclavicular ligament, and the posterior surface of the *manubrium sterni*. The fibres run upwards and slightly medially to attach to the *lower border* of the *body* of the *hyoid bone* (see Fig. 6.10b).

Nerve supply

Sternohyoid is supplied by the *anterior primary rami* of *C1, 2* and *3*, via the ansa cervicalis.

Sternothyroid

Sternothyroid (see Fig. 6.10b) is smaller than, and is situated posterior to, sternohyoid. It arises from the posterior surface of the *manubrium sterni*, below the attachment of sternohyoid, and from the *first costal cartilage*. Being broader than sternohyoid the fibres run upwards and laterally over the trachea and thyroid gland to attach to the oblique line of the *thyroid cartilage*.

Nerve supply

Sternothyroid is supplied by the *anterior primary rami* of *C1, 2* and *3*, via the ansa cervicalis.

Thyrohyoid

Thyrohyoid is a short muscle running between the oblique line of the *thyroid carti-lage* as a continuation of sternothyroid, and the lower border of the body and greater horn of the *hyoid bone*.

Nerve supply

Thyrohyoid is supplied by the *anterior primary rami* of *C1*, which reaches the muscle via the hypoglossal nerve.

Omohyoid

Omohyoid (see Fig. 6.10b) resembles the digastric muscle in that it consists of two bellies united by an intermediate tendon. The inferior belly arises from the *transverse scapular ligament* and adjacent margins of the *suprascapular notch* on the upper border of the scapula, and runs forwards and slightly upwards to an *intermediate tendon*. From the tendon the superior belly runs upwards and medially to attach to the lower border of the *body* of the *hyoid*.

Under cover of sternomastoid the intermediate tendon is bound down to the clavicle and the first rib by a sling of deep cervical fascia, thereby maintaining the angled appearance of the muscle.

Nerve supply

Omohyoid is supplied by the *anterior primary rami* of *C1, 2* and *3* via the ansa cervicalis.

Action

All of these so-called infrahyoid (strap) muscles act to depress the hyoid bone after it has been elevated during swallowing. Alternatively, by fixing the hyoid bone, the suprahyoid muscles can act on the mandible to depress it against resistance.

Thyrohyoid acting by itself raises the thyroid cartilage towards the hyoid, thereby pulling the larynx upwards under the root of the tongue. In this way thyrohyoid is responsible for closing the laryngeal inlet and prevents food from entering the larynx during swallowing. Acting by itself, sternothyroid opens the laryngeal inlet by pulling the thyroid cartilage away from the hyoid. During forced inspiration sternothyroid probably acts to keep the laryngeal inlet open.

MASTICATION AND SWALLOWING (DEGLUTITION)

Mastication is the name given to the process involved in chewing and grinding food between the molar and premolar teeth in order to break it down into smaller fragments so that it can be moulded into a softer, more manageable bolus and swallowed. The requisite movements of the mandible occur at the temporomandibular joints (see p. 656) and involve opening and closing of the mouth, together with protraction and retraction of the mandible.

Initially, food is bitten off by the incisor teeth by means of the contraction of masseter, medial pterygoid and temporalis. Chewing movements are essentially produced by the alternate contraction of the pterygoid muscles first on one side and then the other. The elevators (masseter and medial pterygoid) of the side on which the pterygoids are functioning are also active to keep the teeth opposed. On the opposite side, temporalis is active to retract that side of the mandible, particularly if the food is sticky. There may also be activity in digastric, mylohyoid and geniohyoid to help separate the teeth momentarily when the bolus is sticky. During these swinging movements of the mandible the food is prevented from escaping between the teeth by the action of various other muscles intimately involved in the masticatory process. If food passes into the vestibule of the mouth it is returned by the contraction of buccinator. If it escapes medially into the oral cavity it is ground against the hard palate and pushed back between the teeth by the action of the tongue. Contraction of mylohyoid helps keep the tongue against the hard palate, while orbicularis oris around the mouth prevents food escaping through the lips.

Once a suitable consistency has been achieved the bolus of food is collected from the anterior part of the mouth by the tip of the tongue and pressed back towards the soft palate by mylohyoid, digastric and stylohyoid. At the same time the elevators of the mandible and the mylohyoid contract, and the hyoid bone is elevated, carrying with it the larynx. Geniohyoid then pulls the hyoid forwards to widen the pharynx in anticipation of receiving the bolus. The soft palate is raised so closing off the nasopharynx and preventing food entering the nose. Elevation of the tongue and the hyoid bone closes the laryngeal inlet so that food does not enter the airways. The food bolus slides over the surface of the epiglottis into the laryngopharynx. Respiration is reflexly inhibited as the constrictor muscles of the pharynx contract successively to push the bolus of food towards the oesophagus. When the bolus has passed the laryngeal inlet, the hyoid bone and the larynx are pulled down to their resting positions by contraction of sternohyoid, sternothyroid and omohyoid. Breathing is once again resumed and another mouthful can be dealt with.

Swallowing fluids is essentially similar, except that in the initial stages the tongue forms a tube. The fluid is then forced backwards by the tongue flowing down over the sides of the epiglottis, thereby avoiding the laryngeal inlet.

Application

Painful spasm of the muscles of mastication is frequently seen following traumatic overstretching, a situation which can arise during dental extraction. The resulting 'trismus' responds well to gentle heat and soft tissue techniques applied to the muscles.

Joints

THE TEMPOROMANDIBULAR JOINT

Introduction

The temporomandibular joint is the means whereby the mandible (lower jaw) articulates indirectly with the skull. It is one of the few joints in the body which contains a complete intra-articular disc thereby dividing the joint space into upper and lower compartments. This feature facilitates the movements which are possible at the joint in such a way that the combined gliding and hinge action produces rotation of the mandible around a transverse axis which passes between the two lingulae. The position of this axis means that during mandibular movements the structures entering the mandibular foramen, i.e. the inferior alveolar nerve and vessels, are not put under tension.

The articular surfaces of the two components of the joint are not congruent. Indeed, they are highly incongruent; it is the function of the intra-articular disc to improve congruence between the surfaces. However, it is probably a functional advantage to have highly incongruent joint surfaces at the temporomandibular joint because of the growth changes associated with the mandible, and therefore the changing demands made upon the joint.

At birth the two halves of the mandible are separate, with the body being a shell of alveolar bone enclosing the developing teeth. The ramus is short and the angle it makes with the body is obtuse, about 175°, so that the condyle lies nearly in line with the body (Fig. 6.11a). During the first year the two bodies begin to fuse at the symphysis, with union being complete by the end of the second year. The ramus gradually enlarges, with there being a corresponding decrease in the angle between the body and the ramus so that by about the age of four it has decreased to 140° (Fig. 6.11b). Progressive changes within the mandible continue so that in the adult this angle has decreased to 110° or less (Fig. 6.11c). With the loss of the teeth in old age, the alveolar sockets are absorbed and the angle between body and ramus now increases, due to bony remodelling, to 140° (Fig. 6.11d). The condyle becomes bent backwards so that the mandibular notch is widened.

The mandible grows in width between its angles, as well as in length, height and thickness. The condylar process grows not only upwards, but also backwards and sideways, thus contributing to its increase in total length, as well as height and width. Modelling maintains the shape of the condyle and the curves of the anterior margin of the ramus and coronoid process.

In the adult, the long axis of the condyle is directed medially and backwards, forming an angle of some 30° with the frontal plane (Fig. 6.12). This angle is not, however, always consistent from side-to-side. If prolonged, the two axes would meet in the median plane at the anterior margin of the foramen magnum.

The temporomandibular joint, together with its associated ligaments and muscles, as well as the occluding surfaces of the teeth limits the forcible opposition of the jaws during biting. However, this is only one aspect of normal function which includes mastication, suckling, swallowing, yawning and speaking, although this latter activity involves little force at the joint.

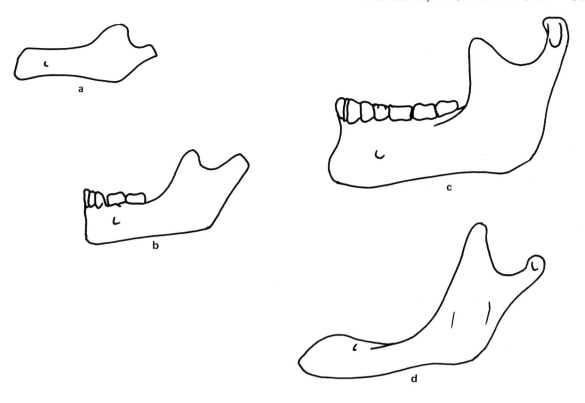

Fig. 6.11   Age changes in the mandible: **a** = at birth, **b** = age 4, **c** = adult and **d** = old age.

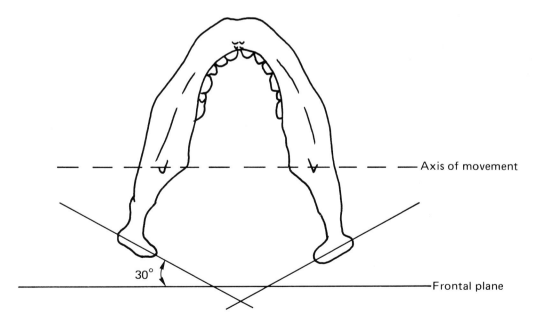

Fig. 6.12   Inferior view of mandible.

Articular surfaces

The temporomandibular joint is a synovial condyloid joint between the mandibular fossa of the temporal bone on the base of the skull, and the condyle of the mandible. Intervening between these two joint surfaces is a complete intra-articular disc. Both bony articular surfaces are covered by fibrocartilage, with the superficial part having a large fibrous element with only the deeper parts containing cartilage.

Mandibular fossa

The temporal articular surface is concavoconvex from behind forwards (Fig. 6.13), and extends from the squamotympanic fissure to the anterior margin of the articular eminence. The fossa is oval, being wider mediolaterally than anteroposteriorly (average values being 23 and 19 mm respectively). At birth this surface is more or less plane, with the lateral part higher than the medial. Changes in the surface during childhood result in the sinuous shape seen in sagittal section. Mediolaterally the surface becomes more horizontal. In the adult the fossa consists of a continuous plate of compact bone with no underlying spongy bone. Remodelling occurs throughout life in this bony plate, and may lead to deviations from the usual joint shape.

Condyle of the mandible

The spindle-shaped condyle is at right angles to the ramus of the mandible, with its long axis passing posteromedially. It is slightly smaller than the mandibular fossa, being on average 20 mm long (mediolateral dimension) and 10 mm wide (anteroposterior dimension). The articular surface of the condyle is curved and is displaced slightly posteriorly with respect to the highest point of the condyle (Fig. 6.13). Mediolaterally there is a great degree of symmetry.

Intra-articular disc

An articular disc separates the incongruent bony articular surfaces moulding itself upon them during movements at the joint (Fig. 6.13). The disc is thought to be derived from the tendon of lateral pterygoid, which in the embryo passes posteriorly between the head of the mandible and the temporal bone to attach to the malleus. That part of the tendon compressed between the two bones is said to form the disc. In the adult when viewed from above it is an avascular oval plate of fibrous tissue. In the newborn it is relatively flat, but with development of the bony constituents of the joint becomes shaped rather like a 'jockey's cap', so that its upper surface is concavoconvex to fit the mandibular fossa and articular eminence, and its undersurface is concave over the condyle.

The central region of the disc, although the most dense, is the thinnest, about 1.1 mm, while anteriorly and posteriorly its thickness varies up to 2.0 and 2.8 mm respectively. Very rarely is the disc perforated in its central region. Although essentially avascular the extreme periphery of the disc, which is attached all the way round to the inside of the capsule, is highly vascularized and innervated. Anteriorly the disc attaches near the condyle, and receives, together with the adjoining capsule, the attachment of the upper fibres of lateral pterygoid. Posteriorly it attaches nearer to the temporal bone than the mandible, and is therefore not so freely mobile as elsewhere. This region of the disc is less dense than in other parts, with the fibres having a crinkled arrangement enabling a small degree of elongation and recoil.

At birth the central region consists of relatively soft collagenous tissue, which becomes coarsened with age and use. The functional wear that occurs is thought to be a major factor in the conversion of the region into a disc of fibrocartilage.

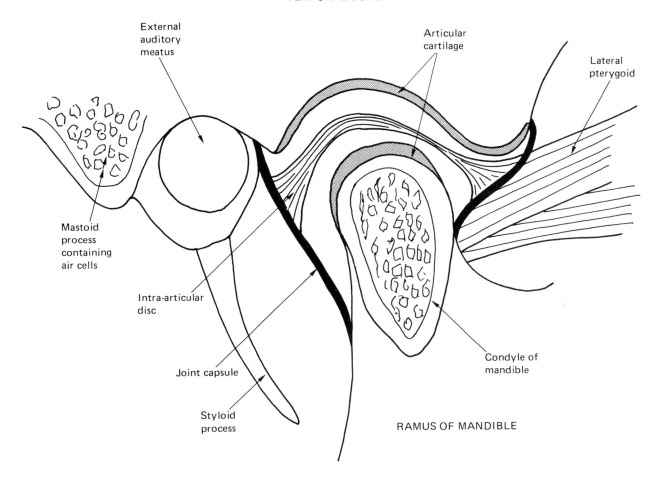

TEMPORAL BONE

External
auditory
meatus

Articular
cartilage

Lateral
pterygoid

Mastoid
process
containing
air cells

Intra-articular
disc

Joint capsule

Styloid
process

Condyle of
mandible

RAMUS OF MANDIBLE

Fig. 6.13 The articular surfaces of the
temporomandibular joint.

Joint capsule and synovial membrane

The strong, fibrous capsule of the joint is thin and loose, surrounding the articular surfaces and enclosing the intra-articular disc. It is attached above to the margins of the mandibular fossa as far anteriorly as the transverse prominence of the articular eminence. Below, the capsule attaches to the neck of the mandible (Fig. 6.14). To the inner aspect of the capsule is attached the intra-articular disc (see Fig. 6.13). Above this attachment, the capsule is loose thereby permitting free movement of the disc with respect to the mandibular fossa; below, the capsule is much more taut with the fibres of the medial and lateral parts of the capsule being so short that the disc appears to be attached directly to the medial and lateral ends of the condyle. Part of the tendon of lateral pterygoid inserts into the front of the joint capsule, and therefore indirectly to the intra-articular disc.

The capsular attachments are such that they allow a rotatory movement to occur between the condyle and the undersurface of the disc, as well as enabling the disc and condyle to move backwards and forwards as one unit against the mandibular fossa.

Two synovial membranes are associated with the joint, one for each compartment, i.e. above and below the disc. Each lines all the non-articular surfaces and fuses with the periphery of the disc.

Ligaments

Associated with the joint are three ligaments, two of which are accessory. However, these latter ligaments have an important role in guiding the movement of the mandible against the base of the skull under the influence of muscular activity. The lateral ligament blends with the capsule, while the sphenomandibular and stylomandibular ligaments are accessory to the joint. To a large extent the pterygomandibular raphe also acts to guide the movements of the mandible.

Lateral ligament

The lateral ligament has a broad attachment to the lower border and tubercle of the zygo-matic bone. From here the fibres pass downwards and backwards blending with the joint capsule to attach to the lateral and posterior parts of the neck of the mandible (Fig. 6.14a). It reinforces the lateral aspect of the joint capsule.

Sphenomandibular ligament

The sphenomandibular ligament is a strong, thin flat band lying on the medial side of the joint. It passes downwards and forwards from the spine of the sphenoid to the lingula and adjacent area on the medial side of the ramus of the mandible (Fig. 6.14b). The sphenomandibular ligament develops from the sheath of that part of the cartilage of the first pharyngeal arch (Meckel's cartilage) lying between the base of the skull and the mandibular foramen.

Stylomandibular ligament

The stylomandibular ligament is a thickening of deep cervical fascia, which separates the parotid (posterior) and submandibular (anterior) salivary glands. It extends from near the apex of the styloid process to the lower part of the posterior border of the ramus of the mandible near the angle (Fig. 6.14).

Blood and nerve supply

The arterial supply to the temporomandibular joint is from branches of the middle meningeal and anterior tympanic branches of the maxillary artery, and the superficial temporal and ascending pharyngeal arteries. The superficial temporal and maxillary arteries are the terminal branches of the external carotid artery, while the ascending pharyngeal arises from the external carotid lower down in the neck. Venous drainage is to the retromandibular vein and thence to the jugular system within the neck. The lymphatic drainage of the joint is to the deep parotid lymph nodes.

The nerve supply to the joint is by twigs from the auriculotemporal and masseteric branches of the mandibular division of the *trigeminal* (fifth cranial) *nerve*.

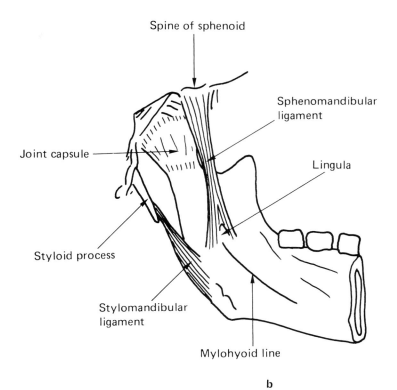

Fig. 6.14 **a** = Lateral, **b** = medial views of the temporomandibular joint showing the ligaments associated with the joint.

Relations (Fig. 6.15)

The joint is relatively superficial, being covered only by skin and subcutaneous tissue. The condyle can be palpated immediately below the middle third of the zygomatic arch. Posteriorly crossing the zygomatic arch, but in front of the external auditory meatus, are the superficial temporal vessels. Pressure applied in this region reveals the pulse.

Anteriorly is the tendon of lateral pterygoid as it passes from its anterior and deep attachments to insert partly into the anterior joint capsule and neck of the mandible. Also anteriorly is the tendon of temporalis, lying superficial to lateral pterygoid, as it passes deep to the zygomatic arch from the temporal fossa to attach to the anterior and medial aspects of the coronoid process.

The root of the styloid process is posteromedial to the mandibular fossa, which has medial to it the carotid sheath and its contents.

Stability

Stability at the joint depends to a considerable extent as to whether the mouth is open or closed, being greater with the mouth closed and the teeth occluded.

With the mouth closed the teeth themselves stabilize the mandible on the maxilla and take any strain if a blow is received on the chin. Furthermore, forward movement of the condyle is discouraged by the articular eminence and contraction of the posterior fibres of temporalis. Backward movement is prevented by the lateral ligament and by contraction of lateral pterygoid.

With the mouth open the joint is less stable, because the condyle has moved forward onto the articular eminence as well as rotating. Backward dislocation is opposed again by the lateral ligament and lateral pterygoid, while forward dislocation is restricted by the articular eminence, tension in the lateral ligament and contraction of masseter, temporalis and medial pterygoid. However, with the mouth open there is little to prevent an upward dislocation through the thin roof of the mandibular fossa. In practice this injury is extremely rare as a blow to the drooping mandible usually causes the mouth either to close or open more fully.

The most common dislocation is one in which one or both condyles ride forwards beyond the articular eminences, i.e. a forward dislocation (Fig. 6.16a). This may occur in yawning or opening the mouth too widely. Reduction of the dislocation is often prevented by spasm of the posterior deep fibres of masseter, which tend to hold the dislocated jaw open because these fibres now pass down behind the axis of rotation due to the forward position of the condyles. To reduce the dislocation the spasm must be overcome, with or without anaesthetic. If the dislocation is on one side only it can be reduced by placing the thumb on the back teeth of the dislocated side and pushing downwards and backwards. This releases the condyle and the mandible springs back into place; care must be taken to quickly remove the thumb. If the dislocation is bilateral then the angles of the mandible have to be gripped tightly with one hand and pulled downwards and backwards, while the other hand pushes the chin upwards (Fig. 6.16a). The mandible should, on release of the condyles, spring back into position (Fig. 6.16b). Occasionally the dislocation tends to recur, particularly on yawning. With loss of permanent dentition the joint is less stable and anterior dislocation occurs more readily. It is also more easily reduced because of the relative lengthening of the ligaments of the joint due to tooth loss.

Fig. 6.15 Relations of the temporomandibular joint, with part of the mandible removed.

Fig. 6.16 Relationship of the temporomandibular joint in (**a**) bilateral dislocation and (**b**) with the mouth closed.

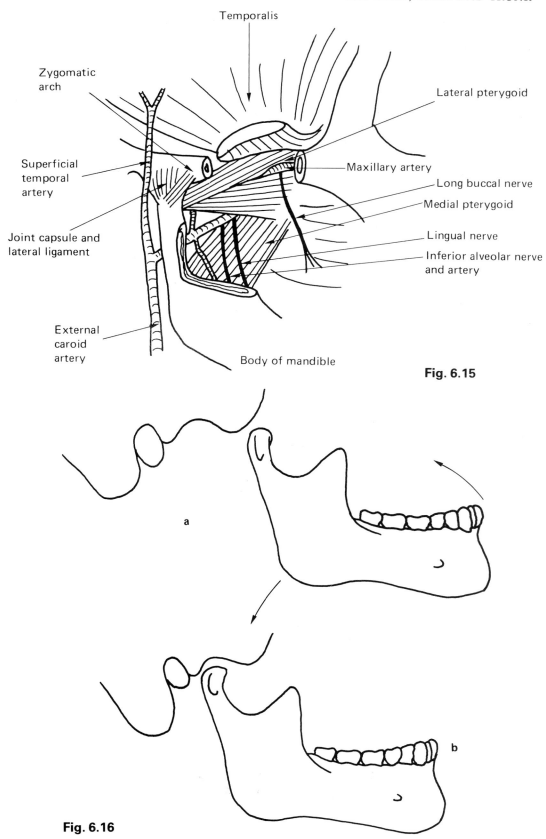

Temporalis

Zygomatic arch

Lateral pterygoid

Superficial temporal artery

Maxillary artery

Long buccal nerve

Medial pterygoid

Joint capsule and lateral ligament

Lingual nerve

Inferior alveolar nerve and artery

External caroid artery

Body of mandible

Fig. 6.15

a

b

Fig. 6.16

Movements

The movements of the mandible can be described as lowering (depression) and raising (elevation) of the jaw, protraction (forward movement), retraction (backward movement) and side-to-side movements. All of these movements are used to some extent during chewing. However, to fully understand and appreciate the movements which occur at the temporomandibular joint, some knowledge of the relationship between the upper and lower teeth with the mouth closed is necessary. With the teeth in contact (occluded) the upper incisors lie in front of the lower ones, there usually being some contact between their opposing surfaces (Fig. 6.17b). When the mouth is opened from this position the edges of the lower incisors pass downwards and forwards until the edges of both sets of incisors are directed towards each other. The downward and forward movement of the mandible, in initiating opening of the mouth, indicates the compound movement of forward gliding and rotation that occurs at the temporomandibular joint.

The form of the articular surfaces of the joint enables a hinge-like rotation to occur between the condyle and the inferior surface of the articular disc in the lower compartment of the joint, while in the upper compartment the condyle and disc glide forwards (and slightly downwards) against the mandibular fossa as a single unit. It is the sinuous form of the mandibular fossa and articular eminence which ensures that the teeth become separated by direct downward movement of the mandible as well as by its hinge action.

Throughout this combined gliding and hinge action the mandible tends to rotate about a transverse axis through the two lingulae (Fig. 6.17a). The position of this axis is determined by the sphenomandibular and stylomandibular ligaments acting as stays, while various muscles are contracting to produce the movements.

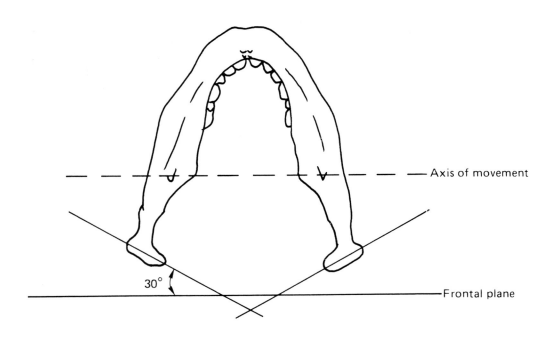

Fig. 6.17a The axis of movement of the mandible, which passes through the two lingulae.

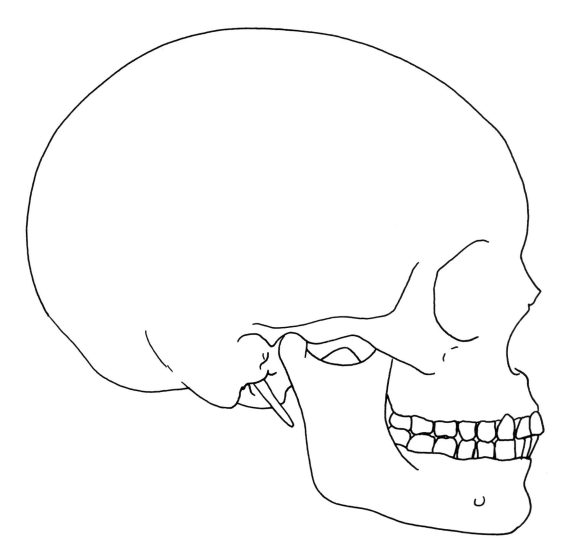

Fig. 6.17b The normal relationship of the teeth with the mouth closed.

Protraction and retraction (Fig. 6.18a, b)

Protraction and retraction are the actions whereby the condyle and disc move as one unit against the mandibular fossa. In protraction the condyle and disc glide forwards so that the condyle rides on the articular eminence. Retraction is the opposite movement whereby the condyle is relocated in the mandibular fossa. Protraction is primarily produced by contraction of lateral pterygoid pulling on the disc and neck of the mandible. It is helped by medial pterygoid and the superficial fibres of masseter. Retraction is produced by the posterior almost horizontal fibres of temporalis, assisted by the suprahyoid muscles. Lateral pterygoid may contract eccentrically during retraction to control the movement.

Elevation and depression (Fig. 6.18a, c)

Elevation and depression of the mandible involve the hinge-like rotation of the condyle against the intra-articular disc, and this occurs in the lower compartment of the temporomandibular joint. Depression of the mandible usually involves the eccentric contraction of temporalis to give a controlled opening of the mouth under the influence of gravity. If there is resistance to opening, as when chewing sticky buns, then geniohyoid, mylohyoid and digastric contract pulling on the mandible from a fixed hyoid.

Closing the mouth (elevation) is a very powerful action produced by the combined action of masseter, medial pterygoid and temporalis, the two former holding the mandible in a sling. Temporalis is considered to be the antigravity muscle contracting to keep the mouth closed under normal conditions.

Side-to-side (grinding) movements

In chewing and grinding movements, the mandible is alternately protracted and retracted with the two sides usually moving in opposite directions so that one side is protracted while the opposite side is retracted. These movements are combined with elevation and depression with the result that the mandibular teeth move diagonally across the maxillary teeth with the intervening food being crushed and ground. Consequently, all of the so-called 'muscles of mastication' are called into action, working rhythmically and alternately. Medial pterygoid is of particular importance in this respect as it plays a major role in producing the oblique movement of the mandible. However, to keep the food between the teeth and to prevent it lodging in the vestibule of the mouth or returning to the oral cavity proper, buccinator and the muscles of the tongue respectively are also working hard and so must therefore be included in any discussion of mastication.

Accessory movements

A number of accessory movements are possible at the temporomandibular joint, however only two of them will be described here. With the subject lying supine and the head turned through 90° so that the face looks laterally, a downward directed pressure on the mandibular condyle (using the thumb) causes it to move transversely within the mandibular fossa. Keeping the subject's head in the same position, pressure applied behind the lobe of the ear to the back of the condyle, and directed forwards, produces forward movement of the condyle.

Surface marking and palpation

The line of the temporomandibular joint can be clearly and easily identified by placing the tip of the finger immediately in front of the tragus of the ear. As the subject opens his or her mouth the mandibular condyle moves forwards, and a large depression can then be felt; this is the cavity of the joint.

Fig. 6.18 Movements of the mandible: **a** = the closed position of the mouth, i.e. retracted and elevated; **b** = protraction; **c** = depression.

Bones

THE VERTEBRAL COLUMN

The vertebral column, extending from the base of the skull to the pelvis, is composed of a series of irregularly-shaped bones which increase in size from above downwards. The individual vertebrae are bound together by ligaments and have intervertebral discs between their bodies. In young children, 33 separate vertebrae can be identified, however, by the time adulthood is reached five have fused to form the sacrum and four to form the coccyx. Of the remaining 24, seven are found in the neck (cervical vertebrae), twelve articulate with the ribs (thoracic vertebrae) and five are found in the lower back (lumbar vertebrae). Within each group the vertebrae have similar features, some of which are distinctive, regarding shape and the orientation of their articular processes.

With the exception of the first and second cervical vertebrae, all vertebrae possess a large weight-bearing body anteriorly and vertebral arch posteriorly, which consists of a series of bony processes (Fig. 6.19a). The body varies in shape and size depending on its location in the vertebral column, but is roughly cylindrical with flattened upper and lower surfaces. On these surfaces, the markings of the attachment of the intervertebral disc around the periphery can be seen surrounding a roughened central area. The front and sides of the bodies are roughened, particularly at their upper and lower edges, and concave from top-to-bottom. The posterior surface is fairly smooth and has a large foramen for the passage of the basivertebral vein. The vertebral arch arises from the posterolateral aspect of the body, and with the body surrounds the vertebral foramen. *In situ* adjacent vertebral foramina, together with the intervertebral discs and the ligamenta flava form the vertebral canal which houses the spinal cord and its various coverings.

The vertebral arch consists of two *pedicles* and two *laminae*. Each pedicle passes from the upper part of the posterolateral aspect of the vertebral body to join with the anterolateral extremity of the corresponding lamina. The laminae slope backwards to meet in the midline posteriorly, where they are continuous with the posterior projecting spinous process. Because the pedicles are not as deep as the vertebral bodies, the opening formed between adjacent pedicles (the intervertebral foramen) enables the spinal nerves and supporting blood vessels to enter or leave the vertebral canal. The intervertebral foramen is closed anteroinferiorly by the intervertebral disc, an important relation to note in some pathologies of the vertebral column and spinal nerves.

Arising from the junction of each pedicle and lamina are three processes: the transverse process projecting laterally, and the articular processes, one directed upwards and one directed downwards. In adjacent vertebrae, superior and inferior articular processes make contact with each other by small synovial joints—the *zygapophyseal joints*. It is the shape and orientation of the articular facets on these processes which largely determines the range and type of movement possible between adjacent vertebrae.

With a few exceptions, each part of a vertebra is potentially presented in every other vertebra; the main features of which are shown in Fig. 6.19a. The body is the only part of a vertebra that is represented throughout the whole series of vertebrae, even so, that of the atlas has been displaced as the dens of the axis. The major differences between cervical, thoracic, lumbar and sacral vertebrae is related to the size of their costal elements (Fig. 6.19b). In the cervical region, the medial end of the costal element fuses with the side of the vertebral body. The presence of the vertebral vessels lying anterior to the true transverse process prevents complete fusion of the costal element with the transverse process. Instead, a costotransverse lamella (bar) joins the two parts together laterally, leading to the formation of the *foramen transversarium*. Consequently, the anterior tubercle of the transverse process is the lateral end of the costal element, while the posterior tubercle represents the lateral end of the transverse process. The first and second cervical vertebrae have no anterior tubercles.

In the thoracic region, the costal element remains separate giving rise to the rib, which articulates directly with the body and transverse process of its corresponding vertebra.

In the lumbar region, the costal element has again been incorporated into the ver-

tebra. So complete is its incorporation that apart from the root of the transverse process (lateral process) the remainder is composed of costal element. The true transverse process in the lumbar region gives rise to the accessory and superior processes as well as the lateral.

Even in the sacrum, the costal elements have been incorporated and form the major part of the lateral masses.

a

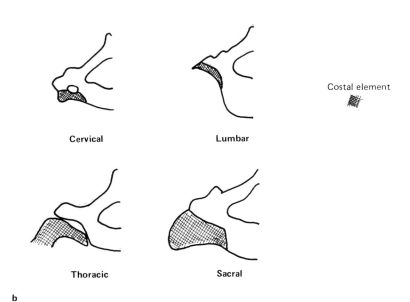

b

Fig. 6.19 **a** = Schematic representation of a vertebra; **b** = fate of the costal element in each of the vertebral.

Cervical vertebrae
(Fig. 6.20a)

The characteristic feature of all cervical vertebrae is the presence of a foramen transversarium in each transverse process. They tend to be small as they do not carry much weight. The third, fourth, fifth and sixth cervical vertebrae are sufficiently similar to be considered together. The *body* is relatively small, appearing kidney-shaped when viewed from above. Its superior surface projects upwards at the sides, while its inferior surface is correspondingly bevelled. Between the sides of adjacent surfaces of the bodies, each side of the intervertebral disc, are small synovial joints (uncovertebral joints, see p. 738). The anterior surface is marked by the attachment of the anterior longitudinal ligament, while laterally the body is hollowed. The posterior surface of the body is flat.

The short *pedicles* pass laterally and backwards, which is why the vertebral canal in the cervical region is triangular and larger than elsewhere. The long and narrow *laminae* pass posteromedially joining together to form the spinous process. The short, bifid *spine* projects backwards from the centre of the vertebral arch.

The composite *transverse processes* are stout projections arising from the lateral side of the body and pedicle. Each transverse process ends in prominent *anterior* and *posterior tubercles*, joined by the costotransverse lamella. Within each process is a *foramen transversarium*, bound posteriorly by the pedicle, and anteriorly and laterally by the various parts of the transverse process. It transmits the vertebral artery and vein.

The large *superior* and *inferior* articular processes project from the articular mass, which is located at the union of the pedicle and lamina on each side.

Each process bears an articulated facet. The slightly convex superior facet faces upwards and backwards while the reciprocally concave inferior facet faces downwards and forwards. The facets become more vertical in the lower part of the cervical spine.

The atlas (C1) (Fig. 6.20b)

This ring of bone bears very little resemblance to a cervical, or for that matter any other vertebra. It has no body or spine, but consists of slender anterior and posterior arches joined on each side by a lateral mass, which bears articular facets superiorly and inferiorly and a transverse process laterally. The concave superior facets articulate with the condylar processes of the occipital bone, while the concave inferior facets articulate with the second cervical vertebra. The inferior articular facets are segments of a sphere thereby facilitating rotation, which occurs between the atlas and axis. Each lateral mass is marked on its medial side by a small tubercle to which the transverse ligament of the atlas attaches.

Passing between the lateral masses anteriorly is the short flattened anterior arch, which has in the middle of its anterior surface the anterior tubercle and posteriorly a facet for articulation with the dens of the axis. The posterior arch, which represents the pedicles and laminae of typical vertebrae is a long, curved bar of bone joining the lateral masses and the roots of the transverse processes. Posteriorly, the posterior tubercle represents the spinous process. On the superior surface of the posterior arch, running medially from the back of each lateral mass is a shallow groove for the vertebral artery before it enters the foramen magnum. This groove may be converted into a foramen by cartilaginous or bony tissue.

The strong transverse processes are large and wide. They may also be bifid, even though they represent only the posterior tubercle of a typical cervical vertebra. The foramen transversarium, lying close to the lateral mass, transmits the vertebral vessels as well as sympathetic nerves.

a

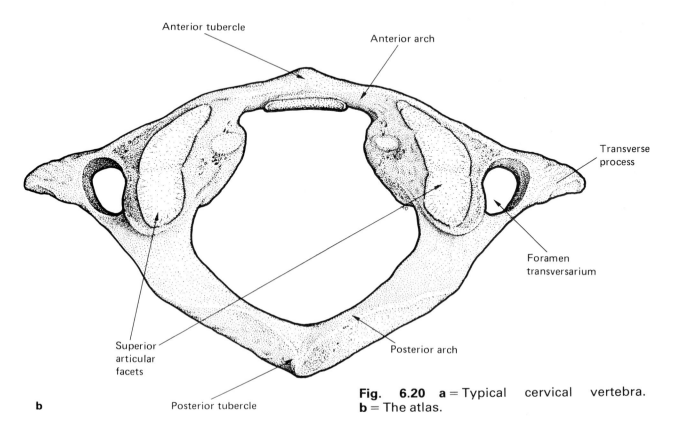

b

Fig. 6.20 a = Typical cervical vertebra. **b** = The atlas.

The axis (C2) (Fig. 6.21a)

The axis, the second and strongest of the cervical vertebrae, bears many of the features of a typical cervical vertebra. It has, however, the separated body of the atlas fused with the superior surface of its body giving an upward tooth-like projection known as the *odontoid process* (dens). The dens is slightly pointed at its apex, where the apical ligament attaches it to the anterior margin of the foramen magnum. From the sloping sides of the apex, alar ligaments pass to tubercles on the medial sides of the occipital condyles. Its anterior surface has a small smooth facet, concave from above down and convex transversely for articulation with the facet on the back of the anterior arch of the atlas. Posteriorly is a smooth, constricted horizontal surface where the transverse ligament crosses. Above this constriction there is a slightly expanded area known as the head.

The large superior articular facets lie at the junction of the body and pedicle, and transmit the weight of the head to the body of the axis, leaving the dens free to rotate with respect to the atlas. The articular facets are slightly convex resembling a segment of a dome, and face upwards and laterally. They allow the gliding forwards of one lateral mass whilst the other glides backwards when the atlas rotates on the axis. The slightly concave inferior facets face downwards and forwards and are situated just behind the transverse processes at the junction of the pedicles and the laminae on either side.

The transverse processes are small and rounded, projecting laterally from the sides of the vertebral body. As there are no anterior tubercles, the front of the foramen transversarium is closed by the costotransverse lamella.

The thick and strong laminae pass backwards and medially joining together to form the strong stout spine which is usually bifid. The spine projects almost 1 cm further posteriorly than the posterior tubercle of C1 and covers the much thinner spine of C3.

The inferior surface of the axis is very similar to that of a typical cervical vertebra (see Fig. 6.20a).

The seventh cervical vertebra (vertebra prominens) (Fig. 6.21b)

As its name implies, this vertebra is noted for the length of its spinous process, which is not bifid. It is larger than the preceding cervical vertebra and exhibits similarities to the thoracic vertebrae. The body is larger, the pedicles are directed more posteriorly than laterally, the inferior articular facets face more anteriorly than downwards, and the vertebral canal is generally smaller than that of other cervical vertebrae.

The transverse processes have a small foramen transversarium, which only transmits the vertebral vein. Occasionally the anterior costal element of the transverse process is much longer than the posterior part, giving all the appearances of a rudimentary rib as it extends forwards towards the first rib as either a fibrous or bony strip. This may lead to pressure on the eighth cervical nerve root as it passes forwards over the first rib to take part in the brachial plexus.

Fig. 6.21 **a** = The axis. **b** = The eleventh cervical vertebra.

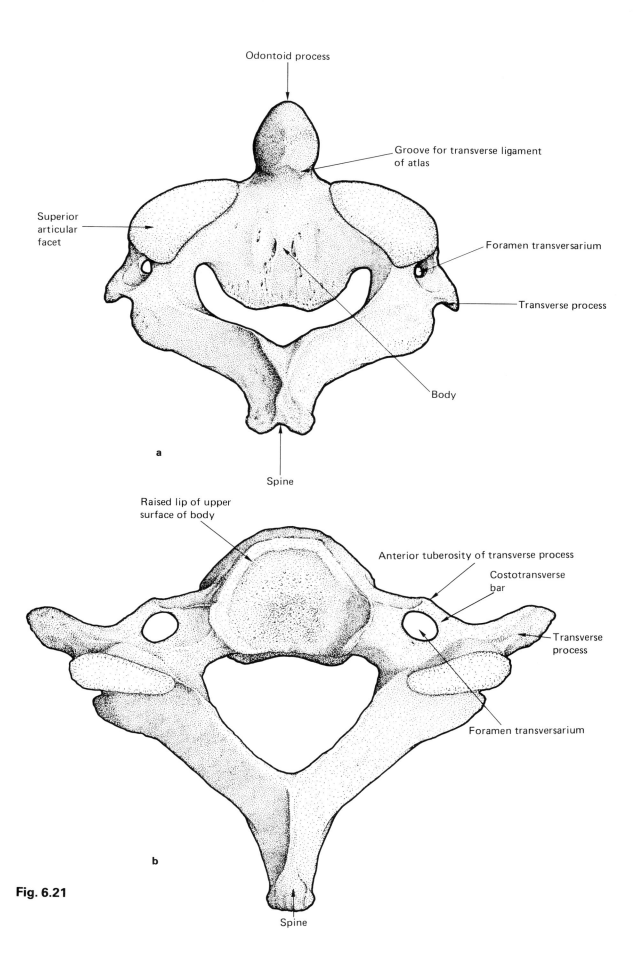

Odontoid process

Groove for transverse ligament
of atlas

Superior
articular
facet

Foramen transversarium

Transverse process

Body

a

Spine

Raised lip of upper
surface of body

Anterior tuberosity of transverse process

Costotransverse
bar

Transverse
process

Foramen transversarium

b

Fig. 6.21

Spine

Thoracic vertebrae (Fig. 6.22)

The distinctive feature of thoracic vertebrae is the presence of articular facets on the sides of the vertebral body for articulation with the heads of at least one pair of ribs. The bodies of thoracic vertebrae are typically heart-shaped, when viewed from above, and on their sides bear articular facets. The bodies of the second to eighth vertebrae have large, almost completely oval facets near their upper borders, and smaller demifacets near their lower borders. Although similar in basic arrangement, the upper facet of the ninth thoracic vertebra is situated at the base of the pedicle. The body of T1 has a complete oval facet near its upper edge and a demifacet at its lower. The tenth, eleventh and twelfth vertebrae have single complete facets located at the junction of the body with the pedicle. Between T10 and T12 the facets gradually move from the upper to lower region of the junction (Fig. 6.22b).

The short pedicles project almost directly backwards from the upper part of the body. They gradually become larger and stronger from above downwards. The laminae are inclined towards the midline, and although narrow from side-to-side they are deep so that they overlap one another from above.

The spinous processes are long and slope downwards, with those in the middle of the series being almost vertical. The upper and lower ones are shorter and generally less sloping. The twelfth is almost horizontal resembling a typical lumbar spine.

The long, thick, rounded transverse processes project laterally, backwards and slightly upwards from the junction of the pedicle with the lamina. They have an oval facet on the anterior surface near the tip which faces anterolaterally, for the tubercle of the corresponding rib. In the upper thoracic vertebrae these facets are concave but gradually become flatter from above downwards. The transverse processes of the eleventh and twelfth thoracic vertebrae have no facets. The transverse process of the twelfth thoracic vertebra is very short and shows features similar to the lumbar vertebrae.

From just medial to the base of the transverse process, the articular processes project almost vertically; the superior upwards and the inferior downwards. The articular facets on the superior process are slightly concave transversely, being flat from above down, and face backwards but also slightly upwards and laterally. The facets on the shorter inferior articular processes are reciprocally curved and face in the opposite direction. The superior articular facets of one vertebra articulate with the inferior facets of the vertebra above. The joints so formed lie on the arc of a circle whose centre lies within the body of the vertebra. Consequently, rotation as well as flexion and extension are favoured in the thoracic region (see p. 766).

The inferior articular processes of T12, although they project vertically, do not lie in the same general plane as the other thoracic articular processes. They are in fact lumbar in type, therefore the articular facets are markedly convex transversely and face anterolaterally.

The vertebral foramen is smaller than that in either the cervical or the lumbar region, and is nearly circular in appearance.

Fig. 6.22   **a** = Typical thoracic vertebra, superior view; **b** = the first, ninth, tenth, eleventh and twelfth thoracic vertebrae, lateral view.

Body

Superior
costal facet

Vertebral
canal

Pedicle

Transverse
process

Superior
articular facet

Lamina

Spine

a

Facet on
transverse
process

First

Ninth

Complete
facet on
side of
body

Tenth

Eleventh

Twelfth

b

Fig. 6.22

Lumbar vertebrae (Fig. 6.23)

The five lumbar vertebrae are much stouter and stronger than those in either the thoracic or cervical regions. They possess neither foramina transversaria or articular facets for the ribs. Each has a large, kidney-shaped body with almost parallel upper and lower surfaces, except for L5 which is deeper in front than behind. The pedicles, which pass almost directly backwards, are short and strong, joining the narrow laminae which pass backwards and medially towards the spine. Adjacent laminae are widely separated from each other, leaving diamond-shaped spaces which contain the ligamenta flava.

The spines of the lumbar vertebrae project almost horizontally backwards, being level with the lower half of the body. They are wider from above downwards with a thickened posterior edge. That of L5 is frequently rounded.

The articular processes project upwards and downwards from the region where the pedicle joins the lamina. The articular facets on the superior process are concave transversely and flat vertically, facing posteromedially. On the posterior edge of the superior articular process is the rounded mamillary process. The inferior articular processes are set closer together than the superior and have facets which are reciprocally curved to face anterolaterally. The superior facets articulate with the inferior facets of the vertebra immediately above. The inferior articular processes of the fifth lumbar vertebra are more widely set apart and flatter than those of other lumbar vertebrae. Their articular facets face anterolaterally to meet the superior articular facets of the sacrum.

The triangular vertebral canal is larger than that in the thoracic region, but slightly smaller than in the cervical region.

With the exception of the fifth lumbar vertebra the transverse processes are short and thin, projecting laterally and slightly backwards from the sides of the vertebral body and base of the pedicles. The third is the longest, while the fourth and fifth are inclined upwards. The transverse processes of L5 are short and stout, and may be fused with the lateral part of the sacrum. From the root of each transverse process, a small tubercle (the *accessory process*) projects posteriorly. The root of the transverse process in known as the *lateral tubercle*.

The sacrum and coccyx

A description of the sacral and coccygeal vertebrae can be found on p. 314, and their ossification on p. 316.

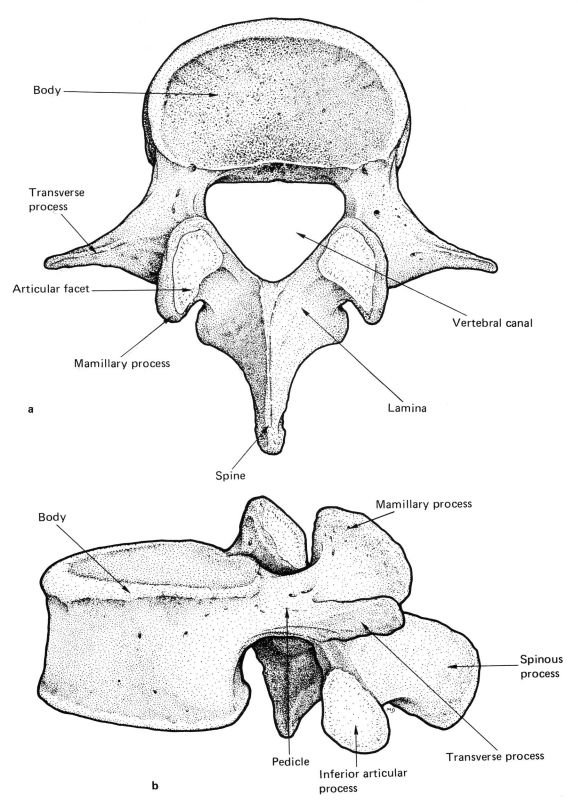

Body

Transverse
process

Articular facet

Mamillary process

Vertebral canal

Lamina

a

Spine

Body

Mamillary process

Spinous
process

Pedicle

Transverse process

Inferior articular
process

b

Fig. 6.23 A lumbar vertebra: **a** = superior
view; **b** = lateral view.

Palpation of the vertebral column

Unfortunately there is considerable variation in the location of bony points from one individual to another and even from side-to-side within the same individual. This is particularly apparent in the region of the trunk, where the length of the spines can vary considerably, be angled differently or occasionally even be absent. The best way of identifying vertebral spines is therefore to count downwards or upwards from known bony landmarks and cross check with other surface markings. Considerable time and practice is involved in developing palpation techniques, but once mastered it will prove to be an invaluable asset in the future.

The most obvious surface markings are the posteriorly directed spines. However, their palpation can vary considerably, due to the lordosis (convexity forwards) in the cervical and lumbar regions and the kyphosis (concavity forwards) in the thoracic and sacral regions of the vertebral column.

Cervical region

This is most easily examined with the subject prone and the forehead supported on the hands with the chin slightly tucked in. Even so, the central area (C3–5) may be quite difficult to distinguish. There are, however, two unmistakable landmarks, these being the spines of the second and seventh cervical vertebrae.

First find the external occipital protuberance on the occipital bone; this should be almost directly below the most prominent part of the back of the skull. Approximately 2 cm below this, the large prominence of the spine of C2 will be encountered. There is a deep hollow between the two landmarks because C1 has no spinous process, just a relatively small tubercle. Moving down the neck some 10 cm, the long spinous process of C7, also known as the vertebra prominens, is the next large prominence to be encountered. Usually two prominences can be felt in this region as the spinous process of T1 is just below that of C7. Occasionally, a third prominence, the spinous process of C6 can also be felt. If there is any doubt as to the differential identification of C7, the subject should be asked to raise the forehead from the hands, in which case the spines of C7 and T1 remain under the fingers, whilst that of C6 moves forwards and may not be palpable. If the cervical spine is flexed, the spinous processes may be a little easier to identify, but this depends, to a large extent, on the tautness of the ligamentum nuchae.

Deep palpation lateral to the muscle mass, on either side of the spinous processes, reveals another line of bony projections running up the side of the vertebrae. These are the tips of the transverse processes. They appear blunted because the fingers are feeling both anterior and posterior tubercles at the same time (see Fig. 6.20a). Near the top of the neck a series of cord-like structures can be felt running downwards and laterally from the tubercles, these are the *scalene muscles*. The large transverse process of C1 can easily be felt below the mastoid process of the skull. At the lower end of the cervical region, the tubercles become more pronounced with the seventh nearly always projecting further laterally than the rest. It may also be quite tender to the touch. In some subjects the costal element of C7 may be longer than normal and also slightly mobile giving the appearance of a rudimentary rib consequently it is termed a 'cervical rib'. Occasionally, this may lead to pressure on the eighth cervical nerve root leading to neurological signs and symptoms in the area of its distribution.

Thoracic region

In the thoracic region the spinous processes are much easier to identify, particularly if the subject is sitting with the trunk flexed. The spines of the seventh cervical and the first thoracic vertebrae are even more prominent than when lying prone. It is now easy to identify the spines of individual thoracic vertebrae. Identification is made easier, however, if one finger is placed on the spine above to mark it whilst that below is determined. Each spinous process appears to be quite pointed as far as T11. That of the twelfth thoracic vertebra, on the other hand, is flattened and similar to that of a lumbar vertebra.

With the subject lying prone, a line of smaller tubercles can be felt approximately 2 cm either side of the spines. These are the posterior aspects of the transverse processes, and as they are usually covered by the long back muscles they are less easy to palpate. The transverse processes pass slightly upwards and laterally, being in line with the upper part of the body of the corresponding vertebra. The spinous processes, however, pass downwards and backwards approximately 3 cm below the transverse process of the same vertebra. This is important to remember when palpation is being used for diagnostic purposes.

Just beyond the transverse process each rib can be felt passing downwards and laterally around the chest wall.

Lumbar region

The lumbar region of the vertebral colum has a lordosis similar to that of the cervical region. Consequently, it is not easy to ident-ify the spinous processes. With the subject lying prone, and with sufficient support under the abdomen to raise the lumbar region so that it is level, the whole lumbar region can be examined. The spinous processes of the lumbar vertebrae can be palpated in a central cleft down the midline. About 3 cm each side of the midline a small dimple can be seen on the posterior superior aspect of the buttock. This marks the location of the posterior superior iliac spine, which can be easily palpated and acts as an important landmark for the identification of other structures. From these spines the crests of the ilium can be traced upwards and forwards. The spinous process of L5 can be felt in a deep hollow, just above the sacrum, approximately 2 cm above a line drawn between the posterior superior iliac spines. From here the spinous process of L4 is easily recognizable above that of L5. With care, the small gaps between the spinous processes of L4 to T12 can be palpated, and each process identified. The centre of the spinous processes of each vertebra, unlike that in the thoracic region, lies at a level just below the centre of the body of its corresponding vertebra. On either side of the midline is a powerful column of muscle tissue running from the posterior part of the sacrum up towards the thoracic region.

On deep palpation, lateral to this bulk of muscle, small pointed tubercles can be felt, running down either side. These are the tips of the transverse processes each one being located just above the level of the centre of its corresponding spinous process. Higher up, level with the spinous process of L1, the tip of the twelfth rib can be palpated, being level with the ninth costal cartilage in front and lying in the transpyloric plane.

Ossification

A typical vertebra ossifies in cartilage from the three primary centres and five secondary centres.

The primary centres appear in the vertebral body and in each half of the vertebral arch. That for the centrum, the larger median part of the body, appears between the second and fifth month *in utero*, being present first in the lower thoracic region and then spreading sequentially up and down the column. The centres for the coccygeal vertebrae appear between birth and puberty, with ossification spreading without the formation of secondary centres. Because each centrum is usually ossified from two centres, anomalies may arise in that they may fail to unite and remain as two separate halves, or only one may ossify giving rise to a hemivertebra.

The primary centre in each half of the vertebral arch appears at the junction of the pedicle and lamina at two months *in utero* in the upper cervical region, spreading down to the sacrum by the fifth month. From each centre, ossification spreads into the lamina and pedicle where it extends into the centrum to complete the body, and into the root of the transverse process.

At birth, the centrum and each part of the vertebral arch are separated by cartilage.

That between the centrum and each arch begins to ossify in the cervical region during the third year, extending to other regions by the seventh year. The laminae begin to unite soon after birth in the lumbar region, spreading to the cervical region by the second year. This process is not complete in the sacrum until the seventh to tenth year. Once the laminae have fused, ossification spreads into the root of the spinous process.

The multiple secondary centres for the upper and lower surfaces of the bodies appear during the ninth year. They fuse to form flat rings of bone around the periphery of these surfaces. Secondary centres appear in the tips of the transverse processes during the eighteenth year. Fusion of all of these secondary epiphyses with the rest of the vertebra begins at 18, for the bodies, and should be complete by the age of 25.

The lumbar vertebrae also have secondary centres for the mamillary processes. In addition, the first lumbar vertebra may have separate primary centres for its transverse processes, which may remain separate to form a lumbar rib. In the fifth lumbar vertebra there may be two primary centres in each half of the vertebral arch, united by cartilage between the superior and inferior articular processes. Consequently, there is a temporary risk of separation between the two parts.

The upper two cervical vertebrae cannot be considered typical in their pattern of ossification and therefore are dealt with separately. In the atlas a primary centre appears during the second month *in utero* for each half of the vertebral arch and the associated lateral mass, the two halves usually unite during the third or fourth year. Occasionally, a secondary centre may appear in the intervening cartilage. At birth the anterior arch is cartilaginous, but an ossification centre appears by the end of the second year to fuse with the lateral masses, and includes the anterior part of the superior articular surface, during the seventh year. An epiphysis for each transverse process appears and unites with the rest of the bone during puberty.

In the axis, primary centres for each vertebral arch appear during the second month *in utero*, one for the lower part of the body and two more side-by-side for the dens and upper part of the body during the fifth month. Those for the dens fuse together 2 months later so that at birth the axis consists of four parts which unite between the third and sixth year. Secondary centres appear in the tip of the dens between 2 and 6 years to fuse with the dens by the age of 12, and for the lower surface of the body which fuses during puberty between 18 and 25. Occasional additional ossification centres may be present.

Bifid cervical spinous processes each have a secondary ossification centre, in addition to which the sixth and seventh cervical vertebrae may have separate primary ossification centres for their costal elements. If present, these usually fuse with the rest of the bone during the fifth year. However, there may be a tendency for that of the seventh to remain separate as a cervical rib.

With so many ossification processes and patterns occurring simultaneously it is not surprising, therefore, to find some variations in the total number of vertebrae present. This is usually due to a reduction, or rarely, an increase in the number of coccygeal vertebrae.

The number of cervical vertebrae is constant in number at seven. However, the number of thoracic vertebrae may be increased by the presence of ribs associated with L1. Similarly the number of lumbar vertebrae may be reduced as above, or by incorporation of L5 into the sacrum. Such sacralization may be partial or complete. The sacrum may gain or lose additional segments.

Many congenital conditions of the vertebral column are due to incomplete fusion of its constituent parts. Hemivertebrae can cause an abnormal lateral curvature (scoliosis) of the vertebral column. The laminae may fail to fuse or meet in any region, but most commonly in the lumbosacral region, giving rise to spina bifida. The spine, laminae and inferior articular processes of L4 and L5 may be joined to the rest of the vertebrae by cartilage and not completely fused. Under certain loading conditions this can lead to a separation whereby the vertebral body, most commonly that of L5, slides forwards. This condition is known as *spondylolisthesis*.

THE THORACIC CAGE
(Fig. 6.24)

The thoracic cage is a bony and muscular structure which surrounds, protects and supports the heart and lungs amongst other structures. It is egg-shaped with the narrower end superior towards the neck and the wider end inferior. However, the upper and lower parts of the thoracic cage are cut off obliquely so that the superior opening slopes downwards and forwards at approximately 45°, while the inferior opening slopes downwards and backwards. The openings so formed are known as the thoracic inlet and outlet respectively.

The thoracic inlet is bounded by the anterior surface of the body of the first thoracic vertebra posteriorly, the medial border of the first rib and its costal cartilage on either side, and the superior surface of the manubrium sterni anteriorly. Through this opening pass the oesophagus and trachea, as well as the vessels and nerves which enter or leave the thorax. In the lateral part of the inlet, the apex of the lung is found and is supported and covered by the suprapleural membrane. The thoracic outlet is much larger and is bound by the anterior surface of the body of the twelfth thoracic vertebra posteriorly, the twelfth and the anterior half of the eleventh rib on either side, together with the sixth to tenth costal cartilages and the xiphisternal junction anteriorly. The diaphragm covers most of the outlet, but has in it openings for the passage of the aorta, oesophagus and inferior vena cava. Other, smaller structures also pierce the diaphragm to pass between the thorax and abdomen.

The bony components of the thoracic cage are the 12 thoracic vertebrae posteriorly, 12 pairs of ribs laterally and the sternum anteriorly. In general, the ribs pass from behind forwards connecting the thoracic part of the vertebral column to the sternum. The ribs are so arranged that as they pass forwards they also slope downwards. Consequently, the anterior end of the rib is at a lower level than the posterior part. The space between adjacent ribs, the *intercostal space*, is filled by muscles, among which are found the intercostal vessels and nerves. The sixth intercostal space is probably the longest, with those above and below gradually decreasing in length. The upper spaces are wider than the lower ones, which tend also to be narrower posteriorly. The articulation of these bony parts is such that the thorax is flattened anteroposteriorly so that its transverse diameter is larger than its anteroposterior diameter. In children the anteroposterior and transverse diameters are more or less equal because the ribs run more horizontally around the thorax.

Fig. 6.24   a = Thoracic cage, anterior view; **b** = thorax, showing thoracic inlet and outlet.

The ribs

The ribs are long, flat bones which ossify from a cartilage model, part of which persists anteriorly as the costal cartilage of the rib. The costal cartilage of the first rib is very short and often ossified, particularly late in life, whereas the remainder gradually increase in length from above downwards, with the tenth costal cartilage being the longest. The costal cartilages of the upper seven ribs articulate directly with the sternum, while the eighth, ninth and tenth do so via the costal cartilage above. The eleventh and twelfth ribs merely have cartilage caps at their anterior ends, and end within the abdominal wall musculature. They are often referred to as floating ribs. Each rib has a head, neck, angle and shaft. Some ribs exhibit certain features which distinguish them from the rest. These are the first, tenth, eleventh and twelfth ribs. The remainder are known as typical ribs.

A typical rib (Fig. 6.25)

The rib has an enlarged head at its posterior end, which presents two flattened articular facets with a ridge between them, which articulate with the upper border of the body of its own vertebra and the lower border of the body of the vertebra above.

The head is joined to the shaft by a short flattened neck, which has upper and lower borders, and anterior and posterior surfaces. The neck continues laterally as the shaft, being marked on its posterior aspect at the junction by the tubercle of the rib, which has a small oval articular facet on its medial part and is roughened laterally. The shaft is flattened having smooth medial and lateral surfaces, a rounded upper and a sharp lower border. The lower border forms the outer margin of the subcostal groove, the inner margin being higher on the medial surface of the rib about one-third of the way up. Some 3 cm or so lateral to the tubercle, the shaft turns downwards and inwards giving it a twisted appearance. This is the angle of the rib. Only the second rib does not show this twisting of the shaft, in addition to which its outer surface faces upwards and outwards. The anterior end of the rib widens and ends as a roughened hollow where it becomes continuous with its costal cartilage.

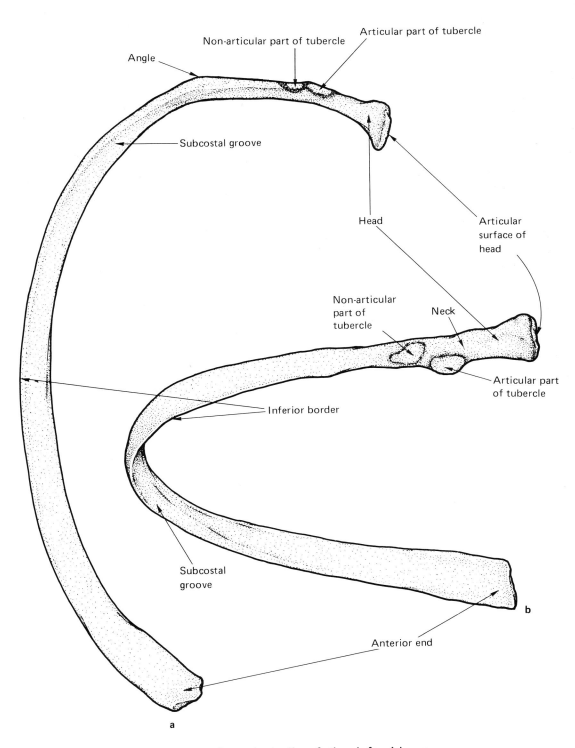

Angle

Non-articular part of tubercle

Articular part of tubercle

Subcostal groove

Head

Articular surface of head

Non-articular part of tubercle

Neck

Articular part of tubercle

Inferior border

Subcostal groove

Anterior end

a

b

Fig. 6.25 A typical rib of the left side: **a** = viewed inferiorly; **b** = viewed posteriorly.

The first rib (Fig. 6.26a)

This is short and sharply curved, giving it a C-shape. Its head has only one facet for articulation with the body of the first thoracic vertebra. Joining the head to the shaft is a relatively long, narrow neck. The tubercle of the rib is large and situated on the outer border, and from here the rib slopes downwards and forwards. The shaft has superior and inferior surfaces, and medial and thickened lateral borders. It is not angled and remains broad throughout its length. Its lower surface has a shallow subcostal groove running longitudinally while the upper surface has two shallow transverse grooves either side of the scalene tubercle which projects from the inner border. The anterior groove transmits the subclavian vein and the posterior the subclavian artery and the first thoracic nerve, the two vessels being separated by scalenus anterior attaching to the scalene tubercle. Anteriorly, it articulates with the manubrium sterni by its costal cartilage.

The tenth rib

This shows many of the features of a typical rib, being long with a definite angle. It has, however, only one facet on the head for articulation with the body of the tenth vertebra.

The eleventh rib (Fig. 6.26b)

This is about half the length of the tenth rib, and also possesses only one facet on its head for articulation with its corresponding vertebral body. It does not, however, have an articular facet on its tubercle for articulation with the transverse process.

The twelfth rib (Fig. 6.26c)

This is very short and 'dagger-like' in appearance. Its head has one complete articular facet for articulation with the body of the twelfth thoracic vertebra, but there is no tubercle or articular surface for articulation with the transverse process, angle or subcostal groove. Its anterior end is tapered in contrast to the widening of the other ribs.

Costal cartilages

The hyaline costal cartilages are continuous with their respective ribs and connect them either directly (one to seven) or indirectly (eight to ten) to the sternum. The perichondrium of the cartilage is continuous with the periosteum of the rib. It is thus possible to rupture the cartilage within the perichondrium without obvious displacement of the cartilage.

Ossification

A primary ossification centre appears near the angle of the rib at six weeks *in utero*. All secondary centres appear at puberty, fusing with the remainder of the bone by the age of 25. In the second to sixth ribs, secondary centres appear in the head and in each part of the tubercle, while the eleventh and twelfth ribs only have a secondary centre in the head.

Fig. 6.26 a = The first rib, left side, superior surface; **b** = the eleventh rib, left side, superior surface; **c** = the twelfth rib, left side, medial surface.

The sternum (Fig. 6.27)

The sternum is an elongated, flat bone situated in the midline of the anterior chest wall. It extends from the root of the neck to the abdominal wall and is composed of three parts: the manubrium superiorly, the large body and the small irregular xiphoid process inferiorly. All three parts have anterior and posterior surfaces, and lateral, superior and inferior borders. Adjacent parts articulate by secondary cartilaginous joints.

The *manubrium* is the widest part of the sternum, being roughened on its anterior surface and smooth posteriorly. On its superior border is the jugular (suprasternal) notch, with the smaller clavicular notches either side for articulation with the clavicles. Below the clavicular notch on the lateral border is a roughened area for articulation with the first rib costal cartilage, and lower down a half facet for the second rib costal cartilage. The oval inferior surface is roughened for the attachment of the fibrocartilaginous disc of the manubriosternal joint.

The *body* is composed of four fused segments, again it is roughened on its anterior surface and smooth posteriorly. It does not lie directly in line with the manubrium, but forms an obtuse angle of 160° which can easily be palpated, and so forms a useful landmark even in obese individuals. The superior surface receives the fibrocartilaginous disc, while the lateral borders show articular facets for the costal cartilages of the second to seventh rib. The second and seventh facets are demifacets, while those in between are full facets. Inferiorly the body is continuous with the irregularly-shaped *xiphoid process* at the secondary cartilaginous xiphisternal joint. The xiphoid process may be perforated or bifid, nevertheless it is thinner than the body of the sternum, being flush with its posterior surface.

The jugular notch is level with the lower border of the body of the second thoracic vertebra, the sternal angle with the lower border of the body of the fourth, and the xiphisternal junction with the ninth thoracic vertebra.

Ossification

Primary ossification centres appear in the manubrium during the fifth month *in utero*, and then in the four sternebrae in the sixth, seventh, eighth and ninth months from above downwards. They fuse in sequence from below upwards in childhood, at puberty and at age 21. The manubrium usually does not fuse with the body until old age. Ossification of the xiphoid process can begin any time after the age of 3, however it does not fuse with the body until middle age.

Palpation

With the subject seated, a deep hollow can be seen at the base of neck. The inferior margin of this hollow is the jugular (suprasternal) notch, either side of which the medial end of the clavicle can be palpated. Following the clavicle laterally, both its anterior and superior convex surfaces can be easily distinguished. Further laterally the now concave anterior border can be traced to the end of the bone. Beyond this the anterior, lateral and posterior borders and the superior surface of the acromion process can be palpated (see p. 56).

Two fingers' breadth below the suprasternal notch can be felt a ridge of bone beyond which the sternum changes direction. This is the sternal angle at the level of the manubriosternal joint. Either side can be palpated the costal cartilage of the second rib. The space below the second rib and its costal cartilage is the second intercostal space.

At the lower end of the sternum, the pointed xiphoid process can be identified with the costal cartilages of the seventh to tenth ribs running laterally away from it. At the junction of the ninth costal cartilage, there is a marked angle on the anterior rim of the rib cage. This angle is level with the tip of the twelfth rib and the spinous process of the first lumbar vertebra posteriorly, and the pylorus of the stomach internally. A transverse plane at this level is thus referred to as the transpyloric plane. The lateral bor-

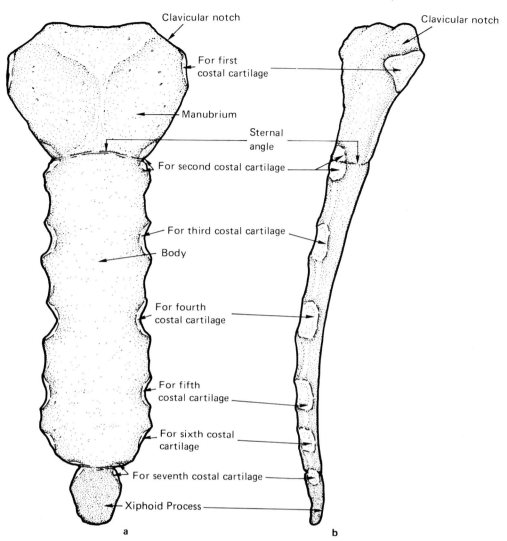

Fig. 6.27   The sternum: **a** = anterior aspect; **b** = lateral aspect.

der of the rectus abdominis also crosses the costal margin at this level. At this junction on the right hand side, the fundus of the gall bladder may be palpated.

The upper two ribs are difficult to palpate. The first is almost completely covered by the clavicle anteriorly, and by thick muscle posteriorly. However, on deep pressure applied to the anteromedial part of the supraclavicular fossa, the superior surface of the first rib can be identified. It should be remembered that this manoeuvre may be painful to the subject because pressure is put on the structures running over the rib at this point.

The second rib is easily identifiable at the sternal angle, but soon becomes lost in thick muscle as it passes posteriorly. The third to eighth ribs are easily identified throughout most of their length, except that they are covered to a variable extent by the scapula. Posterolaterally, the angles of the ribs are quite clear, particularly if the scapula is drawn forwards in protrusion, lateral to the paravertebral gutter. The anterior half of the eleventh rib is quite clear, running anteriorly to the mid-axillary line, whilst the tip of the twelfth rib can be palpated just beyond the bulk of the long back muscles lying on the transpyloric plane.

Muscles

MUSCLES OF THE NECK

The region of the neck is one of the most complex areas within the body. Several named regions can be identified with respect to areas bound by specific muscles. Some of these regions contain important structures, e.g. the carotid arteries. However, the regions so described often have no functional basis.

Many of the muscles in the neck are extremely small and impossible to palpate. Nevertheless their actions, either individually or in groups, are important in the alignment and correct carriage of the head and neck. Although many of the smaller muscles can be shown to have specific actions, their main role appears to be one of balancing the head on the vertebral column. The following muscles have been described in groups according to the prime movements they produce, without regard to their relative positions within the neck. The movements detailed below include both those of the neck, i.e. the cervical spine, and those of the head on the neck. Consequently, subgroupings of muscles are given depending on whether their action is exclusively on the neck, on the head and neck together, or exclusively on the head with respect to the neck.

MUSCLES WHICH FLEX THE NECK

Longus colli
Sternomastoid
Scalenus anterior (see pp. 684–686)

Longus colli (Fig. 6.28a)

Longus colli is a muscle in three parts which lies on the front and sides of the upper thoracic and cervical vertebral bodies. The lowest part runs obliquely upwards from the front of the bodies of the *first, second* and *third thoracic vertebrae* to the anterior tubercles of the transverse processes of the *fifth* and *sixth cervical vertebrae*. The middle part runs vertically from the front of the bodies of the *upper three thoracic* and *lower three cervical vertebrae* to attach to the front of the bodies of the *second, third* and *fourth cervical vertebrae*. The upper part of longus colli arises from the anterior tubercles of the transverse processes of the *third, fourth* and *fifth cervical vertebrae* to attach to the anterior tubercle of the *atlas* (Fig. 6.28a).

Nerve supply

Longus colli is supplied by the *anterior primary rami of C3, 4, 5* and *6*.

Action

The main action of the longus colli muscles, acting either singly or together is to flex the neck. It is possible that when working singly the lowermost part of longus colli could aid lateral flexion to the same side and rotation to the opposite side, but the central position of both origin and insertion make this questionable.

Sternomastoid (sternocleidomastoid)
(see Fig. 6.29a)

Sternomastoid is a long strap-like muscle, arising from two heads, which runs obliquely around the side of the neck close to the midline anteriorly. The *sternal head* is via a narrow, rounded tendon from the upper part of the *anterior surface* of the *manubrium sterni*, whereas the broad *clavicular head* is by a flattened muscular attachment from the upper surface of the *medial third* of the *clavicle*. The fibres from the two heads are initially separated by a small gap, with the clavicular head passing deep to the sternal head, but then unite to form a relatively thick muscle belly. Above, sternomastoid inserts by a short, strong, flat tendon into the lateral surface of the *mastoid process* of the *temporal bone*, and a thin aponeurosis which runs to the lateral third of the *superior nuchal line* of the *occipital bone*.

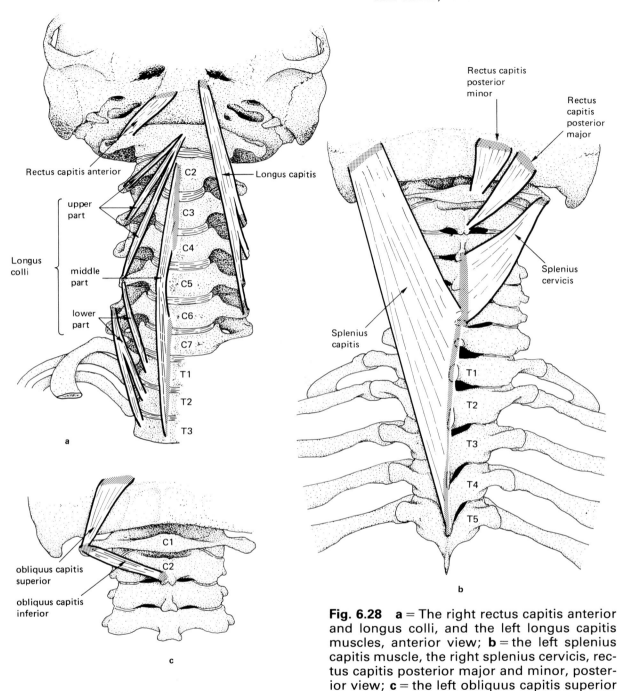

Fig. 6.28 **a** = The right rectus capitis anterior and longus colli, and the left longus capitis muscles, anterior view; **b** = the left splenius capitis muscle, the right splenius cervicis, rectus capitis posterior major and minor, posterior view; **c** = the left obliquus capitis superior and inferior muscles, posterior view.

Nerve supply

The motor supply of sternomastoid is by the spinal part of the *accessory* (eleventh cranial) *nerve*. It receives sensory fibres from the anterior rami of C2 and C3. The skin over the muscle is supplied by roots C2 and 3.

The spinal part of the accessory nerve enters the deep surface of the upper third of the muscle and leaves it about halfway down its lateral border. The sensory fibres may join with the accessory nerve.

Action

Contraction of sternomastoid tilts the head to the same side and produces lateral flexion of the neck. At the same time there is rotation of the head to the opposite side. The anterior fibres of the muscle are said to flex the head on the neck, while the posterior fibres (those to the superior nuchal line) may extend the head at the atlanto-occipital joint.

When both sternomastoid muscles contract they produce flexion of the neck by pulling the head forwards. If the head and neck are fixed then it is possible for these muscles to raise the clavicle and manubrium sterni, and hence the ribs, so that they act as accessory muscles of respiration.

Palpation

The sternomastoid can be easily palpated if the subject is asked to laterally flex the neck to the same side and then rotate the head to the opposite side against resistance. Both the sternal and clavicular heads can be gripped between the fingers with the gap between them easily identifiable. The round muscle belly is palpable throughout its length, as is the flat tendon at its attachment to the mastoid process.

MUSCLES WHICH FLEX THE HEAD AND NECK

Sternomastoid (see pp. 682–684)
Longus capitis

Longus capitis (see Fig. 6.28a)

Longus capitis is a long narrow muscle which runs from the anterior tubercles of the transverse processes of the *third, fourth, fifth* and *six cervical vertebrae*, passing upwards and medially to attach to the basilar part of the *occipital bone* lateral to the pharyngeal tubercle.

Nerve supply

Longus capitis is supplied by the *anterior primary rami* of *C1, 2, 3*, and occasionally, *4*.

Action

Longus capitis flexes the head on the neck, as well as flexing the upper cervical spine. However, such a movement is usually achieved by relaxation of the extensor muscles, so that active flexion is only needed against resistance.

MUSCLES WHICH FLEX THE HEAD ON THE NECK

Rectus capitis anterior

Rectus capitis anterior (see Fig. 6.28a)

Rectus capitis anterior is a short strap muscle lying deep to longus capitis. It passes from the *anterior surface* of the *lateral mass* of the *atlas*, upwards and medially to the basilar part of the *occipital bone* between longus capitis and the occipital condyle.

Nerve supply

Rectus capitis anterior is supplied by the *anterior primary rami* of *C1* and *2*.

Action

Rectus capitis anterior flexes the head on the neck. However, its main function is probably to stabilize the atlanto-occipital joint during movement.

MUSCLES WHICH LATERALLY FLEX THE NECK

Scalenus anterior
Scalenus medius
Scalenus posterior
Splenius cervicis
Levator scapulae (see p. 82)
Sternomastoid (see pp. 682–684)

Scalenus anterior (Fig. 6.29c)

Scalenus anterior is the anterior of the three scalene muscles, being found deep to sternomastoid but in front of scalenus

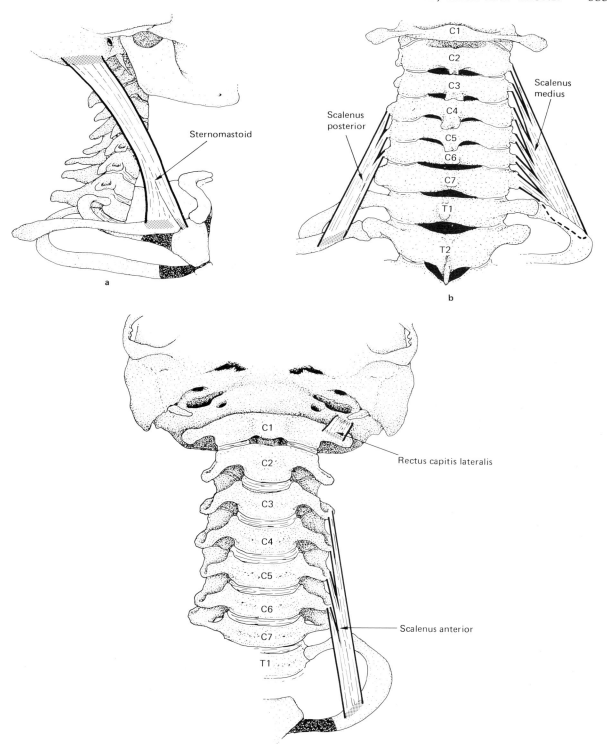

Fig. 6.29 **a** = The right sternomastoid muscle, lateral view; **b** = the right scalenus medius muscle and left scalenus posterior muscle, posterior view; **c** = the left scalenus anterior and rectus capitis lateralis muscles, anterior view with the clavicle removed.

medius. It arises from the *anterior tubercles* of the transverse processes of the *third* to *sixth cervical vertebrae*. The muscle fibres run downwards almost vertically, deep to the prevertebral fascia, and form a narrow tendon which attaches to the prominent *scalene tubercle* on the inner border of the *first rib* (see Fig. 6.29c).

Nerve supply

Scalenus anterior is supplied by the *anterior primary rami* of *C4, 5* and *6*.

Action

Singly, scalenus anterior laterally flexes the neck to the same side together with a limited amount of rotation to the opposite side. When both scalenus anterior muscles contract they produce flexion of the neck. If, however, their upper attachment is fixed they act to steady the first rib during respiration, and may assist in its elevation.

Scalenus medius (see Fig. 6.29b)

Scalenus medius is the middle and largest of the three scalene muscles. It arises from the *transverse processes* of the *first* and *second cervical vertebrae*, and from the *posterior tubercles* of the *third* to *seventh cervical vertebrae*. The muscle fibres run downwards and laterally to attach to a rough impression on the upper surface of the *first rib* behind the groove for the subclavian artery.

Nerve supply

Scalenus medius is supplied by the *anterior primary rami* of *C3* to *C8* inclusive.

Action

Working singly, scalenus medius produces strong lateral flexion of the neck to the same side. If its upper attachment is fixed, then

this strong muscle is very effective in steadying or elevating the first rib during respiration.

Scalenus posterior (see Fig. 6.29b)

Scalenus posterior is the smallest and most posterior of the three scalene muscles, arising from the *posterior tubercles* of the transverse processes of the *fourth, fifth* and *sixth cervical vertebrae*. Its fibres run downwards and laterally to attach to the outer surface of the *second rib* behind the attachment of serratus anterior.

Nerve supply

Scalenus posterior is supplied by the *anterior primary rami* of *C6, 7* and *8*.

Action

Scalenus posterior laterally flexes the neck to the same side and may assist in steadying the second rib during respiration.

Splenius cervicis (see Fig. 6.28b)

Splenius cervicis arises from the *spinous processes* of the *third* to *sixth thoracic vertebrae* from where its fibres run upwards and laterally to attach to the *posterior tubercles* of the transverse processes of the *upper three* or *four cervical vertebrae* in front of levator scapulae.

Nerve supply

Splenius cervicis is supplied by the *posterior primary rami* of *C5, 6* and *7*.

Action

Acting on its own, splenius cervicis laterally flexes and slightly rotates the neck to the same side. Together, both muslces extend the neck.

MUSCLES WHICH LATERALLY FLEX THE HEAD AND NECK

Sternomastoid (see also pp. 682–684)
Splenius capitis
Trapezius (see pp. 76, 82)
Erector spinae (see pp. 705–706)

Sternomastoid

Application

Spasm or contracture of one sternomastoid muscle produces the characteristic deformity of lateral flexion of the neck to the same side with rotation of the head to the opposite side. This position is often seen in patients with acute neck pain, or in infants with torticollis (wry neck). Frequently, these conditions require that the muscle be stretched into its longest position by extending and laterally flexing the neck, coupled with rotation of the head in the appropriate direction.

Splenius capitis (see Fig. 6,28b)

Splenius capitis lies deep to the rhomboids, trapezius and sternomastoid. It arises from the lower half of the *ligamentum nuchae* and the *spinous processes* of the *seventh cervical* to *fourth thoracic vertebrae*. The muscle runs upwards and laterally to attach to the posterior aspect of the *mastoid process* of the *temporal bone* and the lateral third of the *superior nuchal line* deep to sternomastoid.

Nerve supply

Splenius capitis is supplied by the *posterior primary rami* of C3, 4 and 5.

Action

Acting individually splenius capitis extends the head and neck. However, this action is usually accompanied by lateral flexion of the neck and rotation of the face to the same side. Only when both splenius capitis muscles act together is pure extension of the head and neck achieved.

MUSCLES WHICH LATERALLY FLEX THE HEAD ON THE NECK

Rectus capitis lateralis

Rectus capitis lateralis (see Fig. 6.29c)

Rectus capitis lateralis is a short strap-like muscle running upwards from the upper surface of the *transverse process* of the *atlas* to the *jugular process* of the *occipital bone*.

Nerve supply

Rectus capitis lateralis is supplied by the *anterior primary rami* of *C1* and *2*.

Action

Rectus capitis lateralis produces lateral flexion of the head to the same side. Its main action, however, appears to be stabilizing the atlanto-occipital joint during movement.

MUSCLES WHICH EXTEND THE NECK

Levator scapulae (see p. 82)
Splenius cervicis (see p. 686)

MUSCLES WHICH EXTEND THE HEAD AND NECK

Trapezius (see pp. 76, 82)
Splenius capitis (see p. 687)
Erector spinae (see pp. 705–706)

MUSCLES WHICH EXTEND THE HEAD ON THE NECK

Rectus capitis posterior major
Rectus capitis posterior minor
Obliquus capitis superior

Rectus capitis posterior major
(see Fig. 6.28b)

This small muscle arises from the *spinous process* of the *axis* and runs to attach to the lateral part of the *inferior nuchal line* of the *occipital bone*, deep to obliquus capitis superior and semispinalis capitis.

Nerve supply

Rectus capitis posterior major is supplied by the *posterior primary ramus* of *C1*.

Action

Rectus capitis posterior major extends the head on the neck. Working singly it may produce some rotation of the head to the same side. However, stabilization of the atlanto-occipital joint during movement is probably its main role.

Rectus capitis posterior minor
(see Fig. 6.28b)

This small muscle arises from the *posterior tubercle* of the *atlas* and inserts into the medial part of the *inferior nuchal line* of the *occipital bone*, medial and deep to rectus capitis posterior major.

Nerve supply

Rectus capitis posterior minor is supplied by the *posterior primary ramus* of *C1*.

Action

Rectus capitis posterior minor extends the head on the neck, and like the major muscle, stabilizes the atlanto-occipital joint during movement.

Obliquus capitis superior
(see Fig. 6.28c)

This muscle arises from the upper surface of the *transverse process* of the *atlas* and inserts in the *interspace* between the *superior* and *inferior nuchal lines* of the *occipital bone* lateral to semispinalis capitis.

Nerve supply

Obliquus capitis superior is supplied by the *posterior primary ramus* of *C1*.

Action

Obliquus capitis superior extends the head on the neck, as well as having an important stabilizing role during movement.

MUSCLES WHICH ROTATE THE NECK

Semispinalis cervicis (see p. 702)
Multifidus (see p. 702)
Scalenus anterior (see pp. 684–686)
Splenius cervicis (see p. 686)

MUSCLES WHICH ROTATE THE HEAD AND NECK

Sternomastoid (see pp. 682–684)
Splenius capitis (see p. 687)

MUSCLES WHICH ROTATE THE HEAD ON THE NECK

Obliquus capitis inferior
Rectus capitis posterior major (see p. 688)

Obliquus capitis inferior (see Fig. 6.28c)

Obliquus capitis inferior is the largest of the so called suboccipital muscles. It arises from the *spinous process* of the *axis* and runs upwards and laterally to the posterior aspect of the *transverse process* of the *atlas*.

Nerve supply

Obliquus capitis inferior is supplied by the *posterior primary ramus* of *C1*.

Action

Obliquus capitis inferior turns the face to the same side. Due to the lever arm afforded by the atlas this is quite a strong movement. The muscle also acts as an extensile ligament stabilizing the atlanto-axial joint during movement.

Nerve supply

THE CERVICAL PLEXUS
(Fig. 6.30)

The cervical plexus is formed from the anterior primary rami of the upper four cervical nerves and consists of a series of loops between adjacent nerves. The first cervical nerve emerges between rectus capitis anterior and rectus capitis lateralis. It then descends in front of the transverse process of the atlas to join the ascending branch of the second cervical nerve. As it does so, it sends a large branch to join the hypoglossal nerve. The second, third and fourth nerves divide into upper and lower parts, with adjacent parts joining together. The lower part of the fourth cervical nerve may participate in the brachial plexus. The loop communications of the plexus lie close to the vertebral column in front of levator scapulae and scalenus medius behind the prevertebral muscles. The branches arising from these loops lie posteromedial to the internal jugular vein under cover of sternomastoid. The branches given off can, for descriptive purposes, be grouped into superficial and deep. The former all supply the skin of the lower part of the skull and neck, while the latter separate again into medial and lateral divisions, which go on to supply muscles or communicate with other nerves.

Superficial branches (Fig. 6.30a)

There are four cutaneous nerves which all appear in the posterior triangle just above the midpoint of the posterior border of sternomastoid before piercing the deep fascia to supply the skin of the head and neck.

Lesser occipital nerve

The lesser occipital nerve (C2, 3) hooks below the accessory nerve to emerge above the other three and ascends along the posterior border of the sternomastoid to pierce the deep fascia at the apex of the posterior triangle. It then divides into branches to supply the skin and fascia on the upper lateral part of the neck, the cranial surface of the auricle and mastoid process, and adjacent part of the scalp. Occasionally, the nerve is double.

Great auricular nerve

The great auricular nerve (C2, 3 or sometimes just C3) is the largest of the cutaneous branches. It emerges below the lesser occipital nerve and passes upwards and forwards over the superficial surface of sternomastoid, deep to platysma, towards the lower part of the auricle. During its course, it divides into a number of branches. Anterior branches pass through the substance of the parotid gland and over the angle of the mandible to supply skin and fascia over the posteroinferior surface of the face. Within the parotid gland these branches communicate with the facial nerve. Intermediate branches supply both surfaces of the lower part of the auricle. Posterior branches supply an area of skin and fascia over the mastoid process. These posterior branches communicate with the lesser occipital nerve and the posterior auricular branch of the facial nerve.

Tranverse cutaneous nerve

The transverse cutaneous nerve of the neck (C2, 3) passes horizontally forwards around the posterior border of sternomastoid, deep to platysma and the external jugular vein. As it passes across sternomastoid it divides into upper and lower branches, which supply the skin and fascia over the anterior triangle of the neck from the mandible to just above the clavicle near the midline.

Supraclavicular nerves

The supraclavicular nerves (C3, 4) appear as one large nerve at the posterior border of sternomastoid just below its midpoint. This large nerve passes down through the lower part of the posterior triangle, dividing into lateral, intermediate and medial supraclavicular nerves. They all pierce the deep fascia above the clavicle to supply skin and fascia over the lower part of the side of the neck and anterior chest wall as far as the sternal angle. The lateral nerve also supplies the acromioclavicular joint, while the medial supplies the sternoclavicular joint. Branches from the intermediate and lateral nerves may groove or pierce the clavicle.

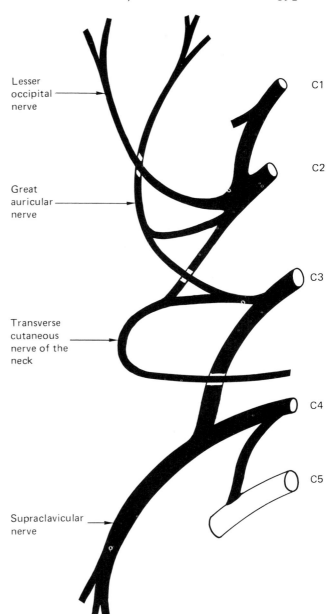

Lesser occipital nerve

Great auricular nerve

Transverse cutaneous nerve of the neck

Supraclavicular nerve

C1

C2

C3

C4

C5

Fig. 6.30a Superficial branches of the cervical plexus.

Deep branches (Fig. 6.30b)

Muscular branches

These arise with other branches of the plexus deep to sternomastoid and can be divided into lateral and medial branches depending on whether they pass into the posterior or anterior triangles respectively.

Lateral branches   From the second cervical nerve, a sensory branch enters the deep surface of sternomastoid. From the third and fourth cervical nerves, a sensory branch crosses the posterior triangle to enter the deep surface of trapezius. Separate fibres from C3, 4 innervate levator scapulae, and scalenus medius and posterior.

Medial branches   The medial branches pass to innervate the prevertebral muscles rectus capitis lateralis and anterior (C1, 2), longus capitis (C1, 2, 3, 4) and longus colli (C2, 3, 4). From the first cervical nerve a branch joins the hypoglossal nerve. A smaller branch of sensory fibres passes superiorly within the hypoglossal nerve to supply the skull and dura mater of the posterior cranial fossa; this is the meningeal branch. The remaining fibres descend in the hypoglossal nerve to be given off in one of three branches, none of which contain hypoglossal fibres. These are the superior root of the ansa cervicalis, which descends in front of the internal and common carotid arteries to join the inferior root, formed by branches from C2 and 3 passing over the anterior surface of the internal jugular vein, to form the ansa cervicalis superficial to the carotid sheath. Branches from the ansa innervate sternohyoid, sternothyroid and omohyoid. The other two branches from the hypoglossal nerve containing C1 fibres are the nerve to thyrohyoid and the nerve to geniohyoid.

Phrenic nerve   The phrenic nerve arises from C3, 4, 5, although its principal root is C4. Branches from C3 reach it either directly or by the nerve to sternohyoid, whereas the C5 fibres may reach it directly or via the accessory phrenic nerve from the nerve to subclavius. The phrenic nerve innervates the diaphragm, being its only motor supply, and has to pass through both the neck and the thorax to reach it.

In the neck each phrenic nerve descends from lateral to medial over the front of scalenus anterior, and lies behind sternomastoid, omohyoid, the internal jugular vein and the suprascapular vessels and is anterior to the cervical fascia. At the base of the neck the phrenic nerve enters the thorax by passing behind the subclavian vein and in front of the subclavian artery.

In the thorax the left and right phrenic nerves are separated from the pleural cavity only by the mediastinal pleura.

Left phrenic nerve   It passes in front of the internal thoracic artery, medial to the apex of the left lung and pleura, between the left common carotid and subclavian arteries to cross the aortic arch anterior to the vagus nerve. It then passes anterior to the root of the left lung having the left ventricle and pericardium medially and the pleura of the left lung laterally. It pierces the muscular part of the diaphragm lateral to the oesophageal opening to supply its under surface mainly on the left.

Right phrenic nerve   This is shorter and more vertical entering the thorax lateral to the right brachiocephalic vein and the superior vena cava; it is not in contact with the vagus nerve. It then passes between the pleura and pericardium across the right atrium to reach the inferior vena cava, having passed anterior to the root of the right lung. It passes through the central tendon of the diaphragm through or beside the inferior vena caval opening to supply the under surface of the muscle mainly on the right side.

In addition to providing the only motor supply to the diaphragm, the phrenic nerves are also sensory to its central part as well

Lateral   **Medial**

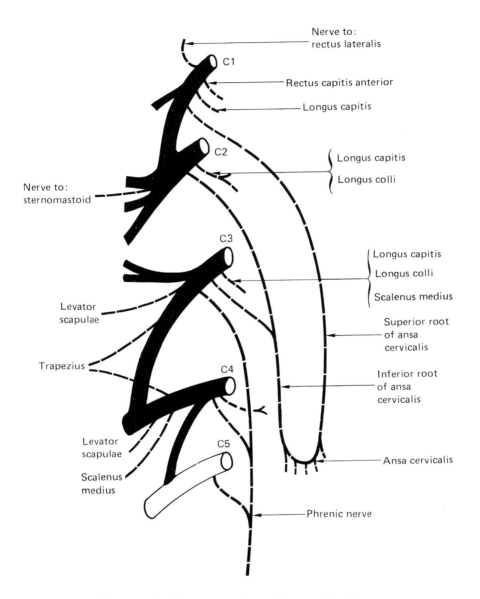

Nerve to:
rectus lateralis

C1

Rectus capitis anterior

Longus capitis

C2

Longus capitis

Longus colli

Nerve to:
sternomastoid

C3

Longus capitis

Longus colli

Scalenus medius

Levator
scapulae

Superior root
of ansa
cervicalis

Trapezius

C4

Inferior root
of ansa
cervicalis

Levator
scapulae

C5

Ansa cervicalis

Scalenus
medius

Phrenic nerve

Fig.6.30b Deep branches of the cervical plexus
(superficial branches cut).

as to the mediastinal and diaphragmatic
pleura, fibrous pericardium, diaphragmatic
peritoneum and probably also to the liver,
gall bladder and inferior vena cava. The
phrenic nerves receive fibres from the sympathetic trunk in the neck and the coeliac
plexus in the abdomen.

Communicating branches (Fig. 6.30b)

The cervical plexus sends fibres to the
vagus, accessory and hypoglossal nerves,
and receives grey rami communicantes from
the superior cervical ganglion of the sympathetic trunk.

Muscles

MUSCLES WHICH PRODUCE MOVEMENTS OF THE TRUNK AND THORAX

For descriptive purposes the trunk includes the lumbar and thoracic parts of the vertebral column, consequently movements of these two regions are considered together. The small degree of movement possible between adjacent vertebrae, when combined across several segments, can produce a considerable range of flexion, extension, lateral bending or rotation of the trunk.

Flexion of the trunk occurs when the lumbar and thoracic parts of the vertebral column bend forwards; movement in the opposite direction is *extension*. These two movements are of considerable functional significance, particularly when they accompany flexion or extension of the hip joint. However, care must be taken when measuring the range of movement of the trunk so that movement at the hip is not included. *Lateral flexion* (side-bending) of the trunk occurs when the level of the shoulders becomes inclined with respect to that of the pelvis and therefore lateral flexion occurs on both the left and right sides. In this movement adjacent parts of the vertebral bodies on one side come closer together, while those on the opposite side become separated. *Rotation* of the trunk is produced by the summation of individual vertebral movements which enable the trunk to be twisted to the right or left whilst keeping the shoulders level. Rotation of the pelvis about the hip joint can increase the rotation of the shoulders. Again care must be taken to fix the pelvis when assessing the degree of trunk rotation.

An important structural component of the trunk is the thoracic cage whereby the ribs, articulating with the thoracic vertebrae and sternum, afford protection to the underlying soft tissues. The muscles of *inspiration* and *expiration* are therefore considered in this section together with the thoracic cage. The anterior abdominal wall muscles, as well as being involved in producing trunk movements, also raise intra-abdominal pressure, this aids expiration and all straining activities, e.g. micturition, parturition, coughing and vomiting.

As in other sections, a detailed description of any muscle is only given with its first described action.

MUSCLES WHICH PRODUCE FLEXION OF THE TRUNK

Psoas major (see pp. 354–356)
External oblique
Internal oblique
Rectus abdominis
Psoas minor

External oblique (obliquus externus abdominis) (Fig. 6.31a)

The external oblique muscle is situated on the anterolateral aspect of the abdominal wall, and has its fibres running downwards and medially from the ribs towards the midline (Fig. 6.31a). It is the most superficial of the three sheets of muscle of the anterior abdominal wall. Its upper attachment is by fleshy slips to the *outer borders* of the *lower eight ribs* and their *costal cartilages*. It interdigitates with serratus anterior above and latissimus dorsi below. From here the muscle fibres sweep downwards and medially, with those from the lower two ribs passing almost vertically to attach to the *outer lip* of the anterior two-thirds of the *iliac crest*, leaving a free posterior border of the muscle running between the twelfth rib and the iliac crest. The remainder of the fibres give rise to a large aponeurosis which is broader below than above. They sweep across rectus abdominis, participating in the formation of the *rectus sheath* (see p. 697), towards the midline to fuse with that from the opposite side at the linea alba. The *linea alba* is a fibrous raphe which runs from the tip of the

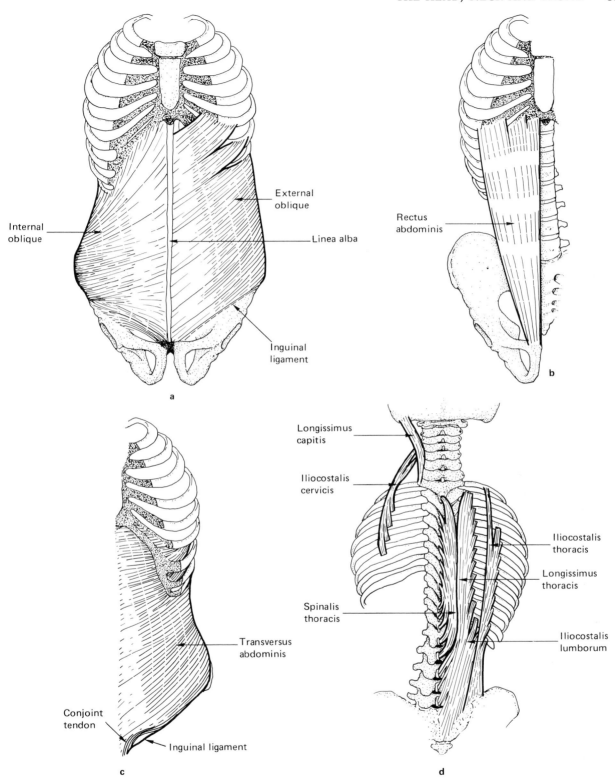

Fig. 6.31   **a** = The right internal oblique and left external oblique muscles, anterior view; **b** = the right rectus abdominus, anterior view; **c** = the left transversus abdominus, oblique view; **d** = the erector spinae muscle, showing its constituent parts.

xiphoid process of the sternum to the symphysis pubis.

The lower, free border of the aponeurosis stretches between the pubic tubercle and the anterior superior iliac spine, and forms the *inguinal ligament*. The inguinal ligament folds back on itself so that it is convex downwards–this is caused by the pull of the fascia lata of the thigh which attaches along its length. The medial part of the inguinal ligament is expanded backwards along the pecten pubis, forming the *lacunar ligament*, (a further extension of the lacunar ligament along the pecten is the *pectineal ligament*). In the anatomical position the lacunar ligament is almost horizontal. Above the pubic tubercle is a triangular cleft in the aponeurosis; this is the *superficial inguinal ring*. Its base is at the pubic crest and its apex is directed upwards and laterally; the sides are bound by the medial and lateral crura.

Nerve supply

The external oblique is supplied by the *anterior primary rami* of the *lower six thoracic nerves, T7 to T12.* The skin over the muscle is supplied by the same nerve roots.

Internal oblique (obliquus internus abdominis) (see Fig. 6.31a)

The internal oblique muscle lies deep to the external oblique, and is the middle of the three sheets of abdominal muscles. The muscle fibres arise from the *lateral two-thirds* of the *inguinal ligament*, the *anterior two-thirds* of the *intermediate line* of the *iliac crest*, and from the *thoracolumbar fascia* (see Fig. 6.33c). From this attachment the fibres fan outwards with the most posterior fibres passing almost vertically to attach to the inferior borders of the *lower four ribs*. The more anterior and lower fibres pass upwards and medially, giving way to an aponeurosis along a line extending downwards and medially from the tenth costal cartilage to the body of the pubis. The aponeurosis has a complex involvement in the formation of the *rectus sheath* (see p. 697) before interlacing with that of the opposite side at the *linea alba*. That part of the muscle arising from the inguinal ligament passes medially and downwards, blending with

the lower part of transversus abdominis to form the *conjoint tendon* which attaches to the *pubic crest* and *pecten pubis*. A few fibres from the inferomedial part of the muscle pass along the spermatic cord to form the cremaster muscle (see p. 701).

Nerve supply

The internal oblique is supplied by the *anterior primary rami* of the *lower six thoracic nerves* (T7 to T12) and also the *first lumbar nerve* (L1).

Rectus abdominis (see Fig. 6.31b)

Rectus abdominis runs vertically on the front of the abdomen, enclosed within the rectus sheath (see p. 697). It arises from the front of the *symphysis pubis* and the *pubic crest*, via two tendons, and passes upwards, widening as it does so, to attach to the anterior surfaces of the *xiphoid process* and the *costal cartilages* of the *fifth, sixth* and *seventh ribs* (see Fig. 6.31b). The slightly convex lateral border of the muscle presents as a groove, the *linea semilunaris*, on lean individuals, while the two muscles are separated by the *linea alba*. Transverse tendinous intersections, usually three in number, are found in the anterior part of the muscle and are firmly attached to the rectus sheath. The lowest of these intersections lies at the level of the umbilicus, the highest at the level of the xiphoid, and the third about midway between the other two.

Each rectus abdominis muscle is enclosed in a fibrous sheath formed by the aponeuroses of the external and internal oblique muscles and transversus abdominis, the two sheaths being fused along their medial borders in the region of the linea alba. The sheath differs in its formation in its upper and lower parts from that in its central, more extensive area. The upper three-quarters of the internal oblique aponeurosis, approximately midway between the pubic symphysis and umbilicus, and the xiphoid process splits into two layers one of which passes anterior and the other posterior to rectus abdominis. The aponeurosis of transversus abdominis fuses with the posterior layer to form the posterior part of the rectus sheath, while that of external oblique fuses with the

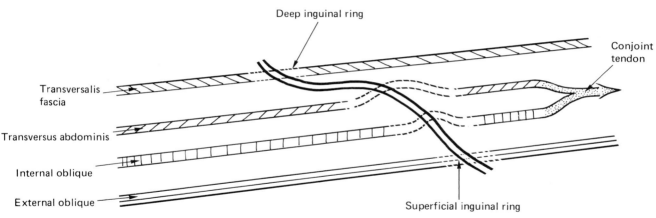

Fig. 6.32 **a** = A section through the rectus sheath, (i) above the level of the umbilicus, and (ii) below the level of the umbilicus, to show the arrangement of the fascia which forms it; **b** = schematic representations to show the structures forming the inguinal canal.

anterior layer (Fig. 6.32a(i)). Below the mid-point between the umbilicus and the symphysis pubis, the aponeuroses of all three muscles pass in front of rectus abdominis so that the posterior wall of the sheath is deficient. The inferior limit of the posterior layer of the sheath is marked by a crescentic border, the arcuate line. Below the arcuate line, the rectus abdominis lies directly on the tranversalis fascia, separating it from extraperitoneal fat (Fig. 6.32a(ii)). Above the costal margin, the posterior layer is again deficient so that rectus abdominis lies directly on the thoracic wall.

Within the sheath is found pyramidalis, when present. This small muscle, supplied by the subcostal nerve (T12), lies anterior to rectus abdominis, arising from the pubic crest and inserting into the linea alba. It tenses the linea alba, presumably to help provide a stable attachment from which the abdominal muscles can work, particularly when the trunk is flexed.

In the latter stages of pregnancy, the linea alba stretches to increase the distance between the two rectus abdominis muscles, a condition called *divarication* (or *diastasis*) *recti*. A separation of five or more centimetres can occur, but postpartum this returns to normal providing undue strains are avoided.

Nerve supply

The rectus abdominis is supplied by the *anterior primary rami* of the *lower six* or *seven thoracic nerves* (T6/7 to T12). The skin over the muscle is supplied by nerves with root values T4 to L1.

Action

Flexion of the trunk is produced by concentric contraction of the external oblique, internal oblique and the rectus abdominis of both sides. If the rib cage becomes the fixed point then these same muscles can lift the anterior part of the pelvis and alter the degree of pelvic tilt. This latter action has a significant effect in decreasing the lumbar lordosis, and as such is advocated by some in the management of low back pain. These muscles are also involved in rotation and lateral flexion of the trunk, as well as in general functional activities involving the abdomen which are discussed later (see pp. 714, 715).

Palpation

The two rectus abdominis muscles can be easily palpated as they run vertically and centrally on the front of the abdomen when the trunk is flexed against resistance. In an athletic subject, it should also be possible to palpate the three transverse tendinous intersections, as well as the linea alba and linea semilunaris at the sides of the muscle.

The flat nature of the oblique muscles makes their palpation difficult in all but the muscular subject. However, a flat hand placed over the lower lateral aspect of the ribs may allow the contraction of external oblique to be felt on resisted flexion. The internal oblique muscle may be similarly palpated if the hand is placed over the lower abdomen just above the anterior half of the iliac crest.

Psoas minor

Psoas minor is a weak muscle not always present. However, when it is present it arises from the sides of the *twelfth thoracic* and *first lumbar vertebrae* and the intervening *intervertebral disc*. The fleshy belly soon gives gives way to a long tendon which lies on psoas major and attaches to the *iliopubic eminence* and the *iliac fascia*.

The muscle is supplied by the *ventral ramus* of *L1*, and acts as a weak flexor of the lumbar spine.

MUSCLES WHICH RAISE INTRA-ABDOMINAL PRESSURE

External oblique (see pp. 694–696)
Internal oblique (see p. 696)
Rectus abdominis (see pp. 696–698)
Transversus abdominis
Cremaster

Transversus abdominis (see Fig. 6.31c)

Transversus abdominis is the deepest of the three sheets of abdominal muscles, and as its name suggests has transversly arranged muscle fibres. It arises from: the *lateral third* of the *inguinal ligament* and the *anterior two-thirds* of the *inner lip* of the *iliac crest* inferiorly, the *thoracolumbar fascia* posteriorly, and the *inner surface* of the *costal cartilages* of the *lower six ribs* superiorly. Here it interdigitates with the attachment of the *diaphragm* (see Fig. 6.31c).

The fibres of transversus abdominis pass horizontally around the abdominal wall to end in an aponeurotic sheet which fuses with the posterior layer of the aponeurosis of internal oblique, to eventually reach the *linea alba*. It is therefore involved in the formation of the rectus sheath (see p. 697).

Those fibres arising from the inguinal ligament arch downwards to join with those from the internal oblique muscle to form the *conjoint tendon* which attaches to the *pubic crest* and the *pecten pubis* behind the superficial inguinal ring.

The lower free border of transversus abdominis, between its attachment to the inguinal ligament and the pecten pubis, is concave downwards. Below this border the fascial covering of the muscle (*transversalis fascia*) comes into contact with both the internal and external oblique muscles and the inguinal ligament. In the lateral part of this fascia is a round opening, this is the *deep inguinal ring*.

Nerve supply

Transversus abdominis is supplied by the *anterior primary rami* of the *lower six thoracic nerves* (T7 to T12) and the *first lumbar nerve* (L1).

Action

The actions of all eight muscles of the abdominal wall (four each side) can be related to the function of raising intra-abdominal pressure. This is achieved by the 'sheet' muscles pulling on the rectus sheath via their aponeuroses, flattening the abdomen and so compressing the abdominal viscera. If the diaphragm maintains its tone and resists upward displacement, the subsequent increase in intra-abdominal pressure is important in producing the so-called 'expulsive' acts. Combined with appropriate sphincter relaxation, the increased pressure on the bladder aids micturition, on the rectum it assists in defaecation, and on the stomach it helps in vomiting. In the final stages of childbirth, the compressive force produced by these muscles helps to expel the fetus from the uterus.

When the diaphragm is relaxed the increase in intra-abdominal pressure presses the abdominal viscera against its lower surface and so pushes the diaphragm upwards. This increases the pressure inside the thorax so that when the glottis is opened air is forced from the lungs in a violent, explosive cough or sneeze. The coughing action is further reinforced by the abdominal muscles acting on the lower ribs by pulling them downwards.

Pain resulting from surgical incision of the abdominal wall frequently causes inhibition of these muscles, thereby making coughing very difficult.

The combined action of the abdominal muscles, together with the diaphragm, can also produce a 'muscular corset' which holds the abdominal viscera in place. This action can be increased during activities, such as lifting, whereby a form of pneumatic cushion is formed in front of the vulnerable lumbar spine. This action is frequently seen when people hold their breath, thus anchoring the diaphragm, prior to and when moving a heavy object.

Palpation

A combined contraction of all the abdominal muscles can be easily felt if the hand is placed over the centre of the abdomen while the subject coughs. The increased tension within the anterior abdominal wall can also be appreciated during any of the 'expulsive' acts described.

Inguinal canal (see Fig. 6.32b)

The inguinal canal is an oblique passage through the anterior abdominal wall, about 4 cm long, which transmits the spermatic cord in the male and the round ligament of the uterus in the female, as well as the ilio-inguinal nerve in both sexes.

It begins at the *deep inguinal ring* (a round opening in the transversalis fascia about 1.5 cm above the mid point of the inguinal ligament) and ends at the *superficial inguinal ring*, a deficit in the aponeurosis of external oblique above the pubic tubercle and medial end of the inguinal ligament. In the fetus and in young children, the deep and superficial rings lie opposite each other, and so facilitate, in the male, the passage of the testis and associated structures into the scrotum from the abdomen. However, with growth the two rings become separated so that in the adult the inguinal canal runs downwards and medially from the deep to the superficial rings. Throughout its course the floor of the canal is formed by the inguinal ligament, with the lacunar ligament in addition medially.

The anterior wall is formed by the external oblique aponeurosis throughout, reinforced in its lateral third by muscular fibres of the internal oblique. Posteriorly the wall is formed throughout by transversalis fascia, which is reinforced by the conjoint tendon in its medial third. These reinforcements of the anterior and posterior canal walls lie opposite the deep and superficial rings respectively. The roof of the canal is formed by the arching fibres of internal oblique and transversus abdominis as they pass from front to back so forming the conjoint tendon.

As the spermatic cord (or round ligament) passes through the canal it acquires coverings from some of the structures forming the canal. On entering the canal, the spermatic cord takes a covering from the margins of the deep inguinal ring—this is the internal spermatic fascia derived from the transversalis fascia. From the lower border of internal oblique a second covering is acquired—this is the cremasteric fascia containing the cremaster muscle. Finally, as the spermatic cord emerges from the canal the third and last covering is acquired from the margins of the superficial inguinal ring—this is the external spermatic fascia derived from the external oblique aponeurosis.

The inguinal canal is a weak point in the anterior abdominal wall. The reinforcements opposite the deep and superficial inguinal rings afford them some protection. Nevertheless, there is a tendency for contraction of the abdominal muscles to push mobile abdominal contents along the canal. However, contraction of these same muscles also narrows the canal and reduces the size of the inguinal rings. In fact internal oblique is in more or less continuous contraction when standing, so will tend to have a protecting as well as supporting role as far as the inguinal canal is concerned. Some activities, such as heavy exertion with the trunk rotated, may actually cause the canal to open.

Because of this weakness it is not surprising that part of the mobile abdominal viscera may be squeezed through the superficial inguinal ring, so forming a hernia. For obvious reasons inguinal hernias tend to be twice as common in men than in women. One of two types of inguinal hernia may occur, indirect (oblique) or direct. An indirect hernia follows the course of the testis in its passage through the abdominal wall to appear at the superficial ring; at the deep ring it is lateral to the inferior epigastric vessels. A direct hernia pushes its way through the posterior and sometimes the anterior wall of the canal following no preformed path. It lies medial to the inferior epigastric vessels, and may also appear lateral to the superficial ring.

Both forms of inguinal hernia can be distinguished from a femoral hernia, which emerges through the femoral canal, because its root lies above the inguinal ligament, whereas in a femoral hernia the root is below the inguinal ligament.

Cremaster

Cremaster is a loose arrangement of muscle fibres that loop around the spermatic cord and testis. It is continuous with the lower edge of internal oblique and the adjacent part of the inguinal ligament, and attaches to the pubic tubercle. It is usually well-developed in the male but sparse in the female. It is supplied by the genital branch of the genitofemoral nerve (L1, 2), although voluntary control over the muscle is not possible. A cremasteric reflex is present which raises the testis when the medial side of the thigh is stroked. The reflex is very active in infants, but is much reduced by puberty.

Cremaster, together with the dartos muscle, helps to form a mechanism whereby the temperature of the testes can be controlled. Relaxation of these muscles allows the testes to hang well down into the scrotum so that their temperature falls. Contraction of the muscles draws the testes towards the superficial inguinal ring so raising its temperature. Precise regulation of the temperature of the testes is important for the proper formation of spermatozoa, which require a constant temperature slightly lower than body temperature.

MUSCLES WHICH PRODUCE ROTATION OF THE TRUNK

Internal oblique (see p. 696)
External oblique (see pp. 694–696)
Multifidus
Rotatores
Semispinalis

Rotation of the trunk to the left is produced by a simultaneous contraction of the right external oblique and the left internal oblique. Conversely, rotation to the right is produced by the left external oblique and the right internal oblique. These movements may be accompanied by some flexion of the trunk.

Multifidus (Fig. 6.33a)

Multifidus lies deep to semispinalis and erector spinae in the gutter between the spinous and transverse processes of the vertebrae at all levels. From below upwards the lateral attachment of multifidus is from the back of the *sacrum* and the *fascia* covering erector spinae, the *mamillary processes* of the *lumbar vertebrae*, the *transverse processes* of the *thoracic vertebrae*, and the *articular processes* of the *lower four* or *five cervical vertebrae* (Fig. 6.33a). From this extensive origin the muscle fibres are arranged in three layers as they pass upwards and medially to attach to the *spines* of all the *vertebrae* from the *fifth lumbar* to the *axis*. The deepest layer attaches to the vertebrae immediately above, the middle layer to the second or third vertebra above, and finally the outer layer to the third or fourth vertebra above.

Rotatores (Fig. 6.33a)

Rotatores are best developed in the thoracic region, being represented by variable bundles in the lumbar and cervical regions. They lie adjacent to the *transverse process* of one *vertebra*, passing upwards to attach to the *lamina* of the *vertebra* above.

Nerve supply

Both multifidus and rotatores are supplied by the *posterior primary rami* of *adjacent spinal nerves*.

Action

Multifidus can produce rotation, as well as extension and lateral flexion, of the vertebral column at all levels, whereas rotatores can only produce rotation in the thoracic region. Both muscles, however, probably have more functional importance in their role as stabilizers of the vertebral column, where they act as extensible ligaments, adjusting their length to stabilize adjacent vertebrae irrespective of the position of the vertebral column.

Semispinalis

Semispinalis extends from the lower thoracic region to the base of the skull and consists of three parts. *Semispinalis thoracis* arises from the transverse processes of the lower thoracic vertebrae (T6 to T10) and attaches to the spinous processes of the lower cervical and upper thoracic vertebrae (C6 to T2). The larger *semispinalis cervicis* runs from the transverse processes of T1 to T6 to the spinous processes of C1 to C6. The largest part of semispinalis is *semispinalis capitis* which runs from the transverse processes of T1 to T6 and articular processes of C4 to C7 to attach to a medial impression between the superior and inferior nuchal lines on the base of the skull. The most medial part of semispinalis capitis may be separated from the remainder, and if so is known as *spinalis capitis*.

Nerve supply

Semispinalis is supplied by the *posterior primary rami* of *adjacent spinal nerves*.

Action

Semispinalis, when acting on both sides, produces extension of the thoracic and cervical parts of the vertebral column. When only one side contracts, it produces rotation of the trunk and neck to the opposite side.

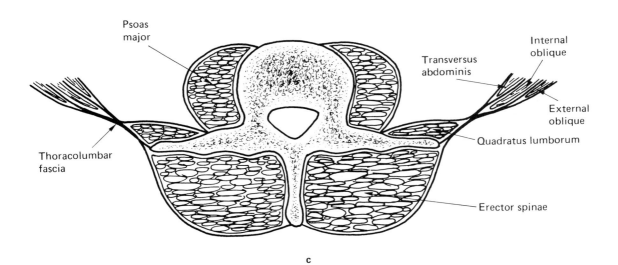

Fig. 6.33 **a** = The lower part of the left multifidus muscle, and the lower four right rotatores muscles, posterior view; **b** = the right quadratus lumborum, the lower interspinalis and left intertransversarii muscles, posterior view; **c** = transverse section through the region of the upper lumbar spine to show the arrangement of the thoracolumbar fascia.

MUSCLES WHICH PRODUCE LATERAL FLEXION OF THE TRUNK

External oblique (see pp. 694–696)
Internal oblique (see p. 696)
Rectus abdominis (see pp. 696–698)
Erector spinae (see pp. 705–706)
Multifidus (see p. 702)
Quadratus lumborum
Intertransversarii

The movement of the trunk to one side is called lateral flexion. Movement to the right is produced by muscles of the right side: rectus abdominis, the external and internal oblique muscles, quadratus lumborum and erector spinae.

Quadratus lumborum (see Fig. 6.33b)

Quadratus lumborum is a large, flat, quadrilateral muscle of the posterior abdominal wall running between the *pelvis* and the *twelfth rib*, deep to erector spinae. It attaches inferiorly to the *iliolumbar ligament* and adjacent posterior part of the *iliac crest*. From here the fibres run upwards and slightly medially to attach to the medial half of the *lower border* of the *twelfth rib*. During its course, the medial border of quadratus lumborum attaches to the lateral part of the anterior surface of the *transverse processes* of all *lumbar vertebrae*. The muscle is enclosed by the anterior and middle layers of the thoracolumbar fascia (see Fig. 6.33c).

Nerve supply

Quadratus lumborum is supplied by the *anterior primary rami* of the *subcostal nerve* and the *upper three* or *four lumbar nerves* (T12, L1, 2, 3 and 4).

Action

Contraction of quadratus lumborum produces lateral flexion of the trunk to the same side. When standing on one leg, quadratus lumborum acts strongly on the non-weight-bearing side to stop the pelvis dropping downwards. It also steadies the twelfth rib during deep inspiration, so that the origin of the diaphragm is fixed. Both muscles acting together help extend the lumbar vertebral column and also give it lateral stability.

Intertransversarii (see Fig. 6.33b)

The intertransversarii are small slips of muscle passing between adjacent *transverse processes* in the cervical and lumbar regions. In the cervical region they are reasonably well-developed, with each muscle consisting of up to four slips running between adjacent transverse processes from the atlas (C1) to T1. In the lumbar region the intertransversarii exist as pairs of muscle slips, the lateral slip running between adjacent transverse processes, and the medial one passing from the accessory process of one vertebra to the mamillary process of the vertebra above. The lateral slips of muscle may extend as far as the transverse process of T10. In the cervical region the slips of the intertransversarii lie both anterior and posterior to the emerging ventral ramus of the spinal nerve, whereas in the lumbar region they lie behind the ventral ramus.

Nerve supply

The intertransversarii in the cervical region and the lateral part in the lumbar region are supplied by the *anterior primary rami* of *adjacent spinal nerves*, while the medial lumbar slips are supplied by the *posterior primary rami* of the *adjacent nerves*.

Action

The intertransversarii on one side can produce lateral flexion to the same side in the lumbar and cervical regions. However, their main function is to act as extensile ligaments, thus stabilizing adjacent vertebral segments during movements of the trunk.

MUSCLES WHICH PRODUCE EXTENSION OF THE TRUNK

Quadratus lumborum (see p. 704)
Multifidus (see p. 702)
Semispinalis
Erector spinae
Interspinales

Erector spinae (see Figs. 6.31d, 6.33c)

Erector spinae is a large, complex, powerful mass of muscle consisting of several parts running alongside the length of the vertebral column.

In the lumbar region, the muscle has a broad belly with a well-defined lateral border, but as it extends upwards it divides into three parallel columns, each of which is divided into three parts according to their relative positions.

Erector spinae arises inferiorly from a strong, thick, flat tendon which is attached along a U-shaped line around the origin of multifidus. The medial limb comes from the *spinous processes* of *T11* to *L5*, spreading onto their *supraspinous ligaments* and the *median sacral crest*. The lateral limb attaches to the *lateral sacral crest*, the *sacrotuberous, sacrococcygeal* and *posterior sacroiliac ligaments*, and the posterior part of the *iliac crest* medial to the internal oblique. Deep to the lateral limb erector spinae has a fleshy attachment to the iliac tuberosity and the inner lip of the iliac crest. From this extensive origin the muscle fibres pass upwards deep to latissimus dorsi splitting into three columns.

Iliocostalis

This is the most lateral of the three columns and can be divided into lumbar, thoracic and cervical parts. The iliocostalis lumborum part inserts by six slips into the inferior borders of the lower six ribs near their angles. Medial to each of these slips arises iliocostalis thoracis which inserts near the angles of the upper six ribs and the transverse process of C7. Finally, iliocostalis cervicis arises medial to the slips of thoracis to insert into the posterior tubercles of the transverse processes of the fourth to seventh cervical vertebrae.

Longissimus

This intermediate column of erector spinae is the longest and thickest. It can be divided into thoracic, cervical and capitis parts. Longissimus thoracis runs from the transverse and accessory processes of the lumbar vertebrae and adjacent thoracolumbar fascia to insert by two sets of slips to the transverse processes of all twelve thoracic vertebrae and adjacent regions of the lower ten ribs. Longissimus cervicis runs from the transverse processes of T1 to T6, medial to thoracis, to the posterior tubercles of the transverse processes of C2 to 6. Longissimus capitis arises from the transverse processes of T1 to T5, in common with longissimus cervicis, and articular processes of C4 to C7, and inserts into the posterior aspect of the mastoid process.

Spinalis

This is the relatively insignificant medial column of erector spinae being divided into thoracic, cervical and capitis parts. Spinalis thoracis, the most clearly demarcated portion, runs from the spinous processes of T11 to L2 to those of T1 to T6. Spinalis cervicis and capitis are poorly developed, and are frequently blended with adjacent muscles (see p. 702 for spinalis capitis).

Nerve supply

The component parts of erector spinae are all supplied by adjacent *posterior primary rami* according to their position.

Action

Erector spinae, when the three muscle columns of both sides act together, extends the lumbar, thoracic and cervical spines, as well as the head on the neck. Consequently, it is the major extensor of the trunk. However, it is also important in controlling flexion of the trunk. When the three muscle columns of one side act together they produce combined lateral flexion and rotation to the same side. When standing on one leg, the lower part of erector spinae on the non-weight-bearing side works strongly to prevent the pelvis dropping. During walking the erector spinae contract alternately to steady the vertebral column on the pelvis.

Because the main mass of muscle is situated in the lumbar region, it (particularly longissimus thoracis) is responsible for maintaining the secondary lumbar curvature when sitting and standing.

Palpation

The two erector spinae can be felt and seen as columns of muscle either side of the lumbar spine, particularly during extension. Each muscle mass can also be felt contracting when alternately standing on one leg and then the other.

Interspinales (see Fig. 6.33b)

The interspinales are short, insignificant muscles of the back extending between *adjacent spinous processes*. They are best developed in the cervical and lumbar regions of the vertebral column where they consist of bundles of muscle fibres either side of the interspinous ligament. In the thoracic region they are poorly developed or absent.

Nerve supply

The interspinales muscles are supplied by the *posterior primary rami* of adjacent spinal nerves.

Action

The interspinales muscles can produce extension of the cervical and lumbar spine but have a more significant role in stabilizing the vertebral column during movement.

MUSCLES WHICH PRODUCE INSPIRATION

Diaphragm
Intercostals
Levatores costorum
Serratus posterior superior

In extreme respiratory distress other muscles, whose primary action is described elsewhere, may assist in increasing the thoracic dimensions in an attempt to draw more air into the lungs. These muscles are often referred to as the *accessory muscles of respiration*. They include serratus anterior, sternomastoid, the scalene muscles, subclavius, pectoralis minor and major. However, to use these muscles effectively their attachment to the ribs and sternum must be free to move with their other attachment becoming the fixed point. Details of these muscles are given in the sections on the upper limb or neck.

Diaphragm (see Fig. 6.34a)

The diaphragm is a musculotendinous sheet separating the thoracic and abdominal cavities. It consists of muscle fibres, attached around the thoracic outlet, which converge to a *central* trefoil-shaped *tendon*. The lumbar part of the diaphragm arises in part from two *crura* which attach to the anterolateral aspects of the *bodies* of the *lumbar vertebrae*: the larger *right crus* from the bodies and intervening discs of L1 to L3, the *left crus* from the bodies and disc of L1 and L2. The *aorta* passes into the abdomen behind the two crura as they cross one another, and in front of the body of T12. At this point the two crura are connected by a tendinous band, the median arcuate ligament. Fibres of the right crus generally pass towards the left, separating to surround the *oesophagus* before inserting into the central tendon. Fibres of the left crus may also pass behind the oesophageal opening, separating it from the aortic opening. From near the oesophageal opening, the suspensory ligament of the duodenum arises from the right crus to attach to the terminal part of the duodenum.

The remainder of the lumbar part of the diaphragm arises from the *medial* and *lateral arcuate ligaments* which are immediately lateral to the crura. The medial arcuate ligament is a thickening of the fascia covering psoas major and runs from the side of the body of L2 to the transverse process of L1. The lateral arcuate ligament is a thickening of the anterior layer of the thoracolumbar fascia covering quadratus lumborum and runs from the transverse process of L1 to the tip of the twelfth rib. Lateral to the arcuate ligaments the costal part of the diaphragm arises from the inner surface of the *lower six ribs* and their costal cartilages, interdigitating with transversus abdominis, to insert into the anterolateral part of the central tendon.

The most anterior sternal part of the diaphragm arises by two slips from the posterior surface of the *xiphoid process* of the sternum (see Fig. 6.27).

All the muscle fibres arch upwards and medially towards their insertion into the central tendon which is situated towards the front of the thorax. Consequently, the short anterior fibres and longer posterior fibres give the appearance of an inverted letter J when viewed from the side. When viewed from the front, two small domes or *cupolae* on either side of the central tendon can be seen, that on the right being at a slightly higher level than that on the left; the central part lies opposite the xiphisternal joint.

The upper surface of the diaphragm is covered with the parietal pleura, which lines the thoracic cavity. A potential space, the costodiaphragmatic recess, separates the parietal and visceral pleurae, the latter covering the lungs. The fibrous pericardium is firmly attached to the central tendon. The inferior surface of the diaphragm is lined by the parietal layer of peritoneum. This surface is related on the right side to the right lobe of the liver and right kidney, and on the left side to the liver, fundus of the stomach, and left kidney.

Several structures pass between the thorax and the abdomen, and they do so by either passing through or behind the diaphragm. The major tubular structures (inferior vena cava, oesophagus and aorta) do so by named openings; they may be accompanied by nerves and/or other vessels. The *caval opening* is in the central tendon just to the right of the midline, and transmits the inferior vena cava and branches of the right phrenic nerve. The opening is level with the lower border of T8, with the wall of the vena cava firmly adherent to its margin. Consequently, the inferior vena cava is constantly held open.

The *oesophageal opening*, at the level of T10, is to the left of the midline surrounded by fibres of the right crus. As well as the oesophagus, the trunks of the vagus nerves (now known as the gastric nerves) and the oesophageal branches of the left gastric vessels pass through this opening. The left phrenic nerve pierces the muscular part of the diaphragm near to the oesophageal opening in front of the left part of the central tendon.

The *aortic opening* lies behind the diaphragm, in front of T12, as the two crura cross each other. The aorta and thoracic duct pass in and out of the abdomen at this opening. The azygos vein is partly covered by the right crus. The greater and lesser splanchnic nerves pass through the crura as they enter the abdomen running to the coeliac ganglion.

Behind the medial and lateral arcuate ligaments pass the sympathetic trunk and subcostal nerve respectively. Anteriorly, between the sternal and costal attachments of the diaphragm, the superior epigastric artery passes to enter the rectus sheath and supply the upper part of rectus abdominis.

Nerve supply

The diaphragm is supplied with motor and sensory innervation by the *left* and *right phrenic nerves*, root value *C3,4* and *5*. Additional sensory fibres to the peripheral part of the diaphragm are supplied by the lower six intercostal (thoracic) nerves.

Action

The diaphragm is the major muscle of inspiration. Downward movement of the diaphragm, elevation of the ribs and forward movement of the sternum all increase the dimensions of the thorax and this then draws in air. From its resting position, sequential contraction of the diaphragm can be described in the following stages. Contraction of the peripheral muscular portion of the diaphragm against the fixed ribs flattens the two cupolae and pulls the central tendon down from the level of T8 to T9. Further descent is prevented by compression of the abdominal viscera which is prevented from bulging outwards by tone in the abdominal muscles and, to a smaller extent, tension on the pericardium. At this point the central tendon becomes the fixed point and further contraction of the muscle fibres causes movement of the ribs and sternum. The lower ribs are lifted upwards and outwards to increase the lateral diameter of the thorax whilst the upper ribs are raised to push the body of the sternum forwards and so increase the anteroposterior diameter. These movements of the ribs are known as 'bucket-handle' and 'pump-handle' respectively (see pp. 724, 725) and occur at the costovertebral, costotransverse, sternocostal and interchondral joints. In shallow respiration the descent of the diaphragm can be as little as 1.5 cm, whereas in deep inspiration it can be as much as 10 cm. This descent, together with movement of the ribs and sternum, produces a very efficient mechanism for drawing air into the lungs. From the position of full inspiration the diaphragm relaxes to control the rate of expiration produced by the elastic recoil of the lungs.

The diaphragm also plays an important role in increasing intra-abdominal pressure, where it resists upward movement of the abdominal contents when the abdominal muscles contract, to produce the expulsive acts (defaecation, vomiting, micturition and parturition). This action is also important in supporting the lumbar spine during lifting activities. It is likely that the compression of the oesophagus by the fibres of the right crus prevents regurgitation of food from the stomach.

The changes in pressure in the thoracic and abdominal cavities, caused by movement of the diaphragm will assist venous and lymphatic drainage from the abdomen to the thorax.

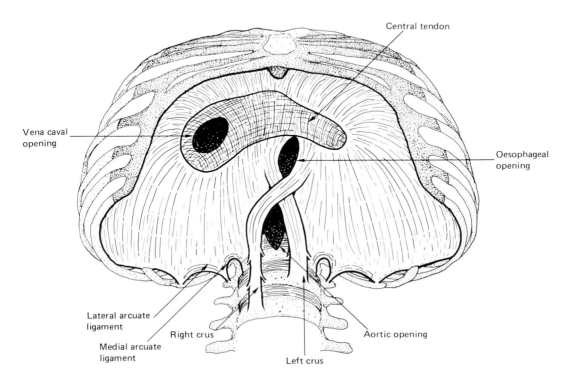

Fig. 6.34a The diaphragm, inferior view.
(Fig. 6.34b–d see p. 711.)

Palpation

The diaphragm is too deep to be directly palpable, but the effects of its contraction can be seen and felt. With the subject sitting and relaxed, the examiners flat hand should be placed over the subcostal angle. After full expiration as a breath is taken the abdominal wall can be felt pushing outwards. If the hands are now placed along the lower ribs these will be felt rising upwards and outwards at the same time as the sternum is being pushed forwards.

Frequently, accessory muscles of respiration are used during breathing. In many instances this leads to apical breathing, in which only the upper parts of the lungs are used. Instruction in the correct method of diaphragmatic breathing greatly increases the efficiency of breathing, and is essential in activities which require breathing control, such as singing.

Intercostal muscles (intercostales)
(Fig. 6.34d)

The intercostal group of muscles pass between adjacent ribs and are arranged in three layers. The region between the ribs in which the muscles are situated is known as the intercostal space.

The outer layer of muscle is the *external intercostal*. Its fibres pass obliquely downwards and forwards from the lower border of the rib above to the upper border of the rib below. It extends from the tubercles of the ribs posteriorly, becoming thinner anteriorly until it is replaced by, and is continuous with, the external intercostal membrane in the region of the costochondral junction. In the lower part of the thorax the fibres of the external intercostals blend with those of external oblique.

The middle layer of muscle is the *internal intercostal*, which extends from the lower border of the costal cartilage and costal groove of the rib above to the upper border of the rib below. It extends from the side of the sternum to the angle of the rib where it is replaced by the internal intercostal membrane. The muscle fibres pass obliquely downwards and backwards from the costal groove on the rib above to the upper border

of the rib below, being at 90° to those of the external intercostal (Fig. 6.34d). The muscle is thicker anteriorly than posteriorly.

The deepest muscle layer is the *innermost intercostal*, which although not complete, runs between the innermost surface of adjacent ribs. It is poorly developed in the upper intercostal spaces. The muscle fibres run in a similar direction to those of the internal intercostals but are separated from them by the intercostal nerve and vessels running in the neurovascular plane between the deep and intermediate muscle layers.

Nerve supply

The intercostals are supplied by the *anterior primary rami* of the *adjacent intercostal nerves* (thoracic). The skin over each intercostal space is supplied by the cutaneous branches of the same nerves.

Action

It is generally accepted that some of the external intercostals are active during inspiration causing elevation of the rib below towards the rib above. The precise role of the internal and innermost intercostals has not been fully established. However, it seems likely that their contraction resists the blowing in and out of the intercostal spaces during respiration and thus produce a more rigid cavity upon which the diaphragm can act. Marked caving in and bulging out of the intercostal spaces occurs when the intercostals are paralysed in quadriplegia. Action in the intercostals has been recorded during many movements involving the trunk. Again, it would appear that their role is one of stabilization of the chest wall.

Levatores costorum (Fig. 6.34b)

Levatores costorum is a small strong, triangular muscle, found between C7 and T11. Each of the twelve muscles of each side runs from the *tip* of the *transverse process* of the *vertebra* above to the *upper border* of the *rib* below, near its tubercle (Fig. 6.34b). The fibres fan out as they pass downwards and laterally.

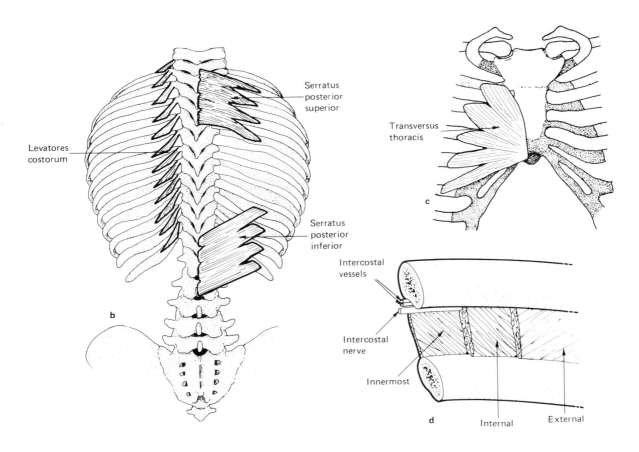

Fig. 6.34b–d   b = The left levatores costorum, and right serratus posterior superior and inferior muscles, posterior view; **c** = the left transversus thoracis muscle on the inner surface of the thoracic cage; **d** = the intercostal muscles, lateral view.

Nerve supply

Levatores costorum is supplied by the *anterior primary rami* of the *adjacent thoracic nerves. nerves*.

Action

These small muscles elevate the ribs during inspiration. However, their position enables them to also produce a slight degree of rotation and lateral flexion of the trunk.

Serratus posterior superior (Fig. 6.34b)

Serratus posterior superior is a thin, flat muscle lying in front of the rhomboids. It

arises from the lower part of the *ligamentum nuchae* and the *spinous processes* of *C7* to *T3*. The fibres pass downwards and laterally to attach lateral to the *angles* of the *second* to *fifth ribs* (Fig. 6.34b).

Nerve supply

Serratus posterior superior is supplied by the *anterior primary rami* of the *thoracic nerves T2* to *T6*.

Action

Their attachment to the ribs causes them to be elevated thus assisting inspiration.

MUSCLES WHICH PRODUCE EXPIRATION

External oblique (see pp. 694–696)
Internal oblique (see p. 696)
Transversus abdominis (see pp. 698–699)
Latissimus dorsi (see pp. 90–92)
Transversus thoracis
Subcostals
Serratus posterior inferior

The role of the abdominal muscles in forced expiration is considered on page 699.

Transversus thoracis (see Fig. 6.34c)

Transversus thoracis is found on the inner aspect of the anterior thoracic wall. It arises from the posterior surface of the *xiphoid process*, lower half of the *body* of the *sternum*, and *fourth* to *seventh costal cartilages*. The lower fibres pass horizontally while the upper ones pass upwards and laterally to attach to the *inner surface* of the *second* to *sixth costal cartilages* (see Fig. 6.34c).

Nerve supply

Transversus thoracis is supplied by the *anterior primary rami* of the *adjacent thoracic nerves*.

Action

Transversus thoracis pulls the costal cartilages articulating with the sternum downwards and so contributes to expiration.

Subcostals

The subcostal muscles are irregular slips extending across one or two intercostal spaces, attaching to the *inner surface* of the *rib* near the angle. They are best developed in the lower thoracic region where their fibres run in the same general direction as those of the innermost intercostal, with which they may be continuous.

Nerve supply

The subcostals are supplied by the *anterior primary rami* of the *adjacent thoracic nerves*.

Action

The subcostals depress the ribs and so aid expiration.

Serratus posterior inferior (see Fig. 6.34b)

Serratus posterior inferior lies deep to latissimus dorsi, arising from the *spinous processes* of *T11, T12, L1, L2* and their *supraspinous ligaments* via the thoracolumbar fascia. The muscle fibres run horizontally to attach to the *lower four ribs* at their angles.

Nerve supply

Serratus posterior inferior is supplied by the *anterior primary rami of T9, 10 and 11.*

Action

Serratus posterior inferior helps to pull the lower four ribs downwards and backwards and so may assist expiration.

FASCIAE OF THE TRUNK

Superficial fascia

The superficial fascia of the back is thick and contains a large amount of fat held within a meshwork of fibres, whereas at the front and sides of the trunk it contains a variable amount of fat. Laterally it is loosely connected to the skin, but in the midline, particularly in the neck, it holds the skin more firmly to the deep fascia. In the superficial fascia of the anterior abdominal wall fat is commonly deposited in middle age; in the upper part of the abdomen in males and the lower part in females.

As the superficial fascia of the trunk passes down towards the thigh it divides into two layers, between which lie the superficial vessels and nerves. It is continuous with the superficial fascia of the thigh. The deeper of these two layers is a thin elastic membrane, which in the lower part of the abdominal wall is loosely attached to the external oblique aponeurosis, and more firmly to the linea alba and symphysis pubis. In the lower abdomen this deeper membranous layer is a substitute for the deep fascia proper, which is very scant. This membranous layer passes superficial to the inguinal ligament to attach to the deep fascia of the thigh (fascia lata) some 2 cm distal and parallel to the inguinal ligament.

Deep fascia

The deep fascia over the anterior and lateral parts of the chest and trunk has no special features. It is relatively thin and elastic to allow both the thorax and abdomen to expand. In the lower part of the abdomen it may be replaced by the external oblique aponeurosis and membranous layer of the superficial fascia. It is attached superiorly to the clavicle and side of the sternum, and inferiorly to the iliac crest.

The back, however, is covered by a layer of deep fascia of variable thickness and strength. In the neck it is dense and strong, becoming relatively thin lower down. It covers and encloses the superficial muscles connecting the upper limb to the trunk. It is attached to the spines of the thoracic and lumbar vertebrae, the spine and acromion process of the scapula, the iliac crest and the back of the sacrum. Laterally it is conti-

nuous with the deep fascia of the axilla, the thorax and the abdomen; it also blends with the deep investing fascia of the arm.

Deep to the superficial muscles of the back is found an extremely strong layer of the deep fascia, the thoracolumbar fascia. However, it is really only well-developed in the lower thoracic, lumbar and sacral regions.

Thoracolumbar fascia (see Fig. 6.33c)

The thoracolumbar fascia consists of three separate layers. The *posterior layer*, which is superficial to erector spinae, is attached medially to the spinous processes of the thoracic, lumbar and sacral vertebrae and their supraspinous ligaments. This layer extends from the sacrum and iliac crest to attach to the angles of the ribs, lateral to iliocostalis; latissimus dorsi partly arises from the strong membranous part of this layer in the lower part of the back.

The *middle layer* of the fascia attaches medially to the tips of the lumbar transverse processes and to the intertransverse ligaments. It extends from the lower border of the twelfth rib and the lumbocostal ligament above, to the iliac crest and iliolumbar ligament below. It is sandwiched between erector spinae and quadratus lumborum, joining the posterior layer at the lateral border of erector spinae.

The *anterior layer* of the fascia lies anterior to quadratus lumborum, and attaches to the front of the lumbar transverse processes medially. Laterally it fuses with the middle layer at the lateral border of quadratus lumborum. It extends from the iliac crest and iliolumbar ligament below, to the lower border of the twelfth rib. Superiorly it is thickened between the twelfth rib and transverse process of L1 to form the lateral arcuate ligament. It is the thinnest of the three layers.

Laterally the single sheet of fascia so formed acts as the point of attachment for transversus abdominis and the internal oblique muscles.

In the lumbar region this thick sheet of fascia is important in filling the gap between the twelfth rib and the iliac crest. It acts as a protective membrane and is considered by some to function as a large ligament.

In the thoracic region the fascia is thinner, being sandwiched between erector spinae and latissimus dorsi, and the rhomboids.

SIMPLE ACTIVITIES OF THE TRUNK

As in previous sections, this short description is included in order to show how different muscle groups cooperate in producing a desired movement. The starting position will be described followed by the sequence of movements involved, together with the joints and muscles responsible, and end by an account of how these muscles work. These general principles can then be applied to any movement.

A sit-up

Starting position

The subject lies on his or her back.

Sequence of movements

The lumbar and thoracic spines are flexed by rectus abdominis and all four abdominal oblique muscles, all working concentrically. Once the trunk has been raised several centimetres from the ground, a position is reached where psoas major can work. With reversed origin and insertion, this muscle pulls on the lumbar spine increasing flexion of both the lumbar spine and the hips. As this occurs there is a tendency for psoas to lift the legs off the floor unless the feet are fixed. This action is opposed by synergic activity in the hamstrings which hold the legs against the floor but which unfortunately tend to flex the knees. This latter unwanted action is opposed by the quadriceps which keep the knees extended.

As the body returns to its lying position from sitting, involving extension of the hips and trunk, these same muscles now work eccentrically to control the downward movement which is produced by gravity. If the sit-up is performed with the hands behind the neck, and rotation of the trunk is also included, e.g. so that the right elbow moves to the left knee, then the left internal and right external oblique muscles will be working strongly to bring about the rotation.

Bending down to touch toes and straightening up again

Starting position

The subject stands in the anatomical position.

Sequence of movements

The thoracic and lumbar spines and the hip joints are all flexed. From the starting position there will be a brief concentric contraction of the trunk and hip flexors to move the trunk forwards; it is then that gravity takes over, being the force producing the movement. Following this, flexion of the trunk is controlled by the eccentric contraction of erector spinae and quadratus lumborum, and that of the hip by eccentric contraction of gluteus maximus and the hamstrings.

The movement of returning to the upright position, in which the trunk and hips are extended, is produced by concentric contraction of these same muscles.

Sideways bending

Starting position

The subject stands in full lateral flexion to the left.

Sequence of movements

The trunk is moved from full lateral flexion to the upright position by concentric contraction of the following muscles on the right side of the body: external and internal oblique, rectus abdominis, quadratus lumborum and erector spinae. Once the trunk has moved past the vertical into right lateral flexion, gravity continues the movement. Corresponding muscles on the left, working concentrically, now take over to control the movement.

Increasing and decreasing lumbar lordosis

Starting position

The subject stands with a deep lumbar lordosis.

Sequence of movements

The lumbar spine is moved from its extended to a more neutral position by rotation of the pelvis. The anterior part of the pelvis is raised by a concentric contraction of the two rectus abdominis muscles, while at the same time the posterior part is pulled downwards by the hamstrings and gluteus maximus, also working concentrically. The pelvis is returned to its neutral position by concentric contraction of the erector spinae and quadratus lumborum. If contraction of these muscles continues then the lordosis may be increased as the posterior part of the pelvis is raised.

MUSCLES OF THE PELVIC FLOOR

Levator ani
Coccygeus

Levator ani (Fig. 6.35)

The two levator ani muscles are broad but thin, stretching to form a gutter-like floor across the lower part of the pelvis, separating the pelvic cavity from the perineum. The two muscles unite in the midline but for most of their extent are separated by the prostate in the male and the urethra and vagina in the female. Each muscle arises in a continuous manner from the inner deep surface of the *pubic body* anteriorly, the *obturator membrane*, and the *pelvic surface* of the *ischial spine* posteriorly. From this extensive attachment the muscle fibres run backwards, downwards and medially towards the midline, inserting into the *perineal body*, the sides of the *anal canal* and the *anococcygeal ligament* between the anal canal and coccyx. Levator ani usually comprises at least two distinct parts: the *iliococcygeus* and the *pubococcygeus*.

The pubococcygeal part of levator ani is that part arising anterior to the obturator canal. The most anterior fibres pass backwards around either the prostate in the male or the vagina in the female to the perineal body. More posterior fibres pass to the prostate or vagina to loop around the upper part of the anal canal holding the anorectal junction towards the symphysis pubis. Some of these fibres fuse with the longitudinal muscle of the rectum and via a series of fibroelastic slips pass through the external anal sphincter to attach to the skin around the anus. The most posterior fibres of pubococcygeus insert into the anococcygeal ligament and sides of the coccyx.

Iliococcygeus, arising from the fascia over obturator internus, inserts into the anococcygeal ligament and sides of the coccyx. It is partly overlapped on its deep surface by the posterior part of pubococcygeus (Fig. 6.35)

Nerve supply

Levator ani has a dual nerve supply, from the *anterior rami* of *S3* and *S4*, and also by a branch from the perineal branch of the *pudendal nerve*, root value *S4*, which enters the muscle on its perineal surface.

Action

Levator ani, together with coccygeus, plays an important role in supporting the pelvic viscera, particularly in the female. It is constantly active.

Contraction of the two levator ani muscles has a constricting effect on the openings in the pelvic floor, either reflexly or voluntarily. For example, when intra-abdominal pressure is raised as in coughing, a reflex contraction of the two levator ani muscles closes the urethra and anus to prevent unwanted micturition or defaecation. This action becomes voluntary when these muscles, supplementing the appropriate sphincters, contract to resist an inconvenient urge to micturate or defaecate.

In the female, the position of levator ani surrounding the vagina, is important in supporting the uterus. It is here that the muscle may become excessively stretched during childbirth or surgically traumatized by episiotomy. This stretching may also adversely affect the action of levator ani on the anus and, more commonly, the urethra, leading to possible stress incontinence. Stress incontinence results in leakage of urine, and possibly faeces, whenever intra-abdominal pressure is raised. Active exercise is neccessary to regain normal tone of levator ani, and consequently pelvic floor exercises are taught to restore normal function. Unfortunately, these exercises can be difficult to teach and electrical stimulation may be necessary. It is possible to test and assess the power of contraction of levator ani by inserting the compressible bulb of a 'perineometer' into the vagina. Failing this the strength of contraction can be felt against a gloved finger placed in the vagina.

In males, the problems of stress incontinence are much less common but are sometimes seen following prostatectomy. Pelvic floor exercises are again necessary to restore the tone of levator ani.

Coccygeus (Fig. 6.35)

Coccygeus lies posterior to, but in the same plane as, levator ani. It is a flat triangular sheet of muscle and fibrous tissue stretching from the *spine* of the *ischium* to the margin of the *coccyx* and lower two parts of the *sacrum*. The more fibrous gluteal surface forms the *sacrospinous ligament*.

Nerve supply

Coccygeus is supplied by the *anterior primary rami of S4.*

Action

Forming the posterior part of the pelvic floor, coccygeus assists levator ani in its role in supporting the pelvic viscera and maintaining intra-abdominal pressure. It also pulls the coccyx forwards after it has been pushed backwards during defaecation or parturition.

Fig. 6.35 The muscles of the female pelvic floor (**a**) inferior view; (**b**) superior view.

Joints

JOINTS OF THE THORAX

Introduction

The bony components of the thorax articulate with one another in such a way as to provide a rigid, yet slightly mobile thoracic cage (Fig. 6.36). Posteriorly, adjacent thoracic vertebrae articulate with one another by both secondary cartilaginous and synovial joints. Anteriorly, the various parts of the sternum are joined by secondary cartilaginous joints, while laterally each rib is joined to its costal cartilage by a primary cartilaginous joint. However, it is the articulation of the rib with the vertebral column posteriorly and with the sternum anteriorly, either directly or indirectly, which provides the mobility necessary during respiration. By the action of muscles, the ribs are moved so as to change both the anteroposterior and transverse diameters of the thorax. The precise nature of rib movement differs in different regions of the thorax, being determined by the form of the articulating surfaces as well as their anterior articulations.

This section considers articulations within a rib (at the costochondral joint) and the sternum (at the manubriosternal and xiphisternal joints) before the articulations of the rib with the vertebrae and sternum. Articulations between vertebrae are considered on page 728.

Costochondral joint

This is a primary cartilaginous joint between the anterior roughened end of a rib and the lateral end of the costal cartilage (Fig. 6.36a). It is surrounded by perichondrium which is continuous with the periosteum of the rib. Movement at these joints is confined to a slight bending of the cartilage at the junction with the rib. The cartilage, however, may show some twisting during movement of the rib.

The costochondral joints can be stressed by applying continuous pressure to the anterior aspect of the chest wall, as in leaning against a table whilst sitting, or against a fence when standing. This continued stress often results in the joint becoming extremely painful and possibly swollen. Depending on its location, the pain may be misdiagnosed as a cardiac problem causing the patient further, unnecessary stress. The condition is known as *Tietze's syndrome/ chondritis*.

Sternal joints

Manubriosternal joint

This is a secondary cartilaginous joint between the inferior surface of the manubrium and the upper surface of the body of the sternum. The opposing surfaces of the two bones are covered with a thin layer of hyaline cartilage, between which there is a fibrocartilaginous disc, often hollow at its centre. The joint is strengthened in front and behind by longitudinal fibrous bands and the adjacent sternocostal ligaments (see Fig. 6.38). Occasionally the joint resembles a primary cartilaginous joint. In later life it may begin to ossify.

A small amount of movement (7°) is permitted at this joint. During inspiration there is a decrease in the obtuse angle between the manubrium and body of the sternum. There is also a very slight shift of the body upwards (Fig. 6.36b). This is particularly noticeable when pressure is applied to the front of the chest.

Xiphisternal joint

The xiphoid process is an irregularly shaped piece of cartilage joined to the body of the sternum by a secondary cartilaginous joint, supported all round by a fibrous capsule. The xiphoid ossifies late in life and with it the xiphisternal joint. While it remains cartilaginous, there is a certain amount of flexibility of the xiphoid process at the joint.

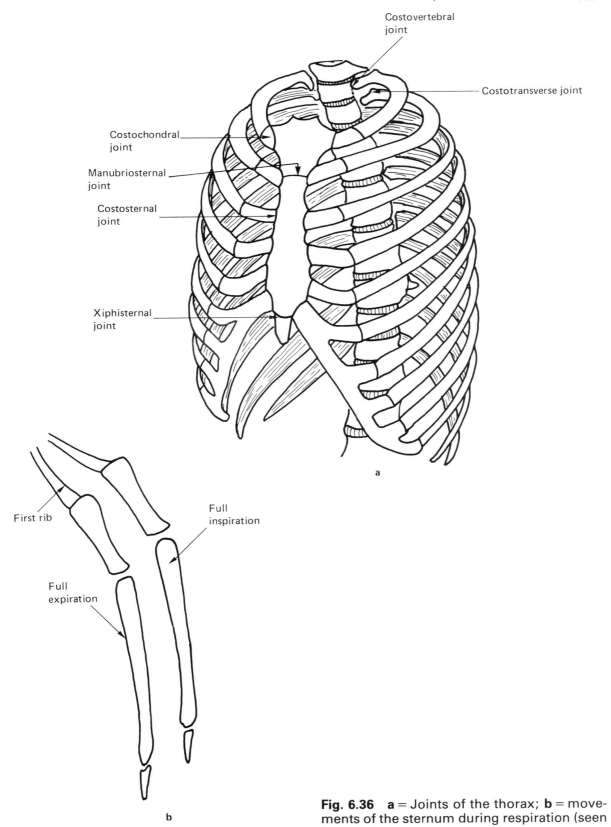

Fig. 6.36 **a** = Joints of the thorax; **b** = movements of the sternum during respiration (seen laterally).

ARTICULATIONS OF THE RIBS AND THEIR COSTAL CARTILAGES

Posteriorly the typical ribs articulate with the sides of the bodies of two adjacent vertebrae via costovertebral joints and with the transverse process of its corresponding vertebra by a costotransverse joint. Anteriorly, the costal cartilages articulate directly with the sternum by costosternal joints or with each other by interchondral joints. The first, tenth, eleventh and twelfth ribs articulate only with one vertebral body, in addition the eleventh and twelfth do not articulate with their transverse process or anteriorly with the preceding costal cartilage.

Costovertebral joints

Articular surfaces

These joints are between the convex articular facets on the head of the rib and a large concave demifacet on the upper border of the corresponding vertebra and a smaller demifacet on the lower border of the vertebra above (Fig. 6.37a). The crest on the head of the rib articulates with a slightly cupped depression on the posterolateral aspect of the intervening intervertebral disc. The joint surfaces are covered with hyaline cartilage.

Joint capsule

A loose fibrous capsule surrounds the joint. Anteriorly it is thickened to form the radiate ligament of the head of the rib (Fig. 6.37a), while posteriorly it blends with, and is reinforced by, the adjacent denticulation of the posterior longitudinal ligament. An intra-articular ligament completely divides the joint space, each part of which is lined by synovial membrane.

Ligaments (Fig. 6.37a)

Intra-articular ligament This short, thick band passes from the crest of the head of the rib to the intervertebral disc and divides the joint cavity into two parts.

Radiate ligament of the head of the rib

This ligament passes medially from the front of the head under cover of the lateral part of the anterior longitudinal ligament. It consists of three bands of fibres radiating upwards to the body of the vertebra above, horizontally to the front of the intervertebral disc and inferiorly to the body of the vertebra below.

Ribs one, ten, eleven and twelve articulate with their own vertebrae only. Consequently, there is a single joint cavity, no intra-articular ligament and a poorly developed radiate ligament.

Costotransverse joint

The costotransverse joints are present only between the tubercles of the upper ten ribs and the transverse processes of their corresponding vertebrae (Fig. 6.37b).

Articular surfaces

The joint is between the articular facet on the front of the transverse process, near its tip, and an oval facet on the posteromedial aspect of the tubercle of the rib. The shape of the joint surfaces changes from above downwards (Fig. 6.37c). In the upper costotransverse joints, the facet on the rib tubercle is convex and that on the transverse process is reciprocally concave. However, this arrangement disappears lower down, with that of the rib facet and of the transverse process becoming flatter. This change in shape is one of the factors responsible for the different movements of the upper and lower ribs during respiration.

Joint capsule

A thin, fibrous capsule completely surrounds the joint. It is strengthened posterolaterally by the lateral costotransverse ligament, which although in contact with the capsule does not fuse with it.

Ligaments

Lateral costotransverse ligament (Fig. 6.37b) The lateral costotransverse ligament is a stout band passing between the tip of the transverse process, beyond the

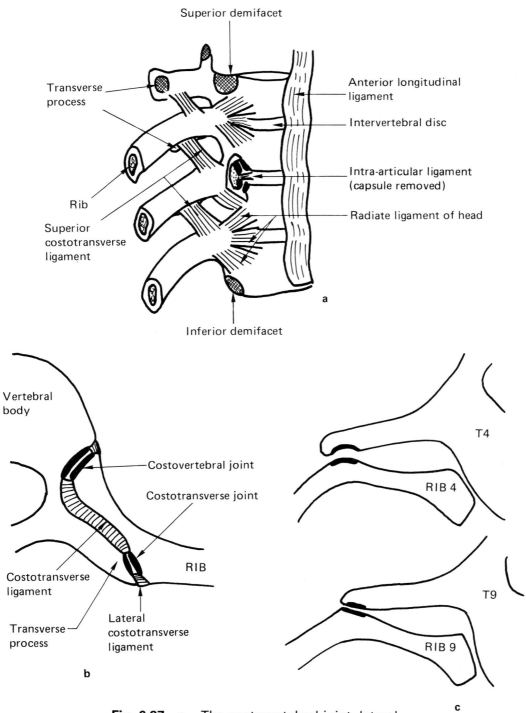

Fig. 6.37 **a** = The costovertebral joint, lateral view; **b** = the costovertebral and costotransverse joints, horizontal section; **c** = shape of the costotransverse joint surfaces at different vertebral levels.

articular facet, and the roughened lateral part of the costal tubercle.

Costotransverse ligament (see Fig. 6.37b) The costotransverse ligament consists of short fibres binding the rib to the transverse process. It passes from the back of the neck of the rib, to the front of the transverse process, medial to the facet.

Superior costotransverse ligament (see Fig. 6.37a) The superior costotransverse ligament consists of an anterior band which passes from the rib upwards and laterally, and a posterior band which passes upwards and medially from the rib. These bands attach to the undersurface of the transverse process of the vertebra above and are separated by the external intercostal muscle. The fibres of the anterior band blend laterally with the internal intercostal membrane.

Movements

The movements at costovertebral and costotransverse joints are dealt with together. Each movement is small, but because of the length of the rib it is considerably magnified anteriorly. As the rib is raised or lowered there is a twisting gliding movement at the costovertebral joints, which is limited by the radiate and intra-articular ligaments.

Concurrently, there is movement at the costotransverse joint. In the lower joints there is gliding and rotation of one plane surface against another. Higher up, because of the curved nature of the joint surfaces, the movement tends to be one of rotation only.

Sternocostal joint

These joints are between the medial end of the costal cartilage of the first to the seventh ribs and the sternum (Fig. 6.38). That between the first costal cartilage and the sternum is a primary cartilaginous joint (synchondrosis), the cartilage uniting with the socket on the upper part of the lateral border of the manubrium sterni. It prevents any appreciable movement between the two components, an important factor in respiration. The remaining joints are synovial, being surrounded by a fibrous capsule and supported anteriorly and posteriorly by radiate ligaments. The joint cavity for the second rib is usually divided into two by an intra-articular ligament. With increasing age, however, these cavities, except for that of the second costal cartilage, become obliterated.

The anterior radiate ligament passes from the medial end of the costal cartilage over the joint to the anterior aspect of the sternum, its highest fibres passing upwards and medially, the middle fibres horizontally, the lower fibres downwards and medially (Fig. 6.38). The fibres interlace with those from the joint above, below and from the opposite side, forming a criss-cross feltwork covering the front of the sternum; this fuses with tendinous fibres of pectoralis major. The posterior radiate ligament of these joints forms a similar pattern over the posterior aspect of the sternum.

The second sternocostal joint is similar to those above except that the anterior and posterior radiate ligaments attach above to the manubrium sterni, horizontally to the fibrocartilaginous pad between the manubrium and body, and below to the body of the sternum (Fig. 6.38). The intra-articular ligament of the joint restricts its movement.

These synovial joints allow the medial end of the cartilage to glide up and down in the sockets on the lateral border of the sternum when the rib is raised and lowered during respiration.

Interchondral joints

The interchondral joints are formed between the tips of the costal cartilages of the eighth, ninth and tenth ribs and the lower border of the cartilage above (Fig. 6.38). The eighth and ninth costal cartilage joints are synovial, while the tenth is more like a fibrous joint. Small synovial joints are also formed between the adjacent margins of the fifth to ninth costal cartilages.

All these synovial joints are surrounded by fibrous capsules, strengthened anteriorly and posteriorly by oblique ligaments. The joints provide a slight gliding movement which adds to the general mobility of the region. The interchondral joints can be strained, under similar circumstances as the

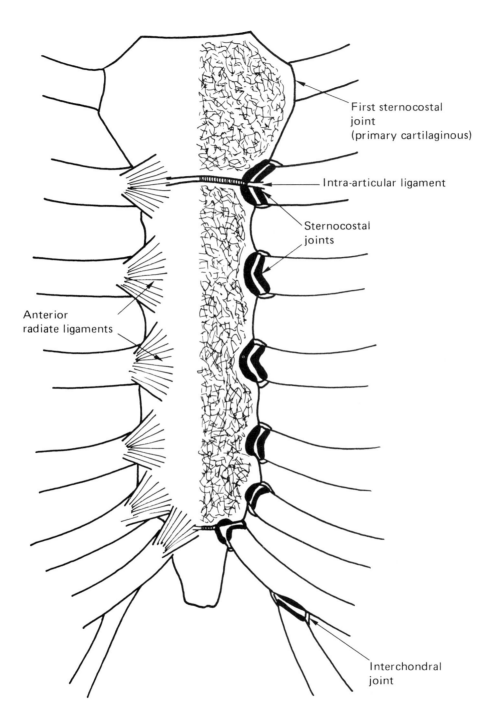

First sternocostal
joint
(primary cartilaginous)

Intra-articular ligament

Sternocostal
joints

Anterior
radiate ligaments

Interchondral
joint

Fig. 6.38   The sternocostal and interchondral
joints.

costochondral joints leading to pain radiating from the area of the costal cartilage.

Movements of the thoracic cage

During respiration the volume of the thoracic cage changes. This is achieved by movement of the diaphragm, and movements of the ribs and sternum. Consequently, the vertical, transverse and anteroposterior diameters of the thorax increase and decrease during inspiration and expiration respectively. Each rib and its costal cartilage can be considered as a lever which moves up and down. The precise nature of the movement depends on several factors including its length and whether it articulates directly with the sternum or not. The ribs that articulate with the sternum gradually increase in length from above down with their anterior ends lying at a lower level than the posterior ends (Fig. 6.39a). Although the eighth and ninth ribs are shorter, the nature of their attachment to the costal margin means that the transverse diameter of the thorax continues to increase as far as the ninth rib, after which it decreases.

The axis about which the rib moves passes along the neck of the rib through the costovertebral and costotransverse joints (Fig. 6.39b). It therefore runs backwards and laterally following the inclination of the transverse processes of the vertebrae. However, the inclination of the transverse processes is less oblique for the upper thoracic vertebrae, gradually increasing as the thoracic vertebral column is descended. Consequently, although the axis of movement relative to each rib remains unchanged, the resultant movement of the upper and lower ribs differs.

Movement of the upper ribs (second to fifth) about an axis along their necks causes their anterior ends to be raised, and with them the body of the sternum. Because the first costal cartilage is firmly attached to the manubrium, as well as the first rib being much shorter, movement of its anterior end is slight, the longer second to fifth ribs lifting the body of the sternum upwards and outwards causing a bending of the manubriosternal joint. In this way the anteroposterior diameter of the thorax is increased

(Fig. 6.39b). There is very little lateral movement of these ribs, except perhaps during the terminal part of a deep inspiration, because the axis of movement is less oblique than lower down. The movement has been likened to that of the handle of a pump when drawing water from a well: it is therefore often referred to as 'pump handle' movement.

Movement of ribs eight to ten result in an outward and upward movement of their anterior ends. This lateral excursion of the ribs and their costal cartilages causes a widening of the infrasternal angle and a consequent increase in the transverse diameter of the thorax (Fig. 6.39b). Because the shape of the costotransverse joints of these lower ribs is flat, there is both rotation and gliding of one bone against the other (see Fig. 6.37c). Consequently, it appears that the axis of movement of the ribs passes through the costovertebral and sternocostal or interchondral joints (Fig. 6.39b). The upward and outward movement of the shaft of the rib has been likened to raising the handle from the side of a bucket: it is therefore often referred to as 'bucket handle' movement.

The intermediate ribs six and seven show both pump handle and bucket handle types of movement. Ribs eleven and twelve are not attached anteriorly and thus have very little influence on increasing the transverse diameter of the thorax. They do, however, give attachment to some of the lower fibres of the diaphragm and, with the aid of quadratus lumborum, provide a firm attachment for the diaphragm.

During expiration the reverse movements of the ribs and sternum occur, with a decrease in both the anteroposterior and transverse diameters of the thorax.

As well as these respiratory movements, the ribs also move passively following changes in the thoracic part of the vertebral column. Flexion of the column causes the ribs to move closer together; extension causes them to move further apart; lateral bending causes those on the concave side to come together and those on the convex side to separate; lateral rotation causes a slight relative horizontal displacement of one rib with respect to its neighbour.

a

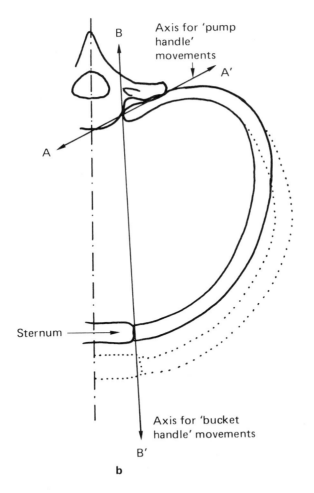

b

Fig. 6.39 **a** = The relationship of the anterior and posterior ends of a rib; **b** = the axes of movement of the ribs during respiration.

ARTICULATIONS OF THE VERTEBRAL COLUMN

Introduction

The function of the human vertebral column, together with a consideration of the adaptations that have occurred in assuming a bipedal posture and gait, have been mentioned in the introductory section to this chapter (see p. 618). Nevertheless it is worth restating that there are 24 free vertebrae in the vertebral column: the five fused sacral and four fused coccygeal vertebrae forming the sacrum and coccyx respectively have already been considered (see p. 314 and 316). Of the free vertebrae, seven are termed cervical, twelve thoracic and five lumbar (Fig. 6.40), there being specific differences between those of each region. Although in the adult the vertebrae are arranged to give specific curvatures to the column (Fig. 6.40), the joints between adjacent vertebrae have a common plan with the exception of the specialized joints between the atlas and the axis (C1 and C2 respectively).

Anteriorly the bodies of adjacent vertebrae are bound together principally by the strong and important intervertebral discs. The more posterior parts of the vertebral arches are united by synovial joints between the articular processes as well as by ligaments. The joints between the vertebral bodies and the vertebral arches are separated by the intervertebral foramina, through which the spinal nerves emerge. The upper and lower boundaries of these foramina are formed by the pedicles of the arches.

The joints between the vertebral bodies and the connections between the vertebral arches are considered separately. However, it must be remembered that functionally they are both concerned with the structure of the vertebral column, interacting to give it a controlled flexibility.

Joints between vertebral bodies

Between the second cervical and first sacral vertebrae the articulations of adjacent vertebral bodies are cartilaginous joints of the symphysis type. The intervening intervertebral discs are composed of fibrocartilage and are separated from the vertebral bodies by a thin layer of hyaline cartilage.

REGION

Line of
gravity

CERVICAL

THORACIC

LUMBAR

SACRUM

Centre of
gravity of
the body

Fig. 6.40   The adult vertebral column, lateral
view.

Intervertebral discs

There are at least 24 intervertebral discs interposed between the vertebral bodies: six in the cervical, twelve in the thoracic and five in the lumbar region, with one between the sacrum and coccyx. (Additional discs may be present between fused sacral segments.) The discs account for approximately one-quarter of the total length of the vertebral column, and are primarily responsible for the presence of the various curvatures. On descending the vertebral column, the discs increase in thickness, being thinnest in the upper cervical region and thickest in the lower lumbar (Fig. 6.41). In the upper thoracic region, however, the discs appear to narrow slightly. In the cervical region the disc is about two-fifths the height of the vertebrae, being approximately 5 mm thick. In the thoracic region the discs average 7 mm in thickness, so that they are one-quarter of the height of the vertebral bodies. The discs in the lumbar regions are at least 10 mm thick, and therefore constitute one-third of the height of the lumbar vertebral bodies. The relative height of the disc to the vertebral bodies is an important factor in determining the mobility of the vertebral column in each of the regions. Individual discs are not of uniform thickness, they are slightly wedge-shaped in conformity with the curvature of the vertebral column in the region of the disc. The curvatures in the cervical and lumbar regions are primarily due to the greater anterior thickness of the discs in these regions.

The overall shape of the discs also varies from one region to another, being similar to the shapes of the adjacent vertebral bodies. Consequently, in the cervical region they tend to be oval, in the thoracic region almost heart-shaped and in the lumbar region kidney-shaped.

It is of considerable practical importance to remember that the intervertebral disc forms one of the anterior boundaries of the intervertebral foramen, and as the spinal nerves pass through the foramina they lie directly behind the corresponding discs. In addition the discs also form part of the anterior wall of the vertebral canal. Consequently, any posterior bulging of the disc may compress the spinal cord as well as the individual spinal nerves.

Fig. 6.41 Relative sizes of the intervertebral discs in cervical, thoracic and lumbar regions.

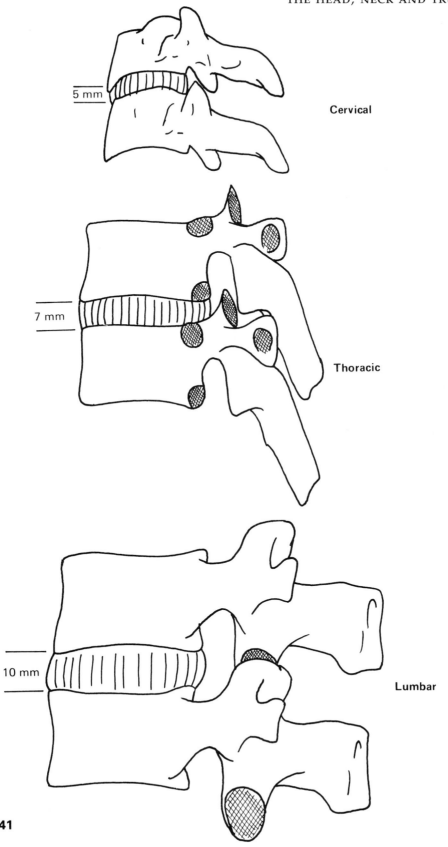

Cervical

Thoracic

Lumbar

Fig. 6.41

Structure

Each disc is structurally characterized by three integrated tissues: the central *nucleus pulposus*, the surrounding *annulus fibrosus* and the limiting *cartilage end plates* (Fig. 6.42a). It is anchored by the annulus fibrosus fibres and the cartilage end plate to the vertebral body.

Nucleus pulposus The nucleus pulposus is the soft, highly hydrophilic substance contained within the centre of the disc. There appears to be no clear division between the nucleus pulposus and the surrounding annulus fibrosus, the main difference being in the density of the fibres contained, with the nucleus having large extrafibrillar spaces containing glycosaminoglycans enabling it to retain fluid. The classical idea, therefore, of a distinct division between the two regions is not true. Furthermore, the concept of the nucleus being round or oval has not been supported by discography, which has shown the nucleus to be more rectangular in the infant and young child, and anything from oval to multilobed in the adult. (Discography is a radiographic technique which allows visualization of the disc in the living subject; clinically it enables the health of the disc to be assessed.) The region between the nucleus and the annulus fibrosus is an area of maximum metabolic activity. It is also sensitive to physical forces as well as to chemical and hormonal regulation of growth processes. Consequently, it may be considered to represent the growth plate of the nucleus pulposus, similar to epiphyseal growth plates, since the nucleus can only increase in size and remodel itself at the expense of the inner part of the annulus fibrosus. The annulus on the other hand increases in horizontal diameter by the addition of new lamellae at the periphery.

The position of the nucleus pulposus within the disc varies regionally, being more centrally located in cervical and thoracic discs and posteriorly located in lumbar discs (see Fig. 6.43). Nucleus position is related to certain aspects of function.

The nucleus pulposus consists of a three-dimensional lattice of collagen fibres in which is enmeshed a proteoglycan gel, which is responsible for the hydrophilic nature of the nucleus. Patchy loss and disappearance of this gel occurs with ageing, which lowers the water content until in advanced degeneration the collagen may be devoid of proteoglycan material (see Fig. 6.43b). This is the major change underlying dehydration of the nucleus in later life. In early life, a water content of 80–88% is usual, however from about the fourth decade onwards this decreases to 70%. These changes in the proteoglycans of the nucleus, both in terms of their loss and composition, change the mechanical behaviour of the disc.

Studies suggest that the nucleus pulposus represents the functional centre of the disc, and that systemic changes within it may be important as a primary cause of pathological change within the disc, and consequently of all pathological change within the intervertebral space. There is, however, the view that in disc degeneration the first morphological change to be observed is the separation of part of the cartilage end plate from the adjacent vertebral body.

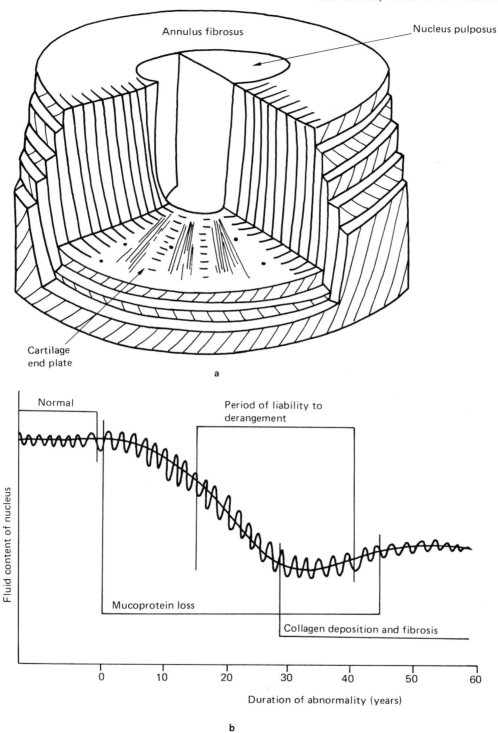

Fig. 6.42 a = Components of the intervertebral disc; **b** = fluid content of the nucleus pulposus and changes with trauma. (Adapted
from Hendry N. (1958). The hydration of the
nucleus pulposus and its relation to the intervertebral disc derangement. *Journal of Bone
and Joint Surgery*, **40B**, 132–44.)

Annulus fibrosus The annulus fibrosus consists of a series of annular bands whose geometry varies as a function of vertebral level and intradiscal region. Each annular band has a roughly parallel course, with its directional arrangement of fibres alternating in adjacent bands (see Fig. 6.42a), with the obliquity of these bands being greatest in the innermost layer of any given disc. The number of lamellae, as well as their size, thickness and obliquity of arrangement, show large variations for any given band within different parts of the same disc, for any particular vertebral level, and from individual to individual. Nevertheless, the average number of lamellae is 20 and in general their thickness varies from 200 μm to 400 μm, increasing from the inside out. Within each lamella the fibrils (0.1–0.2 μm) are uniformly arranged, but the orientation varies considerably from one lamella to another.

Each lamella is composed of obliquely arranged bundles of fibrils, varying in size between 10 and 50 μm. Except for thin fibrils, there is little interconnection between adjacent lamellar sheets, consequently there will be only limited restriction to movement during compression and tension. The question arises as to whether orientation of the collagen bundles is pre-determined or mechanically induced when movement occurs. There are considerable differences in fibril thickness and lamellar organization in the fetus. It is therefore able that mechanical phenomena, particularly torsion are responsible for the arrangement seen in the adult.

The density of the fibrocartilaginous lamellae is a function of the annular region, being more closely packed anteriorly and posteriorly than laterally. The lamella bands do not form complete rings but split intricately or merge to interlock with other bands. The posterolateral regions of the annulus appear to have marked irregularities and are much less orderly. With ageing, the annulus becomes weakest in these posterolateral regions, thereby predisposing to nucleus herniations.

Elastic fibres are present within both the annulus fibrosus and the nucleus pulposus. In the annulus they are circularly, obliquely and vertically arranged, although they are not distributed throughout it but are restricted to the lamellae at the vertebral epiphysis and disc interface. Interlamellar elastic fibres branch and join, freely imparting a dynamic flexibility to the tissue, with obvious implications for function. The intralamellar elastic fibres penetrate the bony vertebrae as perforating fibres.

Fig. 6.43 The relative position of the nucleus pulposus within the intervertebral disc, and its relation to the axis about which movements occur.

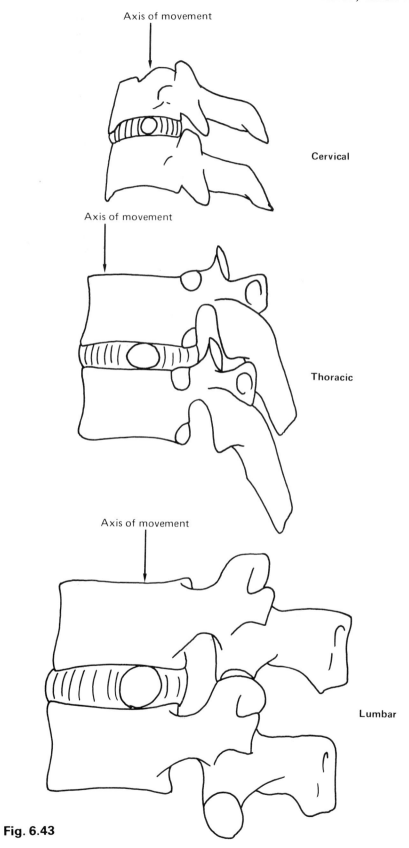

Axis of movement

Cervical

Axis of movement

Thoracic

Axis of movement

Lumbar

Fig. 6.43

Within the annulus the total collagen content is not constant, it decreases from the outer layers towards the nucleus. However, the proportion of type I to type II collagen (which are the principal collagen types within the disc) decreases from the outer layer of the annulus to the nucleus, and also varies from region to region (Fig. 6.44). In other words, type I collagen predominates in the outermost regions of the annulus and type II the innermost; the nucleus pulposus contains type II only. Since type I collagen is typical of tendons and type II of articular cartilage, where large transient compressive forces are generated, the tensile strength of the annulus is probably provided by type I collagen, while the compressive component involves type II. With increasing age, the collagen content of the annulus increases from the inside outwards in the disc, and also downwards from cervical to lumbar regions. However, the proportion of type II collagen does not appear to change with age.

The attachment of the annulus fibrosus to the vertebrae is fairly complicated. The annulus fibres pass over the edges of the cartilage end plate and anchor themselves to and beyond the compact bony zone that forms the outside of the vertebral rim, as well as to the margins of the adjacent vertebral body and its periosteum, thereby forming stable connections between adjacent vertebral bodies. These perforating fibres become interwoven with fibrillar lamellae of the bony trabeculae. This fibrillar anchorage is already present at birth even though the vertebral rim is not ossified.

Cartilage end plate   The hyaline cartilage end plate is found on each surface of the vertebral body and represents the anatomical limit of the disc (see Fig. 6.42a). It is approximately 1 mm thick at the periphery and decreases towards the centre. It can be considered to have three main functions: (1) it appears to protect the vertebral body from pressure atrophy; (2) it confines the annulus fibrosus and nucleus pulposus within their anatomical boundaries, and (3) it acts as a semipermeable membrane to facilitate fluid exchanges between the annulus, the nucleus and the vertebral body via osmotic action. Regarding this third function, however, studies suggest that only the central part of the end plate is permeable.

In the first few years of life, the end plates are loosely attached by a thin layer of calcified material to irregular, radiating, fan-shaped ridges and furrows on the vertebral bodies. Later, a thin layer of calcified material on the end plate firmly adheres to the trabeculae of the porous surface of the vertebral body. It is thought that the end plate is in contact with the bone marrow, through which it receives its nutrients.

In the early part of life, numerous minute vascular channels (cartilage canals) penetrate deeply into the end plate from the vertebral side. However, these channels disappear with increasing age so that by the third decade they are largely obliterated. Following the third decade, retrogressive changes occur in the end plate: it begins to show signs of ossification and there is an increase in calcification. It becomes more brittle, with fimbriation becoming more evident, ranging from thinning to complete destruction of the central end plate zone.

Fig. 6.44   Type and ratio of collagen found within the intervertebral disc. (Adapted from Taylor T. K. F., Ghosh P., Bushel G. R. (1981). The contribution of the intervertebral disc to scoliotic deformity. *Clinical Orthopaedics and Related Research*, **156**, 79–90.)

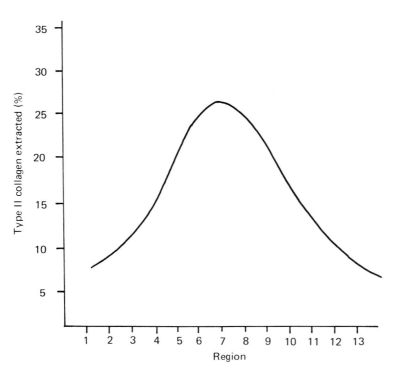

Fig. 6.44

Development The vertebral column begins to develop in the embryonic mesoderm at about 4 weeks, with individual vertebrae developing under the combined inductive influence of the notochord and neural tube. Ablation of either the notochord or the neural tube at an early stage results in failure of sclerotomal and myotomal segmentation. The segmental vessels of aortic origin pass between two sclerotomal zones, which then fuse to form the mesenchymal body of the vertebra (Fig. 6.45). The intervertebral disc therefore develops initially in an environment which contains few blood vessels and is surrounded by a perichondral layer, whose continuity foreshadows the longitudinal vertebral ligaments. The nerves come to lie close to the discs while the intersegmental arteries come to lie either side of the vertebral bodies.

In those regions where the notochord is surrounded by the developing vertebral body it degenerates and disappears. Between the vertebrae, however, the notochord expands as local aggregations of cells within a proteoglycan matrix, forming the gelatinous centre of the disc, the nucleus pulposus. The nucleus is later surrounded by the circularly arranged fibres of the annulus fibrosus, which are derived from the perichordal mesenchyme. The nucleus pulposus and annulus fibrosus constitute the embryonic intervertebral disc. Remnants of notochord may persist in any part of the axial skeleton and give rise to a chordoma. This slow-growing neoplasm occurs most frequently at the base of the skull and in the lumbosacral region.

Following the proliferation and later degeneration of the notochordal cells, there is a fibrocartilaginous invasion of the nucleus pulposus by the orginal mesenchymal intervertebral cells. This invasion occurs at about 6 months *in utero*.

Intervertebral discs lose their embryonic integrity with time, with structural changes occurring in the nucleus throughout adulthood. These normal processes are often considered to be signs of degeneration; they are merely stages in the natural evolution of connective tissue which is being subjected to mechanical stress in the form of combined shear and compression forces. The growth of the intervertebral disc and microscopic changes within it have been correlated with changes associated with weight-bearing in the erect posture. This may be a similar mechanism to that associated with the formation of subcutaneous connective tissue bursae, e.g. housemaid's knee, in which the alternate action of compression forces at right angles to the skin surface and tangential shear stresses induces thickening and delamination of the connective tissue.

Intervertebral discs are subjected to compression, torsion and shear. However, the shear stresses are constantly changing, being dependent on the instantaneous centre of rotation between adjacent vertebrae. Thus the mechanical delamination of the central region of the disc at different vertebral levels could be explained. In other words, the appearance of an irregular cavity in the central region is mechanically induced.

The cartilage end plate also appears to follow this mechanical induction. It is thought to be derived not from the vertebra but from the undifferentiated cells which accumulate in early embryonic life, and develops as an organized structure under mechanical influences. The annular epiphysis of the vertebral body develops in the marginal part of this thin plate of hyaline cartilage, and could therefore be considered to be either part of the disc, or part of the vertebral body.

a

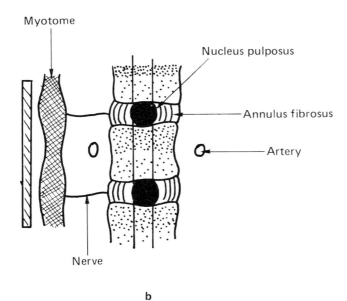

b

Fig. 6.45 Development of the intervertebral disc: **a** = frontal section at 4 weeks showing sclerotome cells around the notochord; **b** = frontal section, adult.

Uncovertebral joints

In the cervical region the intervertebral discs do not extend the full width of the vertebral bodies. Here are found small synovial joints between the lateral parts of adjacent vertebral bodies (Fig. 6.46). The lateral edges of the inferior vertebrae are lipped and fit the bevelled edges of the vertebra above. Consequently, the cartilage-covered superior and inferior articular surfaces face inferolaterally and superomedially respectively. Each joint is surrounded by a capsule which is continuous medially with the intervertebral disc.

Movement at these joints is intimately associated with movements of the cervical spine as a whole, and so, to a certain extent, they help to control these movements, and thus stabilize the neck.

The so-called uncovertebral joints lie anterior to the intervertebral foramen. They can, and do, undergo arthritic changes, which can affect the relevant spinal nerves as well as restrict movement between adjacent vertebrae.

Ligaments

The bodies of the vertebrae are further held together by longitudinal ligaments which extend the whole length of the vertebral column.

Anterior longitudinal ligament The anterior longitudinal ligament supports the anterior aspect of the vertebral column, including the intervertebral discs (Fig. 6.47). It is between 1 and 2 mm thick and consists of three dense layers of collagen fibres: those in the superficial layers extend across several vertebrae, while the deepest fibres join adjacent bones. Superiorly, it has a narrow attachment to the anterior tubercle of the atlas. However, as it descends it becomes wider, terminating by spreading over the pelvic surface of the upper part of the sacrum. In the lumbar region the anterior longitudinal ligament is between 20 and 25 mm wide, giving it a cross-sectional area in this region of between 20 and 50 mm^2.

Above the level of the atlas, the anterior longitudinal ligament is continuous with the anterior atlanto-occipital membrane (see p. 748).

Posterior longitudinal ligament The posterior longitudinal ligament provides the posterior support to the vertebral bodies and is part of the anterior wall of the vertebral canal. It is betweeen 1 and 1.4 mm thick, being composed of two dense layers of collagen fibres: again the more superficial fibres cross several vertebrae, while the deeper ones pass only from one vertebra to the next. The posterior longitudinal ligament is broader above than below.

Unlike the anterior longitudinal ligament the posterior is attached only to the intervertebral discs and the adjacent margins of the vertebral bodies (Fig. 6.47); opposite the middle of each vertebra it is separated from the bone by an interval into which the basivertebral vein passes from the vertebral body. As the ligament narrows in the thoracic and lumbar regions its edges appear serrated (Fig. 6.47). In the lower thoracic and lumbar regions the posterior longitudinal ligament is between 11 and 15 mm wide at the level of the intervertebral disc, whereas at the level of the vertebral body it is only 6 to 8 mm wide. This gives a cross-sectional area for the ligament of between 3 and 11 mm^2 in the lumbar region, which is considerably less than that of the anterior longitudinal ligament. It extends from the posterior surface of the first sacral segment to the back of the body of the second cervical vertebra, where it becomes continuous with the tectorial membrane (see p. 746).

The posterior longitudinal ligament is generally not considered to be as strong as the anterior ligament.

a

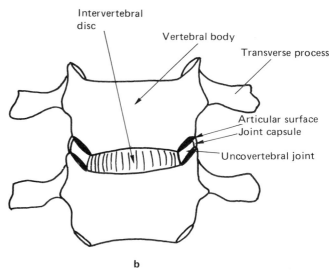

b

Fig. 6.46 **a** = X-ray of the cervical spine showing the uncovertebral joints; **b** = details of the uncovertebral joints.

Fig. 6.47 The anterior and posterior longitudinal ligaments: **a** = lateral view; **b** = posterior view.

a

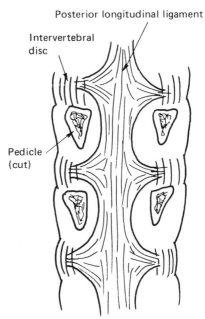

b

Joints between vertebral arches

The vertebral arches are united by synovial joints between their articular processes, as well as by ligaments which pass between the laminae, transverse processes and vertebral spines. In the cervical region, the zygapophyseal joints are behind the transverse processes and form a pillar of bone which is weight-bearing (Fig. 6.48a). In the thoracic region, these joints lie in front of the transverse process, while in the lumbar region they again lie behind them (Fig. 6.48a). Anterior to the zygapophyseal joints in all regions are the intervertebral foramina. Arthritic changes in these joints may give rise to the formation of bony projections (osteophytes) which may press onto the spinal nerve within the foramen.

Zygapophyseal joints

Articular surfaces

Although these synovial joints are of the plane variety, the shape and orientation of the joint surfaces on the articular processes vary in the different regions of the vertebral column (Fig. 6.48).

In the cervical region the articular processes form prominent lateral projections arising from the junction of the pedicles and laminae. They carry flat oval articular surfaces which lie in an oblique plane. The superior facets face upwards, backwards and slightly medially, while the inferior facets face downwards, forwards and slightly laterally (Fig. 6.48). The obliquity of the plane of these joints increases slightly from above downwards.

In the thoracic region the articular processes are thin and more or less triangular, and project almost vertically. The articular surface on the superior processes faces mainly backwards but also slightly upwards and laterally, so that the surface lies on the circumference of a circle whose centre is in the anterior part of the vertebral body (Fig. 6.48a). The inferior processes also have a cir-

cumferential arrangement so that their articular surfaces are directed forwards and slightly downwards and medially. They do not project very far below the laminae.

The lumbar articular processes are strong and have a marked upward and downward projection (Fig. 6.48). The articular surfaces are reciprocally curved in a horizontal plane but virtually straight in a vertical plane. The surfaces on the superior processes are concave and face medially and backwards, while those on the inferior processes are convex, being directed forwards and laterally.

All of the articular surfaces, whether in the cervical, thoracic or lumbar region are covered with hyaline cartilage. The shape and orientation of the articular processes play an important part in determining the type of movement possible within each of the vertebral regions. In the cervical region they are arranged to permit movement in all directions, i.e. flexion, extension, lateral bending and rotation. Those of the thoracic region favour lateral bending and rotation, while in the lumbar region the articular surfaces facilitate flexion, extension and lateral bending. An account of vertebral column movements is given in greater detail on page 762.

Joint capsule and synovial membrane

Each joint is surrounded by a thin fibrous capsule which attaches to the margins of the articular surfaces. The joint capsule is lax, particularly in the cervical region, to facilitate gliding movements between the two bones. Synovial membrane lines the capsule and also attaches to the margins of the articular surfaces.

Accessory ligaments

While there are no ligaments or thickenings associated directly with the joint capsule, a number of accessory ligaments exist which help to stabilize the vertebral arches.

Cervical

Thoracic

Lumbar

a   b

Fig. 6.48 The orientation of the articular facets of the zygapophyseal joints in the cervical, thoracic and lumbar regions of the vertebral column: **a** = superior view; **b** = lateral view.

Ligamentum flavum   The ligamentum flavum passes between the laminae of adjacent vertebrae (Fig. 6.49). Its yellowish appearance is due to the presence of a large amount of elastic tissue within it. It is, in fact, the only true elastic ligament. In each intervertebral interval there are two ligaments, a right and a left. Each is attached to the front of the lower border of the lamina above and passes downwards and backwards to the back of the upper border of the lamina below. The medial borders of the two ligaments meet at the root of the spine, otherwise they are separated by a narrow cleft through which pass veins connecting the internal and external vertebral venous plexuses. Laterally the ligaments extend as far as the joint capsules of the zygapophyseal joints, although they do not blend with them.

Studies in non-human primates have shown that the ligamentum flavum has a cross-sectional area greater than that of the anterior longitudinal ligament. There is no reason to suggest that the same is not true in humans, where they assist the postvertebral muscles in maintaining the upright posture, as well as helping to return the trunk to this position following flexion. Because of their elasticity the ligamenta flava permit separation of the laminae during flexion. This same property prevents them forming folds when the vertebral column returns to the upright position: such folds, if they were present, might become caught between the laminae or press upon the dura mater.

Supraspinous ligament   The supraspinous ligament is a band of longitudinal fibres running over and connecting the tips of the spinous processes (Fig. 6.49). It is continuous with the posterior edge of the interspinous ligament. The deeper, shorter fibres of the ligament connect adjacent spines, while the more superficial and longer fibres extend over three or four spines. In the cervical region it merges with, and to a large extent becomes replaced by, the ligamentum nuchae.

Ligamentum nuchae   The ligamentum nuchae is a triangular, midline, fibroelastic septum extending upwards from the spine of the seventh cervical vertebra to attach to the external occipital protuberance and crest. The deep part of the ligament attaches to the posterior tubercle of the atlas and the spines of all cervical vertebrae (see Fig. 6.55a). In humans the ligamentum nuchae is a rudiment of the well-developed elastic ligament seen in quadrupeds, in which it assists in holding the head erect. Its principal role in humans is perhaps in providing muscle attachments without limiting extension of the neck, as would long cervical spinous processes.

Interspinous ligaments   The interspinous ligaments are thin, membranous, relatively weak bands which pass between and unite adjacent vertebral spines (Fig. 6.49). At cervical levels they are insignificant, but at lumbar levels they are longer and stronger.

Intertransverse ligaments   The intertransverse ligaments are generally insignificant bands connecting adjacent transverse processes. They tend to be absent at cervical levels and really only become obvious in the lumbar region. In the upper part of the vertebral column they are often replaced by intertransverse muscles.

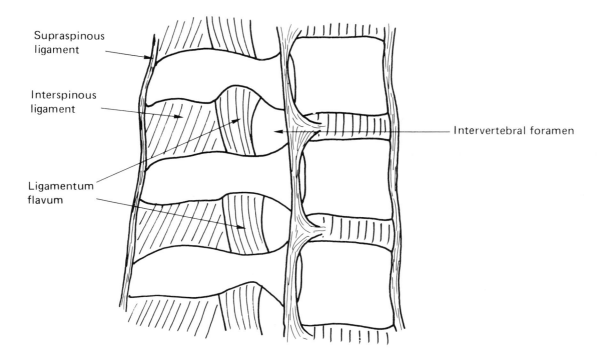

Supraspinous ligament

Interspinous ligament

Ligamentum flavum

Intervertebral foramen

Fig. 6.49 Ligaments accessory to the zygapo-physeal joints.

Atlantoaxial articulations

The joints between the atlas and axis are of two types: bilateral synovial joints between the surfaces of their articular processes, and two median synovial joints formed by the articulation of the dens with the anterior arch and the transverse ligament of the atlas. The median joints are supported by a number of accessory ligaments.

Lateral atlantoaxial joints

Articular surfaces

These joints are between the articular surfaces on the superior articular processes of the axis and those on the inferior lateral masses of the atlas (Fig. 6.50a). The articular surface on the axis is oval with its long axis running from antero-supero-medial to postero-infero-lateral, so that it is inclined obliquely laterally and downwards (Fig. 6.50b). The articular surface is slightly convex about both axes of the oval, with the convexity being greater about its short axis. The atlantal articular surface is also oval with corresponding long and short axes, however it is much flatter showing only a slight concavity if any. Occasionally, this surface may show a slight convexity. Both articular surfaces are covered with hyaline cartilage.

Joint capsule and synovial membrane

Each of the joints is enclosed in a loose fibrous capsule, lined by synovial membrane, which attaches to the margins of the articular surfaces.

Ligaments

Accessory atlantoaxial ligament The accessory atlantoaxial ligament passes obliquely downwards and medially from the back of the lateral mass of the atlas to the back of the body of the axis. In its course it runs in direct contact with the posterior aspect of the joint capsule.

Relations

A membranous expansion from each side of the anterior longitudinal ligament, near its attachment to the anterior tubercle of the atlas, passes to the front of the body of the axis. Posteriorly, bridging the gap between the arch of the atlas and that of the axis is a membrane which is in series with the ligamentum flavum attaching to the vertebral arches of lower levels. The second cervical nerve pierces this membrane and passes behind the lateral atlantoaxial joint, which suggests that these joints are of different morphological origin than the joints between the articular processes of lower vertebrae. Because these joints have the same relationship to the nerve as do the uncovertebral joints, they may be considered to be homologous to them, although they are of course much more specialized.

a

Articular
surfaces of
axis

b

Fig. 6.50 **a** = X-ray of the cervical spine showing the lateral atlantoaxial joint; **b** = articular
surfaces of the axis.

Median atlantoaxial joints

Articular surfaces

The articulation is between a more or less rectangular facet on the front of the dens, which is convex both vertically and transversely, and a reciprocally curved oval facet on the inner aspect of the arch of the atlas (Fig. 6.51). Both of these surfaces are covered with hyaline cartilage.

On the posterior surface of the dens is a further hyaline cartilage-covered surface, concave superoinferiorly and convex transversely, which articulates with the anterior fibrocartilaginous surface of the transverse ligament of the atlas (Fig. 6.51).

Joint capsule and synovial membrane

Each of the median joints is enclosed by a thin fibrous capsule, lined by synovial membrane. Of the joint cavities so-formed, that between the dens and the transverse ligament is the larger.

Ligaments

Transverse ligament of the atlas The transverse ligament of the atlas is a thick strong band arching behind the dens and attaching to a small tubercle on the medial side of each lateral mass of the atlas (Fig. 6.51a). From the middle of the ligament, a small band of longitudinal fibres ascends to attach to the anterior edge of the foramen magnum: a further band of fibres passes downwards to attach to the back of the body of the axis. These two longitudinal bands, together with the transverse ligament constitute the cruciform ligament of the atlas.

Accessory ligaments/membranes

A number of accessory ligaments are associated with the median atlantoaxial joints, which unite the axis with the occipital bone. They therefore serve to increase the stability of the suboccipital region.

Tectorial membrane The tectorial membrane is a broad sheet continuous with the posterior longitudinal ligament, extending from the back of the body of the axis to the occipital bone within the anterior edge of the foramen magnum as far laterally as the hypoglossal canals (Fig. 6.51b). It covers the posterior aspect of the dens, cruciform and alar ligaments, there occasionally being a small synovial bursa between the membrane and the median part of the transverse ligament of the atlas. The lateral parts of the membrane blend with and overlie the accessory atlantoaxial ligament.

As the membrane approaches the foramen magnum it becomes closely applied to and eventually blends with the spinal dura mater.

Alar ligaments The alar ligaments pass obliquely upwards and laterally from each side of the apex of the dens to the medial side of the respective occipital condyle. Each ligament is a short, strong, rounded band (Fig. 6.51b).

Apical ligament of the dens The apical ligament is a slender band lying immediately in front of the upper longitudinal band of the cruciform ligament (Fig. 6.51b). It stretches from the apex of the dens to the anterior edge of the foramen magnum, lying between the diverging alar ligaments.

Fig. 6.51 a = Articular surfaces of median atlantoaxial joint; **b** = ligaments associated with the joint.

Atlanto-occipital joint

Each of the atlanto-occipital articulations is a synovial joint between the occipital condyle and the facet on the upper surface of the lateral mass of the atlas (Fig. 6.52a). The two joints are symmetrical and can be considered as a single ellipsoid joint because functionally they act together, their movements being mechanically linked.

Articular surfaces

The oval articular facets on the atlas are concave about both their long and short axes. Occasionally, these facets may be narrowed in their middle part, or even divided into two separate facets. The long axis of the oval runs obliquely from posterolateral to anteromedial, with that of each side converging to meet in the midline in front of the anterior arch of the atlas (Fig. 6.52a).

The articular surfaces of the occipital condyles are reciprocally curved to those on the atlas, i.e. they are elongated and convex, converging anteriorly. Both articular surfaces are covered with hyaline cartilage.

Joint capsule and synovial membrane

Each of the joints is enclosed in a thin, loose fibrous capsule which attaches to the margins of the articular surfaces and is lined with synovial membrane.

Ligaments/membranes

To a large extent the ligaments and membranes passing between the axis and the occipital bone will confer some stability on the atlanto-occipital joints. However, two membranes connect the arches of the atlas with the occipital bone.

Anterior atlanto-occipital membrane The anterior atlanto-occipital membrane passes between the anterior arch of the atlas to just in front of the anterior margin of the foramen magnum on the base of the skull (Fig. 6.52b). It consists of densely woven fibres, and is thickened in its central portion by an upward prolongation of fibres from the anterior longitudinal ligament. Its lateral margins blend with anteromedial part of the joint capsule.

Posterior atlanto-occipital membrane The posterior atlanto-occipital membrane is attached above to the posterior margin of the foramen magnum, and below to the upper border of the posterior arch of the atlas (Fig. 6.52b). It reaches and blends with the posteromedial aspect of the joint capsule. In the lateral part of its attachment to the atlas, the membrane arches over the vertebral artery and the first cervical nerve as they cross this part of the posterior arch. This lower arched part of the membrane is thickened and may become ossified. (It should be noted that the first cervical nerve passes behind the atlanto-occipital joint).

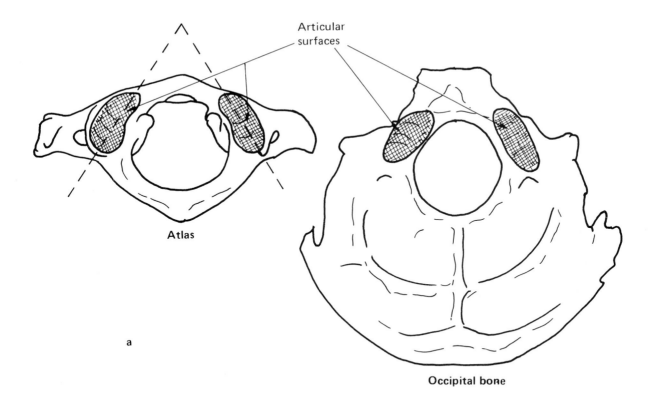

Articular surfaces

Atlas

Occipital bone

a

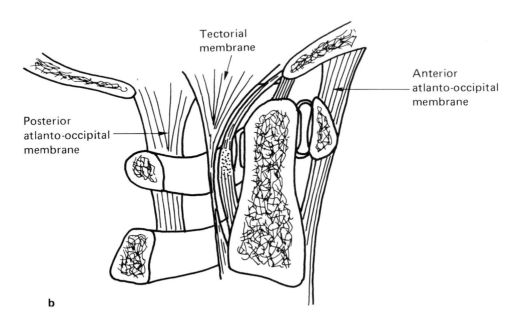

Tectorial membrane

Posterior atlanto-occipital membrane

Anterior atlanto-occipital membrane

b

Fig. 6.52   a = Articular surfaces of the atlanto-occipital joint; **b** = sagittal section to show the ligaments and the median atlantoaxial joint.

Blood and nerve supply

The vertebral column receives its arterial supply segmentally from branches of vessels which lie adjacent to it. In the cervical region these are from the vertebral and ascending cervical arteries; in the thoracic region they are from the costocervical and posterior intercostal arteries; in the lumbar region from the lumbar and iliolumbar arteries, and in the pelvis from the lateral sacral arteries. All of these branches anastomose with and reinforce the anterior and posterior spinal arteries (see p. 853) supplying the spinal cord.

As the branches from all of the above-named arteries pass around the middle of the vertebral body, towards the intervertebral foramen, they give branches to it. Microradiographic studies have shown there to be extensive horizontal and vertical anastomoses between these segmental vessels (Fig. 6.53a).

It is interesting to note that the blood vessels which surrounded the intervertebral disc during the early part of its development subsequently disappear leaving an essentially avascular structure. Except perhaps for its most peripheral part, which receives a supply from adjacent blood vessels, mature discs are supported by diffusion through the spongy bone of the adjacent vertebral surfaces. Consequently, the blood supply to the vertebral body, as well as its possible disruption, is extremely important.

The blood supply to the vertebral body appears to be zoned (Fig. 6.53b). That part of the body immediately adjacent to the disc is a relatively avascular region, with the more central regions being more vascular. However, this central region can be subdivided into that part supplied by the tortuous nutrient artery and that by the metaphyseal arteries. The peripheral region of the vertebral body is supplied by short, straight peripheral arteries. Diffusion of oxygen and nutrients for disc metabolism is also probably zoned because of the arrangement of the lamellae of the annulus fibrosus. Fluid trapped between lamellae is channelled in a vertical plane. Frequent movement of the lamellae probably speeds up diffusion. One of the consequences of ageing is the gradual furring up of arteries, resulting in a reduced, and eventually obliterated, blood flow. The arteries which are affected early on are those which have a tortuous course. As far as the vertebral bodies are concerned, the nutrient and metaphyseal arteries are therefore probably the first to suffer. With increasing age, the peripheral arteries apparently become more numerous, so that the outer sleeve of the vertebral body may get a relatively better blood supply than the central region. Disc degeneration and desiccation has been observed to appear at the centre of the disc earlier than at the periphery. Indeed, the periphery may remain healthy and capable of repair long after disintegration and extrusion of the central part of the disc.

Although disc degeneration and low back pain, due to disc hypoxia and starvation (as a secondary effect of reduced blood supply) is an attractive theory, it is difficult to prove. Nevertheless, symptomatic discs differ from normal in their pH and lactic acid concentrations, suggesting that these biochemical changes are due to anoxic respiration of the disc.

Where the segmental arterial supply to the vertebral column is reduced, e.g. by the natural calibre of the vessels, or jeopardised, e.g. by compression of the vessels, then it might be expected that the intervertebral discs adjacent to this vertebra would be liable to degenerative change at an earlier age than elsewhere. One such region is the lower lumbar where the fifth pair of lumbar arteries are small, and may be subjected to compression by a bulging disc. Consequently, the intervertebral discs either side of the fifth lumbar vertebra might be expected to have reduced nutrition and oxygenation. Ninety-five per cent of disc lesions in one published study* involved one or both discs either side of L5. Although the evidence is circumstantial, reduced blood supply to the vertebrae and consequently to the disc are strongly implicated in disc pathology.

*Weinstein P. R. (1982). Anatomy of the lumbar spine. In *Lumbar Disc Disease.* (Hardy R. W., ed.) pp. 5–15. New York: Raven Press.

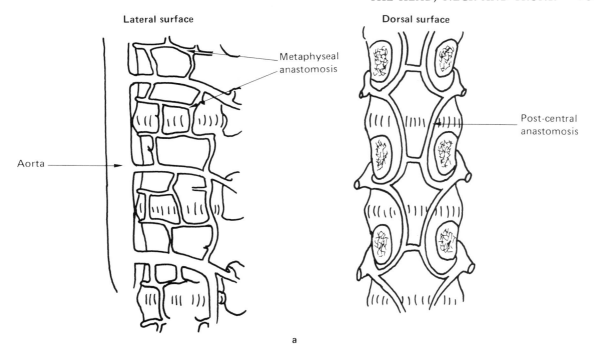

Lateral surface

Dorsal surface

Metaphyseal anastomosis

Aorta

Post-central anastomosis

a

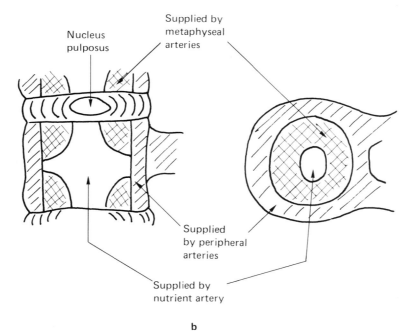

Nucleus pulposus

Supplied by metaphyseal arteries

Supplied by peripheral arteries

Supplied by nutrient artery

b

Fig. 6.53   **a** = Anastomoses between the lumbar arteries and their branches; **b** = zoning of the blood supply to the intervertebral disc. (Adapted from Ratcliffe J. F. (1980). The arterial anatomy of the adult human lumbar vertebral body: a microarteriographic study. *Journal of Anatomy*, **131**, 57–79.)

The veins of the vertebral column form complex, freely communicating plexuses extending the whole length of the column, both inside and out (Fig. 6.54). The plexuses are drained by a series of intervertebral veins which join the vertebral veins in the neck, the posterior intercostal veins in the chest, lumbar veins in the lower back and lateral sacral veins in the pelvis.

The internal vertebral plexuses form a continuous network between the spinal dura and the walls of the vertebral canal (Fig. 6.54b). The two anterior channels lie either side of the posterior longitudinal ligament, anastomosing across the midline, in front of the ligament, and receiving the basivertebral vein (Fig. 6.54b). They communicate above with the basilar and occipital sinuses and the sigmoid sinus within the skull. The posterior internal plexuses lie on the inner surfaces of the laminae and ligamenta flava. Again they anastomose across the midline, with some vessels emerging to join the posterior external plexus by passing between the free medial edges of the ligamenta flava. This latter connection may provide a venous pump mechanism as the vessels become squeezed by the ligamenta flava during movements of the column. The main means of communication between the internal and external plexus, however, is via the intervertebral veins which pass through the intervertebral foramina.

The external plexuses are found along the front of the vertebral column, and around the spinous, articular and transverse processes of the vertebrae.

While the precise arrangement of the venous plexuses associated with the vertebral column may not be of interest per se, it has to be remembered that they form a system of great blood-carrying capacity which extends, with few if any valves, from the pelvis to the cranium, communicating at all levels with the major venous systems of the abdomen, chest, head and neck. This complex venous network almost certainly plays a significant role in the transfer of metastatic cancer cells to widely separated parts of the body under the influence of differences in venous pressure. Indeed, secondary metastases associated with cancer of the breast or of the prostate invariably involve the vertebrae.

The innervation of the intervertebral disc and the existence of nervous tissue within related structures. e.g. ligaments, is of considerable clinical importance. The sinuvertebral nerve is a recurrent nerve of the vertebral canal which supplies the fibrous connective tissue of the spinal canal, i.e. the posterior longitudinal ligament and the periosteum, together with the venous sinuses and the spinal dura. In many respects the sinuvertebral nerve may be considered equivalent to the recurrent meningeal branch of a cranial nerve. It has been described as having a dual origin; one from the spinal nerve and the other from the sympathetic system. The spinal part arises just distal to the dorsal root ganglion and re-enters the spinal canal to reach the midline, giving branches directly towards the discs above and below each level. It is also likely that some fibres innervate the medial aspect of the joint capsule of the zygapophyseal joints.

Numerous fine nerve filaments, as well as encapsulated and non-encapsulated receptors, have been found in the anterior and posterior longitudinal ligaments and the superficial layers of the annulus fibrosus. The innervation of the anterior longitudinal ligament and lateral aspect of the disc appears to be extensive and complex, particularly in the lumbar region, and involves branches from the ventral ramus. The lateral aspect of the zygapophyseal joint capsule probably also receives an innervation from the dorsal ramus as it passes towards the postvertebral muscles.

With both C and A-δ fibres involved in pain transmission, it is clear that structures exist in and around the intervertebral disc whose presence could explain the disc pain caused by mechanical compression of the anterior and posterior nerve fibres in the periphery of the annulus.

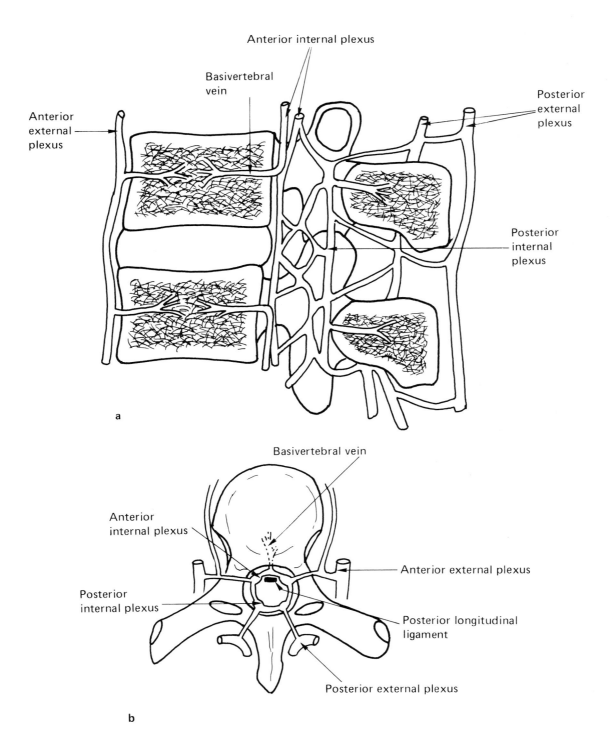

Fig. 6.54 Venous drainage of the vertebral column: **a** = sagittal section; **b** = transverse section.

Relations

Because the vertebral column extends from the base of the skull to the pelvis, and in doing so is associated with several distinct regions of the body, its relations change as various structures at first approach and then move away from it. Consequently, it is not practical to consider in detail all of these relations. However, an attempt is made to illustrate the major relations in each region.

One of the major functions of the vertebral column is to support and protect the spinal cord against physical trauma. Therefore, within the vertebral canal is found the spinal cord and its meningeal coverings (see p. 840 for further details), as well as the internal vertebral venous plexus which is embedded in loose areolar tissue. As the spinal cord ends at the level of the disc between L1 and L2, below this level is found the cauda equina, still within the meningeal coverings as far as the level of S2.

In the neck well-defined fascial sheets and membranes enclose the principal muscle masses, the viscera, and main nerves and blood vessels. These fasciae have continuities and bony attachments which form fascial planes and compartments in which the deeper structures of the neck are confined. The cervical vertebrae are located towards the back of the neck. Posteriorly are the postvertebral muscles, enclosed within the superficial layer of cervical fascia. Anterolaterally is the carotid sheath, enclosing the common carotid artery, internal jugular vein and tenth cranial nerve, with the cervical sympathetic trunk posteromedial to it. The anterior part of the neck comprises essentially two compartments: a superficial muscular compartment, and a deeper visceral compartment enclosing the pharynx, oesophagus, larynx, trachea, thyroid and parathyroid glands. The relationship of the various structures one to another and to the cervical vertebrae at the level of C6 is shown in Fig. 6.55a. There are minor variations concerning the precise arrangement of these structures both above and below this level. Nevertheless, the general plan is similar.

Fig. 6.55   a = Transverse section of the neck at the level of C6; **b** = transverse section of the thorax at the level of T8.

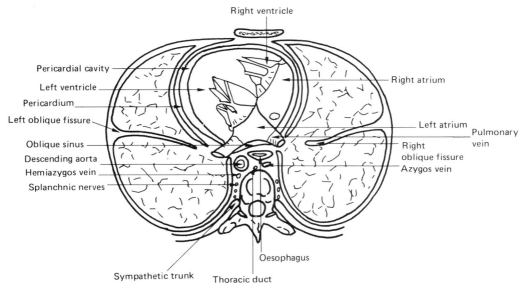

Fig. 6.55

In the thoracic region the anterior relations of the vertebrae differ depending on the level at which the section is taken. In general, above the level of T8, thoracic contents only are seen, i.e. lungs, heart, great vessels and the oesophagus (see Fig. 6.55b). However, below this level, and separated from the thoracic contents by the diaphragm, the liver and stomach become anterior relations (Fig. 6.56a). As in the neck, posterior and lateral to the vertebrae are the postvertebral muscles.

Anterior to the lumbar vertebrae lie the major vessels of the abdomen: the aorta and inferior vena cava. Immediately lateral to the upper three lumbar vertebrae lie the kidneys, with various parts of the gastrointestinal tract generally lying anteriorly (Fig. 6.56a). Once again the main posterior relation, situated between the transverse and spinous processes as in other regions, is the postvertebral muscle mass. At lumbar levels it is difficult to differentiate the components of this large muscle mass. Also in this region the thick and strong thoracolumbar fascia can be readily seen.

Stability

Despite its multisegmental composition, the vertebral column is a relatively stable structure. The ease with which the column can be held erect with a small amount of muscle activity is in contrast to that required to hold the lower limbs in equilibrium against gra-

vity. Many patients after a long illness are able to sit up, with relatively little effort, long before they can stand. This suggests that the arrangement of the various elements of the vertebral column are such that they provide a high degree of inherent stability which requires little, if any, muscle activity to maintain the position of the column. Indeed, it has been shown that a vertebral column devoid of all musculature does not collapse but remains erect, and furthermore can support up to 2 kg placed on its upper end without collapsing. How is this possible when the partial centres of gravity of the various links do not lie in the line of the centre of gravity? Furthermore, the centres of the articulations (except for a few) do not fall into this line. Consequently, rotational stresses between vertebrae must be neutralized otherwise the column would lose its equilibrium and collapse.

What features then contribute to this equilibrium and stability? Of considerable importance is the arrangement and nature of the joints between vertebrae, particularly between their bodies. Being secondary cartilaginous joints they do not permit a large amount of movement. This, together with the fact that the components of the intervertebral disc interact with the adjacent vertebrae, produces a unit (two vertebrae plus the intervening disc) which is self-stabilizing. Whether loaded or at rest the annulus fibrosus fibres are under tension because of

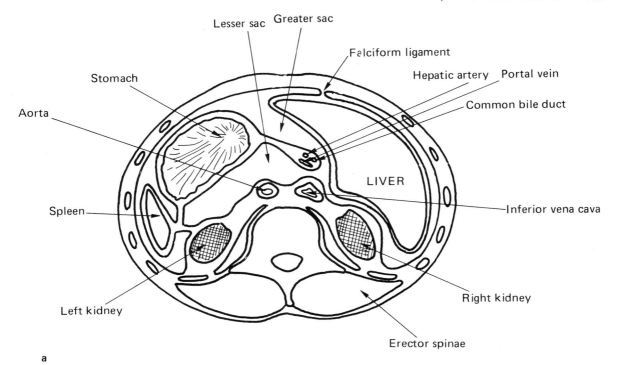

Fig. 6.56 a = Transverse section at T12; **b**
= transverse section at L4.

the preloaded state of the disc, brought about by its water-absorbing capacity. The tension developed in these fibres tends to keep the vertebrae aligned. When a force is applied to the upper vertebrae to cause it to move, say in the direction of extension, the nucleus pulposus moves anteriorly thereby increasing the tension in the anterior part of the annulus, which in turn tends to restore the upper vertebrae to its original position (Fig. 6.57a). Such a mechanism can be seen to work well with asymmetrically applied forces causing movement in the direction of extension, forward flexion and lateral flexion. But what about axial rotation? During rotation the fibres of the annulus running counter to the direction of movement are stretched, while those in the opposite direction become relatively relaxed (Fig. 6.57b). Tension is maximum in the central annulus fibres, consequently the nucleus pulposus is compressed, with its internal pressure rising in proportion to the degree of angular rotation. This compression of the nucleus is such that it pushes back against the annulus with a tendency to put the 'relaxed' fibres under tension. This helps to limit movement and also restore the upper vertebra to its original position. It appears then that no matter what force is applied to the intervertebral disc, it always increases the internal pressure of the nucleus pulposus which stretches the annulus fibrosus. This stretching tends to oppose the movement and restore the system to its initial state.

The unique hydrostatic properties of the intervertebral disc result from the interaction of the annulus fibrosus with the water-binding capacity of the proteoglycans in the nucleus pulposus, and from their interaction with respect to the loading exerted by the longitudinal ligaments binding the vertebrae together. With the intake of water and the subsequent increase in nuclear pressurization, there is an increase in disc height. Not only does this increase in disc height decrease displacement in all directions, it reduces laxity by pushing the adjacent vertebrae apart thereby putting the longitudinal ligaments under tension (Fig. 6.57b). However, if the column is deprived of ligaments as well as muscles it automatically collapses. As long as the ligaments and discs are intact it preserves considerable resistance against deformation, which is the result of the elastic tension resistance of the ligaments and the elastic compression resistance of the discs.

As can be seen from Fig. 6.57b, it is not only the longitudinal ligaments which interact with the disc in providing intrinsic stability, the ligamenta flava, interspinous and supraspinous ligaments are equally important. Consequently, for the system to work efficiently and effectively the neural arches must be firmly attached to the bodies, which of course they are. Experiment has shown, however, that if the entire column of arches is separated from that of the bodies, then the column of arches shrinks by 14%. As long as the arches are joined to the bodies they are spread apart putting the ligaments under tension.

Asymmetrical forces

a

Axial rotation

Supraspinous
ligament

Interspinous
ligament

Ligamentum
flavum

Anterior
Longitudinal ligaments
Posterior

Annulus fibrosus
Nucleus pulposus

b

Fig. 6.57 **a** = Reaction of the intervertebral
disc to asymmetrically applied forces and axial
rotation; **b** = interaction of the intervertebral
disc and vertebral ligaments to provide an
inherent stability to the vertebral column.

The above points regarding inherent stability of the vertebral column have led to a simple mechanical model (Fig. 6.58), whereby adjacent vertebrae move with respect to each other guided by the zygapophyseal joints, with the elastic properties of the disc and ligaments being replaced by springs. Each vertebra can then be considered to act as a first class lever, with the articular process acting as the fulcrum. Within such a model, the vertebral bodies and intervening disc are essentially the supporting structures and therefore have a static role. The articular and spinous processes, together with adjacent ligaments, have the dynamic role of permitting, guiding and limiting movement.

The presence of the thoracic cage and its articulation posteriorly with the thoracic vertebrae confers a certain degree of stability upon the vertebral column in this region. The ribs themselves are forced into the thoracic cage under considerable stress (tearing or rupture of a costal cartilage through trauma results in the rib springing out slightly). In addition the costal cartilages are constantly changing their shape during respiration. In some respects, therefore, the bodies of the thoracic vertebrae are held between the heads of the ribs. Such an arrangement increases the elastic resistance of the thorax, some of which is used in respiration but the greater part of which is exerted against the vertebral column thus contributing to its intrinsic stability.

That the vertebral column has a certain degree of intrinsic stability is of practical and clinical importance: less muscle activity and therefore energy expenditure is required to maintain it in an erect posture. However, as with all joints, ligaments by themselves are not sufficient to maintain stability. They are of necessity reinforced by muscles. Without the presence and intermittent activity of the muscles, the ligaments would gradually stretch and stability would be lost. The large mass of postvertebral muscles play an extremely important role in supporting the ligaments for intrinsic stability. But just as importantly these muscles are primarily responsible for extrinsic stability, i.e. stability during dynamic movements. However, in explosive dynamic movements the post-vertebral muscles by themselves may not be capable of providing the required stability.

With increased dynamic loading of the vertebral column both intra-abdominal and intrathoracic pressures increase (Fig. 6.59). The increase in intra-abdominal pressure and its maintenance acts as a pneumatic cushion which supports the anterior aspect of the lumbar and lower thoracic regions of the vertebral column.

Fig. 6.58 Mechanical model of the vertebral unit.

Fig. 6.59 Increases in intra-abdominal and intrathoracic pressure with increased dynamic loading of the vertebral column. (Adapted from Morris J. M., Lucas S. B., Breslar B. (1961). Role of the trunk in stability of the spine. *Journal of Bone and Joint Surgery*, **43A**, 327–51.)

Fig. 6.58

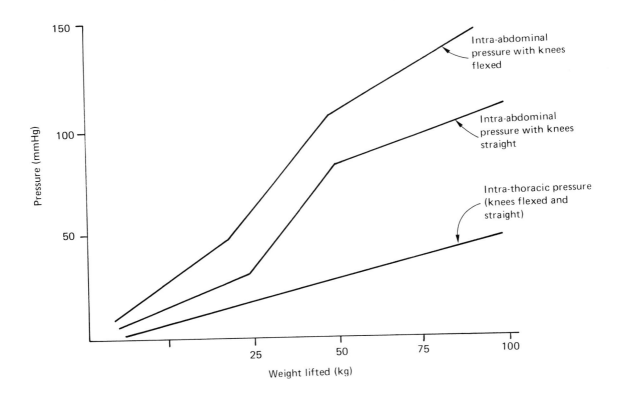

Fig. 6.59

Movements

Movement between vertebrae occurs because the resilient intervertebral discs are slightly flexible, with the type of movement permitted in each region being largely determined by the shape and orientation of the articular processes. Where the discs are thick in relation to the vertebral bodies, i.e. in the cervical and lumbar regions, the range of movement between adjacent vertebrae is increased. Even so the amount of movement between successive vertebrae is slight, being limited by the arrangement of fibres within the intervertebral disc. Nevertheless, when added over the whole of the vertebral column the total range of motion is considerable.

The basic movements of the vertebral column are flexion (forward bending) and extension (backward bending) about a transverse axis, lateral flexion (bending) about an anteroposterior axis and rotation to the right or left about a vertical axis (Fig. 6.60). Of these, lateral flexion and rotation are always associated movements and neither can take place independently of the other. Indeed, it has been shown for the lumbar region that there is always coupling of movements, so that pure movements in any direction do not occur. Even though the coupled movements are small, they are nevertheless important, and probably serve to help maintain the inherent stability present within the vertebral column during movement. All movements are possible in each region of the vertebral column, with the range of motion determined by disc thickness and articular process geometry. The movements of flexion, extension and lateral flexion involve compression of the intervertebral discs at one edge and stretching at the other. During flexion, the anterior borders of the vertebrae come together, while the posterior borders separate. As full flexion is reached, the anterior part of the disc is compressed, tending to push the nucleus pulposus posteriorly. However, the posterior part of the disc, the posterior longitudinal ligament and the ligaments of the vertebral arches all become taut; the principal limiting factor to movement is, however, tension in the post-vertebral muscles. In extension it is the posterior borders of the vertebrae which become approximated, and the anterior separate. Consequently, the anterior longitudinal ligament becomes increasingly taut while all posterior ligaments are relaxed. Extension is freer and has a wider range of movement than flexion, particularly in the cervical and lumbar regions. Much of the apparent movement of flexion is in fact due to flexion of the trunk at the hips and also movement of the head at the atlanto-occipital joints.

The importance of the posterior ligaments and intervertebral discs in limiting movements of the vertebral column has been demonstrated by successive sectioning of these structures and observation and measurement of the movements between adjacent vertebrae. Progressive sectioning of the supra- and interspinous ligaments, the ligamentum flavum, bilateral severing of the articular processes, sectioning of the posterior longitudinal ligament and cutting of the posterior and lateral part of the annulus fibrosus results in a 100% increase in flexion–extension (from 8.4° to 17.3°), a 70% increase in lateral flexion (from 4.9° to 8.3°), and a 650% increase in rotation (from 2.2° to 14.6°) at the thoracolumbar junction. A similar pattern of changes would be expected elsewhere in the vertebral column, although they would be modified by the orientation of the articular processes, particularly regarding the percentage change in rotation.

Fig. 6.60 Movements of the vertebral column.

Movements in the lumbar region

Although the intervertebral discs are thick in this region, and in theory would facilitate relatively large movements between adjacent vertebrae, the orientation of the articular processes (see p. 740) tends to confer a certain degree of stability to this region, restricting rotation in particular. Of the lumbar vertebrae, the lower facets of L5 face mainly forwards to articulate with the superior facets on the sacrum. Consequently, movement between L5 and the sacrum is not the same as that between two typical lumbar vertebrae.

Flexion and extension   Flexion is relatively free in the lumbar region having a total range of 55°, while extension has a range of 30° (Fig. 6.61a). There is less movement at the thoracolumbar junction than between adjacent vertebrae, and there is most movement at the lumbosacral joint. The total range of movement decreases with age so that at 65 years it is between one-half and one-third of the range at the age of 10 years.

In flexion, the vertebrae are tilted forward on each other, so that the lower articular processes of the upper vertebrae glide upwards and forwards on the upper processes of the lower vertebrae (Fig. 6.61b).

Because of the orientation of these joints in space, this allows the upper vertebrae to move forwards slightly over the lower vertebrae. One result of this forward movement is to increase the superoinferior diameter, while narrowing the anteroposterior diameter of the intervertebral foramen. Flexion from the upright position is controlled by the postvertebral muscles on both sides, being limited by tension in the posterior part of the intervertebral disc, the posterior longitudinal ligament, the ligamenta flava, and the inter- and supraspinous ligaments. Flexion from the supine position is brought about by psoas major and the anterior abdominal muscles, particularly rectus abdominis.

During extension, the inferior articular processes of the upper vertebra glide down into the hollowed superior processes of the lower vertebra, causing the upper vertebra to move backwards slightly on the lower vertebra (Fig. 6.61b). The movement is limited by the anterior longitudinal ligament, the anterior part of the intervertebral disc, apposition of the large lumbar spinous process and the 'close-packing' of the facet joints. Extension from the upright position is controlled by psoas and the anterior abdominal muscles, while from the prone position it is produced by the postvertebral muscles.

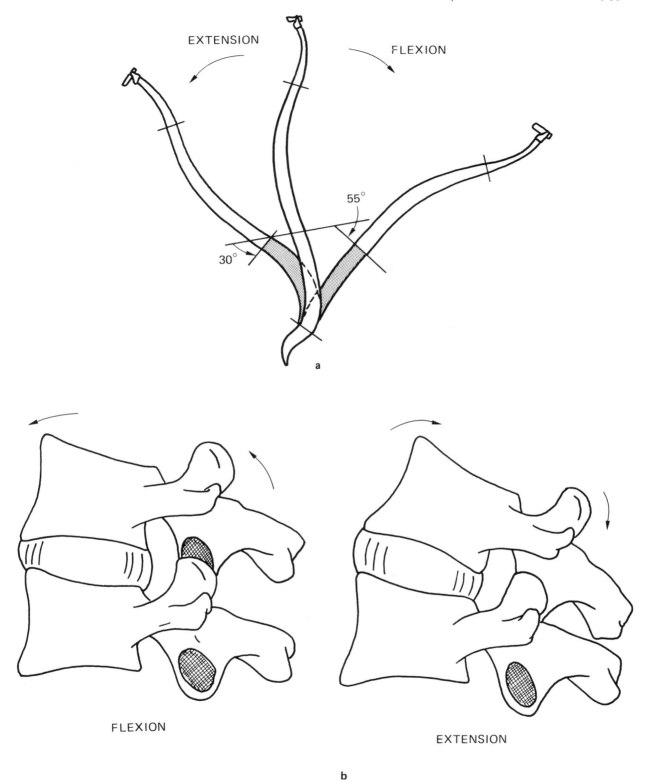

Fig. 6.61 Flexion and extension of the lumbar region. **a** = Range of movement; **b** = movements between adjacent vertebrae.

Lateral flexion The range of lateral flexion, as with that of flexion and extension, varies with the individual and with age. During the preteenage years the range may be as large as 60° either side of the midline; however, by the age of 30 this has been halved. On average, the adult range of movement is between 20 and 30° (Fig. 6.62a). Throughout the total age range lateral flexion at the lumbosacral joint is minimal. Because of the small range of lateral flexion in the lumbar region there is very little associated rotation of the vertebrae. Lateral flexion is greatest in the upright position, and is greatly diminished when the vertebral column is flexed and the lumbar curve is lost.

In lateral flexion, the articular processes of the flexed side become close-packed, while the upper process on the opposite side is withdrawn from that below (Fig. 6.62b). Because the articular surfaces also slope slightly, a narrow gap appears between the articular processes on the unflexed side. As a result the intervertebral foramen on the unflexed side enlarges in all directions, while that on the flexed side narrows. Lateral flexion initially requires active muscle contraction, it is not brought about by controlled relaxation (i.e. eccentric contraction) of the muscles of the opposite side. In other words, lateral bending to the right requires contraction of muscles on the right side, i.e. the anterior abdominal muscles and quadratus lumborum. However, once a certain degree of lateral flexion has been reached (about 10°) then the movement is controlled by the eccentric contraction of the muscles of the opposite side. Movement is limited by the intertransverse ligaments of the opposite side as well as opposing muscle groups.

Rotation Rotation in the lumbar region is extremely small, being of the order of only a few degrees (Fig. 6.62c). The limitation to movement is due to the shape and orientation of the lumbar articular facets. In the erect position there is a narrow gap between opposing articular processes. Consequently, rotation occurs until all these gaps on one side become obliterated. (Narrowing and eventual obliteration of the gaps on one side produce widening of the opposite gaps.)

The rotation possible, however small, depends on the position of the lumbar column. When it is extended no rotation at all is possible because of the close-packed position of the zygapophyseal joints. However, the range of rotation possible increases with increasing flexion.

Accessory movements Rotation is really an accumulation of accessory movements occurring at each of the zygapophyseal joints. It consists of a rocking movement of the inferior articular process of the vertebra above within the hollow of the process of the lower vertebra. These same accessory movements can be demonstrated by applying pressure to one side of a lumbar spinous process when the subject is lying prone with the lumbar column slightly flexed.

A downward pressure applied to the mamillary processes or to the spinous process causes a slight forward gliding of the body of the same vertebra with respect to the body above. At the same time the superior articular processes move forward away from the inferior processes of the vertebra above, while the inferior processes are pushed into the superior processes of the vertebra below.

Fig. 6.62   **a** = Range of movement of lateral flexion;   **b** = movement between adjacent vertebrae during lateral flexion;   **c** = axial rotation.

Lumbosacral junction

Movement at the lumbosacral junction is restricted to flexion and extension, and a small degree of lateral flexion (Fig. 6.63a). In flexion the inferior articular processes of L5 glide upwards over those on the sacrum, with movement being limited by tension in the iliolumbar, inter- and supraspinous ligaments and the postvertebral muscles. Backward and downward gliding of the L5 articular processes on those of the sacrum during extension is arrested by apposition of the spines of L5 and S1.

The intervertebral disc between L5 and S1 is markedly wedged, being thicker anteriorly, and is mainly responsible for the angulation between the lumbar and sacral parts of the vertebral column. Because the lumbosacral junction represents the transition between the mobile (lumbar) and immobile (sacral) parts of the vertebral column, it requires considerable support against potentially damaging stresses. To this end the postvertebral muscle mass is extremely thick in this region, reinforced posteriorly by the lower part of the strong thoracolumbar fascia. It is also worth noting that between L5 and S1 the intertransverse ligaments have been replaced by the much stronger iliolumbar ligaments, which confer additional stability upon this region by restricting lateral flexion (for details of the iliolumbar ligaments see p. 424).

The zygapophyseal joints between L5 and S1 have an important weight-bearing function. Occasionally, there is faulty development of the neural arch of the fifth lumbar vertebra anterior to the inferior articular processes, which may allow separation of the body of L5 from the posterior part of the neural arch. The result is that the body of the fifth lumbar vertebra, together with the trunk above, slides forward and downwards towards the pelvis (Fig. 6.63b), leaving the posterior part of L5 behind articulating with the superior sacral articular processes and tethered by the iliolumbar ligaments. The condition is known as *spondylolisthesis*. The marked angulation at the lumbosacral junction assists this downward and forward movement. The lumbar curvature is accentuated, and the performance of extension exercises is usually extremely painful and dangerous because of the tension on the nerves forming the cauda equina, leading to motor and sensory disturbances along their distribution.

FLEXION EXTENSION

LATERAL FLEXION

a

b

Fig. 6.63 **a** = Movements at the lumbosacral joint; **b** = the forward displacement of L5 in spondylolisthesis.

Movements in the thoracic region

In the thoracic region the intervertebral discs are relatively thin with respect to the vertebral bodies, together with the presence of the ribs and sternum movement is limited. The disposition of the articular processes of the thoracic vertebrae, which lie on the arc of a circle with its centre in the vertebral body, permits flexion, extension, lateral flexion and rotation. However, the inferior processes of the twelfth thoracic vertebra resemble those of the lumbar region and therefore movements at the thoracolumbar junction are similar to those between lumbar vertebrae.

Flexion and extension The combined range of flexion and extension in the thoracic part of the vertebral column is between 50° and 70°, with extension being much more limited than flexion (Fig. 6.64a). Flexion is much freer in the lower half of the region as the lower ribs tend to be longer and more flexible because of their longer costal cartilages.

In flexion the inferior articular processes of the vertebra above slide upwards over the superior processes of the lower vertebra (Fig. 6.64b). The interspace between the two vertebrae opens out posteriorly, compressing the anterior part of the intervertebral disc. Flexion is limited by the presence of the thoracic cage, and by the tension developed in the supra- and interspinous ligaments, the ligamenta flava, and the posterior longitudinal ligament. From the upright position, flexion is controlled by the postvertebral muscles of both sides, while flexion from the supine position is brought about by the anterior abdominal muscles of both sides, particularly rectus abdominis. During flexion all the angles between the various segments of the thorax and between the thorax and vertebral column increase (Fig. 6.64c).

Extension of the thoracic region approximates the vertebrae posteriorly (Fig. 6.64b). It is limited by impact of the articular and spinous processes between adjacent vertebrae, as well as by tension in the anterior longitudinal ligament. The effect of extension on the thoracic cage is to flatten it by decreasing all angles between the various segments of the cage and the vertebral column (Fig. 6.64c). Extension from the upright position is controlled by the anterior abdominal wall muscles and from the prone position it is produced by the postvertebral muscles.

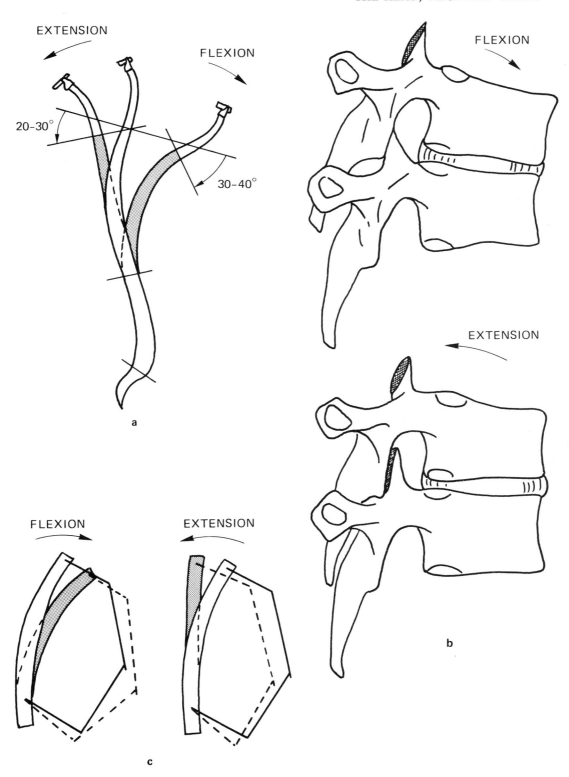

Fig. 6.64 Flexion and extension of the thoracic region: **a** = range of movement; **b** = movements between adjacent vertebrae; **c** = effects on the thoracic cage.

Lateral flexion Lateral flexion in the thoracic region has a range of 20° to 25° to each side (Fig. 6.65a), being freer in the lower half of the region. During lateral flexion the articular processes of the two adjacent vertebrae slide relative to each other, so that those on the contralateral side move as in flexion, while those on the ipsilateral side move as in extension (Fig. 6.65b). Lateral flexion is limited by impact of the articular processes on the side of the movement, and by tension developed in the ligamenta flava and intertransverse ligaments of the opposite side. In the thoracic region lateral flexion is associated with rotation of the vertebrae. In full lateral flexion the degree of rotation is about 20°. In other words for each degree of lateral flexion there is almost 1° of accompanying rotation; the rotation being such that the spinous processes of the thoracic vertebrae point towards the concavity of the curve, i.e. they rotate contralaterally.

As with flexion and extension, lateral flexion modifies the shape of the thoracic cage (Fig. 6.65c). On the contralateral side the thorax is elevated, the intercostal spaces widen, the thoracic cage enlarges and the costochondral angle of the tenth rib tends to open out. On the ipsilateral side the reverse changes occur: the thoracic cage is lowered and shrinks, the intercostal spaces narrow, and the costochondral angle decreases.

As in the lumbar region, lateral flexion is brought about by the contraction of muscles on the same side.

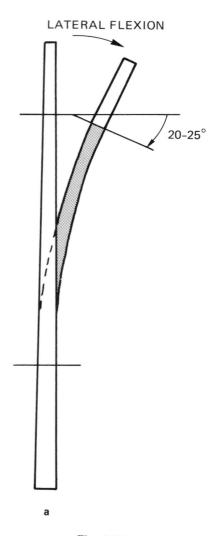

LATERAL FLEXION

20–25°

a

Fig. 6.65

b

LATERAL FLEXION

c

Fig. 6.65 Lateral flexion of the thoracic region: **a** = range of movement; **b** = movements of adjacent vertebrae; **c** = effects on the thoracic cage.

Rotation The orientation of the articular processes in the thoracic region are such as to promote rotation. This may be a necessary adaptation because of the presence of the ribs. Were it not for the presence of the thoracic cage the range of rotation of the thoracic column would be greater. Even so, it is some 35° in each direction (Fig. 6.66a). During the movement, the inferior processes of the upper vertebrae slide sideways outside the superior processes of the lower vertebrae leading to rotation of one vertebral body with respect to the other about a common axis (Fig. 6.66b). This movement of the vertebrae is accompanied by rotation and twisting of the intervertebral disc, which has a tendency to pull the adjacent vertebrae together. A small degree of lateral flexion accompanies this rotation. When the thoracic vertebral column is fully extended both rotation and lateral flexion are greatly reduced, and may be lost completely.

Rotation is limited by tension in the supra- and interspinous ligaments and the ligamenta flava and is brought about largely by the abdominal oblique muscles. For example, rotation of the trunk to the left is achieved by contraction of the right external oblique and the left internal oblique.

Because of the articulation of the ribs with the vertebrae, any rotatory movement of the vertebrae will induce a similar movement in the corresponding ribs. However, such movement is limited due to the articulation of the ribs anteriorly with the sternum. Instead there is a distortion of the ribs in the following manner: an accentuation of the concavity of the rib on the side of rotation, with a flattening of the concavity on the opposite side (Fig. 6.66c). These changes are possible because of the elasticity of the rib and its costal cartilage. These movements of the ribs subject the sternum to shearing forces.

Rotation of the thoracolumbar part of the vertebral column is extremely important during walking. However the rotation is not simple but rather complex, occurring in opposite directions in the upper and lower parts of the region. As one leg swings through ready for the next heel-strike the pelvis rotates about the hip joint of the supporting leg, carrying with it the trunk. In an attempt to keep the head facing forwards the pectoral girdle rotates in the opposite direction. Studies have shown that the intervertebral disc between the seventh and eighth thoracic vertebrae is not subjected to any rotation, while maximum rotation occurs (in opposite directions) in the discs immediately above and below it (Fig. 6.66d). The degree of rotation decreases towards the pelvic and pectoral girdles.

Accessory movements Accessory movements of the thoracic part of the vertebral column are difficult to demonstrate and usually only used therapeutically. Nevertheless, pressure on a spinous process will, because of its length and angulation, produce a slight rocking of the vertebral body and apposition of the articular surfaces of the zygapophyseal joints associated with its articular processes. A localized pressure applied to the posterior aspect of the base of the transverse process just below the zygapophyseal joint will slightly separate the joint by pushing the upper articular process forwards.

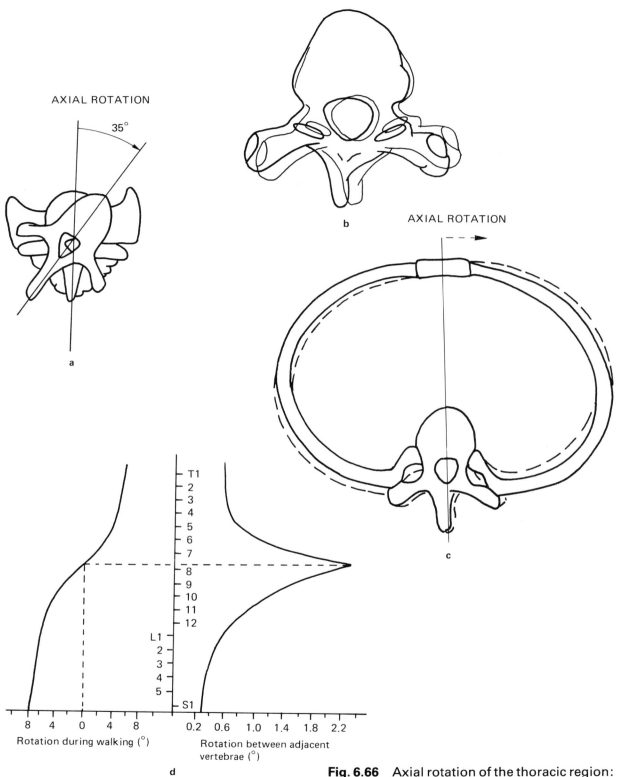

Fig. 6.66 Axial rotation of the thoracic region: **a** = range of movement; **b** = movement between adjacent vertebrae; **c** = effects on thoracic cage; **d** = rotation in the thoracic region during walking.

Movements in the cervical region

Taken as a whole the cervical part of the vertebral column consists of two anatomically and functionally distinct regions. The upper region, known as the suboccipital region, consists of the first and second cervical vertebrae and includes the articulation of this unit with the base of the skull. The lower region extends from the lower surface of C2 down to the superior surface of T1. Although each region is distinct functionally, they are complementary to allow movements of flexion and extension, lateral flexion, and rotation of the head and neck. It is easier, however, to consider each of the regions separately.

Lower cervical region

The intervertebral discs in the lower cervical region are relatively thick, which together with the shape and orientation of the articular facets, means that movements of flexion and extension, lateral flexion and rotation are all fairly extensive. As in the thoracic region, lateral flexion and rotation occur as linked movements.

Flexion and extension   The total range of flexion and extension in the lower cervical region is about 110°, of which only about 25° is flexion (Fig. 6.67a, see also Fig. 6.72a, p. 787). The least movement is between the seventh cervical and first thoracic vertebrae. During flexion the upper vertebral body tilts and slides anteriorly on the lower, compressing the intervertebral space anteriorly (Fig. 6.67b). The tilting of the upper vertebra is facilitated by the anterior ledge on the upper plateau of the lower vertebra, allowing the inferiorly directed projection on the lower plateau of the upper vertebra to move past. Flexion between two verterbrae does not occur about the centre of curvature of the facets on the articular processes. Consequently, the inferior facet of the upper vertebra moves upwards and forwards causing a widening of the joint space posteriorly. Flexion is not limited by bony impact but only by tension developed in the posterior longitudinal ligament, the zygapophyseal joint capsule, the ligamenta flava, the ligamentum nuchae and postvertebral muscles. From the upright position flexion is controlled by the posterior neck muscles of both sides which act against the weight of the head and neck (i.e. trapezius, splenius capitis, longissimus capitis and semispinalis capitis). In the supine position the anterior muscles of both sides flex the cervical column (i.e. sternomastoid, longus capitis, longus colli and the scalene muscles).

In extension the upper vertebra tilts and slides posteriorly over the lower one (Fig. 6.67b). Again, because the movement does not occur about the centre of curvature of the facets, the superior articular facet moves backwards and downwards causing the anterior part of the joint space to widen and the intervertebral foramen to narrow. Extension is limited by tension developed in the anterior longitudinal ligament and by the impact of the superior articular process of the lower vertebra on the transverse process of the upper vertebrae and by the impact of the posterior arches through the ligaments. Extension from the upright position is controlled by the anterior neck muscles as above, while in the prone position, the posterior muscles produce extension.

Movements of the vertebral bodies during flexion and extension is guided to some extent by the uncovertebral joints, otherwise the movements would probably not be as pure as they are.

The fact that there is no bony limitation to flexion predisposes the cervical column to a particular form of dislocation. During car accidents in particular, the vertebral column is strongly extended and then flexed, producing the whiplash injury. Whiplash injuries cause stretching or occasionally tearing of the ligamentous structures limiting flexion. In extreme cases there may be an anterior dislocation of the zygapophyseal joints in which the inferior articular facets of the upper vertebra become hooked on the anterosuperior margin of the superior facet of the lower vertebra (Fig. 6.67c). The dislocation is extremely difficult to reduce as it endangers the medulla oblongata and cervical spinal cord with the risk of paraplegia, quadriplegia or death.

EXTENSION   FLEXION

85°   25°

a

FLEXION

EXTENSION

b

c

Fig. 6.67 Flexion and extension of the lower cervical region: **a** = range of movement; **b** = movements of adjacent vertebrae; **c** = anterior dislocation of the zygapophyseal joints as may occur in severe whiplash injury.

Lateral flexion   Lateral flexion in the lower cervical region has a range of about 40° to each side (Fig. 6.68a, see also Fig. 6.72b, p. 787). However because of the orientation and shape of the articular facets it is impossible to get pure lateral flexion or pure rotation. When the neck is flexed to one side, the lower articular process on that side glides downwards and backwards on the superior process of the vertebra below: on the other side each articular process moves forwards and upwards over the superior process of the vertebra below. Thus flexion to one side is accompanied by a slight rotation to the same side (Fig. 6.68b). If the whole of the lower cervical region is considered rather than the movements between adjacent vertebrae, then there is a slight extension accompanying lateral–rotation of the cervical column.

During lateral flexion, the joint spaces of the contralateral uncovertebral joints widens (Fig. 6.68c). The movement, however, is quite complex because it involves not only lateral flexion of one vertebra with respect to another, but also rotation and slight extension.

As in the thoracic and lumbar regions, lateral flexion of the neck requires muscle contraction on the side of flexion. The movement is arrested in part by opposition of the articular facets and also by stretching of the contralateral zygapophyseal joint capsule and compression of the intervertebral disc.

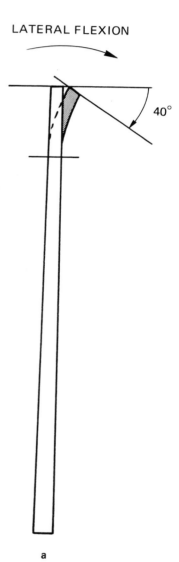

LATERAL FLEXION

40°

a

Fig. 6.68

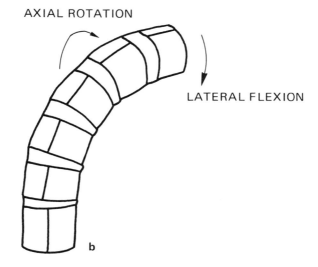

AXIAL ROTATION

LATERAL FLEXION

b

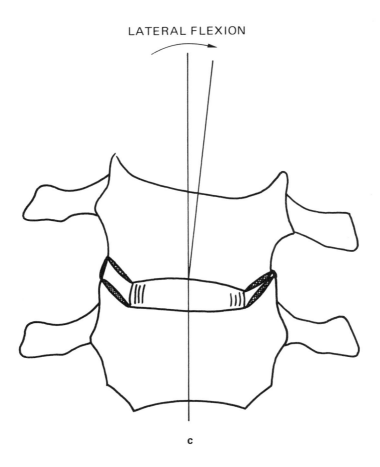

LATERAL FLEXION

c

Fig. 6.68 Lateral flexion of the lower cervical region: **a** = range of movement; **b** = schematic representation of linked lateral flexion and rotation; **c** = movement between adjacent vertebrae.

Rotation Rotation in the lower cervical region amounts to 50° in each direction (Fig. 6.69a). It cannot occur, however, without there being some associated lateral flexion to the same side (Fig. 6.69b). In rotation, the inferior facets on the opposite side of the vertebra above move against the superior facets of the lower vertebra producing a type of camber effect. This results in an increase in the size of the intervertebral foramen on that side. However, on the side to which rotation is occurring, the articular facets separate slightly, thus reducing the size of the intervertebral foramen. The movement is limited by a grinding contact of the opposite side facets, tension within both joint capsules and also torsion of the intervertebral disc. Rotation is produced by posterior muscles which pass upwards and inwards behind the axis of rotation (e.g. semispinalis cervicis), and anterior muscles passing upwards and outwards in front of the axis of rotation (e.g. sternomastoid). This combination of muscle activity produces rotation to the opposite side.

One of the practical consequences of rotation is that it can relieve pressure on the nerve root of the side opposite to the direction of rotation by virtue of the increase in size of the intervertebral foramen. At the same time pressure would be relieved on the same side facet joint, but it would decrease the size of the intervertebral foramen. Practical use is made of these movements in the application of traction in which flexion is combined with rotation to relieve pressure on a nerve root. These movements are also utilized in mobilization and manipulation techniques.

Circumduction Circumduction is a combination of flexion, extension, lateral flexion and rotation, and involves all of the joints in the cervical region. The limiting factors will be those which limit the individual movements. Circumduction is a popular movement in keep fit clubs in which 'clicking' sounds may be sought by the untrained practitioner. Combined movements as in circumduction, particularly when performed towards the extremes of the ranges of movement, bring into play certain 'locking mechanisms' in some of the joints. The 'clicking' sounds that may be heard are often due to forcing a joint beyond one of these locking positions. It commonly leads to severe neck pains, which may be referred to the arm and upper chest, usually appearing within a day or two of performing the activity.

Manipulators often make use of these 'locking mechanisms' practically, even so they must be treated with great care and caution.

Accessory movements Accessory movements are present in the cervical joints, however they are not easy to demonstrate. They fall into two groups: (1) general and (2) local.

(1) Traction of the cervical spine is the most obvious general movement affecting the neck as a whole, producing distraction of the discs and facet joints throughout the region, causing the nerve roots to be drawn back through the intervertebral foramina. With careful positioning traction can be limited to specific areas, however skill in location and handling is essential. In the neutral position an elongation of the neck of several millimeters can be achieved depending on the preparation of the subject. Such an elongation will reduce pressure on the intervertebral disc by some 70% (from $30\,kg/cm^2$ to $10\,kg/cm^2$), as well as distraction of the facet joints.

Traction stretches all of the structures crossing the joints, i.e. capsules, ligamentum nuchae, anterior and posterior longitudinal ligaments, and the muscles. Because of the ligaments passing between C2 and the base of the skull, traction has a negligible effect on the joints between the base of the skull and C1, and C1 and C2. If traction at these joints is achieved it may have undesirable effects, so care and caution should be exercised.

A side-to-side movement can be produced by keeping the head upright and moving it to the left or right. Fixing the lower part of the cervical column and applying some degree of traction increases this movement. It involves a sideways sliding of the vertebral bodies on each other, with a downwards gliding of the facets of the zygapophyseal and uncovertebral joints of one side and an upward gliding on the other.

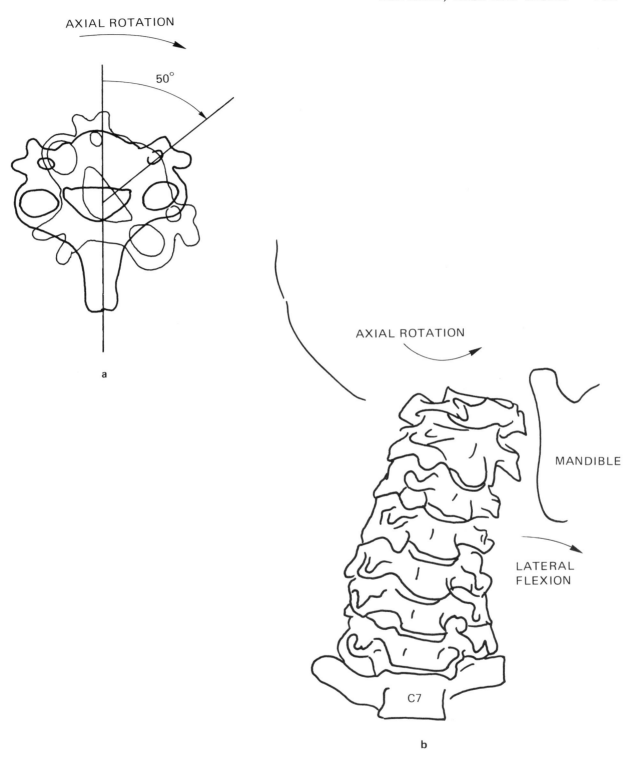

AXIAL ROTATION

50°

a

AXIAL ROTATION

MANDIBLE

LATERAL
FLEXION

C7

b

Fig. 6.69 Axial rotation of the cervical region:
a = range of movement; **b** = combined axial
rotation and lateral flexion.

(2) Local accessory movements can be performed by applying precise pressure to the spines, transverse processes or articular pillars of the vertebrae. Detailed information on the practical application of these procedures is best obtained by consulting the mobilization and manipulation literature.

Suboccipital region

This rather complex unit allows flexion and extension, lateral flexion, and rotation to occur, but because of the nature of the articulations between the bones involved it is perhaps best to consider the movements between the first and second cervical vertebrae, and between the first cervical vertebra and base of the skull separately.

Atlantoaxial (C1–C2) movements

The movements at these joints are extremely complex because all the joints (i.e. the median and lateral two joints) move together. The principal movement at these joints is one of rotation, however a few degrees of flexion and extension may be possible.

Rotation During rotation, the head and first cervical vertebra move as a single unit, with the range of movement being 15° to each side. While the anterior arch of the atlas and the transverse ligament pivot around the stationary dens, the lateral masses of the atlas glide over the articular surfaces of the axis—one forwards and the other backwards (Fig. 6.70a). Because of the oblique orientation of these lateral joint surfaces, together with the slight convexity of the facets on the axis, rotation of the head is accompanied by a slight vertical descent (about 1 mm) of the head. This action slackens the alar ligaments, thus delaying their action in limiting rotation. Rotation can be further increased by tilting the head backwards and to the opposite side.

Rotation is achieved by the action of the suboccipital muscles, sternomastoid and trapezius.

Flexion and extension A few degrees of flexion and extension are possible at the atlantoaxial joints (Fig. 6.70b). The axis about which movement occurs passes more or less through the centre of the dens. Due to the shape of the articular facets of the lateral joints, the lateral mass of the atlas rolls and slides on the superior articular facet of the axis. This movement is only permitted because of the non-rigid transverse ligament, giving some flexibility to the median atlantoaxial joints. During flexion the transverse ligament bends downwards, and during extension it bends upwards.

Accessory movements There are very few accessory movements possible at these joints. Forward and backward movement is prevented by the odontoid process being held between the anterior arch of the atlas in front and the transverse ligament behind. Lateral flexion is prevented by the odontoid process abutting against the medial side of the lateral mass of the atlas. Indeed, all of these movements between the two bones are positively discouraged.

Loss of rotation to one side at the atlanto-occipital joint may lead to compensatory rotation of the rest of the cervical spine to the opposite side often causing pain and discomfort. Restoration of the range can be achieved by fixing the spinous process of the axis and rotating the atlas and the head, the movement can be forced a little beyond the normal. However, it must be stressed that this manouevre should only be performed by a qualified practitioner.

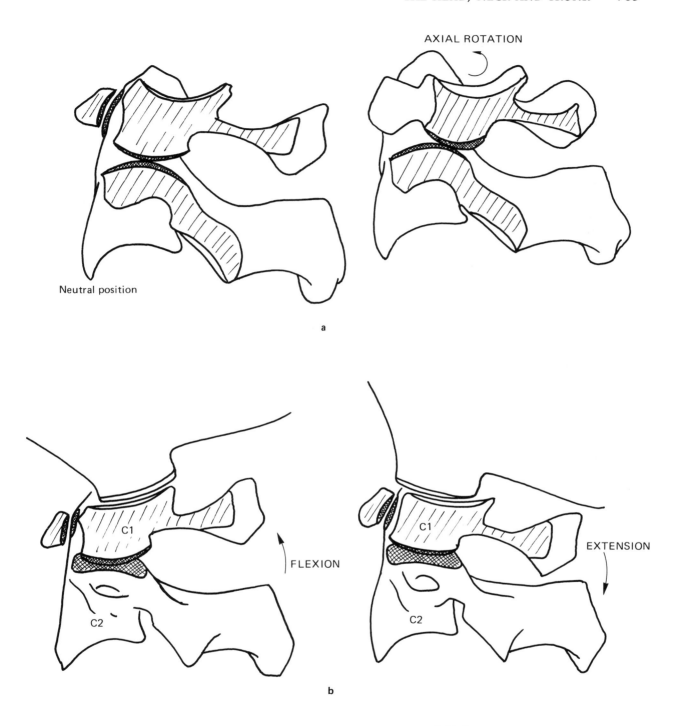

Fig. 6.70   Movement at the atlantoaxial joints:
a = rotation; **b** = flexion and extension.

Atlanto-occipital movements

Movement at the atlanto-occipital joints occurs primarily in two directions: flexion and extension, and lateral flexion. There is, however, slight slipping between the skull and the atlas which constitutes a form of rotation.

Flexion and extension   The total range of flexion and extension is 20° (see Fig. 6.72a, p. 787), the movement being brought about by the occipital condyles sliding on the lateral masses of the atlas. During flexion, the occipital condyles move backwards on the lateral masses; at the same time the occipital bone moves away from the posterior arch of the atlas (Fig. 6.71a). This latter movement causes a slight flexion at the atlanto-occipital joints as the posterior arches of the atlas and axis become separated. Flexion is limited by the tension developed in the joint capsules, the posterior atlanto-occipital membrane, the ligamentum nuchae and the posterior suboccipital muscles. Flexion of the head from the upright position is controlled by the postvertebral neck muscles of both sides acting against the weight of the head (i.e. trapezius, splenius capitis, longissimus capitis, semispinalis capitis and most of the short suboccipital muscles). From the supine position the head is flexed by the anterior muscles of both sides (i.e. sternomastoid, longus capitis, and the short muscles between the atlas and the occiput).

In extension the occipital condyles slide anteriorly on the lateral masses of the atlas (Fig. 6.71b). This brings the occipital bone close to the posterior arch of the atlas, and tends to cause a slight extension at the atlantoaxial joints so that the posterior arches of the atlas and axis are approximated. Extension is limited by the impact of the occipital bone and the posterior arches of the atlas and axis. In a forced extension the posterior arch of the atlas, being caught between the other two bony pieces, may be fractured. Extension is produced in the upright position by the controlled action of the anterior muscles of both sides, and from the prone position by the action of the postvertebral muscles.

Lateral flexion   Lateral flexion in the suboccipital region is limited being no more than 8° to either side (see Fig. 6.72b). It consists of movement of the skull against the atlas (5°), and movement of the axis against the third cervical vertebra (3°). The atlanto-occipital movement consists of a slipping of the occipital condyles so that on the side of the flexion it moves towards the midline and on the opposite side it moves away from the midline (Fig. 6.71c). The movement is limited by tension in the joint capsule and the contralateral alar ligament.

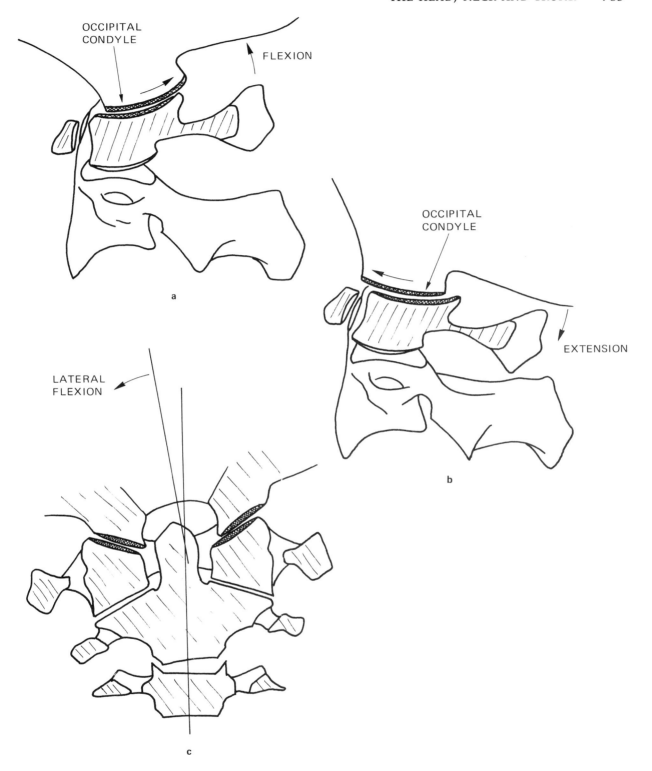

Fig. 6.71 Movement at the atlanto-occipital joints: **a** = flexion, **b** = extension; **c** = lateral flexion.

Rotation The small degree of rotation possible at the atlanto-occipital joints is secondary to the rotation of the atlas around the dens. With respect to the lateral masses of the atlas, one occipital condyle moves forwards while the other moves backwards. Rotation to one side is associated with a slight lateral flexion to the opposite side.

Accessory movements The lateral mass of the atlas can be slid forwards with respect to the occipital bone by applying pressure to the posterior arch when the muscles are relaxed. A forward and backward gliding of the head on the atlas can also be achieved, usually whilst using traction. The head can also be moved sideways producing a sideways gliding of one articular surface against the other. Finally, distraction of the joints can be produced by applying traction to the head; while in distraction a rotatory movement can also be produced.

Application of accessory movements of the vertebral column

A detailed knowledge of the accessory movements of the vertebral column, particularly in the lumbar region, is essential for those using manipulation and movement techniques. There is considerable misunderstanding of how the application of this knowledge can benefit the patient. Although manipulative and movement techniques are not discussed, certain facts are worth stating as they will be of help when consulting the manipulation and movement literature. Because many patients suffer from back problems of one sort or another, comment will be restricted to the lumbar region.

Rotation movements of the lumbar spine, i.e. rotation of the thorax on a fixed pelvis, opens out the zygapophyseal joints on the side to which the thorax is rotating (the degree of gapping and rotation increasing with flexion of the lumbar column). This is similar to that seen in the cervical region upon rotation. However, unlike the cervical region, where the orientation of the articular facets produces an increase in the size of the intervertebral foramen of the opposite side, in the lumbar region the opposite side joints become compressed preventing further movement.

If, as in most cases when these accessory movements are being applied therapeutically, the trunk is fixed and the lower limbs and pelvis are the mobile segments, then rotation of the pelvis to one side has the same effect on the joints as rotating the thorax to the opposite side. Flexing the lumbar column and applying traction to one leg produces a lateral flexion of the lumbar region to the opposite side, which further increases the separation of the zygapophyseal joints on the side of traction. This stretches the joint capsule and the adjacent part of the intervertebral disc thereby increasing the size of the intervertebral foramen, releasing trapped nerve roots.

Fig. 6.72 Total range of movement in the cervical region: **a** = flexion and extension; **b** = lateral flexion.

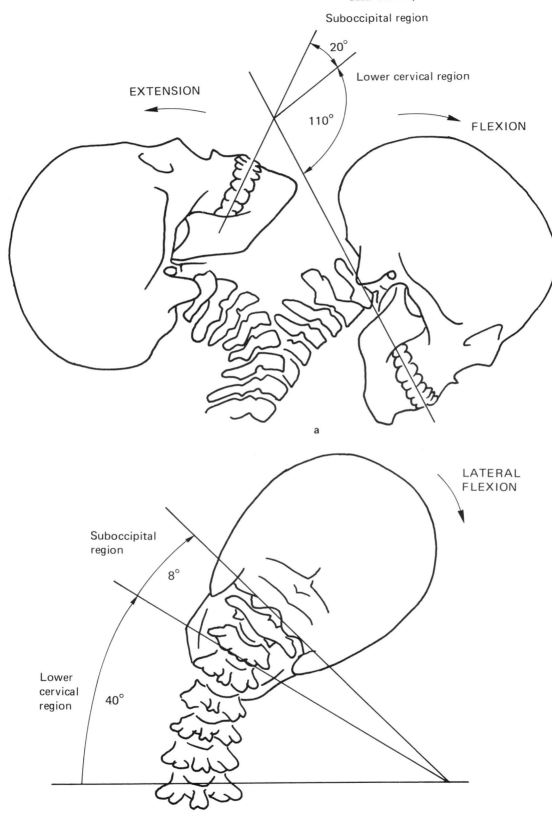

Suboccipital region

20°

Lower cervical region

EXTENSION

110°

FLEXION

a

LATERAL
FLEXION

Suboccipital
region

8°

Lower
cervical
region

40°

b

Fig. 6.72

Biomechanics

Trabecular systems

The trabecular systems within the vertebrae are extensive and complex reflecting the stresses to which each is exposed. Within the body of the vertebra three distinct zones of trabecular bone can be distinguished in a superoinferior direction (Fig. 6.73a). The central zone essentially consists of vertically arranged large-diameter cylinders whose walls are formed by thin solid plates of lamellar bone, with circularly orientated trabeculae arranged around the basivertebral veins. The zones either side, directly beneath the end plate region, are composed of regularly-spaced longitudinal and transverse trabeculae. The anterior superior and inferior regions of the vertebral bodies have decreased trabeculae bone, and are thus regions of mechanical weakness. To a large extent this explains the wedge-shaped compression fracture of a vertebral body (Fig. 6.73b).

Within each vertebral body there is one principal vertical, and several secondary oblique and horizontal systems. Except for the interruption by the intervertebral discs, the vertical system runs throughout the entire column of vertebral bodies from the odontoid process to the sacrum. The oblique accessory systems run in four tracts: a superior and an inferior oblique system on each side. Each superior oblique system runs from the superior articular process of one side downwards through the pedicle to the lower surface of the vertebral body on the opposite side (Fig. 6.73c). The inferior oblique systems run from the inferior articular process of one side upwards via the pedicle to the upper surface of the vertebral body on the opposite side (Fig. 6.73c). These oblique systems do not reach the anterior margin of the vertebral body, so that in this region there are vertical compression trabeculae only (Fig. 6.73a). Posteriorly, behind the articular processes, the oblique systems are continuous with trabeculae within the spinous process (Fig. 6.73c).

Horizontal accessory systems begin in each transverse process and pass into the body of the vertebra where they intersect in the midline (Fig. 6.73d).

In mechanical terms the vertical system sustains body weight and all the jars and shocks which reach the vertebral column in a perpendicular direction. It is the principal trabecular system as stated, and resists atrophy more than the others. In osteoporotic spines the secondary systems atrophy first and their disappearance makes the lines of the vertical system stand out more sharply on radiographs. The spirally wound oblique systems resist torsion, and together with the vertical system, share in the resistance to bending and shear. The horizontal systems are principally tension resistant, as are the minor accessory systems of the transverse and spinous processes, as they resist muscular pull.

It is interesting to note that the compressive breaking strains of lumbar vertebrae, when tested at physiological strain rates, are generally between 7 and 9 kN, with the strength increasing at faster strain rates. However, at least half of the lumbar vertebrae tested in one study were found to have compressive strengths less than the calculated compressive forces.

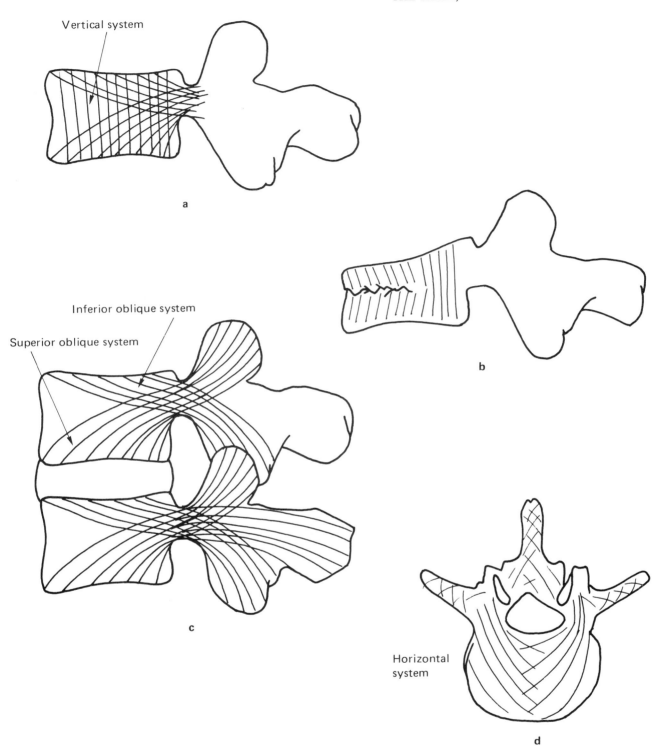

Vertical system

a

b

Inferior oblique system

Superior oblique system

c

Horizontal system

d

Fig. 6.73 Trabecular arrangement within vertebrae: **a** = within body: **b** = compression fracture; **c** = oblique system; **d** = horizontal system.

The vertebral unit

The vertebral unit is a useful concept when modelling of the vertebral column is to be attempted. It consists of two adjacent vertebrae and the intervening intervertebral disc. In terms of its functional components the vertebral column can be considered to consist of an anterior supporting pillar composed of the vertebral bodies and the intervertebral disc, and a posterior pillar comprising the articular processes joined by the vertebral arch. While the anterior pillar plays an essentially static role, the posterior pillar has a dynamic role in vertebral column mechanics.

A further differentiation of the components of the vertebral unit can be distinguished as horizontal layers sandwiched together. The vertebrae themselves form a passive segment, while the intervertebral disc and the posterior ligamentous structures form an active unit, which includes the articular processes. The mobility of this latter segment underlies the movements of the vertebral column.

The oblique trabecular systems described earlier (p. 788) functionally link the anterior and posterior pillars. With these systems as a basis, each vertebra can be compared to a first class lever system with the articular processes acting as the fulcrum (Fig. 6.74). It allows the absorption of axial compression forces applied to the vertebral column by direct and passive absorption by the intervertebral disc, and by indirect and active absorption by the posterior ligaments and paravertebral muscles.

Intervertebral disc mechanisms

At the ultrastructural level, the nucleus pulposus, annulus fibrosus and cartilage end plate appear as a close-packed system, which is postulated to act as a buffer against gravity and torsion and so act as a shock absorber of forces transmitted to the vertebral column. The ability to absorb shock is due to the construction of the disc, in which the soft fluid-like nucleus pulposus is encapsulated within the connective tissue lamellae of the annulus fibrosus. Vertical pressure on the vertebral column results in compression of the disc with deformation of the nucleus pulposus so that it expands radially against the surrounding annulus fibrosus; outward expansion of the annulus fibrosus is necessary in order for the disc to absorb shock.

An examination of lateral, posterolateral and posterior disc bulging under compressive loading and applied movements has shown that the disc may bulge up to 2.7 mm beyond its unloaded state. The largest bulges were associated with lateral flexion. Furthermore, no clear relationship was observed between intradiscal pressure and disc bulge. End plate bulge was found to be negligible (0.1 mm) compared with disc bulge. When degenerated discs were tested they exhibited a greater degree of bulging than non-degenerated discs, presumably because they are less efficient. The clinical manifestation of disc bulging, particularly in degenerating discs, may be the entrapment of the nerve roots as they pass through the narrowed intervertebral foramen.

It has been suggested that the nucleus pulposus plays a major mechanical role in determining the compressive deformation of the disc. However, experiments have shown that the annulus fibrosus appears to be the primary load-bearing structure, capable of performing this function in a near-normal fashion when part or all of the nucleus has been removed. Nevertheless, the efficient functioning of the disc depends to a large extent on the elasticity of the nucleus, which is closely related to its water-binding capacity. Increased pressure within the nucleus (by the imbibition of water) increases the height of the disc, and acts to prestress the disc reducing its laxity, and consequently increasing the vertebral joint stiffness (Fig. 6.75).

Measurements of disc strength and disc pressure show that the tensile strength of the annulus fibrosus is between 15 and 50 kg/cm^2, whilst that of the vertebral bodies varies from 8 to 10 kg/cm^2. In tension, failure is routinely observed at the disc end plate at forces of 850 N at cervical levels and 3000 N at lumbar levels. The vertebral bodies in the cervical region fail in compression at 3000 N and at 5000 N in the lumbar region. The tensile strength of the longitudinal ligaments is approximately 200 kg/cm^2, and

Fig. 6.74 Mechanical model of the vertebral unit.

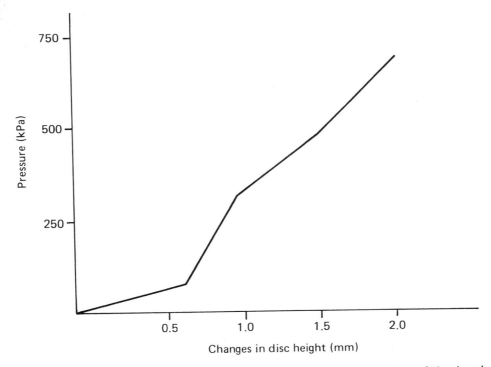

Fig. 6.75 Changes in disc height with increasing nuclear pressurization. (Adapted from Tencer A. F., Ahmed A. M. (1981). The role of secondary variables in the measurement of the mechanical properties of the lumbar intervertebral joint *Journal of Biomechanical Engineering*, **103**, 129–37.)

could therefore provide considerable resistance to disc rupture. The ultimate torsional strength of the intervertebral disc within an intact vertebral column is approximately $40 \, kg/cm^2$. From the foregoing it is possible to appreciate why the vertebral body may fracture without there being any evidence of disc rupture.

Mechanically, the intervertebral disc may be regarded as a viscoelastic structure capable of maintaining very large loads without disintegrating (Fig. 6.76a). The 'end point' of the disc is similar to that of steel. However, when the end point is exceeded the disc still retains some power of recovery after rest, thereby retaining its properties of elasticity. The mechanical efficiency of the disc appears to be improved with use, and the energy lost during recovery is decreased. This is significant in lifting heavy loads, providing a theoretical basis for the custom of 'taking the strain' before a heavy load is lifted. Complete recovery of a disc after loading is modified by the duration of the force application and by the interaction of the various structural elements.

With static loading, deformation of the disc depends on the duration of the loading, becoming stable after approximately 5 min. With loads of up to 130 kg most of the deformation occurs in the first 30 s following loading, even so no absolute equilibrium is reached even after a few hours, i.e. the disc exhibits creep characteristics. The nucleus pulposus appears to act as an incompressible medium of short duration (approximately 1 s), thereafter the nucleus and annulus interact to redistribute, equilibrate and adapt to the load. The creep characteristic is therefore a mechanism by which the disc can distribute the stress, and occurs until the disc adapts or reaches a stable state with respect to a particular load, being governed to a large extent by the zygapophyseal articulation. However, when a dynamic load is applied, the intervertebral disc may begin to vibrate (this occurs in less than 1 s and then dies out) (Fig. 6.76b). In this way the disc acts as a shock absorber by damping the oscillations.

The disc therefore has mechanical properties similar to many elastic and semielastic systems. It is important to be aware of these properties in order to understand the mechanisms of disc damage. For example, when a disc is loaded statically to approach its elastic limit, and then dynamically loaded in addition, the vibrations which occur may, at their peak, exceed the tensile limit of the annulus fibrosus, or the attachment to the bone, resulting in disc damage. The strength and site of failure of the disc appears to be related to the morphology of the nucleus pulposus, however, only when considerable weakness is already present does prolapse occur at a specific site.

a

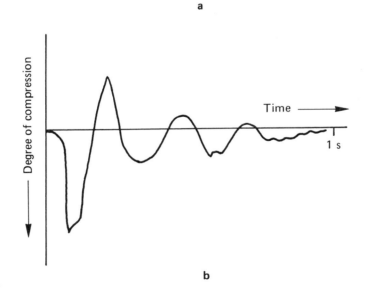

b

Fig. 6.76   **a** = Load-deflection and load-relax-
ation curves of an intervertebral disc. (Adapted
from Markolf K., Morris J. (1974). The structural components of the intervertebral disc.
Journal of Bone and Joint Surgery, **56A**, 675–
87.); **b** = dynamic loading of the intervertebral
disc. (Adapted from Hirsch C. S. (1955). The
reaction of the intervertebral disc to compressive forces. *Journal of Bone and Joint Surgery*,
37A, 1188–92.)

In vivo measurements of intradiscal pressures have shown that the force acting across the L5–S1 joint in a subject lifting loads, is 30% less than calculated theoretically, and more impressively is 50% less in the lower thoracic region. The difference between measured and theoretical findings is thought to be due to absorption of part of the load by the anterior abdominal muscles which contract in response to loading. Increases in disc pressure, compared with quiet standing, have been recorded when coughing (40%), stair climbing (40%) and when walking slowly (15%). The significance of intradiscal pressure is important with respect to discal fluid transport and nutrition. Sustained flexion-loading of a lumbar segment has been shown to produce fluid loss from the disc and a reduction in its height. Therefore sitting postures, which entail flexion of the lumbar column, cause more fluid to be expressed from the lumbar discs than do erect postures; the effect being particularly marked in the nucleus pulposus. The fluid flow in flexed postures is sufficiently large to aid nutrition of the disc. The links between posture, fluid flow and disc nutrition may explain why societies that habitually adopt flexed or squatting postures have a low incidence of lumbar disc degeneration.

With ageing, the mechanical arrangement, and thus the biomechanical response of the intervertebral disc in relation to the zygapophyseal joints, departs from that observed in earlier life. The disc space narrows and the surface contact area of the joints increases. The loss of disc space has been attributed to thinning of the disc, however it equally could be due to sinking of the disc into the vertebral body, which itself weakens with age due to osteoporosis. Whatever the cause, the result is that the anterior and posterior joints of the vertebral column become less protected by the load-attenuating and load-distributing properties of the nucleus with respect to the annulus, decreasing the range of movement as well as the tolerance to impact. A commonly observed radiographic manifestation in disc/joint degeneration is the appearance of bony spurs, ridges or transverse bars along the superior, inferior and lateral margins of the vertebral bodies, invertebral foramen and articular surfaces.

What is not certain is whether these changes are the result of purely mechanical factors causing a disturbance in the equilibrium of the surrounding tissues, or whether it is the result of localized disruption of the periosteum causing alteration in the relationship of normal form and bony contour, or indeed whether still other factors are involved. There does appear to be sufficient clinical and radiological evidence to suggest that the changes in the discs occur with changes in the posterior vertebral column at levels where stresses and strains are greatest (i.e. lower cervical and thoracolumbar areas), adversely affecting vertebral column kinematics. For example, when there is a structural change within the disc, there occurs with time an associated alteration in the zygapophyseal joints, or vice versa, thus affecting local biomechanics. The altered biomechanics of one component of the vertebral column may result in asymmetric motion between the column components, which in turn may cause accelerated damage and degeneration that may eventually affect the entire vertebral region.

Changes in the relative position of the vertebral body also involves changes in the relative positions of the zygapophyseal joints. As nucleus turgor is lost and the disc space decreases, these latter joints become partial weight-bearing elements. Although there is convincing radiographic evidence of osteophyte formation, there is no experimental evidence to confirm that osteophyte presence is indicative of degenerative disc disease.

With the intervertebral disc being indispensable for the normal functioning of the vertebral column, it is not surprising that artificial discs are being developed which could replace a degenerated disc. Although some such discs have been developed they, as yet, do not offer the same degree of efficiency as a replacement hip or knee joint does. There are, of course, fundamental differences in the design of joint prostheses and the design of an acceptable viscoelastic component. In addition, there are major problems associated with the process of removal of the degenerated disc, and implantation of the prosthesis, not least of which is the proximity of the spinal cord posteriorly and the emergence of the nerve roots through the intervertebral foramen. Nevertheless, the further development of such prostheses and their implantation offers tremendous benefits over plating and fixation of vertebral segments. It is to be hoped that it will not be too long before intervertebral disc replacement becomes as common as other joint replacements.

Pathology

The result of spinal fusion to counteract the effects of disc degeneration is to create stress concentrations at either end of the fused segment. These increased stresses increase the chance of degeneration or instability in these regions. Obviously, the greater the number of segments that are fused then the more the remaining segments must move to achieve the same overall range of movement. In the living this is not practically possible, nevertheless the greater the number of fused segments then the higher the stresses in the adjacent unfused segments. Making a section rigid by internal fixation may result in traumatic changes in adjacent segments.

Rotatory injuries of the vertebral column are associated with fractures of the articular facets, which tend to limit excessive rotation. At low levels of the vertebral column the common torsional injury is the facture-dislocation of the thoracolumbar junction. Above this level the thoracic column is relatively stiff by virtue of the presence of the rib cage, and the articular processes offer little resistance to rotation. Below this junction the lumbar region gains increased resistance to deformation by the orientation of the articular processes. The T12–L1 area, being a transitional area, has neither the thoracic supplementary protective elements nor the lumbar protective bony geometry, thus torsional deformation and stress are concentrated at the thoracolumbar junction.

The vertebral column possesses natural curvatures in the sagittal plane. A lateral curvature of the column in a frontal plane is termed a *scoliosis* (Fig. 6.77). In reality this is a three-dimensional deformity consisting of lateral flexion and a rotational abnormality. The curves can be broadly subdivided into two types: non-structural and structural. Non-structural curves have no structural abnormality and can easily be reversed by changing posture or by traction. Included in this group are postural curves which are eliminated on forward flexion and show no fixed vertebral rotation, and compensatory curves which are also devoid of vertebral rotation or structural changes. Compensatory curves develop above and below a single structural curve and maintain the alignment of the body. Structural curves, on the other hand, can be identified by demonstrating rib and vertebral rotation to the convexity of the curve on forward flexion. Radiographs of the curve show vertebral rotation with the bodies rotated to the convexity and the spinous processes to the concavity of the curvature.

In theory, scoliotic curves can occur anywhere along the length of the vertebral column, however in practice they are most commonly found in the thoracic and lumbar regions. Involvement of the thoracic region of the vertebral column is not surprising considering that there is little resistance to rotation in this region. The involvement of the lumbar region is more difficult to account for, although the importance of lordosis in the development of scoliosis has been stressed by some authorities.

One way of classifying scoliotic curves is in terms of the age of the patient. This is particularly important in *idiopathic scoliosis*, which accounts for some 85% of all scolioses, where the side of the convexity of the curve is related to the age of onset. *Infantile*

scoliosis (under the age of 4) is seen most commonly as a left thoracic curve, whereas right thoracic curves are most common in *adolescent scoliosis* (puberty to skeletal maturity). Of these, infantile scoliosis often regresses naturally. Juvenile scoliosis (age 4 to puberty) occurs with almost equal frequency to the right and left sides.

A further, and perhaps more important, classification of scoliosis is in terms of its aetiology and pathogenesis. Three classes of curves are considered:

1. *Congenital*—these arise due to congenital vertebral anomalies which themselves can be classified.
2. *Neuromuscular*—in which there is some obvious neurological or muscular impairment: this type of curve was very common until recently as it frequently developed following poliomyelitis.
3. *Idiopathic*—in which the aetiology is unclear, although many causes have been postulated: within this class there are four main groups, primary skeletal, neuromuscular, metabolic and hereditary.

Although the aetiology of many of the curves is understood, or at least postulated, the mechanisms by which the deformity develops are less certain.

The incidence of clinically evident scoliosis is of the order of 1 to 5 per thousand of the population. However, screening programmes have suggested that as many as 15% of the population show some form of lateral curvature of the vertebral column. Presumably many of these are of the non-structural type or never develop to any significance. Nevertheless, scoliosis is more common in the white population than the black and is more prevalent in females than in males (ratio of 5:1).

Fig. 6.77   A scoliotic spine.

7

The nervous system

Nikolai Bogduk

The nervous system

INTRODUCTION

The nervous system of the body consists of highly specialized cells that are designed to transmit information rapidly between various parts of the body. Topographically it can be divided into two major parts: the *central nervous system* and the *peripheral nervous system* (Fig. 7.1).

The central nervous system is a massive collection of nerve cells connected in an intricate and complex fashion to subserve the higher order functions of the nervous system, such as: thought, language, emotion, the control of movement and the analysis of sensation. It consists of the brain and spinal cord. The central nervous system is isolated from the rest of the body, and its cardinal characteristic is that it is located wholly within the skull and vertebral canal.

The peripheral nervous system consists of cells that connect the central nervous system with the other tissues of the body. These cells are aggregated into a large number of cable-like structures called nerves, which are threaded like wires throughout the tissues of the body.

Fig. 7.1 *The nervous system.* The brain and spinal cord constitute the central nervous system (CNS) which lies within the skull and vertebral canal. The nerves of the peripheral nervous system (PNS) connect the central nervous system with all other parts of the body.

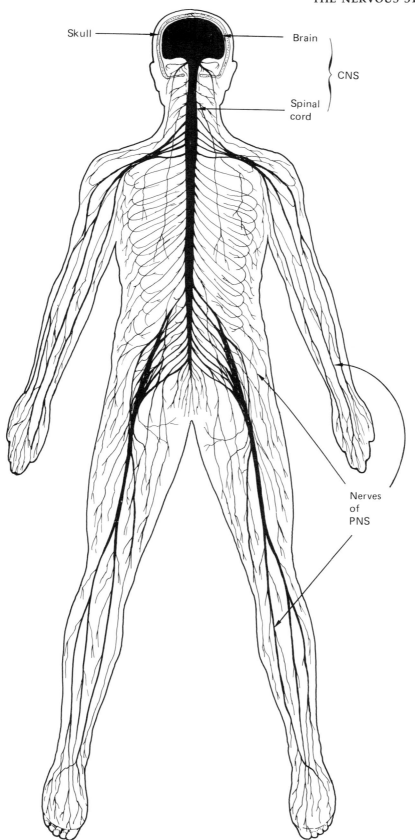

Skull

Brain

CNS

Spinal
cord

Nerves
of
PNS

Fig. 7.1

CELLULAR STRUCTURE

The basic cellular unit of the nervous system is the nerve cell or *neuron*. Neurons differ in size and shape according to their function and location within the nervous system, but all neurons have three characteristic components: a cell-body, an axon, and dendrites (Fig. 7.2).

The *cell body* of a neuron is an expanded portion of the cell which contains the nucleus and the apparatus necessary to sustain the metabolic activities of the cell. The *axon* is a longitudinal, tubular extension or process of the cell membrane and cytoplasm; its function is to transmit information away from the cell body. The cell membrane surrounding the axon is referred to as the *axolemma*. *Dendrites* are processes of the cell membrane that radiate from the cell body in various directions, and are responsible for receiving information and transmitting it to the cell body.

Structurally, dendrites differ from axons as they typically undergo extensive branching very close to the cell body. Axons, in contrast, remain singular for most of their course. They do not branch until their terminal ends are well away from the parent cell body. A neuron has only one axon, but may have several dendrites; the lengths and calibre of axons and dendrites vary, depending on the particular function of the neuron.

INTERNEURAL CONNECTIONS

Individual neurons convey information by conducting electrical action potentials along their cell membrane. Electrical information, however, does not pass from one neuron to another. Communication between separate neurons occurs chemically and involves a specialized structure called a *synapse*.

Synapses are formed by the close approximation of a small discrete area of the cell membrane of one neuron to a reciprocal area of the membrane of a second neuron (Fig. 7.3). The apposed membranes are specially modified in structure and are separated by a narrow gap, measuring about 0.02 µm in width, called the *synaptic cleft*. Across the synapse, one cell communicates with the next, and communication is unidirectional. The membrane of the cell that transmits the information is referred to as the *presynaptic membrane*, and that of the cell receiving the information is the *postsynaptic membrane*.

Near the presynaptic membrane, the cytoplasm of the transmitting neuron contains numerous small vesicles filled with chemicals known as *transmitter substances*. The nature of the transmitter substance varies according to the function of the neuron, but in all cases, when an electrical signal arrives at the terminal end of an axon, the transmitter substance is released from the vesicles through the presynaptic membrane into the synaptic cleft. There it flows across to the postsynaptic membrane where it exerts its effect. This effect can be excitatory or inhibitory depending on the nature of the transmitter substance and the nature of the receptors on the postsynaptic membrane with which it interacts. Excitatory substances generate an action potential in the postsynaptic neuron which can then propagate this potential to its other end. Inhibitory substances alter the electrical potential of the postsynaptic neuron and temporarily reduce its capacity to be stimulated by other neurons.

Synapses typically occur between the axon of one neuron and the dendrite of another. However, they may also occur between axons and cell bodies, axons and axons, and even between dendrites and dendrites. Some neurons receive only a few synapses while others may receive thousands.

The purpose of synapses is not to relieve one neuron of information and simply pass it on to the next, but to allow the interaction of information from perhaps several diverse sources on one cell. The activity of a given neuron may be influenced by many others and, conversely, by having several terminal branches to its axon, a single neuron may influence many other neurons.

By being connected to one another in diverse ways, groups of neurons are organized to subserve different functions of the nervous system. The patterns of connections or circuits vary in complexity and, in

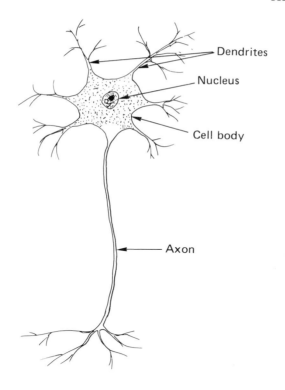

Fig. 7.2   The microscopic appearance of a neuron and its component parts.

Fig. 7.3   A neuron with multiple axo-somatic (as), axo-dendritic (ad) and axo-axonic (aa) synapses. The insets show the detailed structure of the synapse.

general, the more sophisticated the function being subserved, the more complex the circuitry. Only the circuits of a few simple functions are known, and one of the aims of modern research in neuroscience is to resolve the circuitry of more sophisticated functions.

MYELINATION

Myelination is a process whereby certain individual axons are wrapped in a sheath of lipid called *myelin*. The myelin sheath serves as a protective and an insulating coating for the axon, and enhances the speed of conduction of electrical impulses along it.

In the peripheral nervous system, myelination is performed by cells called *Schwann cells*. It is achieved by a Schwann cell curling an extension of its cell membrane around the shaft of the axon in a spiralling fashion (Fig. 7.4). As the extension of the Schwann cell wraps around the axon, the cytoplasm in it is squeezed out until only a double layer of the cell membrane of the Schwann cell remains spiralling around the axon (Fig. 7.4d). In this way the myelin sheath is formed by the lipid and protein of the

cell membrane of the Schwann cell that surrounds the axon. Peripheral to the myelin sheath, the axon is surrounded by the cytoplasm of the Schwann cell, and the outermost cell membrane of the Schwann cell, which acts as a second membrane to the axon, is referred to as the *neurolemma* (Fig. 7.4).

Along its length, a given axon is ensheathed in series by a large number of Schwann cells, but each Schwann cell is related only to a single axon (Fig. 7.4). Junction points where the myelin sheath of one Schwann cell ends and the sheath of the next Schwann cell begins are known as *nodes of Ranvier*. An axon together with the myelin sheath and the Schwann cells that surround it is referred to as a *nerve fibre*.

While many axons in the peripheral nervous system are myelinated a large number remain unmyelinated. Instead of being enveloped by a tightly spiralling sheath of myelin, they run embedded in invaginations of Schwann cell membranes, so that a single Schwann cell may envelope several axons (Fig. 7.5). In lacking a myelin sheath, unmyelinated axons are afforded less physical protection than myelinated ones, but the foremost difference between the two types of axons is that the unmyelinated axons conduct impulses at much slower velocities.

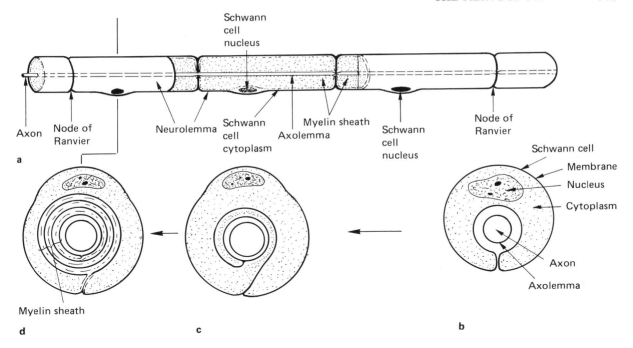

Axon

Node of Ranvier

Schwann cell nucleus

Neurolemma

Schwann cell cytoplasm

Schwann cell nucleus

Axolemma

Myelin sheath

Node of Ranvier

Schwann cell
Membrane
Nucleus
Cytoplasm

Axon
Axolemma

a

Myelin sheath

d   c   b

Fig. 7.4 A myelinated axon of the peripheral nervous system:

a = The microstructure of a nerve fibre. An axon is surrounded by a series of Schwann cells separated from one another by nodes of Ranvier. A segment of the fibre has been sectioned longitudinally to show the internal appearance of the relationships between the axon, its myelin sheath and Schwann cells. Fig. 7.4d depicts the appearance of a transverse section through the nerve fibre taken at the site marked in Fig. 7.4a.

b–d = Stages in the myelination of an axon. Initially the axon is surrounded by the cytoplasm of a Schwann cell (**b**). An extension of the cytoplasm curls around the axon (**c**). Cytoplasmic material is squeezed out of the cytoplasmic extension leaving only a double layer of the Schwann cell membrane spiralling around the axon and forming the myelin sheath (**d**).

Schwann cell membrane

Cytoplasm

Nucleus

Axons

Fig. 7.5 The relationship between unmyelinated axons and Schwann cells.

In the central nervous system, myelination is performed by specialized cells called *oligodendrocytes*. The process is basically similar to that in the peripheral nervous system, except that a given oligodendrocyte is usually involved in the simultaneous myelination of several, separate axons (Fig. 7.6). Unmyelinated axons in the central nervous system run embedded in cytoplasmic extensions, or processes, of oligodendrocytes.

Several diseases may affect myelinating cells, including toxic and metabolic diseases, and most notably multiple sclerosis. In these diseases, neurons are not necessarily directly affected, but the loss of their myelin covering affects the way they conduct action potentials, and this results in disordered neural function.

STRUCTURE OF A PERIPHERAL NERVE

A peripheral nerve is formed by the parallel aggregation of a variable number of axons; the greater the number of axons, the larger the size of the peripheral nerve. Microscopically, within a peripheral nerve, myelinated axons are surrounded by their individual Schwann cell sheaths and unmyelinated axons run embedded in invaginations of the Schwann cell membrane (Fig. 7.7). Furthermore, the axons are held together by sheaths of fibrous tissue which constitute additional coatings that protect them from external mechanical and chemical insults.

Individual myelinated axons are surrounded by a tubular sheath of fibrous tissue called *endoneurium*, whereas clusters of axons are held together by a larger fibrous sheath called *perineurium* (Fig. 7.7). Unmyelinated axons are not enclosed by endoneurium but run in isolated bundles parallel to myelinated axons and are enclosed with them in the perineurial sheath.

A bundle of axons enclosed within a single perineurial sheath is referred to as a nerve *fascicle* (Fig. 7.7). Axons within a fascicle largely remain within that same fascicle throughout the course of the nerve until their peripheral distribution. However, along the course of a peripheral nerve axons may at times leave one fascicle to enter and continue within an adjacent fascicle.

The fascicles within a peripheral nerve are bound together by an external sheath of fibrous tissue known as *epineurium* (Fig. 7.7) which forms the external surface of the macroscopic nerve. As a peripheral nerve passes through the tissues of the body, it gives off branches composed of one or more fascicles of the parent nerve, which leave it to reach their particular destination. Along the course of a nerve, this process is repeated until all the fascicles and axons in the nerve have been distributed to their target tissues.

Fig. 7.6 The relationship between an oligodendrocyte and the several myelinated and unmyelinated axons it ensheaths.

Fig. 7.7 The composition of a peripheral nerve. A peripheral nerve is formed by a variable number of nerve fascicles covered by epineurium. Each fascicle consists of bundles of nerve fibres surrounded by endoneurium and held together by perineurium. Nerve fibres are formed by myelinated axons and unmyelinated axons embedded in Schwann cell cytoplasm.

Oligodendrocyte

Process of
oligodendrocyte

Node of
Ranvier

Myelin
sheath

Axon

Non-myelinated axons

Fig. 7.6

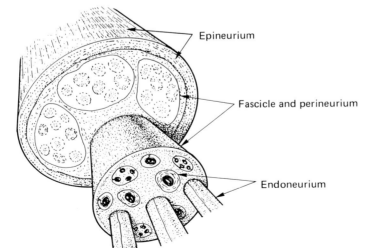

Epineurium

Fascicle and perineurium

Endoneurium

Fig. 7.7

THE CENTRAL NERVOUS SYSTEM

Structure

The central nervous system (CNS) is formed by the aggregation of bundles of axons and clusters of nerve cell bodies. The internal appearance and external form of the central nervous system reflects the manner in which these components are aggregated.

Because axons in the central nervous system are myelinated, clusters of axons take on a whitish appearance. Thus areas in the central nervous system formed mainly by axons are referred to as *white matter* (Fig. 7.8 and 7.9). In contrast, cell bodies are not myelinated, so that areas formed mainly by cell bodies appear grey, and are referred to as *grey matter* (Fig. 7.8 and 7.9).

A collection of cell bodies that forms a prominent, usually rounded swelling is referred to as a *ganglion* (Fig. 7.9). Clusters of axons that form a recognisable bundle within the central nervous system are referred to as a *fasciculus* (Latin meaning bundle) (Fig. 7.9). When bundles of axons form a raised bump or convex contour on the surface of the central nervous system, typically in the spinal cord, the surface resembles the external surface of a tube, and the elevation is referred to as a *funiculus*.

The above-mentioned terms refer simply to the topographic appearance of collections of axons or cell bodies without regard to their function. Other terms are used which carry functional implications. A cluster of axons with a similar function is known as a *tract*, whereas a cluster of cell bodies with a similar function is known as a *nucleus*.

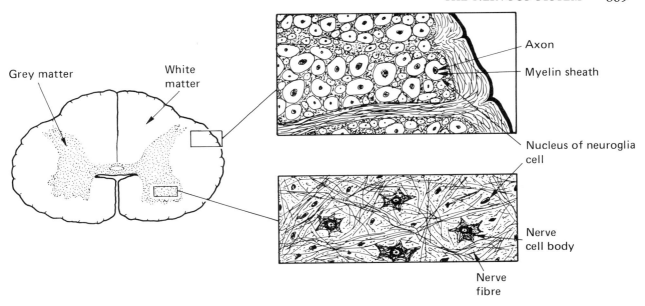

Fig. 7.8 White matter and grey matter as seen in a transverse section of the spinal cord. The central part of the spinal cord is formed by nerve fibres and nerve cell bodies. Such material appears grey on transverse sections. The outer part of the spinal cord consists chiefly of myelinated axons. The myelin endows this material with a white appearance in transverse sections.

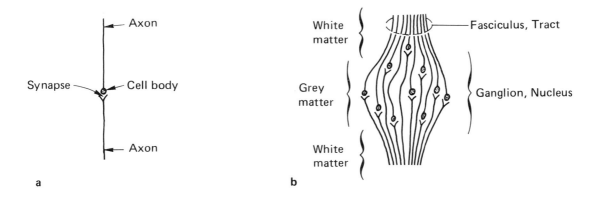

Fig. 7.9 In the central nervous system, neurons are connected in series, with the axon of one neuron forming a synapse with the cell body of the next neuron (**a**). When several axons run together in parallel, they form a fasciculus (**b**), and if they share the same functions the fasciculus is known as a tract. Aggregations of cell bodies form a ganglion, and if the cell bodies share the same functions the ganglion is known as a nucleus. Since cell bodies are not myelinated, ganglia and nuclei form grey matter, while myelinated axons form white matter.

Glial cells

Nerve cells are not the only constituents of the central nervous system. Dispersed between the nerve cells are several types of cells referred to collectively as glial cells (*glia*: Latin meaning glue) for their function, in general, is to hold the neurons of the central nervous system together. As a whole, glial cells outnumber nerve cells, and constitute almost half the total volume of the central nervous system.

Four types of glial cells are found in the central nervous system: *oligodendrocytes, microglia, ependymal cells* and *astrocytes* (Fig. 7.10). Oligodendrocytes have already been mentioned as the cells responsible for myelination in the central nervous system. Indirectly, because they myelinate several parallel axons, oligodendrocytes also serve to hold axons together within the central nervous system. Microglia are the macrophages of the central nervous system, being responsible for removing foreign matter and cellular debris.

Ependymal cells are exclusively found lining the internal surface of the ventricles of the central nervous system. They are epithelial cells arranged side-by-side forming a cellular barrier between the nervous system and the fluid in its cavities.

Astrocytes derive their name from their star-shaped appearance. These cells consist of a cell body with long processes radiating away from it. Two types of astrocyte can be recognized. Microscopically, *protoplasmic astrocytes* occur chiefly in the grey matter of the central nervous system and have thick processes that branch repeatedly. They weave between cell bodies, collectively holding them together, with some processes being attached to small blood vessels (Fig. 7.10). In contrast, *fibrous astrocytes* are found chiefly in white matter and have fewer but longer processes that weave between the axons. The principal role of astrocytes is to provide a framework for the central nervous system by holding the cell bodies and axons in place relative to one another. However, they also play an important role in the nutrition and metabolic activities of neurons by regulating the exchange of chemicals between themselves and blood vessels.

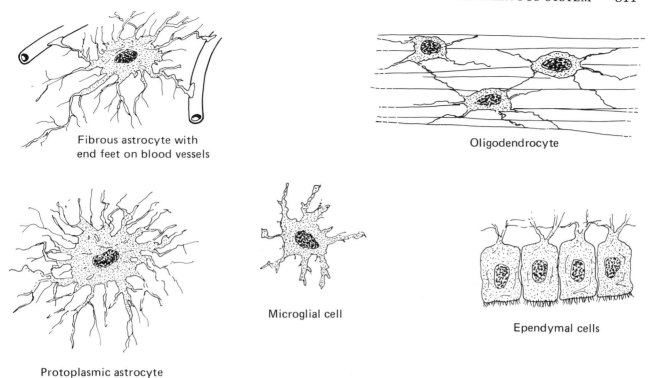

Fibrous astrocyte with
end feet on blood vessels

Oligodendrocyte

Protoplasmic astrocyte

Microglial cell

Ependymal cells

Fig. 7.10   The microscopic appearance of neuroglial cells.

Development

Because it explains many of the features of the adult central nervous system, it is worthwhile briefly considering the development of the central nervous system. In this regard, it is not the intention in this description to cover the entire embryology of the central nervous system, but merely to establish the nomenclature of its major subdivisions and to show how these come to take on their eventual adult form.

The central nervous system develops from a single tubular structure—the *neural tube* (Fig. 7.11a), which forms along the dorsal surface of the embryo, extending from the site of the future head to the tail. Accordingly the tube has two ends: a head end and a tail end. Because the tube eventually bends in the sagittal plane during development of the head and brain, the terms 'anterior, posterior, superior and inferior', as used in gross anatomy, cannot be applied to the nervous system without confusion. For example, although the head lies superiorly in the adult body, it equally lies at the anterior end of the developing embryo. In addition, the ventral surface of the developing neural tube largely comes to face anteriorly in the adult, but the part of it that forms the base of the brain comes to face inferiorly. To circumvent this confusion different terms of reference are therefore used with respect to the central nervous system.

The tail end of the neural tube is called the *caudal end* (Fig. 7.11a). The opposite end, regardless of the direction in which it points with respect to the rest of the body, is called the *rostral end* (Fig. 7.11a). The surface of the neural tube which faces the belly of the embryo is called its *ventral surface*, irrespective of whether the tube is straight or curved in the sagittal plane, while the opposite surface is the *dorsal surface*. These directional terms are equally applicable in descriptions of the adult central nervous system.

The neural tube maintains a narrow cavity along its length, while the thickness of its walls increases as the constituent cells multiply and grow. Most of the caudal part of the neural tube simply grows in length and diameter. Its walls get thicker but its cavity remains narrow. This section of the neural tube forms the future spinal cord, with its cavity becoming the *central canal* of the spinal cord (Fig. 7.11b).

The rostral end of the neural tube undergoes several changes. In various regions the cavity of the tube expands forming dilatations (Fig. 7.11b), and the walls of the tube surrounding these dilatations thicken as a result of nerve cell proliferation. The most rostral end of the neural tube is referred to as the *prosencephalon* (a name derived from the Greek word *encephalon* meaning brain, and *pro* meaning precursor). As the walls of the prosencephalon thicken they expand laterally taking with them a lateral diverticulum of the cavity of the neural tube. These lateral masses of neural tissue constitute the *telencephalon* of the central nervous system (Fig. 7.11c). This name is derived from the Greek words *encephalon* meaning brain, and *tel* meaning far away, referring to the fact that these regions come to lie the furthest away from the centre of the central nervous system. The cavities of the telencephalon on each side are known as the lateral ventricles.

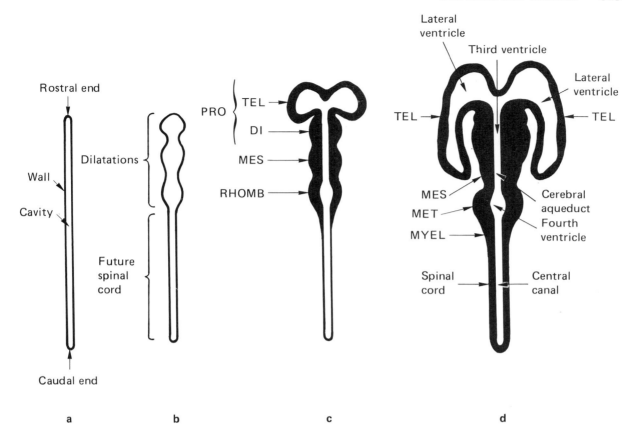

Fig. 7.11   Stages in the development of the central nervous system, as viewed in longitudinal (coronal) sections from a dorsal aspect:

a = The primitive neural tube.

b = Dilatations appear in the rostral end of the neural tube. The remainder forms the spinal cord.

c = Cells in the walls of the neural tube surrounding the dilatations proliferate to form the prosencephalon (PRO), which consists of the telencephalon (TEL) and diencephalon (DI); the mesencephalon (MES), and the rhombencephalon (RHOMB).

d = The telencephalon on each side elongates taking the lateral ventricle with it. The diencephalon surrounds the third ventricle. The mesencephalon surrounds the cerebral aqueduct. The rhombencephalon surrounds the fourth ventricle, and divides into the metencephalon (MET) and myelencephalon (MYEL). The walls of the spinal cord thicken around the central canal.

Gradually, the telencephalon enlarges and grows in a set pattern. There is some growth rostrally on each side, beyond the original rostral limit of the neural tube, but the major growth is laterally and caudally (Figs. 7.11d and 7.12). Cells over the caudo-lateral aspect of the telencephalon eventually grow laterally and then rostrally and ventrally forming an extension that overlaps the lateral aspect of the main mass of the telencephalon (Fig. 7.12d). The lateral ventricles participate in all this growth and elongate in the directions along which the cells of the telencephalon proliferate. Overall, the telencephalon and lateral ventricles assume a curved shape, like that of a ram's horn, extending laterally, then caudally, and eventually curving laterally, ventrally and rostrally.

As the telencephalon develops on each side, it covers and buries the remainder of the prosencephalon (Figs. 7.11d and 7.12). The walls of this part of the tube thicken and form the *diencephalon* (from the Greek *di* meaning between, referring to the fact that this part of the nervous system lies between the telencephalon on each side). The cavity of the diencephalon is known as the *third (III) ventricle* (the two lateral ventricles having constituted the first and second ventricles) (Fig. 7.11d). The third ventricle does not expand laterally. It enlarges only ventrodorsally to become a slit-like cavity at the rostral end of the fully developed central nervous system.

A short distance caudal to the diencephalon, the cavity of the neural tube expands to form the *fourth (IV) ventricle* which assumes a diamond shape when viewed from behind, with lateral angles and tapering rostral and caudal ends (Fig. 7.11d). The tissue surrounding this ventricle proliferates to form the *rhombencephalon* (referring to the rhomboid shape of the fourth ventricle). The rostral part of the rhombencephalon develops into a separate section called the *metencephalon* (Fig. 7.12). The dorsal portion of the metencephalon (that part behind the fourth ventricle) differentiates into a large mass called the *cerebellum* (Latin meaning little brain), and the ventral portion of the metencephalon (in front of the fourth ventricle) forms a bundle of neurons that arch around the ventral surface of the neural tube. Because this arch resembles a small bridge in shape, this section of the central nervous system is called the *pons* (Latin meaning bridge). The caudal portion of the rhombencephalon remains relatively undifferentiated. It is tapered and connects the pons to the spinal cord. It is referred to as the *myelencephalon* (Fig. 7.12).

The section of the neural tube between the diencephalon and the rhombencephalon does not undergo great proliferation. Its walls simply thicken and its cavity remains tubular and narrow. This region is known as the *mesencephalon* (Fig. 7.12), and its cavity is called the *cerebral aqueduct* (Fig. 7.11d).

Collectively, the mesencephalon, pons and myelencephalon constitute a single structural unit that connects the spinal cord to the diencephalon, with the cerebellum attached to it dorsally. It is referred to as the *brainstem*, because it resembles the stalk of a flower or cauliflower with the exuberant mass of the telencephalon representing the flowering part of the 'plant'.

Fig. 7.12 Successive stages in the development of the rostral end of the central nervous system, viewed from the right side:

a = The neural tube differentiates into the prosencephalon (PRO), mesencephalon (MES) and rhombencephalon (RHOMB), and flexes forwards at the junction between the prosencephalon and mesencephalon. **b** = The telencephalon (TEL) first appears as a bulge on the lateral surface of the prosencephalon, leaving the diencephalon (DI) in the midline. The rhombencephalon differentiates into the metencephalon (MET) and myelencephalon (MYEL). **c** = The telencephalon enlarges and grows backwards to cover the diencephalon. **d** = The telencephalon continues to enlarge caudally, and then ventrally, laterally and rostrally, almost completely burying the diencephalon. **e** = Eventually the future adult form of the brain is assumed. The massive telencephalon completely obscures the diencephalon and mesencephalon. The metencephalon forms the future cerebellum.

Nomenclature

The terminology used above with respect to the various subdivisions of the central nervous system is the most formal nomenclature that is in use. It is all based on the Greek word *encephalon*, with each subdivision named by adding a prefix. However, other systems of nomenclature based on Latin words or plain English are also used. Unfortunately, in practice no one system of nomenclature is used consistently, and certain terms are used only in the most formal of circumstances. The various terminologies and their equivalents are given in Table 7.1, with the most commonly used terms highlighted in an italic face. In general, Latin forms or common English forms are used when nouns are required to refer to various parts, but when adjectives are required it is usually the Greek forms that are used.

The term 'prosencephalon' is rarely used; neither is the term 'metencephalon' which refers collectively to the pons and cerebellum. The term 'myelencephalon' is virtually never used outside of an embryological context. Otherwise, this region is referred to by the Latin term *medulla oblongata* which alludes to the tapering shape of this part of the central nervous system as it narrows to the diameter of the spinal cord. The terms 'mesencephalon' and 'midbrain' are equivalent and are used interchangeably and with equal frequency.

Adult morphology

In the fully developed central nervous system most of its subdivisions are clearly recognizable. The spinal cord is long and cylindrical, occupying the rostral three-quarters of the vertebral column. The remainder of the central nervous system lies within the skull (Fig. 7.13). The cerebellum fills the posterior cranial fossa while the brainstem lies behind the clivus. The telencephalon and diencephalon occupy the remainder of the cranial cavity, i.e. the middle and anterior cranial fossae.

Table 7.1   Nomenclature of the division of the central nervous system

Division of central nervous system			
Greek system	*Latin system*	*Common English*	*Related cavity*
Prosencephalon		*Forebrain*	
Telencephalon	*Cerebrum*		Lateral ventricle
Diencephalon			Third ventricle
Mesencephalon		*Midbrain*	Cerebral aqueduct
Rhombencephalon		*Hindbrain*	Fourth ventricle
Metencephalon	*Cerebellum*		
	Pons		
Myelencephalon	*Medulla oblongata*		
	Medulla	*Spinal cord*	Central canal

Cerebrum

Cerebellum

Spinal cord

a

b

Fig. 7.13 The location of the central nervous system within the skull and vertebral canal: **a** = midline section of the head; **b** = lateral view of brain within the skull.

Diencephalon

The diencephalon is not readily apparent in the intact adult brain for it lies buried deep to the telencephalon. It can be demonstrated in dissections in which the telencephalon and cerebellum have been removed (Fig. 7.14). The largest component of the diencephalon on each side is a large mass of nuclei the size of a small egg—the *thalamus*. Each thalamus is continuous caudally with the midbrain, and is separated from the opposite thalamus by the cavity of the third ventricle. The functions of the thalamus are diverse, and include various motor, sensory and emotional processes.

Other components of the diencephalon include the *metathalamus, epithalamus* and *hypothalamus*. The metathalamus consists of two prominences projecting from the posterior, lateral, inferior surface of each thalamus (Fig. 7.14a). These are the medial and lateral geniculate bodies which are involved in certain auditory and visual processes respectively.

The epithalamus consists of a strip of neural tissue that bridges the posterior medial ends of the two thalami (Fig. 7.14b). Projecting from the posterior edge of the epithalamus in the midline is a pea-sized mass known as the *pineal body* or *gland*, a structure concerned with hormonal regulation, particularly of the reproductive hormones.

The hypothalamus forms the rostroventral part of the lateral wall of the third ventricle and is best seen in dissections in which the diencephalon has been split sagittally (Fig. 7.15). It is a thin layer of tissue that drapes from the ventromedial surface of the thalamus and blends with the opposite hypothalamus in the midline, thereby forming a sling of neural tissue across the floor of the third ventricle. Embryologically, the hypothalamus is formed by the ventral and ventrolateral walls of the rostral end of the neural tube while the lateral walls form the thalamus and telencephalon. The rostral end of the hypothalamus is marked by the *lamina terminalis*, a strip of neural tissue bridging the midline and derived from the rostral end of the original neural tube.

Fig. 7.14 The thalamus:
  a = Left lateral view of the brainstem and thalamus with the crus cerebri, optic tract and cerebellar peduncles having been cut (see Fig. 7.16). **b** = A top view of the two thalami astride the rostral end of the brainstem.

Fig. 7.15 A sagittal (midline) section of the brain and brainstem showing the location of the hypothalamus (shaded).

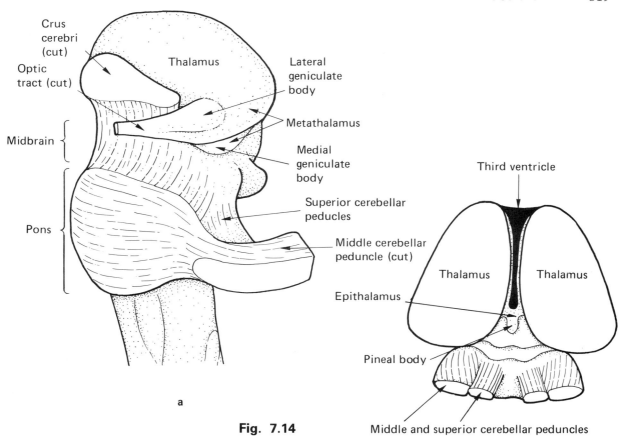

Crus cerebri (cut)

Optic tract (cut)

Thalamus

Lateral geniculate body

Metathalamus

Medial geniculate body

Midbrain

Pons

Superior cerebellar peducles

Middle cerebellar peduncle (cut)

a

Fig. 7.14

Third ventricle

Thalamus

Thalamus

Epithalamus

Pineal body

Middle and superior cerebellar peduncles

b

Anterior column

Corpus callosum

Thalamus

Pineal body

Lamina terminalis

Optic chiasma

Infundibulum

Hypophysis

Hypothalamus

Mammillary body

Oculomotor nerve

Pons

Superior colliculus

Inferior colliculus

Cerebral aqueduct

Cavity of fourth ventricle

Cerebellum

Fig. 7.15

Brainstem and cerebellum

For convenience, the morphology of the brainstem may be studied in specimens in which the cerebellum, telencephalon and diencephalon have been removed (Fig. 7.16). It should be appreciated that in such preparations removal of the cerebellum, which forms the dorsal portion of the hindbrain, opens the fourth ventricle. Therefore, what appears to be the posterior aspect of the brainstem at the level of the pons is actually the ventral wall of the fourth ventricle, referred to by convention as the floor of the fourth ventricle.

The most obvious feature of the ventral surface of the brainstem is the thick bundle of transversely running nerve fibres that constitute the *pons* (Fig. 7.17). Rostral to the pons lies the *mesencephalon* or *midbrain*. Caudal to it lies the *medulla oblongata*.

The ventral surface of the midbrain is marked by two obliquely orientated, semi-cylindrical prominences, each known as a *crus cerebri* or *cerebral peduncle* (Fig. 7.17). The crura cerebri convey motor fibres from the cerebrum to the brainstem.

The fibres of the crura cerebri appear to run under the pons and emerge caudal to it on the ventral surface of the medulla oblongata as two longitudinal prominences either side of the midline. Each of these is known as a *pyramid* (Fig. 7.17); they convey motor fibres to the spinal cord. A shallow midline cleft known as the *anterior median fissure*, separates the two pyramids, but caudally this fissure becomes obliterated for a short distance as the fibres in the pyramids cross the midline before passing into the substance of the spinal cord. This region where the pyramids cross is known as the *pyramidal decussation*. The caudal end of the decussation marks the junction of the medulla oblongata and the spinal cord (Fig. 7.17).

Lateral to each pyramid lies a rounded prominence on the surface of the medulla oblongata which is known as the *olive*. Cells within the olive are involved in the functions of the cerebellum.

The posterior surface of the midbrain is marked by four rounded projections known as *colliculi* (Latin meaning little hills). These are arranged in pairs with a *superior* and an *inferior colliculus* on each side (Fig. 7.17). The superior colliculi mediate certain reflexes involved in turning the head and eyes in response to visual stimuli, while the inferior colliculi mediate similar responses to auditory stimuli.

The caudal end of the medulla oblongata is marked posteriorly by two rounded elevations on each side of the midline. The medial of these is known as the *nucleus gracilis* and the lateral is the *nucleus cuneatus* (Fig. 7.17). These nuclei are responsible for processing sensory information concerning pressure, touch and position sense that passes from the spinal cord to the brainstem and thalamus.

The *cerebellum* is a mass of neural tissue, that outwardly resembles a large clam (Fig. 7.16), the principal function of which is the control of posture, repetitive movements and the geometric accuracy of voluntary movements. It is connected to the brainstem by three pairs of structures known as *peduncles* (Figs. 7.16 and 7.17). The largest of these are the *middle cerebellar peduncles* which run like a belt around the lateral aspect of the brainstem and are directly continuous with the pons. Passing rostrally from the cerebellum into the dorsal aspect of the midbrain are the two *superior cerebellar peduncles* connecting the cerebellum to the rostral portion of the brainstem and the thalamus. Passing caudally from the cerebellum into the dorso-lateral aspects of the medulla oblongata are the two *inferior cerebellar peduncles* which connect the cerebellum with the medulla oblongata and the spinal cord.

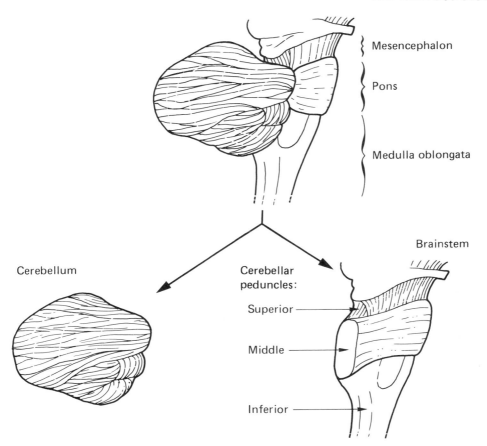

Mesencephalon

Pons

Medulla oblongata

Brainstem

Cerebellum

Cerebellar peduncles:

Superior

Middle

Inferior

Fig. 7.16 The brainstem and cerebellum showing how they can be separated by dividing the superior, middle and inferior cerebellar peduncles.

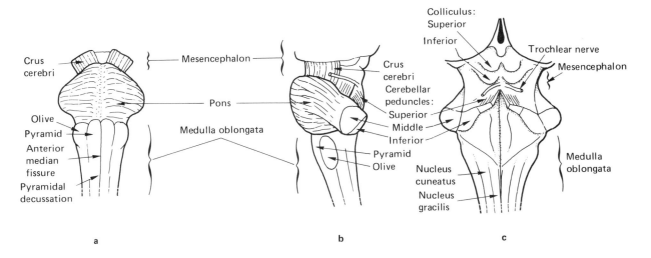

Crus cerebri

Mesencephalon

Olive

Pyramid

Anterior median fissure

Pyramidal decussation

Pons

Medulla oblongata

Crus cerebri

Cerebellar peduncles:

Superior

Middle

Inferior

Pyramid

Olive

Colliculus:

Superior

Inferior

Trochlear nerve

Mesencephalon

Nucleus cuneatus

Nucleus gracilis

Medulla oblongata

a

b

c

Fig. 7.17 Topographical features of the brainstem: **a** = anterior aspect; **b** = lateral aspect; **c** = posterior aspect.

Cerebrum

The cerebrum is divided into left and right halves by a large cleft known as the *longitudinal fissure* (Fig. 7.18a). Each half is referred to as a *cerebral hemisphere*. Deep in the longitudinal fissure the two hemispheres are connected by a large body of transversely running nerve fibres known as the *corpus callosum* (Fig. 7.18a). When the two cerebral hemispheres are separated by a midline incision, their medial surfaces are revealed and the transected surface of the corpus callosum is seen (Fig. 7.18b).

The surface of each cerebral hemisphere is formed by a layer of grey matter, varying between 2–5 mm in thickness, known as the *cerebral cortex*. It contains the cell bodies of the neurons responsible for the various functions of the cerebrum. Deep to the cortex, the cerebral hemispheres are formed by a large mass of white matter that consists of the axons of the neurons in the cerebral cortex, together with axons that enter the cerebrum from the brainstem and diencephalon.

Fig. 7.18 The brain: **a** = Top view of entire brain showing its division into right and left cerebral hemispheres by the longitudinal fissure. **b** = Medial view of the right cerebral hemisphere showing the cut surface of the corpus callosum.

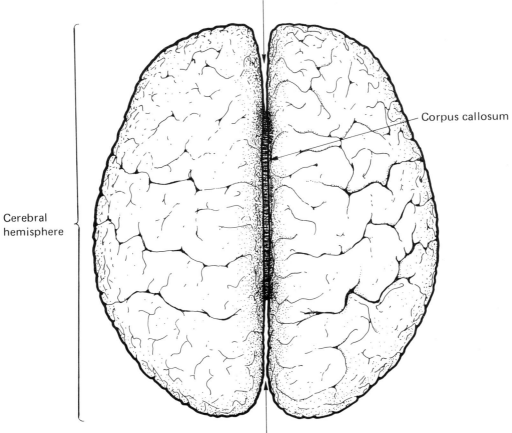

Longitudinal fissure (anterior end)

Corpus callosum

Cerebral
hemisphere

Longitudinal fissure (posterior end)

a

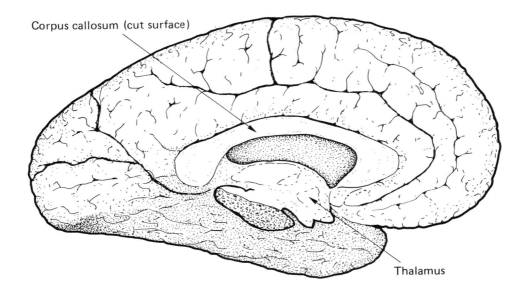

Corpus callosum (cut surface)

Thalamus

b   **Fig. 7.18**

For descriptive purposes, each cerebral hemisphere is divided into four lobes that are named according to the bones of the skull to which they are most closely related (Fig. 7.19). The rostral, or anterior portion of each cerebral hemisphere lies deep to the frontal bone and is known as the *frontal lobe*. The posterior portion lies deep to the occipital bone and is known as the *occipital lobe*. The upper lateral portion of each hemisphere lies deep to the parietal bone and is known as the *parietal lobe*. The lower lateral portion projects laterally and rostrally, lateral to the parietal and frontal lobes. Lying deep to the squamous portion of the temporal bone it is known as the *temporal lobe*. The posterior end of each cerebral hemisphere tapers to a single prominence known as the *occipital pole*. The most anterior ends of the frontal and temporal lobes are known respectively as the *frontal pole* and the *temporal pole*.

The surface of the cerebral cortex is thrown into ridges running in various directions, separated from one another by valley-like depressions. The ridges are referred to as *gyri* (singular: gyrus) and the depressions as *sulci* (singular: sulcus). Each of the gyri and sulci are ascribed a particular name, but these need not be learned until a more detailed study of the central nervous system is undertaken. However, certain sulci and gyri should be recognized because of their significance in subdividing the cerebral hemispheres both topographically and functionally (Fig. 7.20).

The most obvious sulcus is the one that separates the temporal lobe from the parietal and frontal lobes. From the medial aspect of the temporal pole it runs backwards and upwards like a deep valley medial to the temporal lobe, ending at the junction of the temporal lobe with the parietal lobe. Strictly speaking, this sulcus is known as the *posterior ramus of the lateral sulcus*, but, for brevity, it is usually known as the *lateral sulcus*.

Various sulci cross the frontal and parietal lobes transversely (mediolaterally and from above downwards across the surface of the hemisphere). One of these has certain features that allow it to be distinguished from adjacent sulci. It is located near the middle of the cerebral hemisphere and for this reason is known as the *central sulcus* (Fig. 7.20).

It extends from the medial surface of the hemisphere across to its lateral surface, reaching almost as far as the lateral sulcus. Whereas other sulci may extend onto the medial aspect of the cerebral hemisphere, or may reach almost as far as the lateral sulcus, the central sulcus is the only continuous sulcus that does both, and on these grounds it can be recognized unmistakably.

The central sulcus serves to demarcate the frontal lobe from the parietal lobe. All the tissue anterior to the central sulcus therefore constitutes the frontal lobe, with the parietal lobe lying behind it. The sulcus running parallel to the central sulcus and in front of it is known as the *precentral sulcus*, with the gyrus between them known as the *precentral gyrus* (Fig. 7.20). Its significance is that stimulation of the precentral gyrus results in contraction of voluntary muscles, and for this reason this gyrus is referred to as the *motor cortex*.

Similarly, the sulcus immediately behind the central sulcus is known as the *postcentral sulcus*, with the gyrus between the two known as the *postcentral gyrus* (Fig. 7.20). This gyrus receives sensory information from the brainstem and thalamus, and accordingly is sometimes referred to as the *sensory cortex*.

Some distance behind the postcentral sulcus, the medial surface of the cerebral hemisphere is crossed by a clearly marked transverse sulcus that extends onto the upper part of the lateral surface of the hemisphere. This is the *parieto-occipital sulcus* which demarcates the parietal lobe from the occipital lobe (Fig. 7.20). Anteriorly, the parietal lobe is separated from the temporal lobe by the posterior end of the lateral sulcus, but posteriorly no major topographical feature delineates the junction between the temporal lobe and the parietal and occipital lobes.

On the medial aspect of the cerebral hemisphere, the lower end of the parieto-occipital sulcus merges with a longitudinally running sulcus that is known as the *calcarine sulcus* (Fig. 7.20). This name was adopted because the appearance of the parieto-occipital and calcarine sulci together resembles the profile of a bird's foot, with the parieto-occipital sulcus representing the leg and the calcarine sulcus forming the posterior spur

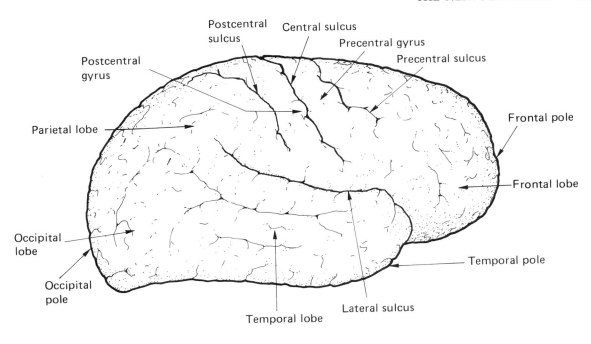

Fig. 7.19   The cerebral hemisphere and its subdivision into lobes, and the principal sulci on the lateral surface.

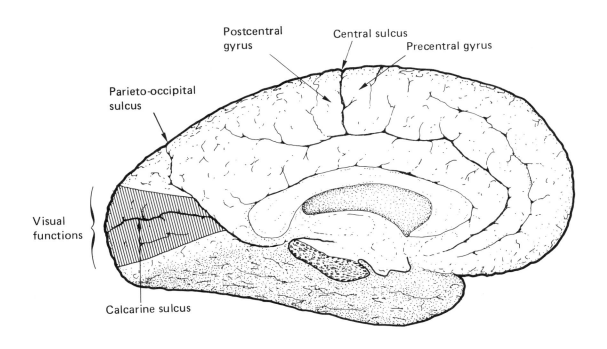

Fig. 7.20   The principal sulci and gyri of the cerebral hemispheres on the medial surface.

(*calcar:* Latin meaning spur). The significance of the calcarine sulcus is that the cortex either side of it is the region of the cerebrum responsible for vision.

All of the occipital lobe, in one way or another, is involved in the function of vision. The parietal lobe is, in general, responsible for sensory functions, such as the perception of touch, pressure, and the position of the body and limbs. It is also responsible for more sophisticated functions such as three-dimensional perception, analysis of visual images, language, geometry and calculations (Fig. 7.21). The frontal lobe subserves motor functions and governs the expression of intellect and personality. The upper part of the temporal lobe opposite the postcentral gyrus is involved in the perception of sound, while the remainder is concerned with memory and various emotional functions.

Base of the brain

The ventral surface or base of the brain is formed largely by the ventral surfaces of the frontal, temporal and occipital lobes of the cerebral hemispheres on each side (Fig. 7.22). The medial edge of the most rostral end of the temporal lobe on each side projects like a blunt hook towards the midline. This region of the cerebral cortex is known as the *uncus* (Latin meaning hook). The uncus subserves the perception of smell.

Anteriorly, neural tissue is absent between the two frontal lobes where they are separated by the longitudinal fissure. Caudal to this space lies the floor of the third ventricle, formed by the junction of the hypothalamus from each side. Most posteriorly, the brainstem projects caudally from the inferior or caudal surface of the diencephalon, which lies buried deep to the cerebral hemispheres.

Projecting in the midline from the floor of the third ventricle is a funnel-shaped extension of neural tissue known as the *infundibulum* (see Figs 7.22 and 7.15). This structure connects the hypothalamus to the pituitary gland and consists of axons from cells in the hypothalamus that regulate the secretion of oxytocin and antidiuretic hormone by the pituitary gland. Caudal to the infundibulum lie two small breast-like prominences known as the mamillary bodies (*mamilla:* Latin meaning little breast), the functions of which are not fully understood (Fig. 7.22).

Applied to the ventral aspect of the diencephalon is an obvious X-shaped structure. It consists of two rostral arms leading to an intersecting region from which two further limbs project caudally to wrap around the crura cerebri and end in the metathalamus (Fig. 7.22). The rostral arms are the terminal ends of the two *optic nerves* which transmit visual information from the retina of the eye. The intersecting region is known as the *optic chiasm* in which certain fibres from each optic nerve cross the midline. The caudal limbs are the *optic tracts* each of which conveys visual information from one half of the visual field to the ipsilateral lateral geniculate body (see Fig. 7.14a).

Analysis of visual
and auditory sensations

Analysis of sensation

Primary sensation

Motor functions (movement)

Intellect,
personality,
memory

Vision

Hearing

Emotions, memory

Fig. 7.21   Principal functions of certain regions of the cerebrum.

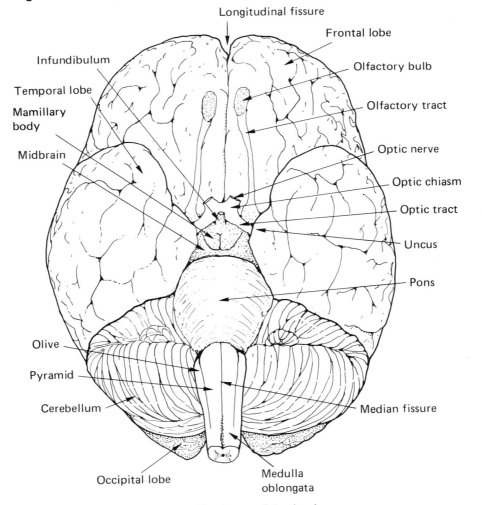

Longitudinal fissure

Frontal lobe

Infundibulum

Olfactory bulb

Temporal lobe

Olfactory tract

Mamillary
body

Optic nerve

Midbrain

Optic chiasm

Optic tract

Uncus

Pons

Olive

Pyramid

Cerebellum

Median fissure

Occipital lobe

Medulla
oblongata

Fig. 7.22   The base of the brain.

Cranial nerves

Certain nerves project from the cranial portion of the central nervous system, i.e. that portion within the skull. These nerves connect the brainstem and diencephalon with various structures and tissues in the head and neck, and with various thoracic and abdominal viscera. While inside the skull, these nerves constitute part of the central nervous system and, as a rule, become peripheral nerves only once they leave the skull. There are twelve pairs of cranial nerves that are known by number or by a name. The name usually reflects the form, function or distribution of the nerve.

The first cranial nerve (*I*) mediates the perception of smell and is known as the *olfactory nerve*. It is in fact composed of a series of short nerves that project from the olfactory epithelium in the roof of the nose through the cribriform plate of the ethmoid bone. Because of their small size they can only be visualized in microscopic dissections or histological preparations of the cribriform plate. The further connections of the olfactory nerves are, however, evident on specimens of the brain. Running along the ventral surface of each frontal lobe is a strip of neural tissue with an expanded rostral end; the whole structure resembles a tiny, flattened spoon or spatula. The expanded end is the *olfactory bulb*, and the long strip is the *olfactory tract* (see Fig. 7.22). Each olfactory nerve synapses on cell bodies that form the ipsilateral olfactory bulb, and the axons of these cells constitute the olfactory tract. The olfactory tract ramifies in the anterior end of the hypothalamus where it has diverse connections, the majority of which eventually pass to the uncus.

The second cranial nerve (*II*) is the *optic nerve* which transmits visual information from the ipsilateral retina to the optic chiasm (see Fig. 7.22). Information from both eyes is transmitted by each optic tract to the lateral geniculate body on each side. After processing this information, cells in the lateral geniculate body eventually relay it to the occipital lobes of the ipsilateral cerebral hemisphere through axons that run in the white matter of the cerebral hemisphere.

The third cranial nerve (*III*) innervates certain muscles of the eye, and is consequently known as the *oculomotor nerve*. It emerges from the ventral surface of the midbrain at the level of the superior colliculus immediately medial to the crus cerebri on each side (Fig. 7.23a and b). It reaches the orbit by passing through the cavernous sinus and then through the superior orbital fissure.

The fourth cranial nerve (*IV*) innervates the superior oblique muscle of the eye and is known as the *trochlear nerve* because the superior oblique muscle acts around a pulley in the orbit (*trochlea:* Latin meaning pulley). The nerve emerges from the dorsal aspect of the midbrain immediately below the inferior colliculus (Fig. 7.23c), and then winds around the crus cerebri to appear on the ventral aspect of the brainstem (Fig. 7.23a and b). It enters the orbit by passing through the cavernous sinus and then through the superior orbital fissure.

The fifth cranial nerve (*V*) divides into three large branches, and is accordingly known as the *trigeminal nerve*. The nerve is mainly sensory with the cell bodies of the sensory fibres located in a swelling on the nerve, the *trigeminal ganglion*, formed at the junction of its three divisions (Fig. 7.23a and b). The part of the nerve between the ganglion and the brainstem is known as the *sensory root* of the trigeminal nerve. It is attached to the lateral aspect of the pons, and demarcates the junction of the pons with the middle cerebellar peduncle.

Although the pons and middle cerebellar peduncle are continuous with one another, being formed essentially by the same nerves, they are by convention demarcated by an imaginary line passing longitudinally through the point of attachment of the trigeminal root to the brainstem. The middle cerebellar peduncle lies dorsal to this line, and the pons ventral to it.

The trigeminal nerve projects ventrally onto the superior surface of the petrous temporal bone, with the trigeminal ganglion resting in a shallow depression on the surface of this bone. Beyond the ganglion the three divisions of the trigeminal nerve leave the skull to supply particular regions of the face and skull.

The first or *ophthalmic division* (V_1) enters the orbit through the superior orbital fissure and its branches supply the ethmoidal air cells, the walls of the nasal cavity, the cornea

Fig. 7.23 The cranial nerves of the brainstem, labelled by number: **a** = anterior view; **b** = left lateral view; **c** = posterior view.

and conjunctiva and the skin of the forehead. The second or *maxillary division* (V_2) leaves the cranial cavity through the foramen rotundum and its branches are distributed to the nasal cavity, the upper teeth, the hard and soft palates and the skin of the face covering the maxilla and zygoma. The third or *mandibular division* (V_3) passes through the foramen ovale and supplies the lower teeth, the temporomandibular joint, the tongue and the skin overlying the lower jaw and temporal regions.

Although largely sensory, the trigeminal nerve is accompanied by a small nerve known as the *motor root* of the trigeminal nerve. This root emerges from the pons just below the sensory root (see Fig. 7.23a and b), and joins the mandibular division of the trigeminal nerve in the foramen ovale, whereafter it supplies the muscles of mastication.

The sixth cranial nerve (*VI*) innervates the lateral rectus muscle of the eye which is responsible for abducting the eye, and for this reason the nerve is known as the *abducens nerve*. It emerges from the brainstem at the caudal border of the pons between it and the commencement of the pyramid (see Fig. 7.23a and b), entering the orbit through the superior orbital fissure.

The seventh and eighth cranial nerves (*VII*) and (*VIII*) emerge as a pair from the lateral aspect of the medulla oblongata immediately below the caudal border of the pons (see Fig. 7.23a and b). They both enter the internal auditory meatus. The seventh cranial nerve is the more medial of the pair, and is known as the *facial nerve* because it innervates the muscles of facial expression after emerging from the stylomastoid foramen. It also contains taste fibres from the anterior two-thirds of the tongue, and parasympathetic fibres destined to innervate the lacrimal, submandibular and sublingual glands.

The eighth cranial nerve has two components: vestibular and cochlear, and is consequently known as the *vestibulocochlear nerve*. The cochlear division arises in the cochlea of the inner ear, and is responsible for hearing. The vestibular division innervates the vestibular apparatus of the inner ear and is responsible for the sense of balance.

The ninth, tenth and eleventh cranial nerves (*IX*), (*X*) and (*XI*) appear as a series of tiny rootlets aligned along the lateral surface of the medulla oblongata (see Fig. 7.23a and b). The uppermost of these rootlets converge to form the ninth cranial nerve, otherwise known as the *glossopharyngeal nerve*; the middle rootlets form the tenth cranial nerve, the *vagus nerve*, and the lowest rootlets form the cranial part of the eleventh cranial nerve, the *accessory nerve*. All three nerves leave the skull through the jugular foramen.

The glossopharyngeal nerve supplies the stylopharyngeus muscle, but principally it is sensory to the pharynx and posterior one-third of the tongue. The vagus nerve, has a diverse distribution including the muscles of the pharynx and larynx, the mucosa of the larynx, the viscera of the chest and much of the abdominal viscera. The ninth and tenth cranial nerves also innervate the carotid body and carotid sinus and are thereby involved in cardiovascular reflexes.

The *accessory nerve* has two components: a cranial and a spinal part. The *cranial accessory nerve* is formed by the lowest rootlets from the lateral aspect of the brainstem. The *spinal accessory* nerve is formed by rootlets that emerge from the lateral aspect of the rostral end of the spinal cord, and which converge to form a single trunk that enters the skull through the foramen magnum (see Fig. 7.23a and b). The spinal and cranial parts of the accessory nerve join for a short distance, but the fibres of the cranial part are rapidly transferred to the vagus nerve through which they are distributed to the muscles of the pharynx, larynx and soft palate. The spinal accessory nerve leaves the skull independently but in company with the glossopharyngeal and vagus nerves through the jugular foramen, and is distributed to the sternomastoid and trapezius muscles.

The twelfth cranial nerve (*XII*) supplies the muscles of the tongue and is known as the *hypoglossal nerve*. It emerges from the brainstem as a series of rootlets attached along the depression between the pyramid and the olive on each side (see Fig. 7.23a and b), leaving the skull through the hypoglossal canal in the occipital bone.

Fig. 7.24 The cranial nerves of the brainstem, labelled by number: **a** = anterior view; **b** = left lateral view; **c** = posterior view.

(This figure has been repeated for convenience.)

Spinal cord

The spinal cord is essentially a long thick cable formed by thousands of longitudinally running axons surrounding a central core of grey matter. It is some 45 cm long and occupies the vertebral canal at cervical, thoracic and upper lumbar levels.

The external surface of the spinal cord has only a few features that have attracted names (Fig. 7.25). Running along the midline on the ventral surface is a pronounced depression known as the *anterior median fissure*. This divides the ventral part of the spinal cord into left and right halves. Dorsally, the spinal cord is marked by several less pronounced longitudinal depressions, one of which lies in the midline, demarcating the left and right halves of the spinal cord, and is known as the *posterior median sulcus*. Another runs along the posterolateral aspect on each side of the entire length of the spinal cord, and is known as the *posterior lateral sulcus*. A further sulcus is present on each side of the rostral half of the spinal cord running longitudinally between the posterior median and posterior lateral sulci. This is known as the *posterior intermediate sulcus*.

Between the three sulci on each side of the rostral half of the spinal cord lie two slightly rounded prominences that extend longitudinally. The medial of the two, between the posterior median and posterior intermediate sulci, is known as the *fasciculus gracilis*, and the other, between the posterior intermediate and the posterior lateral sulci, is the *fasciculus cuneatus*. These fasciculi are formed by bundles of sensory axons destined to synapse in the nucleus gracilis and nucleus cuneatus respectively. Only the fasciculus gracilis is present in the caudal half of the spinal cord, so a posterior intermediate sulcus is lacking in this region.

The width of the spinal cord is not uniform along its length. It is expanded a short distance below its rostral end and again near its caudal end (Fig. 7.25). These expansions occur at levels of the spinal cord responsible for the innervation of the upper and lower limbs. They are formed by the relatively larger number of cell bodies and axons located at these levels to deal with limb functions, and are called respectively the *cervical* and *lumbar enlargement*. The caudal end of the spinal cord tapers to a pointed tip, and this tapering portion is known as the *conus medullaris* (Latin meaning the cone of the spinal cord).

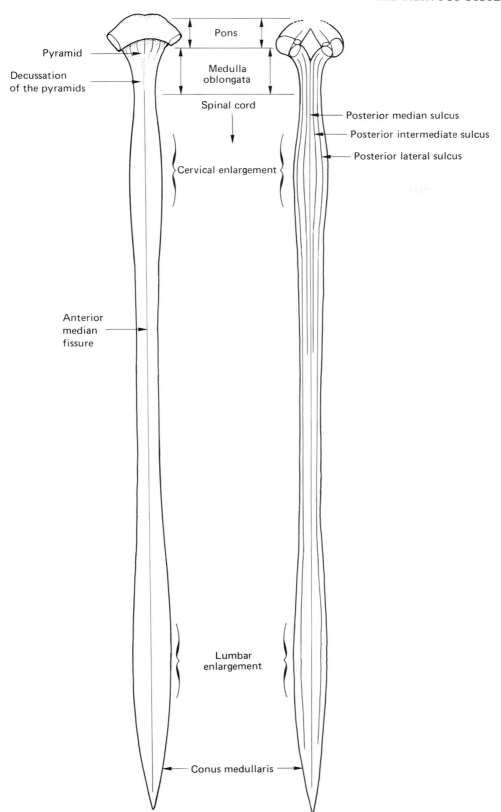

Fig. 7.25 The appearance and surface features of the spinal cord.

Spinal nerves

The spinal nerves are short nerves that lie in the intervertebral foramina of the vertebral column (Fig. 7.26). Outside the vertebral column they form elements of the peripheral nervous system, but within the vertebral canal each spinal nerve is connected to the spinal cord by ventral and dorsal *nerve roots* which are components of the central nervous system.

There are 31 pairs of spinal nerves, each being named according to the vertebra to which it is related. There are eight cervical spinal nerves named C1 to C8, each of which lies *above* the cervical vertebra with the same segmental number except for C8 which lies *below* the C7 vertebra. The remaining spinal nerves take the name of the vertebra that lies above them. Thus, the nerve below the T6 vertebra, for example, is the T6 spinal nerve, and the nerve below the L2 vertebra is the L2. In all, there are 8 cervical (C1–C8), 12 thoracic (T1–T12), 5 lumbar (L1–L5), 5 sacral (S1–S5), and one pair of coccygeal (Co1) spinal nerves.

The ventral roots of all the spinal nerves attach in a longitudinal series to the ventro-lateral aspect of the spinal cord on each side (Fig. 7.27). Similarly the dorsal roots attach to the posterolateral aspect of the spinal cord along the posterior lateral sulcus. As each dorsal root approaches the spinal cord it divides into a series of small branches called *rootlets* which form the junction with the spinal cord. Correspondingly, each ventral root is formed by a series of rootlets which emerge from the spinal cord and gather to form the ventral root proper.

The dorsal roots convey only sensory fibres from the spinal nerves to the spinal cord. The ventral roots convey motor fibres from the spinal cord to the spinal nerves, but they also contain some sensory fibres. Near its junction with the ventral root and the spinal nerve, each dorsal root bears a swelling known as the *dorsal root ganglion* (Fig. 7.27). It is formed by the cell bodies of all the sensory fibres that run in the related spinal nerve.

Each spinal nerve is attached by its roots to a discrete section of the spinal cord called a *spinal cord segment*. The limits of each segment are demarcated by an imaginary transverse plane drawn through the spinal cord midway between the sites of attachment of the most rostral of the rootlets connected to one particular spinal nerve and the most caudal rootlet of the nerve next above. Each spinal cord segment is named according to the spinal nerve which attaches to it (Fig. 7.28). Consequently, the spinal cord consists of a continuous series of 8 cervical, 12 thoracic, 5 lumbar, 5 sacral segments and one coccygeal segment.

Fig. 7.26 The spinal cord and spinal nerves viewed from the back. The lamina of the vertebrae have been removed to reveal the spinal cord in the vertebral canal, and the spinal nerves in the intervertebral foramina.

Fig. 7.27 A close-up view of two segments of the spinal cord and their spinal nerve roots and rootlets.

Fig. 7.28 The spinal cord and its division into segments.

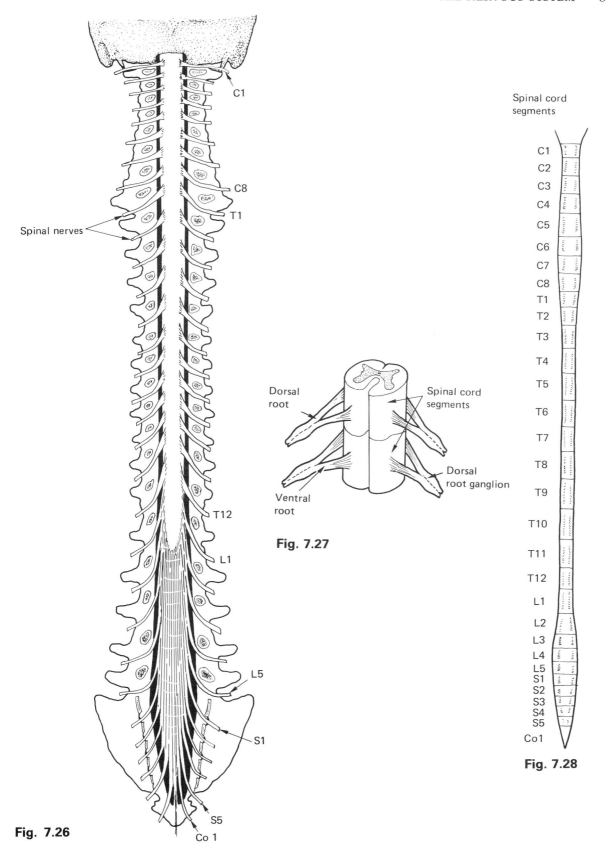

Spinal nerves

C1

C8

T1

T12

L1

L5

S1

S5

Co 1

Fig. 7.26

Dorsal root

Ventral root

Spinal cord segments

Dorsal root ganglion

Fig. 7.27

Spinal cord segments

C1
C2
C3
C4
C5
C6
C7
C8
T1
T2
T3
T4
T5
T6
T7
T8
T9
T10
T11
T12
L1
L2
L3
L4
L5
S1
S2
S3
S4
S5
Co1

Fig. 7.28

Internal structure of the central nervous system

The internal structure of the central nervous system can be studied in a variety of ways. Various dissection and microscopic techniques can be used to determine the location of cell bodies and to trace the course and distribution of axons, but these are used to obtain detailed and specific information. For introductory purposes, it is sufficient to examine the appearance of simple transections of the central nervous system.

Spinal cord

The central core of the spinal cord consists of grey matter which in transverse section has a characteristic appearance (Fig. 7.29). It is distributed in a pattern resembling the shape of a butterfly. The central area surrounding the central canal of the spinal cord is known as the *central grey matter*. Projecting dorsolaterally and ventrally from this central area are extensions of grey matter known as the *dorsal* and *ventral horns.*

The ventral horns on each side are formed by the cell bodies of neurons that innervate voluntary muscles. The axons of these cells leave the spinal cord through the ventral roots. The dorsal horns consist of cells concerned with the processing of sensory information that enters the spinal cord through the dorsal roots. In general, sensory fibres entering the spinal cord synapse on neurons in the dorsal horn, with the axons of these latter cells forming tracts that run upwards or downwards in the spinal cord.

In certain segments of the spinal cord an additional small horn of grey matter is present. It projects laterally in the angle between the dorsal and ventral horns on each side, and is known as the lateral horn (Fig. 7.29b). It contains the cell bodies of neurons, the axons of which constitute part of the autonomic nervous system (see p. 870). Such neurons occur only in the T1 to L2 segments of the spinal cord, and lateral horns are represented only in transverse sections of these segments of the spinal cord.

The peripheral part of the spinal cord consists of white matter formed by axons arranged in tracts that convey information to or from the brainstem or between different segments of the spinal cord. For descriptive purposes three regions of white matter can be identified in each half of the spinal cord. The white matter is divided into sectors by imaginary lines drawn radially through the dorsal and ventral horns (Fig. 7.29c). The white matter between the two horns laterally is collectively known as the *lateral funiculus.* It is formed by descending tracts conveying motor information and ascending tracts concerned with pain, temperature, touch and pressure sensation. The white matter between the dorsal horn and the midline dorsally is called the *posterior funiculus*, and it consists largely of ascending tracts that convey information on pressure, touch and position sense. Finally, the region between the ventral horn and the midline anteriorly is known as the *anterior funiculus*, and is formed by a mixture of descending motor and ascending sensory tracts.

Sometimes the region of white matter embracing the anterolateral aspect of the ventral horn is highlighted as the *anterolateral funiculus.* This is because the axons in this region, overlapping both the anterior and lateral funiculi constitute the largest single collection of ascending sensory fibres that convey the sensations of pressure, touch, pain and temperature.

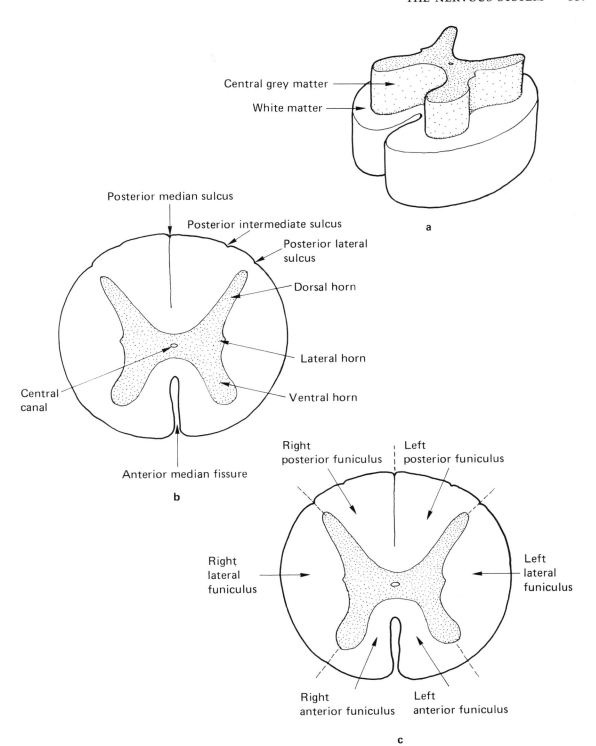

Fig. 7.29a–c   The internal structure of the spinal cord and its appearance in transverse sections.

Brainstem

The appearance of transverse sections of the brainstem is diverse because of the variations in its external shape and internal contents at different levels. However, in general it consists of a central core of grey matter known as the *reticular formation*, surrounded by white matter formed by various motor and sensory tracts, and in which are interspersed various nuclei associated with the cranial nerves. The details of this internal structure are not appropriate at introductory levels and are better addressed when the central nervous system is studied in detail.

Forebrain

The cerebral hemispheres have a characteristic appearance irrespective of whether they are sectioned coronally, horizontally or sagittally. The cerebral cortex is a layer of grey matter that extends over the entire external surface of each hemisphere (Fig. 7.30). The cells of the grey matter are responsible for processing information related to the functions of the particular lobe of the hemisphere in which they lie.

Deep to the cortex, white matter forms the main bulk of each cerebral hemisphere. It consists of axons of cells in the cerebral cortex that communicate with cells in adjacent, distant and contralateral regions of the cerebrum, and also axons that pass out of or into the cerebrum.

Sections cut through the central parts of the cerebral hemisphere reveal the cavity of the lateral ventricle and large collections of grey matter surrounding the lateral and third ventricles (Fig. 7.30). The most posterior large mass of grey matter adjacent to the third ventricle is the thalamus, and the remaining masses of grey matter are collectively known as the *basal ganglia*—a group of nuclei that are involved in the control of movement.

Other features of the internal structure of the cerebral hemispheres are best reserved until a detailed study of the central nervous system is undertaken.

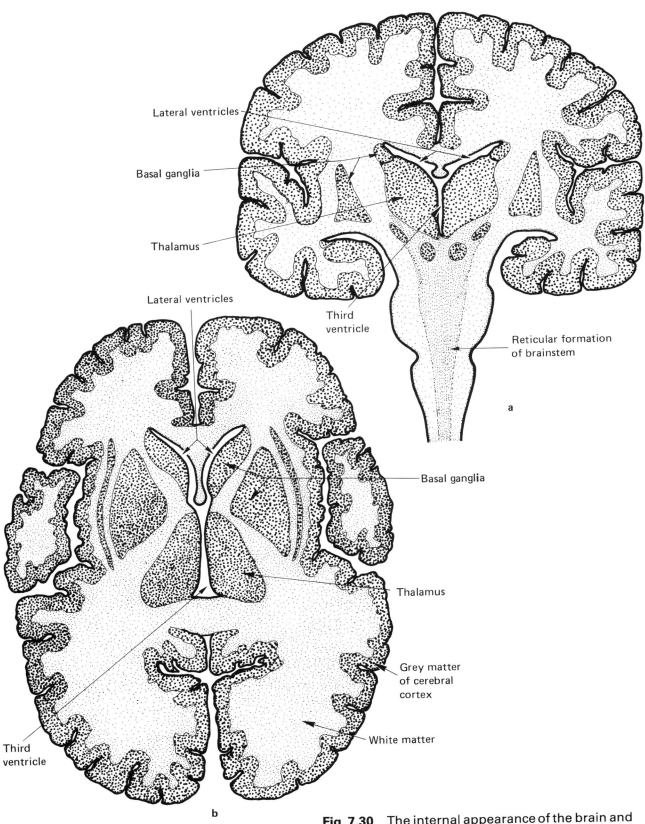

Lateral ventricles

Basal ganglia

Thalamus

Third ventricle

Reticular formation of brainstem

a

Lateral ventricles

Basal ganglia

Thalamus

Grey matter of cerebral cortex

White matter

Third ventricle

b

Fig. 7.30 The internal appearance of the brain and brainstem: **a** = coronal section; **b** = horizontal.

The meninges

Although glial cells hold the neurons of the central nervous system together and afford them protection against metabolic insults, the central nervous system is nonetheless a soft, cellular mass, and as such it is vulnerable to external, mechanical insults which might arise were it freely mobile within the skull or vertebral canal. To protect it against such insults, the central nervous system is surrounded by three membranes, collectively called the *meninges*, and is bathed in a fluid called the *cerebrospinal fluid*.

Meninges of the spinal cord

The outermost of the three meningeal coverings of the central nervous system is a tough fibrous layer: the *dura mater*. In the vertebral canal it forms a long sac, called the *dural sac*, which houses the spinal cord (Fig. 7.31a). Rostrally, the dural sac attaches to the margins of the foramen magnum, but within the vertebral canal it is relatively mobile, being attached to the floor of the vertebral canal only by modest fibrous ligaments. The dural sac is much longer than the spinal cord and reaches as far as the S2 segment of the vertebral column.

The deepest of the three meningeal coverings of the central nervous system is a thin transparent membrane called the *pia mater* (Fig. 7.31b). It intimately invests the entire surface of the spinal cord like a fine skin. From the caudal end of the spinal cord it continues as a thread of tissue devoid of any neural elements, extending through the caudal end of the dural sac, piercing the tip of the sac to attach finally to the coccyx (Fig. 7.31b).

The third of the meningeal coverings of the central nervous system is a shiny membrane called the *arachnoid mater* that, in the first instance, lines the internal surface of the dura mater (Fig. 7.31c). A substantial space thus persists between the arachnoid and dura mater on the one hand and the central nervous system covered by the pia mater on the other. It is called the *subarachnoid space*. It is permeated by a network of threads of arachnoid mater that connect the arachnoid and dura mater to the pia mater. This network resembles the structure of a cobweb and this appearance gives the arachnoid its name (*arachnis*: Greek meaning spider).

Spanning the subarachnoid space surrounding the spinal cord are a series of ligaments formed by the pia mater, called the *denticulate ligaments* (Fig. 7.31d). These ligaments are triangular, tooth-like extensions of the pia mater whose bases are attached at regular intervals along the lateral aspect of the spinal cord, and whose apices are attached to the dural sac. Between the foramen magnum and the tip of the spinal cord, 21 pairs of ligaments project to the dural sac thereby anchoring the spinal cord and protecting it from injury due to violent contact with the walls of the vertebral canal during trunk movements.

Fig. 7.31 The meningeal coverings of the spinal cord:

a = The spinal cord surrounded by the dural sac.

b = The spinal cord ensheathed by pia mater.

c = Arachnoid mater lining the inner surface of the dural sac with threads of arachnoid bridging the subarachnoid space.

d = All three meningeal layers surrounding the spinal cord which is held in place by the denticulate ligaments.

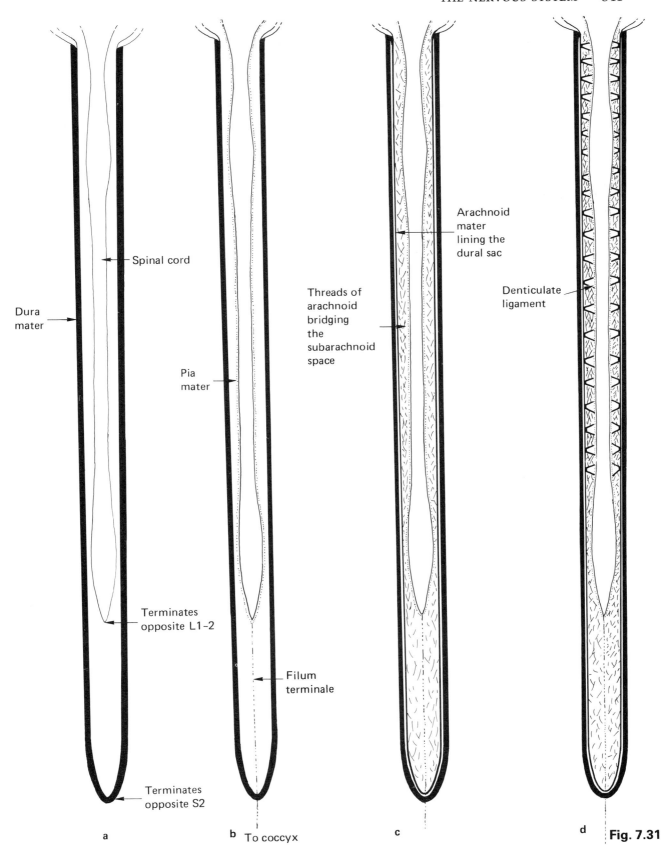

Dura mater

Spinal cord

Terminates opposite L1–2

Terminates opposite S2

a

Pia mater

Filum terminale

b   To coccyx

Arachnoid mater lining the dural sac

Threads of arachnoid bridging the subarachnoid space

c

Denticulate ligament

d   **Fig. 7.31**

Intracranial meninges

The three meningeal layers that surround the spinal cord also surround the brain and brainstem. The pia mater invests the brain and brainstem, following every convolution of its surface, extending into the depths of any sulcus or fissure (Figs 7.32 and 7.33). The pia mater is adherent to the underlying neural tissue, and in an intact specimen, it endows the central nervous system with a smooth surface. Specimens in which the pia mater has been stripped present a granulated surface. The arachnoid mater lines the deep surface of the dura mater and forms a network of fine threads bridging the pia mater and dura (Figs 7.32 and 7.33).

Whereas the dura mater forms a mobile sac around the spinal cord, in the skull it is applied to the internal surface of the cranial cavity where it fuses with the endosteum of the cranium (Figs 7.32 and 7.33). However, at certain sites, the dura mater separates from the adjacent bone to form large folds that project towards the centre of the cranial cavity, and which enclose vascular channels called venous sinuses. These transmit venous blood draining from the central nervous system, cranium and orbit, and are described in more detail in a separate section on p. 854.

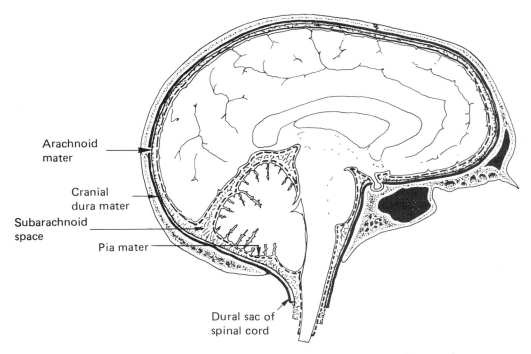

Fig. 7.32 The disposition of the meninges within the cranium.

Fig. 7.33 A close-up view of the meninges in the region of the falx cerebri. The pia mater intimately invests the brain surface. The dura mater is applied to the skull and is reflected to form the falx cerebri, the base of which encloses the superior sagittal sinus. The arachnoid lines the deep surface of the dura, and threads of arachnoid extend across the subarachnoid space to the pia mater. The arachnoid also pierces the dura mater of the superior sagittal sinus to form arachnoid granulations which allow cerebrospinal fluid to drain from the subarachnoid space into the venous blood of the superior sagittal sinus.

The major reflections of dura mater within the skull are the *falx cerebri* and the *tentorium cerebelli* (Fig. 7.34). These are folds of dura mater stretching towards the centre of the cranial cavity. Each fold consists of two layers of dura mater, and presents a free edge, and two surfaces. At the attached edge of the fold, the two layers of dura mater are reflected onto the inner surface of the cranium, being continuous with the rest of the dural lining of the cranial bones.

The falx cerebri projects from the roof of the cranium in the median plane, extending from the crista galli in front to the internal occipital protuberance behind (Fig. 7.34). In profile it is sickle-shaped (*falx*: Latin meaning scythe). The falx projects into the longitudinal fissure and thereby separates the two cerebral hemispheres. Along its attached margin the falx cerebri encloses the superior sagittal sinus, while its free edge encloses the inferior sagittal sinus (see Fig. 7.33).

The tentorium cerebelli lies in a transverse plane projecting from the anterior, lateral and posterior walls of the posterior cranial fossa, forming a partial roof to it (Fig. 7.34). Its peripheral attachments are diverse. Anteriorly, on each side, it attaches to the anterior clinoid process and the postero-superior margin of the petrous temporal bone. Posteriorly, it is attached to the margins of the bony sulcus of the transverse sinus. From these attachments the tentorium cerebelli projects centrally, lying under the basal surface of the occipital and temporal lobes, and covering the top of the cerebellum. Centrally the tentorium forms a U-shaped free edge which extends from one anterior clinoid process to the other. The notch, so formed, transmits the midbrain from the posterior cranial fossa to the diencephalon. Posteriorly in the midline, the posterior end of the falx cerebri fuses with the upper surface of the tentorium cerebelli and encloses the straight sinus.

Cerebrospinal fluid

Running between the threads of arachnoid mater and thereby filling the subarachnoid space is a body of fluid called the *cerebrospinal fluid (CSF)*. The CSF is secreted by strings of capillaries that project into the lateral, third and fourth ventricles of the brain. It fills the cavities of the central nervous system and emerges through apertures in the roof of the fourth ventricle to fill the subarachnoid space of the cranium and spinal cord.

The CSF is secreted continuously, and is continuously reabsorbed into the bloodstream. Reabsorption occurs through fountain-like extensions of the arachnoid mater, called *arachnoid granulations*, that pierce the dura mater of the falx cerebri and project into the superior sagittal sinus (see Fig. 7.33).

Chemically, the CSF protects the central nervous system by maintaining a constant pH environment, while mechanically, it endows the central nervous system with a cushioning fluid environment. Within the cranium the brain is buoyant in a pool of CSF, and within the dural sac, the spinal cord is also suspended in a pool of CSF, being held centrally within it by the denticulate ligaments.

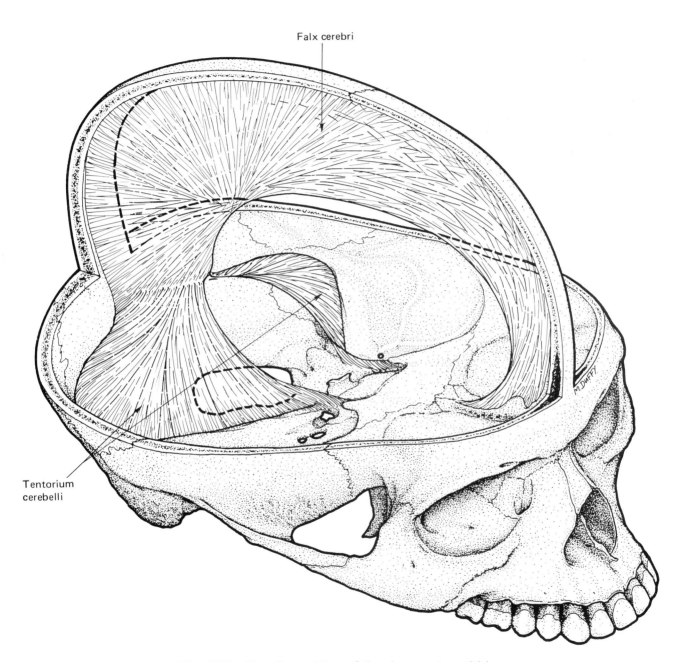

Falx cerebri

Tentorium
cerebelli

Fig. 7.34 The disposition of the dura mater within
the cranium, and its major reflections.

Nerve root sheaths

To reach the peripheral nervous system, the cranial nerves and the spinal nerve roots must penetrate the pia, arachnoid and dura mater. As they leave the brainstem or spinal cord, the proximal ends of the cranial nerves and the spinal nerve roots are invested by the pia mater (Fig. 7.35a), and this is one of the morphological reasons for classifying these nerves as part of the central nervous system. The pia mater spreads like a tubular extension over the surface of each nerve, from its point of attachment to the brainstem or spinal cord as far as the point where the nerve leaves the skull or vertebral canal.

As a rule, the cranial nerves pierce the arachnoid and dura mater at the foramina through which they leave the skull. At these foramina the dura mater and arachnoid mater are drawn into the foramen by the exiting nerve, and eventually the meningeal tissues blend with the fibrous sheath of the peripheral part of the cranial nerve (Fig. 7.35a). Thus, cranial nerves are covered by pia mater and are bathed in CSF as far as their respective foramina.

Modifications to this rule apply to the second to fifth cranial nerves. A dural and arachnoid sheath accompanies the optic nerve as far as the back of the eye, and the nerve is covered by pia mater and is bathed in CSF up to this point. The third, fourth and fifth cranial nerves pierce the dura mater that forms the cavernous sinus, and run outside the dura mater along the walls of the cavernous sinus before passing through the superior orbital fissure. The fifth cranial nerve penetrates the dura mater over the apex of the petrous temporal bone. Its three divisions run extradurally before entering their respective foramina, but the sensory and motor roots are covered by pia mater and bathed in CSF as far as the middle of the trigeminal ganglion, which is where the dura and arachnoid mater blend with the nerve.

The spinal nerve roots are intimately covered by a sleeve of pia mater that is continuous with the pia of the spinal cord (Figs 7.35b and 7.36), and as they leave the dural sac, the spinal nerve roots take a funnel-shaped extension of dura and arachnoid mater with them (Figs 7.35b and 7.36). These extensions are called the *dural sleeves* of the spinal nerve roots, and extend as far as the spinal nerve, so that the entire lengths of the spinal nerve roots are bathed in CSF.

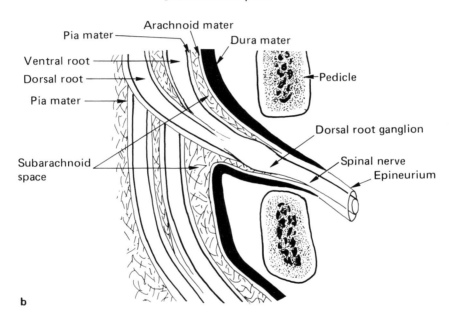

Fig. 7.35 The disposition of the meningeal sheaths of (**a**) cranial nerves and (**b**) spinal nerve roots.

Fig. 7.36 The disposition of the meninges of the spinal cord and spinal nerve roots.

Cauda equina

In the early development of the central nervous system, the spinal cord is the same length as the vertebral column, with each spinal nerve running transversely from the spinal cord to its corresponding intervertebral foramen (Fig. 7.37). However, as the fetus develops, growth of the caudal end of the vertebral column outstrips that of the spinal cord, with the vertebral column becoming substantially longer than the spinal cord. The dural sac is able to grow to accommodate this difference, so that in the adult, the dural sac terminates at the level of the S2 vertebra. The spinal cord, however, ends opposite the L1–2 intervertebral disc.

During the differential growth of the spinal cord and vertebral column, the spinal nerves retain their original relationship with their respective intervertebral foramina, and the spinal nerve roots remain attached to their respective spinal cord segments. The difference in length between the spinal cord and vertebral column is accommodated by elongation of the more caudal nerve roots, which assume an increasingly oblique course within the dural sac (Fig. 7.37).

The cervical spinal cord segments remain related to their ipsisegmental vertebrae, with the cervical nerve roots retaining, more or less, their original transverse course. Some even ascend to their respective intervertebral foramina. However, the upper thoracic spinal cord segments are displaced from their respective intervertebral foramina by about one segmental level, and progressively lower spinal cord segments are displaced from their intervertebral foramina by an increasing margin, until the S5 spinal cord segment lies some 10 vertebral segments short of the S5 intervertebral foramen.

The thoracic, lumbar, sacral and coccygeal nerve roots are therefore progressively longer. Below the caudal tip of the spinal cord, the L2 to S5 and the coccygeal nerve roots form a leash of nerves hanging freely in the dural sac (Fig. 7.38). Each nerve root is ensheathed in its own sleeve of pia mater and is bathed in CSF. This leash of nerve roots resembles the appearances of a horse's tail, and is therefore known as the *cauda equina* (*cauda:* Latin meaning tail; *equus:* Latin meaning horse). As each set of dorsal and ventral nerve roots descends to its respective intervertebral foramen, it passes to the lateral side of the dural sac and penetrates it, as a rule at a level just above the appropriate intervertebral foramen.

Fig. 7.37 The relative disposition of the intervertebral foramina, spinal nerves and spinal cord segments during the development of the spinal cord. In the fetus the spinal cord is the same length as the vertebral column and all nerve roots pass transversely. Growth of the vertebral column outstrips growth of the spinal cord and the lower spinal nerve roots are stretched to assume an oblique course.

Fig. 7.37

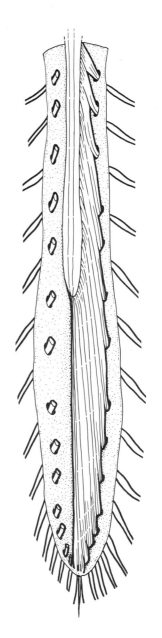

Fig. 7.38   The cauda equina.

Blood supply

The blood supply of the central nervous system is derived from the *vertebral* and *internal carotid arteries*. The internal carotid artery enters the skull through the carotid canal, and then traverses the foramen lacerum and cavernous sinus (Fig. 7.39). It penetrates the dura and arachnoid mater medial to the anterior clinoid process and enters the subarachnoid space over the ventral surface of the brain where it divides into its major branches: the *middle cerebral* and *anterior cerebral arteries* (Fig. 7.40).

Fig. 7.39 The internal carotid and vertebral arteries entering the skull to supply the brain.

Fig. 7.40 The disposition of the arteries of the brain and brainstem on the ventral surface of the brain.

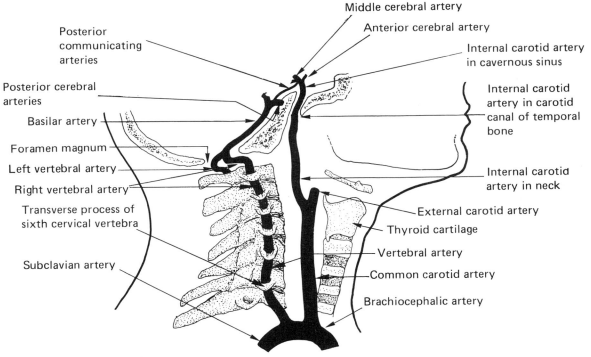

Middle cerebral artery

Anterior cerebral artery

Internal carotid artery in cavernous sinus

Internal carotid artery in carotid canal of temporal bone

Posterior communicating arteries

Posterior cerebral arteries

Basilar artery

Foramen magnum

Left vertebral artery

Right vertebral artery

Transverse process of sixth cervical vertebra

Subclavian artery

Internal carotid artery in neck

External carotid artery

Thyroid cartilage

Vertebral artery

Common carotid artery

Brachiocephalic artery

Fig. 7.39

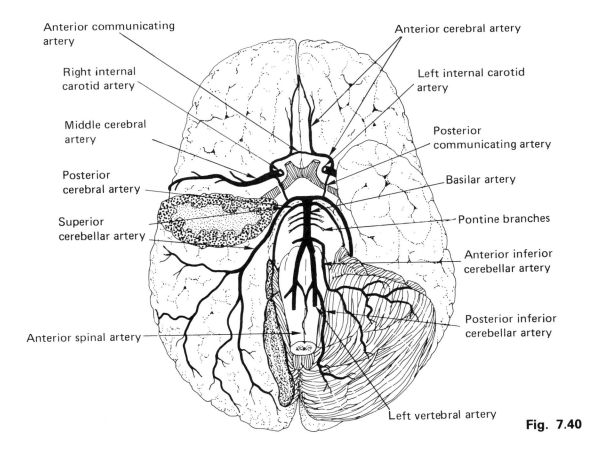

Anterior communicating artery

Right internal carotid artery

Middle cerebral artery

Posterior cerebral artery

Superior cerebellar artery

Anterior spinal artery

Anterior cerebral artery

Left internal carotid artery

Posterior communicating artery

Basilar artery

Pontine branches

Anterior inferior cerebellar artery

Posterior inferior cerebellar artery

Left vertebral artery

Fig. 7.40

The middle cerebral artery passes laterally to gain the floor of the lateral sulcus, and then runs backwards along it. Deep, penetrating branches arise from the proximal part of the middle cerebral artery and enter the cerebral hemisphere from below to supply the region of the basal ganglia. Superficial branches arise from the middle cerebral artery as it runs in the lateral sulcus. These pass in all directions onto the external surface of the cerebral hemisphere, supplying most notably the motor and sensory regions of the cerebral cortex (Fig. 7.41).

Each anterior cerebral artery curves medially, crossing the optic nerve, to enter the longitudinal fissure (see Fig. 7.40). Before doing so, the two anterior cerebral arteries anastomose with one another through a small vessel called the anterior communicating artery. The main trunk of the anterior cerebral artery follows the contour of the corpus callosum and distributes branches to the medial aspect of the cerebral hemisphere (Fig. 7.42).

The vertebral arteries pierce the dural sac and enter the subarachnoid space just above the first cervical vertebra. Each passes forwards and upwards through the foramen magnum to converge in the midline in front of the medulla oblongata (see Fig. 7.40). Their union forms the *basilar artery* which is a single midline vessel that runs upwards in front of the pons. Branches of the vertebral and basilar arteries pass laterally to supply the medulla oblongata, pons and cerebellum.

Each vertebral artery gives off an *anterior spinal artery* that descends obliquely across the front of the medulla oblongata towards the spinal cord (see Fig. 7.40). The two anterior spinal arteries eventually unite to form a single anterior spinal artery that descends along the anterior median sulcus. Most of the blood supply to the spinal cord is derived from this single vessel (Fig. 7.43). Secondary branches of the vertebral artery also descend along the posterolateral aspect of the spinal cord, but these *posterior spinal*

arteries are much smaller than the anterior artery, supplying only the posterolateral corners of the spinal cord (Fig. 7.43). At variable distances along the spinal cord, the posterior and anterior spinal arteries are reinforced by vessels that pass along the spinal nerve roots. In the cervical region these vessels are derived from the second part of the vertebral artery. At thoracic levels they are derived from posterior intercostal arteries, and at lumbar levels from the lumbar arteries (Fig. 7.43).

The terminal branches of the basilar artery are the paired *posterior cerebral arteries* (see Fig. 7.40), each of which wraps around the lateral surface of the midbrain to gain the inferior aspect of the temporal lobe of the cerebral hemisphere (see Fig. 7.42). It supplies the posterior parts of the hemisphere, notably the occipital lobe. Branches from the proximal part of the posterior cerebral artery supply the midbrain, thalamus, metathalamus and epithalamus.

On the ventral surface of the brain, each posterior cerebral artery anastomoses with the ipsilateral internal carotid artery through the *posterior communicating artery* (see Fig. 7.40). These latter vessels allow the vertebrobasilar circulation to communicate with that of the internal carotid arteries. Similarly the anterior communicating artery permits flow between the two internal carotid arteries. The ring of vessels formed by the anterior communicating artery, the anterior cerebral arteries, the internal carotid arteries, the posterior communicating arteries, the posterior cerebral arteries and the end of the basilar artery is known as the *circle of Willis*.

The veins that drain the cerebral hemispheres internally and the region of the basal ganglia and thalamus converge to form a large vessel called the great cerebral vein that passes posteriorly to enter the straight sinus. Veins from the external surface of the cerebral hemispheres drain upwards and downwards towards the superior sagittal and transverse sinuses.

Fig. 7.41 The distribution over the cerebral cortex of the middle cerebral artery.

Fig. 7.42 The distribution over the cerebral cortex of the anterior and posterior cerebral arteries.

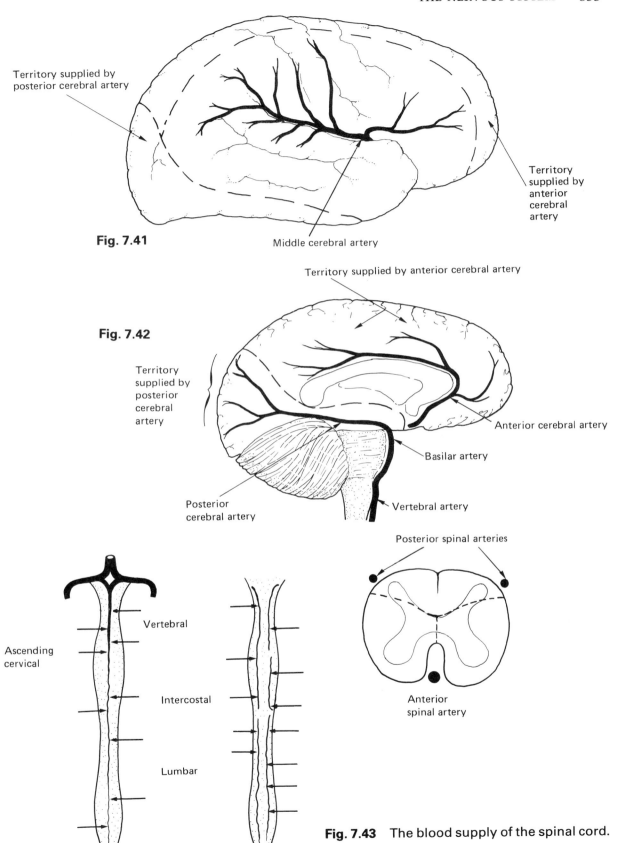

Territory supplied by posterior cerebral artery

Territory supplied by anterior cerebral artery

Fig. 7.41

Middle cerebral artery

Territory supplied by anterior cerebral artery

Fig. 7.42

Territory supplied by posterior cerebral artery

Anterior cerebral artery

Basilar artery

Posterior cerebral artery

Vertebral artery

Posterior spinal arteries

Vertebral

Ascending cervical

Intercostal

Anterior spinal artery

Lumbar

Fig. 7.43   The blood supply of the spinal cord.

The veins that enter the superior sagittal sinus may be injured during blows to the head. They are particularly vulnerable where they penetrate the arachnoid and dura mater (Fig. 7.44). If they are torn at these sites, blood may accumulate between the arachnoid mater and dura mater cleaving the two membranes apart, forming a progressively enlarging collection of blood that slowly compresses the underlying brain. Because of the location of the blood, this condition is known as a *subdural haematoma*.

Dural venous sinuses

The dural venous sinuses are vascular channels that are located at constant sites along the internal surface of the cranium. Most are enclosed by bone on their external aspect, and by a fold of dura mater internally. Others are located wholly within certain folds of dura mater. Some sinuses are small, resembling a small-diameter vein threaded between the dura mater and skull. Others are much larger channels. The cardinal difference between a sinus and a vein is that a sinus lacks the adventitial and muscular layers normally found in the wall of a vein. These are replaced essentially by the bone and dura mater that surrounds the sinus. Consequently, only a layer of endothelial cells separates the blood inside a sinus from its surrounding tissues.

The smaller venous sinuses of the skull are located along the edges of bones that project into the middle and posterior cranial fossae (Fig. 7.44). The superior and inferior petrosal sinuses run along the respective edges of the petrous temporal bone; the sphenoparietal sinus runs along the lesser wing of the sphenoid and the occipital sinus runs along the internal occipital crest. The major venous sinuses of the skull are the paired cavernous, transverse and sigmoid sinuses, and the single superior and inferior sagittal sinuses, and the straight sinus (Fig. 7.44).

The cavernous sinus is formed by the separation of the dura mater from the lateral surface of the sphenoid bone either side of the pituitary fossa (Fig. 7.45). It is a narrow trabeculated space filled with a dense plexus of venous channels. The third and fourth cranial nerves, and the ophthalmic division of the trigeminal nerve pass along the lateral wall of the sinus, running deep to the dura mater but external to the endothelium of the sinus. The sixth cranial nerve runs in company with the internal carotid artery which lies between the endothelium and the bony floor of the sinus. The sinus receives venous blood principally from the sphenoparietal sinus and the superior ophthalmic vein, which drains the orbit, as well as from the middle meningeal vein and veins from the cerebral hemisphere.

The superior sagittal sinus runs posteriorly along the attached edge of the falx cerebri (Fig. 7.44, see also Fig. 7.33). It drains blood from the external surfaces of the cerebral hemispheres, and reabsorbs CSF through the arachnoid granulations. The inferior sagittal sinus is enclosed by the free edge of the falx cerebri.

The straight sinus is enclosed by dura mater along the line of fusion of the falx cerebri with the tentorium cerebelli (see Fig. 7.44). It receives the great cerebral vein and the inferior sagittal sinus. The superior sagittal sinus, the straight sinus and the occipital sinus may meet at the internal occipital protuberance, where the transverse sinuses begin. This region is known as the *confluence of the sinuses* (Fig. 7.44).

Each transverse sinus is located in the like-named bony sulcus running around the posterior and lateral walls of the posterior cranial fossa in the attached margin of the tentorium cerebelli (Fig. 7.44). It drains blood arriving at the confluence of the sinuses and receives veins from the surfaces of the cerebral hemisphere and cerebellum as well as the superior petrosal sinus. It is directly continuous with the sigmoid sinus located in the like-named groove on the mastoid portion of the temporal bone. The sigmoid sinus joins with the inferior petrosal sinus to exit the skull via the jugular foramen and form the internal jugular vein.

Ultimately the majority of the blood in the dural venous sinuses drains to one or other of the internal jugular veins, although some drains through small emissary veins that penetrate the skull at certain sites to reach veins outside the skull.

Fig. 7.44 The venous dural sinuses of the skull.

Fig. 7.45 A coronal section of the cavernous sinus showing its relationships to the sphenoid bone, the internal carotid artery and the third, fourth, fifth and sixth cranial nerves.

THE PERIPHERAL NERVOUS SYSTEM

The peripheral tissues of the body can be classified broadly into the structural components that give the body its shape or external form, and the internal organs, or viscera, of the body. The structural tissues, such as bones, muscles and skin are referred to collectively as somatic structures, and the nerves that supply these tissues are referred to as *somatic nerves*.

The nerves that supply the viscera of the body, such as the heart, lungs and alimentary tract, can be called *visceral nerves*, but by convention, a different term is more commonly applied. Because the nervous functions concerning viscera are largely automatic and subconscious, that part of the nervous system that innervates viscera is referred to as the *autonomic nervous system*. It has components in both the central and peripheral nervous system, and is described separately on p. 870.

Constituents of peripheral nerves

Peripheral nerves are composed of different types of axons that have been classified according to their size, function, or physiological characteristics. The broadest classification of axons recognizes *afferent* (or *sensory*) *fibres* and *efferent* (or *motor*) *fibres*. The terms 'afferent' and 'efferent' refer to the direction in which axons conduct information. Afferent fibres conduct towards the central nervous system and efferent fibres conduct away from the central nervous system. The term 'sensory' refers to axons that convey information to the central nervous system about events that occur in the periphery, while 'motor' fibres cause events in the periphery, usually in the form of contraction of voluntary or smooth muscle.

Axons may also be classified physiologically according to their conduction velocities which in turn are proportional to their sizes (Fig. 7.46). If a peripheral nerve is stimulated electrically and recordings of the evoked activity are taken some distance along the nerve, a wave of electrical activity can be recorded. The wave is generated by the summation of the electrical activity in each of the axons in the nerve. Its size is proportional to the number of axons in the nerve, and its shape reflects the type of axons present.

The wave-form obtained from a nerve containing every known type of axon is represented in Fig. 7.46. The wave has three principal peaks, named by convention as the A, B and C waves. The A wave occurs very soon after the triggering stimulus, for it is produced by rapidly conducting axons with velocities in the range $12–120\,ms^{-1}$. These are classified as *A fibres*. The A wave is broken down into several secondary peaks called A-α, A-β, A-γ, and A-δ waves, each being produced by a particular subgroup of rapidly conducting axons.

The B wave is produced by more slowly conducting, but nevertheless fast fibres classified as *B fibres*. The C wave arrives at the recording electrode much later as it is produced by slowly conducting axons classified as *C fibres* with conduction velocities in the range $0.5–2\,ms^{-1}$.

Not all peripheral nerves contain every type of fibre, and therefore not all nerves will exhibit A, B and C waves. If a particular type of fibre is not represented in the nerve, the wave normally generated by it will not occur. For example, B fibres are not regularly present in all nerves, and B waves are therefore not always recordable.

The conduction velocities of nerve fibres correlate with their morphology. Myelinated axons conduct impulses faster than unmyelinated ones, and amongst myelinated axons those with larger diameters conduct impulses faster than those with smaller diameters. The conduction velocity of a myelinated axon is directly proportional to the total diameter of the axon and its myelin sheath. Numerically, the conduction velocity, in ms^{-1}, is approximately six times the diameter, measured in microns (μm). Thus, the classification of axons into A, B and C fibres correlates with their morphology (Fig. 7.46). A and B fibres are myelinated axons of various diameters and conduction velocities, while C fibres are unmyelinated axons with small diameters and slow conduction velocities.

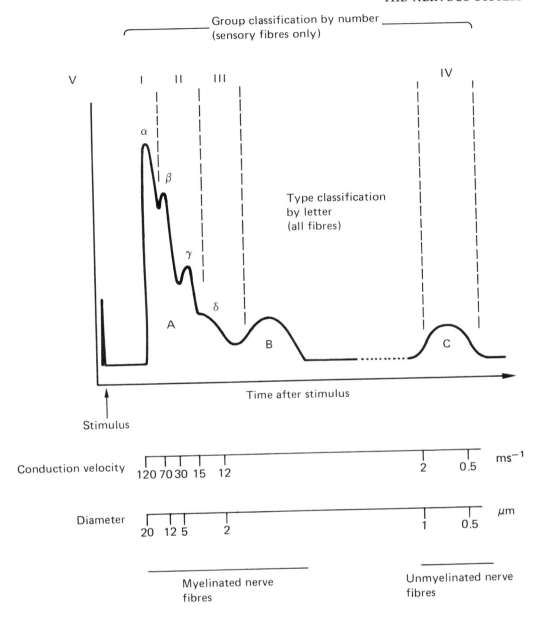

Fig. 7.46 A neurogram of an idealized peripheral nerve. Activity in different types of nerve fibres is reflected by the depolarizations that occur at different times after the delivery of an electrical stimulus to the nerve.

Functionally, A-α and A-γ fibres represent motor fibres to voluntary muscles, and include certain sensory fibres that transmit position sensation from skeletal muscles. A-β fibres mediate sensations of touch, vibration and pressure from skin, and A-δ fibres are sensory fibres that mediate pressure, pain and temperature sensations from skin, pain and pressure from muscle, and pain, pressure and position sensation from ligaments and joints. B fibres are preganglionic sympathetic efferent fibres. C fibres are largely unmyelinated sensory fibres that arise in virtually all tissues of the body and transmit pain, temperature and pressure sensations, but some are postganglionic sympathetic neurons. Because A-β fibres have large diameters they are sometimes referred to as large diameter afferent fibres, while A-δ and C fibres are referred to collectively as small diameter afferent fibres.

Another system of classification of axons relates specifically to sensory fibres. In this system, sensory fibres are classified according to their conduction velocities into groups I, II, III and IV. These groups have the same conduction velocities as type A-α, A-β, A-δ and C fibres respectively, as shown in Fig. 7.46, but do not include the A-α and A-β motor fibres. The fibres of groups III and IV largely mediate pain and temperature sensations. Group II constitutes fibres that mediate pressure and touch, and fibres that form spray endings in muscle spindles (see p. 860). Group I is divided into groups Ia and group Ib. Group Ia fibres are slightly larger and innervate muscle spindles, while group Ib fibres innervate Golgi tendon organs (see p. 860).

Nerve endings

The terminals of axons in peripheral nerves have unique structures depending on their function. Motor axons have terminals designed to deliver a stimulus to muscle cells, while sensory axons have terminals designed to detect particular types of stimuli. These terminals are called receptors, and a diversity of morphological types can be found.

Cutaneous sensory receptors

The nerve endings in skin vary in structure from *simple* to *complex* formations. Simple nerve endings are ones in which the axon terminates without undergoing any branching or other elaboration. Complex endings are ones in which the axons undergo any of a variety of changes, such as forming expansions, assuming a tangled appearance, or becoming surrounded by additional specialized tissue. When an axon terminates simply by losing its myelin sheath and ends as a naked axon, it is known as a *free nerve ending*, and free nerve endings may be simple or complex depending on whether or not they undergo any additional elaboration. Complex endings that are surrounded by a complete capsule of external tissue are classified as *complex encapsulated nerve endings*, while those endings without a complete capsule are referred to as *complex unencapsulated nerve endings*.

The spectrum of nerve endings in skin is illustrated in Fig. 7.47. Simple, *free nerve endings* occur within the epidermis and the dermis. In the epidermis, they run as naked axons between the epidermal cells, and may undergo branching. They are generally orientated perpendicular to the skin surface. In the dermis, free nerve endings run parallel to the skin surface. They are thought to detect stimuli that generate the sensations of pain and temperature, but many are also capable of responding to mechanical stimuli like touch and pressure which deform the skin. Free nerve endings are also found surrounding the roots of hairs. These endings are stimulated by deformation of the hair, and are involved in detecting coarse stimuli that bend the hairs on the skin.

Merkel's discs are complex unencapsulated endings formed when a free nerve ending terminates as a disc-like expansion under a specialized cell in the epidermis called a Merkel cell or a tactile cell. They are found in hairless skin, particularly in the fingertips, and are thought to mediate the sensation of touch.

Meissner's corpuscles are complex encapsulated receptors formed by a spiralling axon surrounded by flattened Schwann cells and encapsulated by fibrous tissue continuous

Free nerve endings

Hair follicle afferents

Merkel's discs

Meissner's corpuscle

Krause's end bulb

Ruffini's corpuscle

Pacinian corpuscle

Fig. 7.47 Types of receptors found in skin.

with the endoneurium of the axon. Meissner's corpuscles are believed to be involved in the sensation of touch. *Krause's end-bulbs* consist of an axon that forms a cluster of multiple short branches surrounded by a fibrous capsule. Simpler varieties occur in which the axon does not undergo branching and only forms a bulbous ending surrounded by a poorly developed capsule. The function of these nerve endings is not known for certain but they occur in the dermis and are believed to respond to mechanical stimulation of the skin.

Ruffini corpuscles consist of an axon that forms a flattened tangle of branches embedded in a bundle of collagen fibres. These nerve endings occur in the dermis and are suitably constructed to respond to stretching of the collagen fibres when the skin is deformed by pressure. *Pacinian corpuscles* are the most complex of sensory nerve endings and consist of a single axon surrounded by several concentric laminae of modified Schwann cells all enclosed in a fibrous capsule. These structures are located in the dermis, and are designed to respond to pressure stimuli.

Receptors in joints and ligaments

Joints and ligaments typically have three types of receptors. These are free nerve endings believed to be responsible for mediating pain; nerve endings that resemble the Ruffini corpuscles and Pacinian corpuscles found in skin. The latter are not as well-developed as Pacinian corpuscles in skin, and are referred to as *paciniform endings*. Ruffini-type and paciniform endings are responsible for detecting stretch and pressure applied to joint capsules or ligaments and so are involved in position sense.

Sensory receptors in muscle

Muscles contain free nerve endings and two types of specialized receptor: Golgi tendon organs and muscle spindles. The free nerve endings are responsible for mediating pain from muscle. They are sparsely scattered throughout the belly of the muscle but tend to occur more densely in the region of the myotendinous junction.

Golgi tendon organs are formed by multiple, terminal branches of an axon weaving between the collagen fibres of the tendon, with the region encompassed by these branches surrounded by a fibrous capsule (Fig. 7.48a). Golgi tendon organs are formed by axons belonging to the Ib class of sensory neurons. When a muscle contracts, the collagen fibres in its tendon are stretched and are brought closer together. This approximation compresses the nerve terminals weaving between them and triggers the axons. In this way, the Golgi tendon organ monitors the extent of muscle contraction and the force exerted by the muscle.

Muscle spindles are highly elaborate structures that have been studied extensively, and much is known about their microstructure and physiology. In essence they consist of two types of modified muscle fibres innervated by group Ia and group II sensory neurons (Fig. 7.48b). Muscle spindles occur throughout the belly of a muscle and are surrounded by a fibrous capsule. They are referred to as 'spindles' because of their fusiform or spindle shape.

The muscle fibres within a spindle are not designed to move the bones to which their muscle is attached. Rather, they are designed to monitor changes in length of the muscle. Because of this difference in function, and because they are located within the fusiform capsule of the spindle, these muscle fibres are referred to as *intrafusal* muscle fibres. The muscle fibres that execute movement upon muscle contraction are known as *extrafusal* fibres.

One type of intrafusal muscle fibre has its nuclei grouped into an expanded region in the middle of the fibre. These are known as *nuclear bag* fibres. The other type of fibre has its nuclei spread along its length. These are known as *nuclear chain* fibres. At their middle, both nuclear bag and nuclear chain fibres are surrounded, in a spiral fashion, by branches of a group Ia sensory neuron. Group II neurons form similar spiral endings around nuclear chain fibres, but form a spray-like ending on nuclear bag fibres (see Fig. 7.48b).

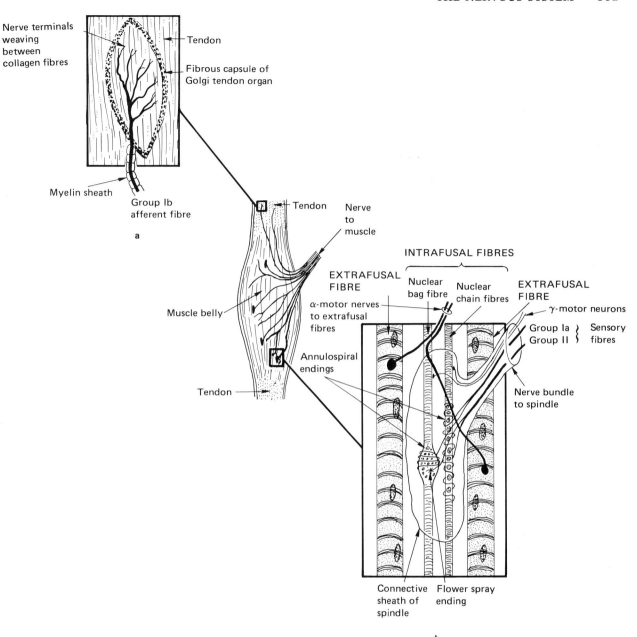

Nerve terminals weaving between collagen fibres

Tendon

Fibrous capsule of Golgi tendon organ

Myelin sheath

Group Ib afferent fibre

a

Tendon

Nerve to muscle

INTRAFUSAL FIBRES

EXTRAFUSAL FIBRE

Nuclear bag fibre

Nuclear chain fibres

EXTRAFUSAL FIBRE

α-motor nerves to extrafusal fibres

γ-motor neurons

Group Ia
Group II } Sensory fibres

Muscle belly

Annulospiral endings

Nerve bundle to spindle

Tendon

Connective sheath of spindle

Flower spray ending

b

Fig. 7.48 **a** = The location and microscopic appearance of Golgi tendon organs; **b** = The muscle spindles.

As a muscle lengthens or shortens, the degree of stretching or relaxation of the intrafusal muscle fibres alters the activity in the Ia and II fibres that innervate them. This activity is relayed to the central nervous system where it is used to determine the length of a muscle and its rate of lengthening or shortening. Indirectly, and in combination with other receptors, joint position is thereby determined. Various subgroups of bag and chain fibres have been identified, and each is responsible for detecting a different component of the change in length, or the rate at which it occurs.

Muscle spindles also receive a motor innervation, and this is from γ-motor neurons. Terminals of γ-motor neurons end on intrafusal fibres either side of the central regions surrounded by the sensory neurons. Activity in the gamma-motor neurons causes the peripheral ends of the intrafusal fibres to contract thereby stretching the central, sensory region. This stretch alters the sensitivity or setting of the central region and allows the sensory functions of the spindle to keep in phase with the overall lengthening and shortening of the whole muscle as it contracts and relaxes.

Without gamma activity, muscle spindles would respond to stretch of the muscle only when it was fully extended. Shortening of the muscle would relieve the stretch, and the muscle spindle would cease signalling the length of the muscle. By contracting, under the control of γ-motor neurons, intrafusal fibres keep the central sensory region of the spindle taut at all times allowing it to keep signalling throughout the total range of movement of the muscle.

Motor nerve endings

Alpha-motor neurons form endings designed to deliver stimuli to extrafusal muscle fibres, and similar but smaller endings are formed by γ-motor neurons on intrafusal fibres. The junction between a motor neuron and a muscle cell involves elaboration of both the neuron and the muscle cell and of certain surrounding tissues, the entire complex being known as a *motor endplate*.

Structurally and functionally, neuromuscular junctions resemble synapses (see Fig. 7.3). As a motor axon approaches its target muscle cell it loses its myelin sheath and forms a flattened expansion that is applied to the surface of the muscle membrane. Once applied, the expansion is covered by a Schwann cell sheath which insulates the neuromuscular junction from the external environment. That portion of the muscle cell to which the nerve is apposed is modified by forming a flattened bump on its surface. This is formed by the focal accumulation of cytoplasm (sarcoplasm) and organelles within the muscle cell that raises its membrane underneath the nerve terminal. That part of the muscle cell membrane applied to the nerve cell is known as the *postjunctional membrane* (Fig. 7.49). Reciprocally, that part of the nerve cell membrane applied to the muscle cell is known as the *prejunctional membrane*.

The postjunctional membrane forms troughs which lodge reciprocal folds of the prejunctional membrane. Within the troughs, the membranes of the nerve cell and muscle cell are separated by a synaptic cleft measuring about 20–50 nm which is filled with an amorphous ground substance. In the floor of the trough, the postjunctional membrane is thrown into further folds known as secondary synaptic clefts which increase the surface area of the receptive muscle membrane (Fig. 7.49).

The terminal expansion of the motor neuron contains vesicles filled with the transmitter substance acetylcholine. When an action potential arrives at the nerve terminal, the vesicles release the acetylcholine through the presynaptic membrane into the synaptic cleft. The transmitter substance then flows across the cleft to react with molecular receptors on the postjunctional membrane which generates an action potential in the muscle membrane. This potential is then propagated into the muscle cell to cause contraction of the muscle fibres.

Fig. 7.49 The microscopic structure of motor end-plates.

The somatic nervous system

The somatic nervous system is formed by the peripheral branches of the cranial and spinal nerves. These branches convey motor axons to the muscles of the body and convey sensory fibres to the central nervous system. The anatomy and distribution of the cranial nerves has been summarized previously in conjunction with the central nervous system (see p. 828). That portion of the peripheral nervous system formed by the spinal nerves is described in the following section.

Each spinal nerve is a bundle of sensory and motor axons connected to the spinal cord by the dorsal and ventral spinal nerve roots. As described previously, the motor fibres have their cell bodies in the ventral horn of the spinal cord, and their axons reach the spinal nerve along the ventral root of the spinal nerve. Sensory fibres have their cell bodies in the dorsal root ganglion, and enter the spinal cord largely through the dorsal root, although some enter via the ventral root. Because the ventral and dorsal roots lie within the vertebral canal and within the dural sac, they are classified as part of the central nervous system. The peripheral nervous system is formed by the branches of the spinal nerves outside the vertebral column.

Immediately beyond the intervertebral foramen, each spinal nerve divides into two branches called the *dorsal ramus* and the *ventral ramus* (Fig. 7.50). With the exception of the first two cervical spinal nerves, the ventral ramus of each spinal nerve is substantially larger than the dorsal ramus.

All dorsal rami pass backwards into the tissues of the back innervating principally the back muscles, and the ligaments and joints of the vertebral arches. Most also supply cutaneous branches to the skin over the posterior aspect of the head, neck, trunk and pelvic girdle (Fig. 7.51). The dorsal rami of C1 and L4,5 lack cutaneous branches, and the cutaneous branches of C4–6 are inconstant. However, that is not to say that these dorsal rami are entirely motor, for although lacking cutaneous branches they nonetheless convey sensory fibres from the muscles, joints and ligaments that they innervate.

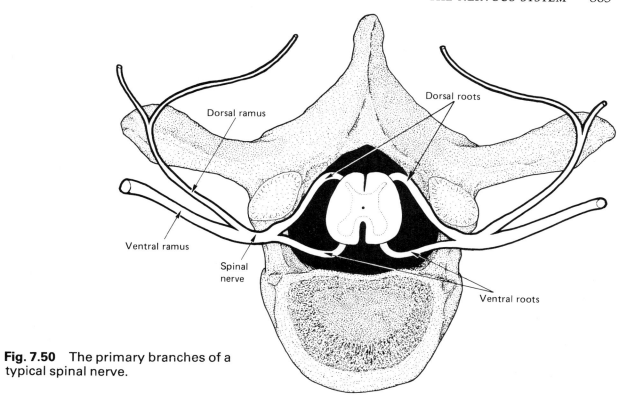

Fig. 7.50 The primary branches of a typical spinal nerve.

Dorsal ramus

Dorsal roots

Ventral ramus

Spinal nerve

Ventral roots

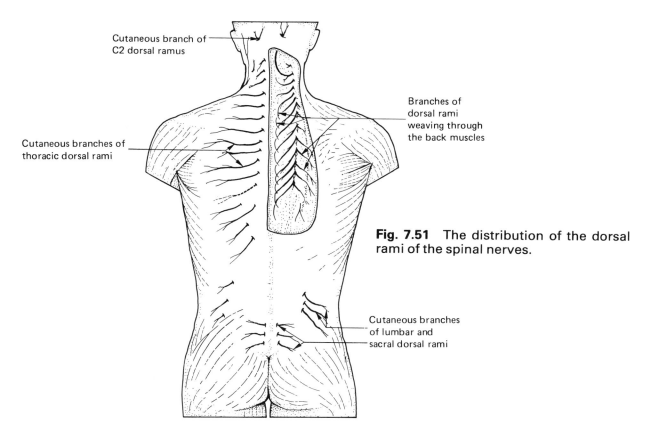

Cutaneous branch of C2 dorsal ramus

Cutaneous branches of thoracic dorsal rami

Branches of dorsal rami weaving through the back muscles

Fig. 7.51 The distribution of the dorsal rami of the spinal nerves.

Cutaneous branches of lumbar and sacral dorsal rami

The ventral rami of the spinal nerves supply the sides and anterior parts of the body wall, the limbs and the perineum. In the thoracic region, the ventral rami, in general, have a simple arrangement. Except for the first, each thoracic ventral ramus forms a typical intercostal nerve that passes laterally from the intervertebral foramen under the rib of the same segment (Fig. 7.52). The first thoracic ventral ramus forms a small branch that constitutes the first intercostal nerve, but the main branch of the ventral ramus passes over the first rib to join in the formation of the brachial plexus (see p. 278). Peripherally, each intercostal nerve innervates the muscles of its intercostal space and the skin overlying that space. The lower six intercostal nerves extend onto the anterior abdominal wall to innervate, in a segmental fashion, the muscles of the anterior abdominal wall and the overlying skin.

At cervical, lumbar and sacral levels, the simple, segmental pattern seen at thoracic levels is modified as the ventral rami form plexuses. A plexus is a network of interconnections between several adjacent ventral rami that allow them to exchange nerve fibres before eventually forming discrete peripheral nerves. The cervical, lumbar and sacral ventral rami form five named plexuses on either side of the vertebral column (see Fig. 7.53):

1. The cervical plexus is formed by the C1 to C4 ventral rami, and the peripheral nerves derived from it are distributed to the prevertebral muscles, levator scapulae, sternomastoid, trapezius, the diaphragm and the skin of the anterior and lateral aspects of the neck from the level of the shoulder to the lower jaw and external ear (see p. 690).
2. The brachial plexus is formed by the C5 to C8 ventral rami together with the main branch of the T1 ventral ramus, and nerves derived from this plexus innervate the musculature and joints of the pectoral girdle and upper limb, and the skin of the upper limb (see p. 479).
3. The lumbar plexus is formed by the L1 to L4 ventral rami with a contribution from the T12 ventral ramus. The smaller nerves derived from this plexus innervate the muscles of the lower anterolateral abdominal wall and the skin of the groin, lateral thigh and anterior parts of the external genitalia. The femoral and obturator nerves are the largest of the lumbar plexus and innervate muscles and skin in the lower limb (see p. 594).
4. The lumbosacral plexus is formed by the L4, L5 and S1 to S3 ventral rami. Branches of this plexus innervate muscles and skin of the lower limb (see p. 605).
5. The sacral plexus is formed by the S3 to S5 ventral rami and gives rise to nerves that innervate the pelvic floor and perineum (see p. 605).

A knowledge of the distribution of the major peripheral nerves is necessary in clinical practice for the diagnosis and assessment of peripheral nerve injuries and other neurological disorders. The course and distribution of the various peripheral nerves are described in more detail in the appropriate chapters dealing with the regions of the body in which they are found. Their cutaneous distribution follows and compliments the segmental dermatome arrangement (see pp. 479, 605). Their muscular distribution constitutes a large body of information, but certain techniques can be used to reduce the burden of learning this information.

A prerequisite for learning the muscular distribution of the major peripheral nerves of the limbs is to appreciate the grouping of muscles into compartments. Within the lower limb there are three muscular compartments in the thigh. The anterior compartment contains quadriceps femoris, pectineus and sartorius muscles. The medial compartment contains the adductor group of muscles and gracilis; while the posterior compartment contains the hamstring muscles and the short head of biceps femoris.

The three compartments in the leg are the anterior compartment containing tibialis anterior, extensor hallucis longus and extensor digitorum longus; the lateral compartment containing peroneus longus and peroneus brevis; and the posterior compartment containing tibialis posterior, flexor hallucis longus, flexor digitorum longus, popliteus, gastrocnemius, soleus and plantaris.

Fig. 7.52 The course and distribution of a typical intercostal nerve.

The muscles of the upper limb are grouped into four compartments. In the arm, there is an anterior compartment containing coracobrachialis, biceps brachii and brachialis, and a posterior compartment containing triceps and anconeus. In the forearm, the anterior compartment contains all the flexors of the wrist, the long flexors of the digits, pronator quadratus, and pronator teres; while the posterior compartment contains the extensors of the wrist and digits, abductor pollicis longus, supinator and brachioradialis.

The innervation of these muscles, and those of the hand and foot, can be summarized by several short rules:

1. The *obturator nerve* supplies all muscles in the medial compartment of the thigh.
2. The *femoral nerve* supplies all muscles in the anterior compartment of the thigh.
3. The hamstrings are supplied by the *tibial* component of the *sciatic nerve*. Lacking an attachment to the ischial tuberosity, the short head of biceps femoris is not a true hamstring and is supplied by the *common peroneal* component of the *sciatic nerve*.
4. The *deep peroneal nerve* supplies all muscles in the anterior compartment of the leg and the extensor digitorum brevis of the foot.
5. The *superficial peroneal nerve* supplies all muscles in the lateral compartment of the leg.
6. The *tibial nerve* supplies all muscles in the posterior compartment of the leg.
7. Of the muscles of the foot, the *medial plantar nerve* supplies flexor digitorum brevis, abductor hallucis, flexor hallucis brevis and the first lumbrical; all the rest are supplied by the *lateral plantar nerve*.
8. All muscles in the posterior compartments of the upper limb are innervated by the *radial nerve*.
9. All muscles in the anterior compartment of the arm are innervated by the *musculocutaneous nerve*.
10. Of the muscles in the anterior compartment of the forearm, the *ulnar nerve* innervates flexor carpi ulnaris and the ulnar half of flexor digitorum profundus; all the rest are innervated by the *median nerve*.
11. Of the intrinsic muscles of the hand, the *median nerve* supplies abductor pollicis brevis, opponens pollicis, flexor pollicis brevis and the lateral two lumbricals; the rest being innervated by the *ulnar nerve*.

The muscles of the pelvic and shoulder girdles are not grouped into compartments and are not covered by such rules. These muscles usually receive a unique nerve supply or a single nerve may supply two or three muscles. These relationships are described in the chapters dealing with the muscles of the pelvic and shoulder regions.

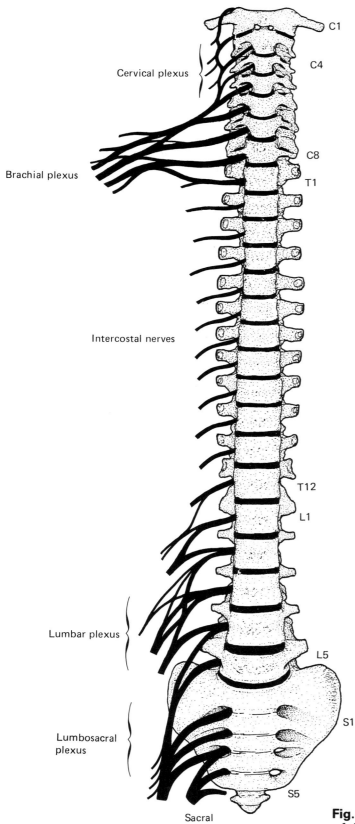

Fig. 7.53 The major somatic nerve plexuses of the body.

THE AUTONOMIC NERVOUS SYSTEM

The autonomic nervous system consists of those nerves that innervate the viscera of the body, its blood vessels, the salivary and lacrimal glands and the sweat glands and muscles of the hairs (arrectores pilorum). On topographical, anatomical, and physiological grounds the autonomic nervous system is divided into two parts: the *sympathetic nervous system* and the *parasympathetic nervous system*.

Topographically, the two systems differ with respect to where they are connected to the central nervous system. Parasympathetic nerves emerge from the central nervous system in cranial nerves III, VII, IX and X, and in the S2 to S4 spinal nerves. Axons of the sympathetic nervous system emerge from the spinal cord in the T1 to L2 spinal nerves. Accordingly, parasympathetic nerves are described as having a cranial–sacral outflow, and sympathetic nerves as having a thoracolumbar outflow.

Anatomically, both systems are similar in that at the microscopic level any target organ is connected to the central nervous system by two neurons in series (Fig. 7.54). The axon of the first nerve emerges from the central nervous system and synapses with the second neuron, and collections of the cell bodies of second neurons form swellings called *ganglia*. Axons conveying information from the central nervous system to such ganglia are called *preganglionic* axons, and the neurons that form the ganglia and whose axons lead from them to the peripheral target organs are called *postganglionic* neurons.

The anatomical difference between the sympathetic and parasympathetic nervous systems is that parasympathetic ganglia lie close to the target organ, while sympathetic ganglia lie some distance away. Consequently, postganglionic parasympathetic fibres are quite short, and postganglionic sympathetic fibres are considerably longer.

Pharmacologically, the parasympathetic and sympathetic nervous systems differ in that parasympathetic postganglionic neur-ons use acetylcholine as their transmitter substance, while sympathetic postganglionic neurons use noradrenaline. However, preganglionic neurons in both systems use acetylcholine as their transmitter.

Physiologically, the autonomic nervous system exerts a variety of effects on different types of tissues, but in general these are all exerted as a result of contraction or relaxation of smooth muscle or of myoepithelial cells in exocrine glands. As a rule, acetylcholine secreted by parasympathetic neurons excites smooth muscle, causing it to contract. Noradrenaline can either excite or inhibit smooth muscle depending on the nature of the molecular receptors found on the smooth muscle membrane. Receptors, known as α-receptors cause smooth muscle to contract; β-receptors cause it to relax. Different tissues are endowed with either α or β receptors, and some tissues contain both types of receptor in different regions or even in the same region. These variations account for the diversity of effects of the sympathetic nervous system.

The sympathetic nervous system stimulates the sino-atrial node of the heart and thereby increases heart rate. It also stimulates cardiac muscle directly to increase the power of cardiac contraction. In the peripheral vascular system the effects of the sympathetic nervous system are variable. Acting on α-receptors, sympathetic nerves cause the smooth muscle of arterioles to contract, resulting in vasoconstriction. Acting on β-receptors, sympathetic nerves cause vasodilatation. In the alimentary tract, the sympathetic nervous system relaxes the smooth muscle of the tract, but stimulates its sphincters to contract. In the respiratory tract it relaxes the smooth muscle of the bronchi. It causes the sphincter of the bladder to contract, and mediates ejaculation in the male by causing contraction of the smooth muscle in the vas deferens, seminal vesicle and prostate gland. In the eye it causes dilatation of the pupil, and in the skin it causes erection of the hairs and sweating.

These diverse effects may be summarized by an aphorism—the effects of the sympathetic nervous system are those that would be evident in the functions of *Fright, Flight, Fight* and *Fill*. The reaction of fright is manifest by pupillary dilatation, hair 'standing on end', sweating and increased heart rate. Flight (running away) and fight involve increased heart rate, increased circulation (vasodilatation) to muscular blood vessels, and diversion (vasoconstriction) of blood from the alimentary tract. All of these actions are mediated by the sympathetic nervous system. The function of 'fill' refers to the relaxation of bronchial smooth muscle to increase air entry, allowing the lungs to fill, and the combination of relaxation of the smooth muscle of the alimentary canal and contraction of its sphincters that results in filling of the lumen of the tract.

In a sense, the parasympathetic nervous system exerts opposite effects. It slows the sino-atrial node, reducing heart rate. In the eye, it causes pupillary constriction and accommodation of the lens. It causes contraction of bronchial musculature, and contracts the smooth muscle of the alimentary and urinary tracts while relaxing their sphincters. Its action on hollow organs is thus designed to empty them. This emptying effect is further evident in the salivary and lacrimal glands, where the parasympathetic nervous system causes secretion of the respective fluids. Its effects on glands is also evident in the respiratory and alimentary tracts where it causes secretion of mucus and acid. The parasympathetic nervous system also has effects on blood vessels. It causes vasodilatation in the genital system to enable erection of the penis or clitoris, and mediates vasodilatation of the internal and external carotid circulations.

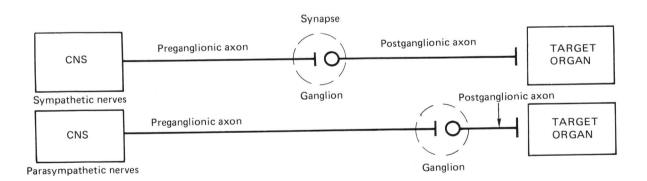

Fig. 7.54 The anatomical similarities and differences between the sympathetic and parasympathetic nervous systems.

The parasympathetic nervous system

The cell bodies of preganglionic parasympathetic neurons are located in special nuclei in the brainstem associated with the nuclei of cranial nerves III, VII, IX and X. The axons of these neurons emerge from the brainstem in these cranial nerves, travelling within them along with their sensory and somatic motor fibres.

Located near the back of the eye is a small ganglion, called the *ciliary ganglion*, formed by postganglionic parasympathetic neurons that innervate the sphincter pupillae and ciliaris muscles of the eye (Fig. 7.55). These postganglionic neurons receive preganglionic neurons from the oculomotor (III) nerve which synapse on them in the ciliary ganglion. Stimulation of the postganglionic neurons by the preganglionic neurons causes the sphincter pupillae to contract, narrowing the pupil, and cause the ciliary muscle to contract, thereby increasing the refractive (focussing) power of the lens.

Located in the pterygopalatine fossa is the *pterygopalatine ganglion* which is formed by postganglionic parasympathetic neurons that innervate the mucus glands of the nose and the lacrimal gland (Fig. 7.55). It receives preganglionic neurons derived from the facial (VII) nerve which stimulate the postganglionic neurons to cause lacrimation and nasal secretion.

The submandibular and sublingual salivary glands are innervated by postganglionic parasympathetic nerves which form a ganglion located in the submandibular region called the *submandibular ganglion* (Fig. 7.55). This receives preganglionic parasympathetic neurons derived from the facial nerve, via the chorda tympani.

The parotid gland is innervated by postganglionic parasympathetic neurons whose cell bodies form the *otic ganglion* located just below the foramen ovale. It receives preganglionic neurons derived predominantly from the glossopharyngeal (IX) nerve with a small contribution from the facial (VII) nerve (Fig. 7.55).

The parasympathetic distribution of the vagus nerve encompasses the heart, the larynx, trachea and bronchi, the pharynx, oesophagus, stomach, small intestine, the large intestine as far as the splenic flexure, as well as the liver, biliary tract and pancreas (Fig. 7.55). Both vagus nerves convey preganglionic axons to these organs. Postganglionic fibres that innervate the sino-atrial node arise from ganglia lying on the surface of the heart, but the postganglionic fibres of the respiratory, alimentary and urinary tracts lie embedded in the walls of these tracts.

The descending colon, sigmoid colon, rectum and pelvic viscera are innervated by parasympathetic neurons that stem from the S2, 3 and 4 spinal nerves. These neurons have their cell bodies in the S2, 3 and 4 segments of the spinal cord, and their axons travel in the ventral roots of the S2, 3 and 4 spinal nerves. As the ventral rami of these nerves emerge from the anterior sacral foramina, the parasympathetic axons leave them to pass directly to their target viscera. These visceral branches of the S2, 3 and 4 ventral rami are known as the *pelvic splanchnic nerves* (Fig. 7.56).

Those fibres destined for the pelvic viscera pass directly into them where they synapse on postganglionic parasympathetic neurons located within the walls of the viscera. Those destined for the descending and sigmoid colon pass upwards out of the pelvis and pass across the left posterior abdominal wall to reach the descending colon, or enter the sigmoid mesocolon to reach the sigmoid colon.

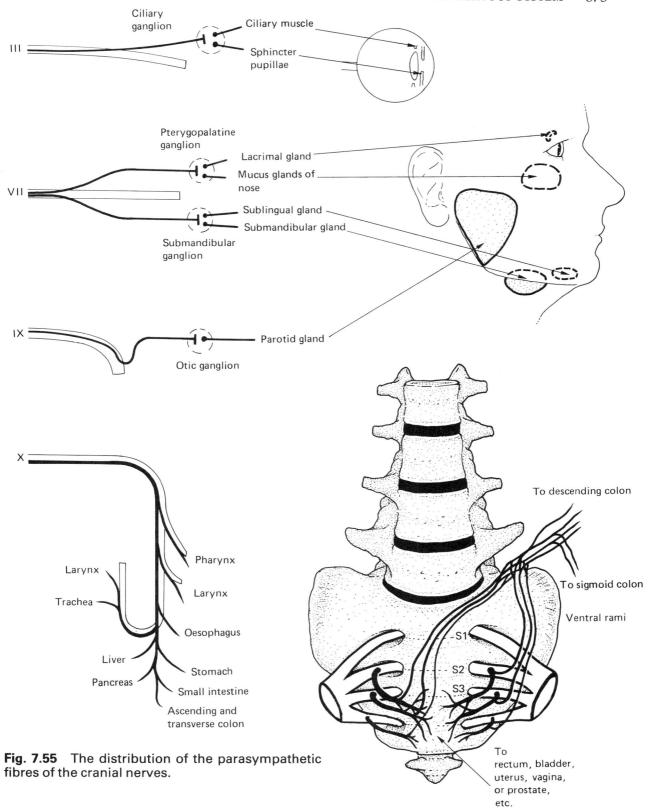

Fig. 7.55 The distribution of the parasympathetic fibres of the cranial nerves.

Fig. 7.56 The pelvic splanchnic nerves.

The sympathetic nervous system

Running longitudinally either side of the vertebral column are two chains of nerve fibres called the sympathetic trunks. They extend from the level of the C1 vertebra to the coccyx. They cross the tips of the cervical transverse processes, the heads of the ribs at thoracic levels, and the anterolateral aspects of the vertebral bodies at lumbar and sacral levels (Fig. 7.57). These trunks are formed by preganglionic and postganglionic neurons of the sympathetic nervous system, and sites along the trunks where preganglionic and postganglionic neurons synapse are marked by swellings called the *sympathetic ganglia*.

Embryologically, a sympathetic ganglion is formed opposite each spinal nerve, but later in development certain ganglia divide and refuse in a variable pattern to form a lesser number of ganglia. Eventually, about eleven thoracic, between one and six, but usually four lumbar, and four sacral ganglia are formed. In front of the coccyx the two sympathetic trunks join to form a single common ganglion known as the ganglion impar. At cervical levels, two main ganglia are formed: a large one at the C1–3 vertebral level, called the superior cervical ganglion, and one at the cervicothoracic level called the cervicothoracic ganglion, or the stellate ganglion because of its star-like shape. A third ganglion is frequently, but not constantly formed at the C6 level. It is known as the middle cervical ganglion.

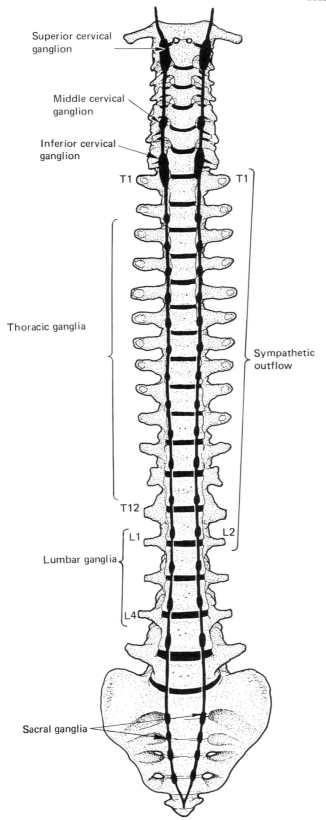

Fig. 7.57 The sympathetic trunks.

The cell bodies of preganglionic sympathetic neurons are located in the lateral horns of the grey matter in the T1 to L2 segments of the spinal cord. Their axons leave the spinal cord in the ventral roots of the spinal nerves at these same levels (Fig. 7.58). Preganglionic sympathetic neurons are not found in spinal nerves or nerve roots at other levels.

After traversing the spinal nerve, preganglionic sympathetic neurons enter the ventral ramus of the spinal nerve, but just beyond the intervertebral foramen they leave the ventral ramus, forming a branch that enters the adjacent sympathetic trunk. This branch conveys preganglionic neurons *from* the ventral ramus *to* the sympathetic trunk (Fig. 7.58). Because it is a branch, it is called a ramus, and because it communicates with the sympathetic trunk, it is called a ramus communicans. Furthermore, because preganglionic neurons are myelinated, in fresh specimens they take on a whitish appearance, and so the branch is formally known as a *white ramus communi-cans* (plural: rami communicantes).

Upon entering the sympathetic trunk, preganglionic sympathetic neurons terminate or assume an upward or downward course within the trunk. Preganglionic neurons from the white rami communicantes derived from upper thoracic ventral rami as a rule, tend to pass upwards in the sympathetic trunk to reach cervical levels before terminating. Those from lower thoracic and lumbar white rami communicantes tend to pass downwards to lower lumbar and sacral levels within the trunk before terminating. Those from mid-thoracic white rami communicantes run only short distances up or down the sympathetic trunk, or terminate at their level of entry into the trunk.

When they terminate, preganglionic sympathetic neurons do so by synapsing with the cell bodies of postganglionic sympathetic neurons located in the sympathetic ganglia. The axons of postganglionic sympathetic neurons then leave the sympathetic trunk, or pass upwards or downwards within it before leaving.

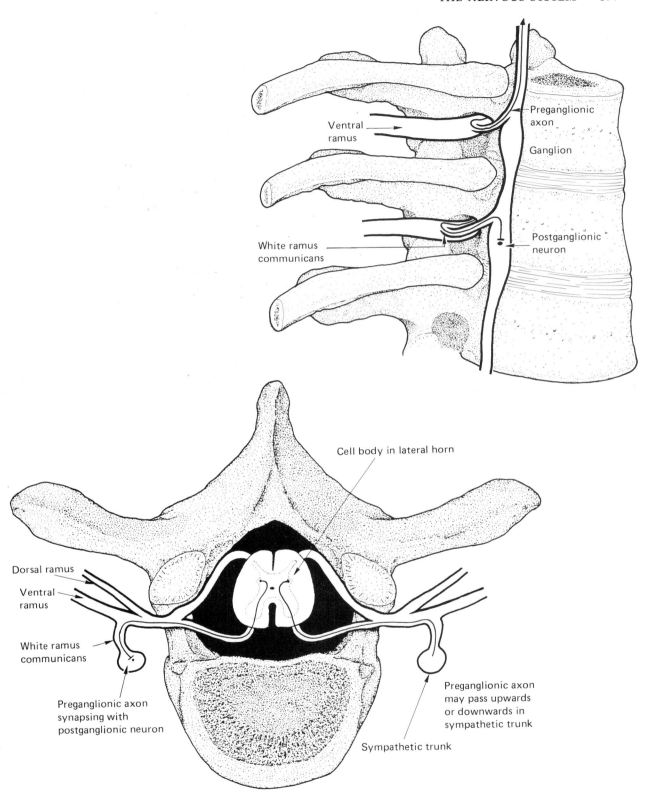

Fig. 7.58 The course of preganglionic sympathetic axons.

Postganglionic sympathetic neurons leave the sympathetic trunk in any of three ways. Most do so by joining a ventral ramus. Others leave the trunk to follow arteries, or form distinct branches of the sympathetic trunk that pass directly to certain viscera or plexuses (Fig. 7.59).

Postganglionic neurons that join a ventral ramus do so by forming a small branch that passes *from* the sympathetic trunk *to* the ventral ramus (Fig. 7.60). Such branches are known as rami communicantes, but because postganglionic sympathetic neurons are unmyelinated, they appear greyish, and the branch to the ventral ramus is known as a *grey ramus communicans*. Grey rami communicantes leave the sympathetic trunk at all levels, so that *every* ventral ramus receives a grey ramus communicans. This is distinct from the pattern exhibited by white rami communicantes which are found only at the T1 to L2 levels. Moreover, it is evident that whereas every ventral ramus is connected to the sympathetic trunk by a grey ramus communicans, those at T1 to L2 levels have *both* grey and white rami communicantes. In dissections, white and grey rami cannot be distinguished by the naked eye, but as a rule, grey rami join the ventral rami slightly proximal to the origins of the white rami.

Once they join the ventral ramus, some of the postganglionic sympathetic neurons assume a short recurrent course to enter the dorsal ramus of the spinal nerve, but the majority pass distally within the ventral ramus. The postganglionic neurons use the course of the dorsal rami and ventral rami to reach their destinations which are principally the blood vessels in the tissues supplied by the ventral and dorsal rami. These include the blood vessels in any muscles or joints supplied by the ventral and dorsal rami, and any blood vessels in skin, if the nerves have cutaneous branches. In addition, some postganglionic sympathetic neurons follow the course of cutaneous branches of the somatic nerves to reach sweat glands in the skin and arrectores pilorum muscles.

Because the skin and deep tissues of the head are supplied by cranial nerves and not by spinal nerves, the blood vessels and sweat glands of the head cannot receive their sympathetic nerve supply via grey rami communicantes. So, a different strategy is used to innervate these structures.

As they run rostrally in the neck, the common, internal and external carotid arteries run close to the cervical portion of the sympathetic trunk. Postganglionic sympathetic neurons destined to supply structures in the head leave the sympathetic trunk and join these arteries. Along the arteries they either form distinct nerves that run parallel to the artery (like the internal carotid nerves), or plexuses that weave around the artery like a vine winding around a tree trunk. The plexuses are named according to the artery around which they wind. Thus, an internal and an external carotid plexus is formed.

The plexuses and nerves follow the course of their respective arteries, giving rise to branches that follow any branches formed by the artery. Thus, ultimately postganglionic sympathetic neurons can reach their destinations by following the artery that also supplies that destination. Consequently, as a rule, any structure in the head derives its sympathetic innervation from the sympathetic plexus on the nearest available main artery.

A modification to this rule relates to the sympathetic innervation of the eye. The internal carotid nerves accompany the internal carotid artery through the carotid canal and foramen lacerum as far as the cavernous sinus. In the sinus some sympathetic nerves leave the internal carotid artery to pass independently through the superior orbital fissure to reach the ciliary ganglion. Others leave the internal carotid artery to join the ophthalmic division of the trigeminal nerve eventually entering its nasociliary branch. Sympathetic nerves reach the eye either through the *short ciliary* branches of the ciliary ganglion or along the *long ciliary* branches of the nasociliary nerve. Within the eye they are distributed to the dilator pupillae muscle and the blood vessels within the eye.

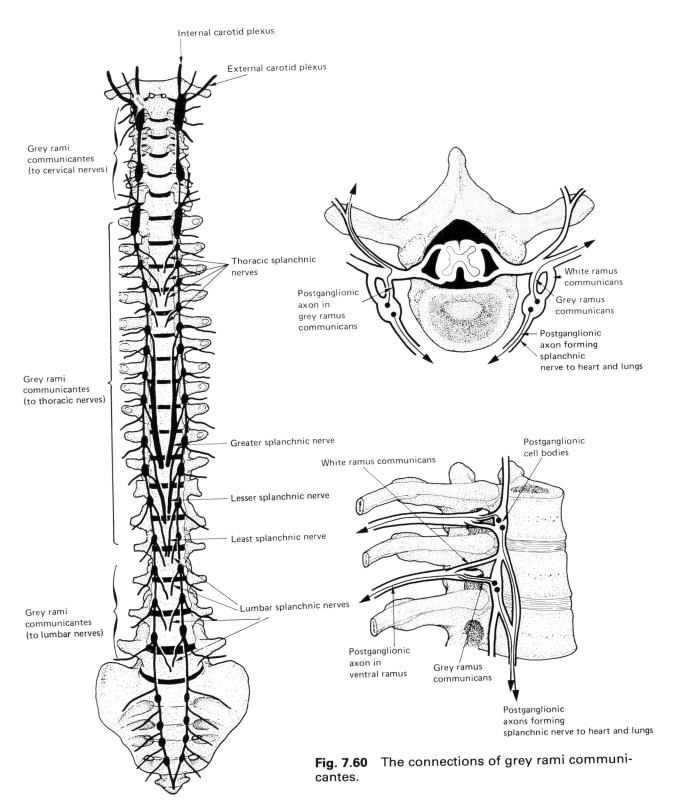

Internal carotid plexus

External carotid plexus

Grey rami
communicantes
(to cervical nerves)

Thoracic splanchnic
nerves

Grey rami
communicantes
(to thoracic nerves)

Greater splanchnic nerve

Lesser splanchnic nerve

Least splanchnic nerve

Grey rami
communicantes
(to lumbar nerves)

Lumbar splanchnic nerves

White ramus
communicans

Grey ramus
communicans

Postganglionic
axon in
grey ramus
communicans

Postganglionic
axon forming
splanchnic
nerve to heart and lungs

White ramus communicans

Postganglionic
cell bodies

Postganglionic
axon in
ventral ramus

Grey ramus
communicans

Postganglionic
axons forming
splanchnic nerve to heart and lungs

Fig. 7.60 The connections of grey rami communicantes.

Fig. 7.59 Branches of the sympathetic trunks.

Sympathetic nerves to thoracic, abdominal and pelvic viscera pass directly from the sympathetic trunk as large, dissectable nerves called *splanchnic nerves*. Splanchnic nerves to the heart and lungs are formed by postganglionic sympathetic axons that arise from the upper four thoracic sympathetic ganglia (see Fig. 7.59). They form plexuses around the bronchi and coronary arteries which they follow to reach their respective destinations.

The abdominal viscera are innervated by the *greater*, *lesser* and *least splanchnic nerves* which have greatly variable origins from the lower seven or eight thoracic sympathetic ganglia. All three nerves enter the abdominal cavity by piercing the ipsilateral crus of the diaphragm, and upon entering the abdomen they form dense plexuses surrounding the coeliac artery, the renal arteries and the abdominal aorta (Fig. 7.61).

The greater, lesser and least splanchnic nerves are formed by preganglionic sympathetic axons that pass through the sympathetic trunk without synapsing. Instead they synapse with postganglionic neurons whose cell bodies form large ganglia surrounding the coeliac and renal arteries, known respectively as the *coeliac* and *aorticorenal ganglia*. The axons of these postganglionic neurons reach their target organs by forming plexuses that surround and follow the arteries to the abdominal viscera, and,

as a rule, any abdominal organ receives its sympathetic nerve supply along the artery that supplies that organ.

One modification to this pattern relates to the adrenal gland. Embryologically, the medulla of the adrenal gland has the same origin as the sympathetic nervous system, and its cells are equivalent to postganglionic sympathetic neurons. The adrenal gland, therefore, is innervated directly by preganglionic neurons from the coeliac plexus, and not by postganglionic neurons.

The pelvic viscera receive their sympathetic innervation from postganglionic neurons that descend from the coeliac plexus along the aorta, forming the abdominal aortic plexus. This plexus is supplemented by postganglionic neurons from the lumbar splanchnic nerves that arise from the lumbar sympathetic ganglia. At the level of the L4 vertebra, the aorta terminates, but its sympathetic plexus continues onto the anterior surface of the L5 vertebra and promontory of the sacrum, where it is known as the superior hypogastric plexus (Fig. 7.61). Leashes of nerves derived from this plexus descend either side of the sacrum in company with the internal iliac arteries, joining the pelvic splanchnic nerves to form the inferior hypogastric plexuses. From these latter plexuses, postganglionic sympathetic neurons enter the bladder, rectum and other pelvic viscera.

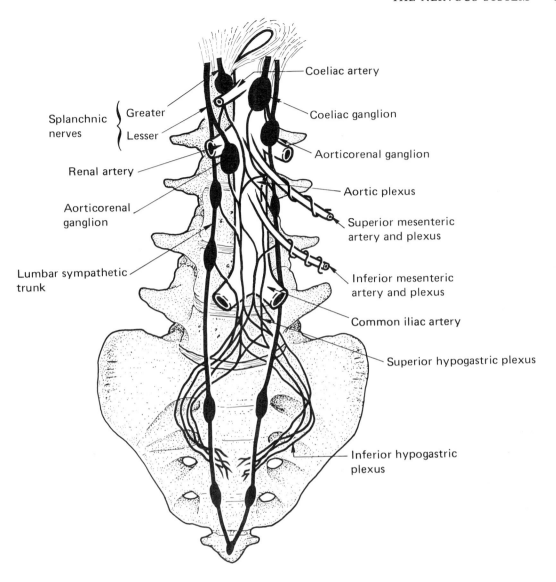

Fig. 7.61 Sympathetic nerves in the abdomen and pelvis.

Index